Evolutionary Biology

VOLUME 6

George Gaylord Simpson

Evolutionary Biology

VOLUME 6

EDITORS:

THEODOSIUS DOBZHANSKY
University of California, Davis

MAX K. HECHT
Queens College

WILLIAM C. STEERE
The New York Botanical Garden

APPLETON–CENTURY–CROFTS
Educational Division/Meredith Corporation
NEW YORK

This volume is dedicated to Dr. George Gaylord Simpson on his 70th birthday, in recognition of his scientific achievements. The articles in this volume are from his students and colleagues who wish to express their appreciation of his contributions to paleontology and evolutionary theory, which have benefited the science as a whole.

Contributors

CRAIG C. BLACK, *Department of Systematics and Ecology, University of Kansas, Lawrence, Kansas*

EDWIN H. COLBERT, *The Museum of Northern Arizona, Flagstaff, Arizona*

THEODOSIUS DOBZHANSKY, *Department of Genetics, University of California, Davis, California*

NILES ELDREDGE, *The American Museum of Natural History, New York, New York*

STEPHEN JAY GOULD, *Museum of Comparative Zoology, Harvard University, Cambridge, Massachusetts*

MAX K. HECHT, *Department of Biology, Queens College, New York, New York*

ROBERT HOFFSTETTER, *Institut de Paléontologie, Muséum National d'Histoire Naturelle, Paris*

I. MICHAEL LERNER, *Department of Genetics and Institute of Personality Assessment and Research, University of California, Berkeley, California*

R. C. LEWONTIN, *Committee on Evolutionary Biology, University of Chicago, Chicago, Illinois*

GILES TERNAN MACINTYRE, *Department of Biology, Queens College of the City University of New York, Flushing, New York*

S. B. McDOWELL, *Rutgers University, Newark, New Jersey*

MALCOLM C. McKENNA, *Frick Curator, The American Museum of Natural History, New York, New York*

JAMES V. NEEL, *Department of Human Genetics, University of Michigan Medical School, Ann Arbor, Michigan*

BRYAN PATTERSON, *Museum of Comparative Zoology, Harvard University, Cambridge, Massachusetts*

ALFRED SHERWOOD ROMER, *Museum of Comparitive Zoology, Harvard University, Cambridge, Massachusetts*

BOBB SCHAEFFER, *The American Museum of Natural History, New York, New York*

WILLIAM J. SCHULL, *Department of Human Genetics, University of Michigan Medical School, Ann Arbor, Michigan*

RICHARD VAN FRANK, *425 Riverside Drive, New York, New York*

S. L. WASHBURN, *Department of Anthropology, University of California, Berkeley, California*

ERNEST E. WILLIAMS, *Museum of Comparative Zoology. Harvard University, Cambridge, Massachusetts*

FLORENCE D. WOOD, *Cape May Courthouse, New Jersey*

Contents

Evolutionary Biology

VOLUME 6

1

George Gaylord Simpson: His Life and Works to the Present

MAX K. HECHT, BOBB SCHAEFFER, BRYAN PATTERSON, RICHARD VAN FRANK, FLORENCE D. WOOD

In 1944 George Simpson wrote that "knowing more and more about less and less may mean that relationships are lost and that the grand pattern and great processes of life are overlooked." Awareness of this problem has had a strong influence on George's career. Without giving up the studies that must precede sound generalizations, he has contributed to almost all aspects of evolutionary biology, and his writings have had a profound effect on modern ideas about the history of life.

George Simpson was born in Chicago in 1902, but most of his childhood was spent in Colorado, where his father was engaged in land development and mining. He attended the Denver public schools and began college at the University of Colorado. After three years he transferred to Yale University, graduating in 1923. While in New Haven he married Lydia Pedroja, and the first of their four daughters was born there.

College opened new vistas and George's original desire for a literary career faded as his interest in science, particularly in the history of life and the principles of evolution, grew. This interest began at the University of Colorado, where, motivated by a distinguished faculty, he plunged with his characteristic intensity into the study of petrology and paleontology. He continued these studies as an undergraduate at Yale and remained there for graduate work. Although generally quiet in class, George could electrify an audience with his erudition. His rapid comprehension and intense concentration were quickly noticed by his fellow students, who recall that his seminars were noteworthy for their depth, comprehensiveness, and length. His student days are also remembered for the penetrating, and occasionally devastating, questions he addressed to his professors.

Early in his graduate career, George began to concentrate in vertebrate paleontology and he soon became involved in working with the Marsh collection of Mesozoic mammals in the Peabody Museum at Yale. By the time he obtained his doctorate in 1926, he had published nearly 20 papers on this collection (and one dealing with ostracoderms). A revised version of his thesis, American Mesozoic Mammalia, was published in 1929 in the Memoirs of the Peabody Museum of Yale University.

In addition to the official graduate curriculum, George undertook a self-imposed regimen of reading in related areas which no doubt was more pleasant and fruitful to him than some of the slow-paced classes. He grasped languages, including Mongolian and Sanskrit, with astonishing facility, and enjoyed them as problems for solution in the same way that some people enjoy crossword puzzles. His linguistic ability was to later serve him well in many parts of the world—not only Europe, but North Africa and South America. Many of the genera and species that he named are based on Arabic and South American Indian words, rather than on Latin or Greek roots.

Upon completion of his graduate work, George was awarded a National Research Council fellowship to study the European collections of Mesozoic mammals. He produced a monographic revision of these forms, basing his work mainly on the collections in the British Museum (Natural History). While Simpson was in England, W. D. Matthew of the American Museum of Natural History invited him to join the staff of that institution. He was appointed Assistant Curator of Vertebrate Paleontology upon his return to the United States in 1927.

As early as 1924 George had collected fossil vertebrates as a field assistant for the American Museum. Later expeditions under Museum auspices took him to the San Juan Basin of New Mexico and to the Pleistocene deposits of Florida in connection with his continuing studies of Mesozoic and Tertiary mammals. Through the generosity of H. F. Scarritt, he led two expeditions to the badlands of Patagonia to collect Tertiary mammals (1930–31 and 1933–34). He was an admirer of the works of the Ameghino brothers, and in Buenos Aires he had several long talks with Carlos Ameghino. The paleontological results of the Scarritt Expeditions were published in a long series of papers during the middle 1930's and culminated in a two-part monograph entitled "The Beginning of the Age of Mammals in South America" (1948 and 1957).

A delightful popular work "Attending Marvels: A Patagonian Journal" was another result of the expeditions. George had developed a great liking for Patagonia and its heterogeneous inhabitants, and he wrote fondly of Indians, gauchos, guanacos, bandits, and fossils. The book reveals a warmth of human interest not evident in George's other writings.

Simpson's field experiences in South America continued. At the invitation of the government he went to Venezuela in 1938–39 to work in the fossil-bearing Tertiary and Pleistocene deposits. The fossil localities lay within the territory of a remote and primitive tribe, the Kamarakoto, whose habits and customs Simpson studied with his characteristic thoroughness and insight. On his return he wrote a comprehensive monograph on the Kamarakoto, which considered everything from artifacts to linguistics. An anthropologist concluded a review of the monograph with these words: "if only I could do as good a job in vertebrate paleontology as this vertebrate paleontologist has done in anthropology, I would consider that I have not lived in vain."

By the middle 1930's Simpson had become interested in new approaches to the study of variation in fossil organisms. A 1937 paper on a Paleocene mammal fauna from Montana included his first published use of statistics to define species of fossil mammals. In the same year he also published a study dealing with the problem of the origin of higher taxa. His concern with variation and quantitative approaches to the study of recent and fossil animals led to the publication of a classic text, "Quantitative Zoology" (1939), written in collaboration with Anne Roe, his second wife, whom he married in 1938. Twenty years later it was revised with R. Lewontin as third author. Dr. Anne Roe Simpson, in her own right an outstanding psychologist has complemented her husband in numerous joint undertakings. Her devotion and understanding have greatly contributed to Simpson's productivity.

Paleobiogeography and the significance of the fossil record in understanding the evolutionary process occupied George's attention during the late 1930's and the early 1940's. His concern with the latter culminated in the highly original volume "Tempo and Mode in Evolution" (1944), written just before he entered military service. Another important project of the same period was his classification of the mammals (greatly expanded from a 1931 version), published along with a famous essay on the principles of classification. Although the primary purpose of the essay was to explain the principles on which his own classification was based, it was the first really modern attempt to analyze the philosophical basis for animal taxonomy and classification.

A short note in Simpson's handwriting, found in the American Museum files and dated December 2, 1942, reads, "I have stepped out, right back after the war." At the bottom of the same sheet he later wrote, "Back to stay, I hope." The latter is dated October, 1944. During most of his military career Simpson served as a captain and a major in army intelligence. He had a harrowing cross to North Africa and took part in the African and Italian campaigns. Some years prior to his army tour he had begun to cultivate a Simpson hallmark—his Van

Dyck beard. This was noted by General Patton during an inspection tour, and in a memorandum forwarded through channels to Simpson's commanding officer, the general demanded removal of the beard. Basing his case on army regulations governing officers, Simpson defended the right to wear his "pink whiskers" (as Patton designated them), and after much through-channels correspondence was allowed to retain them.

Fig. 1. G. G. Simpson in 1944 as a U. S. Army major. (Photograph by Louis Monaco)

In 1944 George Simpson was appointed Chairman of the newly consolidated Department of Geology and Paleontology at the American Museum. In the following year he was also made a Professor of Zoology at Columbia University, where he taught vertebrate paleontology and evolutionary biology in the graduate school.

Summer field work was resumed in 1946. A search for Paleocene and Eocene mammals begun in the San Juan Basin (which was near his summer home in the mountains above Cuba, New Mexico) soon extended to Wyoming and Colorado. George's interest in the history of the neotropical fauna led to a 1956 expedition with the Museu Nacional in Rio de Janeiro to search for late Tertiary and Pleistocene mammals in a remote area along the Jurua River in the Amazon basin. During a camp clearing operation on the return trip, an assistant felled a tree that struck Simpson and injured him severely. In addition to lacerations and

Fig. 2. The discoverer and site of Simpson's Quarry, Fossil Creek, Huerfano Basin, near Gardner, Colorado, in 1954. (Photograph by G. Whitaker)

a concussion, he suffered a compound fracture of the leg. Fortunately for Simpson, one of the expedition members was George Whitaker, a former World War II medical aide. Whitaker improvised a pallet in a dugout canoe and set out with his patient. The nearest adequate medical assistance was at Belém, some 1500 miles downstream. It was possible to transfer to a motorboat, and 48 hours later they reached a jungle landing strip, where they caught a biweekly plane to Belém. Simpson was then flown on to New York where he was immediately hospitalized. He did not become ambulatory until after several operations and a long convalescence. His remarkable recovery was due in part to his stoic unwillingness to allow himself to be incapacitated.

Simpson's myriad published titles are the best testimony to his outstanding intellectual gifts. While actively contributing to the more descriptive aspects of vertebrate paleontology, he produced fundamental publications in organic evolution, historical biogeography, and the interpretation of the meaning of life for a wide audience. "The Meaning of Evolution," published in 1949, is one of the clearest semi-popular expositions of evolution available at the present time. "The Major Features of Evolution" (1953) is a profound treatment of the evolutionary mechanisms from the viewpoint of a paleontologist. It supplements and in some ways replaces his earlier "Tempo and Mode in Evolution." The highly successful college textbook "Life" (1957, 1965), written in collaboration with C. S. Pittendrigh, L. H. Tiffany, and W. S. Beck, is an outstanding synthesis involving all aspects of biology.

Simpson's eminence in biology and paleontology has been recognized by his election to the American Philosophical Society, the National Academy of

Science, and numerous foreign academies. He has received the President's Medal for Science, honorary degrees from Yale, Princeton, Glasgow, Durham, and Oxford, awards from the National Academy of Sciences, the Geological Society of America and the Société Géologique de France, and numerous fellowships and honorary memberships in various societies in this country and abroad.

Fig. 3. Shortly before Simpson left the American Museum of Natural History for Harvard in 1959, the Department of Geology and Paleontology of the AMNH presented him a bronze replica of the first specimen he collected for the AMNH, parts of a Mesohippus, *shown here at the corner of the table in front of a wine glass. (Others in the photo are, left to right, Gilbert Stucker, George Whitaker, Bobb Schaeffer, Norman Newell, Valerie Newell. Photograph by R. van Frank.)*

In 1959 George accepted an appointment as Alexander Agassiz Professor at Harvard University. There his output continued unabated in such titles as "Principles of Animal Taxonomy" (1961) and "This View of Life" (1964), as well as in papers on penguins, South American mammals, and general biology.

For reasons of health, the Simpsons sadly disposed of "Los Pinavetes," their beloved mountain home in New Mexico, where friends and colleagues enjoyed boundless hospitality and exhilarating conversation, along with superb martinis and Spanish songs rendered to George's mandolin accompaniment. In 1967 they moved to Tucson and George became associated with the Department of Geology at the University of Arizona. Official retirement from Harvard followed in 1969. From Tucson the Simpsons have continued their world travels—to Australia, New Zealand, South America, and Antarctica. During 1968 they incorporated the Simroe Foundation for education and research in science. Separately housed behind the Simpsons's Tucson residence, it includes a large research library in evolutionary biology, vertebrate paleontology, and occupational psychology.

George Simpson's achievements represent a sort of spectrum, ranging from descriptive paleontology to evolutionary synthesis and finally to the meaning of science and of life for everyman. Although he is rather shy and retiring his pen has revealed forceful opinions coupled with deep concern for the fate of our world.

BIBLIOGRAPHY (1925-1971)*

George Gaylord Simpson

1925a. American triconodonts. [Abstract.] Bull. Geol. Soc. Amer., 36:229.
1925b. Reconnaissance of part of the Santa Fé formation. [Abstract.] Bull. Geol. Soc. Amer., 36:230.
1925c. Mesozoic Mammalia. I. American triconodonts. Amer. J. Sci., (5)10:145-165, 334-358.
1925d. [Review of: The Downtonian Fauna of Norway. I. Anaspida, with a Geological Introduction, by J. Kiaer.] Science, 62:288-289.
1925e. Mammals were humble when dinosaurs roved. New York Times, Sunday Ed., Special Feature Section, Oct. 18, 1925.
1925f. Mesozoic Mammalia. II. *Tinodon* and its allies. Amer. J. Sci., 5(10):451-470.

*(Does not include various non-scientific publications, unsigned notes, interviews, unprinted lectures, addresses, etc.)

1925g. A Mesozoic mammal skull from Mongolia. Amer. Mus. Novitates, No. 201:1-11.
1925h. Mesozoic Mammalia. III. A preliminary comparison of Jurassic mammals. Amer. J. Sci., (5)10:559-569.
1925i. [Review of: A Nearly Complete Articulated Skeleton of *Camarasaurus*, by C. W. Gilmore.] Amer. J. Sci., (5)10:572-573.
1926a. [Review of: The Osteology of the Reptiles, by S. W. Williston.] Amer. J. Sci., (5)11:96-97.
1926b. [Review of: Geschichte und Methode der Rekonstruktion vorzeitlicher Wirbeltiere, by O. Abel.] Amer. J. Sci., (5)11:97-98.
1926c. Mesozoic Mammalia. IV. The multituberculates as living animals. Amer. J. Sci., (5)11:228-250.
1926d. New reconstruction of *Lasanius*. [Abstract.] Bull. Geol. Soc. Amer., 37:237.
1926e. Pre-Cretaceous evolution of mammalian lower molars. [Abstract.] Bull. Geol. Soc. Amer., 37:238.
1926f. [Personal letter to R. S. Lull, published *in* An Item of Museum History, by J. D. Figgins.] Proc. Colorado Mus. Nat. Hist., 6(4):22-24.
1926g. [Review of: The Origin of Birds, by G. Heilmann.] Amer. J. Sci., (5)11:453-454.
1926h. World's most complete collection of remains of man's mouse-like ancestor in Peabody. Yale Daily News, May 5, 1926:5.
1926i. Are *Dromatherium* and *Microconodon* mammals? Science,(n.s.)63:548-549.
1926j. New reconstruction of *Lasanius*. Bull. Geol. Soc. Amer., 37:397-402.
1926k. The fauna of Quarry Nine. Amer. J. Sci., (5)12:1-11.
1926l. American terrestrial Rhynchocephalia. Amer. J. Sci., (5)12:12-16.
1926m. Mesozoic Mammalia. V. *Dromatherium* and *Microconodon*. Amer. J. Sci., (5)12:87-108.
1926n. The age of the Morrison formation. Amer. J. Sci., (5)12:198-216.
1926o. Cretaceous mammal skulls from Mongolia. [With W. K. Gregory.] Amer. Mus. Novitates, No. 225:1-20.
1926p. Cretaceous mammal skulls from Mongolia. [With W. K. Gregory.] Nature (London), 118:698-699.
1927a. [Remarks on evolution of mammalian molars.] *In* Krogman, W. M., Anthropological aspects of the human teeth and dentition. J. Dental Res., 7:52-53.
1927b. A North American Oligocene edentate. Ann. Carnegie Mus., 17:283-298.
1927c. Mammalian fauna of the Hell Creek formation of Montana. Amer. Mus. Novitates, No. 267:1-7.
1927d. Mammalian fauna and correlation of the Paskapoo formation of Alberta. Amer. Mus. Novitates, No. 268:1-10.
1927e. Mesozoic Mammalia. VI. Genera of Morrison pantotheres. Amer. J. Sci., (5)13:411-416.
1927f. Mesozoic Mammalia. VII. Taxonomy of Morrison multituberculates. Amer. J. Sci., (5)14:36-38.
1927g. Correction. *Tathiodon*, new genus, to Replace *Tanaodon* Simpson non Kirk. Amer. J. Sci., (5)14:71.
1927h. On the cynodont reptile *Tribolodon frerensis*, Seeley. Ann. Mag. Nat. Hist., (9)20:28-32.
1927i. Mesozoic Mammalia. VIII. Genera of Lance mammals other than multituberculates. Amer. J. Sci., (5)14:121-130.
1927j. Mesozoic Mammalia. IX. The brain of Jurassic mammals. Amer. J. Sci., (5)14:259-268.
1928a. A new mammalian fauna from the Fort Union of southern Montana. Amer. Mus. Novitates, No. 297:1-15. [Abstr., Bull. Geol. Soc. Amer., 39:300-301.]
1928b. Mesozoic Mammalia. X. Some Triassic mammals. Amer. J. Sci., (5)15:154-167.
1928c. A Catalogue of the Mesozoic Mammalia in the Geological Department of the British Museum. London, British Museum (Nat. Hist.), 215 pp.
1928d. Mesozoic Mammalia. XI. *Bracantherulum tendagurense* Dietrich. Amer. J. Sci., (5)15:303-308.
1928e. American Eocene didelphids. Amer. Mus. Novitates, No. 307:1-7.

1928f. Multituberculates in the Wasatch formation. [With Walter Granger.] Amer. Mus. Novitates, No. 312:1-4.
1928g. Mesozoic Mammalia. XII. The internal mandibular groove of Jurassic mammals. Amer. J. Sci., (5)15:461-470.
1928h. [Review of: The Downtonian and Devonian Vertebrates of Spitsbergen. Part I. Family Cephalaspidae, by E. A. Stensiö.] Amer. J. Sci., (5)15:529-531.
1928i. Affinites of the Polydolopidae. Amer. Mus. Novitates, No. 323:1-13.
1928j. Pleistocene mammals from a cave in Citrus County, Florida. Amer. Mus. Novitates, No. 328:1-16.
1928k. Further notes on Mongolian Cretaceous mammals. Amer. Mus. Novitates, No. 329:1-14.
1928l. Affinities of the Mongolian Cretaceous insectivores. Amer. Mus. Novitates, No. 330:1-11.
1928m. Paleocene multituberculates from Mongolia. [With W. D. Matthew and Walter Granger.] Amer. Mus. Novitates, No. 331:1-4.
1928n. Hind limb musculature and habits of a Paleocene multituberculate. [With H. O. Elftman.] Amer. Mus. Novitates, No. 333:1-19.
1929a. Pleistocene mammalian fauna of the Seminole field, Pinellas County, Florida. Bull. Amer. Mus. Nat. Hist., 56:561-599.
1929b. A revision of the Tertiary Multituberculata. [With Walter Granger.] Bull. Amer. Mus. Nat. Hist., 56:601-676.
1929c. Third contribution to the Fort Union fauna at Bear Creek, Montana. Amer. Mus. Novitates, No. 345:1-12.
1929d. Some Cretaceous mammals from the Lance formation, Ann. Carnegie Mus., 19, No. 2, Art. V:107-113.
1929e. A collection of Paleocene mammals from Bear Creek, Montana. Ann. Carnegie Mus., 19, No. 2, Art, VI:115-122.
1929f. Paleocene and Lower Eocene mammals of Europe. Amer. Mus. Novitates, No. 354:1-17.
1929g. The extinct land mammals of Florida. Fla. State Geol. Surv., 20th Ann. Report, 1929:229-280.
1929h. Hyracoidea. The Encyclopedia Britannica, 14th Ed., 12:25.
1929i. Multituberculata. The Encyclopedia Britannica, 14th Ed. 15:953. [Revision, 1947c.]
1929j. Tillodontia. The Encyclopedia Britannica, 14th Ed. 22:215-216. [Revision, 1946t.]
1929k. Hunting extinct animals in Florida. Natural History, 29:506-518.
1929l. Additions to the fauna of the Gashato formation of Mongolia. [With W. D. Matthew and Walter Granger.] Amer. Mus. Novitates, No. 376:1-12.
1929m. American Mesozoic Mammalia. Mem. Peabody Mus. Yale University, 3(I):i-xvi, 1-236.
1929n. A new Paleocene uintahere and molar evolution in the Amblypoda. Amer. Mus. Novitates, No. 387:1-9.
1929o. The dentition of *Ornithorhynchus* as evidence of its affinites. Amer. Mus. Novitates, No. 390:1-15.
1930a. Sea sirens. Natural History, 30:41-47.
1930b. Additions to the Pleistocene of Florida. Amer. Mus. Novitates, No. 406:1-14.
1930c. A new specimen of *Eodelphis cutleri* from the Belly River formation of Alberta. Canada Dept. Mines, Bull. No. 63, Geol. Series No. 51, Contributions to Canadian Paleontology, pp. 29-32, 80-81.
1930d. Rodent giants. Natural History, 30:305-313.
1930e. Bibliography of Mississippian and Pennsylvania footprints of North America. [*In* Footprints from the Coal Measures of Alabama, by T. H. Aldrich, Sr., and W. B. Jones.] Geol. Surv. Alabama, Mus. Paper, No. 9:63-64.
1930f. Tertiary land mammals of Florida. Bull. Amer. Mus. Nat. Hist., 59:149-211.
1930g. Post-Mesozoic Marsupialia. Fossilium Catalogus, 1: Animalia, Pars 47:1-87.
1930h. [Extracts from a letter concerning the Scarritt Patagonian Expedition.] Natural History, 30:661-662.

1930i. *Holmesina septentrionalis*, extinct giant armadillo of Florida. Amer. Mus. Novitates, No. 442:1-10.

1930j. *Allognathosuchus mooki*, A new crocodile from the Puerco formation. Amer. Mus. Novitates, No. 445:1-16.

1931a. A new classification of mammals. Bull. Amer. Mus. Nat. Hist., 59:259-293.

1931b. *Metacheiromys* and the Edentata. Bull. Amer. Mus. Nat. Hist., 59:295-381.

1931c. Origin of mammalian faunas as illustrated by that of Florida. Amer. Naturalist, 65:258-276.

1931d. Pleistocene exploration and fossil edentates in Florida. [With W. W. Holmes.] Bull. Amer. Mus. Nat. Hist., 59:383-418.

1931e. A new insectivore from the Oligocene, Ulan Gochu horizon, of Mongolia. Amer. Mus. Novitates, No. 505:1-22.

1932a. Children of Patagonia. Natural History, 32:135-147. Reprinted *in* The West Coast Leader, (Lima, Peru), 20:6-8.

1932b. The supposed occurrences of mesozoic mammals in South America. Amer. Mus. Novitates, No. 530:1-9.

1932c. The most ancient evidences of disease among South American mammals. Amer. Mus. Novitates, No. 543:1-4.

1932d. Fossil Sirenia of Florida and the evolution of the Sirenia. Bull. Amer. Nat. Hist., 59:419-503.

1932e. The supposed association of dinosaurs with mammals of Tertiary type in Patagonia. Amer. Mus. Novitates, No. 566:1-21.

1932f. Enamel on the teeth of an Eocene edentate. Amer. Mus. Novitates, No. 567:1-4.

1932g. Some new or little-known mammals from the *Colpodon* beds of Patagonia. Amer. Mus. Novitates, No. 575:1-12.

1932h. New or little-known ungulates from the *Pyrotherium* and *Colpodon* beds of Patagonia. Amer. Mus. Novitates, No. 576:1-13.

1932i. *Cochilus volvens* from the *Colpodon* beds of Patagonia. Amer. Mus. Novitates, No. 577:1-13.

1932j. Skulls and brains of some mammals from the *Notostylops* beds of Patagonia. Amer. Mus. Novitates, No. 578:1-11.

1932k. A new Paleocene mammal from a deep well in Louisiana. Proc. U. S. Nat. Mus., 82(2):1-4.

1932l. Scarritt Patagonian Expedition [A Report of Progress]. [Signed "G. G. S."] Natural History, 32:559.

1932m. Mounted skeletons of *Eohippus, Merychippus* and *Hesperosiren.* Amer. Mus. Novitates, No. 587:1-7.

1932n. Miocene land mammals from Florida. Bull. Florida State Geol. Surv., No. 10:7-41 [Reprinted in 1956.]

1933a. The supposed fossil marsupial from Africa. Natural History, 33:106-107.

1933b. Late Mesozoic and early Tertiary in Patagonia. [Abstract.] Bull. Geol. Soc. Amer., 44:100.

1933c. Skull of the extraordinary Patagonian Eocene ungulate, *Trigonostylops*. [Abstract.] Bull. Geol. Soc. Amer., 44:198.

1933d. A day in Patagonia. Natural History, 33:187-198.

1933e. Structure and affinities of *Trigonostylops*. Amer. Mus. Novitates, No. 608:1-28.

1933f. The "plagiaulacoid" type of mammalian dentition, a study of convergence. Jour. Mammal., 14:97-107.

1933g. Braincasts of *Phenacodus, Notostylops* and *Rhyphodon.* Amer. Mus. Novitates, No. 622:1-19.

1933h. A new crocodilian from the *Notostylops* beds of Patagonia. Amer. Mus. Novitates, No. 623:1-9.

1933i. A new fossil snake from the *Notostylops* beds of Patagonia. Bull. Amer. Mus. Nat. Hist., 67:1-22.

1933j. Braincasts of two typotheres and a litoptern. Amer. Mus. Novitates, No. 629:1-18.

1933k. A simplified serial sectioning technique for the study of fossils. Amer. Mus. Novitates, No. 634:1-6.

1933l. Stratigraphic nomenclature of the early Tertiary of central Patagonia. Amer. Mus. Novitates, No. 644:1-13.

1933m. Critique of a new theory of mammalian dental evolution. J. Dental Res., 13:261-272.

1933n. Paleobiology of Jurassic mammals. Palaeobiologica, 5:127-158.

1933o. The ear region and the foramina of the cynodont skull. Amer. J. Sci., (5)26:285-294.

1933p. A gigantic fossil snake. Natural History, 33:557-558.

1933q. A Nevada fauna of Pleistocene type and its probable association with man. Amer. Mus. Novitates, No. 667:1-10.

1933r. Glossary and correlation charts of North American mammal-bearing formations. Bull. Amer. Mus. Nat. Hist., 67:79-121.

1934a. Attending Marvels. A Patagonian Journal. New York and London, The MacMillan Company, 295 pp.

1934b. A new notoungulate from the Early Tertiary of Patagonia. Amer. Mus. Novitates, No. 735:1-3.

1934c. The Scarritt Expeditions of the American Museum of Natural History, 1930-34. Science, 80:207-208.

1934d. Patagonian oasis. Natural History, 34:541-553.

1934e. Provisional classification of extinct South American hoofed mammals. Amer. Mus. Novitates, No. 750:1-21.

1934f. [Description and identification of a taeniodont from the Ruby formation.] In Patterson, Bryan: A contribution to the osteology of *Titanoides* and the relationships of the Amblypoda. Proc. Amer. Philos. Soc., 73:97-98.

1935a. Early and Middle Tertiary geology of the Gaiman region, Chubut Argentina. Amer. Mus. Novitates, No. 775:1-29.

1935b. Bibliography [of scientific publications of George Gaylord Simpson]. Privately printed (at the Amer. Mus. Nat. Hist.), issued February 27, 1935. 6 pp.

1935c. Descriptions of the oldest known South American mammals, from the Río Chico formation. Amer. Mus. Novitates, No. 793:1-25.

1935d. The Tiffany fauna, Upper Paleocene. I. Multituberculata, Marsupialia, Insectivora, and?Chiroptera. Amer. Mus. Novitates, No. 795:1-19.

1935e. Notes on the classification of Recent and fossil opossums. J. Mammal., 16:134-137.

1935f. The first mammals. Quart. Rev. Biol. 10:154-180.

1935g. Occurrence and relationships of the Río Chico fauna of Patagonia. Amer. Mus. Novitates, No. 818:1-21.

1935h. The Tiffany fauna, Upper Paleocene. II. Structure and relationships of *Plesiadapis*. Amer. Mus. Novitates, No. 816:1-30.

1935i. The Tiffany fauna, Upper Paleocene. III. Primates, Carnivora, Condylarthra, and Amblypoda. Amer. Mus. Novitates, No. 817:1-28.

1935j. New Paleocene mammals from the Fort Union of Montana. Proc. U. S. Nat. Mus., 83:221-244.

1935k. An animal from a lost world. Natural History, 36:316-318.

1935l. Cylindrical structures in sandstones in Patagonia. [Abstract.] Geol. Soc. Amer., Prelim. List . . . Abstracts . . . 48th Ann. Meeting, December 1935, p. 30. Proc. Geol. Soc. Amer. for 1935, p. 106. [For full text see 1936h.]

1935m. Relationship of local and continental mammalian faunas. [Abstract.] Geol. Soc. Amer., Prelim. List . . . Abstracts . . . 48th Ann. Meeting, December 1935, p. 68. Proc. Geol. Soc. Amer. for 1935, p. 394. [For full text see 1936m.]

1936a. Third Scarritt Expedition of the American Museum of Natural History. Science, 83:13-14.

1936b. The Third Scarritt Expedition. Natural History, 37:90.[Unsigned.]

1936c. Misconstructing a mastodon. Natural History, 37:170-172.

1936d. [Editor.] The Explorers Journal, 14(1):1-28.

1936e. Structure of a primitive notoungulate cranium. Amer. Mus. Novitates, No. 824:1-31.

1936f. A specimen of the Upper Cretaceous multituberculate *Meniscoëssus*. Amer. Mus. Novitates, No. 825:1-4.

1936g. Skeletal remains and restoration of Eocene *Entelonychia* from Patagonia. Amer. Mus. Novitates, No. 826:1-12.

1936h. [Comment on cylindrical structures in sandstone.] Bull. Geol. Soc. Amer., 46, Supplement:2011-2014.

1936i. Notas sobre los mamíferos más Antiguos de la Colección Roth. Inst. Mus. Univ. Nac. La Plata, Obra del Cincuentenario, 2:63-94.

1936j. [Review of A Parade of Ancient Animals, by Harold O. Whitnall.] Natural History, 37:371.

1936k. Census of Paleocene mammals. Amer. Mus. Novitates, No. 848:1-15.

1936l. Additions of the Puerco fauna, Lower Paleocene. Amer. Mus. Novitates, No. 849:1-11.

1936m. Data on the relationships of local and continental mammalian faunas. J. Paleont., 10:410-414.

1936n. [Editor.] The Explorers Journal, 14(2):1-16.

1936o. [Notes on Argentine mastodonts.] *In* Proboscidea, by Henry Fairfield Osborn, Vol. 1, 595. New York, The American Musuem of Natural History.

1936p. A new fauna from the Fort Union of Montana. Amer. Mus. Novitates, No. 873:1-27.

1936q. Studies of the earliest mammalian dentitions. The Dental Cosmos, 78:791-800, 940-953.

1936r. *Carsioptychus*, new name for *Plagioptychus* Matthew, *nec* Matheron. Amer. J. Sci., (5)32:234.

1936s. Horses and history. Natural History, 38:276-288. [See also 1937a, b. Reprinted *In* The Illustrated Library of the Natural Sciences, 2:1313-1325. New York, Simon and Schuster. 1958.]

1936t. A specimen of *Pseudostylops subquadratus* Ameghino. Mem. Ist. Geol. R. Univ. Padova, 11:1-12.

1936u. [Editor.] The Explorers Journal, 14(3):1-16.

1937a. Horses and history. Our Dumb Animals, 70(1):11. [Partial reprint of 1936s, with one illustration, not in the original.]

1937b. El papel del caballo a través de la historia. La Hacienda, 32(1):2-6. [A translation of 1936s, with slight variations in the text and 5 illustrations not in the original, plus 4 reproduced from the latter.]

1937c. [Review of: Restless Jungle, by M. L. J. Akeley.] Natural History, 39:73.

1937d. *Unuchinia*, new name for *Apator* Simpson, not Semenow. J. Paleont., 11:78.

1937e. The beginning of the age of mammals. Biol. Rev., 12:1-47.

1937f. Patterns of phyletic evolution. Bull. Geol. Soc. Amer., 48:303-314. [Abstr., 1937w.]

1937g. [Review of: Explorers Club Tales.] Natural History, 39:220.

1937h. How fossils are collected. Natural History, 39:329-334.

1937i. New reptiles from the Eocene of South America. Amer. Mus. Novitates, No. 927:1-3.

1937j. Super-specific variation in nature and in classification: from the viewpoint of paleontology. Amer. Naturalist, 71:236-267.

1937k. [Review of: Burton of Arabia, by S. Dearden.] Natural History, 40:450.

1937l. The skull in the Multituberculata. [Abstract.] Proc. Geol. Soc. Amer. for 1936:379-380. [For full text see 1937s.]

1937m. [Review of: Wissenschaftliche Ergebnisse der Oldoway-Expedition 1913, neue Folge, Heft 4.] J. Mammal. 18:374-385.

1937n. Additions to the Upper Paleocene faunas of the Crazy Mountain field. Amer. Mus. Novitates, No. 940:1-15.

1937o. The Fort Union of the Crazy Mountain Field, Montana, and its Mammalian Faunas. Bull. U. S. Nat. Mus., 169:i-x,1-287.

1937p. [Review of: Unknown Karakorum, by R. C. F. Schomberg.] Explorers J. 15(2-3):21. [Signed "G. C. Simpson" by misprint.]

1937q. A new Jurassic mammal. Amer. Mus. Novitates, No. 943:1-6.

1937r. Bezoar stones. Natural History, 40:598-602. [See also 1937u.]

1937s. Skull structure of the Multituberculata. Bull. Amer. Mus. Nat. Hist., 73:727-763. [Abstr., 1937l.]

1937t. Notes on the Clark Fork, Upper Paleocene, fauna. Amer. Mus. Novitates, No. 954:1-24.

1937u. Magic bezoar stones. Science Digest, 2(6):84-86. [Condensation of 1937r.]
1937v. An ancient eusuchian crocodile from Patagonia. Amer. Mus. Novitates, No. 965:1-20.
1937w. Patterns of phyletic evolution. [Abstract.] Abstract Papers to be offered . . . 50th Ann. Meeting, Geol. Soc. Amer., p. 64. Same, in Proc. Geol. Soc. Amer. for 1937:126. [For full text, see 1937f.]
1938a. [Review of: Map Makers, by J. Cottler and H. Jaffe.] Natural History, 41:75.
1938b. Review of a discovery of Triassic mammals. Amer. J. Sci., (5)35:144-146.
1938c. [Review of: A Review of the Archaeoceti, by Remington Kellogg.] J. Mammal., 19:113-114.
1938d. Connecticut dinosaurs. Museum-News in Stamford [Connecticut], 2(2):1-2.
1938e. Osteography of the ear region in monotremes. Amer. Mus. Novitates, No. 978:1-15.
1938f. Mongolian mammal names. Amer. Mus. Novitates, No. 980:1-26.
1938g. *Crossochelys*, Eocene horned turtle from Patagonia. Bull. Amer. Mus. Nat. Hist., 84:221-254.
1938h. [Review of: The Making of a Scientist, by R. L. Ditmars.] Explorers J., 16(1):15-16.
1938i. [Review of: Lost Atlantis, by James Bramwell.] Explorers J. 16(1):16-17.
1938j. A new marsupial from the Eocene of Patagonia. Amer. Mus. Novitates, No. 989:1-5.
1939a. Estudio sobre vertebrados fósiles en Venezuela. Rev. Ministerio de Fomento, Caracas, Venezuela, 2(8):275-283.
1939b. Ownership of separates. J. Mammal., 20:111-112
1939c. [Communication on a tillodont tooth, *in* Geology of the Northwest Part of the Red Desert, Sweetwater and Fremont Counties, Wyoming, by R. L. Nace.] Bull. Geol. Surv. Wyoming, No. 27:26-27.
1939d. The development of marsupials in South America. Physis, 14:373-398.
1939e. Quantitative Zoology. Numerical Concepts and Methods in the Study of Recent and Fossil Animals. [With Anne Roe.] New York and London, McGraw-Hill Book Co., 414 pp. [Revised ed., 1960a.]
1939f. Research in Venezuela. Science, 90:210-211.
1939g. Amateur color photography of habitat groups in the Museum. Musecam, 1(4):10-12.
1939h. Types in Modern taxonomy. [Abstract.] Bull. Geol. Soc. Amer., 50:1967-1968. [cf. 1940b.]
1940a. Mammals and land bridges. J. Washington Acad. Sci., 30:137-163.
1940b. Types in modern taxonomy. Amer. J. Sci., 238:413-431. [Cf. 1939h.]
1940c. Minutes of the Section of Vertebrate Paleontology. Proc. Geol. Soc. Amer. for 1939:268-269.
1940d. [Review of: The Wandering Lake, by Seven Hedin.] Explorers J., 18(2):27-28.
1940e. The names *Mesotherium* and *Typotherium*. Amer. J. Sci., 238:518-521.
1940f. Man who made "Dinosaur" a household word. [Review of: O. C. Marsh, Pioneer in Paleontology. by C. Schuchert and C. M. LeVene.] New York Times Book Review, July 14, 1940:5.
1940g. Studies on the earliest primates. Bull. Amer. Mus. Nat. Hist., 77:185-212. [Consists of eight short papers: I. A new apatemyid. II. A new American Lower Eocene anaptomorphid. III. New Designation for a European anaptomorphid. IV. Skeletal remains referred to *Hemiacodon*. V. Classification of the anaptomorphidae. VI. Relationships of Paleocene and Eocene primates. VII. Distribution of Paleocene and Eocene primates. VIII. Indexed bibliography of Paleocene and Eocene primates.]
1940h. The case history of a scientific news story. Science, 92:148-150.
1940i. Antarctica as a faunal migration route. Proc. Sixth Pacific Sci. Cong., 1939:755-768.
1940j. Review of: the mammal-bearing Tertiary of South America. Proc. Amer. Philos. Soc., 83(5):649-709.
1940k. Resurrection of the dawn-horse. Natural History, 46:194-199. [Reprinted *in* The Illustrated Library of the Natural Sciences, 2:1326-1337. New York, Simon and Schuster. 1958.]
1940l. Los Indios Kamarakotos (Tribu Caribe de la Guayana Venezolana.) Revista de Fomento, Caracas, 3:201-660.

1940m. [Two photographs, Jimmie and Marie Angel and plane on Auyán-tepuí, published in connection with: Unchallenged Champion, by E. T. Gilliard.] Natural History, 46(5):262-263.
1940n. Naturalists in Venezuela. [Summary of lecture.] Proc. Roy. Canadian Inst., Ser. IIIA, Vol. 5:38-39.
1941a. [Review of: The Mongol Empire, Its Rise and Legacy, by M. Prawdin.] Explorers J., 18(4):30-31.
1941b. The role of the individual in evolution. J. Washington Acad. Sci., 31:1-20.
1941c. How dost thou portray the simurgh? Introducing the story of animal art through the ages. Natural History, 47:86-96.
1941d. Vernacular names of South American mammals. J. Mammal., 22:1-17.
1941e. [Editor.] News Bulletin, The Society of Vertebrate Paleontology, No. 1, March 20, 1941:1-11. [Contains, among other things, articles by G. G. S.: History of the Society and its predecessors, pp. 1-2; and, legal restrictions on fossil collecting, pp. 5-7.]
1941f. [Review of: A Textbook of Zoology, Vol. II (Vertebrates), by Parker and Haswell, revised edition by C. Forster-Cooper.] Natural History, 47(4):242.
1941g. [Review of: The Social Relations of Science, by J. G. Crowther.] Natural History, 47(4):244.
1941h. Quantum effects in evolution. [Abstract.] Science, 93:463.
1941i. A giant rodent from the Oligocene. Science, 93:474-475.
1941j. [Editor.] News Bulletin, The Society of Vertebrate Paleontology, No. 2, May 20, 1941, pp. 1-13. [Contains, among others, article by G. G. S.: Cretaceous dinosaurs and the age of the Morrison, again. pp. 3-5.]
1941k. How we knew where to dig. In Through Hell and High Water, by members of the Explorers Club, pp. 205-209. New York, Robert M. McBride and Company.
1941l. Paleontology. In The Progress of Science. A Review of 1940, pp. 265-263. New York, The Grolier Society.
1941m. Minutes of the Section of Vertebrate Paleontology, held at Cambridge, Massachusetts, December 27, 28, and 29, 1940. Proc. Geol. Soc. Amer. for 1940:268-271.
1941n. The affinities of the Borhyaenidae. Amer. Mus. Novitates, No. 1118:1-6.
1941o. Some Carib Indian mammal names. Amer. Mus. Novitates, No. 1119:1-10.
1941p. [Review of: The Lungfish and the Unicorn, by Willy Ley.] Natural History, 48(1):59.
1941q. The Eogene of Patagonia. Amer. Mus. Novitates, No. 1120:1-15.
1941r. The species of Hoplophoneus. Amer. Mus. Novitates, No. 1123:1-21.
1941s. The function of saber-like canines in carnivorous mammals. Amer. Mus. Novitates, No. 1130:1-12.
1941t. Discovery of jaguar bones and footprints in a cave in Tennessee. Amer. Mus. Novitates, No. 1131:1-12.
1941u. Large Pleistocene felines of North America. Amer. Mus. Novitates, No. 1136:1-27.
1941v. [Editor.] News Bulletin, The Society of Vertebrate Paleontology, No. 3, August 11, 1941, pp. 1-11. [Contains, among others, article by G. G. S.: Some recent trends and problems of vertebrate paleontological research, Part 1, pp. 2-4.] [See 1941cc.]
1941w. [Review of: New Worlds in Science, edited by Harold Ward.] Natural History, 48(2):123-124.
1941x. Walter Granger. Science, 94:338-339.
1941y. A giant rodent from the Oligocene of South Dakota. Amer. Mus. Novitates, No. 1149:1-16.
1941z. A new Oligocene insectivore. Amer. Mus. Novitates, No. 1150:1-3.
1941aa. [Review of: The Mammalian Fauna of the White River Oligocene, by Scott, Jepsen, and Wood.] Science, 94:416-417.
1941bb. Range as a zoological character. Amer. J. Sci., 239:785-804.
1941cc. [Editor.] News Bulletin, The Society of Vertebrate Paleontology, No. 4, November 10, 1941, pp. 1-12. [Contains, among others, articles by G. G. S.: Walter Granger, pp. 1-2; and, Some Trends and problems . . . , cont., pp. 10-11.] [See 1941v.]
1941dd. Mounted skeleton and restoration of an early Paleocene mammal. Amer. Mus. Novitates, No. 1155:1-7.

1941ee. A Miocene sloth from southern Chile. Amer. Mus. Novitates, No. 1156:1-6.

1942a. [Editor.] The Explorers Journal, 29(4):1-16.

1942b. [Review of: The Second Yearbook of Research and Statistical Methodology Books and Reviews, edited by O. K. Buros.] Amer. J. Sci., 240:155-157.

1942c. The meek inherit the earth. Natural History, 49(2):98-103. [Reprinted in 1942k; also, The Illustrated Library of the Natural Sciences, 3:1672-1691. New York, Simon and Schuster. 1958.]

1942d. Proboscidean dental histology. In, Proboscidea, a Monograph of the Discovery, Evolution, Migration and Extinction of the Mastodonts and Elephants of the World, by Henry Fairfield Osborn. New York, American Museum of Natural History, Vol. 2, pp. 1607-1608, and pls. xxvi-xxx and their legends, after p. 1630. Also short notes in the same volume, not separately listed, pp. 1159, 1222, 1411, 1416, and 1420.

1942e. Memorial to Walter Granger. Proc. Geol. Soc. Amer. for 1941:159-172.

1942f. Society of Vertebrate Paleontology. Proceedings of first annual meeting at Boston and Cambridge, Mass., Dec. 29, 30, and 31, 1941. Proc. Geol. Soc. Amer. for 1941:227-232.

1942g. [Editor.] News Bulletin, The Society of Vertebrate Paleontology, No. 5:1-19.

1942h. The great animal invasion. Natural History, 49(4):206-211, 236. [Reprinted in 1942k.]

1942i. [Review of: A Short History of Science to the Nineteenth Century, by Charles Singer.] Natural History, 49(4):239.

1942j. Paleontology. In The Progress of Science. A Review of 1941, pp. 272-276. New York, The Grolier Society.

1942k. The rise of mammals. Guide Leaflet, Amer. Mus. Nat. Hist., No. 110:1-13. [Reprint of 1942c, h.]

1942l. [Review of: An English 13th Century Bestiary, by S. A. Ives and H. Lehmann-Haupt.] Natural History, 50:111.

1942m. Early Cenozoic mammals of South America. Proc. 8th Amer. Sci. Cong., 4:303-332.

1942n. The first natural history museum in America. Science, 96:261-263.

1942o. The beginnings of vertebrate paleontology in North America. Proc. Amer. Philos. Soc., 86:130-188.

1942p. [With Anne Roe.] A standard frequency distribution method. Amer. Mus. Novitates, No. 1190:1-19.

1942q. [Review of: Hadrosaurian Dinosaurs of North America, by R. S. Lull and N. E. Wright.] Amer. J. Sci., 240:823-825.

1942r. A Miocene tortoise from Patagonia. Amer. Mus. Novitates, No. 1209:1-6.

1943a. The discovery of fossil vertebrates in North America. J. Paleont., 17(1):26-38.

1943b. Mammals and the nature of continents. Amer. J. Sci., 241:1-31.

1943c. Criteria for genera, species, and subspecies in zoology and paleozoology. Ann. N. Y. Acad. Sci., 44(2):145-178.

1943d. Turtles and the origin of the fauna of Latin America. Amer. J. Sci., 241(7):413-429.

1943e. Notes on the mammal-bearing Tertiary of South America. Proc. Amer. Philos. Soc., 86(3):403-404.

1943f. Relationships of the orders of mammals, by William Diller Matthew (edited and annotated by George Gaylord Simpson). J. Mammal., 24(3):304-311.

1943g. Una tortuga del terciario de Venezuela. Rev. Fomento, Venezuela, año 5, nos. 51-52:53-64.

1944a. Osborn, Henry Fairfield. In Dictionary of American biography. Vol. 21, Suppl. 1:584-587. New York, Charles Scribner's Sons.

1944b. A Carib (Kamarakoto) myth from Venezuela. J. Amer. Folklore, 57:263-279.

1944c. [Review of: I went to the Soviet Arctic, by Ruth Gruber. Revised edition.] Natural History, 53(9):389, 427.

1944d. Sir Arthur Smith Woodward. Amer. J. Sci., 242:686-688.

1944e. Tempo and Mode in Evolution. New York, Columbia University Press, 237 pp. [Reprint, New York, Hafner Publishing Co., 1966. Translations: French, 1950a; German, 1951g.]

1945a. [Review of: Thomas Jefferson and the Scientific Trends of His Time, by Charles A. Browne.] Natural History, 54(1):46.
1945b. Notes on Graphic biometic comparison of samples. Amer. Naturalist, 79:95-96.
1945c. [Review of: The World and Man as Science Sees Them, edited by Forest Ray Moulton.] Natural History, 54(3):142-143.
1945d. Comparative scientific strength of universities. Science, 101:506-507.
1945e. Symposium on age of the distribution pattern of the gene arrangements in *Drosophila pseudoobscura*. [3.] Evidence from fossils and from the application of evolutionary rate distributions. Lloydia, 8(2):103-108.
1945f. [Review of: Mammals of the Pacific World, by T. D. Carter, J. E. Hill, and G. H. H. Tate.] Natural History, 54(7):296-297.
1945g. A Deseado hegetothere from Patagonia. Amer. J. Sci., 243:550-564.
1945h. The principles of classification and a classification of mammals. Bull. Amer. Mus. Nat. Hist., 85:i-xvi, 1-350.
1945i. Notes on Pleistocene and Recent tapirs. Bull. Amer. Mus. Nat. Hist., 86(2):33-82.
1945j. [Review of: Mainsprings of civilization, by Ellsworth H. Huntington.] Amer. J. Sci., 243(11):637-641.
1945k. Neotypes. Amer. J. Sci., 243(12):680-694.
1946a. The Duchesnean fauna and the Eocene-Oligocene boundary. Amer. J. Sci., 244(1):52-57.
1946b. [Review of: Vertebrate paleontology, by Alfred S. Romer.] Amer. J. Sci., 244(1):61-63.
1946c. Vertebrate paleontology at Columbia. News Bull. Soc. Vert. Paleont., No. 16:2-3.
1946d. Charles W. Gilmore. News Bull. Soc. Vert. Paleont., No. 16:18-20.
1946e. Tempo and mode in evolution. Trans. N. Y. Acad. Sci., (2)8(2):45-60.
1946f. [Review of: Vertebrate Paleontology, by Alfred S. Romer.] Quart. Rev. Biol., 21(1):78.
1946g. [Review of: The Mammalia of the Duchesne River Oligocene, by William B. Scott.] Quart. Rev. Biol., 21(1):79.
1946h. Amblypoda. The Encyclopaedia Britannica, 1946 edition, 1:740.
1946i. Ancylopoda or Chalicotherioidea. *Ibid.*, 1:893.
1946j. *Anthracotherium. Ibid.*, 2:39.
1946k. *Arsinoitherium. Ibid.*, 2:439.
1946l. *Dinotherium (Deinotherium). Ibid.*, 7:391.
1946m. *Dryopithecus. Ibid.*, 7:690.
1946n. *Eohippus. Ibid.*, 8:634.
1946o. Ganodonta, or Taeniodonta. *Ibid.*, 10:17-18.
1946p. *Hipparion. Ibid.*, 11:583.
1946q. *Mastodon. Ibid.*, 15:42:43.
1946r. Oreodont. *Ibid.*, 16:890.
1946s. *Silvatherium. Ibid.*, 20:724.
1946t. Tillodontia. *Ibid.*, 22:215-216. [Revision of 1929j.]
1946u. Titanothere. *Ibid.*, 22:252.
1946v. Toxodontia. *Ibid.*, 22:337.
1946w. Edward Wilber Berry. Year Book Amer. Philos. Soc. for 1945:346-349.
1946x. *Palaeogale* and allied early mustelids. Amer. Mus. Novitates, No. 1320:1-14.
1946y. Tertiary land bridges. Trans. N. Y. Acad. Sci., (2)8(8):255-258.
1946z. Bones in the brewery. Natural History, 55(6):252-259. [Reprinted, Bull. Nat. Speleol. Soc., 12:18-25(1950).]
1946aa. Fossil penguins. Bull. Amer. Mus. Nat. Hist., 87(1):1-100. [Publications of the Scarritt Expeditions, No. 33.]
1946bb. [Reply to letter on evolution and religion.] Natural History, 55(7):342-343. [Reprinted *In* Ways of Mammals in Fact and Fancy, by Clifford B. Moore, pp. 194-197. New York, The Ronald Press Co.]
1946cc. [Discussion of the occurrence of *Sebecus icaeorhinus*.] *In Sebecus*, representative of a peculiar suborder of fossil Crocodilia from Patagonia, by Edwin Harris Colbert. Bull. Amer. Mus. Nat. Hist., 87(4):224.

1946dd. [Reply to letter regarding pigs and peccaries.] Natural History, 55(10):441.

1946ee. [With Otto Haas.] Analysis of some phylogenetic terms, with attempts at redefinition. Proc. Amer. Philos. Soc., 90(5):319-349.

1947a. [Review of: The Mammals of Michigan, by William H. Burt.] Natural History, 56(1):6.

1947b. Litopterna. The Encyclopaedia Britannica, 1947 edition, 14:218-219.

1947c. Multituberculata. The Encyclopaedia Britannica, 1947 edition, 15:953. [Revision of 1929i.]

1946d. [Review of: Charles Darwin and the Voyage of the Beagle, edited by Lady Nora Barlow.] Natural History, 56(3):101.

1947e. The problem of plan and purpose in nature. Sci. Monthly, 64(6):481-495.

1947f. Holarctic mammalian faunas and continental relationships during the Cenozoic. Bull. Geol. Soc. Amer., 58:613-688.

1947g. A new Eocene marsupial from Brazil. Amer. Mus. Novitates, No. 1357:1-7. [Portuguese version, 1948k.]

1947h. Note on the measurement of variability and on relative variability of teeth of fossil mammals. Amer. J. Sci., 245(8):522-525.

1947i. A continental Tertiary time chart. J. Paleont., 21(5):480-483.

1947j. Haramiya, new name, replacing Microcleptes Simpson, 1928. J. Paleont., 21(5):497.

1947k. Paris conference on paleontology and evolution. News Bull. Soc. Vert. Paleont., No. 21:1-2.

1947l. [Review of: A Yanqui in Patagonia, by Bailey Willis.] Natural History, 56(8):341-342.

1947m. Evolution, interchange, resemblance of the North American and Eurasian Cenozoic mammalian faunas. Evolution, 1(3):218-220.

1947n. A Miocene glyptodont from Venezuela. Amer. Mus. Novitates, No. 1368: 1-10. [cf. 1955a.]

1947o. [A contribution from E. C. Cope.] In News Bull. Soc. Vert. Paleont., No. 22:31-32. [Misprint: for "E. C. Cope" read "E. D. Cope."]

1948a. William Berryman Scott. Amer. J. Sci., 246(1):53-54.

1948b. [Review of: The Horse of the Desert, by William Robinson Brown.] Natural History, 57(2):54, 94.

1948c. A fossil-collecting campaign in New Mexico. Science, 107:207-212.

1948d. Menatotherium, Eocene mammal from France. Amer. J. Sci., 246(3):165-170.

1948e. The Eocene of the San Juan Basin, New Mexico. Amer. J. Sci., 246(5):257-282; 246(6):363-385.

1948f. William Berryman Scott (1858-1947). Year Book Amer. Philos. Soc. for 1947: 295-300.

1948g. Biographical memoir of William Berryman Scott 1858-1947. Biogr. Mem. Nat. Acad. Sci. U.S.A., 25, Mem. 7:175-203.

1948h. [Review of: Evolution of the Horse Brain, by Tilly Edinger.] Quart. Rev. Biol., 23(2):144-145.

1948i. The Beginning of the Age of Mammals in South America. Part 1. Bull. Amer. Mus. Nat. Hist., 91(1):1-232. [Part 2, 1967h.]

1948j. Como Bluff. Guidebook 3rd Ann. Field Confer. Soc. Vert. Paleont. in southeastern Wyoming, Univ. Wyoming, August 1948, pp. 27-36.

1948k. Um novo marsupial do Eocene no Brasil. Notos Prelim. Estudos, Div. Geol. Min., Minist. Agr., Rio de Janeiro, No. 44:1-10. [Portuguese version of 1947g.]

1949a. A fossil deposit in a cave in St. Louis. Amer. Mus. Novitates, No. 1408:1-46.

1949b. Rates of evolution in animals. In Genetics, Paleontology, and Evolution, edited by Glenn L. Jepsen, George Gaylord Simpson, and Ernst Mayr, pp. 205-228. Princeton, New Jersey, Princeton University Press. [Paperback ed., New York, Athen.]

1949c. Essay-review of recent works on evolutionary theory by Rensch, Zimmerman, and Schindewolf. Evolution, 3(2):178-184.

1949d. Continents in the Age of Mammals. Tulsa Geol. Soc. Digest, 17:58-65.

1949e. The Meaning of Evolution. A Study of the History of Life and of Its Significance for Man. New Haven, and London, Yale University Press, xv+364 pp. (paperback ed., 1960).

[British ed., London, Geoffrey Cumberlege, Oxford University Press, 1950. Indian ed., Calcutta, 1965. Revised eds., 1951h, 1967f. Translations: French, 1952j; Italian, 1954i; Persian, 1959n; Danish, 1962j; Dutch, 1962k; Spanish, 1962l; Japanese, 1962m; Portuguese, 1963j; Finnish, 1963m. Shorter version, 1951h. Revised ed., 1971a.]

1949f. [Review of: Historical Geology, by Carl O. Dunbar.] Natural History, 58(8):342.

1949g. [Review of: History of the Primates: an Introduction to the Study of Fossil Man, by W. E. Le Gros Clark.] Science, 110:455-456.

1949h. [With José Luis Minoprio.] A new adianthine litoptern and associated mammals from a Deseadan faunule in Mendoza, Argentina. Amer. Mus. Novitates, No. 1434:1-27. [Cf. 1950n.]

1948i. Periodicity in vertebrate evolution. [Abstract.] Bull. Geol. Soc. Amer., 60, no. 12, pt. 2:1919-1920.

1949j. [Review of: Factors of Evolution, by I. I. Schmalhausen.] J. Hered., 40(12):322-324.

1950a. Rythme et Modalités de l'Evolution. [Translation of 1944e by Pierre de Saint-Seine.] Paris, Editions Albin Michel, 354 pp.

1950b. [Excerpt from letter on the status of the name Neohippus Abel.] In Hoffstetter, R. Algunos observaciones sobre los caballos fósiles de la América del sur Amerhippus gen nov. Bol. Inf. Cienc. Nac. (Quito, Ecuador), 3(26 and 27):449-451.

1950c. [Review of: The Nature of Natural History, by Marston Bates.] Saturday Rev. Literature, April 8, 1950:27.

1950d. [Review of: Death of a Science in Russia, edited by Conway Zirkle.] Natural History, 59(4):186.

1950e. New comprehension, power, guidance. Natural History, 59(4):148.

1950f. Evolution up to date. A review. [Review of Natural Selection and Adaptation, by H. J. Muller, Sewall Wright, Glenn L. Jepsen, G. Ledyard Stebbins, and Ernst Mayr.] J. Hered. 41(4):110-112.

1950g. [Review of: Science and the Moral Life, by Max Otto.] Amer. J. Sci., 248(5):364-367.

1950h. [Review of: The Nature of Natural History, by Marston Bates.] Natural History, 59(5):199.

1950i. Cenozoic formations and vertebrate faunas. Guidebook 4th Ann. Field Confer. Soc. Vert. Paleont. in northwestern New Mexico. Amer. Mus. Nat. Hist., and Univ. New Mexico, May 1950:74-85. [Cf. 1950j.]

1950j. Lower Tertiary formations and vertebrate faunas of the San Juan Basin. Guidebook New Mexico Geological Society, 1st Field Conference in San Juan Basin, New Mexico, November 1950:85-89. [Modified from 1950i.]

1950k. A synopsis of three lectures on evolution and the history of life. Bull. Wagner Free Inst. Sci., 25(2):5-12.

1950l. [Review of: Natural Regions of the U.S.S.R., by L. S. Berg.] Natural History, 59(6):244-245.

1950m. Note on the supposed discovery of Eocene fossils in New Mexico in 1867 or earlier. News Bull. Soc. Vert. Paleont., No. 29:5-6.

1950n. [With José Luis Minoprio.]Fauna del deseadense en Mendoza. An. Soc. Cient. Argentina, 149(6):245-253. [Based on 1949h, but with omissions, emendations, and additions.]

1950o. History of the fauna of Latin America. Amer. Scientist, 38(3):361-389. [Reprinted in Science in Progress, 7th Ser., New Haven, Yale University Press, 1951. Reprinted in Ehrlich, P. R., R. W. Holm, and P. H. Raven, eds.: Papers on Evolution, pp. 333-361.]

1950p. Trends in research and the Journal of Paleontology. Jour. Paleont., vol. 24, no. 4, July 1950, pp. 498-499.

1950q. Are nonflying wings functionless? Science, vol. 112, no. 2908, Sept. 22, 1950, p. 342.

1950r. Evolutionary determinism and the fossil record. The Sci. Monthly, vol. 71, no. 4, October 1950, pp. 262-267.

1950s. [Review of: Lehrbuch der Paläozoologie, by Oskar Kuhn.] Amer. J. Sci., 248(10):749-750.

1950t. The meaning of Darwin. *In* Charles Darwin's Autobiography, edited by Sir Francis Darwin. New York, Henry Schuman, pp. 1-11.
1950u. Organic evolution. Collier's Encyclopedia, 1950 edition, 7:510-516.
1950v. [Review of: Earth Movements and Organic Evolution. Proc. 18. Geol. Cong., Great Britain, 1948 . . .] Amer. J. Sci., 248(11):825.
1950w. Acquired characters. Chambers's Encyclopaedia, 1950 edition, 1:51-52.
1950x. Evolution. Chamber's Encyclopaedia, 1950 edition, 5:493-501.
1950y. Orthogenesis. Chamber's Encyclopaedia, 1950 edition, 10:252.
1950z. Species. Chamber's Encyclopaedia, 1950 edition, 13:65-66.
1950aa. [Two short comments on zoning of the Pleistocene and age of a fauna from Texas, *in* The Vertebrate Fauna and Geologic Age of Trinity River Terraces in Henderson County, Texas, by J. W. Stovall and W. N. McAnulty.] Amer. Midland Naturalist, 44(1):242-243.
1950bb. [Four short articles *in* Paléontologie et Transformisme, by C. Arambourg, L. Cuénot, P.-P. Grassé, J. B. S. Haldane, J. Piveteau, G. G. Simpson, E. A. Steniö, P. Teilhard de Chardin, H. V. Vallois, J. Viret, and D. M. S. Watson. Paris, Albin Michel. Also published in Paris, 1950, by the Centre National de la Recherche Scientifique as Colloques Internationaux, XXI, Paléontologie (Paris, Avril 1947).](1) [Remarks on phenomena and causes of extinction.] Pp. 116-118. (2) L'orthogenese et la théorie synthétique de l'evolution. Pp. 123-163. (3) [Remarks on orthogenesis.] Pp. 178-179. (4) Remarques sur la micro-évolution, la macro-evolution et al méga-evolution. Pp. 225-231.
1951a. [Review of: The Life of Vertebrates, by J. Z. Young.] Science, 113:454-455.
1951b. Hayden, Cope, and the Eocene of New Mexico. Proc. Acad. Nat. Sci. Philadelphia, 103:1-21.
1951c. [Review of: Genesis and Geology. A Study of the Relationships of Scientific Thought, Natural Theology, and Social Opinion in Great Britain, 1790-1850, by Charles Coulston Gillispie.] Natural History, 60(5):197.
1951d. [Review of: The Nature of the Universe, by Fred Hoyle.] Natural History, 60(5):199.
1951e. Some principles of historical biology bearing on human origins. Sympos. Quant. Biol., 15:55-66.
1951f. Horses. The Story of the Horse Family in the Modern World and through Sixty Million Years of History. New York, Oxford University Press, xvi + 247 pp.
1951g. Zeitmasse und Ablaufformen der Evolution. Gottingen, "Musterschmidt," Wissenschaftlicher Verlag, 1951. xi + 331 pp. [German version of 1944e, translated by Gerhard Heberer with new forewords by translator and by author.]
1951h. The Meaning of Evolution. [A specially revised and abridged edition of 1949e.] New York, The New American Library. 192 pp. [German translation, 1957h.]
1951i. American Cretaceous insectivores. Amer. Mus. Novitates, No. 1541:1-19.
1951j. The species concept. Evolution, 5(4):285-298.
1951k. [Review of: Times Arrow and Evolution, by H. F. Blum; and Fall of the Sparrow, by Jay Williams.] The Yale Review, 41(1):275-277.
1952a. For and against uniform endings in zoological nomenclature. System. Zool. 1(1):20-23.
1952b. [Review of: Checklist of Palaearctic and Indian Mammals, by J. R. Ellerman and T. C. S. Morrison-Scott.] Science, 115:431-432.
1952c. Periodicity in vertebrate evolution. *In* Distribution of Evolutionary Explosions in Geologic Time. A Symposium. J. Paleont., 26(3):359-370.
1952d. Evolutionary genetics. [Review of Genetics and the Origin of Species, By Theodosius Dobzhansky.] Evolution, 6(2):246-247.
1952e. Chester Stock (1892-1950). Biogr. Mem. Nat. Acad. Sci., 27(14):335-362.
1952f. Probabilities of dispersal in geologic time. *In* The Problem of Land Connections across the South Atlantic with Special Reference to the Mesozoic. A Symposium. Bull. Amer. Mus. Nat. Hist., 99(3):163-176.
1952g. Notes on British hyracotheres. J. Linnean Soc. London (Zool.), 42:195-206.
1952h. [Review of: A Land, by Jacquetta Hawkes.] Natural History, 61(7):292.

1952i. [Review of: Der Zeitfaktor in Geologie und Paláontologie, by Otto H. Schindewolf.] Amer. J. Sci. 250(9):698-699.

1952j. L'Evolution etsa Signification. [Translation of 1949e by A. Ungar-Levillain and F. Bourlière.] Paris, Payot, 304 pp.

1952k.How many species? Evolution, 1(3):342.

1952l. [Review of: Grundfragen der Paläontologie, and of Der Zeitfaktor in Geologie und Paläontologie, by Otto H. Schindewolf.] Quart. Rev. Biol. 27(4):388-389.

1953a. Otto Falkenbach (1878-1952). News Bull. Soc. Vert. Paleont., No. 37:31-32.

1953b. Acceptance by George Gaylord Simpson [to citation by Glenn L. Jepsen on presentation of Penrose Medal to George Gaylord Simpson]. News Bull. Soc. Vert. Paleont., No. 37:8. [Cf. 1953h.]

1953c. [Review of: Révision de la Faune des Mammifère Oligocènes d'Auvergne et du Velay, by R. Lavocat.] Amer. J. Sci., 251(3):241.

1953d. Life of the Past. An Introduction to Paleontology. New Haven and London, Yale University Press, and Geoffrey Cumberlege, Oxford University Press, xii + 198 pp. [Paperback ed., New Haven, Yale University Press, 1961. Spanish translation, 1967i. Cf. 1968f.]

1953e. Nomen nuda. Saturday Review, 36:23.

1953f. [Review of: Evolution in Action, by Julian Huxley.] Natural History 62(6):244.

1953g. The Baldwin effect. Evolution, 7(2):115-117.

1953h. Response by George Gaylord Simpson [to citation by Glenn L. Jepsen on presentation of Penrose Medal to George Gaylord Simpson.] Proc. Vol. Geol. Soc. Amer., Ann. Report for 1952: pp. 52-53. [Cf. 1953b.]

1953i. Letter to editor [regarding Jefferson-Goforth correspondence.] News Bull. Soc. Vert. Paleont., No. 38:21.

1953j. [Review of: Methods and Principles of Systematic Zoology, by Ernst Mayr, E. Gorton Linsley, and Robert L. Usinger.] Science 118:117-118.

1953k. [Comments, in Symposium: Do We Need More Becoming Words?] Amer. Anthropol. 55(3):399-400.

1953l. How much do fossils tell? Science Digest, 34(3):75-78. [Condensed from a chapter of 1953d.]

1953m. [Review of: Explorations in Science, by Waldemar Kaempffert.] Sci. Monthly, 77(4):214-215.

1953n. [Review of: Man, Time, and Fossils, by Ruth Moore.] The New York Herald Tribune Book Review, November 8, 1953:6.

1953o. Modern concepts in evolution. The Teaching Scientist, 10(2):2-3.

1953p. The Major Features of Evolution. New York, Columbia University Press, xx + 434 pp. [Paperback ed., New York, Simon and Schuster (Clarion Books), 1960.]

1953q. [Review of: Man, Time, and Fossils, by Ruth Moore.] Natural History, 62(10):437.

1953r. Evolution and Geography. An essay on historical biogeography with special reference to mammals. Condon Lectures, Oregon State System of Higher Education, Eugene, Oregon, December 1953, pp. 1-63.

1953s. Horses and evolution. Report of the Brisbane meeting of the Australian and New Zealand Association for the Advancement of Science, 28:160-165.

1954a. [Review of: Historical Aspects of Organic Evolution, by Philip G. Fothergill.] Natural History, 63(1):6.

1954b. An apatemyid from the early Eocene of New Mexico. Amer. Mus. Novitates, No. 1654:1-4.

1954c. [Review of: A List of the Names Proposed for Genera and Subgenera of Recent Mammals from the Publication of T. S. Palmer's Index Genera Mammalium 1904 to end of 1951, by L. R. Conisbee.] Science, 119:134.

1954d. [Review of: Science in Progress. Eighth Series, edited by George A. Baitsell.] Natural History, 63(2):52.

1954e. [Review of: Triassic Life of the Connecticut Valley (Revised), by Richard Swann Lull.] Amer. J. Sci., 252(2):122-123.

1954f. Ermine Cowles Case (1871-1953). Year Book Amer. Philos. Soc. for 1953:329-333.

1954g. The rediscovery of Peale's mastodon. Proc. Amer. Philos. Soc., 98(4):279-281.

1954h. Tendances actuelles de la systématique des mammifères. Mammalia (Paris), 18(4):337-357.
1954i. Il Significato dell'Evoluzione. [Translation of 1949e by Brauna del Bianco.] Milano, Valentino Bompiani & C., 462 pp.
1954j. Origens e desenvolvimento dos mamíferos sulamericanos. An. Acad. Brasileira Ciênc. 26(nos. 3 and 4):xxxii and xxxiii.
1955a. Un glyptodonte del Mioceno de Venezuela. Bol. Geol. (Venezuela),3(8):95-107. [Slightly revised Spanish translation of 1947n.]
1955b. The Phenacolemuridae, new family of early primates. Bull. Amer. Mus. Nat. Hist., 105(5):411-442.
1955c. [With Carlos de Paula Couto.] Os Mastodontes do Brasil (The Mastodonts of Brazil). Bol. Inst. Brasileiro Bibliog. Document; Rio de Janeiro, No. 2:1-20. [Cf. 1957b.]
1955d. [Review of: The Origin of Vertebrates, by N. J. Berrill.] Science, 122:1144.
1955e. [Review of: An Outline of Biometry, by C. W. Bliss, and D. M. Calhoun.] Amer. Scientist, 43(1):153.
1956a. Zoogeography of West Indian Land Mammals. Amer. Mus. Novitates, No. 1749:1-28.
1956b. [Review of: Die Evolution der Organismen. Ergebnisse und Probleme der Abstammungslehre. 2nd ed. Parts 1-4. Edited by Gerhard Heberer.] Quart. Rev. Biol., 31(1):44-45.
1956c. [Review of: Evolution, Genetics, and Man, by Theodosius Dobzhansky, and of Genetics in the Atomic Age, by C. Auerbach.] Natural History, 65(6):284-285.
1956d. [Review of: The Story of Our Earth, by Richard Carrington.] Natural History, 65(6):286.
1956e. [Review of: Some Extinct Elephants, Their Relatives and the Two Living Species, by P. E. P. Deraniyagala.] Science, 124:185-186.
1956f. Symposium on evolution held in Spain. Evolution, 10(3):333-334.
1957a. [Review of: Evolution: The Ages and Tomorrow, by G. Murray McKinley.] Ann. Amer. Acad. Polit. Soc. Sci., 309:182-183.
1957b. [With Carlos de Paula Couto.] The mastodonts of Brazil. Bull. Amer. Mus. Nat. Hist., 112(2):125-190. [Cf. 1955c.]
1957c. [Review of: The Dentition of the Australopithecinae, by J. T. Robinson.] Science, 125:817.
1957d. Australian fossil penguins, with remarks on penguin evolution and distribution. Rec. South Australian Mus., 13(1):51-70.
1957e. [With C. S. Pittendrigh and L. H. Tiffany.] Life: An Introduction to Biology. New York, Harcourt Brace & Co., 845 pp. [2d ed., 1965g.]
1957f. [Review of: Modern Science and the Nature of Life, by William S. Beck.] Natural History, 66(6):286-287.
1957g. [Review of: The Species Concept in Palaeontology. Systematics Association publication No. 2: A symposium. P. C. Sylvester-Bradley, ed.] Science, 125:1151.
1957h. Auf Den Spuren Des Lebens. [Translation of abridged ed. of The Meaning of Evolution, 1951h, by Wolgang and Hildegard Laskowski.] Berlin-Dahlem, Colloquium Verlag Otto H. Hess, 224 pp.
1957i. [Review of: The Liassic Therapsid Oligokyphus, by Walter Georg Kühne.]Science, 126:1250.
1957j. A new Casamayor astrapothere. Rev. Mus. Munic. Cienc. Nat. Tradic. Mar del Plata, Argentina, 1(3):11-18.
1958a. [Review of: The Species Problem, Ernst Mayr, ed.] Science, 127:245.
1958b. How the animals got to where we now find them. [Review of: Zoogeography: the Geographical Distribution of Animals, by Philip J. Darlington, Jr.] Natural History, 67(3):116-119, 166-168.
1958c. [Various short passages in:] Concepts of Biology. A symposium edited by R. W. Gerard. Behav. Sci. 3(2):89-215. [Repr., National Academy of Sciences, National Research Council, Publ. 560. Washington, D. C.]
1958d. Geography of land and freshwater vertebrates. [Reveiw of Zoogeography: the Geographical Distribution of Animals, by Philip J. Darlington, Jr.] Ecology, 39(2):379-380.

1958e. Science by jury. [Review of Six Days or Forever, by Ray Ginger.] The Nation, 186(19):420-421.
1958f. [Review of: The Story of Life, by H. E. L. Mellersh.] Science, 127:1235.
1958g. Memorial to Richard Swann Lull (1867-1957). Proc. Vol. Geol. Soc. Amer., Annual Report for 1957:127-134.
1958h. [Review of: Die Evolution der Organismen. Ergebnisse und Probleme der Abstammungslehre. 2nd Ed. Part 5. Edited by Gerhard Heberer.] Quart. Rev. Biol., 33(2):148-149.
1958i. Man, Still the Unknown. [Review of: In Search of Man, by André Missenard.] Contemporary Psychology, 3(6):155-156.
1958j. [Review of: Morphological Integration, by Everett C. Olson and Robert L. Miller.] Science, 128:138.
1958k. Charles Darwin in search of himself. [Review of: The Autobiography of Charles Darwin, 1809-1882, with Original Omissions Restored. Edited by Lady Nora Barlow.] Sci. Amer., 199(2):117-122.
1958l. [With Anne Roe, coeditors.] Behavior and Evolution. New Haven, Yale University Press, 557 pp.
1958m. The Study of Evolution: Methods and Present Status of Theory. In 1958l, pp. 7-26.
1958n. Behavior and Evolution. In 1958l, pp. 507-535.
1958o. [Review of: The Genetic Basis of Selection, by I. Michael Lerner.] J. Hered., 49(6).
1959a. Letter to editor [on teleology.] Science, 129:672-674.
1959b. Letter to editor [on fossil collecting]. Sci. Amer., 200(4)180-182.
1959c. [Foreword (pp. 5-6). Appendix: note on biometry and systematics (pp. 51-54.] In Matthew W. D., and C. de Paula Couto, The Cuban Edentates. Bull. Amer. Mus. Nat. Hist., 117(1).
1959d. Anatomy and morphology: classification and evolution: 1859 and 1959. Proc. Amer. Philos. Soc., 103(2):286-306.
1959e. [With E. Rabinowitch, R. J. Dubos, H. J. Muller, and J. Huxley.] The Scientists Speak: Biology. New York, Harcourt, Brace & Co. [A phonograph record, HB-SS-1, and accompanying printed students' guide. On the record, the opening and closing talks and the introductions to the four other speakers are by G. G. S. In the printed guide, pp. 6-7 and 25 are by G. G. S.]
1959f. [Foreword to: The Life and Letters of Charles Darwin, pp. v-xvi] New York, Basic Books. 2 vols.
1959g. [Review of: The Mammals of North America, by E. Raymond Hall and Keith R. Nelson.] Science, 129:1353-1354.
1959h. Soricidae? and Primates. In The geology and paleontology of the Elk Mountain and Tabernacle Butte area, Wyoming, by Paul O. McGrew. Bull. Amer. Nat. Hist., 117(3):151-157.
1959i. A new middle Eocene edentate from Wyoming. Amer. Mus. Novitates, No. 1950:1-8.
1959j. [With Malcolm C. McKenna.] A new insectivore from the middle Eocene of Tabernacle Butte, Wyoming. Amer. Mus. Novitates, No. 1952:1-12.
1959k. Mesozoic mammals and the polyphyletic origin of mammals. Evolution, 13(3):405-414.
1959l. [Review of: Traité de Paléontologie, Tome VI, Mammifères, Evolution. Vol. II, edited by Jean Piveteau.] Quart. Rev. Biol., 34(2):149-150.
1959m. A new fossil penguin from Australia. Proc. Roy. Soc. Victoria, 71(2):113-119.
1959n. [Translation into Persian of The Meaning of Evolution (1949e).] Published by Ibn Sina.
1959o. Fossil mammals from the type area of the Puerco and Nacimiento strata, Paleocene of New Mexico. Amer. Mus. Novitates, No. 1957:1-22.
1959p. Two new records from the Bridger middle Eocene of Tabernacle Butte, Wyoming. Amer. Mus. Novitates, No. 1966:1-5.
1959q. [Review of: Just before Darwin: Robert Chambers and "Vestiges," by Milton Millhauser.] Science, 130:158.
1959r. Creatures extinct, living or fictional. [Review of: On the Track of Unknown Animals, by Bernard Heuvelmans.] Natural History, 68(9):492-494, 544-546.

1959s. Before Columbus came. [Review of: No Stone Unturned: An Almanac of North American Prehistory, by Louis A. Brennan.] The New York Times Book Review, 8 Nov.: p. 30.

1959t. [Review of: From Galaxies to Man, by John Pfeiffer.] Science, 130:1105.

1959u. The nature and origin of supraspecific taxa. Sympo. Quant. Biol., 24:225-271.

1959v. Darwin led us. The Humanist, No. 5:267-275.

1959w. [Review of: Hystricomorph rodents from the late Miocene of Colombia, South America, by Robert W. Fields.] Quart. Rev. Biol., 34(4):305-306.

1960a. [with Anne Roe and Richard Lewontin.] Quantitative Zoology, revised edition. New York, Harcourt, Brace and Co., vii + 440 pp. [Revision of 1939e.]

1960b. [Review of: The Phenomenon of Man, by Pierre Teilhard de Chardin.] Sci. Amer. 202(4):201-207.

1960c. The world into which Darwin led us. Science, 131:966-974.

1960d. Notes on the measurement of faunal resemblance. Amer. J. Sci., 258-A (Bradley Volume):300-311.

1960e. [Review of: The Antecedents of Man, by W. E. Le Gros Clark.] Science, 131:1208-1209.

1960f. Man among the primates. [Review of The Antecedents of Man, by Sir Wilfrid E. Le Gros Clark.] Nature (London), 186:665.

1960g. The history of life. In The Evolution of Life. Vol. 1. of Evolution after Darwin, Sol Tax, ed. pp. 117-180. The University of Chicago Centennial, Chicago, University of Chicago Press.

1960h. [Letter to the editor on types and name-bearers.] Science, 131:684.

1960i. [Letter to the editor commenting on two letters to the editor of Science about "The World into which Darwin Led Us."] Science, 131:1822, 1824.

1960j. [Remarks on the Tiffany formation and the occurrence of Ignatiolambda barnesi.] In Simons, E. L., The Paleocene Pantodonta, Trans. Amer. Philos. Soc., (n.s.)50(6):67. [This is part of a manuscript on Ignatiolambda, left incomplete and otherwise unpublished to avoid duplication of effort.]

1960k. Diagnosis of the classes Reptilia and Mammalia. Evolution, 14(5):388-392.

1960l. [Various short passages, without separate titles.] In Issues in evolution. Vol. III of Evolution after Darwin, Sol Tax, ed., pp. 145-174. The University of Chicago Centennial. Chicago, University of Chicago Press.

1960m. Man's evolutionary future. Zool. Jahrbücher Syst., 88(1):125-134.

1960n. [Review of: Paléontologie Stratigraphique, and Atlas de Paléogéographie, by Henri Termier and Geneviève Termier.] Science, 132:1884-1885.

1960o. [Review of: Die Evolution der Organismen, edited by G. Heberer.] Quart. Rev. Biol., 35(4):331-332.

1961a. A recent study of the history and philosophy of modern science. [Review of The Edge of Objectivity, by Charles C. Gillispie.] Natural History, 70(1):5-7.

1961b. Principles of Animal Taxonomy. New York, Columbia University Press. xii + 247 pp.

1961c. Lamarck, Darwin and Butler. Three approaches to evolution. The American Scholar, 30(2)238-249.

1961d. A basic work on evolutionary theory. [Review of: Evolution above the Species Level, by Bernhard Rensch.] Evolution, 15(1):112-113.

1961e. [Review of: Evolution: Process and Product, by Edward O. Dodson.] Amer. Scientist, 49(1):94A-97A.

1961f. [Reviews of: The Wellsprings of Life, by Isaac Asimov; and The Long Road to Man, by Robert L. Lehrman.] Science, 133:1242-1243.

1961g. Roy Chapman Andrews (1884-1960). Amer. Philos. Soc., Yearbook 1960:106-108.

1961h. One hundred years without Darwin are enough. Teachers College Record, 62(8):617-626.

1961i. Some problems of vertebrate paleontology. Science, 133:1679-1689.

1961j. [Review of: The Orion Book of Evolution, by Jean Rostand.] Science, 133:1700.

1961k. [Comments on genetic evolution] and [Comments on Cultural Evolution.] *In* Evolution and Man's Progress. Daedalus, Summer 1961, issued as Proc. Amer. Acad. Arts Sci., 90(3):468-470; 518.

1961l. The supposed Pliocene Pebas beds of the upper Juruá River, Brazil. J. Paleont., 35(3):620-624.

1961m. Horses. New York, Anchor Books, Doubleday and Company, Inc. [Reprint of 1951f with new preface.] xxxvi + 323 pp.

1961n. La evolución de los mamíferos sudamericanos. Estudios Geológicos (Inst. Invest. Lucas Mallada), 17:49-58.

1961o. [Review of: A Classification of Living Animals, by Lord Rothschild.] Science, 134:1745.

1961p. Historical zoogeography of Australian mammals. Evolution, 15(4):431-446.

1961q. [Review of: Vertebrate Speciation. A University of Texas Symposium. W. Frank Blair, ed.] Quart. Rev. Biol., 36(4):286.

1962a. Some cosmic aspects of organic evolution. *In* Evolution and Hominisation. Contributions in honor of Gerhard Heberer on the occasion of his 60th birthday, edited by G. Kurth, pp. 6-20. Stuttgart, Gustav Fischer Verlag.

1962b. The status of the study of organisms. Amer. Scientist, 50(4):36-45.

1962c. Evolution's two components: biological and cultural. [Review of Mankind Evolving: The Evolution of the Human Species, by Theodosius Dobzhansky.] Science, 136:142-143.

1962d. Notes on the nature of science by a biologist. *In* Notes on the Nature of Science, pp. 7-12. New York, Harcourt, Brace & World.

1962e. [Foreword to: The Origin of Species, by Charles Darwin, pp. 5-9.] New York, Collier Books.

1962f. [Review of: A Synthesis of Evolutionary Theory, by Herbert H. Ross.] Science, 136:528.

1962g. Evolution of Mesozoic mammals. International Colloquium on the Evolution of Mammals, Brussels, Sept. 1960, part 1:57-95.

1962h. Biology and the nature of science. Lapham Hall Dedication Lectures, University of Wisconsin, Milwaukee, 17 February 1962 [unpaged].

1962i. The mammalian fauna of the Divisadero Largo formation, Mendoza, Argentina. [With José Luis Minoprio and Bryan Patterson.] Bull. Mus. Comp. Zool., 127(4): 239-293.

1962j. Evolutionen og Dens Perspektiver. [Danish translation of 1949e.] Copenhagen, Gyldendals Uglebger, 220 pp.

1962k. De Betekenis van de Evolutie. [Dutch translation of 1949e.] Antwerp and Utrecht, Aula-Boeken, 250 pp.

1962l. El Sentido de la Evolución. [Spanish translation of 1949e.] Buenos Aires, Editorial Universitaria de Buenos Aires, 319 pp.

1962m. The Meaning of Evolution. [Japanese translation of 1949e.] Tokyo, Yammamoto Shoten, 373 pp.

1962n. Genesis of cancer. Science, 137:460-462. [Discussion of inheritance of acquired characters; title supplied by editor is misleading.]

1962o. Genetic composition and cultural structure (a reply to Anthony Leeds). Science, 137:917-918.

1962p. The course of evolution. *In* White, J. F., ed., Study of the Earth, pp. 291-301. Englewood Cliffs, New Jersey, Prentice-Hall, Inc. [Extract from 1949e.]

1962q. Theories of evolution. *In* White, J. F., ed., Study of the Earth, pp. 301-309. Englewood Cliffs, New Jersey, Prentice-Hall, Inc. [Extract from 1953d.]

1962r. The study of evolution: methods and present status of theory. *In* Howells, W., ed., Ideas on Human Evolution, Selected Essays, 1949-1961. pp. 1-19. Cambridge, Massachusetts, Harvard University Press. [Extract from 1958l.]

1962s. Primate taxonomy and recent studies of nonhuman primates. Ann. New York Acad. Sci., 102(2):497-514.

1963a. Biology and the nature of science. Science, 139:81-88.

1963b. [Review of: Aus Jahrmillionen. Tiere der Vorzeit, by Arno Hermann Müller.] Science, 139:900.

1963c. [Review of: The Origin of Races, by Carleton S. Coon.] Perspect. Biol. Med., 6(2):268-272.
1963d. [Review of: Problèmes Actuels de Paléontologie, ed. by J.-P. Lehman.] Science, 139:1044.
1963e. [Review of: Anatomie et Biologie des Rhinogrades, by Harald Stümpke.] Science, 140:624-625.
1963f. [Letter to the editor in reply to letters to the editor on Science article, Biology and the nature of science.] Science, 140:762-766.
1963g. Notes on the names of some Argentine fossil mammals. Rev. Mus. Argentino Cienc. Nat. "Bernadino Rivadavia," Cienc. Zool., 8(2):15-26. [Dated 1962, probably issued in 1963.]
1963h. [Review of: Cerveaux d'Animaux Disparus, by Colette Deschaseaux.] Science, 140:798.
1963i. [Review of: Traité de Paléontologie: Mammiferès. Tome 6, Vol. 1, ed. by Jean Piveteau.] Quart. Rev. Biol., 38(1):82-83.
1963j. o Significado da Evolucão. [Portugese translation of 1949e.] São Paulo, Livraria Pioneira Editora, 355 pp.
1963k. Historical science. In The Fabric of Geology, ed. by C. C. Albritton, Jr., pp. 24-48. Reading, Mass., Palo Alto, and London, Addison-Wesley.
1963l. A new record of Euceratherium or Preptoceras (extinct Bovidae) in New Mexico. J. Mammal, 44(4):583-584.
1963m. Kehitys Luonto ja Ihminen. [Finnish translation of 1949e] Helsinki, Weilin & Goos, 184 pp.
1964a. Earth, air, fire, and water. [Review of: The Five Ages of Man, by Gerald Heard.] Saturday Revue, Feb. 29, 1964:36-37.
1964b. The nonprevalence of humanoids. Science, 143:769-775.
1964c. This View of Life: The World of an Evolutionist. New York, Harcourt, Brace & World, Inc., ix + 308 pp. [Paperback ed., 1966. Dutch translation, 1968n. Swedish version, 1970o.]
1964d. The meaning of taxonomic statements. In Classification and Human Evolution, ed. by S. L. Washburn. New York, Wenner-Gren Foundation, Viking Fund Publications in Anthropology, No. 37:1-31. [Dated 1963, issued in 1964. Reprint, 1966l.]
1964e. Barzun: The glorious entertainer. [Review of: Science: The Glorious Entertainment, by J. Barzun.] Science, 144:38-39.
1964f. Letter to the Editor [Space Flights and Biology.] Science, 144:246.
1964g. Agassiz: End of an Era. [Review of The Intelligence of Louis Agassiz, by G. Davenport.] The Humanist, 24(2):62.
1964h. Letter to the Editor [Life on Other Planets: Some exponential speculations]. Science, 144:614.
1964i. Numerical taxonomy and biological classification. [Review of: Principles of Numerical Taxonomy, by Sokal and Sneath.] Science, 144:712-713.
1964j. [Review of: Essays of a Humanist, by Julian Huxley.] The New York Times Book Review, May 24, 1964:10, 12.
1964k. Science v. the humanities. [Review of: The Role of Science in Civilization, by R. B. Lindsay; and: Science: The Glorious Entertainment, by J. Barzun.] Natural History, 73(6):4, 5.
1964l. [With Anne Roe.] The evolution of behavior. In The behavioral sciences today, Bernard Berelson, ed., pp. 89-100. New York, London, Basic Books, Inc. Also issued earlier as a separate by Voice of America, U. S. Information Agency, Washington, D. C., Behavioral Sci. Series 8:1-8; updated.
1964m. Alfred Russel Wallace. [Review of: Biologist Philosopher. A Study of the Life and Writing of Alfred Russel Wallace, by Wilma George.] Science, 144:1209-1210.
1964n. Species density of North American Recent mammals. System. Zool., 13(2):57-73.
1964o. Organisms and molecules in evolution. Science, 146:1535-1538. Also in Protides of the Biological Fluids, H. Peeters, ed. Sect. A. Phylogeny, pp. 29-35. Amsterdam, Elsevier Publishing Co.

1964p. Mammalian evolution on the southern continents. Synthesis and summing-up. Proc. 16th Int. Cong. Zool., 15, Specialized Symposia, pp. 63-65.

1965a. Zoology. *In* Listen to Leaders in Science, A. Love and J. S. Childers, eds., Chapter 10, pp. 121-139. Atlanta, Tupper & Love; New York, David McKay Co.

1965b. [Review of: Heredity and the Nature of Man, by Th. Dobzhansky.] Science, 147:392.

1965c. [Foreword to: Olduvai Gorge 1951-1961, Fauna and Background, by L. S. B. Leakey, pp. ix-x.] London, Cambridge University Press.

1965d. Description of *Galago senegalensis* E. Geoffroy, 1796. *In* Olduvai Gorge 1951-1961, Fauna and Background, by L. S. B. Leakey, pp. 15-16. London, Cambridge University Press.

1965e. Long abandoned views. [Letter to the Editor.] Science, 147:1397.

1965f. Paleontology: handbook of techniques. [Review of: Handbook of Paleontological Techniques, by B. Kummel and D. Raup, eds.] Science, 148:354.

1965g. [With William S. Beck.] Life: An Introduction to Biology. 2nd (revised) ed. New York, Harcourt, Brace & World, Inc., xviii + 869 pp. [1st ed., 1957e. Shorter ed., 1969a.]

1965h. Races in animal evolution. Int. Social Sci. J. (UNESCO) 17(1):139-141. Also as: Les races dans l'évolution animale, in French version of same issue, Rev. Int. Sci. Soc., 17(1):pp. 148-150.

1965i. Polytypism, monotypism and polymorphism. Int. Social Sci. J. (UNESCO), 17(1):142-144. Also as: Polytypisme, monotypisme et polymorphisme, in French version of the same issue, Rev. Int. Sci. Soc., 17(1):151-153.

1965j. Teilhard de Chardin Biography—The nomination of a saint? [Review of: Teilhard de Chardin, a Biographical Study, by Claude Cuénot.]New Haven Register, May 2, 1965.

1965k. The Geography of Evolution. Collected Essays. Philadelphia and New York, Chilton Books, x + 249 pp.

1965l. Attending Marvels. A Patagonian Journal. Modified reprint of 1934a, with new introduction by L. M. Gould. New York, Time Reading Program, Time Inc., xxv + 289 pp.

1965m. [Remarks.] *In* DeVore, P. L., ed., The Origin of Man, pp. 45-47, 51. transcript of a Symposium, distributed through *Current Anthropology* for the Wenner-Gren Foundation for Anthropological Research.]

1965n. [Review of: Phenetic and Phylogenetic Classification, edited by V. H. Heywood and J. McNeill.] Science, 148:1078.

1965o. A review of masterometry. Evolution, 19(2):249-255.

1965p. Los mamíferos casamayorenses de la colección Tournouër. Rev. Mus. Argentino Cienc. Nat. "Bernardino Rivadavia," Paleont., vol. 1 (1):1-21.

1965q. Biological sciences. *In* The Great Ideas Today 1965, pp. 286-319. Chicago, Encyclopedia Britannica, Inc.

1965r. The problem of problems. *In* The Mystery of Matter, edited by Louise B. Young, pp. 527-530. New York, Oxford University Press.

1965s. A fundamental treatise. [Review of: The Origin of Adaptations, by Verne Grant.] The American Scholar, 34(3):500-502.

1965t. Science and the culture of our time. The South Atlantic Quarterly, 64(4):478-495.

1965u. Réponse. [Unauthorized French translation of a reply to a questionnaire on evolution and religion; whole issue of journal titled "Teilhard et la Science."] Itinéraires Chroniques et Documents, No. 96:124-126.

1965v. End of an era in biology. [Review of: Ideas in Modern Biology," edited by John A. Moore.] Science, 150:1142-1143.

1965w. Note on the Fort Ternan beds of Kenya. Amer. J. Sci., 263(10):922.

1965x. [Introduction] *in* Logbook for Grace, by Robert Cushman Murphy, pp. xvii-xxi. New York, Time Reading Program, Time Inc.

1965y. New record of a fossil penguin in Australia. Proc. Roy. Soc. Victoria, 79(1):91-93.

1966a. Naturalistic ethics and the social sciences. Amer. Psychol. 21(1):27-36.

1966b. Ages of experimental animals. [Letter to the editor.] Science, 151:517.

1966c. Ages of experimental animals. [Letter to the editor.] Science, 152:16.

1966d. Creeping coeducation. [Letter to the editors.] Yale Alumni Magazine, Feb. 1966:7.

1966e. The biological nature of man. Science, 152:472-478. [Repr., Perspectives on Human Evolution, 1:1-17 (1968). Japanese transl., 1966m.]
1966f. Individual adaptation. [Review of: Man Adapting, by René Dubos.] Science, 152:1049.
1966g. [German version of Remarks on Father Teilhard, in Teilhard de Chardin, by J. Hemleben, pp. 166-167.] Hamburg, Rowoholt.
1966h. Mammalian evolution on the southern continents. N. Jahrb. Geol. Paläont. Abh., 125:1-18.
1966i. Organic evolution. [Review of: Processes of organic evolution, by G. Ledyard Stebbins.] Science, 152:1364.
1966j. The world into which Darwin led us. In Readings in anthropology, compiled by J. D. Jennings and E. A. Hoebel. New York, McGraw-Hill, pp. 6-13. [Modified reprint of 1960c.]
1966k. The nonprevalence of humanoids. In Extraterrestrial life: An Anthology and Bibliography, compiled by E. A. Shneour and E. A. Ottesen. Washington, NAS-NRS Pub. 1296A, pp. 269-281. [Reprint of 1964c.]
1966l. The meaning of taxonomic statements. Bobbs-Merrill Reprint Series in the Social Sciences, A-347:1-31. [Reprint of 1964d.]
1966m. The biological nature of man [Japanese transl. of 1966e.] Japan-America Forum, No. 12:45-63.
1966n. Good enough for Moses? [Review of: D-Days at Dayton: Reflections on the Scopes Trial, edited by Jerry R. Tomkins.] Nature (London), 210:5042.
1966o. Mammals around the Pacific. The Thomas Burke Memorial Lecture 1965. Memorial Washington State Museum, 1966.
1966p. Die Evolution des Pferdes. Naturwissenschaft und Medizin, No. 14, Jahrg. 3:349.
1966q. A scientific system of ethics. [Review of: Science and Ethical Values, by Bentley Glass.] The American Scholar, Autumn, 1966:782.
1966r. [Review of: The Act of Creation, by Arthur Koestler.] Isis, 57(1):187.
1966s. [Review of: The Nomenclature of the Hominidae, by Bernard G. Campbell.] Man, (n.s.)(1):4.
1966t. Interpretations of DNA. [Letter to the editor.] Science, 154:1120.
1967a. The crisis in biology. American Scholar, 36(3):363-377.
1967b. Biology and the public good. Amer. Scientist, 55(2):161-174.
1967c. Evolution. Merit Encyclopedia, 6:501-510.
1967d. The Tertiary lorisiform primates of Africa. Bull. Mus. Comp. Zool., 136(3):39-61.
1967e. The Ameghinos' localities for early Cenozoic mammals in Patagonia. Bull. Mus. Comp. Zool., 136(4):63-76.
1967f. The Meaning of Evolution. Revised edition. New Haven, Yale University Press, 364 pp. [Paperback. A completely revised, reset updating of 1949e. Hardbound issue, 1968.]
1967g. On science and scientists. [Review of: The Art of the Soluble, by P. B. Medawar.] Science, 158:246.
1967h. The beginning of the age of mammals in South America. Part 2. Systematics: Notoungulata, concluded (Typotheria, Hegetotheria, Toxodonta, Notoungulata incertae sedis); Astrapotheria, Trigonostylopoidea; Pyrotheria; Xenungulata; Mammalia incertae sedis. Bull. Amer. Mus. Nat. Hist., 137:1-259. [Pt. 1, 1948i.]
1967i. la Vida en el Pasado. Madrid, Alianza Editorial. [Spanish version of 1953d.]
1967j. Master and pupil. [Review of: Darwin and Henslow. The Growth of an Idea. Letters 1831-1860, edited by Nora Barlow.] Nature (London), 215:1417.
1967k. Readings in anthropology. [Review of: Human Evolution. Readings in Physical Anthropology, edited by Noel Korn and Fred W. Thompson, second edition.] Nature (London), 216:309.
1968a. African prehistory. [Review of: Background to Evolution in Africa, edited by W. W. Bishop and J. D. Clark.] Science, 159:182-183.
1968b. Vertebrate zoology. [Review of: Structure and Habit in Vertebrate Evolution, by G. S. Carter.] Science, 159:295.
1968c. What is man? [Review of: The Naked Ape, by Desmond Morris.] New York Times Book Review, Feb. 4, 1968:16-20.

1968d. A didelphid (Marsupialia) from the early Eocene of Colorado. Postilla (Peabody Mus. Nat. Hist.), No. 115:1-3.
1968e. The cochlea in multituberculates. System. Zool., 17:98.
1968f. Life of the Past. An Introduction to Paleontology. New York, Bantam Books, 194 pp. [A slightly modified paperback issue of 1953d.]
1968g. The scope and limits of biology. University of Denver Magazine, 5(3):21-25.
1968h. Recommended summer reading. American Scholar, Summer 1968:544, 546.
1968i. Premature citations of zoological nomina. Science, 161:75-76.
1968j. Some cosmic aspects of organic evolution. In Kurth, G. ed., Evolution und Hominisation, 2 ed., pp. 1-16. Stuttgart, Gustav Fischer Verlag. 1968, [Revised version of 1962a. German transl., 1968l.]
1968k. Evolutionary effects of cosmic radiation. Science, 162:140-141.
1968l. Kosmische Aspekte der organischen Evolution. Naturwiss. Rundschau, 21:425-434. [German translation of 1968j by Dr. Gertrud Mordhorst.]
1968m. Fossil mammals. In Moore, R. C., et al., Developments, Trends, and Outlooks in Paleontology, J. Paleont., 42:1375-1377.
1968n. Het Wereldbeeld van een Evolutionist. Utrecht & Antwerp, Aula-Boeken, 415 pp. [Dutch translation of This View of Life, 1964c.]
1969a. [With W. S. Beck.] Life. An Introduction to Biology. Shorter edition [of 1965g.] New York, Harcourt, Brace and World.
1969b. Biology and Man. New York, Harcourt, Brace & World. (Cf. 1970n.]
1969c. Organization. [Review of: The Art of Organic Forms, by P. C. Ritterbush.] Science, 164:683.
1969d. The present status of the theory of evolution. Proc. Roy. Soc. Victoria, 82(2):149-160.
1969e. South American Mammals. In Biogeography and Ecology in South America, E. J. Fittkau, J. Illies, H. Klinge, G. H. Schwalbe, and H. Sioli, editors, vol. 2, pp. 879-909. The Hague, Dr. W. Junk N. V. Publishers.
1969f. The Kamarakoto Indians. A Carib Tribe of Venezuelan Guayana. pp. i-ix, 1-335, in 3 vols. Human Relations Area Files (Yale Univ.). Reference: 5:Simpson, N-5, (1939) 1940. SS16 Pemon SS16 Kamarakoto. [This is a photocopy printing of the unpublished English original of 1940l,a Spanish translation. The present H.R.A.F. printing is not technically published, but its availability is noted.]
1969g. Aquatic chordates. [Review of: Fundamentals of Paleontology. vol. XI. Agnatha and Pisces, Y. A. Orlov and D. V. Obruchev, editors, English translation by Israel Program.] Earth Science Reviews, 5:A139-A140.
1969h. La Geographie de l'Evolution. Paris Masson, 204 pp. [Translation of 1965k.]
1969i. [With Anne Roe, eds.] Evolution und Verhalten. Frankfurt am Main, Suhrkamp.
1969j. Evolution: Methoden und derzeitigen Stand der Theorie. Ibid.:7-35.
1969k. Verhalten und Evolution. Ibid.; 212-253.
1969l. On the term brachydont. System. Zool., 18:456-458.
1969m. The first three billion years of community evolution. In Diversity and Stability in Ecological Systems. Brookhaven Symposia in Biology, No. 22:162-177.
1970a. The Argyrolagidae, extinct South American marsupials. Bull. Mus. Comp. Zool., 139:1-86.
1970b. [Selected passages from previous works:] Purpose arises only in man, pp. 172-173. The world into which Darwin led us, p. 226. The fallacy of aggregation ethics, pp. 366-369. The importance of genetic variety. pp. 528-529. Epilogue. p. 620. In L. B. Young, ed., Evolution of Man. New York, Oxford University Press.
1970c. Horses. New York, Oxford University Press. [Slightly modified reprint of 1951f.]
1970d. Darwin's philosophy and methods. [Essay review of: M. T. Chiselin, The Triumph of the Darwinian Method.] Science, 167:1362-1363.
1970e. Uniformitarianism. An inquiry into principle, theory, and method in geohistory and biohistory. In Hecht, M. K., and W. C. Steere. editors, Essays in Evolution and Genetics in Honor of Theodosius Dobzhansky, pp. 43-96. New York, Appleton-Century-Crofts.
1970f. Ages of fossil penguins in New Zealand. Science, 168:361-362.
1970g. On Sarles's views on language and communication. Current Anthropology, 11:71-72.

1970h. Miocene penguins from Victoria, Australia, and Chubut, Argentina. Mem. Nat. Mus. Victoria, 31:17-24.
1970i. On randomness and determinism: discussion. Bull. Geol. Soc. Amer., 81:3185-3186.
1970j. Mammals from the early Cenozoic of Chubut, Argentina. Breviora, No. 360:1-13.
1970k. Additions to knowledge of the Argyrolagidae (Mammalia, Marsupialia) from the late Cenozoic of Argentina. Breviora, No. 361:1-9.
1970l. Addition to knowledge of *Groeberia* (Mammalia, Marsupialia) from the mid-Cenozoic of Argentina. Breviora, No. 362:1-17.
1970m. Drift theory: Antarctica and Central Asia. Science, 170:678.
1970n. The biological nature of man. *In* Cloud, P., ed., Adventures in Earth History, pp. 932-943. San Francisco, W. H. Freeman and Co. Also *in* Jackson, W., ed., Man and the Environment, pp. 3-18. Dubuque, William C. Brown Co., 1971. [Modified reprints of 1969b, chap. 6.]
1970o. Slump, Urval, Utveckling. Stockholm, Rabén & Sjögren. [Modified Swedish version of 1964c.]
1971a. The Meaning of Evolution. Revised ed. New York, London, and Toronto, Bantam Books. [Paperback ed. of 1949e.]
1971b. Fossil penguin from the late Cenozoic of South America. Science, 171:1144-1145.
1971c. Biologist and generalist. [Review of: Memories, by Julian Huxley.] Science, 173:135.
1971d. A review of the Pre-Pliocene penguins of New Zealand. Bull. Amer. Mus. Nat. Hist., 144:319-378.
1971e. Status and problems of vertebrate phylogeny. *In* Alvaredo, Gadea, and de Haro, eds., Simposio Internacional de Zoofilogenia, pp. 353-368. Universidad de Salamanca, Facultad de Ciencias.

2

Phylogeny and Paleontology

BOBB SCHAEFFER, MAX K. HECHT, AND NILES ELDREDGE

The American Museum of Natural History
New York, N. Y. 10024

INTRODUCTION

Paleontologists have traditionally regarded the temporal sequence of fossils as central to the concept of phylogeny. In recent years the significance of the time aspect has been questioned by a number of systematists who argue that the fossil record can offer only a very incomplete picture of phylogeny and that temporal criteria are generally less reliable than morphologic ones in working out relationships. We intend to explore these different opinions by considering both the nature of paleontological data and some methodological generalizations concerning their use.

Incisive comments on the more traditional point of view have been provided by Simpson (1961, p. 83):

> Data on recent animals have no time dimension, or one too short to be of much real use. Since evolutionary taxonomy has a time dimension, these data [from recent animals] are deficient in an important way. They are not themselves historical, yet must serve for drawing historical inferences. That is a basic problem as regards homology, and also in many other aspects of taxonomy. The method of approach must be comparative, and conclusions must be drawn as to sequences in which we have only the final terms. Some recent animals are more primitive in some respects than others. It is therefore often possible to form a sequence among recent animals that approximates one that occurred in time. It is essential to remember that the two are not the same thing and that it is always most improbable that one exactly corresponds with the other. When properly interpreted, such sequences essentially supplement the evidence of characters in common..Paleontological studies are often based on contemporaneous fossils, and they are just as comparative and based on just as nonhistoric data as those on recent animals. However, when based on sequences in geological time or when relatable to recent faunas, paleontological studies do have a true time dimension and the data are directly

historical. In spite of deficiencies in other respects (biased samples, incomplete anatomy, no physiology, etc.), fossils provide the soundest basis for evolutionary classification when data adequate in their own field are at hand.

Criteria for providing a hypothesis of relationships in terms of character states (primitive to derived) have been proposed by many systematists. Following the introduction of the cline concept by Huxley (1938), in which he emphasized progressive change in morphological characters in a geographic sequence of contemporaneous populations, Simpson (1943, p. 174) coined the term "chronocline" for a sequence of successive populations arranged temporally. He regarded geographical clines (which he called "choroclines") as analogous in every way to chronoclines. As an example of a chronocline he cited the "vertical species" of the early Tertiary mammal *Ectocion*, and he interpreted the successive changes in tooth dimensions as indicating a "genetically continuous, ancestral-descendant, series of populations gradually changed in morphology, most noticeably in size . . . " (*ibid.*).

Nearly two decades later, Simpson (1961, p. 179) defined a cline as "an arrangement of characters, not or organisms or of populations," and he noted that the cline concept is "extremely useful in arranging the data of classification and in understanding and defining individual taxa . . . " He employed the term chronocline "for successional clines" or for the "actual ancestral sequence" (p. 102).

Maslin (1952) was the first to use the term "morphocline," implying that it is a contemporaneous series of character states arranged in a primitive to derived sequence. He called this sequence "polarity." He believed that a morphocline among a series of recent taxa can be used to approximate the chronocline, despite the absence of the fossil record. His main criterion for determining the primitive condition within a morphocline is that it is "found in the less modified members of related groups of the same rank."

In a more recent discussion of chronoclines, morphoclines and polarity, Kluge (1971) emphasized that the reconstruction of a phylogeny "must be based on (1) degree of relationship between populations, (2) relative position of divergent lines, and (3) direction of evolutionary change" (p. 27). In his opinion, time, which can be determined only from the fossil record, is not necessary for the reconstruction of a phylogeny. Kluge's synthesis clearly involves the ideas of Maslin, Simpson and others. But it also seems to include the concepts of Hennig (1966) and Brundin (1966, 1968), particularly in emphasizing that time is not an essential, or even a desirable parameter in working out phylogenies.

It is obvious that these and other authors have used the term chronocline in several different ways. Although we believe that an actual sequence, even in the sense of the one Simpson (1943) described for *Ectocion*, can rarely, if ever, be recognized, we prefer to define a chronocline as he did (1961, p. 179).

Throughout the present paper, then, a chronocline simply means the real (as opposed to a hypothetical) sequential change in character states.

It is reasonable to ask whether any fossil record is ever complete enough, and the preservation good enough, to regard a chronocline as an actual ancestral-descendant sequence. Paleontologists who are working with "good" records (e.g., for horses, camels) are emphatically affirmative. But for the vast majority of invertebrate and vertebrate records any attempt in this direction is not realistic. We simply wish to point out that it is dangerous to assume at the outset that a chronocline is a pure reflection of an ancestral-descendant sequence, no matter how complete the record may seem to be.

Some neontologists have expressed the opinion that paleontologists can contribute little to the development of a phylogenetic classification. Various reasons for this attitude include (1) the generally "poor" fossil record; (2) inadequate knowledge of related living taxa on the part of the paleontologist; (3) the lack of diagnostic characters in the preserved hard parts of many extinct taxa; (4) the possibility that paleontological data may tend to reduce or eliminate the "real and evident discontinuities which will provide an objective basis for the divisions of our hierarchy" (Crowson, 1970, p. 67). Because of these and other opinions about the nature of the fossil record, Crowson proposes that organisms represented only by fossils should be classified separately from living ones.

In regard to (1) above, an estimate of quality for a particular fossil record in terms of "poor" to "good" is clearly relative and mostly subjective. In our frame of reference, a good record is one that provides enough character data to make a choice between alternative hypotheses of relationship at a particular power of resolution (e.g., the Amphibia undoubtedly arose from the rhipidistian fishes, but their ancestry within the Rhipidistia remains controversial).

In regard to (2), we believe that most paleontologists seriously interested in the phylogeny of a group are conversant with its living members. The third and fourth points are discussed below, mainly in support of the contention that data from both living and fossil animals may provide the basis for a common, phylogenetic classification. The possibility of evaluating the nature of the relationship will depend, in part, on the kind and number of characters that may be compared in both the living and fossil representatives.

It is our opinion that the spectrum of primitive-derived character states, or polarity, must be worked out (and, in fact usually is worked out), at least initially, on the basis of morphologic criteria. The reason for this conclusion is that the sequence of fossils in the rocks may not offer a true picture of polarity. Primitiveness and apparent ancientness are not necessarily correlated. In order to provide a "reasonable" hypothesis of phylogeny it is necessary to propose a morphocline for each character under consideration, and following that, to arrive at some conclusion (however tentative) regarding the direction of evolutionary change. By supporting the contention that time per se cannot be employed in hypothesizing relationships, we are, in effect, disagreeing with the concept that a chronocline necessarily provides the closest approximation of an actual phylogeny. The time dimension *should not* be ignored, but, as discussed below, should be relegated to a different role in attempting to understand the history of organisms.

Our dispute with the notion that a chronocline approaches a real phylogeny can be most easily explained on the basis of the model in Fig. 1. Much of what

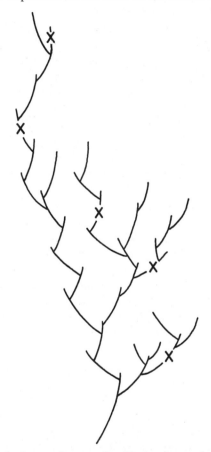

Fig. 1. An actual phylogenetic tree. Fossil samples are indicated by an "X." The vertical axis is absolute time; the horizontal axis represents morphological differences among the taxa. Though an apparent chronocline is formed by the sequence of fossil samples, the fossil taxa do not form an ancestral-descendant sequence.

we know about the evolutionary process indicates that it proceeds within limits imposed by the ancestral genotype, morphogenetic canalization and selection pressure. Most phylogenies resulting form this process probably resemble that in Fig. 1 and differ only in being more or less complicated. In spite of some apparently excellent fossil records that seem to show well-defined ancestral-descendant lineages at the specific level (as in the horses), it is probable that the detailed phylogenetic sequence and ramifications for most groups of organisms can never be worked out from the fossil record. If we consider, for example, the hypothetical recovered samples indicated in Fig. 1, it is apparent that no two have an ancestral-descendant relationship, and, in fact, that they belong to different lineages. Relatively low diversity groups that have evolved for a long interval in one geographical area and have a good fossil record will provide the closest approximation of a phylogeny—not because we know the temporal sequence in which the fossils occur, but because we have a relative abundance of morphological characters that may be used to set up a hypothesis of relationships. The chronocline concept implies, wrongly, we believe, that the temporal sequence is, in itself, meaningful in evaluating relationship.

NATURE OF PALEONTOLOGICAL DATA

In lieu of analyzing the entire, integrated organism, systematists have always been forced to compare selected samples of the whole—characters or character complexes—in order to produce a hypothesis of relationship. The neontologist can obviously select from a far wider range of characters than can the paleontologist. The apparent subjectivity of this selection and the desire to work with as much of the total organism as possible have been major arguments for the development of numerical taxonomy. But the question can be fairly asked, How much or what parts of the total organism must be compared in order to produce a reasonable hypothesis of relationships? The fact that deductions based on the skeleton, either endo- or exo-, or parts thereof, are more frequently than not supported by data derived from soft tissues, physiology, or biochemistry, has enhanced the use of hard parts in nearly all Recent groups possessing them—and it follows, in fossil groups as well. A high level of adaptive specificity may permit identification and consideration of relationships based on a relatively small number of characters—as in the case of mammalian molar teeth.

The point is that there is no basic difference between the data of the neontologist and that of the paleontologist. The problem is rather whether or not the paleontologist has enough phylogenetically meaningful characters to make a reasonable judgment of affinity. The most interesting and potentially useful characters, at least in the vertebrates, are those which can be studied in relation to some major function—feeding, locomotion, reproduction, perception—primarily because they give meaning to any consideration of adaptation. The form of the skeleton is clearly related to the first two functions, and it may provide some information on the last two. Muscle scars on trilobite glabellae (Eldredge, 1971a) and hinge lines on pelecypod shells are also subject to function interpretation and may be treated in the same way. However, the functional meaning of changes in the dermal skull pattern of fishes, in the centra of amphibians and in the coiling of gastropods, still defy understanding. They are, nonetheless, empirically useful for purposes of comparison and classification.

If we agree that (1) the degree of relationship (as defined by recency of common ancestry) should be determined initially on the basis of morphology alone, and (2) that time and geographical distribution per se (which are also attributes of organisms) would not be used as comparative data for evaluating relationships, then animals of different geologic ages, including living ones, can be compared as though they were contemporaneous. This, in fact, is the way comparisons have usually been made—either consciously or subconsciously.

For groups with living representatives the inclusion of extinct taxa may be regarded as providing a closer approximation of the actual diversity of the entire group. The contention of Hennig (1966) and of Brundin (1966) that phylogenetic analysis must start with living representatives is believed by us to be unnecessary if the fossil record is to have any meaning or usefulness—simply because to do otherwise is to throw away potentially valuable data—a scientifically unsound procedure. Extinct and living representatives must be compared on the basis of the same characters, regardless of whether or not additional (unpreservable) characters are used for reinforcing conclusions about the relationships of the living (and indirectly of the fossil) ones. It is our belief that all taxa, fossil or recent, must initially be treated equally—to the extent that this is possible in actual practice.

HOMOLOGY AND POLARITY

Character analysis, which underlies any consideration of phylogeny, involves two problems. One of these is homology and the other is morphocline polarity. As Jardine (1969) has stressed, character homology in extinct groups can be dealt with operationally only on the basis of topography (i.e., relative position and relationships of skeletal components). In groups with living representatives, morphogenesis may play an essential role in establishing homology, as between certain reptilian jaw elements and the mammalian ear ossicles, or between the vertebral components in the major vertebrate groups. In practice, most paleontologists (like most neontologists) assume specific homologies, and question their validity only if no phylogenetic sense can be made of the data. As such, there are no absolute criteria for establishing homology—topographically similar structures are merely presumed to be homologous until reasons emerge to cast doubt on the assumption. It is possible to work out a morphocline without detailed understanding of homology as long as enough data are available to eliminate any serious morphological gaps in the series. We are commonly dealing with problems of pattern analysis, where detailed homologies of individual elements, or parts of elements, are difficult or impossible to ascertain.

The distinction between homologous and homoplastic characters may require evidence from both fossil and living animals. The atlas-axis complex in birds and mammals includes an odontoid process that permits rotation of the skull. The developmental pattern and topographic relationships of this complex indicate that it is homologous in both groups. The fossil record, however, shows that the functional odontoid process is absent in pelycosaurs and primitive archosaurs. It is evident, therefore, that the odontoids of birds and mammals are homoplastic (not homologous) structures demonstrating parallel evolution independently resulting from developmental and topographic homologues that were present in primitive reptiles.

The development of a phylogenetic scheme is dependent primarily on the determination of a morphocline and its polarity for each characters under consideration. Neozoologists may determine the primitive state of a morphocline by: (1) common occurrence of a character within a particular group and its closest relatives; and (2) similarities in morphogenesis and organogenesis. Some neozoologists also use biogeographic data to support their opinion regarding polarity within a morphocline. This approach is unreliable, however, as all organisms with either relict or continuous distributions are mosaics of different character states that range from primitive to advanced. Similarly, the fossil record for most groups of organisms is too incomplete to allow the assumption that relative stratigraphic position is necessarily indicative of morphocline polarity. It therefore seems to us that polarity, at least initially, should be determined on the basis of comparative morphology, even within such a well-documented series as *Hyracotherium*-to-*Equus*. The resulting morphocline might initially be interpreted as either *Hyracotherium-Equus* or *Equus-Hyracotherium*. By comparing this spectrum of equid morphology with similar spectra exhibited by related perissodactyl families it is evident that the one digit character state is derived. *Hyracotherium*, with its four front and three rear functional toes, is not the most primitive equid merely because it is the oldest taxon referred to that family, but because many of its character states are shared with other perissodactyl groups.

PHYLOGENY AS A THEORY OF RELATIONSHIPS

To most paleontologists a phylogeny consists of a series of statements of the form: Taxon A gave rise to Taxon B; Taxon B gave rise to Taxon C and also to Taxon D; etc. In other words, the relationships among taxa are expressed in terms of a series of ancestors and descendants, with qualifications inserted for dubious cases. Neontologists, of course, are faced with the difficulty (some would say impossibility) of recognizing ancestral-descendant relationships among Recent taxa. This leads to a contrasting view of phylogeny: that the history of a group of taxa can be expressed by a series of statements such as: Taxon A is more closely related to Taxon B than either is to Taxon C; etc. Here relationships are expressed strictly in terms of recency of common ancestry. Of necessity the neontologist's view is purely cladistic (in the sense that all organisms being classified exist at one time level), no matter what formal schooling of systematics is being followed.

Many neontologists, however, share the paleontologist's view that the fossil record is the only real way of discovering phylogeny. Statements to the effect that phylogeny, except at the highest taxonomic levels, is unknowable in the absence of an adequate fossil record, but that a comparative study of serology, morphology, behavior, etc., in Recent organisms provides some understanding of relationship, are frequent. Such statements are usually expressed as a *pro forma apologia* in the introduction to many studies of Recent biota (e.g., Sokal and Sneath, 1963, p. 227; Silvestri and Hill, 1964, p. 89; Inger, 1967, p. 369; Moss and Webster, 1969, p. 423). Recently this point of view has been explicitly attacked by Wilson (1965, p. 214), Colless (1967, p. 293). Hull (1967, p. 180) and Nelson (1970, p. 375). The point here is that there seems to be a lingering belief among some neontologists that absence of fossil data prohibits any reasonably definitive statement on phylogeny. This belief stems directly from the notion that phylogeny must be expressed in terms of ancestral-descendant sequences in order to be proper.

The notion of ancestry and descent is, of course, implicit in the concept of phylogeny and is a logical concomitant to the entire idea of organic evolution. But there exists a large information gap between what we know *must have* happened and knowledge of what actually *did* happen. The idea that the fossil record provides documentation for the actual course of phylogeny has followed as an almost axiomatic corollary to the adoption of evolutionary theory as the key to understanding the diversity of life. In this view the only drawback that has kept the fossil record from answering most questions in systematics is its notorious incompleteness. Proponents of this view have failed to grasp an essential point: an actual phylogeny is not capable of outright discovery; it is a system of relationships that needs to be analyzed. The fossil record is clearly no panacea to students of phylogeny. The reason for this is not really that the record is "incomplete," but that many neontologists and paleontologists have assumed that if enough rocks are split the record of past life will reveal itself.

The frequent assumption that "evolution can be read directly from the rocks" is itself intricately bound with the belief that evolution is a gradual, generally phyletic, phenomenon. Indeed, the standard picture of species level evolution among paleontologists calls for slow, steady *in situ* transformation of an entire stock; this concept can be conveniently labelled "phyletic gradualism" (Eldredge and Gould, Ms.). Such a model of the evolutionary process maximizes the probability that the course of phylogeny could, at least in theory, be fossilized and revealed simply by good biostratigraphic data. Phyletic gradualism as an operative model for interpreting the fossil record has recently been criticized by Eldredge (1971b) and Eldredge and Gould (Ms.). All that needs to be noted here is that this picture of the evolutionary process has served to justify the view that the fossil record is a source of direct information, however distorted, on the course of phylogeny. A good example of these intermingled beliefs was penned by W. D. Matthew (1926, p. 454) at a time when the Scopes trial was fresh in memory:

> Stratigraphic studies and exact records of geological level were developed in the nineties, and added a new and fascinating interest to the work, as one could actually trace in the succession of strata the progressive evolution of the different races, verifying in specimen after specimen the primitive characters of those from the lower layers, the progressive character of those from the upper layers, and the intermediate conditions in specimens from the middle beds.[1] No one carries a more solid conviction of the truth of evolution than the field paleontologist. He has seen it with his own eyes, and it is quite useless for learned pundits of the pulpit or laboratory to tell *him* that evolution is only a hypothesis, or that paleontology does not prove anything about it. He knows better; he has seen it himself ineffaceably inscribed in the records of the past.

Identification of a fossil taxon as the ancestor of another taxon involves both a comparative study of the morphology and a proper sequence of occurrence in the sedimentary column. The prime difficulty with the use of presumed ancestral descendant sequences to express phylogeny is that biostratigraphic data are often used in conjunction with morphology in the initial evaluation of relationships, which leads to obvious circularity. By maintaining that biostratigraphic data should be ignored when evaluating relationships, we are simply arguing that phylogenies must be based on comparative morphology. Data concerning relative stratigraphic position necessarily bias the results by narrowing the range of possible relationships held by the taxa in question. Obviously Taxon A cannot be ancestral to Taxon B, if the latter is some two million years older than Taxon A. But a penchant for recognizing ancestor-descendant sequences may result in ignoring the possibility that Taxa A and B, rather than possessing an ancestor-descendant relationship, actually possess a common ancestor, i.e., neither is ancestral to the other.

A further difficulty is that morphocline polarity in one character may be different from that in another character. All organisms are bound to be relatively primitive in some respects, and relatively derived in others (the concept of mosaic evolution: DeBeer, 1954). The probability of finding a fossil taxon that

[1] Matthew had his specialty—fossil mammals—in mind, which came closer to substantiating this statement than any other group of organisms.

is primitive in all respects to another, younger taxon, is small. These problems must be dealt with in the same manner as conflicting directions of morphoclines among Recent organisms (Maslin, 1952).

If phylogenetic affinity is assessed on the basis of comparative morphology, it follows that a cladogram of the sort illustrated in Fig. 2A represents the best possible expression of relationships. This is because the cladogram is based on fewer assumptions (regarding ancestor-descendant relationships) than the usual phylogenetic tree, which is a highly specific statement, and is frequently but one of several that could be derived from the same morphologic and stratigraphic data (Fig. 2B-D). In other words, a cladogram claims less than, but actually says as much as, a phylogenetic tree. Thus we feel that for most purposes, a

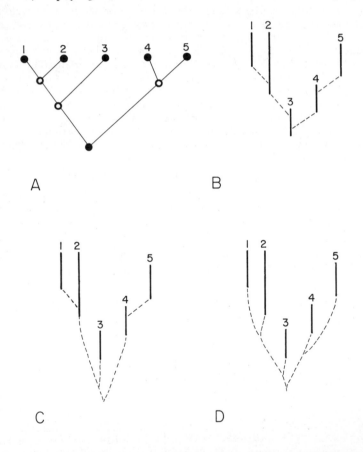

Fig. 2. A. Cladogram expressing relationships among two living taxa (1, 2) and three extinct taxa (3, 4, 5). B, C. Two of the many phylogenetic trees that could be constructed from the data used to develop the cladogram A. D. A phylogenetic tree derived from the cladogram A. In B-D the fossil taxa are shown in their proper biostratigraphic sequence of occurrence.

statement of relative recency of common ancestry (as represented pictorially by the cladogram) is the simplest and most accurate representation of phylogeny possible, given the kinds of information available to either the paleontologist or the neontologist. A phylogeny, then, is a theory of relationships expressed in the form: Taxa A and B are more closely related to each other than either is to Taxon C. When defined in this way a phylogeny is of exactly the same form whether it involves fossils, Recent organisms, or a mixture of both.

DETERMINATION OF RELATIONSHIPS

A phylogeny in the form of a theory of relationships can ultimately be constructed from the totality of morphoclines for all of the characters studied for all of the taxa under consideration. General procedures for elucidating the simplest phylogenetic scheme from such an array of data have been discussed by many authors (e.g., Simpson, 1961: Hennig, 1966; Mayr, 1969; Farris et al., 1970). It is not our intent to offer a detailed presentation of a formal methodology here, but rather to discuss specific aspects of the problem that are relevant to paleontology.

We here accept a basic tenet of the "phylogenetic cladists" (Hennig, Brundin, Nelson, etc.) that assessments of affinity are most reliably based on shared, derived characters. In other words, relationships are most easily grasped when viewed in the context of morphological specializations held in common by two taxa. The hypothetical condition of the ancestor (the morphotype) of two derived taxa can then be used comparatively to determine the next most closely related taxon. In this context the morphotype is not only an abstraction but also a best estimate of the actual ancestral condition. The reader is referred to the papers of Zangerl (1948) and Nelson (1970) for more extended discussions of the concept.

It will be argued below that, for certain purposes, it may be desirable to identify actual fossil taxa with hypothetical morphotypes. However, such a procedure should be avoided in the preliminary construction of a theory of relationships. The reasons for this have already been mentioned. Foremost among them is the very low probability that any older fossil taxon may be found to possess all the combinations of features of the hypothesized morphotype. To "correct" or "adjust" the hypothesized morphotype in order to take into account the actual combination of features found in the older taxon is to abandon the internal logic of the comparative procedure. The significance of the Class Monoplacophora in relation to problems in early molluscan phylogeny is instructive in this regard. The several species of the living monoplacophoran *Neopilina* all possess possibly metameric series of ctenidia, pedal musculature (plus associated nerves), nephridia, atria, and gonads. Fossils unquestionably allied to *Neopilina* have long been known from sediments ranging in age from Cambrian to Devonian. *Neopilina* corresponds admirably with most renditions of the ancestral molluscan morphotype, with the conspicuous exception that the morphotype was not ·generally thought to have possessed any metamerically arranged organs. For example, there was supposed to be but one pair of ctenidia, arranged symmetrically in a posterior mantle cavity. Exceptions to this condition among Recent molluscs (the multiple "ctenidia" in the Amphineura; the two pairs of ctenidia in *Nautilus*) were supposed to have been secondarily derived duplications not representative of the primitive condition (however, see Naef, 1926).

Two related questions now face malacologists interested in the form of the ancestral mollusc: (1) are the serially arranged organs of *Neopilina* primitive or derived from a simpler molluscan condition? (2) if they are primitive, does this imply that the.hypothesized ancestral mollusc should be changed to include a similar metamerically arranged series of organs? There seem to be four basic approaches which may be taken to answer these two questions: (1) an intensive study of the complexity and regularity of the interrelationships among the serially repeated structures in *Neopilina* to provide an estimate of the likelihood that the arrangement is "truly" metameric or only superficially so: (2) a detailed study of the ontogeny of those organs, for the same reason; (3) comparison with other taxa within the Mollusca, including a reevaluation of the multiplication of comparable structures in the Amphineura and Cephalopoda; and (4) comparison with other protostomous phyla. Some such studies have indeed already been made (most notably, those by Lemche and Wingstrand, 1959), although the conclusion that metamerism is primitive in *Neopilina* and for the Mollusca as a whole is still actively contested (see, for example, Vagvolgyi, 1967).

The stratigraphic occurrence of fossil Monoplacophora is notably absent from the above list. Indeed, the fossil record tells us only that (1) there are fossil taxa closely related to *Neopilina*, and (2) these fossils first appear before any other well-known molluscan class, with the exception of the Gastropoda. This information demonstrates only that the Monoplacophora have been "segmented" at least since the Cambrian and that *Neopolina* is not a unique organism. Such data, however, do not tell us whether or not we should revise the hypothetical ancestral morphotype. Furthermore, should the hypothetical ancestral mollusc be re-defined as a metameric creature, it is totally unreasonable to identify any one fossil monoplacophoran as *the* ancestral mollusc, especially in view of the diversity and obvious specialization seen even among Cambrian species. One true value of the fossil record, in this light, is that a minimum age can be assigned to the differentiation of the Monoplacophora from the other molluscan classes. Another aspect is that a perceptive student of fossil molluscs, J. B. Knight (1952), was able to establish, prior to the announced discovery of *Neopilina*, that a group of univalved fossil molluscs later referred to the Monoplacophora were probably untorted and possibly metameric. Had *Neopilina* not been discovered, or had the Monoplacophora truly become extinct sometime between the Devonian and the Holocene, paleontological data might still have forced a reevaluation of the question of metamerism in the primitive mollusc, though without the impetus and with fewer data than are forthcoming from the living *Neopilina*. But biostratigraphy has nothing to say about primitive vs. derived conditions in this or any other case.

A further problem attendant to the identification of actual fossil taxa with hypothetical morphotypes is the frequent discovery that a morphologically "primitive" taxon may occur quite high in the stratigraphic range of a group for which it is supposed to be ancestral. This problem has vexed most paleontologists at one time or another, particularly in relation to groups with a poor fossil record. The usual procedure is to deemphasize the anomolous stratigraphic position and continue to regard the seemingly primitive taxon as truly primitive, an approach we regard as generally valid. Even when a taxon is discovered that is both primitive and low in the stratigraphic range of its referred higher taxon, it is almost invariably derived (specialized) in some feature(s). It follows, therefore, that biostratigraphy is rarely relevant to the problem of working out relationships because it may add a distorting bias, and that identification of an actual fossil taxon with an ancestral morphotype is unnecessary for the delimitation of relationships.

SUMMARY AND CONCLUSIONS

Up to this point we have attempted to provide the basis for a theory of relationships that may involve paleontological as well as neontological data. We are well aware that the purposeful omission of biostratigraphic information during the initial comparison of the morphology will meet with disfavor on the part of many paleontologists.

It has been our intention to outline a consistent methodology applicable to all studies of relationship among both fossil and Recent taxa, regardless of the relative completeness of the fossil record in any particular case. Such a methodology simply cannot be based on an abstract, ideal situation; though primitiveness and ancientness may in fact be found to coincide, it is simply wrong to use biostratigraphy to determine polarity *a priori*. It should not be incorporated into the methodology just because it *may* be right. Biostratigraphy and polarity often do seem to correspond, but this is something to be demonstrated, not assumed.

It should be recalled that the methodology involved in arriving at a theory of relationships emphasizes the comparison of character states at or near the "derived" end of a morphocline, mainly because primitive states may be shared by quite distantly related organisms. It therefore follows that the higher the number of primitive character states held in common by a group of organisms, the closer we may come to defining a hypothetical common ancestor. Similarity among organisms, in the sense of primitive *or* shared derived character states, is thus not excluded from consideration, but the objective of the analysis must be carefully defined. On the basis of all these "rules," including initial avoidance of the time factor, the operational routine leading to a theory of relationships permits little or no compromise.

In spite of all that has been discussed above, it would be foolish indeed to view the fossil record merely as a dimensionless source of additional information regarding the total diversity of a group. As noted in several plâces, we do *not* recommend that time be ignored, but rather that it be given a different role in the analysis. The temporal aspect of paleontological data, which Simpson and others have written about so penetratingly, provides the one additional element that makes the fossil record the only "laboratory" where evolutionary experiments may be studied against the actual time scale.

A theory of relationships represents a precise series of predictions for a partially discernable series of actual evolutionary events. In order to attempt a comparison of theory and historical record, we may assume that the cladogram in Fig. 2 includes living Taxa 1 and 2 and extinct Taxa 3, 4, and 5. By combining the implications of this cladogram with the available biostratigraphic data, it is possible to construct several different phylogenetic trees. In many such cases there will be a high degree of correlation between the inferred sequene of phylogenetic events and the biostratigraphy of the taxa under study. This simply reflects a tendency toward a direct relationship between time, evolution, and deposition of sediments.

In order to study evolutionary tempo and mode on the basis of the above deliberations, one of several possible phylogenetic trees must be accepted as the "best-fit" estimate of relationships. The best-fit is determined by recognizing the fossil taxa that resemble most closely the conditions of the morphotype. Because some fossil taxa will come closer to the morphotypes than others— mostly because of differences in hypothetical and actual character states—the phylogenetic tree will necessarily represent a mixture of ancestor-descendant and cladistic relationships. There is no way of formally testing a phylogenetic tree, but the congruence of morphocline and chronocline polarities increases our confidence in the hypothesized phylogeny. Once a tentative but acceptable tree is available, it may form the basis for studies on evolutionary trends, adaptive radiation, and evolutionary rates.

Perhaps the most important conclusion that may be derived from these deliberations is that paleontologists, like neontologists, will find it rewarding in systematic studies to distinguish between primitive and derived characters. This distinction is, in fact, often made intuitively, but the reasons for concentrating on derived characters in framing a diagnosis or in formulating a hypothesis of relationship are too frequently not appreciated. Because of a fragmentary fossil record it may be impossible to postulate a morphocline even in terms of a single primitive and a single derived character state. In spite of this difficulty, we believe that there is a compelling internal logic in this general approach to particular problems of relationship and phylogeny.

Acknowledgments

The authors wish to thank Drs. Walter Bock, Karl F. Koopman, Malcolm C. McKenna, Gareth J. Nelson, Norman D. Newell, Richard H. Tedford, and Ernest E. Williams for critical comments on the manuscript. Unanimity of opinion was not anticipated, and the final version, although influenced by the readers' comments, is the sole responsibility of the authors.

REFERENCES

Brundin, L. 1966. Transantarctic relationships and their significance, as evidenced by chironomid midges, with a monograph of the subfamilies Podonominae and Aphroteniinae and the austral Heptagyiae. K. Svenska Vet. Akad. Handl., 11:1-472.

——— 1968. Application of phylogenetic principles in systematics and evolutionary theory. *In* Ørvig, T., ed., Current Problems of Lower Vertebrate Phylogeny. Nobel Symposium 4, pp. 473-495. New York, John Wiley and Sons.

Colless, D. H. 1967. The phylogenetic fallacy. Syst. Zool., 16:289-295.

Crowson, R. A. 1970. Classification and Biology. London, Heinemann Educational Books, Ltd.

DeBeer, G. A. 1954. *Archaeopteryx* and evolution. Advance. Sci., 42:1-11.

Eldredge, N. 1971a. Patterns of cephalic musculature in the Phacopina (Trilobita) and their phylogenetic significance. J. Paleont., 45:52-67.

——— 1971b. The allopatric model and phylogeny in Paleozoic invertebrates. Evolution, 25:156-167.

——— and S. J. Gould. (Ms.). Speciation and punctuated equilibria: an alternative to phyletic gradualism. *In* Schopf, T. J. M., ed., Concepts and Models in Paleobiology.

Farris, J. S., A. G. Kluge and M. J. Eckardt. 1970. A numerical approach to phylogenetic systematics. Syst. Zool., 19:172-189.

Hennig, W. 1966. Phylogenetic Systematics. Urbana, University of Illinois Press.

Hull, D. L. 1967. Certainty and circularity in evolutionary taxonomy. Evolution, 21:174-189.

Huxley, J. S. 1938. Species formation and geographical isolation. Proc. Linn. Soc. London, 1937-1938:253-264.

Inger, R. F. 1967. The development of a phylogeny of frogs. Evolution, 21:369-384.

Jardine, N. 1969. The observational and theoretical components of homology: a study based on the morphology of the dermal skull-roofs of rhipidistian fishes. Biol. J. Linn. Soc., 1:327-361.

Kluge, A. G. 1971. Concepts and principles of morphologic and functional studies. *In* Waterman, A. J., ed., Chordate Structure and Function, pp. 3-41. New York, MacMillan Co.

Knight, J. B. 1952. Primitive fossil gastropods and their bearing on gastropod classification. Smithsonian Misc. Coll., 117:1-56.

Lemche, H., and K. G. Wingstrand. 1959. The anatomy of *Neopilina galatheae*. Galathea Report, 3:9-72.

Maslin, T. P. 1952. Morphological criteria of phyletic relationships. Syst. Zool., 1:49-70.

Matthew, W. D. 1926. Early days of fossil hunting in the high plains. Natural. Hist., 26:449-454.

Mayr, E. 1969. Principles of Systematic Zoology. New York, McGraw-Hill.

Moss, W. W., and W. A. Webster. 1969. A numerical taxonomic study of a group of selected strongylates (Nematoda). Syst. Zool., 18:423-443.

Naef, A. 1926. Studien zur generellen Morphologie der Mollusken. 3. Ergeb. Zool. (Jena), 6:27-124.

Nelson, G. J. 1970. Outline of a theory of comparative biology. Syst. Zool., 19:373-384.

Silvestri, L. G., and L. R. Hill. 1964. Some problems of the taxometric approach. *In* Heywood, V. H., and J. McNeill, eds., Phenetic and phylogenetic classification. Syst. Assoc. Publ., 6:87-103.

Simpson, G. G. 1943. Criteria for genera, species, and subspecies in zoology and paleozoology. Ann. N. Y. Acad. Sci., 44(2):145-178.

    1953. The Major Features of Evolution. New York, Columbia Univ. Press.

    1961. Principles of Animal Taxonomy. New York, Columbia Univ. Press.

Sokal, R. R., and P. H. Sneath. 1963. Principles of Numerical Taxonomy. San Francisco, W. H. Freeman and Co.

Vagvolgyi, J. 1967. On the origin of molluscs, the coelom and coelomic segmentation. Syst. Zool., 16:153-168.

Wilson, E. O. 1965. A consistency test for phylogenies based on contemporaneous species. Syst. Zool., 14:214-220.

Zangerl, R. 1948. The methods of comparative anatomy and its contribution to the study of evolution. Evolution, 2:351-374.

3

The Origin of Faunas. Evolution of Lizard Congeners in a Complex Island Fauna: A Trial Analysis

ERNEST E. WILLIAMS

Museum of Comparative Zoology
Harvard University
Cambridge, Massachusetts 02138

INTRODUCTION

The history of faunas, whether studied by paleontologists and zoogeographers or by systematists, has customarily been described in terms of phylogeny or colonization—in terms, therefore, of the origin or arrival of species. However, a major element permitting the build-up of faunas has been the coadaptation of their species—the fact that they are ecologically fitted together. Study of this coadaptation among living species is, in fact, a major part of modern ecology. Yet ecologists have, on their part, avoided history; they have avoided any attempt to look closely, theoretically or empirically, at the historical sequence of events in the build-up of a complex coadapted fauna.

In order to test whether a historical ecology for complex faunas is possible, I here endeavor to provide the necessary analysis in one well-documented case, taking as my starting point some empirically determined rules of size change in a lizard genus that has colonized many islands and has radiated on some of them to form complexly coadapted congeneric faunas.

Schoener (1970) has provided evidence that in the lizard genus *Anolis* species living without congeners—"solitary anoles"—on the Lesser Antillean islands tend to fall within a characteristic small size range. Again he has shown that, when two anole species occur on any Lesser Antillean island, there is always marked difference in size. His unpublished data also show that, in general, the greater the diversity of island anole faunas, the greater the disparity between the largest and smallest species. I shall call these empirically discovered relationships the *Schoener rules.*

Schoener has discussed these phenomena in terms of competition for resources, primarily food (Schoener, 1969a, 1969b, 1969c, 1970), and has proposed an elaborate model (Schoener, 1969a) predicting optimal sizes for solitary predators, and, as well, convergence and divergence of size changes in complex faunas.

He has not, however, attempted to trace or explain the historical sequence of events in any complex fauna. In all his explicitly predictive statements he has avoided anything beyond simple interactions (species pairs or, more rarely, trios).

I shall here endeavor to explore the possibility of expanding the Schoener rules and their proposed ecological explanation into a model of the historical sequence of size change that can be matched against the probable history of an actual fauna—that of the island of Puerto Rico. The model will be as simple as possible. It will take the classical expectations of character displacement for species pairs and, carrying these forward for increasingly larger faunas, will endeavor to explain some of the complexities in evolution (not only of size) in complex island faunas with as few supplementary assumptions as possible. The proposed model will derive directly from the empirical base of the Schoener rules. What Schoener has shown to be true for the Lesser Antilles—islands of small to moderate size and all of modest age—I here extrapolate in quite literal fashion to an island—Puerto Rico—of much greater size and age.

The choice of Puerto Rico as the test of the proposed model is an inevitable one. For this island, far better than for any other, there exists a phylogeny of the anoline lizards constructed in classical fashion on morphological and other grounds independently of any ecological hypothesis whatever. This phylogeny therefore provides a framework not susceptible to manipulation or distortion to which any ecological hypothesis must be fitted.

WEST INDIAN ANOLES, SIZE, AND ECOLOGICAL PRINCIPLES

West Indian anoles provide good data to an extent that is only beginning to be appreciated. They are taxonomically well known (although new species are probably still to be discovered on the two largest islands, Cuba and Hispaniola). Ecologically their study has begun to be quite sophisticated. Large museum collections exist for most species, permitting collection of accurate metrical data.

Beyond this, however, the distribution of so many species (more than 70) over so many islands (Fig. 1) with varying degrees of diversity allows one to treat the island faunas as "experiments of nature," testing each hypothesis as it is devised.

One other fact makes West Indian *Anolis* especially favorable for ecological discussion. They occupy the diurnal arboreal lizard niche in the West Indies essentially alone. They came to the Antilles from the complex faunas of the mainland, where they primitively occupied the tree crown, and where they share this niche with some other lizards and also birds and mammals. In the West

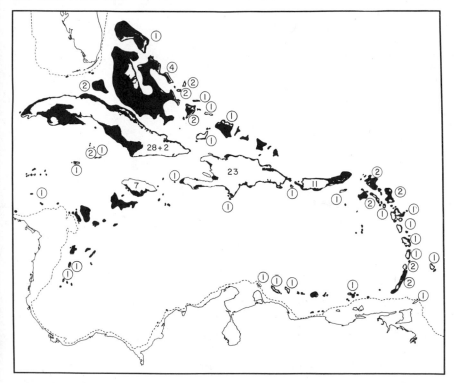

Fig. 1. The West Indian islands and the number of Anolis *species per island or island bank. (The additional two on Cuba are species of the related genus* Chamaeleolis.*)*

Indies they have usually no lizard competitors in vegetational niches, and there are far fewer birds and even fewer mammals. On these islands all erect vegetation from grass to trees—everything that provides a perch—is essentially the domain of *Anolis*. In consequence, competition is almost wholly intrageneric, and West Indian *Anolis* can be treated as if they were evolving alone. Figure 2 indicates some of the most common niches filled by *Anolis* on the largest, most complex islands (cf. Rand and Williams, 1969).

For West Indian *Anolis* we have the addtional good fortune that Schoener has done the basic work of measurement. He has tabulated measurements for the largest third and the largest sixth of the available samples and also maxima of head length, snout-vent length, and tibial length for all West Indian species

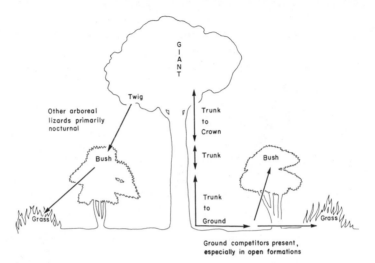

Fig. 2. The most common ways in which the vegetation of the larger Caribbean islands may be utilized by members of the genus Anolis. *Niches are named according to the usage of Rand and Williams (1969). It is shown that the bush and grass niches can be reached from two directions.*

(specimens in the Museum of Comparative Zoology, supplemented when desirable by other major collections). Schoener's tabulations are the solid base upon which all discussions of size in this paper are built.

Schoener has preferred in his own analyses (Schoener, 1969c) to use the mean of the largest third. In the present paper, with access to his original tabulations, I shall most often use maxima. My choice rests on the following considerations: (1) Schoener's tables make clear that the maxima do not differ in trend or significance from the means of the largest third. (2) The maximum is a convenient datum easily obtainable when Schoener's tables require to be suplemented. (3) Maxima, as an additional statistic, test for the inclusion of taxa that have been mistakenly ignored. (The very few extreme individuals that initially seemed out of line with the rest of certain species samples have proved in one case to be representative of a distinct, and at the time of measurement, unrecognized species, and in another of a valid subspecific difference—see below.)

Schoener's data on species difference in size is supplemented by limited evidence on the sizes of insect prey taken by size classes within species (primarily from stomach analyses of two competing species, *A. aeneus* and *A. richardi*, on the Lesser Antillean island of Grenada (Schoener and Gorman, 1968)). The data, though meager, are quite suggestive. The following conclusions are well-supported by the present evidence:

(1) Adults of species that differ in adult size eat prey of different average size. The range of prey size is always great, but larger species eat significantly larger prey than smaller species (Schoener and Gorman, 1968).

(2) Smaller size classes within a species in general take smaller prey than the larger size classes of the same species (Rand, 1967; Schoener, 1967, 1968; Schoener and Gorman, 1968).

(3) Equally sized juveniles of species that differ in adult size already differ in prey-size preferences in the same way that the adults differ (Schoener and Gorman, 1968).

(4) The sexes of dimorphic species differ in prey size preference (Schoener, 1967; Schoener and Gorman, 1968).

(5) Equally sized juveniles of the two sexes tend already to differ in prey size preference in the same way that the sexes of the adults differ (but special growth or energy requirements in differing seasons may complicate this simple statement; see Schoener and Gorman, 1968).

These observations provide functional background for the interpretation of the size relationships seen in the Schoener rules as classical character displacement by divergence. Hence they provide also the empirical foundation for the edifice of inference erected in this paper.

THE LESSER ANTILLES: MODEL FOR A MODEL

I am here deliberately choosing the anoles of the Lesser Antilles as the model for a model. I am postulating that the mechanism which resulted in the Schoener rules accurately mirrors that which operated in the first stages of the more diverse faunas of the Greater Antilles. The Schoener rules provide quantification and example; we go beyond them to analysis of more complex faunas by step-by-step employment of the same rules. However, we will first need to look closely at the Lesser Antillean data to determine whether the causal explanation I propose does in fact fit the data in all regards. Figure 3 maps the area and names the islands and species discussed.

Schoener's First Rule: The Size of Solitary Species

Schoener's Rule 1 states that an anole occupying an island without congeneric

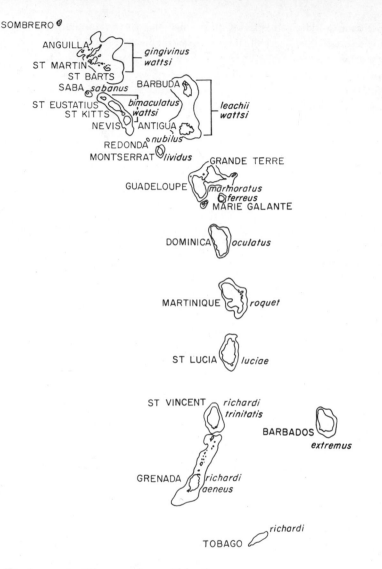

Fig. 3. The Lesser Antilles: species and islands.

competition tends to a range of sizes with maximal head lengths of between 20 and 25 mm and maximal snout-vent lengths of between 65 and 95 mm. Table 1 records the maximal sizes for the solitary anoles in the Lesser Antilles for which the Schoener rule was formulated. The two phyletic groups—*Anolis roquet* and *bimaculatus*—are treated separately. Inspection shows immediately (1) there is strong sexual dimorphism; (2) head sizes are similar in magnitude and range in both phyletic groups; (3) body length (snout-vent length minus head length) is greater by 8 mm in the *roquet* group than in the *bimaculatus* group; (4) the spread between largest and smallest is very similar in both groups and for both measurements (5 mm for head size in the *bimaculatus* group, 3 mm for the same measurement in the *roquet* group; 13 mm for snout-vent length in the *bimaculatus* group, 17 mm for the same measurement in the *roquet* group).

In Table 1 I have, however, carefully omitted those species and islands which pose some difficulty for the Schoener rule. These, unquestionably, are crucial. Let us first propose a mechanism explaining the Schoener rules and then see whether the anomalous examples are reconcilable with this explanation.

Table 1. Maximal Sizes for Solitary Species of *Anolis* in the Lesser Antilles

A. roquet Group (Omitting *richardi* on Tobago
and *aeneus* on the Grenadines)
(See Below in Text)

Island	Species	Head Length	Snout-Vent Length	N
Martinique	*roquet*	20♂/15♀(1.3)	79♂/59♀ (1.3)	50/20
St. Lucia	*luciae*	25/16 (1.6)	91/62 (1.5)	49/13
Barbados	*extremus*	20/15 (1.3)	74/60 (1.2)	43/18

A. bimaculatus Group (Omitting *marmoratus* on Guadeloupe)
(See Below in Text)

Island	Species	Head Length	Snout-Vent Length	N
Saba	*sabanus*	20♂/14♀ (1.4)	67♂/51♀ (1.3)	70/34
Montserrat	*lividus*	21/15 (1.4)	69/51 (1.3)	55/41
Redonda	*nubilus*	23/15 (1.5)	79/52 (1.5)	21/5
Dominica	*oculatus oculatus*	23/16 (1.4)	75/55 (1.4)	21/10
	o. cabritensis	22/16 (1.4)	75/57 (1.3)	24/11
	o. winstoni	23/18 (1.3)	77/61 (1.3)	23/7
	o. montanus	25/17 (1.5)	95/64 (1.5)	15/12

I assume, out of hand, that size is under the control of natural selection and always tends to an optimum for each species, maintaining it if reached, pushing toward it if not yet attained. The explanation, then, for similar sizes in solitary anoles should be intraspecies competition, leading to similar selective forces acting upon species with similar but not necessarily identical initial adaptations.

Note that the anoles that populated the Lesser Antilles came from complex faunas (Puerto Rico to the north, South America to the south; Gorman and Atkins, 1969), which were diverse in sizes as in other features. There is thus no ground for predicting for an invader at the time of invasion any particular size.[1]

[1] Schoener (1969c) has discussed the possibility that "solitary size" is itself significant for colonization, pointing out that *carolinensis, grahami* and *cristatellus*, colonists of islands satellite to the Greater Antilles, are of solitary size on their home islands. But, as he also points out, *sagrei*, one of the two major colonizers (the other is *carolinensis*, of Williams, 1969) is smaller than solitary size on its home island (Cuba) but has apparently evolved to solitary size on Swan Island, where it may have been long resident. Two colonists of the Bahamas—*angusticeps* and *distichus*—are also smaller than solitary size on their respective ports of origin, Cuba and Hispaniola.

In any event, selection for a new size optimum begins with the fact of invasion. Attainment of a size optimum will, however, take time. Some cases, therefore, should exist in which the time since invasion has not been long enough, the size optimum has not been reached, and the first Schoener rule is apparently violated.

Problem Cases Under the First Schoener Rule:
Solitary Species That Are Too Large

We have admitted a considerable range for solitary species. The largest species, indeed, may in snout-vent length be almost one-and-one-half times the smaller, or in head length 1.3 times the smaller. Most solitary anoles do in fact fall in the range 65 to 80 mm in body length. Two populations fall 11 and 15 mm respectively beyond this, *luciae* with a maximum body length of 91, *oculatus montanus* with a maximum of 95 mm. As Table 1 shows, *montanus* is only one exceptional population within a species which otherwise falls near the center of the size range of solitary anoles. I have no ready explanation for the size of *luciae* or *montanus*. It would be facile but no real explanation to ascribe the size discrepancy of the aberrant population of *oculatus* to the fact that it is montane. We must apparently acknowledge the existence of unknown accessory factors that spread out the size range that is adaptive for solitary species.

However, two other populations have body size maxima 24 and 33 mm respectively beyond the extremes already set by *luciae* and *montanus*. To admit these as falling under the first Schoener rule would seem destructive of the rule itself. I propose that both in fact have only recently become solitary.

Recall that we have not regarded the size of solitary anoles as primitive but as something evolved. If, therefore, a species not of solitary size either has arrived on a land mass that has no congeners or if its competing congeners have, for whatever reason, gone extinct, that species will be under selection to become of solitary size. Evolution, however, takes time and, if the present time transect finds the newly arrived or newly solitary species in the initial stages of its evolution, it will not yet have undergone evolution. It will still be of nonsolitary size.

The explanation that it is newly arrived seems the plausible explanation for the size of *Anolis richardi*, solitary on Tobago. This population has a maximum head length of 32 mm and a maximum snout-vent length of 128 mm.[2] These measurements are far out of line with the ranges of 20 to 23 mm for head length and 74 to 91 for snout-vent length found in other solitary anoles of the *roquet* group. However, *A. richardi* on Tobago is judged by taxonomists to be subspecifically identical with a population on Grenada that is a member of a species pair. As Table 2 indicates, *richardi* on Tobago is comparable in size with

[2] Lazell (1971) reports a male with a snout-vent length of 140 mm. This exceeds all known dimensions for the larger of a species pair. I must admit again that I have no ready explanation for this.

Table 2. Male and Female Maxima for Solitary and
Paired Populations of Anolis richardi

	♂	N	♀	N
Tobago (solitary)	32 – 128	(42)	21 – 80	(20)
Grenada (paired with *aeneus*)	28 – 108	(49)	19 – 73	(25)
St. Vincent (paired with *trinitatis*)	34 – 122	(38)	23 – 84	(27)
Bequia (paired with *aeneus*)	31 – 108	(30)	20 – 71	(9)
Carriacou (paired with *aeneus*)	31 – 120	(13)	19 – 71	(5)

those populations of *richardi* which are members of a species pair. If we may infer that *A. richardi* evolved its size as a member of a species pair and has only recently colonized Tobago, no anomaly exists. Much other data fit this hypothesis. Gorman and Atkins (1969) have shown that the direction of colonization for the *roquet* group in this part of its range has been *from* north to south. *Anolis richardi*, according to this, came from Grenada to Tobago. Since the Tobago population does not differ in squamation, color, or in the electrophoretic properties of those of its proteins which have been tested from the Grenada population, we may safely say that it appears to have undergone very little evolution in situ. We may then reasonably infer that the Tobago population has not had time to evolve to the solitary optimum and find in this an adequate explanation of its failure to conform to the Schoener rule.

It is worth noticing (Table 3) that *A. aeneus*, one of the smaller species pairs with *A. richardi*, does occur alone on some of the Grenadines and in these cases keeps the same size that it has on Grenada. Again, the historical explanation seems adequate: the solitary populations of *aeneus* in the Grenadines have not been isolated long enough.

In the Guadeloupean microarchipelago, on Guadeloupe itself, and on Desirade and Les Saintes, there is a series of populations differing strikingly in color and also in some scale characters. All these populations (maximal snout-vent lengths 71 to 80 mm) conform to the first Schoener rule for the size of solitary anoles. Off the Guadeloupe bank to the southwest is the island of Marie Galante. The only species collected there by recent expeditions—*A. ferreus*—has a size, like that of Tobago *richardi*, corresponding to that of the larger of a species pair (Fig. 4) and very unlike the related adjacent populations. Schoener (1969c) and Williams (1969) have commented on this problem. Schoener (1969c) suggests

Table 3. Maximal Size of *Anolis aeneus* on the Grenada Bank

Paired with *richardi*	Head Length	Snout-Vent Length	N
Grenada	19♂/14♀	71♂/51♀	49♂/19♀
Bequia	18/13	68/49	36/3
Carriacou	18/13	70/48	29/12
Solitary			
Mayreau	17♂/13♀	65♂/48♀	22♂/7 ♀
Petite Martinique	17/12	61/45	24/12
Petite St. Vincent	19/13	70/48	9/4
Union	18/13	69/50	13/8

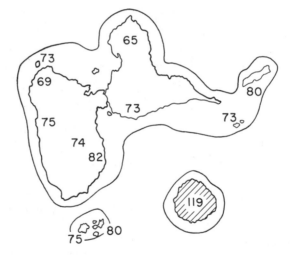

Fig. 4. The Guadeloupean microarchipelago. Numbers are maximum adult male size in each of the named populations. (Data corrected according to Lazell, 1971.)

several hypotheses but characterizes as "*ad hoc*" and "unfalsifiable" the hypothesis favored by Williams (1969) of the former presence of a second species on the island.

Clearly, if the second species is not now present (and there is no current evidence that it is) the idea of its former presence may seem merely an *ad hoc* escape from a conclusion damaging to the hypothesis. But the belief that all ecological conditions must be explained by present conditions *only* is itself fallacious, and historical explanations cannot safely be disregarded out of hand. The postulation of a second species is not literally unfalsifiable: it could be demonstrated by fossils or by old collections. In the present case, the hypothesis might be reinforced by evidence on vegetational history: Marie Galante is an arid island; was it always so, or has climatic deterioration eliminated the wet-adapted of two species?

One fact about Marie Galante may speak against the hypothesis of a second species: Marie Galante is on its own bank, and Williams (1969) has postulated that two species have been established in the Lesser Antilles only on emerging complex banks that permit both species to have a secure foothold before coming into contact and competition. However, Williams (1969) has also suggested that even failed invasions might leave their mark upon a resident species. (Schoener, 1969c has suggested for *ferreus* an explanation which might apply as a reason for the failure of *ferreus* to return to solitary anole size after extinction of the putative second species: "It may be just as advantageous for species to have females at the size normal for males, which they are in *richardi* or *ferreus*, or at least not feasible to move them off on adaptive peaks in favor of males.")

A still unresolved question is crucial to the second species hypothesis. The second species would on the grounds of proximity have to be a member of the *marmoratus* complex, while *ferreus* on Marie Galante, clearly related to that complex, must be supposed to have reached species status. If *ferreus* were not a full species, competition would not "nudge" it (Williams, 1969) into larger size. Instead, gene flow should reduce any trend to large size. Lazell (1964), the last reviser of the *marmoratus* complex, is vehement that *ferreus* is merely a subspecies of *marmoratus* and in fact he sees it as a participant in a size cline with adjacent island populations. The cline is less obvious on its face than Lazell makes out, but the issue is not easily settled. In such a case, biochemical taxonomy may very well assist; if *ferreus* is a species, it may plausibly differ from the other members of the *marmoratus* complex when studied by electrophoretic analysis of proteins.

The Marie Galante anole is on any hypothesis a special case; there are no genuine parallels. It is on its own bank and thus ought to have the characteristics of a solitary anole; however, its bank is special in that it is very close (almost uniquely close) to another larger bank. Compare, however, the similar proximity of the St. Vincent and Grenadan banks which (Williams, 1969) is involved in the major evolutionary events in the *roquet* group (Gorman and Atkins, 1969). It is tempting to seek the explanation of the one special feature in the other: the distance may be just far enough to have permitted *ferreus* to reach species status and just close enough to permit a high frequency of failed invasions. (Baskin and Williams [1966] have suggested similar "threshold" invasions as the explanation of the striking difference in neighboring island *Ameiva*.)

Schoener's Second Rule: Coadjustment of Species Pairs

Schoener's second rule predicts that, if two anole species occur on an island, one will be smaller and the other larger, the ratio of the two sizes ranging from

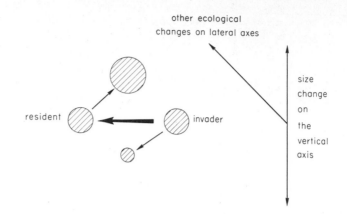

Fig. 5. Diagram of the possible effect on a resident solitary anole of an invader of the same size.

1.5 to 2. A simple model of classical character displacement provides a mechanism for this result: assume the invasion of the domain of a solitary anole by successful propagules of another solitary anole. The two are initially *ex hypothese* similar in size (Fig. 5). They compete for food and other resources. The classic expectation is divergence (character displacement) in order to avoid or lessen the effects of competition. Among the possible kinds of divergence will be size divergence, which has been shown to correlate with utilization of different sizes of food (Schoener and Gorman, 1968). Other modes of divergence are, of course, possible, but as a simplifying assumption we will *at first* ignore these. Our model and our prediction then is that, as a result of interspecies competition, one species will become larger and the other smaller.

No prediction is made in this model regarding the magnitude of size change. The striking empirical discovery of the Schoener rule for Lesser Antillean anoles is the extent of size difference.[3] In all cases in which two species are truly syntopic, i.e., both found widely dispersed and intermixed all over an island, the species differ in size by an impressive factor. Physically adjacent species in complex anole faunas may differ by much less or may not differ at all.

In most cases—taking mean solitary anole size as the initial size—both members of a species pair have changed size. As in the case of solitary anole size, there appears to be a phyletic factor in size change (Table 4).

---

[3]The size differences found by Schoener for *Anolis* are impressively greater than those found empirically for birds, as Schoener has himself commented. There is, however, an obvious difference in life history between birds, which characteristically exercise parental care of their young and lead or actively feed them, and reptiles, in which their young may be active competitors. All the discussion in this paper is in terms of adult sizes. In order genuinely understand the competitive significance of size for *Anolis* and other reptiles, we should know sizes and their food from hatchlings to old adults. No data adequate to this issue exist.

Table 4. Divergence from Average Solitary *Anolis* Species Size in Two-Species Islands (Figures Rounded; Males Only. Unpublished Data from Schoener.)

Head Length

1. *bimaculatus* group (average solitary size ca. 22 mm head length)

	Larger	Smaller	Larger/Smaller
Anguilla bank	−1, −2, −2	−8, −8	1.4, 1.4
St. Kitts bank	+4, +7, +9	−7, −7, −7	1.7, 1.9, 2.1
Antigua bank	+9, +11	−6, −6, −6	1.9, 2, 1

2. *roquet* group (average solitary size ca. 21 mm head length)

	Larger	Smaller	Larger/Smaller
St. Vincent	+13	−3	1.9
Grenada bank	+7, +10	−3, −3	1.6, 1.7

Snout-Vent Length

1. *bimaculatus* group (average solitary size ca. 71 mm snout-vent Length)

	Larger	Smaller	Larger/Smaller
Anguilla bank	−3, −6, −7	−25, −24	1.4, 1.4
St. Kitts bank	+17, +31, +35	−20, −22, −22	1.8, 2, 2.1
Antigua bank	+31, +42	−17, −19	1.8, 2.2

2. *roquet* group (average solitary size is 81 mm snout-vent length)

	Larger	Smaller	Larger/Smaller
St. Vincent	+41	−10	1.7
Grenada bank	+27, +39	−10, −11	1.5, 1.7

In the *bimaculatus* species group in the northern Lesser Antilles, the smaller of the species pair diverges from solitary size substantially and rather uniformly, the larger to a variable degree, on one bank to an extreme degree, on another variably. In one case (*wattsi-gingivinus* on the Anguilla bank), there is no departure by larger species from solitary size. This is a special case, to be discussed below as a problem.

In the southern Lesser Antilles, the very distinct *roquet* species group (Underwood, 1959; Gorman and Atkins, 1969) has its smaller species relatively little reduced from solitary anole size (there is near overlap with the lower range of solitary species of *roquet* or *bimaculatus* groups) and the larger is much larger in absolute terms (always more than 50% greater than solitary size).

One other fact is of importance: Schoener and Gorman (1968) have shown that on Grenada, in addition to substantial size divergence between the two syntopic species, there is real if less striking difference in thermal habitat and hence physiological adaptation. There is anecdotal evidence for similar climatic difference (or difference in climatic range) between other pairs of Lesser Antillean anoles. Thus, *wattsi* on St. Kitts and on Barbuda is known to include in its habitat darker areas than any utilized by *bimaculatus* on St. Kitts or *leachii* on Barbuda.

This is a noteworthy phenomenon: though the Lesser Antillean data demonstrate in two distinct phyletic groups that one of the first adjustments between syntopic anoles is size divergence (and substantial size divergence at that), probably in all cases there is divergence also in another parameter. Thus, if we view size divergence as movement on a vertical scale to avoid competitive collision, there is apparently always movement also sideways in another ecological dimension. Clearly, to fully fit our model to the Lesser Antillean facts, we must amend it to include the possibility (in fact, high probability) of ecological adaptations in factors other than size. Nevertheless, we shall as a matter of method always look *first* for size change as the adaptive reply to interspecies competition—finding something of an empirical justification in the striking extent of size change in the adaptive shift from Lesser Antillean solitary species to Lesser Antillean species pairs.

A Problem Case Under the Second Schoener Rule:
A Member of a Species Pair That Is Too Small

Anolis gingivinus of the Anguilla bank, as already mentioned, has the size of a solitary anole, although a second species, *A. wattsi*, occurs on the same bank. On St. Martin, *A. gingivinus* males have a maximum head length of 22 mm and a maximum snout-vent length of 68 mm. They are, in fact, at the lower end of the range of size for solitary species. *A. wattsi* on the same island is indeed smaller (the same maxima, 14 and 47 mm, respectively) and hence there is not in a strict sense a violation of the Schoener rule. However, the ratio between larger and smaller species is the lowest (1.5) in any Lesser Antillean species pair and *wattsi* is as large on St. Martin as on the St. Kitts or the Antigua banks. There should be some special aspect of the relations of the two species on the Anguilla bank that explains the anomalous ratio.

Anolis wattsi, which on the other banks on which it occurs is widely syntopic with a larger species, is on St. Martin strikingly localized. *Anolis gingivinus*, like the larger species of the other banks, is widespread over all the island, but *A. wattsi* is restricted to certain ravines (Lazell, Ruibal, personal communications). In fact, the restriction of *A. wattsi* on St. Martin corresponds to its general tendency on other islands (see above) to occur most frequently and abundantly in damper and shadier places than the larger species, whichever that may be. But the restriction on St. Martin is severer, more complete, such that *wattsi* does not occur outside the damper, shadier places. It is impressive for our argument that though this special sort of overlap implies minimal size change, there is still size change. *Anolis wattsi* is a derivative of *A. acutus*, solitary and of solitary size on St. Croix; the most impressive change externally in *wattsi* is size.

From the Lesser Antilles to Large Complex Islands: The Model Stated

According to the hypothesis here set forward, the size ratios seen on the two-species islands of the Lesser Antilles give us the correct image of the magnitude and nature of the size differences that evolved between the first two species of any of the Greater Antilles.

Again, the thermal difference so clearly demonstrated on Grenada by Schoener and Gorman is a model of sorts of alternative differences to be expected in the two species stage of the colonization of the Greater Antilles.

The two-species stage on the Greater Antilles is long past. The Lesser Antillean story is the only clue we have to it. Contrariwise, the one-, two-, three-, or four-species islands that we see among the Caribbean satellites to the Greater Antilles (cf. Williams, 1969) do not provide any comparably useful model of these earliest stages in the evolution of the fauna of the large islands. *All* these satellite islands have animals that are too recently arrived and too little evolved since their arrival to provide any light on the radiation within the large islands.

We must begin then with the Lesser Antillean model. We can, as a thought experiment, add to a fauna (coadapted as in the Lesser Antilles) various sizes of new colonizers (Fig. 6).

Thus (1) if we add a new anole of appropriately solitary size, it will be intermediate between the two resident species. The easiest adjustment would seem to be change in size of one or both resident species—a spread of extremes. (We assume, according to the Lesser Antillean model of the species pair, that after evolution of size adaptation, the largest of the series of three will be about twice the size of the invader and the smallest about half its size; i.e., that syntopic species adjacent in size will, whenever possible, differ in size by a ratio of 2 to 1.) Note that in the simplified competitive scheme that we have set up the invader will *not* change size. If it were to do so, it could only come closer in size to one or the other of the two resident species.

(2) If we postulate a single invader as large as the larger of the pair (and we allow only size change), we again expect a spread of extremes. The amount of change and whether one or all will change will depend upon the genetic potentialities of each. An essentially similar result is expected if the invader is as small as the smaller of the resident pair.

(3) We will expect no size change—all other things being equal—only if the single newly arrived species is sufficiently larger or sufficiently smaller than the resident species to avoid or relieve competition on that ground alone. Such size disparity is to be expected in the colonizer only if it comes from a complex fauna where alone extreme sizes, according to our hypothesis, will have evolved.

In any event, with three species present we expect a graded series of

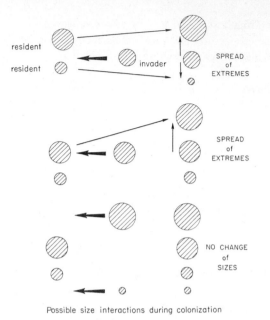

Fig. 6. *Possible size interactions during colonization of a two-anole island by invaders of various sizes.*

sizes—large, middle, and small—such that they are far enough apart in physical dimensions to be noncompetitors. I emphasize again that as a first hypothesis we assume the size ratio seen in two species islands of the Lesser Antilles to apply to adjacent species in multispecies series.

We are ignoring here, again deliberately, some real possibilities of size convergence (Schoener, 1970). We may be compelled to invoke size convergence or at least limitation of size divergence later under special conditions of resource distribution. We set this aside here as not a *first* expectation.

If now, following our simplified model, we add still another species, we see that again unless it fits at the extremes it will compete in size with some resident and indeed the more the size series is spread, the more difficult will it be for a new invader to avoid competition by change of its own size. Again we expect size change only at the extremes.

THE MODEL TESTED

The First Test: A General View of Size in the Greater Antilles: The Model Elaborated

To test and amplify these hypotheses, we have only to look at the largest and smallest species on each of the four Greater Antilles Table 5. The extremes are indeed further apart the larger the fauna. This we have in fact defined as the third Schoener rule.

Table 5.

Island	Faunal Size	Males of Largest Species	Males of Smallest Species	Size Spread
Cuba	28 species	191[a]	38	−153
Hispaniola	23 species	175	38	−137
Puerto Rico	11 species	137	40	− 97
Jamaica	7 species	124	57	− 74

[a]Data not from Schoener but from Schwartz and Garrido (1971). Dealing with much larger samples than those available to Schoener, they divide the *equestris* complex into five species, the maxima of which are 191, 190, 188, and 172.

But note that some constraint seems to exist at the lower end of the scale: on Cuba the smallest species is not significantly smaller than the smallest on Hispaniola or Puerto Rico. Only on Jamaica is there a difference. Here the smallest species is 17 mm larger, thus appearing to imply that the pressure toward small size is not as great as on the larger, faunally richer islands.

Apparently, however, there is some floor at ca. 38 to 40 mm male snout-vent length; below this size, change is not possible to an anole: no pressure of adjacent species can push the smallest species further. Note also that size change *upward* does not have a simple and direct relation to the number of species; it is slowed in the larger islands.

What, then, are the factors that provide upper and lower limits to size change?

Obviously one upper limit is provided in energetic terms by available food resources. We find, therefore, that giants tend to be allopatric (the "races" of *A. ricordii* or species of *A. equestris*). In addition, Schoener has provided evidence that giant anoles may extensively supplement their insect diet with fruits. It is reasonable to suspect that this may be a general phenomenon. Note, however, that the *equestris* complex on Cuba is larger than any anolines on any part of North, Central, or South America. Clearly, on the mainlands constraints on large anoline size are greater than on the islands. Presumably, mainland anoles are affected by the competition of other arboreal forms such as other lizards but probably also birds and mammals. (Some birds compete with anoles in the West Indies, but critical groups present on the mainland are absent.)

Lower limits—which seem in anoles to be even more rigid than the upper limits and are *the same on the mainland and the islands*—are perhaps provided by competition with insects and by vulnerability to insect and other arthropod predation.

In any event, such constraints apart, we expect and find the spread of extremes. But on the Greater Antillean islands, the spread of extremes does not keep pace with the size of the fauna. The initial distance as exemplified on two species islands in the Lesser Antilles was considerable: the larger species might be half again the size of the smaller. Clearly, between adjacent middle sized species in large faunas, this distance has been severely compressed and, if we look at actual faunal sizes on each of the Greater Antilles, we find much duplication of middle sizes.

We should expect this on our model. The extremes clearly have a free direction in which to move. The middle, however, is always crowded (Fig. 7). An animal at the middle cannot readily adapt in size. It cannot easily grow larger because a range of upper sizes is already preempted; it cannot grow smaller because a range of smaller sizes is already preempted. For it, adaptation (coadjustment) must involve another ecological dimension.

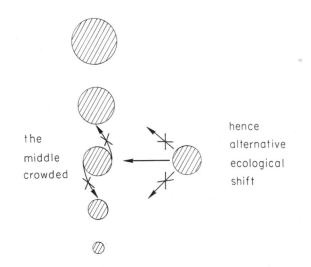

the
middle
crowded

hence
alternative
ecological
shift

Fig. 7. The "crowded middle" in the later stages of colonization or radiation.

In fact, we have already seen on two species islands of the Lesser Antilles that even two species do coadjust in other regards than size. They move apart on other ecological dimensions as well—in the analyzed case in a microclimatic dimension.

We emphasize then again the two phenomena—vertical movement on the size scale with spread of extremes and sidewise movement on other ecological dimensions.

If we look at the vertical movement on the size axis, we see that this is freest for extreme species. Until there are other constraints, these species need not move sidewise: the larger may become larger and the smaller smaller. If this be true, the largest and the smallest species should have retained their original microhabitat. They will be syntopic because their adjustment has been in absolute size.

This is not true at all, however, for the middle-sized species. The crowded middle requires that these species must move apart in some ecological dimension other than size. We must expect these species of intermediate size, then, to be ecologically very diverse; we may also expect some of these species to be allotopic or allopatric.

Let us now test these hypotheses against an actual fauna.

Puerto Rico: The Test By Reconstruction of History

On the basis of the model just constructed, it should be possible to set up a series of sequential steps which lead to a fauna of any desired complexity—5, 10, 20, 25. But how shall we test these presumptive patterns? They are historical patterns not directly verifiable. Obviously we can test our model and the patterns it generates only if we have some solid independent ground for inferring the sequence of events in faunal history, some island fauna for which we are confident that we know phyletic relationships, know which species are primitive and which derived, know in fact the total sequence.

Very fortunately the Puerto Rican anole fauna is known and understood to the desired degree. No other of the Greater Antilles fits the stringent requirements of the test. Jamaica, with seven species, all the result of a single radiation, might rival Puerto Rico, but the sequence of phyletic branching among the endemic species is so unclear that several phylogenies might be proposed with no grounds for choice among them. In Cuba and Hispaniola, there are still a number of species incompletely known and probably also species still to be discovered. Their faunas also are mixtures of more than one phyletic group and involve endemic radiations complicated by one or several later invasions. Certainly we can only hesitantly speak of the phyletic sequences in either of these islands.

Even for the Puerto Rican bank (Fig. 8) there is still one species which is very poorly known. Ten species are ecologically well studied on the mainland of Puerto Rico (Fig. 9): *A. cuvieri*, a giant anole; *A. occultus*, a dwarf; *A. evermanni*, a green tree anole; *A. stratulus*, a grey-brown smaller tree anole; *A. gundlachi, A. cristatellus, A. cooki*, brown or grey anoles of the lower tree

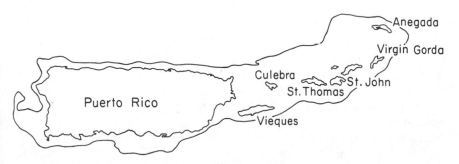

Fig. 8. The Puerto Rican bank, showing the Puerto Rican mainland and the smaller Virgin Islands to the east.

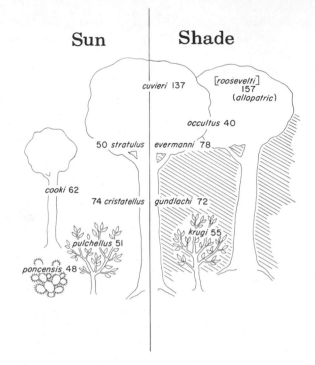

Fig. 9. The 10 Anolis *of the mainland of Puerto Rico placed diagrammatically according to their spatial and climatic niches. Number is maximum male size. In brackets is an eleventh species, A.* roosevelti, *isolated on the small island of Culebra (see Fig. 8).*

trunk; and *A. krugi, A. pulchellus* and *A. poncensis,* striped anoles of bushes and grasses. These can be discussed with confidence. However, on the small island of Culebra to the east, an eleventh species is known from two specimens: *Anolis roosevelti.* It may now be extinct. Fortunately its relationships and phyletic position are clear (it is a giant, related to but more primitive than the common giant species of Puerto Rico—*A. cuvieri*) and, though nothing is directly known of its ecology, much may be inferred from its structure, so very similar to *A. cuvieri.* The incompleteness of our knowledge is in this instance minimally inconvenient. (See further below.)

Before going on, let us establish unmistakably that we have all the information needed to determine and verify the historical sequence of ecological change in the Puerto Rican anole fauna that we are attempting to reconstruct. For our purpose we need:

(1) *Detailed information on the ecology of the Recent species.* This we have for Puerto Rico from Rand (1964), Schoener and Schoener (1971b) and Webster (1969) as well as unpublished notes on *Anolis cooki* by Webster.

(2) *A clue to the ecology primitive for the group.* We can infer this from the

basic adaptations of the genus. The adhesive toe lamellae which define the genus are devices for arboreal life high in the trees on leaves and branches. *Anolis* came to the islands from the complex faunas of the mainlands; it was there primarily and primitively an animal adapted to the tree crown. Of the modern niches on Puerto Rico, therefore, the crown niche should be most like (but not identical to) the niche of the anole that first invaded Puerto Rico.

(3) *A clue to the first stages of complexity.* At a minimum we must know the two species stages and the rules for transformation from the one species stage. We have this, of course, in the Lesser Antilles in Schoener's rule 2. It would help, no doubt, if we had direct empirical evidence on stages of three or four species, but in *Anolis*, as I have pointed out above, we have no such stages, evolved *in situ*, available to us. Our model is the device by which we bridge this gap in our evidence.

(4) *A test of the temporal sequence in ecology that we are endeavoring to set up.* The usual test will be phylogeny. It would be best were there a fossil sequence that would really give us in successive layers and ages the sequence of sizes that did occur. But no such sequence is known for *Anolis* in Puerto Rico—or anywhere. We must operate, therefore, in the customary way by inference from the morphology of Recent species. Fortunately, in Puerto Rico the morphological evidence seems unusually solid and unambiguous. As we shall see below, there are few loose ends. For Puerto Rican anoles we can construct an exceptionally believable phylogeny.

Figure 10 constructs this phylogeny in terms of the evidence provided by the investigations of Etheridge (1960, 1965) on osteology, of Gorman and Atkins (1969) on karyotypes, and of Maldonado and Ortiz (1966) on electrophoretic patterns. This evidence is discussed in some detail below.

However, Fig. 10, like most dendrograms, does not carry on its face all the information that is needed to justify or even to construct such a phyletic diagram. In addition to the specific features cited above and labeled in Fig. 10, there are two sorts of background information utilized that are always implicit for the specialist who makes and is competent to make such a phyletic diagram:

(1) *Narrow relationships.* Always in a phyletic study some species appear on the totality of obvious external characters and on habitus and often on geographic proximity to be so closely similar, that any more elusive character—skeletal, chromosomal, biochemical, or behavioral—that contradicts that relationship is itself put in question. We deal in such cases with species pairs and species series, in which the problem is *not* a problem of establishing affinity but may involve, instead, a problem of finding valid differential characters.

In Puerto Rico the narrow relationships of the anoles are easy to recognize. To the experienced eye and especially in life, all Puerto Rican anoles are readily distinguishable by conventional external characters: dewlap and body color, scale size, etc., but despite the differences, species pairs and series are obvious: *A. cristatellus* and *A. cooki* are such an obvious pair and have in the past been

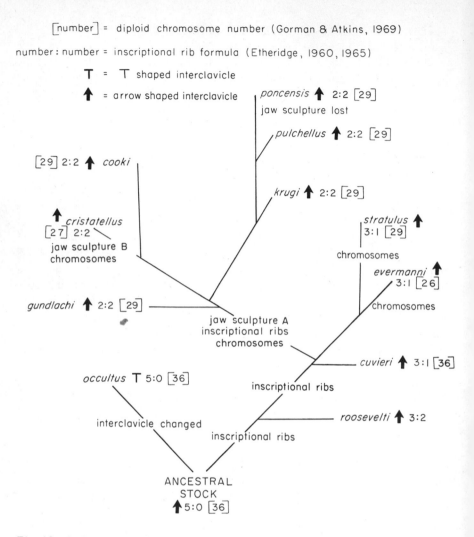

[number] = diploid chromosome number (Gorman & Atkins, 1969)

number : number = inscriptional rib formula (Etheridge, 1960, 1965)

T = T shaped interclavicle

↑ = arrow shaped interclavicle

Fig. 10. A dendrogram for Puerto Rican Anolis *indicating the points at which chromosomes and skeletal morphology change.*

confused; *A. gundlachi* is similar to them in habitus, including tail crest, but quite distinct in body color and especially scale size. *A. cuvieri* and *A. roosevelti* are as clearly similar to each other in their middorsal and tail crests but they differ in color and in smaller details. *A. evermanni* and *stratulus* are not so obviously paired, differing strikingly in color. They are united as much by the absence of the scale specializations of the other series as by any positive feature. *A. krugi, A. pulchellus,* and *A. poncensis* form an obvious series, similar in habitus but differing sharply in scale size and dewlap color.

Many of the characters ("character states") that unite such species pairs and series reflect direct ecological adaptations to the environment in which they live. Thus, *poncensis, pulchellus,* and *krugi* are strikingly similar in their relatively slender body habitus and in the dorsolateral light lines that further emphasize their slenderness. Both features are directly adaptive (cryptic) in the grass-bush habitat of these three species. It would seem reasonable to suspect circularity in any phylogenetic hypothesis that uses groups partly defined on ecological grounds in such a test as we propose of the *origin* of ecological adaptations. But such ecological adaptations by themselves neither affirm nor deny phyletic relationships. Clearly the unity and validity of groups partly recognized on directly adaptive features needs to be confirmed by independent evidence, i.e., the evidence of characters *not* directly adaptive. However, ecological adaptations may be those of a common ancestor or they may have been separately acquired by diverse phyletic lines. If, however, the independent evidence—karyotypic, biochemical, osteological—is congruent with the hypothesis of common ancestry, there will be no ground for discarding groups partly ecological in nature from our test phylogeny. What we will seek in the phyletic parallel to our ecological diagram is a *sequence* of morphological adaptation to be compared with a *sequence* of ecological adaptations, and a sequence is given by the connections *between* "narrow" groups not by the groups themselves.

How do we connect these narrow groups with one another? Clearly again by similarity. Of any species pair or series, one member is closer to other species in the relevant complex. Here ecological adaptations are no longer involved; we deal strictly with characters that transgress at least minor ecological boundaries: we here use evidence such as that labeled in Fig. 10, not in despite of "narrow relationship" but as a complement to it. We use karyotypic, biochemical, or osteological evidence for whatever leads they provide. Thus, no habitus or ecological features make obvious a particularly close relationship between *gundlachi* and the *poncensis-pulchellus-krugi* series; however, the electrophoretic evidence of Maldonado and Ortiz insists on this relationship. Chromosomal evidence (Gorman, Thomas, and Atkins) again shows a closer resemblance of *gundlachi* with the grass-bush series than with *cristatellus,* which in habitus and habits would seem a closer relative. Similarly, jaw sculpture suggests that the grass-bush series may form a larger unit with *cristatellus, gundlachi,* and *cooki,* and even with *Anolis cybotes* on the adjacent island of Hispaniola.

(2) *Wider relationships.* Just as the evidence of narrow relationship is not explicit in Fig. 10 and yet was essential to its making, so there is another side of background evidence of as great importance but again not explicit on the diagram itself. Figure 10 was not constructed *in vacuo* on evidence provided by Puerto Rican anoles alone; implicit in it are many stated judgments on the phylogeny of *Anolis,* of iguanids, and of lizards. This is necessarily true. In the present stage of taxonomic biology, it cannot be successfully pretended that any scheme of classification or any phyletic diagram, however restricted in scope, is

independent of the thousands of analyses that have gone before it. We necessarily (and despite pretensions to the contrary) examine all cases in the context of accumulated knowledge. Only from such wider viewpoints can we get clues to primitive character states whether in Puerto Rican anoles or in other groups. Etheridge (1960) assessed the phyletic sequence of skeletal features *within Anolis* on the basis of a careful consideration of the interrelationships of all iguanids (and for certain features, all lizards). His analysis itself relied heavily upon the prior work of Cope and Boulenger—and of others of lesser competence. Similarly, the judgment central to the discussion below of karyotype evolution, that the karyotype with 12 macrochromosomes and 24 microchromosomes is primitive *within Anolis*, rests upon considerations derived from a review of known iguanid and other lizard karyotypes (Gorman, Atkins, and Holzinger, 1967). Such overviews of the information on one or several higher levels are imperative preconditions for phyletic analysis. In analysis of the Puerto Rican anoles we would have no firm foundation for our phylogeny except that we have such overviews. Direction of evolutionary change is never unequivocally indicated within any narrow group; it only begins to be indicated by the connections between narrow groups and may only be satisfactorily indicated by the *congruence* of trends in a wide-ranging comparison going far beyond the level of the narrow groups.

Let us consider for a moment one character state peculiar to one species—the body scales of *poncensis*. They are larger and more heavily keeled than in any other Puerto Rican anole. Are they primitive, i.e., temporally antecedent to the other compared character states, or derived, i.e. the result of relatively recent divergence? Clearly the condition is at one end of a series of evolutionary stages, but which end? Clearly there is a sequence *poncensis-pulchellus-krugi* in which *krugi* is more similar to other Puerto Rican anoles than are the other grass-bush anoles, but what is the direction of the sequence? There is no answer within the sequence itself. The answer comes from the evidence of inscriptional ribs and of karyotypes, and especially from the *congruence* of these two quite independent kinds of evidence, each of which depends on information not only outside the Puerto Rican radiation but outside the genus *Anolis*. On this evidence, quite outside the *poncensis-pulchellus-krugi* series, there can be no question but that *poncensis* is an extremely specialized animal, the most specialized species of the whole Puerto Rican radiation.

I emphasize that Fig. 10 has built into it as background information much that derives from both the wider and the narrower view. With this understanding, the specific characters most used in the construction of the figure can now be commented upon.

The characters used in the construction of Fig. 10 deserve brief comment:

(1) *Number of inscriptional ribs* (Etheridge, 1960, 1965). "Inscriptional ribs" are the endochondral abdominal skeleton of lizards, and in *Anolis* involve numbers of fixed and floating abdominal "chevrons" that are species- and

species-group-specific. South American *Anolis* of the alpha section, to which all Puerto Rico anoles belong, have high numbers of such chevrons (5 to 6), all of which are fixed. (High numbers are believed to be primitive; see Etheridge, 1960, pp. 110-115). In the West Indies, most species have reduced numbers of chevrons, some of which become free in advanced forms. On the basis of inscriptional ribs, Puerto Rican anoles sort into the following groups, arranged in the order of increasing specialization (data on *A. occultus* [undescribed in 1960] and *A. cooki* [not then recognized as a full species] have not previously been published and derive from Etheridge, in litt.):

I	*A. occultus*	5 to 6 fixed; 0 free
II	*A. roosevelti*	3 fixed; 2 free
III	*A. cuvieri*	
	A. evermanni	3 fixed; 1 free
	A. stratulus	
IV	*A. cristatellus*	
	A. cooki	
	A. gundlachi	2 fixed; 2 free
	A. krugi	
	A. pulchellus	
	A. poncensis	

Anoles on other islands would be included in each of these groupings except I, e.g., *A. ricordii* of Hispaniola in group II, and many species on Hispaniola, Cuba, and Jamaica in group III, fewer on each of the islands in group IV. Occurrence of groups III and IV o Jamaica, all the anoles of which belong to the beta section of Etheridge (1960), demonstrates that groups III and IV have separately evolved in these two sections. Since these groups have evolved twice, they may have evolved independently still other times. It requires other evidence to settle the point.

But the sequence from primitive to specialized seems clear, however many times it may have occurred; and this evidence is of primary importance for the placement of *occultus* and *roosevelti* in the dendrogram of Fig. 10 and puts them clearly at the base of the phyletic tree.

(2) *Interclavicle type* (Etheridge, 1960). All Puerto Rican anoles belong to the alpha section as distinguished by Etheridge (1960, 1965)—the autonomic caudal vertebrae are without or have only very small transverse processes. Within the alpha section, two major subsections differ in the shape of the interclavicle and its relationship to the clavicle. The two kinds of interclavicle have been distinguished as "arrow" and "T"—a convenient phraseology which somewhat exaggerates the actual difference. An "arrow" interclavicle has the lateral arms divergent from the clavicle in their whole extent; a "T" interclavicle has these arms proximally closely applied to the clavicle. The phyletic sequence within the alpha anoles is clearly from "arrow" to "T." Nonanoline iguanids have the arms

of the interclavicle more widely divergent from the clavicle than in any anole, and among anoles most of those which are primitive in regard to inscriptional ribs have arrow-shaped interclavicles.

Within Puerto Rico, only *occultus* has a T-interclavicle. In inscriptional ribs it is quite primitive and it is a plausible hypothesis that the first anoline split within Puerto Rico occurred between the ancestors of *occultus*, which evolved the T-shaped interclavicle, and the ancestors of *roosevelti-cuvieri*, which retained the primitive arrow-interclavicle.

(3) *Jaw sculpture* (Etheridge, 1960). Jaw sculpture occurs only in adult anoles of a few species in Puerto Rico and Hispaniola, and one in Cuba. Etheridge distinguished three types of sculpture, two of which occur in Puerto Rico: (a) the *cristatellus* type (B of Fig. 10): "the outer and lower parts of the dentary are swollen and irreguarly scored with deep horizontal excavations." This is known in *cristatellus* (and the very similar species *scriptus* from the Caicos, Inagua and Mariguana banks west of Puerto Rico).

(b) the *krugi* type (A of Fig. 10): "along the ventral surface of the dentary there is a series of from seven to ten large, deep, semi-lunar excavations." This occurs in *A. krugi, A. gundlachi,* and *A. pulchellus.*

The groupings here are clearly minor ones, but the specific kind of sculpture seen is distinctive enough to be probably monophyletic and hence useful at the species group level. *Anolis cooki*, not distinguished as a species at the time Etheridge wrote, has the *krugi* type jaw sculpture (MCZ 93434).

(4) *Electrophoretic patterns.* A. A. Maldonado and Evelina Ortiz (1966) subjected blood sera from *A. cristatellus, A. gundlachi, A. krugi, A. pulchellus, A. evermanni*, and *A. cuvieri* to electrophoresis. Patterns of mobility and of concentration of four globulins and of albumin were obtained. The most similar patterns were those of *A. pulchellus* and *A. krugi*, and *A. gundlachi* was next in its resemblance to these. *Anolis cristatellus* was distinctive among Puerto Rican anoles in the relatively slower mobility of its third globulin. *A. cuvieri* and *A. evermanni* were distinctive in the higher mobility and greater concentration of the first globulin. These results are readily interpretable in terms of our dendrogram, and, like karyotypes and in contrast to external morphology, indicate a closer relation of *A. gundlachi* to the grass anoles (*A. krugi, A. pulchellus, A. poncensis*) than to *A. cristatellus.*

(5) *Karyotypes* (Gorman and Atkins, 1969). A karyotype with 6 pairs of macrochromosomes and 12 pairs of microchromosomes has been regarded as primitive for lizards generally and specifically for the family Iguanidae (Gorman, Atkins, and Holzinger, 1967). This pattern is retained in only two Puerto Rican anoles but the other rather diverse karyotypes in Puerto Rican anoles may be derived from this most primitive one (Gorman and Atkins, 1969). The karyotypes sort into the following groups:

I   (primitive): *A. occultus, A. cuvieri*, $2N = 36$
II   (advanced): $2N$ reduced from 36:
   a. *stratulus, gundlachi, krugi, pulchellus,*
       poncensis, cooki $2N = 29$
   b. *cristatellus* $2N = 27$
   c. *evermanni* $2N = 26$

Analysis at this level (diploid number only) is, of course, very incomplete and includes in one group karyotypes not closely related.

Further analysis (Gorman and Atkins, 1969) sorts II into 2 series: (a) a *cristatellus* group with a primitive subseries containing *gundlachi, cooki, krugi, pulchellus*, and *poncensis*, and a more advanced subseries including only *cristatellus* on Puerto Rico plus *scriptus* in the Bahamas; (b) an *acutus* group (named after a related species on St. Croix) with only *stratulus* and *evermanni* as Puerto Rican members.

The *cristatellus* series is well defined: all have a sex trivalent $(X_1 X_2 Y)$. The diploid number is therefore odd in males, but *cristatellus* and *scriptus* lack two microchromosomes present in more primitive members of the series (Gorman, Thomas, and Atkins, 1968).

The *cristatellus* group differs from *stratulus* in having 6 macro-, *2 intermediate*, and 5 microbivalents and the sex trivalent; whereas *stratulus* has 6 macro-, *one* intermediate, and 6 microbivalents; and the sex trivalent—i.e. the 8th chromosome—is metacentric in the *cristatellus* group, acrocentric in *stratulus*. *Anolis evermanni* differs from both the *cristatellus* series and *stratulus*. It lacks the sex trivalent but has a heteromorphic pair of sex chromosomes. As in *stratulus* there is a sharp break between 6 macrobivalents and the seventh (intermediate), which is metacentric. The 8th chromosome pair (acrocentric) are the sex chromosomes. There are only 26 chromosomes in both males and females.

Clearly in the advanced Puerto Rican species certain of the original 12 pairs of microchromosomes have undergone fusion to produce intermediate metacentric and sex chromosomes, and there apparently has been loss of chromosomes as well. The intermediate steps are missing in these rather impressive changes, and it is not on the face of the evidence possible to determine at what point the *cristatellus* group branched off relative to *stratulus* and *evermanni*. If, as Etheridge (1960) believes on osteological grounds, *A. cybotes* of Hispaniola is a member of the *cristatellus* series, then, since the karyotype of *cybotes* is primitive (6 pairs of macro-, 12 pairs of microbivalents), the sex trivalent must have evolved twice. The dichotomy between *cristatellus* and *acutus* would have been very early and *evermanni* may have diverged before the sex trivalent evolved in the *acutus* group. Alternatively, if, as Gorman and Atkins believe, the sex trivalent evolved only once, *cybotes* cannot be part of the *cristatellus* series (see their dendrogram, 1969, p. 77) and *evermanni* may have lost its sex trivalent secondarily.

The important point appears to be that the *cristatellus* series is very much a small radiation on Puerto Rico, compact and clearly delineated, and quite separate now from the *acutus* group, which is relict on Puerto Rico but achieved its own flowering out in the *bimaculatus* and *wattsi* series of the northern Lesser Antilles. Whether the *cristatellus* series branched off *before* the *acutus* series or at some point *from* the *acutus* series cannot now be determined. Figure 10 rather arbitrarily chooses the point of divergence early, following the osteological rather then the karyotypic evidence.

The several kinds of evidence are in very good agreement and the dendrogram can be taken to be a highly probable representation of real relationships.

Compare now Fig. 11, which indicates the ecological and size changes correlated with the phyletic branching. Inspection of this diagram leads to the following comments:

(1) The first dichotomy within the dendrogram involves size change primarily. The two species that are the surviving representatives of that dichotomy in the modern fauna are basically in the same habitat and climatic niche.[4] They both may crudely be described as crown animals of the shaded forest. It is possible to quibble a bit about this but the same modal situation describes both. A giant anole such as *cuvieri*, though it is, in fact, seen some of the time at every level (personal observation), is most often seen high in the crown. A dwarf anole such as *occultus* is seen on branches and twigs of small diameter (Webster, 1969) and therefore not infrequently on bushes and vines, but certainly its modal structural niche includes the crown.

The size ratio between these two species is the most extreme seen within the whole Puerto Rican sequence. It far exceeds the size differential seen on the two-species islands of the Lesser Antilles. We may reasonably doubt that the size differential seen now is the original size differential when these species first coadapted; rather it must represent the "spread of extremes."

The dendrogram of Fig. 10 now appears to require that there be a second dichotomy derived from the *cuvieri-roosevelti* stock and resulting in (1) the *evermanni* sequence (which gave rise to the *bimaculatus* sequence in St. Croix and the Lesser Antilles) and (2) the *gundlachi* sequence (more important in Puerto Rico). However, the apparent implication of Fig. 10 that there was a true dichotomy (appearing to imply simultaneity of origin of the *evermanni* and *gundlachi* stocks) is not necessary in terms of our model.

Our model, based as it is on the primary importance of size, implies that the next step in the sequence would be the addition of only *one* new species. Such an addition would have the result suggested in Fig. 6—a species of middle size

---

[4] *A. occultus* and *A. cuvieri; roosevelti* is here ignored since it is an isolated relict not syntopic with *occultus.* See below.

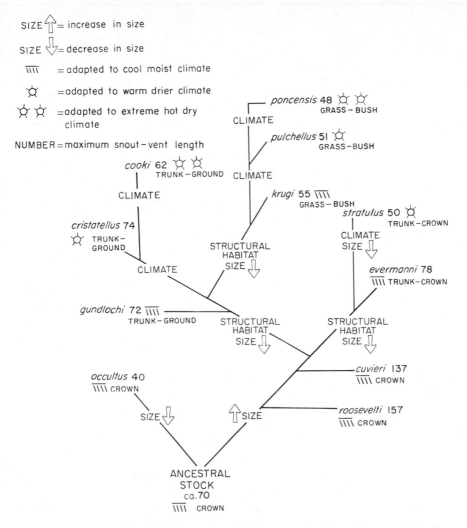

Fig. 11. A dendrogram for Puerto Rican Anolis *showing the points at which size or other ecological change have occurred.*

inserting between two already divergent species, which thus become more extreme in size ("spread of extremes").

Anolis evermanni fits our expectation for this third species. It is intermediate in size between *cuvieri* and *occultus* and it is again basically a crown animal of the shaded forest. When now we examine the size ratios of these three crown species, we find that the size ratios between adjacent species (i.e., those most similar in size) are quite within the range of the ratios of the anoles of two species islands in the Lesser Antilles:

cuvieri	137	
ratio *cuvieri:evermanni*		1.8
evermanni	78	
ratio *evermanni:occultus*		1.95
occultus	40	

Let us at once admit that *evermanni* as the third species was not at its first origin ecologically equivalent to *evermanni* in the modern fauna any more than the giant and dwarf were at the time of their dichotomy identical to modern *cuvieri* and *occultus*. In size *evermanni* may have been essentially what it is now; but it may have used more of the tree trunk then than it does in the presence of the additional species of the Recent fauna.

It must again be emphasized that, while we are here stressing size adjustment to every extent possible, other adjustments to the presence of competing species do in fact always occur. Thus, although in the crown size change was primary, other ecological adjustments did in fact occur in the trio *occultus, evermanni, cuvieri* and are seen in the trio today:

(1) Giant species such as *cuvieri* cannot, as adults, utilize the finer twigs and branches of the crown; they are necessarily confined to the more central area of the crown, the heavier branches, and they do use the trunks of their trees and do descend not infrequently to the ground. We unfortunately know extremely little about the habitat of smaller individuals and hatchlings.[5] However, hatchling *cuvieri* are already larger than adult *occultus*. The species may therefore always be confined to larger perches than those characteristic of *occultus*. Neither adults nor juveniles of *cuvieri* have even been found sleeping on low perches readily accessible to the human eye.

(2) Dwarf species such as *occultus* do use very small twigs, vines and stems. We have the advantage for *occultus* of the detailed observations of T. P. Webster (1969), who provides the following summary: "*Anolis occultus* appears to be an inhabitant of the peripheral vegetation. Branches and bushes along trails have characterized all the productive collection localities discovered to date; these somewhat artificial conditions give the collector access to vegetation continuous with the more or less high canopy characteristic of Puerto Rico's montane forest." *Occultus* has most frequently been collected sleeping, again on twigs and branches and at or a little above eye height. (It may also sleep high in the canopy but this has not been observed.)

In essence then, *cuvieri* occupies the central, and *occultus* the peripheral, parts of the tree crown. Their habitats then are contiguous but not broadly overlapping.

The situation appears to be different with *evermanni*. *Anolis evermanni* belongs to the group of anoles that Rand and Williams (1969) have called "trunk-crown" anoles. These are often seen high on the trunk and also use the

[5]We do know for *cuvieri* that very young specimens have a radically different (banded = cryptic?) pattern from that of the uniform green adults.

crown, and sometimes emerge into the sun at the top of the crown. The young are found occasionally on twigs and small branches. They thus appear to broadly overlap both *occultus* and *cuvieri* and, as we have suggested, the size of all three seems to have been adapted to alleviate resource competition.

Interaction between the three species has not been seen, but there may be some behavioral adaptation also. Thus (1) Webster (1969) reports that, despite the occasional use of small perches already mentioned, juvenile *evermanni* seem to prefer perches of large diameter, a preference tending to minimize overlap with *occultus*. (2) If *cuvieri*, like *equestris* and *richardi*, is partially frugivorous (Schoener and Gorman, 1968; Schoener, personal communication; Lazell, 1971), competition with the other two species is further reduced. (3) *Anolis occultus* may differ behaviorally also in its more frequently slow mode of locomotion, capable though it is of quick jumps and leaps. It may in correlation with this stealthy habit be more of a searcher than a pursuer than the other two to some degree are, at least.

All three species live in shaded forest. *Anolis occultus* may be the most restricted by shade and humidity; *evermanni*, which is by far the commonest, may be the most versatile and require shade least; *cuvieri* is intermediate. Even museum data on distribution demonstrate this; it is not tied at all strictly to montane or wet habitats. The three are certainly not different enough to be categorized as occurring in different climatic niches. Whether they are said to use different structural niches is a matter of definition. All use the tree crown. If we choose to subdivide the crown niche, we might usefully speak of a twig or dwarf niche, a giant niche and a trunk-crown niche.

But with these three the primitive crown niche—the higher level of vegetation of the shaded forest—however broadly conceived, is full. An additional species no longer adapts primarily to size. It uses some additional ecological parameter—structural or climatic or both.

The statement that the crown niche of the shaded forest is full is empirical, not theoretical. There appear to be three and only three subniches to the crown. This is true not only for Puerto Rico but for the two larger islands—Cuba and Hispaniola—as well. There are indeed on Puerto Rico and on each of the larger islands more than three crown species, but the additional species are allopatric or allotopic over most or all of their ranges; there may be overlap but there is never regular and total syntopy. On each island the situation is, in fact, complex, but its complexity may reflect the difficulty of achieving stable syntopy for even three species (Table 6). Note that in Jamaica there is *not* syntopy of three crown species. There is a giant (*garmani*) and a near-dwarf in the forest but a third (*grahami*) is a species of more open country. There is even a fourth crown species (*valencienni*), partly syntopic with *grahami* but differing in foraging behavior from all other Jamaican species. Except for *valencienni*, the Lesser Antillean relationship roughly holds in all cases between adjacent sizes *within the same climate*.

Table 6. Differentiation of *Anolis* spp. With in the Three Subniches of the Crown Niche in the Greater Antilles[a]   F = Forest;   O = Open Situations.   Numbers = Maximum Male Size.

Giant Niche	172-191 *equestris* complex (several, probably 5 *allopatric* species) (F)	175 *ricordii* complex (possibly 3-4 *allopatric* species) (F)	137 *cuvieri* (F) 157 *rooseveltii* (F?) (allopatric)	124 *garmani* (F)	86 *valencienni* (O) (differing in foraging behavior from all other Jamaican species)
Trunk-Crown Niche	78 *porcatus* (FO) 91 *allisoni* (O) (mostly allopatric but differing in climatic niche where sympatric)	80 *chlorocyanus* (F) 84 *coelestinus* (F) (=a parapatric lowland pair) 60 *aliniger* (O) 52 *singularis* (F) (= allopatric montane pair)	78 *evermanni* (F) 50 *stratulus* (O) (differing in climatic niche)	57 *opalinus* (F) 72 *grahami* (O) (differing in climate and hence usually allotopic to *garmani* and *opalinus*)	
Dwarf Niche	46 *isolepis* (F) *angusticeps* (O) (these differ in climatic niche)	40 *insolitus* (F)	40 *occultus* (F)		

[a]Classification into these categories is primarily by size but also partly by habitat, e.g., *opalinus*, *stratulus*, and *singularis* are nearly of dwarf size but are not twig anoles. *Anolis singularis* (recently collected specimens) appears to be larger than here recorded when allopatric to *coelestinus*.

How does it happen that the crown niche becomes full? A possible explanation is the following: Recall again the size relationships between the three crown species: they differ in size according to a relationship by which the largest is almost twice the size of the second, and the second approximately twice the size of the third. This spread of sizes is that which we saw in most Lesser Antillean species pairs, and the Lesser Antillean ratio is that which *ex hypothese* we expect whenever species are coadapted by size. Let us now try to insert into the crown another species. Wherever we try to insert it, if the size ratio of nearly 2X for adjacent species is maintained, the spread of extremes becomes improbably great: if the new species is nearest the small end of the series, by spread of extremes, the smallest would pass the floor, which we have seen empirically limits size change in this direction: the smallest species would be impossibly small. If the new species is inserted nearer the large end of the series, the largest species would by the same phenomenon far exceed the largest anole known: the largest species would be implausibly large (perhaps more on biochemical than on bioenergetic grounds). Clearly a definite floor prohibits size change in one direction, and evident resistance impedes size change in the other. Within the crown, therefore, we should see a maximum of three size classes.

Once the crown is full, whatever the reason, it follows that when *gundlachi* is added to the faunal complex as its fourth species, it inserts itself *below* the high arboreal niches of the three previous species. It takes its place in the lower levels of vegetation, the males on the lower tree trunk, the females and juveniles on adjacent bushes and shrubs and saplings. This is a change of structural niche. Climatically, *gundlachi* is, like the other three species, an animal of the shaded wet forest. Indeed, as Schoener and also Webster have emphasized, *gundlachi* is in deeper shade than the other species because its habitat under the closed canopy is so far from the crown's access to the sun.

The station of male *gundlachi* is, as we have said, on the lower tree trunk and, more important still, its attention is focused downward; its foraging area is on the ground.[6] It is probably for this reason that, though male *gundlachi* abuts in the higher parts of its territory on the lower (trunk) parts of the range of *evermanni*, there is effectively little competition between the two species and hence no requirement at all for size adaptation: *gundlachi* is as large as or a little larger than *evermanni*.

It is necessary to note here that empirically—from the evidence of Recent *gundlachi* and of its analogues on other island—the adaptations to the lower trunk and ground are not as simple as statement of the change in behavioral terms only would seem to imply. Trunk-ground are morphologically as well as behaviorally different from crown species; there is a difference in length of limbs, in general habitus, a reduction in number of adhesive lamellae under the toes. There is in fact a complex assortment of morphological changes, which it is

---

[6] Hence the term "trunk-ground" for its niche (Rand and Williams, 1969).

plausible to assume were more difficult to accumulate genetically and therefore took longer to attain than the adjustments empirically seen as minor in size change, the change seen in the crown species. Here is another reason to believe, quite aside from our model, that *gundlachi* was not, as the dendrogram might suggest, contemporaneous in origin with *evermanni*.

Add now a fifth species. Where will it go? We have shown that it is not likely to be added to the crown. Can it be added in the basic niche of *gundlachi*? An accurate answer here requires more careful scrutiny of the *gundlachi* niche. It includes the lower tree trunk but also the peripheral grasses and bushes. There is obvious here a possible coadjustment analogous to that which resulted in *occultus* and *cuvieri*—one species specializing on the center, the other on the periphery of the niche. In Puerto Rico the fifth species—*krugi*—does stand in relation to *gundlachi* much as *occultus* does to *cuvieri*. It is in the same level of vegetation as *gundlachi*, but it occurs peripherally in grasses and bushes and on these extends a bit beyond the shaded forest into the sunnier edges. It has begun to emerge from the forest.

Anolis krugi is smaller than *gundlachi* but the ratio between the two is 1.3, not 2. Why is *krugi* not smaller? Very probably because it has begun to emerge from the forest. It is so far peripheral to *gundlachi* that it has begun to emerge into a different climatic zone: it is spatially *and* climatically distinct from *gundlachi*; unlike *occultus-cuvieri-evermanni* the overlap is not intimate and extensive. Size reduction there may be, but it need not be of the maximal kind seen in most Lesser Antillean pairs. One can instead see in *krugi-gundlachi* a parallel to the relation of *wattsi* and *gingivinus*, where also there is a strong spatial and climatic displacement compensating for or allowing a less than maximal size displacement.

With *krugi* the shaded forest (and its edge) appears to have been filled in Puerto Rico. All further evolution of Puerto Rican anoles is the evolution of climatic vicariants[7] of anole types already represented in the shaded forest:

(1) *Anolis stratulus* is the dry country trunk-crown vicariant of *evermanni*. It finds its place in more open situations, more isolated or sunnier trees. Schoener and Schoener (1971b) have shown, however, that it does overlap peripherally with *evermanni*—sometimes extensively—and hence they have suggested that its small size (ratio *evermanni* 78:*stratulus* 50 = 1.5) is an adaptation to alleviate competition between the two species. Here Schoener and Schoener (1971b) consider the size adaptation secondary to the climatic, and I agree. I assume that *stratulus* achieved its climatic adaptation in dry and open forests (perhaps in southwest Puerto Rico) but acquired its small size after contact with *evermanni*.

(2) *Anolis cristatellus* and *cooki* are respectively the dry adapted and the dryer adapted trunk-ground vicariants of *gundlachi*. Schoener and Schoener (1971b) have shown there is minimal overlap between *cristatellus* and *gundlachi*. It is not

[7]Vicariant: an ecological analogue (=ecologue) of a species, characteristically allotopic or allopatric.

surprising then that they are of equivalent sizes. *Anolis cooki*, on the contrary, though its range is small (in portions of southwest Puerto Rico only), does overlap with *cristatellus* over a significant part of its very limited range, and it is in fact smaller. The ratio, however, is not as high as is usual in anole size adaptations (*cristatellus:cooki* = 1.2) and this accords with a suspicion that the contact and overlap of the two species are relatively recent.

(3) *Anolis pulchellus* and *poncensis*—dry country grass-bush anoles—are strict parallels to *cristatellus* and *cooki* and ecologues of *krugi*. Again, *poncensis* is slightly smaller than *pulchellus*. Again, there is known to be overlap. The size ratio is again low. Does this mean recent contact or does it mean only minimal overlap? Or has it some physiological reason quite apart from competition?

These two climatic vicariants, it is obvious, parallel in a much more radical way the thermal difference which Schoener and Gorman demonstrated for the two anoles of Grenada. They again reinforce our proposition that size adaptations have severe limits as means of coadaptation and at some point must be supplemented or replaced by other ecological shifts.

A LOOK BACK FROM THE NEW VANTAGE POINT

We have now completed our review of the Puerto Rican radiation. How well does it fit our theoretical expectations? Astonishingly well. Recall that we have insisted on size change as primary and, following Schoener, as a consequence only of the need for partitioning of food resources. We have resisted all other explanations until they have been forced upon us. Such requirements are, we must confess, unrealistically stringent. That they have not defeated us is testimony that size divergence may really have been a major *initial* factor in the radiation of West Indian anoles.

It is first necessary, however, to be quite clear about what we have done. We have *not* demonstrated a *phylogeny* of size change; we have only demonstrated the theoretical predictability of certain *sequences* of changes in size and in other aspects of ecology. The distinction is an important one: the size/ecology sequence does not require that the relation of the members of the sequence be ancestor-descendant. In this case we believe them to be so, because the probable sequence of sizes as derived from a simple ecological model is in agreement with a probable phylogeny as derived from other evidence. But the sequence originates in the exigencies of an ecological situation quite apart from the origin or phylogeny—whether by radiation *or perhaps by invasion*—of the species that are *fitted together* in the size sequence.

In point of fact, on the two larger islands the phyletic evidence requires that the same sequence which we have constructed here be built from phyletically diverse components: thus on Cuba the crown anoles are alpha anoles in the sense of Etheridge (1960) and have come into Cuba from Hispaniola, while the trunk-ground anoles are betas in the sense of Etheridge and have arrived from

Jamaica. The bush-grass anoles of Cuba have come from both sources. In Hispaniola the same ecomorphs[8] are the results of three different invasions.

Thus, though we have here on Puerto Rico compared a hypothetical size sequence with a putative phylogeny, we were never in fact interested in the genetic ancestor-descendant aspect of that phylogeny; we were only interested in the fact that the phylogeny affirmed a certain sequence of species, which we could then compare with our postulated sequence of the *fitting together* of species ecologically. For the size/ecology sequence we did not care how—or where—the species were produced which were and *had to be* fitted together in a certain way: so long as the actors in the drama were somehow available, the drama could proceed.

Indeed, from a conventional point of view, there have been two notable omissions in our discussion of the history of Puerto Rico. I have, first of all, nowhere attempted a chronology. I have not done so because no evidence permits even a tentative and imperfect chronology. A sequence appears to imply some sort of chronology, but even as to this I will not agree to any postulation of a given time interval between events; any appearance of accuracy implied by such a statement would be false.

Again I have here nowhere discussed the topic of the geography of species origin on the Puerto Rico bank. I have, in fact, attempted this analysis but without results that satisfy me. As we have seen, it has not been essential to the portion of the story that has concerned us. We know that the whole Puerto Rican bank, including the present Virgin Islands, was available for species origins; we infer from the localization of certain species in southwest mainland Puerto Rico that some area here promoted species differentiation. We have, therefore, sufficient complexity to generate the required species, and we need not for our present purpose look behind this fact of sufficient complexity to the actual geography of history.

The limited story that I have attempted here is an ecological history told strictly in ecological terms: given certain ecological facts, certain consequences should have taken place and should have done so sequentially. In this limited history there has been no need for geography to intrude.

In the real world of Puerto Rico, geography does intrude at one point. In all of the previous discussion we have treated one species—*A. roosevelti*—as outside the story, a dangling irrelevancy. It is, in fact, a reminder that not all islands will be as simple as Puerto Rico has *appeared* to be. On all islands the populations that become syntopic species were once geographic isolates. The frequent dual process of isolation and then reunion may sometimes be interrupted, and an isolate may remain allopatric to the close relative from which it has diverged. This is the process by which the climatic series which we have described as the

---

[8] species with the same structural habitat/niche, similar in morphology and behavior, but not necessarily close phyletically.

climax of the Puerto Rican radiation came into being. On the two largest islands these vicariants (cf. Table 6)—sometimes climatically differentiated and hence able to exist sympatrically but also sometimes not obviously ecologically different and holding extensive parapatric or minimally overlapping distributions—make up a substantial element of the high species diversity of these islands. Even on Puerto Rico the anoles of the arid southwest—*A. cooki* and *A. poncensis*—were certainly at some not too distant time allo- or parapatric to the widespread species *A. cristatellus* and *A. pulchellus*. *A. roosevelti*—perhaps already extinct—seems clearly to be such a residual population, perhaps a Culebra autochthon, but perhaps only a relict there. On the Puerto Rican bank *A. roosevelti*, however, is only a detail that complicates the story without disturbing its flow.

For other islands, not only the two larger Greater Antilles but also for Jamaica, relictual populations may be essential elements both in history and in the present. For all the islands it is probably essential to the full story that isolation and reunion of populations results *each time* in the extinction of some local populations that do not coadjust and that at a maximum are able only to achieve a brief stand-off with their newly-met ecological equivalents. The largest islands have permitted survival of numbers of local isolates as well as many coadjusted species.

I have written about the evolution of Puerto Rico anoles as though the remarkable coadjustment of species we observe was achieved without difficulty and without carnage. Extinction has not been mentioned. This is an artifact permitted by the invisibility of the prior process of competition. No transitional or disappearing species—except *roosevelti* (which may be already gone)—seem exposed to our view. But this may be an erroneous judgment. *Anolis cooki* is even now a species of very limited range (Fig. 12) and at all the terrestrial borders of that range and on the offshore island of Cajo de Muertos (not mapped) it is intimately in contact with *cristatellus*. It is clearly ecologically somewhat different; it clearly survives as of now. But is this a stable situation? It is easy to see climatic change wiping *cooki* out. But even without climatic change is *cooki* holding its own? It is not possible to answer this question on any current evidence, but the existence of *cooki* may already be marginal. It may be the very model of a species about to submerge.

Anolis poncensis may be little better. In its very limited range, *A. cooki* is often abundant. *Anolis poncensis* is nowhere as abundant, though it has a substantially greater total range. Again it is clearly restricted by climate. Climatic oscillation one way might expunge it; in the other direction it would expand its range.

For either of these species it is not possible now to visualize how in the event of extinction they could be replaced. Clearly lizard species diversity in Puerto Rico is a fragile thing. Extinction for certain species has a perhaps low but quite

Fig. 12. **The present distribution of** Anolis cooki.

evident probability; replacement has no probability calculable in terms of human ability to see it happen.

Anolis roosevelti is larger than *cuvieri*. Clearly it is a product of the spread of extremes, and thus, though it is more primitive than *cuvieri*, it is no relict of any very ancient stage; probably it belongs to the stage just before the present. Nothing more can be guessed about it. Such relicts provide us little new information. They are, along with such local species as *A. cooki* and *A. poncensis*, however, very important as reminders of the invisible part of history—of the real but usually unrecorded role of extinction.

FROM THE SPECIAL TO THE GENERAL: THE ORIGIN OF FAUNAS

Puerto Rico is a special case—as I have admitted—an exceptionally favorable case. Dare we generalize from it?

I have already stated that no other island provides at this time as good a case as Puerto Rico that each other of the Greater Antilles has its own special problems and difficulties. Still we may attempt to generalize, to look at the faunas of islands abstractly and generally but with as much realism as abstraction permits.

I have written above about the intraisland radiation in Puerto Rico in terms of "adding" species. This obviously, when we deal with intraisland radiation, is only a device that permits us to ignore for the moment the geography and chronology of speciation. I have used such a device only because, as we have seen above, ignorance does not at the moment permit us to do more.

But realistically, what did happen? At least in general terms can we describe the process we believe to have occurred?

Let us treat intraisland radiation in terms of geographic speciation. Though other modes of speciation may sometimes occur, may have occurred in the Greater Antilles, we know very little about the processes and mechanisms involved. In contrast, enough cases of apparent geographic speciation have been analyzed—including some complex cases—that we may comfortably think of the geographic origin of species in general terms, rather than in terms of some individual, perhaps special case.

If radiation is a result of geographic isolation resulting in species difference, then clearly the formation of faunas is a matter of repeated secondary contacts—first isolation and then reunion. Theoretically at least, this has an interesting consequence. If isolation is continued long enough to permit differentiation to go to species level and this process is continually repeated, then clearly the original number of species held in common between an isolate and its parent population has each time an opportunity to double.

Think of this in its simplest terms (Fig. 13).[9] Imagine an island inhabited by a single species. Let this island be divided by any barrier—a physiographic one for simplicity's sake. Given time enough—and we need not initially define time enough—one species may become two. Theoretically this process could be indefinitely repeated. But clearly, faunas do not increase by N^2 with time.

Two factors must be involved in the limitation on increase: it must be difficult to achieve syntopy (only certain syntopic coadjustments are achieved with ease) and extinction must be a frequent phenomenon. Looking carefully at the phenomenon of faunal build up, we can list the following set of expected events if geographic speciation and then secondary contact occurs:

(1) *Syntopy by coadaptation*: Any species that are able to coadapt syntopically by differences in structural habitat survive. In the Puerto Rico forest five anole species have achieved syntopy: *cuvieri, occultus, evermanni, gundlachi,* and *krugi.* If the arguments previously made have been valid, syntopic coadjustment was achieved sequentially and *in an apparently inevitable sequence.* In the genus *Anolis,* in the absence of the competition of noncongeners and given the ecological adaptations possible to it, the sequence of five syntopic states is, we predict, a preferred sequence, a *main* sequence, readily and almost inevitably attained—given space and time enough. And in fact, on the two larger Greater Antillean islands this sequence of five syntopic states is in fact present—with additions and complications. On the smaller Jamaican bank only four syntopic states of this sequence are achieved. The latest and fifth state, the grass-anoles state, is missing. Since differentiation requires space, we may look

---

[9] Compare with this Fig. 10 of Bock (1970) or Fig. 4 of Moore (1960) for demonstration of the inevitability of diagrams such as this in the geographic analysis of sequences in speciation.

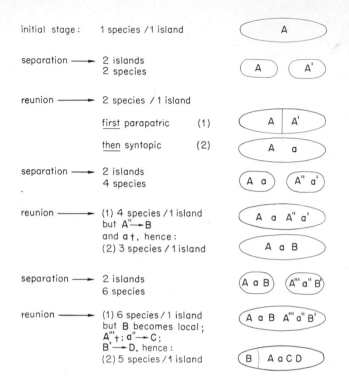

initial stage :   1 species /1 island

separation ──►   2 islands
                  2 species

reunion ──►   2 species / 1 island

                  first parapatric   (1)

                  then syntopic   (2)

separation ──►   2 islands
                  4 species

reunion ──►   (1) 4 species / 1 island
                  but A"──►B
                  and a†, hence :
                  (2) 3 species / 1 island

separation ──►   2 islands
                  6 species

reunion ──►   (1) 6 species / 1 island
                  but B becomes local ;
                  A"'†; a"──►C ;
                  B'──►D, hence :
                  (2) 5 species / 1 island

Fig. 13. A diagram of the possible origin and evolution of a fauna of moderate complexity generated by the subdivision and reunion of an island.

first to Jamaica's smaller area as an explanation. (But the Jamaican phenomenon requires careful analysis on its own in a paper consecrated to it.)

(2) *Syntopy by special adaptations:* Any species that achieves a radical innovation, not part of such a preferred sequence described above, but adequate to avoid syntopic competition will again survive. The anoline faunas of the two largest Antilles and also Jamaica have species or series of species, not readily compared from one island to another, which locally or over the entire island have achieved syntopy by strategies which take them largely out of the competitive framework which by character displacement has produced the main syntopic sequence. Anole species that appear to fit this category do not exist in Puerto Rico but on Cuba include the *lucius-argenteolus-bartschi-vermiculatus* series, on Hispaniola the *monticola* series, and on Jamaica *valencienni*. In one or another way, distinctive for each set, these have ecologies which set them up alongside the main sequence anoles without competitively disturbing them.

(3) *Sympatry without syntopy:* Species that differ in climatic preference may coexist. In Greater Antillean anoles there thus result syntopic series that are partial analogues of the original syntopic sequence of the forest. Thus in Puerto

Rico, to the five syntopic species of the forest there correspond the three roughly syntopic species of dryer areas—*stratulus, cristatellus,* and *pulchellus,* and in still drier areas the two, again roughly syntopic species *cooki* and *poncensis.* (The climatic borders for the different structural habitats are not the same and hence *cristatellus* is not strictly syntopic with *stratulus* nor *cooki* with *poncensis.*)

(4) *Parapatry*: Species with otherwise similar adaptations may achieve a stand-off if the point of contact is a transition point in climate or ecology permitting one to be *locally* superior in one climate or ecology and the other *locally* superior in the other. No clear case of this exists in Puerto Rico but classic parapatry is seen in such geographically replacing species as *argenteolus, lucius, bartschi* in Cuba, and *coelestinus-chlorocyanus* in Hispaniola.

(5) *Allopatry*: Any species protected by barriers that minimize contact may survive locally. In Puerto Rico the relevant case is *A. roosevelti* isolated on Culebra.

(6) All species unprotected by barriers and not superior in any ecology, even a local one, go extinct. *Anolis cooki* in Puerto Rico is not protected by a barrier and is superior only in and limited to very hot dry areas. Should climatic change eliminate its present climatic zone, the species would also go. More interestingly, there must in the past have been many evanescent species, locally differentiated, but unable to hold their own on secondary contact.

It is in the aspect of extinction after secondary contact that intraisland radiation in lizards compares best with the faunal turnover that ornithologists (e.g. Mayr, 1965) have so much emphasized. Because the process is much slower in lizards, it is not evident in the way that is true of faunal change during colonization in birds (MacArthur and Wilson, 1963) or insects (Simberloff and Wilson, 1969). This aspect of faunal build-up is largely invisible (Williams, 1969). What is obvious is an accumulation of coadapted species with a relatively stable community structure, i.e., a fauna.

CONCLUSIONS

The relevant data for a historical ecology of Puerto Rican anoles has been provided (1) by the phyletic studies of Etheridge, and the zoogeographic data of Gorman and Atkins, and (2) by the work of Schoener, and of Schoener and Gorman on the ecology of solitary anoles and species pairs. On this as a base, with very few subsidiary assumptions, it has been possible to erect a necessary sequence of ecological changes: Primitively and primarily adapted to the tree crown in shaded forest, the anoles of Puerto Rico, as they radiate with the island bank, are first able to utilize size difference as a major means to syntopic coexistence. Beyond the stage of the third species, however, size ceases to have the same importance, and spatial shift, and the use of parts of the tree other than the crown, and climatic shift, and use of open rather than shaded situations, become essential elements in the adaptations that permit the addition of species to the fauna.

SUMMARY

Historical ecology is possible. In a test case utilizing the anoline lizards of Puerto Rico, it is demonstrated (1) that, given some ecological rules derived from simple cases in living animals, it is possible to reconstruct the historical sequences by which species are fitted together into the coadapted units that are called faunas, and (2) that this postulated ecological sequence can be tested against and receive confirmation from a phyletic sequence erected on quite independent evidence. The case chosen is an exceptionally favorable one in terms of completeness of the evidence. Presumably, however, such sequences, once established, may be extrapolated to cases in which less evidence now exists and at least illuminate the problem and perhaps, in the happiest event, lead on to the solutions.

Historical ecology such as this is independent of the precise geography or chronology of the faunal build up. The only prerequisites for the achievement of any grade of ecological complication are geography complex enough and time long enough to permit the origin (or establishment) and coadjustment of appropriate species. Such a process, however, is not simple and involves much experimentation and extinction.

Acknowledgments

I have benefited from the comments of Thomas Schoener, Robert Trivers, Jonathan Roughgarden, and Bryan Patterson. Albert Schwartz has provided certain information. A lizard ecology discussion group at Harvard University provided some of the destructive criticism that reveals weaknesses and hidden assumptions. Support for this research came from National Science Foundation grant B 019801X and previous grants dealing with the evolution of *Anolis* in the West Indies.

REFERENCES

Baskin, J., and E. E. Williams. 1966. The Lesser Antillean *Ameiva* (Sauria:Teiidae). Re-evaluation, zoogeography, and the effects of predation. Studies on the Fauna of Curacao and other Caribbean Islands, 23:144-176.

Bock, W. J. 1970. Microevolutionary sequences as a fundamental concept in macroevolutionary models. Evolution, 24:704-722.

Etheridge, R. 1960. The Relationships of the Anoles (Sauria, Iguanidae): an Interpretation Based on Skeletal Morphology. Madison, University Microfilms.

———1965. The abdominal skeleton of lizards in the family Iguanidae. Herpetologica, 21:161-168.

Garrido, O. H., and A. Schwartz. 1968. Cuban lizards of the genus *Chamaeleolis*. Quart. J. Florida Acad. Sci., 30:197-220.

Gorman, G., and L. Atkins. 1969. The zoogeography of Lesser Antillean *Anolis* lizards–an analysis based upon chromosomes and lactic dehydrogenases. Bull. Mus. Comp. Zool., 138:53-80.

_____L. Atkins, and T. Holzinger. 1967. New karyotypic data on 15 genera of lizards in the family Iguanidae, with a discussion of taxonomic and cytological implications. Cytogenetics (Basel), 6:286-299.

_____R. Thomas, and L. Atkins. 1968. Intra- and interspecific chromosome variation in the lizard *Anolis cristatellus* and its closest relatives. Breviora (Mus. Comp. Zool.), No. 293:1-7.

Lazell, J. 1962. Geographic differentiation in *Anolis oculatus* of Dominica. Bull. Mus. Comp. Zool., 127:466-478.

_____1964. The anoles (Sauria, Iguanidae) of the Guadeloupéen Archipelago. Bull. Mus. Comp. Zool., 131:359-401.

_____1971. The anoles (Sauria, Iguanidae) of the Lesser Antilles. Bull. Mus. Comp. Zool. (In press).

MacArthur, R., and E. O. Wilson. 1963. An equilibrium theory of insular zoogeography. Evolution, 17:373-387.

Maldonado, A. A., and E. Ortiz. 1966. Electrophoretic patterns of serum proteins of some West Indian *Anolis* (Sauria, Iguanidae). Copeia, 1966:179-182.

Mayr, E. 1965. Avifauna: turnover on islands. Science, 150:1581-1588.

Moore, J. C. 1960. Squirrel geography of the Indian subregion. Syst. Zool., 9:1-17.

Rand, A. S. 1964. Ecological distribution in Anoline lizards of Puerto Rico. Ecology, 45:745-752.

_____1967. Ecology and social organization in the iguanid lizard *Anolis lineatopus*. Proc. U. S. Nat. Mus., 122:1-79.

_____and E. E. Williams. 1969. The anoles of La Palma: Aspects of their ecological relationships. Breviora (Mus. Comp. Zool.), No. 327:1-19.

Schoener, T. 1967. The ecological significance of sexual dimorphism in size in the lizard *Anolis conspersus*. Science, 155:474-477.

_____1968. The *Anolis* lizards of Bimini: resource partitioning in a complex fauna. Ecology, 49:704-726.

_____1969a. Models of optimal size for solitary predators. Amer. Natural., 103:277-313.

_____1969b. Optimal size and spcialization in constant and fluctuating environments. Brookhaven Sympos. Biol., 22:103-114.

_____1969c. Size patterns in West Indian *Anolis* lizards. I. Size and species diversity. Syst. Zool., 18:386-401.

_____1970. Size patterns in West Indian *Anolis* lizards. II. Correlations with the sizes of particular sympatric species–displacement and convergence. Amer. Natural., 104:155-174.

_____ and G. Gorman. 1968. Some niche differences in three Lesser Antillean lizards of the genus *Anolis*. Ecology, 49:819-830.

_____ and A. Schoener. 1971a. Structural habitats of West Indian *Anolis* lizards I. Lowland Jamaica. Breviora (Mus. Comp. Zool.) 368:1-53.

_____1971b. Structural habitats of West Indian *Anolis* lizards II. Puerto Rican highlands. Breviora (Mus. Comp. Zool.) 375:1-39.

Schwartz, A., and O. H. Garrido. 1971. The lizards of the Anolis equestris complex (Sauria: Iguanidae) in Cuba. (In press)

Simberloff, D. S., and E. O. Wilson. 1969. Experimental zoogeography of islands. The colonization of empty islands. Ecology, 50:278-296.

Underwood, G. 1959. The anoles of the eastern Caribbean (Sauria:Iguanidae). Part III. Revisionary notes. Bull. Mus. Comp. Zool., 121:191-226.

Webster, T. P. 1969. Ecological observations on *Anolis occultus* Williams and Rivero (Sauria, Iguanidae). Breviora (Mus. Comp. Zool.), No. 312:1-5.

Williams, E. E. 1969. The ecology of colonization as seen in the zoogeography of anoline lizards on small islands. Quart. Rev. Biol., 44:345-389.

4

Allometric Fallacies and the Evolution of *Gryphaea*: A New Interpretation Based on White's Criterion of Geometric Similarity

STEPHEN JAY GOULD

Museum of Comparative Zoology
Harvard University
Cambridge, Massachusetts 02138

OF OYSTERS AND ORTHOGENESIS

I have often imagined that La Gioconda's enigmatic smile is directed towards the scholars who write turgid books to explain her beauty. In length alone, literature about Shakespeare must exceed the Bard's works by an order of magnitude usually reserved for interstellar distances. Yet if every profession must have its *Drosophila*, shall we begrudge a Jurassic oyster yet one more article?

The literature on *Gryphaea* is replete with biometrical errors, both standard and subtle. I have three aims here: (1) to describe these errors; (2) to show that the available data, when properly interpreted, indicate no change in coiling for the basal Liassic gryphaeas of Great Britain; (3) to apply a new measure both to the old debate and to Hallam's recent work on later Liassic gryphaeas. I cannot solve the substantive issue of whether *Gryphaea* really did alter its coiling during the Lower Lias. This is an essay on method.

In 1922, Trueman proposed an evolutionary sequence leading from *Liostrea irregularis* to *Gryphaea arcuata incurva* and spanning the *Planorbis* to *Semicostatum* Zones (Hettangian to Lower Sinemurian) of the British Jurassic. "It is doubtful," he wrote, "whether any better example of a lineage of fossil forms

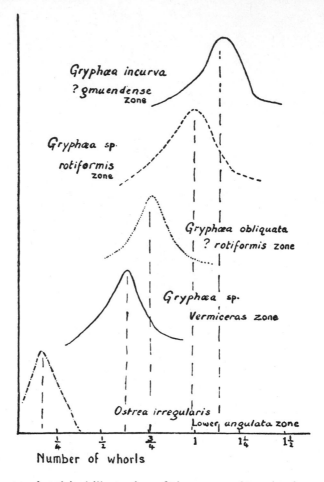

Fig. 1. Trueman's original illustration of the supposed trend to increased coiling in lower Liassic gryphaeas. From Trueman, 1922, Fig. 5, p. 263.

could be found" (1922, p. 258). He detected six trends in the sequence, three of which, as Joysey notes (1959, p. 299), fired the subsequent debate: increase in coiling of the left valve (Fig. 1), increase in size of the shell, and reduction in the area of juvenile attachment.

Hallam (1959) redefined the problem as follows: *Liostrea irregularis* and *Gryphaea arcuata*, he claims, are two good Linnaean species. There is no gradual transition between them, nor does *Liostrea* show any "gryphaeoid" trend. *Gryphaea* "sharply replaced" *Liostrea* "just below the top of the Angulata Zone" (1959, p. 107). Somewhere and at some time, *Gryphaea* evolved from a flat liostraeid oyster, but this is not recorded by gradual *in situ* evolution in Britain. The uppermost *Angulata* gryphaeas either migrated from elsewhere or speciated rapidly as an isolated local population. *Liostrea* was then replaced by competition (Hallam, 1963, p. 574). This interpretation has been challenged, and Trueman's reasserted, by Swinnerton (1959) and Philip (1962). I follow Hallam and treat *Gryphaea* only as he defines it (uppermost *Angulata* to *Semicostatum* Zone). This reflects no substantive preference on my part; good data exist only for *Gryphaea* (attached liostraeids are hard to collect and measure).

Gryphaea entered the general literature (and even assaulted popular consciousness) via Trueman's assertion (1922, p. 265) that the coiling trend of *Gryphaea arcuata* reached a stage "when the coiled apical portion pressed against the opercular right valve. Thus in such advanced *Gryphaeas* the shell would be kept closed . . . It is obviously difficult to account for evolution in a direction that inevitably leads to the extinction of the lineage, if evolution is the result of the operation of natural selection" (see also Trueman, 1930 and 1940; and Lang, 1923). Moreover, since the gryphaeoid trend is a recurrent, or iterative, event in the evolution of oysters (Sylvester-Bradley, 1959), Trueman believed that this path to destruction was followed several times.

In applying Eimer's term "orthogenesis" to this recurrent inadaptive trend, Trueman (1940) carefully disavowed any of the mystical, teleological, or predeterministic uses of that phrase. He ascribed such trends to "internal" effects, to "some physiological or chemical factor" (1940, p. 85) and wrote (1940, p. 93): "Excessive development implies that the evolution was out of the control of the environment and it may be presumed that some internal factor was responsible." He cited a mutation pressure greater than that of natural selection as a possible cause for orthogenesis (1940, p. 90). Lang (1923, p. 11) had suggested overly-rapid rates of shell secretion as the ultimate executioner: "These trends, even if at first encouraged by the environment because they are of use to the organism, are soon out of the environment's control; they are lapses which may overtake *Ostrea* at any moment of its evolution—trends which having once started continue inevitably to the point when their exaggeration puts the organism so much out of harmony with its environment as to cause its extinction."

Although these proposals for internally driven momenta seem naive today, they were reasonable and even resourceful within evolutionary theory of the 1920's. For the synthesis of population genetics had not yet been wrought, and traditional doubts about the importance of natural selection were still common and appropriate. This produced a dilemma: if all trends were adaptive and natural selection could not sustain them, what alternative was there to the Lamarckian impetus of creative response to felt needs with direct inheritance of features so acquired? (Neo-Lamarckism, despite Osborn's attempts, had lost its earlier popularity by the 1920's.) Lang (1923, p. 11) sought to avoid a resurgent Lamarckism by asserting the inadaptive nature of many trends: "Lamarckism . . . must be accepted if definite variations are regarded as necessarily useful. But need they be so regarded? ... In the extreme in-rolling of *Gryphaea's* shell there appears to be a trend carried sometimes to a positively harmful conclusion. For specimens of *Gryphaea* occur with the left umbo so pressed against the right valve that, even if thus the valves could show a chink, further growth of an infinitesimal amount would effectively seal the shell and immure the organism." Moreover, Trueman's notion of mutation pressure is both credible in theory and capable of sustaining trends outside the control of natural selection; it does not work in fact because observed mutation rates are simply not high enough to overpower the influence even of small selective pressures.

In any event, Trueman's view created an important anomaly within Darwinian theory. In a major work of the early synthesists, Haldane (1932, p. 141) admitted that "the exaggerated coiling of *Gryphaea* cannot at present be explained with any strong degree of likelihood." Neo-Darwinians have labored ever since to incorporate Trueman's notion into the orthodoxy of the Modern Synthesis. Westoll (1950) and Simpson (1953) pointed out that overcoiling would kill only the oldest individuals—perhaps only the postreproductive genetic ciphers—and thereby benefit the population. Haldane (1956) even made the wry suggestion that death by overcoiling illustrated the excellent adaptation of *Gryphaea*; for how often do animals obtain the privilege of meeting their end "from slowly operating physiological causes, rather than a 'sudden' death due to predation, acute infection, cold, burial in mud, or other possible causes"? I take this as a statement of sophisticated frustration.

But amidst the twists and turns of elaborate verbal resolutions, a more basic and obvious question was rarely posed: Is it true? Is Trueman's idea correct? For if it were not, an impressive edifice of theory, exegesis, and apologetics would topple upon a discredited foundation even weaker than that supporting the "great image" of Nebuchadnezzar's dream.

Charles Darwin wrote in the Descent of Man that "false facts are highly injurious to the progress of science, for they often endure long; but false views, if supported by some evidence, do little harm, for every one takes delight in proving their falseness." Trueman's interpretation of overcoiling did not survive the modern synthesis; his facts have endured to challenge the theory of him who issued the warning cited above. We may, however, challenge Trueman's "facts" on two counts.

(1). Did coiling ever produce a shell that could not open? I have never seen any study of this claim. Trueman merely asserted (in a footnote) that the type specimen of *G. incurva* had overcoiled to this extent; his suggestion was followed by all later workers. Yet a variety of compensatory mechanisms—the concavity of the right valve, the migration of the body from the umbo (Joysey, 1959, p. 317), and the reduction of coiling by terminal flaring in adults (the last illustrated by Trueman himself 1922, p. 254; reproduced here as Fig. 2)—indicate that coiling to occlusion may not have occurred. Oysters, after all, do not open very widely in feeding or respiring (Galtsoff, 1964, p. 169).

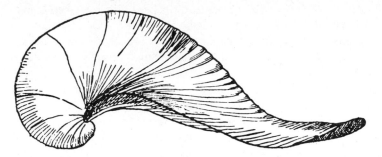

Fig. 2. A compensatory mechanism to prevent overcoiling. Drawn from Trueman's original illustration of a large individual that reduced its tightness of coiling with a terminal flare. From Trueman, 1922, Fig. 6, p. 264.

(2). Did a trend to increased tightness of coiling (or even to intensified coiling only as a concomitant of phyletic size increase) occur at all? I shall devote the rest of this paper to showing that it did not according to data now available.

ALLOMETRIC FALLACIES

I have defined allometry broadly as "the study of size and its consequences" (Gould, 1966, p. 587). Since size increase is the one uncontested trend in *Gryphaea's* evolution, any study must consider the concomitant changes in shape that such an increase entails. This has never been done properly. The debate on *Gryphaea* has displayed three major errors, each more subtle than the last.

Trueman's Claim: Direct Comparison of Nonstandardized Data

Since *Gryphaea* begins its postlarval life as a flat, attached juvenile, its total coiling must increase continuously through ontogeny. In comparing the coiling of two populations, differences due to growth must be separated from true variation in "tightness" of coiling—differences measured at a common standard that eliminates ontogenetic variation. If size increase in phylogeny proceeds as an extension of ontogeny, then larger oysters must coil further than their smaller ancestors and we do not know whether this increase be a simple concomitant of growth (as it must in part) or a true variation in tightness as well. Of course, if greater coiling is due entirely to increase in size, it occurs nonetheless and overcoiling to occlusion may still ensue. But, in this case, Trueman would have been wrong in citing increase in coiling as a separate trend in the evolution of *Gryphaea*. Indeed, Trueman (1922, p. 261) clearly advocated an increase in tightness: "Measurement of the spirals of the *Gryphaeas* studied has shown that the spiral angle α is the lowest in the most primitive members, and increases to about 80° in *G. incurva.*" All later authors have discussed the coiling trend in terms of tightness.

Unfortunately, Trueman used a method that permits no distinction of the two reasons for differences in coiling. He characterized each sample as a frequency distribution for number of whorls in supposedly adult specimens (Fig. 1). But, as Joysey (1959) points out, these curves are not really age-standardized; moreover, they rely on differing criteria, for, due to phylogenetic increase in size, shells accepted as adults at one level would be rejected as juvenile at a higher one. But the most telling criticism is that they do not correct for differences in size—the "? *gmuendense*" gryphaeas (Fig. 1) may average $1\frac{1}{8}$ whorls simply because they are larger than the $\frac{5}{8}$-whorled gryphaeas of the *Vermiceras* Subzone. Trueman showed remarkable foresight in anticipating by 10 years the methods of the modern synthesis (the consideration of populations and their statistical analysis, not individuals and the compendia of their differences); it is unfortunate that he chose an inadequate technique.

Philip (1962, p. 333) defended Trueman's method, arguing that variation in tightness so exceeded variation due to growth that the latter could be ignored. He based his conclusion on the assumption that *Gryphaea* grew as a logarithmic spiral—which it manifestly did not (as Trueman stated both in his original article [1922, p. 261] and in the work used by Philip for this analysis [Maclennan and Trueman, 1942, p. 214] and as every one of Philip's own graphs show by their negative *y*-intercept [explained on p.   ]). Philip gives the following equation for log-spiral growth:

$$\theta = (\log r)\,(\tan \alpha) \tag{1}$$

where θ is the total coiling, r is the right valve length, and α is the spiral angle. Using Maclennan and Trueman's ranges for a sample from Loch Aline ($r = 24$ to 50 mm; $\alpha = 71°$ to $82°$), Philip concluded that total coiling would vary by 145% over this range of α at constant size, but only by 23% for this range of size at a constant spiral angle. But the spiral angle of *Gryphaea* increases during ontogeny, often to an extent greater than the entire range of α among the Loch Aline adults (Maclennan and Trueman, 1942, p. 214). Growth entails *both* an increase in r and in α; their combined effect upon total coiling can be much larger than 145%—and this will be due to growth alone.

We have, in conclusion, two examples (Trueman's claim and Philip's defense) that illustrate the most basic of allometric errors—a failure to recognize the correlation of size and shape at all.

The Hallam-Philip Debate: Misinterpretation of Parameters in Growth Equations

Once we identify a correlation between size and shape, we usually fit a regression to ontogenetic data and characterize our sample by the parameters of this regression—its slope and intercept. Although this is a fine approach, its application is often marred by errors in the interpretation of these parameters. These errors mark the next stage of the *Gryphaea* debate—a series of articles in the *Geological Magazine* that had all the attributes of epic drama, from Swinnerton's (1959) righteous indignation, replete with charges of "sin" and "monstrous" error, to Joysey's (1960) existential despair of finding any solution.

Another potential problem with this approach lies in the inference of ontogeny from "mass" data—samples of individuals that died at various stages of growth (Cock, 1966). In *Gryphaea*, the potential difficulty is natural selection; for if individuals dying young differed systematically from the juvenile stages of adults, then a mass curve would distort ontogeny by treating the dead juveniles as if they were the youthful stages of survivors. Joysey (1959) suggested that dead juveniles be compared with the corresponding stages of adults as a test for natural selection. Philip (1962, p. 335) claimed evidence for just such an effect, but he later retracted this assertion (Philip, 1967, p. 330). Meanwhile, Hallam (1968), in an extensive study of attachment areas and shell shape, found no differences between individual and mass curves. We may therefore conclude, with Hallam (1968, p. 99), that mass curves "give a reliable [I would say rough] indication of the growth of individual specimens."

The *Gelogical Magazine* debate began with Hallam's claim (1959) that two aggregated *Gryphaea* samples, one from the *Angulata* Zone, the other from the higher *Bucklandi-Gmuendense* Zones, showed no difference in tightness of coiling. Hallam based his analysis upon "mass" plots of *P* (periphery of the coiled left valve) vs *R* (length of the flat right valve—see Fig. 3); since

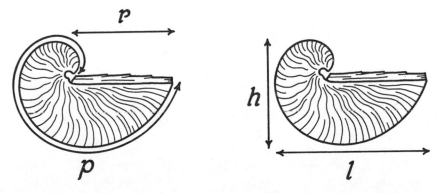

Fig. 3. The measurement of coiling in gryphaeas. Left: Hallam (1959), Philip, and Burnaby plotted the periphery of the coiled valve (P) against the length of the flat right valve (R). Right: Hallam (1968) plotted the length (L) of the shell against its height (H). The ratios P/R or L/H measure the tightness of coiling at any given size.

tightly-coiled oysters have a relatively long periphery, the ratio of P/R is a good measure of coiling in any individual. Subsequent analysts of Hallam's data (Philip and Burnaby) did not dispute this measure, and I assume, with all parties to the debate, that plots of P vs R do express the inferred ontogeny of coiling in *Gryphaea*.

Gryphaea does not grow as a logarithmic spiral, the only curve that maintains its shape as it expands (D'Arcy Thompson, 1942, p. 757). Tightness of coiling increases during growth (Trueman, 1922; Maclennan and Trueman, 1942); hence the ratio of P/R increases as well. Growth, therefore, is allometric and the simplest linear equation

$$P = bR \tag{2}$$

cannot apply. Hallam fit the power function

$$P = bR^a \quad \text{or} \tag{3}$$
$$\log P = a \log R + \log b \tag{4}$$

to his data and calculated the following equations for his two samples (where a is the slope and $\log b$ is the y-intercept):

$$\log P = 1.61 \log R - 0.50 \text{ for the } \textit{Angulata} \text{ Zone} \tag{5}$$
and
$$\log P = 1.57 \log R - 0.39 \qquad \text{for the } \textit{Bucklandi-} \tag{6}$$
$$\textit{Gmuendense} \text{ Zones.}$$

Hallam (1959, p. 101) then proposed a test of Trueman's hypothesis: "The slope 'a' gives information on the tightness of coiling. If Trueman is to be proved right 'a' should be significantly greater for the higher horizon." Since the slopes of (5) and (6) do not differ, Hallam concluded that both samples displayed the same tightness of coiling. But 'a' expresses the rate of increase in tightness during growth; it does not measure differences in tightness between samples. One sample may increase its ontogenetic rate of coiling much more rapidly than another and still remain less tightly coiled at any comparable size within the actual range. A regression is defined by two parameters—its slope *and* its y-intercept. Two P-R regressions may have the same slope and still differ in tightness of coiling because one is located above or below the other. This, indeed, is what Hallam's data show.

Hallam's regressions are plotted as Fig. 4. Due to a difference in y-intercepts, the line for *Angulata* gryphaeas lies below that for the later *Bucklandi-Gmuendense* shells. Thus, at any common size, later oysters are more tightly coiled (higher ratio of P/R) than their ancestors. The very data that Hallam cites to refute an increase in tightness actually support Trueman's original view.

At 1.61, the slope for *Angulata* gryphaeas is higher (though not significantly) than that for *Bucklandi-Gmuendense* shells (1.57). Therefore, the two lines will cross at some point (Fig. 4) and, beyond a certain size, ancestral oysters would,

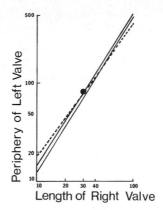

Fig. 4. Plots, on logarithmic scales, of Hallam's equations. Solid lines represent Hallam's regressions as he reported them: the lower line for Angulata *gryphaeas, the upper for* Bucklandi-Gmuendense *specimens. Hallam found no significant difference in slope and concluded that both samples had the same tightness of coiling. But* Angulata *gryphaeas have a lower y-intercept and, hence, are less coiled than their descendants at any common size in gryphaea's range (the largest* Angulata *individual has a right valve 38 mm long). Philip (1962) showed that Hallam made an error in calculating the* Angulata *regression. The correct equation is shown as a dotted line. The curves now intersect at R ∼ 30 mm. In smaller gryphaeas, ancestors are more tightly coiled than descendants; in larger specimens, descendants are more tightly coiled than ancestors.*

in theory, be more tightly coiled than their descendants. The crossing point can be calculated by setting the right-hand sides of (5) and (6) in equality; it occurs at a right valve length of 564.3 mm. Since maximum R is only 46 mm, this extrapolation is biologically meaningless (at 564.3 mm, *Gryphaea* would look like an ammonite). According to Hallam's regressions, descendants are more tightly coiled than their ancestors at any common size actually reached by *Gryphaea*.

Philip (1962, p. 340) recognized that Hallam's slope did not provide a comparison for tightness of coiling among samples. Nevertheless, he perpetuated the same error by assuming that the slope of a linear equation

$$P = aR + b \qquad (7)$$

would somehow measure this elusive "tightness." (Philip believes that this linear equation provides a better fit to Hallam's data than a power function.) But it does not matter what equation you fit: the definition of a straight line still requires a measure of slope and of position. The same objections raised against Hallam's method apply with identical force here.

Philip did not just ignore b, the y-intercept of his equation; he even presented a rationale for not considering it: "b is not independent of a, so the factors contained in a must influence b. For this reason b is disregarded in the following treatment" (Philip, 1962, p. 330). There is, indeed a correlation between the parameters: low intercepts tend to accompany high slopes when intercepts are calculated, since they almost always are, at a value of x below the range of actual data (White and Gould, 1965; Mayrat, 1966). But a correlation is not an identity. Series of parallel lines have identical slopes and different intercepts; obviously, the parameters can vary independently.

Philip treated each of Hallam's samples separately (four from the *Angulata* Zone, three from the *Bucklandi-Gmuendense* Zones). He then showed (1962, table 2, p. 331) that slopes for gryphaeas from the higher zone are usually greater (and significantly so) than those for *Angulata* samples. From this information alone, he concluded (1962, p. 331): "in general throughout the country there is an increase in the tightness of coiling in the Gryphaeas of the higher *bucklandi* and *gmuendense* Sub-zones."

But Philip's method does not resolve the issue at hand. Let us calculate the actual P/R ratios from Philip's equations for each sample at several common sizes. These data are presented as Table 1 along with similar calculations for Hallam's amalgamated samples. Common sizes are chosen as 20, 30, and 40 mm right valve length. Mean right valve lengths for Hallam's seven samples range

Table 1. Expected Values of P/R (Tightness of Coiling) at 20, 30, and 40 mm, Calculated from Equations of Hallam and Philip. Hallam Fitted a Power Function, Philip a Linear Equation.

Sample	Slope	Intercept	P/R at 20 mm	P/R at 30 mm	P/R at 40 mm
(A) From Philip (1962)					
Yorkshire *Angulata*	3.59	−19.1	2.64	2.95	3.11
Glamorgan *Angulata*	2.89	− 9.65	2.41	2.57	2.65
Dorset *Angulata*	3.43	−19.1	2.48	2.79	2.95
Somerset *Angulata*	3.36	−18.3	2.45	2.75	2.90
Yorkshire *Bucklandi*	4.44	−42.7	2.31	3.02	3.37
Glamorgan *Gmuendense*	3.63	−26.0	2.33	2.76	2.98
Skye *Gmuendense*	3.91	−37.6	2.03	2.66	2.97
Angulata *(average)*			2.50	2.77	2.90
Bucklandi-Gmuendense (average)			2.22	2.81	3.11
(B) From Hallam (1959)					
Angulata	1.61	.3162	1.97	2.52	3.00
Bucklandi-Gmuendense	1.57	.4074	2.25	2.83	3.35
(C) Hallam (1959) as corrected by Philip (1962)					
Angulata	1.37	.8035	2.43	2.83	3.15
Bucklandi-Gmuendense	1.57	.4074	2.25	2.83	3.34

from 18.2 to 33.2; the largest *Angulata Gryphaea* has a right valve 38 mm in length. Extrapolation to common sizes beyond 40 mm would be biologically meaningless and even this value is a bit too large since it exceeds the actual measure of any *Angulata Gryphaea*.

I note, parenthetically, that the *y*-intercepts for each of Philip's equations are negative (column 2 of Table 1). This indicates yet again that *Gryphaea* increases its tightness of coiling during growth. In Hallam's logarithmic equation (3), values of *a* unequal to 1 indicate allometry; for when *a* = 1, (3) becomes

$$y = bx \tag{8}$$

and *y*/*x* has the same value at any size. In Philip's linear equation (7), *y*-intercepts different from zero denote allometry since only a zero *y*-intercept yields an invariant *y*/*x*. When the *y*-intercept of (7) is negative, *y* increases faster than *x* (for *y*/*x* must equal zero at the *x*-intercept and increase thereafter). Thus, both Hallam's and Philip's equations show positive allometry and increased tightness of coiling during the ontogeny of *Gryphaea*.

How shall we interpret the data calculated from Philip's equations (Table 1)? At small sizes, ancestors are more tightly coiled than descendants (Fig. 5); at the largest sizes, they are less tightly coiled. (Philip, 1967, reaches the same conclusion in his new analysis based upon *P/R* ratios of actual specimens divided into 10 mm size classes). At a value of about 30 mm (above the mean value of *R* in all but one of Hallam's samples and well within the range of *Angulata* adults), ancestors and descendants have the same ratio of *P/R* and, hence, the same tightness of coiling (Fig. 5). These are the facts; interpretation then becomes a

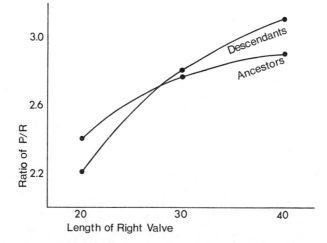

Fig. 5. Tightness of coiling (as predicted by Philip's equations) vs size in Angulata (ancestral) vs Bucklandi-Gmuendense (descendant) gryphaeas. For most of the size range, ancestors are more coiled than descendants at a common shell size; for large specimens, descendants are more coiled than ancestors.

matter of preference. Philip (1967) still insists that Trueman's contention is valid because the largest sizes illustrate the original hypothesis. But the reverse of Trueman's claim holds in most of the size range (beginning of coiling to 30 mm of a 38 mm range) and the point of equality for the two sample-groups occurs at an adult size. These ambiguities led me to the ironic conclusion (Gould, 1970, p. 100) that Hallam's data uphold Philip's interpretation, while Philip's calculations support Hallam's claim.

One disturbing point remains: why should there be such discrepancy between the equations of Hallam and Philip (with points of equality at 564 and 30 mm respectively)? Fortunately, this difficulty is easily (and happily) resolved. As Philip (1962) showed, Hallam made an error in calculating his equation for the *Angulata* gryphaeas. (5) Should read:

$$\log P = 1.37 \log R - 0.095 \qquad (9)$$

Using this equation, (Fig. 4) the point of equal coiling (calculated by setting the right-hand sides of [6] and [9] in equality) occurs at 29.84 mm. This accords excellently with Philip's calculation. The facts of the case are not in dispute.

Burnaby's Paradox: Improper Standardization

In a fine example of what we have come to call "British understatement," Burnaby (1965, p. 257) opened his paper on *Gryphaea* by writing: "Since 1922, an imposing fabric of evolutionary theory has been built upon premises whose factual basis—the fossil record of change in *Gryphaea*—is evidently not unchallengeable." I should now like to challenge Burnaby's reading of these facts.

Burnaby's paper is not easy to follow and his points are often lost in a statistical morass. But what he did, in essence, is this:

(1). He wanted to avoid the inference of ontogeny from "mass" data and, therefore, decided to characterize each sample by the average growth of an actual individual. To do this, he randomly selected 30 individual gryphaeas, 15 from each of Hallam's *Angulata* and *Gmuendense* samples from Glamorgan. Using Hallam's power function (3), he determined values of the slope a for each individual shell from pairs of P-R measures at an early and late growth stage.

(2). He found no significant difference in mean a between the two subsamples and used the joint mean ($a = 1.766$) as a best value for both. "In the absence of evidence to the contrary" (p. 271), he took 1.766 as an estimate of the slope for average individuals in each of Hallam's seven samples.

(3). Of all (P,R), the joint mean of a sample is most likely to occur on the ontogenetic curve of an average individual in that sample. Therefore, he passed a line of $a = 1.766$ through the joint mean for each of Hallam's samples and calculated the seven resulting values of the intercept, $\log b$.

(4). He found that values of $\log b$ were generally smaller for samples from the higher zones. Now, in any pair of parallel lines fitting (3)—i.e., in regressions of equal slope—the ratio of y-values for the two lines is the same at all common values of x (Gould, 1966, p. 597 and in press). Thus, the ratio of y-intercepts is a "growth invariant" (Burnaby, 1965, p. 268) measure of differences in shape between two power functions of constant slope. (The supposed size-independence of log b figured in the first, and still most famous, use of power functions in biometrics. Dubois [1897] assumed, quite incorrectly, a common slope of $\frac{5}{9}$ for brain vs body weight in all mammals. He then established a scale of improving "cephalization" measured as increasing values of log b.)

Since descendants have lower values of log b than ancestors, they also have smaller P/R ratios at any value of R—that is, descendants are less tightly coiled than ancestors at all common sizes! Thus Burnaby reached the "curious" and "astonishing" conclusion (Philip, 1967, pp. 329 and 333) that Trueman's story should be reversed—that *Gryphaea* became less tightly coiled as it evolved.

I question Burnaby's work on two counts:

(1). I fear that it is a classic example of statistical rigor inappropriately applied to inadequate samples. Burnaby's logic is impeccable; his calculations are flawless. But, as in all deductive arguments, the conclusions are only as good as their premises; and a fallacious premise early in the sequence brings accumulating error later on. His pitfall is a common one: the confusion of statistical with biological significance. Thus, early in the argument, he worried that a might vary systematically with shell size. He divided each of his Glamorgan subsamples into small and large shells and tested (p. 270) for differences in a. In each subsample, small shells had a mean a lower than large shells, but the difference was statistically significant in neither case. This is undeniable, but is it the best biological procedure then to assume that there *are* no differences and to continue using 1.766 as a common value for all? Each Glamorgan subsample contained but 12 shells. My suspicions would have been aroused by the smaller mean a for small shells in each case. Knowing that I had insufficient material to assess biological significance, I would have measured more specimens and performed my test on a larger sample. "Insignificance" is often an artifact of too small a sample size. The assumption of a constant slope is the weakest link in Burnaby's sequence; yet the size-invariance of log b, and hence the entire argument, depends upon it.

(2). We can accept all Burnaby's data, including the constancy of slope, and still question his contention that *Gryphaea* uncoiled as it evolved. This conclusion rests upon the comparison of an average ancestor with an average descendant *of the same size*. Burnaby (1965, p. 271) justifies his size-standardization by formulating Trueman's original claim in these terms: "The hypothesis under test is that for a specified fixed radius, the shells tend to have a longer peripheral length and a greater total angle of coiling in the higher zone." In criticizing Trueman (p. 95), I maintained that comparisons must be standardized to eliminate spurious differences in coiling due to growth. All previous discussions—Burnaby's (above), Van Valen's procedural note (1968), and my own résumé of the Hallam-Philip debate—have assumed that common size is the proper standard. But there are other possibilities, common age and the elusive concept of common developmental stage for example. There are good grounds for rejecting common size as an appropriate biological standard when the subjects both differ in adult size and grow with strong allometry.

To illustrate the point with an equine example: baby horses have relatively longer legs than adults; fitting (3) to an ontogenetic leg length vs. body length plot yields a slope less than 1 and a condition of negative allometry. Walton and Hammond (1938) performed breeding experiments between Shetland ponies and considerably larger Shire horses. Forelimb length vs body-length plots yielded constant slopes but increasing intercept values for the following series: pure Shetland, Shire father and Shetland mother, Shetland father and Shire mother, and pure Shire. This is also the sequence of final adult size. Walton and Hammond (1938, p. 329) took common size as a standard and interpreted the increasing intercepts thus: "This implies that the pure Shetland is relatively shorter in the limb than the pure Shires and the crosses are intermediate and that this is true at any body size." By using common size, adult Shetlands are compared with juvenile Shires; since juvenile horses have relatively long legs, this yields the spurious conclusion that Shetlands are shorter limbed. But Walton and Hammond's own data show that *adult* Shires have the same ratio of forelimb length/body length as adult Shetlands. The size standard is "true" but biologically inappropriate because it reintroduces a growth artifact into a technique designed to eliminate it; the biological question requires that tests be made at a common developmental stage.

We have the same situation in *Gryphaea*. At common sizes, ancestral adults are compared with subadult descendants. Since tightness of coiling increases during growth, Burnaby's "evolution" to looser coiling could be the artifact of an improper comparison between tightly coiled adults and more loosely coiled juveniles. Would it not be better to compare shells at a common developmental stage—at, for example, their average adult or maximal sizes? The following section develops the consequences of this standard when applied to series of power functions with constant slope. I will argue that large descendants, according to data now available, had the same shape as large ancestors—that geometric similarity marked the phylogenetic size increase of *Gryphaea*.

THE EVOLUTION OF *GRYPHAEA*: A NEW INTERPRETATION

White's Criterion of Geometric Similarity

Ever since Huxley's classic work of the 1920's, culminating in *Problems in Relative Growth* (1932), the power function,

$$y = bx^a \qquad (10)$$

(often called the "equation of simple allometry" or just the "allometric equation") has been applied to thousands of correlations between size and shape (Gould, 1966; Cock, 1966). Several years ago, I became impressed with the frequency of recorded cases in which allometric regressions for related animals had the same slope but differing intercepts (forming sets of parallel lines). German authors, Meunier (1959a and b) in particular, had observed the same phenomenon and dubbed it "transpositional allometry." I then noticed a correlation among size ranges, the sequence of intercept values and the type of allometry—and became intrigued by the pattern (Fig. 6). When slopes are less than 1, larger intercepts (*b*-values) are associated with larger animals; when slopes are greater than 1, larger animals lie on regressions with smaller values of *b*. I have been able to make sense of this correlation only in the following way:

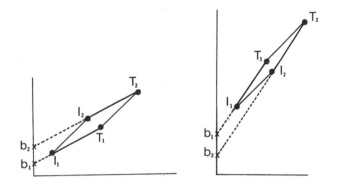

Fig. 6. Correlation of size ranges and b-values for the preservation of geometric similarity in power functions of the same slope. I_1 *and* T_1 *are beginning and end points of growth for smaller animals,* I_2 *and* T_2 *the same points for larger animals on a parallel regression.* b_1 *And* b_2 *are the b-values associated with the corresponding regressions.* I_1 *and* I_2 *are joined by a line of slope = 1. This means that animals at the beginning points of both curves have the same shape (y/x). Since a line of slope = 1 joins the 2 end points as well,* T_1 *and* T_2 *have the same shape.*

Case 1, left: when the slope is less than 1, the regression with larger animals has a higher b-value than that with smaller animals, when corresponding points on the two curves have the same shape.

Case 2, right: when the slope is greater than 1, the regression with smaller animals has the larger b-value.

suppose that an animal grows with ontogenetic allometry of slope a; suppose that, in the course of its evolution, it increases (or decreases) in size but continues to grow with a slope of a; suppose, finally, that selection operates to maintain the same shape at corresponding stages (both hatchlings, both adults): suppose, in other words, that evolution proceeds in geometric similarity—change in size with no alteration of shape. There is only one way to satisfy these conditions: by transposing the descendant's line of allometry. And the direction of transposition satisfies the correlation noted above: when $a < 1$, larger descendants must have larger b-values in order to retain the same shape as their smaller ancestors at comparable stages; when $a > 1$, larger animals need smaller b-values. (This can be seen graphically in Fig. 6; remember that lines of $a = 1$ join points of equal shape, i.e., of equal y/x).

When we note a transposition satisfying this correlation of size and b-value (as does Burnaby's for ancestral and descendant gryphaeas), we should suspect that the maintenance of geometric similarity lies behind it. There is an obvious test for this suspicion: does the actual difference in size between corresponding stages equal the difference in size at which shells on the two regressions have the same shape? Two transposed regressions differ only in b; the difference in size for points of equal shape must be implicit in this parameter. In 1962, White derived such a measure (in White and Gould, 1965); here, I name it "White's criterion of geometric similarity."

The following derivation is a simplified version of the original (see Gould, 1971b, for a long compendium of its application for body shape in gulls, brain weight in felids and primates, tooth shape in canids and ursids, skull form in bovids, growth of horses, and differentiation of local races in lobsters and mollusks). Consider two regressions of constant $a \neq 1$. (When $a = 1$, all points on any one curve and no corresponding points of two curves have the same shape, since y/x is a constant for each curve.) For any point on regression 2, there is one and only one point of the same shape on regression 1, such that:

$$\frac{y_1}{x_1} = \frac{y_2}{x_2} \tag{11}$$

and

$$\frac{y_1}{y_2} = \frac{x_1}{x_2}. \tag{12}$$

At these points, the two regression equations are

$$y_1 = b_1 x_1^a$$

and

$$y_2 = b_2 x_2^a. \tag{13}$$

Therefore

$$\frac{b_1}{b_2} = \frac{\dfrac{y_1}{x_1^a}}{\dfrac{y_2}{x_2^a}} \tag{14}$$

and from (12)

$$\frac{b_1}{b_2} = \frac{\dfrac{x_1}{x_1^a}}{\dfrac{x_2}{x_2^a}} \tag{15}$$

or

$$\frac{b_1}{b_2} = \left(\frac{x_1}{x_2}\right)^{1-a} \tag{16}$$

Now x_1/x_2 is the desired quantity—the relative difference in size at which shape on the two regressions is the same. Let us call this quantity s. Finally:

$$s = \left(\frac{b_1}{b_2}\right)^{\frac{1}{1-a}} \tag{17}$$

s is White's criterion; if $s = 5$, for example, an animal on regression 1 will have the same shape as one on regression 2 when it is five times as large. If White's criterion equals the actual difference in size, then geometric similarity has been preserved in evolution.

The Data of Burnaby and Hallam (1968) Suggest That *Gryphaea* Did Not Change Its Tightness of Coiling During the Basal Lias

I shall now connect two previously-developed ideas to form a new, and rather surprising, interpretation of *Gryphaea's* evolution in coiling: (1) standardization by common developmental stage is more appropriate than standardization by common size (the latter is misleading because it involves the comparison of juveniles with adults); (2) White's criterion, s of (17), provides a test for evolution in size with no change of shape in cases of transpositional allometry (regressions of common slope and differing intercepts).

Burnaby (1965, p. 276) reports the following mean equations (his figures differ from these because he leaves his equations in logarithmic form and figures in centimeters and natural logarithms; I use mm and common logarithms in conformity with all Burnaby's predecessors and successors):

$$P = 0.237R^{1.766} \quad \text{for } \textit{Angulata} \text{ samples} \tag{18}$$

$$P = 0.210R^{1.766} \quad \text{for } \textit{Bucklandi-Gmuendense} \text{ samples:} \tag{19}$$

These regressions form a transposition in accord with the usual correlation: the slope is greater than 1, and larger descendants have smaller b-values than their ancestors. Applying White's criterion, from (17):

$$s = 0.886076^{-1.3055}$$

$$s = 1.17. \tag{20}$$

Thus, an average *Bucklandi-Gmuendense Gryphaea* has the same tightness of coiling as an average *Angulata Gryphaea* when it is 1.17 times as large. (Burnaby believed that the Glamorgan *Angulata* sample had been distorted and performed some doubtful corrections upon it [p. 276]; if this sample is eliminated, $s = 1.24$.) Now, if 1.17 were also the rate of phyletic size increase, then descendants would have the *same* tightness of coiling as ancestors at corresponding stages of development. The shift of intercepts which Burnaby, through improper standardization, interpreted as phyletic decrease in coiling, would actually have occurred, in order to preserve in larger descendants the same shape as their smaller ancestors.

Hallam (1959) measured the extent of size increase between the two times. His ratio of maximum sizes is 1.21 (38 and 46 mm for right valve length), an excellent agreement with White's criterion of 1.17. (The ratio of actual mean sizes is 1.18, but this is an unstandardized figure easily biased by differing frequency distributions among size classes.) Moreover, Hallam (1959, p. 104) claims that this difference in size is remarkably uniform: "Size indeed appears constant over a wide area . . . geographic variations seem negligible." His values for Yorkshire are almost identical to those cited above for southwestern England (37 and 45 mm for a maximum size ratio of 1.22). He finds the same order of difference in Loch Aline, Gloucestershire and even in Würtemberg, Germany. I therefore take 20% as an approximate measure of size increase between *Angulata* and *Bucklandi-Gmuendense* times; this yields a ratio of about 1.20 between descendants and ancestors. Since this value accords admirably with White's criterion, Burnaby's equations indicate that descendant gryphaeas are geometrically scaled-up models of their smaller ancestors: there was no change in tightness of coiling at all.

This leaves an unanswered question: do Burnaby's equations accurately represent his data? I have stated some doubts (p. 103) based on the assumption of constant slopes; Philip (1967) has raised other objections. These are considered below in the appendix; there I conclude (or inconclude) that each reason given for rejecting Burnaby's equations can be countered in theory, though any one may be valid in fact.

Burnaby's equations indicate no change in coiling, but the equations may be wrong. Fortunately, Hallam's most recent work (1968) contains extensive new data that yield the same conclusion. Hallam, moreover, fits his equations directly to data; he does not impose any *a priori* constraint upon the values of parameters. We may accept his equations with confidence.

Hallam (1968) used a new bivariate measure of coiling as accurate as P/R, but much easier to measure (Fig. 3b). He compared total shell height with total length; the greater the relative height, the tighter the coil. D'Arcy Thompson showed that this ratio measures the tightness of a spiral (Hallam, 1968, p. 99). Hallam extended his study beyond the lithic and verbal morass of the basal Lias to include gryphaeas of the entire lower and middle Liassic sequence. He plotted length against height and fitted the power function (10) to 12 samples. Since the more slowly growing length is now upon the ordinate, the slope of this function will be less than 1 (it was greater than 1 in the *P-R* plots because the more rapidly growing periphery was plotted upon the ordinate; when both variables are subject to error, the choice of ordinate is arbitrary).

The calculated slopes are remarkably constant: eight of twelve samples are within 0.03 of the mean value, 0.799; among the remaining four, the maximum difference from the mean is 0.10. Since the use of White's criterion requires constant slopes, I disregarded the four samples differing by more than 0.03 from the mean. I shall use 0.799 for the other eight samples (as a permissible approximation based on actual data, not an *a priori* assumption); no calculated value differs significantly (I would say biologically as well as statistically) from this mean. Values of b, the y-intercept, must then be recalculated by passing a line of slope 0.799 through the joint mean of the sample. (Hallam's original b-values cannot be used since measures of slope and intercept are interrelated, and even small variation in slope can produce large differences in intercepts when the latter are calculated, as they are in this case, at a value of x far from the range of actual data—see White and Gould, 1965.) Through Dr. Hallam's kindness in supplying the original data, I performed these calculations and present the results as Table 2.

Table 2. Parameters for Length-Width Plots in 8 Samples. From Hallam (1968). Note Continuous Increase of Intercept Through Time.

ample (Zone and Locality)	Intercept Using Slope as Calculated by Hallam	Common Mean Slope = 0.79865	N
ʋinatum, Raasay	.8062	4.6752	20
ex, Warwickshire	.7931	4.5015	38
mesoni, Yorkshire	.8076	4.2723	54
ʋtusum, Scunthorpe (Lincolnshire)	.7737	3.3730	91
micostatum, Skye	.7994	3.2867	158
micostatum, Glamorgan	.8225	3.2400	86
ʋcklandi, Redcar (Yorkshire)	.7696	3.2293	97
ngulata, Redcar	.8171	3.1225	190

Of Hallam's eight samples, four are from the debated basal Lias: one from the *Angulata* Zone, three from the *Bucklandi-Semicostatum* Zones (lines 5 to 8 of Table 2—*Gmuendense* is the first subzone of the *Semicostatum* Zone). Calculating White's criterion from (17), and remembering that 1.20 is our estimate of actual size increase, relative size differences for equal tightness of coiling are as follows: for a comparison of *Angulata* and *Bucklandi* gryphaeas from the same locality at Redcar, Yorkshire, $s = 1.18$; for the *Angulata* sample and the average of all three descendant samples, $s = 1.22$. Again, ancestors have *the same* tightness of coiling as comparable descendants! The evolution of the ontogeny of *Gryphaea* is marked by a shift in b-values. I propose that this shift occurred in order to maintain the ancestral shape in larger descendants.

Can we provide a biological interpretation for the shift in b-values? I argued previously (p. 106 of this work and Gould, in press) that a shift of allometry lines is the only way to achieve complete geometric similiarity in scaling up or down. This complete identity is achieved simply, by allowing descendants to begin the allometric process at a different size than ancestors (Fig. 6): i.e., the same initial shape is reached at a different size and the sequence of shapes then proceeds through ontogeny, each step of the sequence being attained at the same relative difference in size (equal to White's criterion).

In many cases, the concept of "initial size" is a mathematical artifact since growth must begin at (0,0) in all instances. But as Angleton and Pettus (1966) show, this need not hold: in many cases, it is biologically reasonable to speak of growth beginning at large body sizes (egg masses, secondary sexual characters). In *Gryphaea*, coiling does not begin when the shell first forms, but only after it has broken its juvenile attachment. The first point of a *P-R* or *L-W* plot is the size at which attachment ceases, not (0,0). If descendant gryphaeas are geometrically scaled-up models of their ancestors, they must have attained this condition simply by breaking the attachment at a larger size and proceeding through the same ontogeny to a correspondingly bigger final size.

Yet such a speculation is inconsistent with another of Trueman's original claims: that the area of juvenile attachment decreases during evolution. I am pleased to report that more recent evidence indicates an *increase* in size of attachment during the evolution of *Gryphaea* in the basal Lias. In a late article, Swinnerton (1964, p. 420) reversed his long-held opinion (1939, 1940) and argued that the attachment area increased through time: "Out of 658 grown shells from the *Angulata* Zone, only 19 had areas more than 1 centimetre in diameter; but out of 302 grown shells from the Lower *Bucklandi* Zone the corresponding number was twenty-two, thus showing a tendency towards an increase in size of area." Hallam (1968) provided an extensive set of measurements. For three samples (288 specimens) of *Angulata* gryphaeas the attachment scar averages 2.03 mm in length; for four *Bucklandi-Semicostatum* samples (402 specimens), it averages 2.54 mm. The ratio of these means is 1.25. Not only did the length of attachment increase, it increased to the same extent as both adult size and White's criterion. Descendant gryphaeas seem to be geometrically scaled-up models of their ancestors.

White's Criterion and the Later Liassic Evolution of *Gryphaea*

Hallam's latest work (1968) abounds with irony and "teems," as Gilbert said, "with quiet fun." In it he shows that whatever happened in the basal Lias (only three of the fourteen lower and middle Liassic zones—in fact only two and a fraction since *Gryphaea* enters at the top of the *Angulata* Zone), the prevailing trend through the entire lower and middle Lias proceeded, in every respect but size, in reverse order to Trueman's claims for the basal Liassic gryphaeas. In the zones above those involved in the great debate, *Gryphaea* increases in size, decreases in tightness of coiling, decreases in thickness of the valve, and increases in size of the attachment area.

Hallam believes that the transition from a flat liostreid to an incurved gryphaea occurred rapidly. Since this transformation requires little more than a strong relative increase in the transverse component of growth (sensu Owen, 1953), its genetic basis might be quite simple. Coiling is clearly adaptive because it allowed *Gryphaea* to colonize the waters in or near estuaries that were rich in suspended organic matter. While these waters provide the benefit of greater nutrition, they also presented the problems of turbidity and high sedimentation rate. Coiling confers two advantages: it raises the mantle margin higher above the sea bed, reducing thereby the chance of suffocation; and it opens a new environment to exploitation—"the muddy sea bed with only minute amounts of shell or other hard surface available for colonization" (Hallam, 1968, p. 125). But, at the same time, the tightly-coiled spiral presents a great disadvantage: it reduces the stability of the shell (see Hallam's report of flow channel experiments, 1968, pp. 119-122). Hallam sees the subsequent evolution of *Gryphaea* largely in terms of selection to improve stability as the shell increases in size. Gradually, the shell becomes relatively broader and reduces its curvature by decreasing the transverse component of growth. The attachment area increases as the transverse component weakens since the action of that component pulls the shell up from its original adhesion. As stability increases, the need for a massive shell diminishes and the metabolic drain involved in producing so much lime is reduced by thinning the shell. "The end product was a thin-shelled, saucer-shaped *Gryphaea* which expressed a good balance between stability and the need to keep the mantle margin above the muddy bottom" (Hallam, 1968, p. 126).

This plausible story (Fig. 7) can also be viewed in the light of White's criterion (Fig. 8). The evolution of coiling proceeded via a series of transpositions or shifts in allometry lines (Fig. 8). At first, the shift was just great enough to prevent a further reduction of stability by greater coiling at comparable stages in descendants: the transposition retained the original shape at new and larger sizes (portion of Fig. 7 marked "shape maintained"). But Hallam has demonstrated

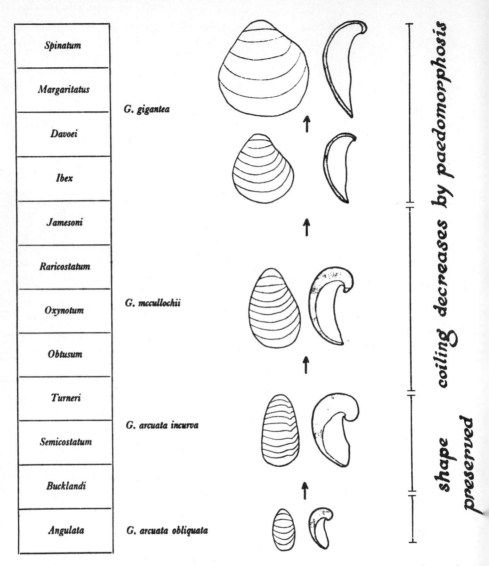

Fig. 7. Hallam's representation of the evolution of Gryphaea *throughout the Lias. Note continual increase in size and initial preservation of adult shape followed by decreased coiling and shell thickness in the higher beds. Adapted from Hallam, 1968, Fig. 26, p. 124.*

that shells of the same shape become more unstable as they grow larger (his Fig. 25, p. 121 shows that an adult *Gryphaea* from the *Semicostatum* Zone is more unstable than a smaller adult *Angulata* shell and much more unstable than its own juveniles). Thus, as size continues to increase, the maintenance of

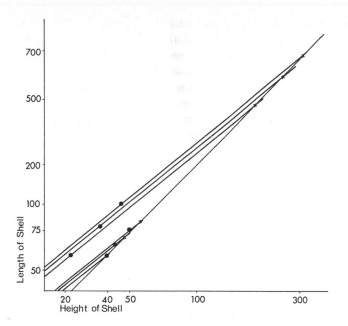

Fig. 8. Length vs height of shell for six of Hallam's gryphaea samples. Slope = 0.799 in each; logarithmic scales. From bottom to top: Angulata *Zone from Redcar; combined line for three* Bucklandi-Semicostatum *samples (Redcar, Glamorgan, and Skye) not distinguishable at this scale;* Obtusum *from Scknthorpe;* Jamesoni *from Yorkshire;* Ibex *from Warwickshire; and* Spinatum *from Raasay. Points represent phyletic size increase in shell length (each represents the mean length of the five largest shells in the sample). Crosses represent hypothetical points on each curve at which tightness of coiling equals that of the ancestral* Angulata *sample. (All crosses lie on a line of slope = 1.) At first, evolution proceeds very nearly in geometric similarity (correspondence of points and crosses for first three lines). Later, the actual rate of size increase falls far behind the rate needed for preservation of shape and coiling decreases by paedomorphosis. These curves alone are subject to the alternate interpretation of two evolutionary sequences, each preserving geometric similarity. (The three top points fit very closely to a line of slope = 1.)*

ancestral shape no longer provides adequate stability. I continue to be impressed with the number of cases in which size increase seems to provide a primary impetus for changes in shape (Gould, 1971a).

Evolution by shift of allometry lines continues, but now the extent of shift begins to outstrip the rate of size increase, and geometric similarity is no longer preserved in descendants: the rate of increase in size has fallen below the rate of increase in White's criterion. Now, the size at which descendants would have the same shape as ancestors is never reached in fact; adult descendants cease to grow at a shape that characterized a juvenile stage of their ancestors (compare dots and crosses on Fig. 8; portion of Fig. 7 marked "coiling decreases by paedomorphosis"). When the actual increase in size lags White's criterion, evolution proceeds via paedomorphosis. Moreover, the comparison of actual increase with White's criterion provides a measure of this paedomorphosis. The ratio of maximum sizes for the earliest and latest gryphaeas (lines 1 and 8 of Table 2) is 1.76 (1.72 for the average of the five largest in each sample, or 1.95 for the ratio of attachment lengths). From the data of Table 2, White's criterion, from (17), is 7.42. The *Spinatum* gryphaeas would have attained the same shape as *Angulata* shells had they grown to be 7.42 times as large; in fact, they are not even twice as large.

SUMMARY

(1). In 1922, Trueman proposed that the evolution of *Gryphaea* during the basal Lias of Britain had been marked by increase in size, increase in tightness of coiling and decrease in the area of juvenile attachment. He believed that *Gryphaea* had perpetrated its own demise by coiling past the point of utility to a stage at which the shell could no longer open. He described this evolution as orthogenetic, claiming that it had been driven by an internal factor capable of swamping the effect of natural selection. I have tried to show that the basis of this proposal may be pure fiction.

(2). Although Trueman's interpretation of coiling was not accepted by the modern synthesists, his facts were not disputed. This produced an anomaly within Neo-Darwinism that many authors tried to counter with *ad hoc* proposals.

(3). A variety of biometric errors, by Trueman and later interpreters, has placed the "facts" of coiling in great doubt. These errors resulted from a failure to deal properly with the allometric consequences of phyletic increase in size in *Gryphaea.*

(4). Trueman based his claim upon a series of histograms for total coiling in adults. But coiling increases in ontogeny; if phyletic size increase proceeds as an extension of ontogeny, descendants will be more coiled than ancestors simply because they are larger. Comparisons must be standardized to eliminate the effects of growth.

(5). Hallam and Philip used bivariate regressions to compare their samples. They both erred in assuming that Trueman's claim could be tested by a comparison of slopes alone; but y-intercepts must be considered as well. When both parameters are analyzed, Philip's equations support Hallam's conclusion (no change in coiling), while Hallam's equations uphold Philip's interpretation (that Trueman's claim is correct).

(6). Burnaby reanalyzed Hallam's data and concluded that *Gryphaea* had decreased its tightness of coiling through time. But Burnaby made *a priori* assumptions that may be unwarranted, used too small a sample size in several tests, and standardized his data improperly. He tested Trueman's hypothesis by comparing gryphaeas of the same size. This contrasts an adult ancestor with a juvenile descendant; since coiling increases in ontogeny, the apparent decrease in tightness may be an artifact of growth.

(7). The comparison of corresponding developmental stages (juveniles at point of detachment, average adults) yields an appropriate biological standard for the separation of size-correlated coiling from true tightness.

(8). When power functions have the same slope and different intercepts, we can derive a figure, here named White's criterion, that measures the relative difference in size at which specimens on two curves have the same shape. If White's criterion equals 5, for example, a shell on regression 1 has the same ratio of y/x as one on regression 2 when it is five times as large. If White's criterion equals the actual extent of size increase, then evolution has proceeded in geometric similarity—with change in size but no alteration of shape.

(9). The equations of Burnaby (1965) and Hallam (1968) are power functions with a common slope and differing intercepts. White's criterion, calculated from these equations, equals the actual extent of size increase as recorded by Hallam (about 20%); this comparison of ancestors with their enlarged descendants meets the criterion of standardization in point (7). These data indicate that *Gryphaea* increased in size, *but did not change its coiling*, during the lower Lias.

(10). Hallam (1968) has shown that gryphaeas of the later Lias decreased their coiling while continuing to increase in size. Regression lines continue to maintain the same slope, but White's criterion begins to outstrip the actual rate of size increase. Descendants now cease to grow before they reach the incoiling of their ancestors, and evolution to decreased coiling proceeds via paedomorphosis.

APPENDIX: ON PHILIP'S CRITIQUE OF BURNABY'S EQUATIONS

Philip (1967) attacked Burnaby's contention that the y-intercept is a growth-invariant measure of coiling when two power functions of P vs R have the same slope (Burnaby assumed a constant slope of 1.766 for all samples). Philip calculated an intercept value for individual specimens in the Somerset or Dorset *Angulata* sample (his Fig. 3, p. 335 says Somerset, but the caption reads Dorset). He did this by passing a line of slope 1.766 through the (P,R) value of each specimen at its final size. He plotted these intercepts against final size and calculated a significant negative correlation: large specimens have lower intercepts. (Actually, the correlation exists only because the smallest specimens have high intercepts; for all shells above 20 mm in R, the correlation disappears.)

I should first point out that Philip, though he raises a serious point, has formulated his criticism improperly. When two power functions have the same slope, their intercepts must record a size-independent difference in Burnaby's sense—that the ratio of y-values for the two regressions is constant at any x. This is a necessary mathematical consequence of the equations. Burnaby used 1.766

as an estimate for each of Hallam's seven samples and passed a line of this slope through each joint mean in order to calculate intercepts. If this slope is now applied to all individuals within a sample and if the resulting intercepts depend upon shell size, this can only mean that 1.766 is an inadequate estimate of slope for the massed sample.

There are many ways to produce a correlation between intercept and shell size; I can think of only two that have some claim to represent the actual growth of *Gryphaea* (Fig. 9). Let us examine these and ask how each affects Burnaby's contention that 1.766 is an adequate estimate for the slope of an average ontogeny.

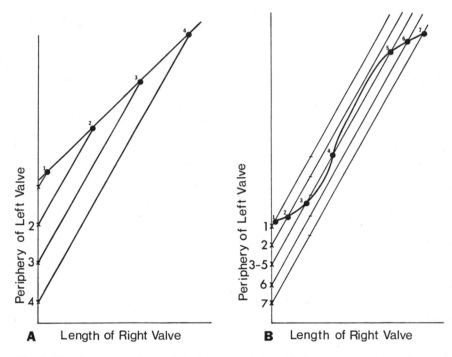

A   Length of Right Valve   B   Length of Right Valve

Fig. 9. Two interpretations of the inverse relationship between specimen size and b-value.

9a (left). Larger specimens have lower b-values at slope = 1.766 because this slope is higher than that of the "mass" curve joining points 1 to 4.

9b (right). Individual growth is sigmoidal. When a slope of 1.766 is fit to each specimen, larger forms have lower b-values.

In Fig. 9a, the correlation ensues simply because 1.766 is too high an estimate for individual growth *as inferred from mass data.* If the mass slope is smaller, the imposition of 1.766 upon each specimen produces lower intercepts in larger specimens. In fact, Hallam (1959, 1960) fitted power functions to mass data and never measured a slope as high as 1.766 (his values range from 1.32 to 1.57; Philip [1962] showed that his 1.61 for *Angulata* gryphaeas was in error). If mass data do represent individual ontogeny (as I argued on p. 97), then 1.766 is too high and Burnaby's equations must be rejected. But if the mass slopes are too low because highly coiled individuals tended to die when young, then 1.766 might be a good estimate for individual growth. Burnaby determined his value of 1.766 as a mean for individuals measured from Hallam's Glamorgan samples; in passing this slope through the joint means of other samples, he did not claim to fit a mass curve thereby, but merely to represent the growth of an average individual.

In Fig. 9b, the correlation is a consequence of sigmoidal growth for P vs R in individuals (in this case we do assume that mass data represent an average ontogeny). If juveniles grow with $a < 1.766$, adolescents with $a > 1.766$ and adults, again, with $a < 1.766$, then larger specimens will tend to have lower intercepts (the slight reversal of correlation during adolescence is swamped in mass plot of intercept vs size). But is this not an absurdly *ad hoc* suggestion? It is not because we have tentative evidence for each portion of the curve. When Burnaby split his two Glamorgan samples into small and large shells, the mean for small shells was less than 1.766 in each case, for larger ones more. (The differences were statistically insignificant, but the biological question is unresolved because Burnaby's samples were too small.) The adult reduction in slope corresponds to the terminal flange that many shells produce; Trueman recognized this as a device to decrease coiling (Fig. 2). Should Burnaby's equations be rejected in such a case? This depends upon the acceptable degree of simplification for a given study; if 1.766 is the best-fitted single slope (I do not know whether it is), then it might serve as an adequate estimator in general studies.

POSTSCRIPT

It is with greatest pleasure that I dedicate this work to George Gaylord Simpson. I did not have the privilege of knowing him as a teacher; for I am only his "grandchild." But I had the joy of finding his books at an unjaded age. I shall never forget the thrill of staying up past bedtime learning, by a dim and unobstrusive lamp, that life had a history and evolution a meaning.

REFERENCES

Angleton, G. M, and D. Pettus. 1966. Relative-growth law with a threshold. Perspect. Biol. Med., 9:421-424.

Burnaby, T. P. 1965. Reversed coiling trend in *Gryphaea arcuata*. Geol. Jour., 4:257-278.

118   Stephen Jay Gould

Cock, A. G. 1966. Genetical aspects of metrical growth and form in animals. Quart. Rev. Biol., 41:131-190.

Dubois, E. 1897. Ueber die Abhängigkeit des Hirngewichtes von der Körpergrösse bei den Säugethieren. Arch. Anthrop., 25:1-28.

Galtsoff, P. S. 1964. The American oyster *Crassostrea virginica* Gmelin. Fishery Bull. U. S. Dept. Int., 64:1-480.

Gould, S. J. 1966. Allometry and size in ontogeny and phylogeny. Biol. Rev. Cambridge Philos. Soc., 41:587-640.

_____ 1970. Evolutionary paleontology and the science of form. Earth-Sci. Rev., 6:77-119.

_____ 1971a. Fortuitous convergence in Pleistocene land snails from Bermuda. Jour. Paleont., 45.

_____ 1971b. Geometric similarity in allometric growth: a contribution to the problem of scaling in the evolution of size. Amer. Natural. 105:113.

Haldane, J. B. S. 1932. The Causes of Evolution. London, Longmans, Green and Co., Ltd.

_____ 1956. The biometrical analysis of fossil populations. J. Paleont. Soc. India, 1:54-56.

Hallam, A. 1959. On the supposed evolution of *Gryphaea* in the Lias. Geol. Mag., 96:99-108.

_____ 1960. On *Gryphaea*. Geol. Mag., 97:518-522.

_____ 1963. The evolution of *Gryphaea*. Geol. Mag., 99:571-574.

_____ 1968. Morphology, palaeoecology and evolution of the genus *Gryphaea* in the British Lias. Philos. Trnas. Roy. Soc. London [B], 254:91-128.

Huxley, J. S. 1932. Problems of Relative Growth. London, MacVeagh.

Jones, John. 1865. On *Gryphaea incurva* and its varieties. Proc. Cotteswold Nat. Field Club, 3:81-95.

Joysey, K. A. 1959. The evolution of the Liassic oysters *Ostrea-Gryphaea*. Biol. Rev., 34:297-332.

_____ 1960. [untitled]. Geol. Mag., 97:522-524.

Lang, W. D. 1923. Evolution: a resultant. Proc. Geol. Assoc., 34:7-20.

Maclennan, R. M., and A. E. Trueman. 1942. Variation in *Gryphaea incurva* (Sow.) from the Lower Lias of Loch Aline, Argyll. Proc. Roy. Soc. Edinburgh [B], 61:211-232.

Mayrat, A. 1966. Les variations des taux d'allométrie et des indices d'origine dans une série, et leurs relations supposées. C. R. Soc. Biol. (Paris), 160:470-471.

Meunier, K. 1959a. Die Allometrie des Vogelflügels. Z. Wiss. Zool., 161:444-482.

_____ 1959b. Die Grössenabhängigkeit der Körperform bei Vögeln. Z. Wiss. Zool., 162:328-355.

Owen, G. 1953. The shell in the Lamellibranchiata. Quart. J. Micr. Sci., 94:57-70.

Philip, G. M. 1962. The evolution of *Gryphaea*. Geol. Mag., 99:327-344.

_____ 1967. Additional observations on the evolution of *Gryphaea*. Geol. J., 5:329-338.

Simpson, G. G. 1953. The major features of evolution. New York, Columbia University Press.

Swinnerton, H. H. 1939. Palaeontology and the mechanics of evolution. Quart. J. Geol. Soc. London, 95:xxxiii-lxx.

_____ 1940. The study of variation in fossils. Quart. J. Geol. Soc. London, 96:lxxvii-cxviii.

_____ 1959. Concerning Mr. A. Hallam's article on *Gryphaea*. Geol. Mag., 96:307-310.

_____ 1964. The early development of *Gryphaca*. Geol. Mag., 101:409-420.

Sylvester-Bradley, P. C. 1959. Iterative evolution in fossil oysters. Proc. Int. Zool. Congr., 1:193-197.

Thompson, D'Arcy. 1942. On Growth and Form. Cambridge, Cambridge Univ. Press.

Trueman, A. E. 1922. The use of *Gryphaea* in the correlation of the Lower Lias. Geol. Mag., 59:256-268.

_____ 1930. Results of some recent statistical investigations of invertebrate fossils. Biol. Rev., 5:296.

_____ 1940. The meaning of orthogenesis. Trans. Geol. Soc. Glasgow, 20:77-95.

Van Valen, L. 1968. "*Gryphaea*," evolution and natural selection. Evolution, 22:424-425.

Walton, A., and J. Hammond. 1938. The maternal effects on growth and conformation in shire horse-Shetland pony crosses. Proc. Roy. Soc. London [B], 125:311-335.

Westoll, T. S. 1950. Some aspects of growth studies in fossils. Proc. Roy. Soc. London [B], 137:490-509.
White, J. F., and S. J. Gould. 1965. Interpretation of the coefficient in the allometric equation. Amer. Natural., 99:5-18.

5

The Vertebrate as a Dual Animal - Somatic and Visceral

ALFRED SHERWOOD ROMER

Museum of Comparative Zoology
Harvard University
Cambridge, Massachusetts 02138

INTRODUCTION

In the study of vertebrate anatomy and embryology, one frequently encounters the terms "somatic" and "visceral." Musculature is somatic or visceral; there is a somatic skeleton and a visceral skeleton; a somatic nervous system and a visceral nervous system. Are these terms merely descriptive, as regards external or internal position? I believe not. The anatomical and structural differences between the two elements in each organ system and, in great measure, the differences in embryological origin are so marked that the contrasts appear to be basic in the make-up of a vertebrate.

In many regards the vertebrate organism, whether fish or mammal, is a well-knit unit structure. But in other respects there seems to be a somewhat imperfect welding, functionally and structurally, of two somewhat distinct beings: (1) an external, "somatic," animal, including most of the flesh and bone of our body, with a well organized nervous system and sense organs, in charge, so to speak, of "external affairs," and (2) an internal, "visceral," animal, basically consisting of the digestive tract and its appendages, which, to a considerable degree, conducts its own affairs, and over which the somatic animal exerts but incomplete control.

A consideration of what evidence can be gathered from our knowledge of living vertebrate relatives among chordates or hemichordates suggests that this dichotomy has a historical background; that the remote chordate ancestor, as exemplified by pterobranchs, acorn worms and tunicates, was essentially a small, sessile, simply built animal that included in its structure little but a food-gathering and digestive apparatus; that in the developmental stage of more advanced chordates there was added to this, for better distribution of the young, a locomotor "unit" with muscles, supporting structures, and brain and sense organs; that this newly acquired "somatic animal" was at first restricted to the larval period, and resorbed for adult existence; but that, eventually, in progressive chordates, the new, somatic unit was retained throughout life.

The whole story of vertebrate evolution from protochordate ancestors has been one of the elaboration of this active somatic unit, which gave the possibility of immense progress in evolutionary advance. The new somatic and older visceral structural units have been combined into a single animal; but the dichotomy is still apparent in many features of developmental processes and adult structure, and the functional welding of the two units is still imperfect, even in the most advanced of vertebrates.

The thesis just set out includes no new data, but represents a synthesis in a new pattern of many facts long since known to embryologists, comparative anatomists, and students of the lower chordates. I have on several occasions, in 1955 and later years, spoken on this subject and suggested this point of view briefly in texts (as 1959, 1962, 1970) and general discussions (e.g., Romer, 1958a, b, 1967, etc.). As a result, much of the thesis outlined above has become rather widely spread among members of the zoological community, but I think it is perhaps worth-while to lay out the theme of somatic-visceral contrasts more fully than I have done in the past. And it will be clear that my conclusions based on vertebrate anatomy and embryology agree well with the emphasis placed by Garstang (1928) and Berrill (1955) upon the crucial importance of the tunicate larva in the story of vertebrate evolution.

SOMATIC VS. VISCERAL MUSCULATURE

Histologically, vertebrate musculature can be divided into the striated type, which makes up the "flesh" of the body, and smooth musculature, with simpler fibers, which is mainly confined to the gut tube, although with "outliers" (particularly in higher vertebrates) in the vascular system and so forth (it is generally agreed that heart muscle is a derivative of the smooth muscle type). One would expect, therefore, that the embryological origins of muscular materials would correspond to the histological distinctions. In great measure this is the case. The smooth musculature of the gut and vascular system arises from mesenchyme derived from the mesodermal layer of the splanchnopleure surrounding the embryonic gut. Quite in contrast is the site of origin of the greater part of the striated musculature. One of the most obvious features of any vertebrate embryo is the series of mesodermal somites which develop as a paired series on each side of the notochord at an early stage of development. These structures give the first and major indication of such segmentation as a vertebrate possesses (and, in fact, the segmentation of vertebrae, ribs, and spinal nerves occurs as a functional adaptation to this primary segmentation). Part of the material of the somites later breaks up into mesenchyme, forming axial skeletal materials and connective tissues of the dermis. A major part of each somite, however, develops into striated muscle. In every group of vertebrates, from lampreys to mammals, the major muscle-forming part of the somites—the myotomes—can be seen to extend down the flanks and form part or all of the axial musculature of the trunk and tail (Fig. 1). Anteriorly, progress down the

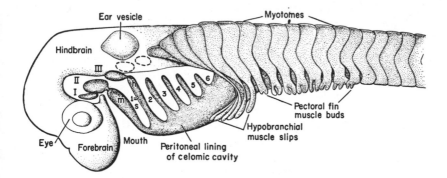

Fig. 1. A diagrammatic view of a shark embryo to show the development of the muscles. Skin and gut tube removed; the brain and eye and ear vesicles are included as landmarks. Posteriorly, the myotomes have extended downward to form myomeres; in the region of the pectoral fin, paired buds are forming from neighboring myotomes as potential fin muscles. Anterior to this, buds from anterior myotomes extend ventrally to form hypobranchial muscles. In the ear region, myotomes (broken lines) are rudimentary or absent, but farther forward three myotomes (I to III) persist to form eye muscles. The position of the spiracular slit (s) and normal gill slits (2 to 6) is indicated. These interrupt the continuity of the coelom and its peritoneal epithelium. Buds of this project upward between the gill slits; from the splanchnopleure there arise the visceral muscles of the mandibular arch (m), the hyoid arch (h), and the more posterior gill arches, in continuity posteriorly with the mesoderm forming the smooth muscles of the remainder of the gut. (In part after Braus. This and later figures are mainly from, or modified from, figures from The Vertebrate Body [Romer, 1962, 1970], courtesy of the W. B. Saunders Co.)

flanks is interrupted by the gill apparatus, but even so, slips from anterior trunk myotomes can be seen in the embryo to make a circuitous passage back around the gills, and down and forward to form the musculature of the tongue and floor of the throat. (The hypoglossal nerve, which innervates much of this musculature in amniotes, follows the same embryonic course.) The typical mesodermal somites run forward only to the level of the occipital region of the skull. There are, however, more anterior outposts of the somite system. In the future otic region of the skull, somites are not represented in the late embryonic or adult structure, but a transitory appearance of somites has been reported here in some instances. Still farther forward, in the orbital region, however, somites are again found, although in reduced form. They are thin-walled little cavities, three in number, the "head cavities," described by a long series of authors in various animals (most recently well described by Gilbert, 1947, 1952, etc.). They do not, apparently, give rise to skeletal or other mesenchymatous structures; but they do give origin to the six small striated muscles (recti, obliqui) which move the eyeball and are innervated by three special little cranial nerves—III, IV, and VI.

It appears that primitively, as seen, for example, in selachians and cyclostomes, the entire series of somatic muscles is formed directly from the myotomes. In more advanced vertebrates, however, somatic derivation may be indirect and in part the somatic musculature may arise from the somatic mesoderm of the embryonic lateral plate—mesoderm which, however, is in turn of somite origin. This indirect origin is known to be true for part of the flank musculature in mammals (Straus and Rawles, 1953, for example). More striking is the situation with regard to the musculature of the paired limbs. It is believed that in sharks and certain other fish types the paired fin muscles arise directly from buds derived from the ventral margins of the myotomes in the region of the fin base, as shown diagrammatically in Fig. 1. A similar direct origin from myotomes was claimed in earlier years for the limb muscles of tetrapods (for example, Mollier, 1895). But this is certainly not the case in most if not all land vertebrates and even in some fishes (Harrison, 1895). Observation and transplantation experiments, particularly of the Harrison School on *Ambystoma*, show that the limb bud musculature arises in situ from masses of mesenchyme lying in place in the flank external to the somatic mesoderm layer of the lateral plate and derived from this mesodermal layer. The origin is from the somites, but the origin is indirect (cf., for example, Harrison, 1918).

Thus far we have seen that there appears to be a clear distinction in origin of smooth and striated muscles—the former derived from mesenchyme of the splanchnopleure surrounding the gut, the latter from the myotomes, in primitive forms directly, in more advanced types partially derived indirectly via the parietal mesoderm. One would assume that the contrast in embryological derivation would agree with the contrast between histological types.

Not so. There is one very striking exception.

In every vertebrate there is a set of well-developed striated muscles associated with the anterior part of the digestive tract, most notably the pharynx. In all fishes there is an important series of muscles, lying along the walls of the pharyngeal region, which effect opening and closing of the gill slits. In jaw-possessing fishes there are powerful muscles associated with jaw movements; it is universally agreed that the jaws represent a modified and enlarged series of gill bars, and these jaw muscles are clearly a special part of the pharyngeal series.

In tetrapods the jaw muscles remain prominent, but the gills are lost; much of the original gill musculature disappears, but a few small muscles persist in the throat and ear region, the trapezius muscle system of the neck is a further persistent relic, and in mammals the muscles of expression are an outgrowth of the same set of muscles.

We have thus, in all vertebrates, an important series of striated muscles primarily associated with the pharyngeal region and visceral in position and function. What of their embryonic origin? One would assume that they are, like all the rest of the striated series, derived from the myotomes, directly in primitive forms, or possibly indirectly via somatopleural mesoderm in advanced types. Not at all, however; they arise—as do the smooth muscles of the more posterior part of the gut—from mesenchyme derived from the gut walls. More posteriorly the splanchnopleure forms a continuous sheet along the gut. In the pharyngeal region its continuity is interrupted by the developing gill pouches. Finger-like processes of mesoderm, however, project upward between successive gill slits; as long ago shown by Van Wijhe (1882) and Dohrn (1884), it is in the splanchnic mesoderm of this series of processes that the muscles of the jaws and the gill bars are formed in selachians. In most more advanced vertebrates the coelomic cavities of the gill bars are obscured, but the origin of these muscles is comparable.[1]

We thus find that a special group of striated muscles arise in the embryo in the same fashion as do the smooth muscles of the gut. This difference from other striated muscles cannot be laid to any topographic "necessity." The posterior part of the pharyngeal region is adjacent to the most anterior members of the trunk myotome system; farther forward the myotomes termed head cavities are in a position to give origin to the most anterior part of the gill-muscle series; and, were there a functional need, the somites that appear fleetingly in the intermediate region could have been called into play. It seems clear that the pharyngeal group of muscles are a specialized part of a set of visceral muscles, associated with the gut, arising in a fashion similar to the smooth musculature found more posteriorly, but developing as striated fibers in connection with the functional need for more efficient musculature in the mouth and pharynx region. Further evidence that the primary anatomical division of the vertebrate muscular system should be not into smooth and striated types but into somatic and visceral systems is afforded by the fact that the line of division along the gut between striated and smooth musculature is not a fixed point. In many forms all gut musculature back of the pharynx is smooth in nature; but in many fishes, on the one hand, and in mammals, on the other, striated musculature extends back into the esophageal region.

It would still be possible, despite these suggestive facts, to argue that the

---

[1] Edgeworth (1935) claims that these muscles are of myotomic origin. His argument, however, does not seem too convincing, although exceptionally during embryonic development a growing visceral muscle comes to lie adjacent to an eye muscle.

differences in embryonic origin of visceral and somatic musculature are not of great significance; after all, it could be said, the splanchnic mesoderm is of somite origin, just as is the musculature of the myotomes, and one cannot conclusively argue for a basal distinction of visceral from somatic musculature on these grounds—particularly since, as we have seen, much of the somatic musculature in higher vertebrates is not of direct myotomic origin. This is a reasonable counter-argument. Were a claim for the special nature of the pharyngeal visceral muscles based solely on the embryological grounds stated, it could perhaps be brushed aside. But, as will be seen in a later section, the innervation of these pharyngeal visceral muscles is of a very special nature, radically different from that of the axial musculature (Goodrich, 1918). Significant, too, as regards the basically distinctive nature of the pharyngeal region is its skeleton, now to be discussed.

SOMATIC VS. VISCERAL SKELETAL SYSTEMS

Skeletal materials are among the most distinctive of vertebrate features, and the notochord, found among lower chordates as well, is without question an ancient chordate supporting structure. In all vertebrates, however, the notochord is reinforced and generally supplanted by other materials—cartilage and bone. All bone and cartilage are formed from condensations of mesenchymal material, and most are formed quite surely from mesenchyme of orthodox mesodermal origin. It is generally—and reasonably—believed that the vertebrae are derived from mesenchyme materials growing out from the medioventral margins of each mesodermal somite, and appropriately termed the sclerotome; and a great part of the braincase is presumed to arise from sclerotomic materials from the most anterior members of the somite series. Less clear, in most cases, is the derivation of the mesenchyme forming the ribs and limb cartilages, but their origin from mesoderm is unquestioned, although this mesoderm may be that of the lateral plate rather than the sclerotome (cf. Straus and Rawles, 1953).

Quite in contrast is the situation in the pharyngeal region. Here, in fishes, are a series of bars which lie between successive gill slits and aid in pharyngeal movements. These structures are more or less completely ossified in most members of the Osteichthyes, but begin in the embryo as cartilages and remain cartilaginous throughout life in sharks, skates, and chimaeras. More anteriorly, the basic elements of the upper and lower jaws present in all vertebrates above the cyclostome level are the prominent palatoquadrate and mandibular (Meckel's) cartilages. It is generally agreed that these cartilages are modified gill bars, and this whole series of cartilages, basically associated with the pharyngeal region of the gut tube, is universally termed the visceral skeleton.

In the early days of embryological investigation, it was assumed that the elements of the visceral skeletal system arose, as do all other skeletal structures, from the mesoderm. But to the surprise of all—and the dismay of many—it has become clear that, in striking contrast, they are of ectodermal origin. Their source material is a remarkable band of tissue known as the neural crest, lying in the gastrula on the border between the tissues destined to become "normal" ectoderm and those which form the neural tube.

Except for a limited amount of more recent work, all data now known about the neural crest were summarized by Hörstadius (1950). In the gastrula stage there begins, through the inductive influence of the underlying notochord, a rolling-up of a central area of the embryonic ectoderm into the neural tube, from which are derived brain and spinal cord. During this process, in which the tissues on either side rise into a pair of longitudinal crests, it can be demonstrated, both by observation and by experiment, that a band of cells lying along the length of the crests on either side is distinctive in nature and destiny from both the more medial cells, which are to make up the materials of the central nervous system, and the more lateral areas of the embryonic ectoderm, destined in general to become epidermis and normal ectodermal skin derivatives (Fig. 2). At a variable stage, ranging from somewhat before to somewhat after the closure of the tube, these neural crest cells are pinched off from the epithelium of future skin and neural tube, take on a mesenchyme-like appearance, and begin to descend down along the outer walls of the neural tube. They have a varied destiny. As might be expected, most of the neural crest cells are incorporated in the more peripheral parts of the nervous system. Others, surprisingly, appear to be the sole source of pigment cells for the entire body. Still others appear to form ordinary mesenchyme. And—the important and remarkable phenomenon with which we are here concerned—in the "head" region (but not in the trunk), a fraction of the neural crest materials metamorphose into the cartilages of the visceral arches and other skeletal structures.

The neural crest was identified by His at a relatively early stage in the history of embryology as a "Zwischenstrang" between the presumptive epidermis and the neural tube, and he correctly identified the crest as the source of peripheral elements of the nervous system, notably the spinal ganglia and at least part of the ganglia of the cranial nerves. Certain workers early claimed a derivation of mesenchyme from the neural crest, and the development of connective tissues from neural crest mesenchyme in various (mainly superficial) areas has been confirmed by later workers. It was Julia Platt (1894, 1896, 1897), however, who first observed, in a graded series of *Necturus* embryos, mesenchyme descending in the head from the general area of the neural crest and definitely transforming into the cartilages of the jaws and other visceral arches. But she believed that the mesenchyme concerned came from the region of the potential epidermis lateral to the neural crest, rather than the crest itself. It remained for Landacre (1921), in a careful morphological study of the salamander *Ambystoma jeffersonianum*, to definitely show that the neural crest itself was the point of origin of the cells which form the visceral arch cartilages. Numerous later studies both morphologi-

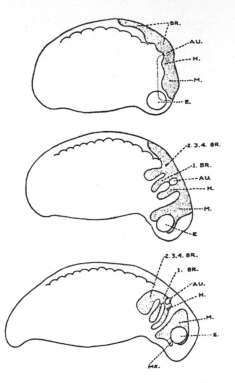

Fig. 2. Side views of salamander embryos to show the downward growth of the neural crest (stippled) to form visceral skeletal structures in the head and throat region. E, eye; AU, auditory capsule; MX, M, H, BR, neural crest downgrowths in maxillary, mandibular, hyoid, and branchial arch regions. (After Stone, from Balinsky, An Introduction to Embryology, W. B. Saunders Co.)

cal and experimental (such as Stone, 1922, 1926, etc.) abundantly demonstrated the origin of the amphibian arches from neural crest materials (Fig. 3); a more recent elaborate study is that of Hörstadius and Sellman (1946). Workers in other groups have found similar conditions, although studies on amniotes are few. Curiously, this origin does not seem to hold in lampreys (Newth, 1951).[2]

Miss Platt's claim of an origin of skeletal materials from the ectoderm was, of course, rank heresy to the embryologists of the period, since the then universally accepted germ layer doctrine assigned the origin of all skeletal materials to the mesoderm; she attempted, it would seem, to soften the blow by coining the term "mesectoderm" for mesenchyme of ectodermal origin, but this did little to calm

---

[2] It is sometimes claimed that the curious externally placed branchial basket of the lampreys is not homologous with the differently situated gill bars of gnathostomes. This was suggested originally by Rathke, who was followed by a number of later writers; but Dohrn (1884) and most recent workers believe the visceral arches homologous throughout the vertebrate series.

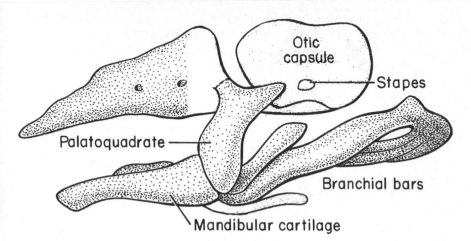

Fig. 3. Side view of the braincase and visceral arches of an amphibian larva. The shaded portions of the braincase and all the visceral arches except the posterior median element are derived from the neural crest; the unshaded portions are of mesodermal derivation. (Modified from Hörstadius and Sellman.)

those with orthodox beliefs. For a time a few embryologists disputed her conclusions (Rabl, 1894; Corning, 1899; Buchs, 1902). Even as late as 1930, when the work of Landacre and Stone had amply confirmed Platt's descriptions, we find that master of vertebrate morphology and morphogenesis, E. H. Goodrich, stating flatly (1930: 396) that the visceral arches "are derived from splanchnic mesoblast," and suggesting that supposed neural crest origins are due to faulty materials or faulty observations. DeBeer, a student of Goodrich, in 1937 (pp. 18, 472-476) tended to avoid the question of neural crest origin of the visceral cartilages, stating that the origin of the visceral arches is "uncertain." However, in 1947 DeBeer, as a result of his own investigations, became converted to the neural crest origin of the visceral arches.

As seen above, most of the work on neural crest skeletal derivatives has been done on amphibians and fishes, and relatively little is known regarding higher vertebrates (but cf. Veit, 1919; Bartelmez, 1923; Holmdahl, 1928, 1934). In this connection, it may be noted that evidence that in mammals the neural crest contributes to the jaw cartilages had been discovered in 1911, by a student working under Professor J. P. Hill of University College, London, but the fact was not published for nearly half a century (Hill and Watson, 1958)—a delay due, it seems, to reluctance of the professor supervising the student's work to commit treason to the germ layer theory!

I have said that the "visceral arches" are the skeletal structures formed by the neural crest. Qualifications must be made to this statement by subtraction and addition.

In urodeles all the gill arches are surely of neural crest origin with one exception—the most ventroposterior element of the series, the second basibranchial (or parahyoid or urohyal of actinopterygians). This seems somewhat puzzling. However, this element may be regarded as developed in an anterior extension of the normal ventral mesodermal mesenchyme which farther back forms the equally midventral sternal element (or elements). We are back of the throat region, to which the neural crest strands descend, and in an area where trunk mesenchyme is present. Further, in amphibians no such element as a urohyal is present in anurans or a considerable fraction of the urodeles; when present in salamanders it generally arises as a discrete structure, often without any close connection with the proper visceral arch apparatus. The urohyal appears to be properly a mesodermal element associated, in origin as in topography, with the hypoglossal or hypobranchial musculature of somite origin.

But in addition to forming the more readily identifiable visceral arches, the neural crest forms the anterior portion of the braincase of the Amphibia. In typical lower gnathostomes the basic structures in braincase formation are two pairs of ventral elements. The *parachordals* develop on either side of the notochord from a point just behind the pituitary back to the occipital region. Farther forward are similarly paired *trabeculae*, from which much of the anterior part of the braincase develops. The parachordals appear, from their position, to be comparable to modified vertebral materials, arising, like vertebral centra, in association with the notochord. Like the vertebrae they arise from mesenchyme derived from normal mesodermal somites. But although the trabeculae include posteriorly mesodermal mesenchyme, most of their substance is derived from the neural crest. That the neural crest should "invade" part of a structure seemingly quite unrelated to the visceral arches seems strange at first sight. Actually, however, such an origin might be expected on other grounds. It is generally believed that in the development of jawed gnathostomes, at least, one (or possibly two) anterior gill slits have been crowded out and eliminated with jaw growth (cf., for example, Allis, 1938; DeBeer, 1937: 375-377), and such a situation is found in the extinct cephalaspids (Stensiö, 1927; Watson, 1954; Wängsjö, 1952) although there is some dispute as to whether one or two "extra" gills and gill arches are represented.

This being the case, one might expect to find some sort of vestiges of the visceral arches associated with the lost premandibular segment or segments. Some have suggested that the shark labial cartilages are such vestiges; it is, however, more probable that they are neomorphs (Goodrich, 1930: 448), essentially "sesamoids" associated with jaw movements. More worthy of consideration has been the suggestion that the trabeculae are remains of an anterior gill arch, secondarily utilized for support of an expanding brain. This hypothesis, first advanced by Huxley, has been supported by Allis (1923, 1925) and other writers. The hypothesis of the visceral nature of the trabeculae was advanced without knowledge of the common embryonic origin of trabeculae and visceral arches, but is in perfect harmony with the facts of embryology showing their relationship.

Beyond the formation of embryonic cartilages, the neurectodermal materials appear to be responsible for hard skeletal structures in later embryonic stages and the adult. It has long been clear that "mesectoderm" is implicated in tooth formation, and recently DeBeer (1947), Andres (1946), Wagner (1949) and others have produced evidence to show that "mesectoderm" is involved in the formation of dermal bone in at least the anterior part of the skull and jaws.

Is this striking and embryologically unique origin of these "visceral" skeletal structures due merely to topographic convenience, or does it represent a basic cleavage between somatic and visceral elements in the vertebrate body? At first sight a plausible argument for the first of these possibilities can be made on the basis that typical mesodermal somites, from which other skeletal structures are formed, do not extend into the anterior part of the head region, and that nature has, so to speak, simply utilized such mesenchymal materials as happen to be at hand here for the formation of these arches. But further reflection shows this to be invalid, as we have seen in the case of the visceral muscles. All the arches posterior to the hyoid lie back of the ear region, in areas in which somite mesenchyme is as readily available as neural crest mesenchyme. Anteriorly, somite development is reduced. But prechordal mesoderm is present in the head region, rolling inward and forward in front of the chordamesoderm, and does, in fact, contribute to trabecula formation posteriorly. Further, mesodermal somites appear to have been developed in early evolutionary stages all the way forward in the head region. They are present in typical vertebrates only in reduced form as the "head cavities" for eye-muscle formation. Unless the method of cartilage formation from neural crest materials had not been early established, one would expect these anterior somites would have remained fully developed as sources of skeletal mesenchyme. All in all, it is clear that the development of the visceral skeleton from mesectoderm is part of an ancient and basic pattern in vertebrate development and history. And this fact, combined with the likewise distinctive nature of the visceral muscles associated with this visceral skeleton, bring forcibly to mind the prominence of the pharynx in the lower chordate relatives of the vertebrates. Of special interest is the fact that in amphioxus, tunicates, and even acorn worms, in which there are no other skeletal structures of any sort, cartilage, or protocartilage, is developed to support the gill region. The visceral skeleton is ancient in its origins—the oldest skeletal structure, in chordate history, far antedating the mesodermal skeletal elements evolving in the "somatic" animal.

SOMATIC AND VISCERAL NERVE COMPONENTS

The distinctive features of visceral musculature and skeletal materials have to do for the most part with the pharynx, emphasizing the presumptive importance of that region in ancestral vertebrates. Equally distinctive features are to be found in the peripheral nervous system; here, however, the distinction of the visceral system is seen not merely in the pharyngeal region, but in the entire gut tract and, indeed, in the innervation of the "viscera" in toto.

In the anatomic and physiological study of the peripheral nervous system, the distinction between motor and sensory—efferent and afferent—systems was clear from early days. But more detailed studies in the latter part of the 19th century made it obvious that further analysis of nerve components was necessary. An early suggestion of this sort came from the side of physiological study (Gaskell, 1886[3]). On the afferent side, there soon developed a concept of distinction between sensory structures of three types, which Sherrington (1906, etc.) termed exteroceptors, proprioceptors, and interoceptors. The main urge for component analysis, however, came from the students of comparative neurology, such as Osborn (1888) and his student Strong (1895). The need first arose because of difficulty in unraveling the complexities of the cranial nerve system, but the analysis is equally applicable to spinal nerves. As developed, the "doctrine" of nerve components has been clearly set forth by Herrick (1903, 1943, etc.), and most fully expounded by Johnston (1902, 1905, 1906), and has contributed greatly to our understanding of nerve structure and classification.

The nerve component doctrine states that nerves may be basically analyzed as constituted by elements that may pertain to any of four components, sensory and motor,[4] both divisible into somatic and visceral elements. Because of the fact that (as noted later) the central connections of elements of the peripheral nerves are generally represented in cord and brain stem in a series of columns with a specific dorsoventral arrangement, the four components may be listed in sequence as (1) somatic sensory, (2) visceral sensory, (3) visceral motor, (4) somatic motor. In each category except the last, "special" as well as "general" subdivisions may be present in the head region.

Somatic sensory components are those carrying impulses inward from sense organs in the "outer tube" of the body (primarily the "exteroceptors" of the physiological classification, which have to do with the "external relations" of the animal, but also the "proprioceptors," the sense organs found in the muscles and tendons of the "outer tube"), structures of some importance in mammals, but little developed in lower vertebrates. Visceral sensory components (volumetrically unimportant) carry inward to the central nervous system impulses arising from the "interoceptors" of the gut and other viscera. Visceral motor elements are those carrying impulses outward to the muscles, smooth or striated, of the

---

[3] Gaskell's work led not only to an excellent volume on the autonomic system (1916) but also to an amusing but highly improbable theory of the origin of the vertebrate nervous system (1908).

[4] More properly, since (for example) excitation of a gland is not technically "motor," one should speak of afferent and efferent rather than sensory and motor components.

visceral system as defined in an earlier section, and to glands as well. The somatic motor components supply the striated somatic musculature.

The cranial nerves show an exceedingly complicated and variable pattern of components, but the spinal nerves as well show clear and seemingly significant distinctions between somatic and visceral components on the motor side of the picture. The classical picture of the composition of a spinal nerve (Fig. 4A) is

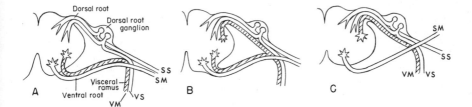

Fig. 4. Diagrammatic views of spinal nerves in (A), a mammal, (B), a lower vertebrate, and (C), a primitive form with separate dorsal and ventral nerves. In mammals most of the autonomic fibers (hatched) emerge from the ventral root; in lower vertebrates part emerge with the dorsal root; primitively, it would appear, all autonomics were part of the dorsal root. Abbreviations: SM, somatic motor; SS, somatic sensory; VM, visceral motor; VS, visceral sensory.

that found in mammals and taught as orthodox in medical and zoological courses. The nerve emerges from the cord in two roots, dorsal and ventral;[5] the dorsal root bears a ganglion a short distance beyond its point of emergence, then turns downward and joins the ventral root. There is thus a two-and-two division of components in the roots. Both sensory components are contained in the dorsal root, and their cell bodies lie in the dorsal root ganglion. The ventral root includes both visceral and somatic motor components. All four come together at the point of union; beyond, both visceral components diverge into the visceral ramus, whereas both somatic components continue out, to muscles and skin, in the main trunk of the nerve.

Up to this point there is no difference in the description of the paths or structure of somatic and visceral elements. Both sensory components emerge in common via the dorsal root, and have their cell bodies (mainly, if not entirely, derived from the neural crest) in the dorsal root ganglion; both motor components have their cell bodies in the dorsal root ganglion; both motor

[5] The BNA terminology generally used in medical teaching for decades caused mental confusion by terming the two roots "posterior" and "anterior" in relation to the (abnormal) posture of *Homo sapiens.*

components have their cell bodies in the gray matter of the cord and both have fibers emerging via the ventral root. However, distinctive features separating somatic and visceral components are to be found in (1) the central connections of the components; (2) the structure of visceral motor as compared with somatic motor elements; (3) the phylogenetic history of the nerve roots.

Within the nerve cord (Fig. 5A), the cell bodies of the motor neurons of both types are situated in the ventral part of the gray matter of the cord. In the adult

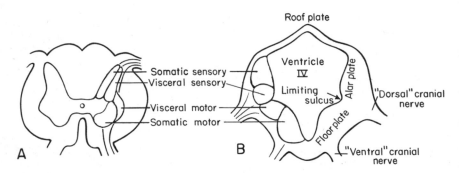

Fig. 5. Diagrammatic cross section of: (A), the spinal cord in an embryonic vertebrate, and (B), the medulla, to show the arrangement of the "visceral" and "somatic" cell areas in the grey matter of the cord and brainstem.

mammal a variety of "nuclei"—clusters of cell bodies—may be distinguished here, but in the embryo and even to a considerable extent in the adult, the somatic motor cells are concentrated in the most ventral part of the area and, particularly in the region of the limbs, cause a pronounced "bulge" in the gray matter—a ventral "horn" or, more properly, a ventral column. Cell bodies of the visceral motor fibers are fewer in number, but are present in all trunk segments in mammals. They are invariably situated more dorsally and laterally, and in some cases cause a slight lateral bulging, as a lateral column or horn. The sensory neurons have, of course, no cell bodies within the cord; however, their axons, entering the white matter dorsally and sending rami anteriorly and posteriorly, typically send branches to series of intercalated or internuncial cells situated in the dorsal "horn" or dorsal column. The topographic distinction between somatic and visceral elements is not generally as distinct as in the case of central motor areas, but to some degree even in the adult and more clearly in embryos two subdivisions can be made out in the dorsal column, with clusters of cells associated with somatic sensory elements situated toward the more dorsal and medial part of the area, those associated with visceral sensory fibers being more laterally and ventrally placed. There is thus established the dorsoventral sequence: somatic sensory - visceral sensory - visceral motor - somatic motor. This same distinctive sequence, as mentioned later, is apparent in the brain stem, and strongly suggests that the somatic-visceral contrast is an ancient one in the history of the vertebrate nervous system.

As regards the pattern of the components in the peripheral nerves, there is no significant difference in structure between the somatic and visceral sensory elements: both enter the cord through the dorsal root, both have their cell bodies in the dorsal root ganglia. The two components, to be sure, are divergent distally, but that is merely a matter of topography, since the somatic fibers naturally run outward in the main stem of the nerve, whereas the majority of the visceral fibers necessarily plunge downward through visceral rami to reach their visceral termini. But as regards motor components, the story is different. The somatic motor fibers course outward and run directly to their termini on motor end-plates, with no nonsense about the matter. Not so for the visceral motor elements. As will be seen later, special visceral motor patterns will be found in the cranial nerves. But in the trunk two neurons in sequence are involved before the smooth musculature or gland is reached and stimulated.[6]

In great measure due to the importance of the visceral system in medicine, this nerve component has been the subject of considerable work in mammals. The visceral system has in the past often been termed the "vegetative" nervous system or "sympathetic" in a broad use of that term. The visceral motor component was early termed the "involuntary" system, but this has generally been replaced by "autonomic." Excellent general accounts of this system, particularly in mammals, can be found in any standard text on human anatomy or physiology. From the lateral column of the gray matter of the cord, where the cell bodies are located, fibers run out through the ventral nerve root in mammals and leave the main trunk of the nerve to descend into the visceral ramus. They do not, however, run directly to the muscle or gland concerned. At some point along this course the fiber of this first neuron—termed the preganglionic neuron—enters a ganglion containing numerous cell bodies of a second series of neurons—postganglionic neurons (Fig. 6). Here each preganglionic fiber makes connections with postganglionic neurons, from which, in turn, fibers extend to the muscle or gland concerned. In mammals this autonomic nerve system can be separated (although far from perfectly) into two units on both physiological and anatomical grounds—a thoracolumbar or sympathetic system (in the narrower usage of the latter term) and a craniosacral or parasympathetic system. The fibers of the sympathetic system are confined to the thoracic and lumbar regions of the column; those of the parasympathetic

---

[6]The sole exception is the adrenal medulla, in which generally only a single neuron is concerned. But, as is well known, the adrenalin-producing cells are actually modified neurons corresponding to the second neuron in the typical two-neuron visceral motor system. Even so, the elasmobranchs show a two-neuron innervation of this organ (Young, 1933).

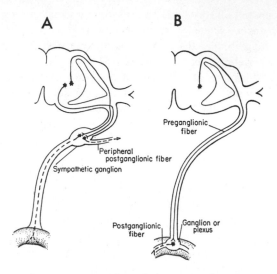

Fig. 6. The autonomic system as found in most lower vertebrates. (A), sympathic components; the relay to the postganglionic neurons takes place in ganglia below. The vertebral column and the postganglionic axons are long. (B), parasympathic components; the cell bodies of the postganglionic neurons are embedded in the gut or other organs.

emerge with cranial nerves (most notably the vagus), on the one hand, and to a lesser extent from a limited number of nerves in the sacral region, on the other. In mammals both series ramify extensively so that all the viscera have a double innervation by both sympathetic and parasympathetic fibers.

A second point of anatomical distinction in the autonomic system lies in the point at which the relay occurs. In the case of the sympathetics, the ganglia concerned are relatively proximally situated, either in close proximity to the origin of the visceral ramus (in the sympathetic chain characteristic of higher vertebrates), or, at the farthest, in the mesenteries leading toward the viscera. They never lie in the substance of the organs to be innervated, and there is always a postganglionic fiber of considerable length. In contrast is the situation in the parasympathetic system. The preganglionic fibers run the entire distance from cord to organ concerned; the relay takes place close to or actually within the substance of the organ innervated. Within the mammalian intestine, there are two conspicuous nerve nets, the myenteric plexus and the submucous plexus, containing a network of cells and fibers. The parasympathetic preganglionic axons penetrate directly to neurons in these plexuses, which are hence to be considered as postganglionic in nature. For our purposes we are less concerned here with the "applied" physiology of the autonomic system, but may note that in general (but with exceptions!) the sympathetic system tends to stimulate the organism, the parasympathetic in contrast, tends toward a calm, "digestive" state. More specifically, it is of interest that while it is now accepted doctrine that the action of most nerve fibers is exerted on end organs through the production of acetylcholine, the postganglionic fibers of the sympathetic system give off an adrenalin-like material.

The situation just described is that found in mammals, with a strong cleavage of the autonomics into sympathetic and parasympathetic subdivisions. It would be of interest to trace the history of the autonomics back down through the vertebrate series. Unfortunately our knowledge of the system in lower classes is very fragmentary, despite such useful studies as those of Young (1933), Yntema and Hammond (1947) and Nicol (1952). Both anatomical and physiological studies of this sort are exceedingly difficult to carry out, and even the mammalian situation would not have received much attention had it not been for its practical medical importance. Some general features of this history, however, seem clear. In lower classes the cleavage between sympathetic and parasympathetic systems is much less clear, and as we descend the scale there is much less evidence of double innervation of organs. There appears to be, on the whole, much less innervation from the spinal cord; on the other hand, in lower classes there is a well-developed branch of the vagus extending backward the entire length of the gut. At the cyclostome level this vagal innervation is present, but there is no autonomic innervation from the spinal nerves except in the rectal and cloacal region (Johnels, 1956). It thus would appear that the autonomic system has undergone gradual elaboration and differentiation during the course of vertebrate history. And, extrapolating backward, one may suspect that this system did not exist in the early ancestors of the vertebrates.

Why a two-neuron chain in autonomic innervation? It cannot be attributed to the distance to be covered; limb muscle axons of the somatic system are often of greater length, and parasympathetic preganglionic fibers extend nearly the whole length of the course to be covered. In the case of the sympathetics, the fact that the postganglionic neurons produce noradrenalin rather than being of the normal "cholinergic" type furnishes a possible raison d'être for a two-chain system. But this argument does not hold for the parasympathetics, where both pre- and postganglionic neurons are cholinergic.

It is not unreasonable to speculate on the possibility that the ancestor of the vertebrates may have had, like many invertebrate types, an essentially independent visceral nerve net; that the development of the autonomic system represents an attempt by the central nervous system at gaining control over visceral activity; and that possibly in the peculiar two-neuron system seen here, the postganglionic neurons may be representatives of the original visceral nerve net system, the preganglionics representatives of attempts at domination by the central nervous system.

This is, of course, highly speculative. As regards the embryonic origin of postganglionic neurons, there is considerable evidence to show that those of the sympathetic division are derived, like sensory neurons, from the neural crest. But as regards the secondary neurons of the parasympathetic system, most prominently those of the plexuses of the digestive tract, the situation is less clear. An origin of these deep neural structures from the neural crest has been claimed, but the evidence is not too strong. On the other hand, certain workers, mainly of an early date, have claimed that these cells arise in situ. But again, there is little assurance of this; problems of differential staining, among other factors, are involved.

Some further suggestive evidence of enteric independence is present. It is commonly stated that all motor or glandular activity set up by the secondary neurons of the autonomic system is controlled by the central nervous system, acting through the preganglionic neurons (e.g., Hill, 1927, etc.). But it is known that isolated gut segments, lacking any innervation, are capable of peristaltic movement, suggesting local "initiative" via nerve net connections. Again, histological studies of gut plexus in mammals show that many of the neurons here, which one assumes offhand to be merely secondary neurons of the parasympathetic system, send axons not only to muscles and glands, but to other neurons in the plexus. Such evidence suggests that we are possibly dealing with retention of an original visceral nerve net of primitive character, now partially controlled by the central nervous system but still retaining some initiative.

A further feature of interest regarding the distinctive nature of visceral motor elements has to do with the history of their mode of exit from the spinal cord (Fig. 4). As already mentioned, in mammals they typically emerge from the cord via the ventral roots, as do the somatic motor axons, and this is often taught as characteristic of vertebrates in general. This is far from the case. Even in mammals there is some evidence that a small fraction, at least, of autonomic fibers emerge via the dorsal root, and, as we pass to lower vertebrates, there is scattered evidence to show that a considerable fraction of the autonomic fibers utilize the dorsal root. In cyclostomes, as we have noted, autonomic elements appear to be rare; but where definitely traced, they appear to use either dorsal or ventral root, indiscriminately (Johnels, 1956). This is suggestive of the possibility that they may have been, when first developed, fully associated with the dorsal roots; and this suggestion receives support from the fact that in amphioxus all visceral components are part of the dorsal root nerves.

Parallel to this possible shift is the evidence suggesting that the presence in a segment of a single nerve with dorsal and ventral roots is a secondary condition (Fig. 7). In all higher vertebrate groups each spinal nerve is a well-fused unit. In sharks, however, the two roots do not completely fuse; rather, they interchange branches, so that the two components in each root separate and combine with their complements of somatic and visceral types. In lampreys we find distinct dorsal and ventral nerves in each segment, the ventral root nerve almost completely composed of somatic motor fibers, the dorsal root mainly sensory, with somatic sensory fibers dominating. In amphioxus, likewise, there are

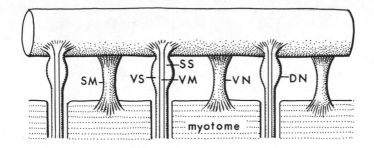

Fig. 7. Diagram of the spinal cord and nerves of the left side of a lamprey seen in dorsal view, to show the alternating arrangement of separate dorsal and ventral spinal nerves, related to intersegmental spaces and myotomes, respectively. In a primitive stage the dorsal root presumably consisted solely of somatic sensory neurons, the ventral root of somatic motor neurons. As control over the viscera developed, visceral fibers, both sensory and motor, presumably formed at first in connection with the dorsal root; the motor fibers later shifted mainly to the ventral root. DN, dorsal nerve; VN, ventral nerve; SM, somatic motor component; SS, somatic sensory; VM, visceral motor; VS, visceral sensory.

completely separate dorsal and ventral roots, the ventral including only somatic motor fibers, the dorsal composed of somatic sensory plus all visceral fibers, as far as they are present. Furthermore, in cyclostomes and amphioxus these discrete nerves are not "in line" with one another dorsoventrally, but alternate in position. This staggered position is functionally reasonable. The sole function of a ventral root in a nerve of this sort is the innervation of the muscles of a myotome, and hence the logical place for its emergence from the cord is in the middle of a segment. On the other hand, a dorsal nerve should be so placed that its components do not need to burrow through a myotome, and an intersegmental position is proper.

Consideration of this series of nerve structures suggests that the history of nerves emanating from the central nervous system might well have been as follows: the primary structures arising from the central nervous system were intrasegmental ventral nerves formed of somatic motor fibers running to the myotomes and intersegmental dorsal nerves formed of somatic sensory fibers; as connections between central nervous system and viscera developed, visceral fibers, both sensory and motor, emerged (as in amphioxus) with the dorsal nerve; but, during the course of vertebrate evolution, there was a trend for the visceral motor fibers to shift down to the ventral root.

The complexity and variability of the cranial nerve situation was a major factor in the development of the dogma of nerve components, and resulted in such valuable analyses as, for example, the early work of Strong (1895) on the tadpole, that of Herrick on the teleost *Menidia* (1899), or (to cite one of many valuable later works) that of Norris and Hughes (1920) on *Squalus*. In the cranial region all four components present in the trunk are present, and in three of the four component areas special categories are found. Three types of nerves are present.

(1) There are special sensory structures that have special nerves quite distinct from any found in the trunk. Nerves I and II for nose and eye are quite unlike any other nerves in the body and seem significant evidence of the antiquity and individuality of these sense organs. Nerve VIII, for the ear, plus the nerves associated with the lateral line organs (from which it is generally agreed that the ear is basically derived) show rather more normal structure, with a proper sensory ganglion, and give a suggestion that we are dealing here with sensory systems of somewhat later development than in the case of eye and nose. It is noteworthy that in the brain the central connections of the nerves adhere closely, in adult as well as embryo, to the series of dorsoventral columns (Fig. 5B) found in the cord and that the special sensory structures are primitively associated with special dorsal sensory regions of the brain: telencephalon, diencephalic roof, and the upper margin of the medulla, from which the cerebellum develops. (2) Turning to the other end of the dorsoventral series, ventral somatic motor nerves, innervating myotome derivatives, are present as nerves III, IV, and VI, for the eye muscles, and XII, the hypoglossal (or the essentially homologous occipital nerves in fishes), innervating hypobranchial or hypoglossal muscles derived from the most anterior trunk myotomes. These nerves are purely somatic motor (except that afferent proprioceptor fibers may be present and that there is an "association of convenience" of eye autonomics with nerve III in many forms). (3) A series of nerves corresponding to the dorsal trunk nerves of lampreys or amphioxus, including V_1 (profundus), $V_{2,3}$ (trigeminal proper), VII (facial), IX (glossopharyngeal), X and XI (vagus plus accessorius), and possibly the tiny nervus terminalis (0). The composition of these nerves is somewhat variable, but they may include part or all of the three components which, it was suggested above, may have been present in a primitive dorsal trunk nerve—somatic sensory, visceral sensory, and visceral motor. A special feature of these cranial nerves, however, is the fact that the visceral motor components are of two sorts: (1) "general" visceral motor components, part of the parasympathetic system, which are two-neuron chains to smooth muscles and glands, and (2) "special" visceral motor neurons, which supply the striated visceral muscles discussed in an earlier section. Despite the specializations found in the head, due to the presence of organs of special sense and of the visceral arch muscles, one gains the impression that we are here dealing with a part of the peripheral nervous system that in some regards—notably the clear distinction between dorsal and ventral root nerves—is more primitive than that found in the trunk.

There is one further difference between dorsal root nerves in the trunk and those of the head region. The discrete dorsal nerves of a lamprey are segmentally arranged in relation to mesodermal segmentation, one to each gap between successive myotomes. This is not the case in the head. Here the arrangement is segmental, but the segmentation concerned is that of the gill slits and intervening gill arches—one nerve for each arch, but with the vagus supplying all the posterior arches. It is the gills and gut which set the pattern, in relation to visceral sensory and visceral motor components, and the distribution of somatic sensory components is brought into line with the pattern of the visceral components.

Since the time of Balfour, there have been attempts to interpret cranial structures, and particularly cranial nerves, in a pattern conformable with trunk segmentation; most notable of these attempts is that of Goodrich (1918). By Goodrich, dorsal and ventral cranial nerves, myotomes, and gills are lined up, in theory, in a segmental series along the length of the head. On analysis, however, the scheme seems surely an artificial one. Vertebrates exhibit segmentation, to be sure, but segmentation of two different sorts: (1) one based on mesodermal somites, from which is derived skeletal segmentation and that of spinal nerves related primarily to the position of the myotomes; (2) gill slit segmentation, from which is derived the segmental arrangement of the visceral arches, of the muscles that move them, and the dorsal, "branchial," nerves that supply this region. It may happen by chance that during development some one gill bar and its musculature may lie below some one specific myotome and its derived musculature. But there is no *a priori* reason to think that the two segmental systems—one basically mesodermal and related to the "somatic" animal, the other basically endodermal, "visceral" in origin—have any necessary relationship to one another. Gill slits and somites arise quite independently of one another in the embryo. And phylogenetically, one may note that a gill slit segmentation is highly developed in acorn worms, in which the somite system is not developed at all.

To sum up the phylogenetic suggestions gained from a consideration of the structure of the nervous system in living vertebrates, high and low, and of their chordate and protochordate "ancestors," one tends strongly to gain the impression that the remote "visceral" ancestral form had a simple superficial nerve net and, at some early stage, acquired a visceral nerve net as well; that, with the development of the "somatic" animal, there developed the central nervous system, with segmental nerves including a ventral root of somatic motor type and a distinct dorsal root at first composed merely of somatic sensory neurons; but that there was a strong tendency for the somatic animal to attempt neural control over the visceral animal, first, perhaps, by a direct connection with the important visceral muscles of the pharynx, later by an attempt to dominate the gut by autonomic fibers, originally by way of dorsal nerve roots, running to the postganglionic neurons, which represent the elements of the original gut nerve net. The development of visceral centers in brain and cord was associated with this attempt at domination of the visceral by the somatic animal. But, as we are ourselves aware, the integration of the visceral animal into the dominant nervous system of our somatic being is still far from perfect.

LOWER "CHORDATES"

In earlier years it was frequently assumed that, since vertebrates are essentially active animals, the vertebrate ancestors had been, from at least an early metazoan stage, free-living and equally active forms (Willey, 1894). The discussion above strongly suggests that this was not the case. The evidence from comparative anatomy suggests that there has been, during the history of the group, increasing dominance of an active "somatic" being over a primitive ancestral "visceral" form which was of a simple nature—this ancestral form consisting of little but a digestive tract, with main emphasis (as shown by the evidence of muscles, skeleton, and nerves) on food gathering functions in the mouth-pharyngeal region. Such an ancestral form would quite surely have been a sessile rather than an active animal. If we turn to such living animals as appear to be related to the ancestry of vertebrates, this conclusion appears to be fully justified. The prevertebrates are, with few exceptions, sessile and often attached microfeeders, which do not actively seek food, but wait for food to come to them; most appear to be essentially the sort of "visceral" animal which the earlier discussion tended to arrive at—forms with a very simple structure except for specializations related to food-gathering.

Such are, in descending sequence, "amphioxus," the tunicates, the acorn worms, and the pterobranchs—more formally the Cephalochordata, Urochordata, Enteropneusta, and Pterobranchia. The first two are universally recognized as vertebrate relatives, and included with them in a common phylum, Chordata; the latter two, more distantly related, are sometimes included in the Chordata, but currently are generally considered as members of a separate, though related, phylum Hemichordata (Van der Horst, 1939; Hyman, 1959: 72-79).[7] Quite surely none of these forms, as they exist today, are ancestral to vertebrates, but are presumably variably specialized survivors of ancestral groups. From their structure, development, and functions clues as to the vertebrate pedigree may be gained. A full account of these forms is given by Dawydoff, Brien, Drach, and Dalcq in the *Grassé Traité de Zoologie* (1948); a more compact survey is that by Barrington (1965) and a very elementary account is contained in Chapter II

---

[7] The Pogonophora (Caullery, 1944; Dawydoff, 1948, etc.) are marine organisms only recently recognized, which are presumably chordate relatives, but degenerate in character and need not concern us here. Nor need we discuss: *Planctosphaera*, apparently a neotenic tornarian larva (Spengel, 1946); a most curious little creature from the Silurian of Scotland, *Ainiktozoon*, which may be an aberrant chordate (Scourfield, 1937); the interesting theory of Jefferies (1967, 1968) that certain echinoderms are true chordates; the problematical conodonts.

of my *Vertebrate Body* (1970). Pterobranchs and acorn worms are adequately described by Hyman (1959).

Pterobranchs

Simplest and lowliest in structure of such forms are the pterobranchs; typical members, *Rhabdopleura* and *Cephalodiscus*, are deep sea forms, which, due to tiny size and rarity of collection, are but poorly known. These are essentially sessile and, to at least some degree, colonial; they secrete about themselves protective tubules.[8] Above a stalk (or peduncle) is a blob of body, above which a "collar" region sends off ciliated arms, or lophophores. Between the bases of the lophophores is a mouth opening; above it is a projecting "nose," a preoral lobe; the digestive tract is doubled on itself, so that the anus opens on the "back" of the body just below the lophophores. There are coelomic cavities representing three segments—preoral lobe, collar, and body—the first single, the other two paired. A small outpocket from the gut tube, not far from the mouth, is comparable to a similar, but larger pocket in acorn worms which has been (very dubiously) considered as an incipient notochord (Komai, 1951; Newell, 1952; Silén, 1954). There are (of necessity) gonads, a rather simple circulatory system, a limited amount of smooth muscle, a glomerulus which functions in excretion. For a nervous system there is a central ganglion from which branches run to the lophophores and other superficial parts of the body, and a diffuse subepithelial nerve net. No nervous elements have been described in the interior of the body. There are sensory cells in the skin, but no formed sense organs of any sort.

These sessile organisms merely sit, quiescently, and obtain their living by collecting food particles from the passing water currents by means of their outflung ciliated arms. In one genus a pair of openings (gill slits) from "throat" to surface—a feature of evolutionary significance—aid in the inflow of food.

We have here as close an approach as one can conceive of to a simple "visceral" animal. To be sure, there is (and has to be) a skin covering; and there is a simple superficial nerve net making sensory contact with the environment and forming the basis from which the somatic nervous system was to develop. But for the most part, we have here a digestive system, specialized anteriorly for food gathering, and very little else. Perhaps the ultimate metazoan ancestor may not have resembled the living pterobranchs. But here we are very close to what might have been theoretically arrived at as such an ancestor.

While this is apart from our major thesis, we may briefly speculate as to the relationship and ancestry of this "visceral" chordate ancestor. If we look about among marine metazoans, we find that the pterobranchs are but one of a number of types with similar habits which make their living in a similar way, as

---

[8] Kozlowski (1947, etc.) has argued for the relationship to pterobranchs of the graptolites, ancient forms represented in the fossil record by rather comparable tubules.

sessile, usually stalked, animals feeding on food particles collected by extended ciliated arms—the lophophores. A similar mode of life is seen in bryozoans (of both types), brachiopods (despite the deceptive shell covering), and phoronids. Furthermore, although most echinoderms show different types of adaptations, the crinoids amongst the existing members of this phylum are likewise stalked sessile forms, which live by gathering food particles along ciliated arms, and the presence in the fossil record of other, ancient echinoderms of a sessile stalked type strongly suggests that the echinoderm phylum originated as forms with a similar mode of life. Are the pterobranchs related to any of these other arm feeders? In some instances morphological and embryological arguments can be marshalled in opposition, but it is not impossible that all of the lophophore-bearers may be to some degree related. In the case of the echinoderms, a good argument can be made for relationship with the hemichordates. Although Berrill has suggested that some similarities betwen pterobranchs and echinoderms are due to convergence, there are basic features in common in embryological development, in larval types (as regards echinoderms and balanoglossids), in certain biochemical characters, in mode of coelom formation, and so forth, that strongly suggest echinoderm-hemichordata affinity (Hyman, 1955: 691-705; 1959: 197-199; Barrington, 1964; 1965: 9-11, etc.). Certainly pterobranchs were not descended from echinoderms, with their various specialized structures (Fell, 1948). But both may have descended from a common lophophore-bearing ancestor of a simple sort. And I may suggest (as one or two others have done before me) that it is not impossible that the pterobranchs themselves may represent—or be very close to—this common ancestor.

Acorn Worms

A step above the pterobranchs in structural complexity and in advance toward vertebrate structure are the Enteropneusta, popularly called acorn worms because in some cases the prominent proboscis with a distinct collar behind it gives much the appearance of an acorn in its cup. Behind the collar is a rather elongate worm-like body, and one tends to think of enteropneustans as active worm-like animals. This, however, is not the case; the acorn-worms are not active forms, but spend most of their existence in sessile fashion in burrows. They are not attached by a stalk, as are some pterobranchs, and in relation to this fact the intestine is not "looped up" as in that group; in some forms, however, a remnant of a stalk persists at the end of the body. They feed, like pterobranchs, by drawing in food particles from the surrounding water. But they do this in a different fashion, and one which gives them a very different superficial appearance. Gone are the primitive ciliated arms. In contrast, the food particles are drawn into the mouth by a current of water, which then passes out on either side of the "throat" through a series of gill slits, the food being strained out in the process. We have noted that in one of the pterobranchs there was a single pair of gill slits; here a whole series is present: this makes for a much more efficient method of filter feeding than the antique lophophore system. We customarily think of gills as respiratory structures. But although some respiration may well go on in the enteropneustan gill passages, their primary function was alimentary.

Some workers, incidentally, have tended to cast doubts upon the relationship of hemichordates to the true chordates (and hence the vertebrates); but it seems highly significant that the development of the gill slits in this group follows in exact detail the complicated mode of development of the gill structures seen in amphioxus.

In the acorn worms we are dealing with creatures still very "visceral" in nature. Of superficial structures of a potentially "somatic" nature there is little to be seen. The superficial nervous system (Bullock, 1945; Knight-Jones, 1952; Silén, 1950) is somewhat more advanced than in pterobranchs, with a nervous center, branches in various directions, and a diffuse subepithelial nerve net. There is, however, one seemingly significant advance. Central in the nervous system is a collection of nerve material in the short "collar" region. Here, during embryological development, a pair of short longitudinal ridges curve upward over a central dorsal area and meet to form a tube, which may remain open or may become a solid structure. This strongly suggests the beginning of the chordate nerve tube; but this is a short structure, its organization is not too similar to that of the vertebrate spinal cord, there is no proper brain, and almost nothing in the way of sense organs.

Apart from this superficial skin sensory system and a certain amount of superficial smooth musculature, we are still dealing mainly with an essentially "visceral" animal, little farther advanced in structure (save for the presence of gill slits) than a pterobranch. One interesting feature, however, is that (as one would postulate for a fairly early stage in protochordate development) a nerve net is present in the gut walls. There appears to be some slight connection of this deep nerve net with the superficial nervous system.

Urochordata

The tunicates, or ascidians, using these terms broadly, are a moderately successful group of marine organisms which are universally held to be chordates and in some fashion related to vertebrate origins, whereas the hemichordates—pterobranchs and acorn worms—are often looked upon with suspicion and often thought (as by Berrill, 1955: 110-118) to be only distantly connected with the story of vertebrate ancestry.

I find such an attitude puzzling. Looked at broadly, the typical adult tunicate marks not the beginning of an evolutionary story, but, in a fashion, its climax. The pterobranchs were in a sense, filter feeders, but not too successful in this mode of life. With the Enteropneusta there came into the picture a new and potentially very successful method of feeding—the development of gill slits, which enable the food-bearing water currents to enter the mouth. In the tunicates the gill apparatus has been used to the full, to function as a very efficient filtering device for the food particles constantly drawn into the mouth. In typical tunicates the complex gill structure makes up the greater part of the bulk of the animal.

Living tunicates are highly varied—colonial or solitary, free-floating or fixed. Not improbably the most primitive and generalized types are to be found among the solitary forms, such as *Molgula* or *Ciona*. These little forms, not uncommon in shallow marine waters, are sessile, attached to the substrate, and it is reasonable to believe that the fixed (often stalked) condition is a direct inheritance from the most primitive chordate stage, the unattached (although essentially sessile) condition found in the Enteropneusta being somewhat aberrant in this regard.

Such a simple tunicate externally looks like a formless lump of tissue, the only visible features of which are an opening at the upper end into which water flows, and a second, lateral opening, through which the water current makes its exit. If a tunicate of this sort is dissected, it will be seen that the greater part of the body consists of a greatly enlarged pharynx with a complex filtering gill-slit apparatus, a much smaller digestive tube of stomach and intestine behind the pharynx—and (apart from gonads) little else. The tunicate, again, is almost a purely "visceral" animal; its external relations are reduced to simplicity by its covering of a stout tunic. Significant, as regards vertebrate relationships, in the complex pharynx there is present an endostyle, a food gathering structure present in amphioxus and preserved in the larval lamprey. The somatic nervous system of the adult consists of a small ganglion from which radiate a few nerves. There is some development of a visceral nerve net around the digestive tract and (again as in enteropneustans) there is a possible forerunner of the autonomic system in that one of the nerves is thought to connect with this visceral nerve net.

The adult tunicate is the logical end form of an evolutionary line of filter-feeders, beyond which little further evolutionary progress would seem probable. However, the developmental history of tunicates shows the presence of a larval type in which, as emphasized by Garstang (1928) and Berrill (1955), we see the possibility of the initiation of a startlingly different line of evolutionary development destined to lead to the vertebrates. Much of tunicate reproduction is of a budding, asexual type; in still other forms sexual reproduction is of an essentially direct type, with little development of a larval form. But in many tunicates there is present a type of larva, the significance of which is of the highest importance.

This tiny larva, shaped much like a tadpole, bears within its anterior end the materials from which the pharyngeal basket and other simple components of the adult are to be derived. But in addition there is a whole series of structures that are normally lost in the adult; their mission is to transport the little creature by active swimming to a spot suitable for adult life. Once this mission is accomplished (sometimes in a very short period of time), the individual attaches and the larval structures disappear. The larval structures are comparable to those of the "somatic" animal which was to become dominant in later vertebrate history.

In this larva we have an animal capable of active locomotion, in contrast to the essentially sessile life of the primitive adult chordates, and, unlike them, alert to its environment. It is endowed with sense organs, albeit of a rudimentary sort. And there is a spinal cord, enlarged anteriorly into a precursor of a brain. There is here a definite notochord of vertebrate type, running the length of the body, and a muscular swimming tail is developed (although the musculature is not segmented). It is of interest that the whole digestive tract is confined to the anterior portion of the embryo, so that we have here a definite true tail contrasting with the so-called tail of some invertebrates, in which internal organs persist. In this "tadpole" larva we have, in simplified form, the basic structures which in the vertebrates are the dominant "somatic" features of the body.

What is the phylogenetic position of this simplified "model" of a vertebrate? At one time it was believed that the ascidian ancestor was an active swimmer, that the tadpole larva represents a reduction of ancestral structures, and that the adult tunicate is a degenerate end form. Much more acceptable, I believe, is the thesis advocated by Garstang—that the ascidian ancestor never had been an active form and that in this "somatic" type of larva we have a new development from which, by paedogenesis and the retention of the "tadpole" condition to sexual maturity, a new evolutionary sequence was to begin. The old adult type, patterned in the general fashion of its "visceral" chordate ancestors, was dropped out of the picture, and a new evolutionary line, dominantly "somatic" in structure, began a progress toward the vertebrate condition (Fig. 8).

Where did this larval type originate and when did its paedogenetic independence begin? Garstang produced ingenious arguments for the view that this larva had been transformed from the ciliated larva of the enteropneustans; but such a derivation is none too certain, and the tadpole larva may have been a new product in primitive urochordates. It is possible that the independence of the tadpole began by paedogenetic development from a full-fledged tunicate stage, as Medawar (1951) suggests, and as Berrill implies, but it is rather generally believed that this was initiated before the ascidians reached their full development, and it has been even suggested that it originated far down the hemichordate series (Whitear, 1957; Bone, 1960).

Amphioxus

Amphioxus represents a stage structurally intermediate in many regards between the tunicate larva and the full-fledged vertebrate, but presents nearly as many problems as it solves. We have here an animal in which many of the "somatic" features foreshadowed in that larva are retained in a sexually mature animal, and carried far toward the vertebrate condition—for example, the highly

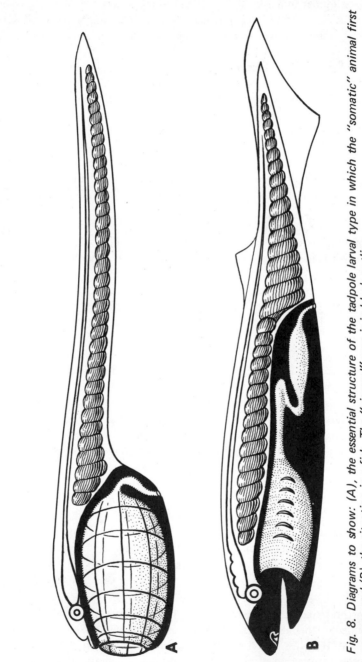

Fig. 8. Diagrams to show: (A), the essential structure of the tadpole larval type in which the "somatic" animal first appears, and (B), the situation in a fish. The "visceral" area is in black outline.

developed series of striated muscle segments, a complex peripheral nervous system, and so on. But amphioxus is rather surely aberrant from a direct line leading upward toward the vertebrates in various regards; for example, the excessive multiplication of gill slits, asymmetrical development, and the presence of a nephridial type of excretory structure.[9] Further, it seems certain that this little creature is degenerate, to some extent at least in, for example, the lack of any development of "brain" and almost complete absence of sense organs—structures at least incipiently present in the tunicate larva. Gregory (1951) suggested that amphioxus was, in fact, a degenerate ostracoderm. This is, quite surely, too extreme a view. But it certainly does seem to be an aberrant and, possibly paedogenetic, laggard, which had started along the path from tunicate larva to vertebrate and failed to progress further (Berrill, 1955; Medawar, 1951).

Other chordates did progress and attain the vertebrate status seen, to begin with, in the oldest of fossil vertebrates, the ostracoderms of the Ordovician and Silurian periods, whose degenerate descendants are the lampreys and hagfishes of today. The ancient ostracoderms, like their lower chordate ancestors, were still filter-feeders (as are the unmetamorphosed lampreys today). Such forms as the cephalaspids among the ostracoderms possessed an enormous pharyngeal gill-filtering basket, behind which was an apparently short gut. The retention and elaboration of the pharynx as a feeding structure in early vertebrates is not improbably responsible for the high development of visceral structures that we have discussed for this region as regards skeleton, muscle, and nerves. The duty of the somatic animal was obviously that of transporting this feeding device to favorable spots for its activity.

The somatic animal, by the time we reach the base of the vertebrate scale in ostracoderms and cyclostomes, was already highly developed and dominant over the visceral apparatus which it transported, and had already progressed far toward this status in amphioxus. A nerve cord of vertebrate type is present in the most primitive vertebrates, and from the "brain" vesicle of the tunicate larva there had developed a brain which, albeit still of small size and relatively simple structure in jawless vertebrates, already had the basic vertebrate pattern. Spinal nerves, with both somatic and visceral components, are already developed in the lowest of vertebrates, and visceral motor nerves are already, in cyclostomes, beginning the process of taking over more direct control of the viscera. The tunicate larva had rudimentary sense organs; cyclostomes and apparently the ancient ostracoderms had nose, eye, and ear highly developed. Supporting structures were well developed. There is an excellent notochord and, in cyclostomes, the beginnings of the vertebral column; cyclostomes have well-developed gill bars and head cartilages, while ostracoderms had even considerable

[9] Homer Smith (1953: 225, family tree, etc.) disliked amphioxus as a close relative of the vertebrates, apparently because of the lack of a vertebrate type of kidney. I would think, however, that he would have welcomed amphioxus, on the ground that, as a presumably primitively marine form, it should not have developed a type of kidney adapted for fresh waters.

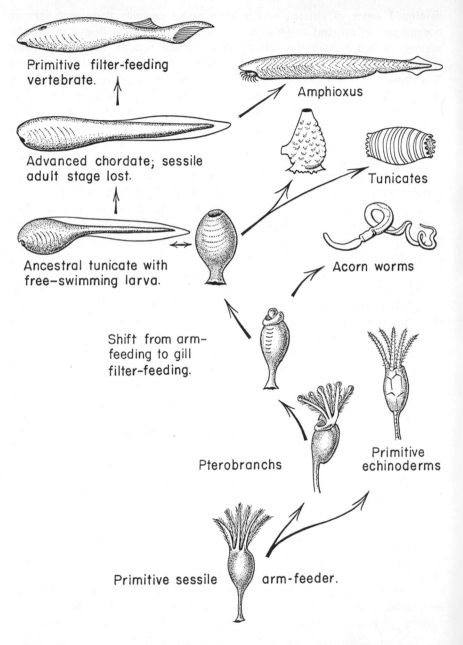

Primitive filter-feeding vertebrate.

Amphioxus

Advanced chordate; sessile adult stage lost.

Tunicates

Ancestral tunicate with free-swimming larva.

Acorn worms

Shift from arm-feeding to gill filter-feeding.

Pterobranchs

Primitive echinoderms

Primitive sessile arm-feeder.

Fig. 9. Diagram to show the probable course of chordate evolution. From a primitive sessile arm-feeder to the tunicates, there evolved successive improvements in the "visceral" animals. With the free-swimming larva of the tunicate type, there began a second evolutionary series, with emphasis on the dominant "somatic" animal.

development of bone (mainly dermal). The locomotor apparatus of strong segmental musculature, already present in amphioxus, continues highly developed and since, in ostracoderms particularly, the viscera appear to be confined to a relatively short anterior portion of the body, there is a high degree of development of that unique chordate feature, a true tail.

Even if, then, amphioxus fell by the wayside, other descendants of forms which retained as adults the tunicate larval structure did progress far, to gain, as primitive fishes, the basic stage in the structural development that has made vertebrates a dominant group. When and how did this advance come about?

Berrill (1955: 156-157) advances the very reasonable idea that the successful evolution of a vertebrate occurred as a result of the ancestral forms being able to invade fresh waters and carry out much of their progress toward the vertebrate condition in that environment where they were relatively free from competition.

It seems quite clear that plants, starting in the sea, had begun to invade inland waters well back in the Paleozoic; by the Devonian they had gone further, and progressed onto the land, so that, as the fossil record tells us, forests had formed by the end of that period. Their progress into fresh waters would, obviously, result in the presence in the streams of organic debris which could yield a new source of food for aquatic animals. What forms could utilize this? Only active animals, capable of resisting the constant trend of currents toward the sea. Most animal phyla are not notable for active swimming potentialities, and even today the faunas of inland waters are none too varied.

Two phyla that have such potentialities are the arthropods and the chordates, and when, in the late Silurian, we first find any appreciable occurrences of continental deposits in the geological record of the Paleozoic era, we find that almost all animal remains consist of members of these two phyla. The arthropods are mainly represented by the eurypterids, scorpion-like forms; the vertebrates are represented by a variety of primitive jawless fishes, the ostracoderms. The eurypterids were not too successful, for they were predaceous types, for whom the vegetable debris was not a suitable food source (and it has been suggested that they fed upon the little primitive fishes found with them [Romer, 1933]). For filter-feeding chordates, however, this sort of food was excellent, and Berrill believes that from near-shore waters they followed this source of food upstream and inland, and underwent most of their evolution into true vertebrates in this new environment, where competition was almost absent.

This theory, however, encounters the much-disputed question as to whether or not the fresh waters were actually the place of origin and early evolution of vertebrates. In the 1930's Homer Smith began a series of studies (Smith, 1932, 1953, etc.) leading to the conclusion that the most primitive type of vertebrate kidney was one which, to put it crudely, had as a prime function the pumping out of the excess water which in a fresh water environment would tend to over-dilute the body fluids of a vertebrate. Since oceanic fishes show a variety of adaptations to counteract this type of kidney function and enable a fish to avoid supersaturation in a salty environment, it is more reasonable to believe that the evolution of the vertebrate kidney (and of the vertebrate to which it pertained) took place in fresh water. At about the same time that Smith began his work, Grove and I (Romer and Grove, 1935) studied the fossil record of early vertebrates in North America as objectively as possible, and, like Smith, concluded that fresh waters were the early vertebrate home.

Neither Smith's conclusions nor mine, however, have remained unchallenged. Basing their argument mainly on the condition in the hagfish, the only vertebrate that fails to regulate the salt content of its body fluids, Robertson (1954, 1957) and others have maintained that the hagfish is primitive, that various devices for salt regulation are secondary, and that the primitive vertebrates were marine. But the arguments for this theory, it seems to me, have a Rube Goldberg-like complexity which does not well withstand an application of Occam's Razor. Following my early work on the paleontological evidence, a number of my colleagues (Gross, 1950; White, 1958; Denison, 1956; cf. Romer, 1955) have pointed out that a large fraction of the earliest fish finds, pertaining to the heterostracan group of ostracoderms, are in deposits suggesting near-shore marine conditions. The problem of the early habitat of the vertebrates is thus an unsettled one, and one for which I see no prospect of a clear solution in the near future. However, the dearth, before the late Silurian, of preservation of freshwater deposits in the geological record and the sudden appearance in freshwater beds of fully developed members of groups for which there is no previous marine record, tend to make me continue to believe that the freshwater story is the correct one.

If we attempt to summarize the history of vertebrates recounted above, it seems to me reasonable to believe that it began with simple attached "visceral" animals like the surviving pterobranchs, but with the development of the gill system progressed to forms that made the most of filter feeding—the tunicates, still simply built and essentially purely "visceral" forms. Then, with the invention of the tunicate tadpole larva, there appeared an active "somatic" animal; this, retaining its structure into the adult state, began a new evolutionary series that, quite probably in fresh waters, resulted at long last in the development of true vertebrates. Our past history has been a long and complicated story.

REFERENCES

Allis, E. P. 1923. Are the polar and trabecular cartilages of vertebrate embryos the pharyngeal elements of the mandibular and premandibular arches? J. Anat., 58:37-51.
——1925. Is the ramus ophthalmicus profundus the ventral nerve of the premandibular segment? J. Anat., 59:217-223.
——1938. Concerning the development of the prechordal portion of the vertebrate head. J. Anat., 72:584-607.

Andres, G. 1946.Über Induktion und Entwicklung von Kopforganen aus Unkenektoderm im Molch (Epidermis, Plakoden und Derivate der Neuralleiste). Rev. Suisse Zool., 53:502-510.

Barrington, E. J. W. 1964. An endocrinological approach to the problem of the origin of the vertebrates. Ann. Soc. Zool. Belgique, 94:161-178.

____1965. The Biology of Hemichordata and Protochordata. San Francisco, W. H. Freeman & Co.

Bartelmez, G. W. 1922. The origin of the otic and optic primordia in man. J. Comp. Neurol., 34:201-232.

____1923. The subdivisions of the neural folds in man. J. Comp. Neurol., 35:231-247.

Berrill, N. J. 1955. The Origin of Vertebrates. Oxford, Clarendon Press.

Bone, Q. 1960. The origin of the chordates. J. Linn. Soc. (Zool.), 44:252-296.

Buchs, G. 1902. Über den Ursprung des Kopfskeletes bei *Necturus*. Morph. Jahrb., 29:582-613.

Bullock, T. H. 1945. The anatomical organization of the nervous system of the Enteropneusta. Quart. J. Micr. Sci., 86:55-111.

Caullery, M. 1944. *Siboglinum* Caullery 1914, type nouveau d'invertébrés, d'affinités à préciser. Leiden, E. J. Brill, Siboga Expeditie, 25 bis: 1-26.

Corning, H. K. 1899. Ueber einige Entwicklungs-Vorgänge am Kopfe der Anuren. Morph. Jahrb., 27:173-242.

Dawydoff, C. 1948. Contribution á la connaissance de *Siboglinum* Caullery. Bull. Biol. France-Belgique, 82(2-3):141-163.

DeBeer, G. R. 1937. The Development of the Vertebrate Skull. Oxford, Clarendon Press.

____1947. The differentiation of neural crest cells into visceral cartilages and odontoblasts in *Amblystoma*, and a re-examination of the germ-layer theory. Proc. Roy. Soc. London [B], 134:377-398.

Denison, R. H. 1956. A review of the habitat of the earliest vertebrates. Fieldiana: Geology, 11:359-457.

Dohrn, A. 1884. Studien zu Urgeschichte des Wirbeltierkörpers. Mitt. Zool. Sta. Neapel, 5:1-95.

Edgeworth, F. H. 1935. The Cranial Muscles of Vertebrates. London, Cambridge University Press.

Fell, B. 1948. Echinoderm embryology and the origin of chordates. Biol. Rev., 23:81-107.

Garstang, W. 1928. The morphology of the Tunicata and its bearing on the phylogeny of the Chordata. Quart. J. Micr. Sci., 72:51-187.

Gaskell, W. H. 1886. On the structure, distribution and function of the nerves which innervate the visceral and vascular systems. J. Physiol., 7:1-80.

____1908. The Origin of the Vertebrates. London, Longmans, Green & Co.

____1916. The Involuntary Nervous System. London, Longmans, Green & Co.

Gilbert, P. W. 1947. The origin and development of the extrinsic ocular muscles in the domestic cat. J. Morph., 81:151-194.

____1952. The origin and development of the head cavities in the human embryo. J. Morph., 90:149-188.

Goodrich, E. S. 1918. On the development of the segments of the head in *Scyllium*. Quart. J. Micr. Sci., 63:1-30.

____1927. The problem of the sympathetic nervous system from the morphological point of view. J. Anat., 61:499-500.

____1930. Studies on the Structure and Development of Vertebrates. London, Macmillan & Co.

Grassé, P.-P. (ed.) 1948. Traité de Zoologie. 11. Echinodermes, Stomocordés, Procordés. Paris, Masson et Cie.

Gregory, W. K. 1951. Evolution Emerging. Volumes I and II. New York, Macmillan & Co.

Gross, W. 1950. Die paläontologische und stratigraphische Bedeutung der Wirbeltierfaunen des Old Reds und der marinen altpaläozoischen Schichten. Abh. Deutsch. Akad. Wiss. Berlin, Math-Nat. Kl., 1949. No. 1: 1-130.

Harrison, R. G. 1895. Die Entwicklung der unpaaren und paarigen Flossen der Teleostier. Arch. Mikr. Anat., 46:500-578.

_____1918. Experiments on the development of the fore limb of *Amblystoma*, a self-differentiating equipotential system. J. Exp. Zool., 25:314-462.

Herrick, C. J. 1899. The cranial and first spinal nerves of *Menidia*: a contribution upon the nerve components of the bony fishes. J. Comp. Neurol., 9:153-455.

_____1903. The doctrine of nerve components and some of its applications. J. Comp. Neurol., 13:301-310.

_____1943. The cranial nerves. A review of 50 years. Denison Univ. Bull., J. Sci. Labs., 38:41-51.

Hill, C. J. 1927. A contribution to our knowledge of the enteric plexuses. Philos. Trans. Roy. Soc. London, 215:355-388.

Hill, J. P., and K. M. Watson. 1958. The early development of the brain in marsupials. J. Anat., 92:493-497.

Holmdahl, D. E. 1928. Die Entstenhung und weithere Entwicklung der Neuralleiste (Ganglienleiste) bei Vogel und Saugetieren. Z. Mikr. Anat. Forsch., 14:99-298; 15:191-203.

_____1934. Neuralleiste und Ganglienleiste beim Menschen. Z. Mikr. Anat. Forsch., 36:137-178.

Hörstadius, S. 1950. The Neural Crest. London, Oxford University Press.

_____and S. Sellman. 1946. Experimentale Untersuchungen über die Determination des knorpeligen Kopfskelettes bei Urodelen. Nova Acta Reg. Soc. Sci. Upsaliensis, (4)13:1-170.

Hyman, L. 1955. The Invertebrates. IV. Echinodermata. The Coelomate Bilateria. New York, McGraw-Hill Book Co.

_____1959. The invertebrates. V. Smaller Coelomate Groups. New York, McGraw-Hill Book Co.

Jefferies, R. P. S. 1967. Some fossil chordates with echinoderm affinities. Sympos. Zool. Soc. London, 20:163-208.

_____1968. The subphylum Calcichordata (Jefferies 1967), primitive fossil chordates with echinoderm affinities. Bull. Brit. Mus. Nat. Hist. (Geol.), 16:241-339.

Johnels, A. G. 1956. On the peripheral autonomic nervous system of the trunk region of *Lampetra planeri*. Acta Zool., 37:251-286.

Johnston, J. B. 1902. An attempt to define the primitive functional divisions of the central nervous system. J. Comp. Neurol., 12:87-106.

_____1905. The morphology of the vertebrate head from the viewpoint of the functional divisions of the nervous system. J. Comp. Neurol., 15:175-275.

_____1906. The Nervous System of Vertebrates. Philadelphia, Blakisten.

Knight-Jones, E. W. 1952. On the nervous system of *Saccoglossus cambrensis* (Enteropneusta). Philos. Trans. Roy. Soc. London [B], 236:315-354.

Komai, T. 1951. The homology of the "notochord" found in pterobranchs and enteropneusts. Amer. Natural., 85:270-276.

Kozlowski, R. 1947. Les affinités des graptolithes. Biol. Rev., 22:93-108.

Landacre, F. L. 1921. Fate of neural crest in urodeles. J. Comp. Neurol., 33:1-44.

Medawar, P. B. 1951. Asymmetry of larval amphioxus. Nature (London), 167:852-853.

Mollier, S. 1895. Die paarigen Extremitäten der Wirbeltiere. II. Das Cheiropterygium. Anat. Hefte, 5:435-529.

Newell, G. E. 1952. The homology of the stomochord of the Enteropneusta. Proc. Zool. Soc. London, 121:741-746.

Newth, D. R. 1951. Experiments on the neural crest of the lamprey embryo. J. Exper. Biol., 28:247-260.

Nicol, J. A. C. 1952. Autonomic nervous systems in lower chordates. Biol. Rev., 27:1-49.

Norris, H. W., and S. P. Hughes. 1920. The cranial, occipital and anterior spinal nerves of the dogfish *Squalus acanthias*. J. Comp. Neurol., 31:293-395.

Osborn, H. F. 1888. A contribution to the internal structure of the amphibian brain. J. Morph., 2:51-96.

Platt, J. B. 1894. Ontogenetische Differenzirung des Ektoderms in *Necturus*. Arch. Mikr. Anat., 43:911-966.

_____1896. Ontogenetic differentiations of the ectoderm in *Necturus*. II. On the development of the peripheral nervous system. Quart. J. Micr. Sci., 38:485-547.

_____1897. The development of the cartilaginous skull and of the branchial and hypoglossal musculature in *Necturus*. Morph. Jahrb., 25:377-464.

Rabl, C. 1894. Ueber die Metamerie des Wirbeltierkopfes. Verh. Anat. Ges. Jena, 6:104-135.

Robertson, J. D. 1954. The chemical composition of the blood of some aquatic chordates, including members of the Tunicata, Cyclostomata and Osteichthyes. J. Exp. Biol., 31:424-442.

_____1957. The habitat of the early vertebrates. Biol. Rev., 32:156-187.

Romer, A. S. 1933. Eurypterid influence on vertebrate history. Science, 78:114-117.

_____1955. Fish origins–fresh or salt water? Deep-Sea Research, Suppl. 3:261-280.

_____1958a. Phylogeny and behavior with special reference to vertebrate evolution. *In* Roe, A., and G. G. Simpson, eds., Behavior and Evolution. New Haven, Yale University Press.

_____1958b. The vertebrate as a dual animal–visceral and somatic. Anat. Rec., 132:496.

_____1959. The Vertebrate Story. Chicago, Univ. Chicago Press.

_____1962. The Vertebrate Body. Third Edition. Philadelphia, W. B. Saunders Co.

_____1967. Major steps in vertebrate evolution. Science, 158:1629-1637.

_____1970. The Vertebrate Body. Fourth Edition. Philadelphia, W. B. Saunders Co.

_____and B. H. Grove. 1935. Environment of the early vertebrates. Amer. Midl. Natural., 16:805-856.

Scourfield, D. J. 1937. An anomalous fossil organism, possibly a new type of chordate, from the upper Silurian of Lesmahagow, Lanarkshire–*Ainiktozoon loganense*, gen. et sp. nov. Proc. Roy. Soc. London, [B], 121:533-547.

Sherrington, C. S. 1906. The Integrative Action of the Nervous System. New Haven, Yale University Press.

Silén, L. 1950. On the nervous system of *Glossobalanus marginatus*. Acta Zool., 31:149-176.

_____1954. Reflections concerning the "stomochord" of the Enteropneusta. Proc. Zool. Soc. London, 124:63-67.

Smith, H. W. 1932. Water regulation and its evolution in the fishes. Quart. Rev. Biol., 7:1-26.

_____1953. From Fish to Philosopher. Boston, Little, Brown & Company.

Spengel, J. W. 1946. *Planctosphaera pelagica*, eine in der Verwandschaftskreis der Enteropneusten gehörige Larve aus dem Tiefenplancton des Golfes von Biscaya. Rep. Scient. Res. "Michael Sars" N. Atl. Deep-Sea Exped. 1910, 5 (5).

Stensiö, E. A. 1927. The Downtonian and Devonian vertebrates of Spitzbergen. Pt. 1. Family Cephalaspidae. Norske Vidensk.-Akad. Oslo, Skrifter om Svalbard og Nordishavet, No. 12:1-391.

Stone, L. S. 1922. Experiments on the development of the cranial ganglia and the lateral line sense organs in *Amblystoma punctatum*. J. Exp. Zool., 35:421-496.

_____1926. Further experiments on the extirpation and transplantation of mesectoderm in *Amblystoma punctatum*. J. Exp. Zool., 44:95-131.

Straus, W. L., Jr., and M. E. Rawles. 1953. An experimental study of the origin of the trunk musculature and ribs in the chick. Amer. J. Anat., 92:471-510.

Strong, O. S. 1895. The cranial nerves of Amphibia. J. Morph., 10:101-230.

Van der Horst, J. C. 1939. Hemichordata. *In* Brown's Klassen und Ordnungen des Tierreichs, 4 Bd., 4 Abt. Leipzig, Akademische Verlagsgesellschaft.

Van Wijhe, J. W. 1882. Ueber die Mesoderm segmente und die Entwickelung der Nerven des Selachier Kopfes. Nat. Verh. Akad. Wet. Amsterdam, 22:1-50.

Veit, O. 1919. Kopfganglienleisten bei einem menschlichen Embryo von 8 Somitenpaaren. Anat. Hefte, 56:305-320.

Wagner, G. 1949. Die Bedeutung der Neuralleiste für die Kopfgestaltung der Amphibien-larven. Untersuchungen an Chimaeren von *Triton* und *Bombinator*. Rev. Suisse Zool., 56:519-620.

Wängsjö, G. 1952. The Downtonian and Devonian vertebrates of Spitzbergen. IX. Morphologic and systematic studies of the Spitzbergen cephalaspids. Norsk. Polarinst. Skrift., No. 97:1-611.

Watson, D. M. S. 1954. A consideration of ostracoderms. Philos. Trans. Roy. Soc. London, [B], 238:1-25.

White, E. I. 1958. Original environments of the craniates. *In* Westoll, T. S., ed., Studies on Fossil Vertebrates. London, The Athlone Press.

Whitear, M. 1957. Some remarks on the ascidian affinities of vertebrates. Ann. Mag. Nat. Hist., (12) 10:338-348.

Willey, A. S. 1894. Amphioxus and the Ancestry of the Vertebrates. New York, Columbia University Press.

Yntema, C. L., and W. S. Hammond. 1947. The development of the autonomic nervous system. Biol. Rev., 22:344-359.

Young, J. Z. 1933. The autonomic nervous system of selachians. Quart. J. Micr. Sci., 75:571-624.

6

Lystrosaurus and Gondwanaland

EDWIN H. COLBERT

The Museum of Northern Arizona
Flagstaff, Arizona 86001

INTRODUCTION

Gondwanaland, that hypothetical supercontinent composed of what are now the continents of Africa, South America, Australia, and Antarctica, and the subcontinent of peninsular India, has been the subject of much lively discussion among geologists, paleontologists, and biologists for more than half a century. Likewise, the inferred phenomenon of continental drift, involving the rifting of Gondwanaland into several large fragments, which are the continents listed above, and the subsequent drifting of those continental blocks to the positions they now occupy, has likewise occupied the attention of many interested authorities, as well as other people, through the past six decades. (It might be added that there has also been a correlative concept of Laurasia, a supercontinent of what are now the northern hemisphere land masses, with its rifting, and the drifting of its several parts to their present positions. Furthermore, many authorities have envisaged a still larger land mass, Pangaea, embracing both Gondwanaland and Laurasia.) According to most students of the problem, Gondwanaland and Laurasia (or Pangaea) are supposed to have existed during at least the latter part of the Paleozoic and the beginning of the Mesozoic eras, the rifting and drifting having taken place at some time subsequent to the middle or final stages of Triassic history.

Many paleontologists have favored the ideas of ancient supercontinents and continental drift, and a great many have until recently been opposed to these concepts. Numerous vertebrate paleontologists have looked with disfavor upon the ancient continents of Gondwanaland and Laurasia, and upon continental drift, in part because they could see no good evidence among the fossils for former supercontinents and drift, and in part because they have felt that such were not necessary to explain the distributions of the ancient faunas that came under their scrutiny. In fact, as late as 1945 Romer could say that "the only favorable evidence for this theory (of Gondwanaland) furnished by the vertebrates is the presence of *Mesosaurus* on both shores of the South Atlantic." (Romer, 1945, p. 529.) And *Mesosaurus* was somewhat suspect, because it was a highly adapted aquatic reptile (Figure 1). Furthermore, it seemed that the distributions of extinct faunas logically could be explained by intercontinental movements along connections that now exist, or have existed in the recent past, the most notable being a trans-Bering bridge between the eastern and western hemispheres, and the Panamanian isthmus connecting the two Americas.

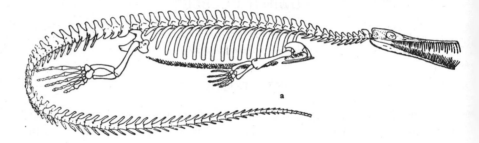

Fig. 1. Mesosaurus *skeleton, as reconstructed by McGregor; the original about 40 cm in length. Note the supple vertebral column, the long tail, and the paddle-like limbs, all adaptations for swimming; and the elongated rostrum set with numerous, long teeth, as adaptations for catching fish. This genus is found in the Permian of South Africa and southern Brazil.*

Within the past decade or so the premises which for so long governed the thinking of many vertebrate paleontologists have been to a large extent modified, so that today the climate of vertebrate paleontological opinion, as well as that among other students engaged in the earth and life sciences, has changed to one of active support of former supercontinents and continental drift. This is nicely exemplified by Romer's paper of 1968 entitled "Fossils and Gondwanaland," in which he argues strongly in favor of the existence of a former Gondwanaland, and elucidates various aspects in the distributions of extinct tetrapods to bolster this view (Romer, 1968, pp. 335-343). Of course a theory that supposes the existence of a Gondwanaland and Laurasia almost automatically supposes the phenomenon of rifting and drifting, in order to explain the breakup of the ancient continents and the movement of their several fragments to their present positions.

What has led to this reversal of opinion among many experienced vertebrate paleontologists, not to mention other paleontologists, paleobotanists, and numerous geologists of all persuasions? Why should Gondwanaland, Laurasia, Pangaea, and Continental Drift now be so widely accepted, when a few years ago these ideas were widely opposed? The answers to these questions are to be found in the profound revolution in geological thinking that has taken place during the past decade or so, and in addition in very important fossil discoveries that have been made during this same time.

THE MODERN GEOLOGICAL REVOLUTION

The science of geology has during recent years been going through a period of revolution as profound as that which swept through the science of biology after the publication of Darwin's "Origin of the Species" in 1859. In some respects the geological revolution shows similarities to the biological revolution of a century ago; in some respects it is different. It is different in that it is being brought about not by one or two men, as was the biological revolution by the observations and by the writings of Darwin and of Wallace, but rather by a considerable number of authorities, working in many geological disciplines, often with the assistance of highly sophisticated technological aids. It is parallel in that, just as Darwin and Wallace changed the concept of the species and of life from a static to a dynamic force, so the geological revolution has changed the large-scale concept of the earth from that of a rather static and stable planet to that of a very active, and in certain respects, an unstable globe.

Several disciplines, some of them of recent development and application, have contributed to this revolution in the study of the earth, with its consequent understanding of our planet in modern terms. These may be mentioned at this place, even though they cannot be discussed at length; such has been done in great detail in a body of recent literature that is truly stupendous.

As long ago as the days of Francis Bacon, when the seafaring expeditions of Spanish, Portuguese, and British sailors were making known some of the details of a thitherto unknown earth, it was noted that there was a remarkable correspondence between the western coast of Africa and the eastern coast of South America. This correspondence became increasingly apparent with the passing of the years and the improvement of surveys and maps, so that by the time the theory of continental drift was developed by Alfred Wegener, during the early years of the present century, the similarity of the coasts on the two sides of the South Atlantic was one of the prime facts used to support his argument. Such similarities on a grand scale were too close, reasoned Wegener, to be merely fortuitous. And this correspondence in the South Atlantic coastlines has been continually cited, ever since the days of Wegener, as a phenomenon supporting the theory of a mobile earth.

Within recent years the study of the "fits" between continents has taken a new turn, and has been transformed from a matter of simple trial and error inspection, made on large and accurate globes, to a detailed computerized analysis of continental margins, based upon deep geophysical surveys. Sir Edward Bullard and his associates, who have been particularly active in the development of such studies, made the comparison between the margins of Africa and South America at the 500 fathom isobath, and found that the correspondence was much too perfect to be the result of chance. Other workers have applied the method, using in some cases the 500 fathom line, in others the 1,000 fathom isobath, and have extended it to all of the southern continents, as well as peninsular India. It has been found by Dietz and Sproll (1970) using the 1,000 fathom isobath and by Smith and Hallam (1970) using the 500 and 1,000 fathom isobath, that not only do Africa and South America fit together in a remarkable fashion, but also that Antarctica, from the Weddell Sea to the Princess Martha coast, fits closely against the southeastern border of the African continent, that the opposite side of Antarctica fits into the Great Australian Bight, and that peninsular India and Madagascar fit closely between the northeastern edge of Africa and that edge of the Antarctic continent between its reconstructed junction with Africa and Australia. Moreover, further computerized studies have shown that the Mauretanian-Moroccan edge of Africa fits against the eastern edge of North America, from Florida to Nova Scotia, that the Moroccan-Algerian edge of Africa fits against the southern border of Spain, and that western Europe, Greenland, and the Newfoundland, Labrador and Baffin Island portions of North America come together much as if they were the pieces of a jig-saw puzzle. Thus has the computer reconstituted not only Gondwanaland but also Laurasia, and in a sense have combined them into a greater Pangaea.

Resemblances extend beyond the matter of continental "fits" to include many aspects of geologic structure. Thus the Samfrau Geosyncline, as envisaged by Du Toit, Wegener's great successor, has been to a large degree confirmed by the modern evidence of fold belts extending from southern South America, across Antarctica, and across eastern Australia. Moreover, there are remarkable geological resemblances between Brazil and western Africa, while the accumulations of essentially horizontal Permo-Triassic sediments, cut and capped by Jurassic dolerites, so characteristic of the great Karroo Basin of south Africa, are matched by similar features in the Transantarctic Mountains of the South Polar continent.

The study of paleomagnetism, and of paleomagnetic reversals, so vigorously prosecuted during the past two decades, has yielded a large body of data that point to the probability of continental drift. The mirror image patterns of paleomagnetic reversals on the opposite sides of the mid-oceanic ridges are indeed remarkably cogent phenomena in support of the concept of drift. In fact, the modern study of the mid-oceanic ridges, combined with studies of paleomagnetism and reversals, would seem to make clear the method and the mechanism of continental drift—matters that were severe stumbling blocks to earlier students of the problem. It now seems reasonably well established that upwelling magmas along the mid-oceanic ridges have intruded themselves between the continental plates, to push them apart at rates that may be on the order of several centimeters per year.

Finally, these various studies have been correlated with the truly grand concept of plate tectonics, which views the surface of the earth as consisting of a number of large plates, some edges of which are being forced apart by sea-floor spreading along the mid-oceanic ridges, other edges of which are descending into the depths along the great oceanic trenches. In totality the view of the earth as based upon these modern geophysical and geological studies provides us with a theory of earth structure and earth history on a monumental scale, a theory the supporting parts of which are integrated in a remarkably satisfactory manner. It is logical; it is elegant.

PALEONTOLOGICAL DISCOVERIES

It is a truism that any hypothesis or theory must be tested on all points of observational fact. How do the distributions of fossils accord with this modern view of earth history, resulting from the recent revolution in the study of geology?

In past years the evidence of the fossils, especially that of pertinent land-living vertebrates, was on the whole rather inconclusive. As mentioned above, about the only fact that seemed to bear with any degree of meaning upon this problem was the occurrence of the Permian reptile, *Mesosaurus*, in South Africa and in Brazil, and nowhere else in the world. But could this distribution of *Mesosaurus* be accepted as evidence for a close geographical relationship between Africa and South America? Might not *Mesosaurus* have been elsewhere in the world, and not as yet discovered, owing to the accidents of preservation and discovery? Moreover, since *Mesosaurus* was so obviously well adapted for swimming, might it not have made its way between the two continents across an intervening ocean (perhaps studded with insular way stations), even though it probably was an inhabitant of fresh water? Certain modern reptiles can do this—for example, the salt-water crocodile, which ranges widely through the tropics of the eastern hemisphere.

Also as mentioned above, up until a few years ago upon the basis of evidence available, the distributions of land-living vertebrates, including those of Permo-Triassic age, might be explained by invoking a world with the continents arranged as they are today, with intercontinental connections that are or recently have been available. The past distributions of some faunas in such a world might have involved immensely long intercontinental movements—from Africa or from western Europe, for example, across the extent of Asia, across a trans-Bering bridge, and thence into North or South America—but such movements would not have been impossible or even particularly unusual. We know, for instance, that during Plio-Pleistocene times various mammals, such as horses, camels, and proboscideans, did just this.

Consequently the discovery of closely related Permian reptiles in South Africa and in Russia, or of very closely related Triassic reptiles in South Africa and China, were facts that could easily be explained upon the basis of modern continental arrangements. They did not have any particular bearing upon Gondwanaland or upon continental drift.

But within the past few years Triassic reptiles of African affinities have been discovered in Argentina and Brazil. One might imagine these animals as having made the long trek from South Africa through Asia, across the Bering region, down through North America, across the Panamanian isthmus, and thence into southern South America, but the close relationships of the reptiles involved, frequently involving generic identities, would seem to make such a route rather improbable. It seems more likely that there was a direct interflow of such animals between Africa and South America, a supposition made all the more probable in the light of the various aspects of geophysical-geological evidence that indicates an intimate connection between the two southern hemisphere continents during past geological ages. Perhaps even more telling than the occurrence of certain Karroo reptiles in South America as evidence for Gondwanaland and drift, has been the finding within the past year of early Triassic Karroo reptiles and amphibians in Antarctica.

In 1967 a single fragment of a labyrinthodont amphibian jaw was found in sediments of early Triassic age about 400 miles from the South Pole, at Graphite Peak, near the Beardmore Glacier, in the Transantarctic Mountains. The specimen was too incomplete for a close identification, but at least it indicated the presence of early Mesozoic tetrapods on the antarctic continent. On the strength of this discovery a search was organized specifically for Triassic tetrapods, to be prosecuted during the 1969-1970 antarctic field season. This fossil hunt, carried on at a locality known as Coalsack Bluff, also near the Beardmore Glacier, but about 60 miles from Graphite Peak, resulted in the collection of about 500 specimens, most of them of a fragmentary nature, of Lower Triassic tetrapods. These fossils, like the single fragment from Graphite Peak, were collected in the Fremouw Formation, one of a sequence of Permo-Triassic sediments exposed in the Transantarctic Mountains, and obviously are closely related to the tetrapods found in the South African Middle Beaufort *Lystrosaurus* Zone, of early Triassic age. It was decided to follow up this initial discovery with a second season of discovery and collecting, this time at McGregor Glacier, some 150 miles from Coalsack Bluff. Again, work would be carried on in the Fremouw Formation. The second field season in Antarctica, still in progress as this is being written, has been successful beyond the wildest dreams of all concerned. Reasonably abundant and complete materials of early Triassic Karroo type amphibians and reptiles have been discovered and collected, to constitute a fossil record that will afford much detailed knowledge of tetrapod life in Antarctica during the early phases of Mesozoic history.

The significance of the antarctic discoveries needs no lengthy elucidation at this place. Suffice it to say for the moment that there is obviously a well documented *Lystrosaurus* fauna in the Transantarctic Mountains, a fauna in many aspects identical to the tetrapod fauna found in the *Lystrosaurus* zone of South Africa. As such it betokens a close connection between Africa and Antarctica—a connection of much more intimate nature than would be afforded by any kind of a land bridge, such as the trans-Bering bridge of much of Cenozoic history, or the Panamanian isthmus of this present age. (And for Antarctica there seems to be not the remotest possibility for a northern connection, and intercontinental movement "the long way around," as may be imagined—not very realistically—for South American reptiles of African complexion.)

Simpson has amply demonstrated that bridges, like those just named, generally act as zoological filters, allowing some animals to make the crossing from one continental mass to another, but excluding other animals from crossing the bridge. Consequently the faunas on the two ends of a filter bridge will show certain similarities, but at the same time they will exhibit many differences as well. The effects of a filter bridge are apparent. The close overall correspondence of the Fremouw tetrapod fauna of Antarctica to the *Lystrosaurus* fauna of South Africa is so marked that, as mentioned above, one must reconstruct more than a bridge to account for the resemblances. In short, the evidence of the fossils, as well as that of continental fits, geological resemblances and the like, show that Antarctica was intimately connected with Africa during early Triassic times, just as South America similarly was connected with Africa. These continents, now so widely separated from each other, almost assuredly were parts of a single land mass, the supercontinent known as Gondwanaland.

Let us look at the tetrapod evidence in more detail.

THE *LYSTROSAURUS* FAUNA IN AFRICA

In the great Karroo Basin is a thick series of Permo-Triassic sediments, essentially of horizontal aspect, intruded and frequently capped by extensive dolerites of Jurassic age (Table 1). These beds, indicating a long history of continental sedimentation, are famous for their successive, remarkably rich, and varied tetrapod faunas. Indeed, the Karroo beds and their contained fossils furnish an unexcelled record of terrestrial tetrapod life in the southern hemisphere during the later phases of Paleozoic history and the beginning years of Mesozoic history. The Karroo beds are divided into two series, the Upper Permian-Lower Triassic Beaufort Series below, and the Middle and Upper Triassic Stormberg Series above. The Beaufort beds have been further distin-

Table 1. The Permo-Triassic Sequences in Southern Africa and Antarctica

	Africa	Antarctica
Triassic	Drakensberg Volcanics	Kirkpatrick Basalts
	Cave Sandstone	Prebble Formation
	Red Beds	
	Molteno	Falla Formation
	Upper Beaufort	
	Cynognathus zone	
	Middle Beaufort	Fremouw Formation
	Lystrosaurus zone	
	(+ *Procolophon* zone)	
	Lystrosaurus fauna	*Lystrosaurus* fauna
Permian	Lower Beaufort	
	Cistecephalus zone	
	Endothiodon zone	Buckley Formation
	Tapinocephalus zone	
	Glossopteris	*Glossopteris*
	Ecca	Fairchild Formation
		Mackellar Formation
	Dwyka tillites	Pagoda tillites

guished and zoned by their characteristic tetrapod faunas, each zone having been designated by some characteristic fossil. Thus the Lower Beaufort beds, of Permian age, have been subdivided from bottom to top into the *Tapinocephalus*, *Endothiodon*, and *Cistecephalus* Zones; the Middle Beaufort beds of early Triassic age are constituted by the *Lystrosaurus* Zone, while the Upper Beaufort beds, also of early Triassic age but slightly younger than the underlying Middle Beaufort, are also composed within a single zone, the *Cynognathus* Zone. Another horizon, the *Procolophon* Zone, has in former years been distinguished as occupying a position intermediate between the *Lystrosaurus* and *Cynognathus* Zones, but recent work indicates that this supposed zone is actually a facies of the *Lystrosaurus* Zone.

The Karroo sediments are sandstones, mudstones, and siltstones such as one might expect as the result of deposition on elevated lands, in streams, in ponds, and in lakes. So it is that the *Lystrosaurus* Zone is composed in large part of grayish and greenish and varicolored mudstones, with associated crossbedded sandstones. Fossils skulls and skeletons occur in remarkable abundance in the siltstones; fragments are found in the stream-channel sands.

By far the most abundant fossils in the *Lystrosaurus* Zone are the remains of *Lystrosaurus* itself (Fig. 2). Probably 90% of all the fossils collected consist of the remains of this interesting reptile. *Lystrosaurus* is a therapsid or mammal-like reptile, belonging to that large subdivision of the therapsids known as the dicynodonts. These were highly adapted reptiles, the largest individuals as large

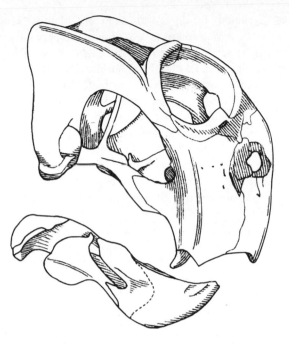

Fig. 2. Lystrosaurus, *a dicynodont therapsid, skull and lower jaw in lateral view;* *the original being about 10 or 15 cm in length. This represents a rather young* *individual, with the tusk beginning to erupt, and is typical of the first* Lystrosaurus *found in Antarctica. Adapted from Crompton (1970).*

as sheep, in which the skull, although retaining almost all of the bones of the primitive reptilian skull, was none the less quite open—the temporal region being composed of long, bony arches. The front of the skull was specialized into a sort of turtle-like beak, in many genera devoid of teeth, except quite commonly for a pair of large upper tusks, one in each maxilla. In *Lystrosaurus* this front part of the skull carrying the two tusks was strongly downturned, so that the profile of the snout, as seen in side view, was almost at, or often quite at, right angles with the line of the skull roof. The eye was in a high position, often with the upper border of the orbit projecting above the top of the skull roof, while the nostril immediately in front of the eye also was rather superior in its position. The edentulous jaws were in life obviously covered with a horny beak. The body was stout, the limbs were rather short and very strong, and the tail was short. All in all, the adaptations of *Lystrosaurus*, taken in conjunction with the sediments in which it is found, show that it probably was an aquatic reptile, ecologically comparable on a small scale with a modern hippopotamus. It seems probable that *Lystrosaurus* was herbivorous, and because of its abundance it would seem likely that it formed the base of the southern African tetrapod food pyramid during early Triassic times.

As might be expected within a genus so abundantly represented as is *Lystrosaurus* in South Africa, there is a considerable range of variation in size and morphology to be seen. The significance of the observable differences in *Lystrosaurus* is a moot point. Inevitably a considerable array of species has been described over the years—some two dozen, in fact. Certainly there is repetition here; perhaps a half dozen or so species are valid, perhaps even fewer. It is obvious that some of the differences ascribed in the past to speciation within *Lystrosaurus* may more properly be assigned to differences due to ontogenetic growth, perhaps in some degree to sexual dimorphism, and most certainly in a considerable degree to individual variability. Also, some of the differences are clearly those resulting from distortion during fossilization. Therefore the problem of species within *Lystrosaurus* is still open, and even now it is being studied in detail.

Suffice it to say at this place that much of the *Lystrosaurus* material would seem to center about the generic type, *L. murrayi*. Perhaps it is valid to consider this species as generally typical of *Lystrosaurus*; therefore comparisons of *Lystrosaurus* in other regions will here be referred back primarily to the species *Lystrosaurus murrayi*.

Two other reptiles occurring within the *Lystrosaurus* Zone are *Thrinaxodon*, a small, weasel-sized mammal-like reptile, and *Chasmatosaurus* (or *Proterosuchus*), a moderate-sized thecodont reptile—an active carnivore belonging to the large group that was in later time to give rise to the dinosaurs. *Thrinaxodon* is a theriodont, one of the very active mammal-like therapsids of carnivorous habits; a reptile so far advanced toward the mammalian condition that it may have been to some degree endothermic, with perhaps even an outer covering of hair. There are about 15 other genera of theriodonts in the *Lystrosaurus* fauna, all of them, like *Thrinaxodon*, of comparatively small size. (See Fig. 3)

There are also some other small reptiles in this fauna; namely *Procolophon* (Fig. 4), a procolophonid, which were persistent cotylosaurs (the cotylosaurs being those primitive reptilian derivatives from labyrinthodont amphibian ancestors), and some protolizards represented by the genera *Prolacerta* and *Pricea*. Finally there are labyrinthodont amphibians, some small, as represented by the common genus *Lydekkerina*, and some quite large, as represented by the genus *Rhinesuchus*, or more properly *Uranocentrodon* (See Table 2.)

This assemblage of tetrapods is sufficiently large and varied so that it probably represents to a fair degree a tetrapod *fauna*; that is, an ecologically balanced assemblage of land-living vertebrates, living in harmony with their environment. That environment must have been one of numerous streams, rivers, ponds, and lakes, of abundant vegetation, forming the food supply for what were probably herds of roaming *Lystrosaurus*, and of tropical or subtropical, or very possibly warm-temperate climates. The record of plant life shows, among other things, large trees, such as *Dadoxylon*. These trees have definite growth rings, which is evidence of the alternation of seasons in the world of that age and at that

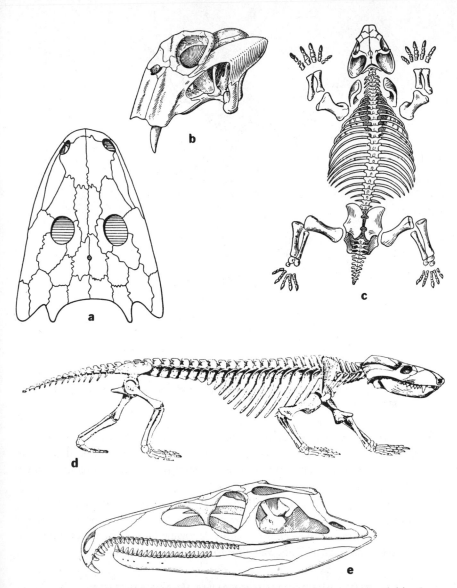

Fig. 3. Prominent constituents of the Lystrosaurus *fauna. a.* Lydekkerina, *a labyrinthodont amphibian, dorsal view of skull; the original about 10 cm in length. b.* Lystrosaurus murrayi, *a dicynodont therapsid, lateral view of skull; the original about 20 cm in length. Note the strongly downturned rostrum, with a tusk in the maxilla; the highly placed orbit, with the naris anterior to it. c.* Lystrosaurus murrayi, *dorsal view of skeleton; the original about 150 cm in length. d.* Thrinaxodon, *a theriodont therapsid, lateral view of skeleton; the original about 45 cm in length. e.* Chasmatosaurus (or Proterosuchus), *a thecodont, lateral view of skull and jaws; the original about 45 cm in length. (a, After Romer; b anc c, after Broom; d, after Brink; e, after Broili and Schroeder.)*

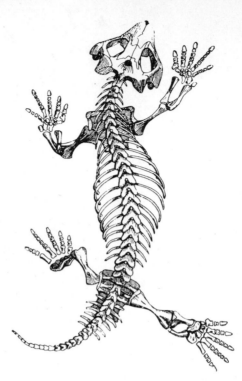

Fig. 4. Procolophon, *a cotylosaur, dorsal view of skeleton; the original about 30 cm in length. After Watson.*

latitude, but not necessarily evidence of cold or even cool winter seasons. The abundant reptilian-amphibian life of the *Lystrosaurus* Zone would seem to militate against inordinately cold or cool temperatures; it was probably a rather bland and amenable climate.

This is a picture of early Triassic life in one part of the southern hemisphere, as recorded by the fossils of the *Lystrosaurus* Zone. It is a very definite type of tetrapod association, and as such is readily recognizable—all of which make the fossils of the *Lystrosaurus* Zone valuable to the paleontologist.

THE *LYSTROSAURUS* FAUNA IN ANTARCTICA

The *Lystrosaurus* fauna in the Lower Triassic Fremouw Formation of the Transantarctic Mountains, recovered from sediments that show many parallels to those of the Karroo Basin by reason of their horizontal expression and their intrusion by extensive dolerites, reflects to an uncanny degree the fossils composing the *Lystrosaurus* fauna of Africa. In Antarctica *Lystrosaurus* is certainly the most abundant of the tetrapods within the Fremouw formation—an

Table 2. *Lystrosaurus* Fauna in Gondwanaland and Laurasia

Africa	Antarctica	India	China
Lystrosaurus Zone	Fremouw Formation	Panchet Formation	Tunghunyshan Formation and Wuhsiang Beds
Lystrosaurus *Thrinaxodon*	*Lystrosaurus* *Thrinaxodon* Thecodonts	*Lystrosaurus*	*Lystrosaurus*
Chasmatosaurus *Procolophon* *Lydekkerina* *Uranocentrodon*	*Procolophon*	*Chasmatosaurus*	*Chasmatosaurus*
	Small Labyrinthodonts	*Labyrinthodonts*	
	Large Labyrinthodonts		

indication that here, as in Africa, this strange reptile probably formed the base of a tetrapod food pyramid, and as such must have been a primary feeder, with an abundant supply of plant food to sustain it. Moreover, as the evidence would seem to show, there is every reason to believe that the antarctic *Lystrosaurus* will prove to be *L. murrayi*. Associated with *Lystrosaurus* in Antarctica there have been found several partial skeletons of the small theriodont, *Thrinaxodon*. In addition, *Procolophon* is present. These genera in themselves give a strong African cast to the antarctic Fremouw fauna.

But in addition there are various other tetrapods, which although not as yet closely identified, nevertheless add to the resemblances that link the Antarctic fauna to the *Lystrosaurus* fauna of the Karroo. Mention can be made at this time of other theriodonts, of small prolacertids that may prove to be close to *Prolacerta* itself, and of thecodonts. Again there are in the Fremouw assemblage large and small labyrinthodont amphibians. Finally there would appear to be, as of this date, certain tetrapods in the Fremouw sediments that are unlike any found in the African *Lystrosaurus* Zone—an indication that the Antarctic fauna is perhaps somewhat more varied than the African fauna.

Whatever the exact identifications of the Antarctic fossils may prove to be, it seems quite apparent at the present time that here, within a few hundred miles of the South Pole, we see a repetition of the African *Lystrosaurus* fauna. And as has been maintained, such a full faunal representation in the South Polar continent probably means that the continental connection was close and was of wide extent—as is indicated by the computerized studies of continental fits. In fact, it would appear that we are looking at parts of a faunal continuum—which is something quite different from faunal expressions at the two ends of a filter bridge. All of which, taken in conjunction with the physical evidence, is very strong evidence indeed in confirmation of a former Gondwanaland.

THE PROBLEM OF SOUTH AMERICA

One would think, in view of the evidence for a close fit between Antarctica and Africa and the full representation of the *Lystrosaurus* fauna in these two continents, that because of the very close and even more remarkable fit between Africa and South America, there would be a representation of the *Lystrosaurus* fauna in this latter continent, also. But no indications of a South American *Lystrosaurus* fauna have as yet come to light. It seems strange that such should be the case.

Although the absence of *Lystrosaurus* in South America may be real, at this date it seems equally probable that such absence is merely a reflection of the imperfection of our knowledge—perhaps in part the result of an imperfection in the paleontological record, perhaps in part a result of the incompleteness of paleontological explorations. It will be interesting to see what the work of future years may reveal in Lower Triassic sediments in the southern portions of South America.

LYSTROSAURUS IN INDIA

The Panchet Formation is a brownish-red siltstone of continental origin that is exposed in the northern part of the Indian peninsula, particularly in the Raniganj coal field, about 150 miles northwest of Calcutta. *Lystrosaurus* is found in the Panchet beds, associated with *Chasmatosaurus*, and with several labyrinthodont amphibians all generically distinct from the amphibians of the South African *Lystrosaurus* Zone. The fossils that have been found to date in the Panchet beds are not sufficiently varied for the assemblage to be considered as truly a fauna, but certainly they are an indication of a *Lystrosaurus*-type fauna that lived in what is now northern India during the beginning of Mesozoic times.

Even with this partial representation of early Triassic tetrapods in India, it is evident that once again we are encountering an assemblage of land-living tetrapods that are very closely related to those of the African *Lystrosaurus* Zone. Indeed, the Indian *Lystrosaurus* is remarkably similar to the generic type-species, and has been so identified.

THE RANGE OF THE *LYSTROSAURUS* FAUNA

From the foregoing remarks it can be seen that the *Lystrosaurus* fauna, so characteristic of the lowest Triassic sediments in South Africa, also occurs in full panoply in the Fremouw Formation of the Transantarctic Mountains, while good indications of it are to be found in the Panchet Formation of peninsular India (Fig. 5). These regions are widely separated today, the Antarctic locality being almost 5,000 miles on a great circle line from the Karroo Basin, with the Indian locality even more distantly removed—at a distance of about 6,000 miles from South Africa. But when the several continents are brought together in the pattern on which Gondwanaland has been reconstituted, then these three areas containing the *Lystrosaurus* fauna are not unduly far apart. In fact, they are separated each from the other by a matter of about 2,000 miles. Such a pattern of localities would very easily come within the range of numerous modern species of reptiles.

For example, if the occurrences of the *Lystrosaurus* fauna in Antarctica, South Africa, and India are plotted on a map of North America, with the distances between them being those that would exist on a reconstruction of Gondwanaland, the antarctic locality could be in Florida, the South African region in the vicinity of Chihuahua, Mexico, and the Indian locality in northern Maine. This scatter of localities falls essentially within the range of the modern North American snapping turtle, *Chelydra serpentina*. Consequently it is not beyond reason to think that *Lystrosaurus* as it occurs in Antarctica, Africa, and India may be a single species, now found in the drifted fragments of what was once a continuous range. And of course what applies to *Lystrosaurus* in this respect equally may apply to the tetrapods associated with *Lystrosaurus*, such as *Thrinaxodon* and *Chasmatosaurus*. This reconstruction of a continuous range for the *Lystrosaurus* fauna in Gondwanaland appears to be eminently logical. It explains the close correspondence of the fauna as it is found in Africa and Antarctica, and probably in India as well.

LYSTROSAURUS IN CHINA

The reconstitution of the range of the *Lystrosaurus* in early Mesozoic Gondwanaland is all very well, but how are we to interpret the presence of this fauna in China? This is a problem that requires some careful consideration.

Lystrosaurus, associated with *Chasmatosaurus*, has been found in two regions of China; in Sinkiang, where it occurs in sediments belonging to the Tunghungshan Series, and in Shansi where it occurs in the triassic sediments of Wuhsiang. As in the case of the occurrences in India, these Chinese records, limited essentially to *Lystrosaurus* and *Chasmatosaurus*, can hardly be considered as representing elements of a fauna; they are too restricted for that. Nevertheless they are definite clues, and it is reasonable to think that they indicate an extension of the *Lystrosaurus* fauna, at least in part, to localities far beyond the limits of what we might call the "home range." On our present-day Earth the Chinese localities are some 8,000 miles or so from South Africa. In a Triassic world, with Gondwanaland occupying the southern hemisphere and

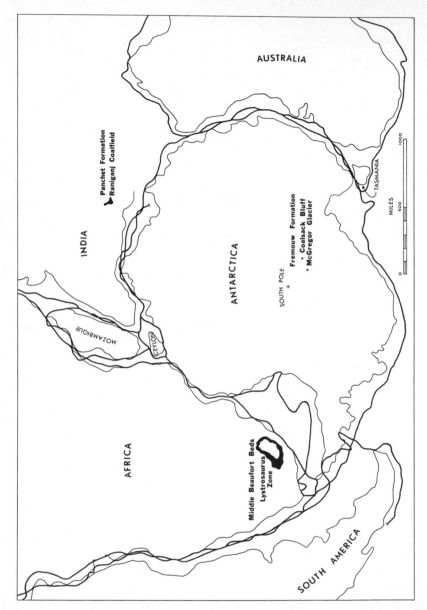

Fig. 5. A reconstruction of a part of Gondwanaland with the continents fitted at the 500 fathom contour, except for Antarctica, which is fitted at the 1,000 meter contour. Adapted from Smith and Hallam, 1970. The heavy outlines show the 500 fathom and 1,000 meter contours; the light lines are the modern coastlines. The Middle Beaufort beds, the Fremouw Formations, and the Panchet Formation contain the Lystrosaurus fauna.

Laurasia the northern, the occurrences of *Lystrosaurus* in China are still far removed from the reconstituted range for the *Lystrosaurus* fauna.

In fact, the elements of the *Lystrosaurus* fauna found in China would have been in Triassic times far beyond the limits of Gondwanaland, and would have been living in an eastern extremity of Laurasia. On the basis of our present knowledge, *Lystrosaurus* and *Chasmatosaurus* in China appear to have been wanderers that entered Laurasia from their Gondwanaland homeland. This would have been quite possible, because if Gondwanaland and Laurasia were joined to form an immense Pangaea (and the physical evidence points to this) there would have been a route for active reptiles to follow, north through Africa, into Laurasia where the southern border of Spain was joined to the Moroccan edge of Africa, and eastwardly from there to China. It was admittedly a long route, covering a distance of perhaps 12,000 miles, but is no longer than the wanderings followed by other long-range migrants, such as those mentioned earlier in this paper.

The fact that only *Lystrosaurus* and *Chasmatosaurus* have been found as representatives of the *Lystrosaurus* fauna in the Chinese region may reflect upon the accidents of preservation and discovery. In this instance, however, the presence of these isolated elements from the *Lystrosaurus* fauna in China may very well indicate the movements of certain faunal elements across a filter bridge and their extension to regions far beyond the natural limits of the fauna. A modern parallel to this might be the presence of *Alligator* in southeastern North America and in China—a separation of some 8,000 miles or more along a great circle line, representing intercontinental migrations across a trans-Bering connection during Cenozoic times.

A NEW WORLD

The *Lystrosaurus* fauna in Gondwanaland epitomizes in many ways the nature of early Triassic tetrapod faunas on that ancient continent. These were, in short, faunas dominated by therapsid reptiles (among which the dicynodonts were particularly numerous), and with small cotylosaurs, eosuchians, certain thecodonts, and varied labyrinthodont amphibians making up the other elements within the faunas. Such assemblages of land-living tetrapods were quite different, it would seem, from the early Triassic tetrapod faunas of Laurasia—faunas in which thecodonts and labyrinthodonts were the dominant elements, and in which therapsid reptiles generally were absent. Thus there would seem to have been in those days a faunal dichotomy among the tetrapods, reflecting the geographical dichotomy as seen in a northern hemisphere Laurasia and a southern hemisphere Gondwanaland. Of course the dichotomy among faunas was not rigid, just as the two supercontinents were not completely isolated one from the other. As we have seen, certain elements of the *Lystrosaurus* fauna may have invaded Laurasia. Moreover, future discoveries may very well show that the incursions of Gondwanaland tetrapods into the northern hemisphere were even more extensive than what is now indicated. Also it seems evident that there were movements from the northern into the southern hemisphere, as well. None the less, early Triassic time, like previous Permian time, would appear to have been a time of two separate faunal expressions, one in the northern and one in the southern half of the earth.

With the onset of late Triassic history, profound changes took place across the face of the earth (Fig. 6). It would seem that this was the time when the rifting of Pangaea was initiated. There was a beginning of separation of South America and of peninsular India from Africa. The disintegration of the continental range of the *Lystrosaurus* fauna had commenced.

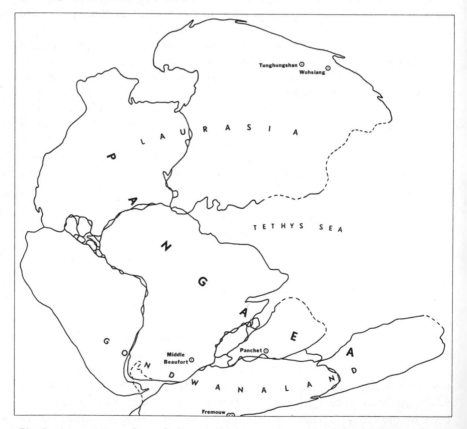

Fig. 6. A reconstruction of the continents at the end of the Permian and the beginning of the Triassic periods. Adapted from Dietz and Holden, 1970. Note the clustering of the Lystrosaurus *fauna as it occurs in the Beaufort, Fremouw, and Panchet beds, and the distant separation of elements of the* Lystrosaurus *fauna as they are found in the Tunghungshan and Wuhsiang beds.*

Even though the breakup of Gondwanaland had begun, there remained avenues for the intercontinental movements of land-living tetrapods. This was the time when the distributions of terrestrial tetrapods became cosmopolitan, rather than being limited as they had been previously, to Gondwanaland and Laurasian moieties. This was the beginning of a new world—geographically and faunally.

The Triassic period is noteworthy as being an age of tetrapod transitions—a time when the old faunas which had been divided between Gondwanaland and Laurasia, and which contained many elements held over from late Paleozoic time, gave way to the influx of new faunas of world-wide aspect. The advent of these new faunas was marked by the rapid rise of the dinosaurs, which were to become the dominant land animals of Jurassic and Cretaceous history. These active and ecologically aggressive reptiles replaced the therapsids, which for so long had abundantly dominated the faunas of Gondwanaland. In the sediments of the Stormberg Series in South Africa the dinosaurs appear in considerable array; the therapsids are present mainly as remnants of a once highly varied group. Many of the therapsids—theriodonts and dicynodonts—were then in the last throes of their long phylogenetic histories, as were the labyrinthodont amphibians. But in one respect, certain therapsids did not truly become extinct; rather they evolved into the first mammals, the ancestors of the tetrapods that eventually were to inherit the earth. In Mesozoic times, however, the mammals were confined to secondary roles in the constitution of faunas; the dinosaurs and some of their archosaurian relatives, especially the crocodilians and the pterosaurs, ruled the continents.

So it was that a new world came into being—a world antecedent to the one in which we live. It was a world in transition, and during long geologic ages the several fragments of Gondwanaland were drifting away from the southern continental center of which they had been integral parts. It was owing to the rifting of Gondwanaland and the drifting of its continental fragments toward their present positions that the distribution of the fossils which represent the *Lystrosaurus* fauna became established in the pattern in which we find them today. It is a fragmented pattern, and only when we reconstruct the *Lystrosaurus* faunal range as it probably existed in an ancient Gondwanaland would the relationships of the fauna seem to assume a distributional pattern accounting for the abundant occurrences of this fauna in regions that now extend from the tropics to the South Pole.

REFERENCES

Barrett, P. J. 1971. Stratigraphy and palaeogeography of the Beacon Supergroup in the Transantartic Mountains, Antarctica. Proc. 2nd Gondwana Symposium, South Africa (in press).

_____ R. J. Baillie, and E. H. Colbert. 1968. Triassic amphibian from Antractica. Science, 161:460-462.

Bonaparte, J. F. 1966. Chronological survey of the tetrapod-bearing Triassic of Argentina. Breviora (Mus. Comp. Zool.), no. 251:1-13.

_____ 1967. New vertebrate evidence for a southern transatlantic connexion during the lower or middle Triassic. Palaeont., 10(4):554-563.

Brink, A. S. 1951. On the genus *Lystrosaurus* Cope. Trans. Roy. Soc. S. Afr., 33(1):107-120.

_____ 1954. A bibliographical list of reptilia from the Karroo beds of Africa. Palaeont. Afr., 2:1-187.

_____ 1959. Note on a new skeleton of *Thrinaxodon liorhinus.* Palaeont. Afr., 6:15-22.

Bullard, E. 1969. The origin of the oceans. Sci. Amer., 221:66-75.

Chowdhury, T. R. 1970. Two new dicynodonts from the Triassic Yerrapalli formation of central India. Palaeont., 13(1):132-144.

Colbert, E. H. 1970. Paleontological investigations at Coalsack Bluff. Antarct. J. U. S., 5:86.

Cox, C. B. 1967. Changes in terrestrial vertebrate faunas during the Mesozoic. The Fossil Record, Geol. Soc., London, p. 77-89.

Crompton, A. W. 1970. Continental drift and a strange fossil reptile. Discovery, 5(2):105-108.

Darlington, P. J. 1965. Biogeography of the Southern End of the World. Cambridge, Mass., Harvard University Press.

Dietz, R. S. and J. C. Holden. 1970. The breakup of Pangaea. Sci. Amer., 223(4):30-41.

_____ and W. P. Sproll. 1970. Fit between Africa and Antarctica: a continental drift reconstruction. Science, 167:1612-1614.

Du Toit, A. L. 1937. Our Wandering Continents. Edinburgh, Oliver and Boyd.

_____ 1954. Geology of South Africa, 3rd ed., Chaps. 12 and 13, pp. 264-359. Edinburgh, Oliver and Boyd.

Elliot, D. H., E. H. Colbert, W. J. Breed, J. A. Jensen, and J. S. Powell. 1970. Triassic tetrapods from Antarctica: evidence for continental drift. Science, 169:1197-1201.

_____ 1971. Antarctic geology and drift reconstructions (in press).

Hallam, A. 1967. The bearing of certain paleozoogeographic data on continental drift. Palaeogeogr. Palaeoclimatol. Palaeoecol., no. 3:201-241.

Haughton, S. H. 1969. Geological History of South Africa. Capetown, Geological Society of South Africa.

Heirtzler, J. R. 1968. Sea-floor spreading. Sci. Amer., 219(6):60-70.

Huene, F. von. 1940. Die saurier der Karroo- , Gondwana- und verwandten Ablagerungen in Faunistischer, biologischer und phylogenetischer Hinsicht. N. Jahrb. Mineral. Geol. Paläont., Beil.-Bd., 83 Abt. B:246-347.

Hurley, P. M. 1968. The confirmation of continental drift. Sci. Amer., 218(4):53-64.

King, L. C. 1965. Geological relationships between South Africa and Antarctica. Geol. Soc. S. Afr. Annex, 68:1-32.

Kitching, J. W. 1968. On the *Lystrosaurus* zone and its fauna with special reference to some immature Lystrosauridae. Palaeont. Afr., 11:61-76.

Matthew, W. D. 1915. Climate and evolution. Ann. N. Y. Acad. Sci., 24:178-318.

Plumstead, E. P. 1962. Fossil floras of Antarctica. Trans. Antarct. Exped., Scientific Reports, no. 9:1-154.

Robinson, P. L. 1958. Some new vertebrate fossils from the Panchet series of West Bengal. Nature (London). 182:1722-1723.

_____ 1967. The Indian Gondwana formations—a review. First Symposium on Gondwana Stratigraphy, pp. 202-268.

Romer, A. S. 1945. Vertebrate Paleontology. Chicago, University of Chicago Press.

_____ 1968. Fossils and Gondwanaland. Proc. Amer. Philos. Soc., 112(5):335-343.

Schopf, J. M. 1970. Gondwana Paleobotany. Antarct. J. U. S., 5(3):62-66.

Simpson, G. G. 1940. Mammals and land bridges. J. Washington Acad. Sci., 30(4):137-162.

_____ 1947. Holarctic mammalian faunas and continental relationships during the Cenozoic. Bull. Geol. Soc. Amer., 58:613-688.

_____ 1953. Evolution and geography. Condon Lectures, Oregon State System of Higher Education, pp. 1-64.

Smith, A. G., and A. Hallam. 1970. The fit of the southern continents. Nature (London), 225:139-144.

Sproll, W. P., and R. S. Dietz. 1969. Morphological continental drift fit of Australia and Antarctica. Nature (London), 222:345-348.

Tripathi, C., and P. P. Satsangi. 1963. *Lystrosaurus* fauna from the Panchet Series of the Raniganj Coalfields. Palaeont. Indica, (N. S.) 37:1-53.

Wegener, Alfred. 1966. The Origin of Continents and Oceans. New York, Dover Press. (Translated from the 4th revised German edition by John Biram).

Young, Chung-Chien. 1935. On two skeletons of Dicynodontia from Sinkiang. Bull. Geol. Soc. China, 14(4):483-517.

____1957. The significance of the lower Triassic reptilian fauna from Wuhsiang of Shansi. Sci. Rec., 1(4):265-270.

7

Was Europe Connected Directly to North America Prior to the Middle Eocene?

MALCOLM C. MCKENNA

Frick Curator
The American Museum of Natural History
New York, N. Y. 10024

"In dealing with paleogeographic problems, the geologic evidence must be regarded as fundamental so far as it goes." W. D. Matthew (1939, p. 168).

"The way of the bridge-builder is strewn with pitfalls." A. L. Du Toit (1944, p. 152).

The title of this paper asks a question that is primarily for the geologist and geophysicist to answer. The data of paleontology utilized here, mainly fossil mammalian evidence, is of secondary but not insignificant importance. I shall try to follow the advice of the first quotation given above, and attempt to avoid the fate implied by the second.

Fossil mammals have always played a crucial part in the almost endless and sometimes silly biological literature about former Atlantic transoceanic dispersal routes, especially "land bridges." My purpose is not to review all that here; one can read Simpson (e.g., 1953 and references cited therein) for the biogeographical principles involved. Such principles broadly hold with little modification today, even though originally developed under a stabilistic tectonic philosophy. But the 1960's have seen a revolution in geological thought as far reaching as the Darwinian one in biology, and it is of interest to see how current ideas of global tectonics interact with evidence from fossil mammals to modify the Simpsonian mammal dispersal model, a model which supplies so much muscle to present concepts of Cenozoic paleobiogeography.

Students of fossil mammals have been influenced greatly by the arguments of Matthew (1915, 1939) and especially those of Simpson (1940, 1943, 1946,

1947a, 1947b, 1952, 1953) against biologically motivated proposals of ad hoc land bridges and in favor of stable continents, the latter being viewed as essentially in their present positions relative to each other and to the earth's rotational axis for all time in the past. Simpson listed (e.g., 1943, p. 2) alternatives for the possible world tectonic framework, as it was then conceived:

1. ... Continents are permanent crustal segments but ... their positions relative to each other have changed radically—the hypothesis of continental drift. [For this view see Taylor (1910), Wegener (1924, etc.), Du Toit (1937), and almost any major tectonic synthesis published since about 1965.]

2. ... The relative positions of points on the globe have not changed significantly but ... the configuration of land and sea has been radically altered and specifically ... continental areas have extended right across the present major ocean basins—this may be called the hypothesis of transoceanic continents. [See for example J. W. Gregory's (1929) history of the Atlantic Ocean.]

3. ... The present relationships of major lands and great sea basins have been approximately constant, aside from rather local changes of contour and changes of relative level—the hypothesis of stable continents. [This view, which goes back at least to Dana (1846, p. 353; 1847), received strong support from American geologists until about 1965.]

Matthew (1915, 1939) was strongly for the third alternative, was totally opposed to the second one for isostatic reasons now confirmed, and was only briefly concerned with the first (mainly in 1939). His ideas on waif dispersal were most important and influential and his discussions of the distribution of Tertiary fossil mammals, as well as more detailed arguments such as that of Simpson (1947a), have been widely used to show that the timing, at least, of Wegener's various versions of continental separation was wrong for southern continents and therefore perhaps wrong in general. Southern continents have been separate throughout the Cenozoic; Wegener had them together too late in time to fit the evidence from fossil mammals.

With the exception of Quarternary intercontinental connections involving eustatic changes and glacial rebound and possibly an early Tertiary northern transatlantic bridge in the general vicinity of Greenland, the prevalence of new land bridges in the minds of paleogeographers in recent years has dropped to a low level, beneath sea level so to speak, largely because of the stout defense of the stabilist faith by American geologists and because of the biogeographical arguments of Matthew and Simpson. With regard to the North Atlantic Simpson worte (1943, p. 6), "The latest connection [directly] between North America and Europe was perhaps Pleistocene, but probably Tertiary and possibly well down in the Tertiary." Three years later he stated (1946, p. 258), " ... no good evidence is found for any Atlantic, direct European-North American, bridge during the Cenozoic, contrary to my former opinion and that of most paleogeographers. The evidence throughout is consistent with a single Siberian-Alaskan bridge, as adequate to explain all the known facts." Similar biogeographically-based statements were made in later papers (Simpson, 1947a, p. 686; 1947b, p. 219). A few years later Mayr (1952, p. 85) wrote, " ... the biogeographic evidence against Tertiary trans-Atlantic connections is sufficiently overwhelming to make it seem unprofitable to pursue the subject further."

By the 1950's the stabilist geological view prevailed in North America, at least for the Cenozoic, and the hypothesis of continental drift was, if regarded by any as true, too remote in operation to affect the known distribution of fossil mammals. The hypothesis of transoceanic continents was even less likely than continental drift, having failed to meet the geological test of isostasy. A few authors, reviewed by Lindroth (1957), still favored Cenozoic North Atlantic transoceanic connections of one sort or another, but in general these were of the biological ad hoc type so ably dealt with by Simpson (e.g., 1943).

During the 1960's it has become increasingly clear, however, primarily on the basis of studies in two distinct branches of paleomagnetic work, that the ocean floor moves (e.g., Vine and Matthews, 1963; Le Pichon, 1968; Morgan, 1968). Large simatic lithospheric plates are generated at mid-ocean rifts and consumed later in trenches, carrying continental sialic fragments passively along on top. "Continental drift" has been confirmed to the satisfaction of all but a few die-hards. The rationale of drift is not (for biologists) just a remote Mesozoic or earlier possibility having nothing to do with Cenozoic distributions. On the contrary, there is now persuasive geophysical evidence (e.g., Avery et al., 1968; Vogt et al., 1970; and references cited in those papers) that the North Atlantic opened, creating a new central simatic floor starting in the south and working generally northward. The North Atlantic south of the position of Iceland seems to have been oceanic or at least marine throughout a longer time during the Mesozoic, but the opening of the ocean north of Iceland, in De Geer's (1912) Scandic "Sea" (Greenland and Norwegian seas), and possibly in the whole area, now appears to be mainly a late Mesozoic to early Tertiary event (Saito et al., 1967; Vogt et al., 1970; Hallam, 1971; Wright, 1971). Where was the final break between northern continental blocks and when did it occur?

Other than vague gropings for "Atlantis," the earliest detailed proposal of a former northern transatlantic connection that I have been able to find is that of Forbes (1859, p. 56), which was amplified by Godwin-Austen in later pages of the same volume, edited by him after Forbes' death. Godwin-Austen cited, in addition, earlier ideas of Sir John Richardson, but I have not found the reference. Strauch (1970) traced the idea back to Alexander von Humboldt, and Harland (1967), traced the idea to Owen in 1857. I have not searched the literature but have no doubt that the concept goes back even further. Godwin-Austen's map and his text (pp. 254, 286-287) attempted to show the limits of this northern transatlantic connection: its southern coast, at the north end of the ancient North Atlantic, stretched from Newfoundland to Cape Farewell at the southern tip of Greenland, from there to Iceland, and then to the Faeroe Islands, finally reaching Denmark via a shore that passed north of the

Shetland Islands. The north shore of the transatlantic connection was more vaguely stated to have stretched "from Nordland to North Greenland (p. 286)." The antiquity of operation of this route was not stated, but a few years later Godwin-Austen (1866, p. 240) had it connect Europe with America as late as the Pliocene. During the early part of this century the location of the postulated northern North Atlantic land connection tended to become more narrowly fixed. Thus, Gregory (1929, p. lxxiv) believed that two locales in the Greenland area were likely dispersal routes: (1) a Greenland-Iceland-Faeroe route, through the Thulean basaltic province (Brito-arctic province) of H. S. Washington (1922, p. 780), and (2) from northern Norway via Spitsbergen to Greenland. Gregory regarded the Thulean route as the more likely route and thought that it had operated as recently as the Pleistocene. The Thulean route, as opposed to a more northern transatlantic connection, appeared on a paleogeographic map in a geologic textbook by F. X. Schaffer (1924). Schaffer's map bears a certain similarity to, and was no doubt influenced by, the maps of Arldt (1919), compiled from still earlier sources. This sort of vague rationale seems to be the principal "geologic" evidence for Kurtén's (1966) adoption of the Thulean route for Sparnacian (early Eocene) northern transatlantic dispersal of terrestrial vertebrates.

The crest of the Greenland-Iceland-Faeroe ridge is generally less than 1200 feet (~400 m.) deep, but in the Denmark Strait between Greenland and Iceland it reaches a depth of 2000 feet. South of the Faeroe Islands a depth of 2700 feet is found (Dietrich, 1964). These depths are two to three times greater than those of the epicontinental Barents Sea and present a formidable problem for proponents of a Thulean land bridge. A more serious embarrassment for Thulean bridge builders, though not an absolutely fatal one, is the young age of igneous rocks on Iceland itself. Radiometric dates (Gale et al., 1966) from present-day western and southeastern Iceland do not exceed 10 million years. No fossil molluscs known from Iceland are older than latest Pliocene (Durham and MacNeil, 1967). Reports of earliest Tertiary or Cretaceous plants appear to be incorrect. Presumably, older igneous rocks, if once at the present Icelandic site, have been carried oceanward and downward into isolating waters as the result of symmetrical spreading from the complex and wide Icelandic rift, but whether in the past this was in all cases subaerial rather than submarine is doubtful. In any case, the present anomalously elevated landmass of Iceland has been a site of oceanic spreading later in time than the Mesozoic emplacement of lavas in the Faeroe Islands, 150±20 million years ago and 86±4 million years ago (Rasmussen and Noe-Nygaard, 1966), in East Greenland, 49±2 million years ago (terminal Sparnacian), or in Scotland, 50 to 60 million years ago. The Greenland-Iceland-Faeroe ridge may in some measure represent symmetrical spreading tracks comparable to the submarine Walvis and Rio Grande ridges of the South Atlantic. There is no geological evidence that subaerial conditions have ever prevailed on the Greenland-Iceland-Faeroe ridge away from the originating rift zone of Iceland. A few judiciously chosen coring sites along the crest of the ridge would no doubt provide enough marine sediment of Tertiary age to put an end to the Thulean land bridge concept.

Although evidence from advances in marine geophysics has weakened the foundations under the Thulean bridge, geophysical considerations strongly support Gregory's second connection in the far north, near Spitsbergen. Wegmann (1948), in a refreshingly profound but now seldom cited analysis of the geological problems of continental separation in the north, drew attention to the importance of De Geer's (1912) line, which runs from northern Norway past the south side of Spitsbergen and along the north side of Greenland and beyond, recognizing it as a major right lateral offset between continental blocks. Wilson (1965) took the further step of explaining how this right lateral motion could be reconciled with left lateral offset of the mid-ocean ridge, provided oceanic crust spreads. Both Wegmann and Wilson envisioned Spitsbergen and the Barents Shelf to have been against northern Greenland at some former time, separation having occurred later along what Wilson recognized to be a right lateral ridge-ridge transform fault. Harland (1967, and earlier work cited therein) reached the same conclusion. The De Geer line is now recognized to be complex (Vogt et al., 1970), and is in part often called the Spitsbergen Fracture Zone. According to Vogt, Ostenso, and Johnson, a major spreading phase began about 60 million years ago south of Iceland with an initial half-spreading rate from the Reykjanes ridge of 1.7 cm/year, dropping to 0.8 cm/year by 40 million years ago. The Labrador rift was active at the same time. North of Iceland, separation of Norway from Greenland at a half-rate of 1.2 cm/year began 60 million years ago but, because of the irregular shape of the two continental plates, the two blocks took some time to slide past one another along the De Geer line, as no doubt was also the case between northern Brazil and West Africa when Africa separated from South America. At this rate of continental separation (2×1.2 cm/year), total Tertiary separation of the two continental blocks along the De Geer line would have been about 1400 km, comfortably more than the present distance along the Spitsbergen Fracture Zone between the Nansen ridge and Spitsbergen. Presumably, spreading between Norway and Greenland therefore slowed during the mid-Tertiary, as it did south of Iceland. Assuming the maximum rate of separation initially, about 260 km of motion along the De Geer line would have taken place by the end of the Sparnacian. This is approximately the distance from the northwest corner of Spitsbergen to the point where the Eurasian and Greenland-North American plate boundary turns directly southward, away from the De Geer line. It seems reasonable, therefore, that Spitsbergen and Greenland parted company at the end of the Sparnacian.

The Barents Shelf is not regarded here as a major problem. It is currently somewhat below sea level, but is apparently epicontinental and everywhere shallower than the deepest parts of the crest of the Greenland-Iceland-Faeroe ridge. The deepest point along the present route from Spitsbergen to northern Europe is about 1000 feet (~300 m.) Perhaps the Barents Shelf has sagged slightly as the Nansen ridge has retreated northward from it. Nor are the present straits between various of the Canadian Arctic islands regarded as serious impediments. Tectonic analysis of the Arctic islands is far from secure, but that animals could make their way from Greenland to Ellesmere Island and then to the Canadian mainland, or disperse in the opposite direction, is accepted here as very probable. Transform faulting between Greenland and Ellesmere Island has occurred in the past, though such motion is not active at present. Obviously, both the sinking of the Barents Shelf and the separation of the Canadian islands need to be explained, but this will be a matter for geophysics, not paleontology, to elucidate.

The Sparnacian and earlier northern land connection, assuming the Barents Shelf to have been above water level, is what I have called the De Geer route (McKenna, 1971) after the De Geer line, where the northern Greenland "Sea" terminated against the transform fault zone until connection with the Arctic Ocean was attained. The rationale of the De Geer route is geological, derived from current concepts of world tectonics. It is, however, also in harmony with biogeographical ideas.

From a biological standpoint Simpson (1947a), Kurtén (1966), Russell (1968), Szalay and McKenna (1971), Savage (ms), and many others have remarked on the very impressive similarity at the generic level of assemblages of Sparnacian fossil mammals in the London-Paris Basin of Europe to those of various Sparnacian deposits in the Rocky Mountains of North America. Russell (1968, table 1) gives the most useful and current information. About 50% of the genera of the two areas, now separated by the Atlantic, are held in common. Additional generic "cousins" are closely related to one another, which suggests evolution *in situ* from forms that dispersed earlier, in the Paleocene. Such a high proportion of genera in common is indicative of a corridor with little filter action and is compatible with, but does not in itself prove, dispersal of northern species across the De Geer route. But by Cuisian and especially Lutetian (middle Eocene) time generic similarities dropped to a low level, about 10% or so, all inherited from Sparnacian or earlier interchange, as Russell's table clearly shows. Had the De Geer route existed in Lutetian time, some mammals would surely have crossed it, yet it appears probable that by that time none did. One can, on biological grounds therefore, deny Lutetian (and later) transatlantic dry-land dispersal, for reasons developed fully by Matthew and by Simpson. Such evidence is closely in accord with the previously presented nonbiological evidence.

Szalay and McKenna (1971) recently attempted to assess the significance of a peculiar late Paleocene mammalian fauna found originally at Gashato, Mongolia, but now also known from additional Asian sites. In agreement with Kurtén (1966), the Gashato fauna and other early Cenozoic and late Mesozoic faunas suggested to our satisfaction that isolation of Eastern Asia from Europe in the Paleocene and early Eocene was nearly complete via Western Asia, but was not complete, especially in Sparnacian time, via Beringia, North America, and the De Geer route (McKenna, 1971). Clearly both the Bering and De Geer routes were possible during the Sparnacian, but the Bering route was the stronger filter. These conditions were accentuated during the Paleocene, apparently mainly because of a cooler climate. Eastern Asia was isolated from Europe by an epicontinental sea (Turgai Straits, Obik Sea).

If we are persuaded that the De Geer route existed in the Sparnacian and earlier, we may now ask, why was it a less effective filter than the Bering route to Asia? An answer is only partially available and may be substantially modified as more data are collected, but geophysical results are again essential for progress in understanding and seem to point to a small but perhaps significant shift in polar position and therefore latitudinal inclination.

All early and many recent paleogeographers or biogeographers omitted polar wander from their maps, depicting such matters as continental drift reconstructions or past distributions of organisms on maps whose meridians and parallels correspond with those of the present earth. Polar wander, however, is almost certainly more fruitfully regarded as lithosphere wander instead, relative to the earth's mantle and core. Continental drift can be regarded as *differential* lithosphere wander, i.e., motion of plates relative to one another as well as to the mantle and core. So long as there was reasonable doubt about continental drift it was justifiable to plot past distributions of animals upon maps resembling those of the "Times Atlas," but at present and in the future *both* general lithosphere wander (polar wander) and differential lithosphere wander (relative plate motion) should be taken into account; in other words, future paleogeographic maps should show recalculated latitude belts as well as relocated crustal blocks. This is easier said than done, of course, because of the paucity of reliable data, but surely such attempts are worthwhile and potentially instructive. Sloan (1969) has attempted to construct palinspastic latest Cretaceous and Paleocene maps of North America and parts of Europe and northeastern Asia, on which the latitude belts are shifted to correspond to calculated former rotational pole positions. Szalay and McKenna (1971) have attempted somewhat similar reconstructions, based upon more refined data (Fig. 1). Such maps, with all their drawbacks and vagueness, are nevertheless potentially more useful than other maps in depicting past distributions of organisms. Their rationale is in essence geophysical and geological, not biological, and therefore significant configurations of biological data are not based upon circular reasoning.

In our recent paper on the Paleocene of Asia (Szalay and McKenna, 1971) we attempted to show the paleogeography of a reassembled Holarctica on the basis of recent geophysical conclusions by others, based on magnetic anomaly studies of the ocean floor, coupled with polar wander data. The rotational pole has been within the Arctic Basin since somewhat before Cenozoic time, but the evidence

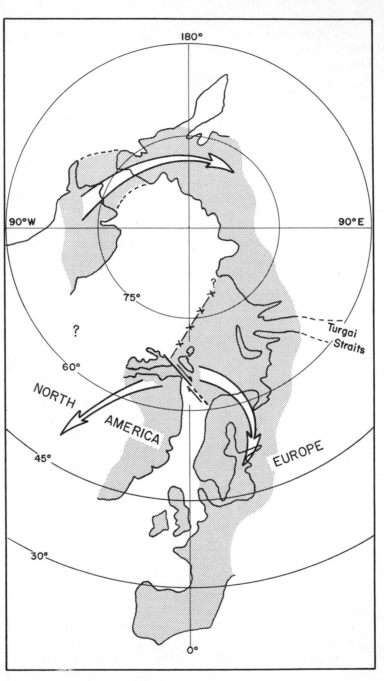

Fig. 1. Palinspastic reassembly of part of Holarctica prior to final northern connection of the Atlantic with the Arctic Ocean. Right lateral motion along the De Geer line later separated the land mass of Europe from that of Greenland-North America. Latitudes are re-located on the basis of paleomagnetic results. The epicontinental Turgai Straits would have extended to the Tethyan seaway. The approximate edge of the Barents Shelf is shown by the line -x-x-x. The large arrows show the Bering and De Geer dispersal routes. See Szalay and McKenna (1971, text and fig. 3) for further details.

we cited and that accepted by Creer (1970) indicates that the rotational pole was formerly nearer Beringia than it is at present, suggesting that Beringia, because of its higher paleolatitude, would have been on that account a stronger filter for terrestrial organisms than the De Geer route. No matter how equable the climate as indicated by paleobotany, near the rotational pole there is no known geophysical way around winter darkness associated with axial tilt relative to the ecliptic.

The De Geer route, until its demise at the end of the Sparnacian, was intrinsically a more equable route than the Bering route, no matter what the climatic zonation. Until the close of Sparnacian time the De Geer route was a major Holarctic corridor.

REFERENCES

Arldt, Theodor. 1919. Handbuch der Palaeogeographie. Band I: Palaeaktologie. Leipzig, Borntraeger, pp. 679.

Avery, O. E., G. D. Burton, and J. R. Heirtzler. 1968. An aeromagnetic survey of the Norwegian Sea. J. Geophys. Res., 73:4583-4600.

Creer, K. M. 1970. A review of palaeomagnetism. Earth Sci. Rev., 6:369-466.

Dana, J. D. 1846. On the volcanoes of the moon. Amer. J. Sci., (2)2:353.

——— 1847. A general review of the geological effects of the earth's cooling from a state of igneous fusion. Amer. J. Sci., (2)4:90-92.

De Geer, Gerald. 1912. Kontinentale Niveauveränderungen im Norden Europas. C. R. Cong. Geol. Int., Stockholm, 1910: 849-860.

Dietrich, G. 1964. Oceanic polar front survey in North Atlantic. In Odishaw, H., ed., Research in Geophysics, Vol. 2, Solid Earth and Interface Phenomena, pp. 291-308 Cambridge, Mass., Massachusetts Institute of Technology.

Durham, J. W., and F. S. MacNeil. 1967. Cenozoic migrations of marine invertebrates through the Bering Strait region. In Hopkins, D. M., ed., The Bering Land Bridge, pp. 326-349. Stanford, Stanford University Press.

Du Toit, A. L. 1937. Our Wandering Continents, an Hypothesis of Continental Drifting. Edinburgh and London, Oliver and Boyd.

——— 1944. Tertiary mammals and continental drift. A rejoinder to George G. Simpson. Amer. J. Sci., 242(3):145-163.

Forbes, E. 1859. The Natural History of the European Seas. London, John Van Voorst, viii ⁻ 306 pp. [Edited and contineud by Robert Godwin-Austen.]

Gale, N. H., S. Moorbath, J. Simons, and G. P. L. Walker. 1966. K-Ar ages of acid intrusive rocks from Iceland. Earth and Planetary Sci. Letters, 1:284-288.

Godwin-Austen, R. A. C. 1866. On the Kainozoic formations of Belgium. Quart. J. Geol. Soc. London, 22:228-254.

Gregory, John Walter. 1929. The geological history of the Atlantic Ocean. Quart. J. Geol. Soc. London, 85:lxviii-cxxii.

Hallam, A. 1971. Mesozoic geology and the opening of the North Atlantic. J. Geol., 79(2):129-157.

Harland, W. B. 1967. Early history of the North Atlantic Ocean and its margins. Nature (London), 216:464-467.

Kurtén, Björn. 1966. Holarctic land connexions in the early Tertiary. Comment, Biol. Soc. Sci. Fennica, 29(5):5 pp.

Le Pichon, X. 1968. Sea-floor spreading and continental drift. J. Geophys. Res., 73:3661-3697.

Lindroth, C. H. 1957. The Faunal Connections between Europe and North America. New York, John Wiley and Sons, 344 pp.

Matthew, W. D. 1915. Climate and evolution. Ann. New York Acad. Sci., 24:171-318.

1939. Climate and Evolution. Second edition, revised and enlarged. Spec. Publ. New York Acad. Sci., 1:xii - 223 pp.

Mayr, Ernst. 1952. Introduction. In Mayr, E., ed., The Problem of Land Connections across the South Atlantic, with Special Reference to the Mesozoic. Bull. Amer. Mus. Nat. Hist., 99(3):85.

McKenna, Malcolm C. 1971. Fossil mammals and the Eocene demise of the De Geer North Atlantic dispersal route. Program, Ann. Meeting, Geol. Soc. Amer., November 1971:1 p. (abstr.).

Morgan, W. J. 1968. Rises, trenches, great faults and crustal blocks. J. Geophys. Res., 73:1959-1982.

Rasmussen, J., and A. Noe-Nygaard. 1966. New data on the geological age of the Faeroes. Nature (London), 209:1229-1230.

Russell, Donald E. 1968. Succession, en Europe, des faunes mammaliennes au début du Tertiaire. Mém. Bur. Rech. Géol. Min., No. 58:291-296.

Saito, T., L. H. Burckle, and D. R. Horn. 1967. Paleocene core from the Norwegian basin. Nature (London), 216:357-359.

Savage, Donald E. [ms]. The Sparnacian-Wasatchian mammalian fauna, early Eocene, of Europe and North America. 7 pp.

Schaffer, F. X. 1924. Lehrbuch der Geologie. II. Teil. Grundzüge der Historischen Geologie (Geschichte der Erde, Formationskunde). Leipzig and Vienna, Franz Deuticks.

Simpson, George Gaylord. 1940. Mammals and land bridges. J. Washington Acad. Sci., 30(4):137-163.

1943. Mammals and the nature of continents. Amer. J. Sci., 241(1):1-31.

1946. Tertiary land bridges. Trans. New York Acad. Sci., (2)8(8):255-258.

1947a. Holarctic mammalian faunas and continental relationships during the Cenozoic. Bull. Geol. Soc. Amer., 58:613-688.

1947b. Evolution, interchange, and resemblance of the North American and Eurasian Cenozoic mammalian faunas. Evolution, 1(3):218-220.

1952. Probabilities of dispersal in geologic time. In Mayr, E., ed., The Problem of Land Connections across the South Atlantic, with Special Reference to the Mesozoic. Bull. Amer. Mus. Nat. Hist., 99(3):163-176.

1953. Evolution and Geography. Condon Lectures, Oregon State Syst. Higher Educ., pp. 1-64.

Sloan, Robert E. 1969. Cretaceous and Paleocene terrestrial communities of western North America. Proc. North Amer. Paleont. Convention, pt. E:427-453.

Strauch, Friedrich. 1970. Die Thule-Landbrücke als Wanderweg und Faunenscheide zwischen Atlantik und Skandik im Tertiär. Geol. Rundschau, 60(1):381-417.

Szalay, Frederick S., and Malcolm C. McKenna. 1971. Beginning of the age of mammals in Asia: the late Paleocene Gashato fauna, Mongolia. Bull. Amer. Mus. Nat. Hist., 144(4):269-318.

Taylor, F. B. 1910. Bearing of the Tertiary mountain belt on the origin of the earth's plan. Bull. Geol. Soc. Amer., 21:179-226.

Vine, F. J., and D. H. Matthews. 1963. Magnetic anomalies over ocean ridges. Nature (London), 199:947-949.

Vogt, P. R., N. A. Ostenso, and G. L. Johnson. 1970. Magnetic and bathymetric data bearing on sea-floor spreading north of Iceland. J. Geophys. Res., 75(5):903-920.

Washington, H. S. 1922. Deccan traps and other plateau basalts. Bull. Geol. Soc. Amer., 33:765-804.

Wegener, Alfred. 1924. The Origin of Continents and Oceans. London, Methuen and Co. [Translation of 3rd German edition. A French translation of the 5th edition was published in 1937.]

Wegmann, C. E. 1948. Geological tests of the hypothesis of continental drift in the Arctic regions, scientific planning. Meddelelser om Grønland, 144(7):1-48.

Wilson, J. T. 1965. A new class of faults and their bearing on continental drift. Nature (London), 207:343-347.

Wright, J. B. 1971. Comments on "Timing of Break-up of the continents round the Atlantic as determined by Palaeomagnetism" by E. E. Larson and L. La Fountain. Earth and Planetary Sci. Letters, 10:271-272.

8

The Evolution of the Tongue of Snakes, and its Bearing on Snake Origins

S. B. MCDOWELL

Rutgers University
Newark, New Jersey 07102

INTRODUCTION

The form and texture of the tongue has long been one of the major bases for the classification of lizards, as evidenced by such herpetological catalogues as de Rooij (1915) that base the "synopsis of families" principally on the tongue, and by the "-glossa" names for higher groups of lizards in the older literature (e.g., Pachyglossa, Leptoglossa, Thecaglossa, Diploglossa, all used by Cope, 1900, but taken by him from earlier authors). I can find no case where a lizard was referred to a particular group on the basis of tongue structure but subsequently found, from other evidence, to be unrelated. On the other hand, in two cases families of lizards have been referred to higher groups against the evidence of the tongue, and subsequent study of the osteology has shown such reference to be in error: the Pygopodidae were referred by Camp (1923) to the same group as that containing Anguidae, Xenosauridae, Anniellidae, Helodermatidae, and Varanidae, in spite of a very different tongue; but McDowell and Bogert (1954) and Underwood (1957) showed that the Pygopodidae are most closely related to the Gekkonidae, with which they agree in tongue structure as well as many other features. (See Table 1.) Camp (1923) also referred the Zonuridae (=Cordylidae) to the group containing the Anguidae, etc., in spite of a quite different tongue, but McDowell and Bogert (1954) and Estes (1962) have shown that the African Cordylidae are most closely related to the African and Malagasy Gerrhosauridae, with which they agree in tongue structure as well as cranial and osteodermal structure and method of tooth replacement.

Table 1. Classification of Squamata mentioned in this paper.

Class Reptilia
  Order Squamata
    Suborder Eolacertilia (Triassic fossils only; regarded as an Infraorder of the Lacertilia
      by previous authors)
    Suborder Lacertilia (Lizards)
      Infraorder Leptoglossa (=Scincomorpha)
          Family Tejidae (*Tupinambis, Cnemidophorus*, and others)
          Family Scincidae (*Mabuya* and others)
          Family Cordylidae (*Cordylus* [=*Zonurus*], *Gerrhosaurus*, and others)
          Family Lacertidae
      Infraorder Nyctisauria (=Gekkota)
        Superfamily Xantusoidea
          Family Xantusiidae (*Klauberina, Xantusia*, and others; referred to
            Leptoglossa by some authors)
        Superfamily Dibamoidea
          Family Dibamidae (*Dibamus* and *Anelytropsis*; referred to Leptoglossa by
            others)
        Superfamily Gekkonoidea
          Family Eublepharidae (*Coleonyx* and others)
          Family Gekkonidae (*Uroplatus, Hemidactylus*, and others)
          Family Sphaerodactylidae
          Family Pygopodidae
      Infraorder Annulata (Amphisbaenia)
          Family Amphisbaenidae (*Amphisbaena* and others; the Annulata are
            sometimes ranked as a suborder or even order!)
      Infraorder Iguania (=Pachyglossa + Rhiptoglossa)
          Family Iguanidae (*Ctenosaura, Sceloporus, Holbrookia*, and others)
          Family Agamidae
          Family Chamaeleontidae
      Infraorder Anguimorpha
        Superfamily Anguoidea (=Diploglossa)
          Family Anguidae (*Anguis, Gerrhonotus, Ophisaurus*, and others)
          Family Xenosauridae (*Xenosaurus* and *Shinisaurus*)
          Family Anniellidae (*Anniella*)
        Superfamily Varanoidea (=Platynota)
          Family Helodermatidae (*Heloderma*)
          Family Varanidae (*Varanus*)
          Family Dolichosauridae (Cretaceous fossils: *Pontosaurus, Acteosaurus*
            [=*Adriosaurus*] and others)
          Family Lanthanotidae (*Lanthanotus*; it is suggested in this paper that this
            "family" be included in the Dolichosauridae)
          Family Aigialosauridae (Lower Cretaceous ancestors of the next family)
          Family Mosasauridae (Upper Cretaceous fossils)
    Suborder Serpentes (=Ophidia) (Snakes)
      Infraorder Cholophidia
          Family Pachyophidae (Cretaceous fossils)
          Family Dinilysiidae (*Dinilysia* of Upper Cretaceous)
          Family Palaeophidae Eocene fossils)

Infraorder Scolecophidia (Blind snakes)
    Family Anomalepididae (*Anomalepis, Liotyphlops, Helminthophis,* and
        Typhlophis)
    Family Typhlopidae (*Typhlops*)
    Family Leptotyphlopidae (*Leptotyphlops*)
Infraorder Alethinophidia (Typical snakes)
    Superfamily Booidea
    Family Aniliidae (*Loxocemus, Xenopeltis, Cylindrophis, Anilius
        Rhinophis, Uropeltis,* and others)
    Family Boidae (*Python, Boa, Eryx, Tropidophis,* and others)
    Superfamily Colubroidea
    Family Acrochordidae
    Family Colubridae (*Atretium, Dasypeltis, Diadophis, Elaphe, Masticophis,
        Natrix, Psammophis, Thamnophis, Xenochrophis,* and others)
    Family Elapidae (*Naja, Aipysurus,* and others)
    Family Viperidae (vipers and pit vipers)

Unfortunately, in lizards the study of the tongue must be confined to living forms, for the hyobranchial skeleton is only loosely involved in the structure of the tongue and the osteology reveals almost nothing about tongue structure. Thus, for the fossils, the structure of the tongue must be inferred from taxonomic relationships rather than the taxonomic relationships deduced from the structure of the tongue. The hyobranchial skeleton has some taxonomic value in its own right, however, and has been used by both Cope (1900) and Camp (1923) in the classification of lizards.

Camp (1923) further extended the characters used in classification by utilizing the throat muscles, and Gnathamuthu (1937) found a number of potentially useful taxonomic characters in his survey of a small but broadly representative series of lizards.

Camp (1923) further extended the characters used in classification by utilizing the throat muscles, and Gnathamuthu (1937) found a number of potentially useful taxonomic characters in his survey of a small but broadly representative series of lizards.

The tongue of snakes is quite different from that of the vast majority of lizards and (if the lizard *Varanus* is forgotten for the moment) the tongue structure of snakes is one of the most striking differences between this group and the lizards, the group from which snakes undoubtedly are derived. Among snakes, the form of the tongue is so nearly uniform that it is of almost no use in snake classification. However, the form of the hyobranchial skeleton and the pattern of throat muscles do offer some taxonomic characters, most recently discussed by Langebartel (1968).

A study of the tongue in lizards and snakes is incomplete unless it includes also the openings on the roof of the mouth for the vomeronasal (Jacobson's) organ; for the tongue functions partly (most lizards) or entirely (snakes) to obtain air samples for the organ of Jacobson and the structure of the tip of the tongue and of the openings of the Jacobson's organ are intimately related functionally.

A survey of the structure of the tongue, hyobranchial skeleton, throat muscles, and openings of Jacobson's organ in snakes and anguimorphan lizards leads me to believe that the peculiarities of the snake tongue can be explained as part of the adaptation to their method of feeding, and that this adaptation involved a series of functional stages each preadaptive to the next but quite viable in itself and by no means an inadaptive transition stage (indeed, for each of these stages there is a living lizard genus that is succeeding today and defending its ecologic niche, as attested by its survival, even in competition with snakes). The evolution of the highly peculiar (almost unique) tongue of snakes thus offers a case history of the modification of a character complex by adaptive means without the total replacement and extinction of more primitive stages by the more progressive derivatives.

THE GENERALIZED LIZARD STAGE

Oelrich (1956) has given a complete account (aside from minor veins) of the head of the iguanid *Ctenosaura*, and because of the usefulness of having a single system of anatomical terms, Oelrich's terminology is used here throughout, even when his usage differs from that of a vast body of previous literature (e.g., he uses the term *hypohyal* for the median process called entoglossal or cultriform process of the hyoid by others).

In *Ctenosaura*, as in most lizards, the tongue is fleshy, broadly triangular in form, and fully exposed on the floor of the mouth. The anterior end is free of the floor of the mouth and is here called the *foretongue*. In *Ctenosaura* the foretongue is only nicked terminally on the midline, as in other iguanids, and as seen also in agamids, gekkotans, and scincids; however in lacertids, tejids, and amphisbaenids the fore-tongue is more deeply cleft into a pair of pointed tines.

The ventral surface of the foretongue of *Ctenosaura* has a pair of smooth and rather hard *pallets* (term used by Cope, 1900). In the normal and retracted position of the tongue, these pallets rest upon the dorsal surface of a pair of lumps on the floor of the mouth (the *sublingual plicae*), which contain the *sublingual glands*, secreting a sticky material onto the pallets. Presumably this secretion allows the pallets to act as adhesive traps for small particles to be tested by the organ of Jacobson. Pygopodidae have similar pallets on the ventral surface of the foretongue, and Underwood (1957) has figured a tongue of the pygopod *Lialis burtonis* that was preserved with the tongue-tip naturally doubled over, so that these ventral pallets faced the roof of the mouth; this inverting of the tip of the tongue would seem the only possible method of transferring material from the pallets to the openings of the organ of Jacobson (*fenestrae vomeronasales externae*) on the palate and is probably characteristic of iguanians, gekkotans, and skinks, where there are ventral pallets. In some lizards, such as lacertids and tejids, the smooth, hard covering of the underside of the tongue-tip curls up onto the dorsal surface of each of the terminal tines and the latter rest *between* the sublingual plicae rather than on top of them; in such lizards it is likely that doubling over of the tip of the tongue is unnecessary for wiping the pallets against the roof of the mouth.

The *hind-tongue* (my term) of *Ctenosaura* is connected to the floor of the mouth by a fold of oral mucosa containing the *genioglossus* muscles. This fold, the *frenulum*, is not macroscopically different from the other oral mucosa or from the ventral surface of the tongue aside from the pallets, and it is the genioglosus musculature contained within the frenulum which distinguishes it; however, the mucosa of the frenulum tends to fall into a lengthwise pleat parallel to the attachment of the frenulum to the hind-tongue. The rear of the hind-tongue of *Ctenosaura*, as in most lizards, is developed into a pair of backwardly directed *posterior limbs*, which are free of the floor of the mouth and lie flanking the larynx at the opening of the esophagus. It would appear that these posterior limbs act as pushing plungers for tamping food backward into the gullet, for *Cnemidophorus tesselatus* and *Sceloporus cyanogenys* that I have observed feeding dart the tongue in and out when swallowing, an action in keeping with a plunger action for the posterior limbs, and difficult to explain otherwise.

The entire dorsal surface of the tongue of *Ctenosaura*, as well as the lateral margins, is clothed with soft papillae that are shortest on the anterior foretongue and longest on the posterior limbs. These papillae make up what is here called the *frictional surface* and increase the frictional drag of the tongue upon food and thus increase the ability of the tongue to manipulate food in the mouth Gekkotans and iguanians have a papillose frictional surface, but in scincids, lacertids, cordylids (including gerrhosaurs), tejids, and amphisbaenids the frictional surface is modified into a field of imbricate scales by keratinization and flattening of the papillae.

The *fenestra vomeronasalis externa* or palatal opening of Jacobson's organ is a small transverse slit in *Ctenosaura*, much too small to admit the broad tip of the tongue. The fenestra vomeronasalis externa lies near the center of a broad but shallow triangular fossa on the roof of the mouth; this fossa is defined laterally by a fold (the *lateral palatine stripe*) that runs just medial to, and parallel with, the maxillary tooth row. The broad and parabola-shaped fossa defined by the lateral palatine stripes agrees closely with the shape of the tongue, and the fossa receives the tongue when the mouth is closed and the floor of the mouth elevated. However, at the front end this fossa is divided longitudinally by a narrow median ridge (the *vomerine raphe*), thus defining a pair of triangular, smooth, and nonglandular areas, each of these areas containing, near its center, the fenestra vomeronasalis externa. Although Oelrich (1956: 111) says, "These two triangular areas reflect the shape of the dorsal tip on the tongue" this does not seem quite correct, for in *Ctenosaura* (as in Iguania generally) the tongue is only feebly nicked terminally and there is no median fissure on the dorsal tip of the tongue to reflect the vomerine raphe. However, the groove between the pallets on the *ventral* surface of the tip of the tongue does reflect the vomerine raphe. This is further evidence that the tip of the tongue is inverted when placed against the fenestrae vomeronasalis externae in *Ctenosaura*. Iguania seem to be unusual in the broadness of the tip of the tongue and in many, perhaps most, other lizards the fenestra vomeronasalis externa is a longitudinal, rather than transverse, slit and the fossa in which it lies is narrower as a result of a broader vomerine raphe (this, in turn, reflecting the deeper and more triangular terminal cleft of the tongue).

Behind the fenestra vomeronasalis externa and well separated from it by soft tissue is the choanal opening, functionally closed over anteriorly by a flap on its lateral margin, the *ectochoanal fold.* The ectochoanal fold is stiffened by a cartilage that is bound to the maxillary bone (the *ectochoanal cartilage*) and extends horizontally to overlap the lateral edge of the very broad and padded vomer, concealing the slit-like anterior portion of the choanal opening except behind the level of the vomer. Just dorsal to the ectochoanal fold, and concealed from ventral view by the latter, is the choanal groove, into the anterior end of which the *lachrymal duct* opens. In *Ctenosaura* the broad opening of lachrymal duct and the anterior end of the ectochoanal fold are close to the fenestra vomeronasalis externa (see Pratt, 1948 for review).

In the hyobranchial skeleton, the *body of the hyoid* of *Ctenosaura* is a rather narrow element, fused laterally to the ventralmost segment of the hyoid arch, which forms the *anterior process of the body of the hyoid*, following Oelrich's terminology. On the midline, the body of the hyoid is extended forward in a long spike, here called the *hypohyal process* to conform with Oelrich although it is called the entoglossal process by almost every other author. The hypohyal process enters the tongue and lies within the tissue of the hind-tongue for most of the length of the latter. The fusion of the body of the hyoid with hyoid arch in *Ctenosaura* probably represents an iguanian specialization rather than a primitive feature, for it does not occur in many other lizards. The extension of the hypohyal process into the hind-tongue is a general feature, seen in almost all lizards, even when this hypohyal process becomes dissociated from the body of the hyoid except for a ligamentous connection, as in some Tejidae (see Jollie, 1960).

The *hyoid arch*, including the anterior process of the body of the hyoid, is Z-shaped, with a long and slender *ceratohyal* running backward from its attachment to the distal end of the anterior process of the body of the hyoid. The posterior end of the ceratohyal is attached to a distalmost element, the *dorsal process of the hyoid arch* (following Oelrich; the epihyal of most authors), which is strongly bent upward and forward to run to the neighborhood of the tympanic membrane (just behind the tympanic membrane and deep to the depressor mandibulae). As in lizards generally, the hyoid arch receives no muscles from the shoulder girdle and is not attached to any of the muscles of the tongue itself. Its chief muscular attachment is to a branchiohyoideus that connects the first ceratobranchial and the ceratohyal. In *Ctenosaura* the ceratohyal also received the attachment of a part of the mandibulohyoideus (=geniohyoideus), the mandibulohyoideus III of Oelrich, running from the lower jaw lateral to the main body of the hypoglossal nerve; but the mandibulohyoideus III does not seem to be of general occurrence in lizards (cf. Gnanamuthu, 1937) and appears to be an iguanian specialization.

The *first branchial* arch of *Ctenosaura* is represented by a long *first ceratobranchial* extending backward (approximately parallel to the lower jaw and to the ceratohyal) to become bent upward abruptly at its rear into a *dorsal process of the first branchial arch* (first epibranchial of most authors). The dorsal process receives no muscles and lies in the posterolateral wall of the middle ear cavity, along with the dorsal process of the hyoid arch and the dorsal process of the second branchial arch (see below). The first ceratobranchial, however, receives more muscles than does any other element of hyobranchial skeleton: the mandibulohyoideus I (=geniohyoideus of most authors) from the lower jaw; the "mandibulohyoideus II" of Oelrich from a median tendon of the throat (see discussion of hyoglossus below); the hyoglossus, forming most of the tongue; the branchiohyoideus from the ceratohyal; and the omohyoideus and sternohyoideus muscles from the shoulder girdle.

The second branchial arch of *Ctenosaura* is represented by two dissociated parts: (1) a long *second ceratobranchial* running backward from the body of the hyoid, with which it is fused, parallel to the trachea and near the midline; and (2) an isolated *dorsal process* (=second epibranchial of most authors), lying in the wall of the middle ear cavity with the other dorsal processes. The dorsal process of second branchial arch agrees with those of the hyoid and first branchial arch in receiving no muscles, but the second ceratobranchial receives fibers from the omohyoideus and sternohyoideus (the muscles from the shoulder girdle principally inserted on the first ceratobranchial). This pattern may be more characteristic of a group within the Iguanidae than of lizards in general, and many iguanids (as well as other lizards) have the second ceratobranchials short and well separated from the midline, and many lizards have no second ceratobranchials at all.

Much variation exists among lizards in the degree of development of the parts of the hyobranchial skeleton (see Cope, 1900; Camp, 1923; and Gnanamuthu, 1937 for summaries with figures of the range in structure of the lacertilian hyobranchium). From a functional standpoint, the dorsal processes of the hyobranchial arches probably should not be considered part of the tongue complex at all; some observations of living lizards lead me to believe they may be of functional importance in the ear.

The anguid *Gerrhonotus*, like iguanids and geckoes, has the tympanic membrane sunk in a distinct pit, and can narrow—or even close—this pit by drawing forward the tissue just behind the external ear. Since this can be done with the mouth closed, it is more likely the dorsal process of the first branchial arch than the depressor mandibulae muscle which acts to close the external ear (the dorsal process of the hyoid arch is essentially fixed in position by ligature of its tip to the region of the tip of the paroccipital process). Probably the branchiohyoideus pulls the first branchial arch forward, thus causing its dorsal process to move forward and close the external ear pit; the fixation of the hyoid in the ear region would increase its efficiency as a fulcrum for such movement of the first branchial arch. *Gerrhonotus* has sturdy dorsal processes on the first branchial and hyoid arches. In the related *Xenosaurus* the tympanum is superficial, without a pit to permit closure, and the dorsal process of the hyoid arch is reduced to a thread-like curvature of the distal end of the ceratohyal. In the related *Anguis* and *Anniella* the tympanic membrane is absent, and so is the dorsal process of the first branchial arch, while the hyoid arch is nearly (*Anguis*) or quite (*Anniella*) absent. All of these lizards have similar tongues, and the presence or absence of dorsal processes on the hyobranchial arches would seem to correlate much better with ear structure than with tongue structure.

In the throat musculature, the *intermandibularis* (mylohyoideus of Camp, 1923) is innervated by the trigeminal nerve and has its fibers oriented transversely across the throat between the jaws. Its origin does not quite extend forward to the anterior end of the mandible, and so in *Ctenosaura*, as in the great majority of lizards, the hypoglossal-innervated genioglossus muscles are the most anteriorly attached muscles of the lower jaw (Fig. 1) The intermandibularis of *Ctenosaura* is divided into a series of transverse strips by the interdigitating slips of the mandibulohyoideus (hypoglossal-innervated), running to the lower jaw between the intermandibularis slips, so that the musculature of the floor of the mouth is rather like a woven basket, with the lower jaw serving as the rim of the basket. The posteriormost part of the intermandibularis of *Ctenosaura* and other lizards is entirely superficial to the mandibulohyoideus, thus resembling the entire intermandibularis of gnathostomes other than Squamata, and is conspicuously broader than the other parts of the muscle; it is designated the *intermandibularis posterior* (=mylohyoideus posterior of Camp). The other parts of the intermandibularis are deep to slips of the mandibulohyoideus, at least at their lateral attachments to the lower jaw; these parts collectively make up the *intermandibularis anterior* (=mylohyoideus anterior of Camp). The anteriormost part of the intermandibularis anterior is in two layers: (1) a broad principal portion, formed of transverse fibers and in obvious replicative sequence with the more posterior parts of the intermandibularis anterior; and (2) a narrower, more superficial bundle of fibers that slant diagonally backward and inward to attach to the raphe of connective tissue on the midline of the throat (this is the *intermandibularis anterior, superficial group* of Oelrich, and the mylohyoideus anterior superficialis of Camp). In *Ctenosaura*, the mandibulohyoideus has three

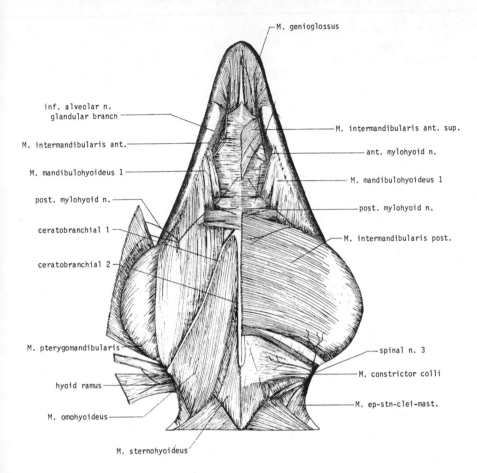

inf. alveolar n.
glandular branch

M. intermandibularis ant.

M. mandibulohyoideus 1

post. mylohyoid n.

ceratobranchial 1

ceratobranchial 2

M. pterygomandibularis

hyoid ramus

M. omohyoideus

M. sternohyoideus

M. genioglossus

M. intermandibularis ant. sup.

ant. mylohyoid n.

M. mandibulohyoideus 1

post. mylohyoid n.

M. intermandibularis post.

spinal n. 3

M. constrictor colli

M. ep-stn-clei-mast.

Fig. 1. Throat muscles of Ctenosaura pectinata. *(From Oelrich, 1956) Abbreviations: M. intermandibularis ant., intermandibularis anterior muscle; M. intermandibularis ant. sup., superficial portion of last; M. intermandibularis post., intermandibularis posterior muscle; M. ep-stn-clei-mast., episternocleidomastodeus muscle.*

slips that divide the intermandibularis into four transverse portions, with the intermandibularic anterior superficial group forming a fifth portion of the muscle.

Camp (1923) concluded that the primitive condition for lizards is for the intermandibularis to be divided into numerous (eight or more) serially replicative divisions by interdigitating insertions of the mandibulohyoideus. (This interweaving of the mandibulohyoideus and intermandibularis is unique to Squamata, however, and in other gnathostomes the intermandibularis is wholly superficial to the hypoglossal-innervated muscles.) This pattern of numerous interdigitations is best seen in some Gekkota, some Scincidae, *Gerrhosaurus* (now referred to the Cordylidae), *Lacerta*, and some Tejidae. Independently, various evolutionary lines of lizards have simplified this pattern by reducing the number of interdigitations. Thus, in the gecko *Uroplatus* the intermandibularis is divided into only an anterior and a posterior portion, even though the gekkotan *Coleonyx* has numerous interdigitations; within the agamids there may be from four (*Liolepis*) to one (*Draco*) interdigitation of the intermandibularis and mandibulohyoideus. Among iguanids, *Ctenosaura* would appear specialized by reduction in number of interdigitations as compared to *Anolis* (as figured by Gnanamuthu, 1937).

Camp also concluded that the superficial bundle of fibers of the intermandibularis anterior seen in *Ctenosaura* was evolved independently within the Iguanidae, since *Holbrookia* and its close relatives lack a distinct superficial group of fibers. This now seems questionable, since *Holbrookia* (R. Etheridge, personal communication) is not the most primitive of the iguanids and may rather be specialized in loss of a distinct superficialis portion. Among nonanguimorphan lizards, the following families (*fide* Camp's descriptions and figures) have a superficial (or cutaneous) group of fibers overlying the principal portion of the intermandibularis anterior: Iguanidae, Scincidae, Dibamidae (to judge from cranial structure, also including *Anelytropsis*), Cordylidae (*Gerrhosaurus*, but not *Cordylus*), Lacertidae. In the following families there is no indication of a superficial group of fibers of the intermandibularis anterior: Gekkonidae (including Uroplatidae), Eublepharidae, Pygopodidae, Xantusiidae, Feyliniidae, Tejidae, Amphisbaenidae, Agamidae, Chamaeleonidae (in these last two families, the intermandibularis anterior is in two layers, but through the differentiation of a new portion, deep to the principal portion). Comparing these lists, it seems possible, perhaps even probable, that a superficial bundle of the intermandibularis anterior is a primitive feature of lizards that has been lost in Gekkota, Tejidae, Amphisbaenidae, the agamids (and their probable derivatives, the Chamaeleonidae), and a few other lizards. This superficial bundle, in fact, seems more nearly comparable to the intermandibularis anterior of nonsquamatan gnathostomes than does the "principal" portion, in being wholly superficial to hypoglossal-innervated musculature.

The throat muscles innervated by the facial nerve are the *constrictor colli* and *cervicomandibularis*. In *Ctenosaura*, as in most lizards, the constrictor colli is a thin sheet of muscle around the neck, just behind the intermandibularis and just beneath the skin.

Ctenosaura is probably specialized in the poor differentiation of the cervicomandibularis. Oelrich regards a posteriormost part of the depressor mandibulae, inserted on the fascia of the intermandibularis posterior near the angle of the jaw, as the homolog in *Ctenosaura* of the cervicomandibularis of most lizards; however, he notes that the posteriormost fibers of his "intermandibularis posterior" are innervated by the facial nerve and it seems reasonable to consider these fibers as also part of the cervicomandibularis. This weak distinction of the cervicomandibularis is a peculiarity of *Ctenosaura* and its close relatives, rather than a general feature of nonanguimorphan lizards. According to Camp (1923), the cervicomandibularis is particularly strong in burrowing lizards, but his illustrations do not bear out such a broad generalization. To judge from Camp's figures, it is most frequent for the cervicomandibularis to end upon the fascia of the intermandibularis posterior, but the amphisbaenids are peculiar in the enormous development of the muscle, which reaches the mandibular symphysis.

Of the muscles innervated by the hypoglossal (Fig. 2), the *hyoglossus* is the most intimately associated with the tongue, forming most of the fleshy mass of that organ. In *Ctenosaura* this muscle is broad and flat, arising from most of the length of the first ceratobranchial. Gnanamuthu (1937) found that all the lizards he examined except *Chamaeleon, Varanus,* and *Mabuia* (=*Mabuya*), but

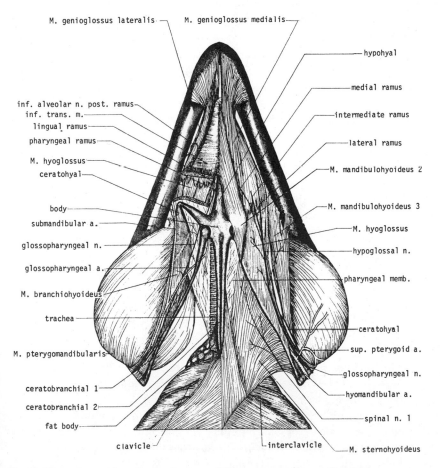

Fig. 2. Throat muscles, deeper layers, of Ctenosaura. *(From Oelrich)*

including the iguanid *Anolis*, had two portions of the hyoglossus, an inner and an outer. Oelrich (1956) does not describe any such division in *Ctenosaura*, but he describes as the "mandibulohyoideus II" a muscle attached posteriorly to the medial end of the first ceratobranchial and extending forward dorsal to the intermandibularis to attach to the midline raphe of the throat, this attachment to the midline raphe sometimes being continued forward by a thin ligament to the symphysis between the genioglossi mediales. Camp (1923) figured a similar muscle in the iguanid *Brachylophus* and identified it as a part of the geniohyoideus (i.e., the mandibulohyoideus of Oelrich and the present work). Furthermore, Camp noted (p. 373): "In *Zonurus* [=*Cordylus*] as in the Iguania the Geniohyoideus is divided, the median half inserting on the mid-ventral raphe and the external half in the usual position on the mandible . . . " It seems likely that this supposed portion of the mandibulohyoideus is actually the "inner hyoglossus," perhaps modified in Iguania to act as a downward and forward rotator of the hyobranchium to aid in erecting the throat fan possessed by the more primitive members.

In *Ctenosaura*, as in most lizards, there are two pairs of genioglossus muscles, the *genioglossus medialis* and the *genioglossus lateralis*, only imperfectly separated from each other. The *genioglossus medialis* is relatively broad and extends from an origin on the symphysial region of the dentary to an insertion on the ventral surface of the hyoglossus muscle. The genioglossus lateralis originates just posterolateral to the genioglossus medialis and inserts on the lateral border of the hind-tongue (not upon the hyoglossus); in lacking an additional insertion upon the mucosa of the buccal floor, *Ctenosaura* differs from most of the lizards examined by Gnanamuthu (1937), including the Iguanid *Anolis*, but resembles the gecko *Hemidactylus*. The genioglossus medialis acts to protract the entire tongue, while the genioglossus lateralis is primarily a protractor of the posterior limbs of the tongue.

The *branchiohyoideus* of *Ctenosaura* extends from a broad origin on the ceratohyal to a narrower insertion on the more distal portion of the first ceratobranchial.

The *mandibulohyoideus* (geniohyoideus of Camp and most authors, ceratomandibularis of Langebartel, 1968) of *Ctenosaura* interdigitates at its mandibular attachment with the intermandibularis anterior, as noted above in the discussion of the latter muscle. Oelrich (1956) recognizes three parts of this muscle in *Ctenosaura*: his mandibulohyoideus I runs from the first ceratobranchial to the lower jaw, interdigitating with the intermandibularis; his mandibulohyoideus II from the medial end of the first ceratobranchial to the median raphe just beneath the tongue and dorsal to the intermandibularis is here regarded as the homolog of Gnanamuthu's (1937) "inner hyoglossus," discussed above; Oelrich's mandibulohyoideus III runs from the middle of the lower jaw to the middle of the ceratohyal. Gnanamuthu (1937) found a muscle in *Anolis* similar to the mandibulohyoideus III of *Ctenosaura* and gave this muscle the name "genioceratoideus" (but that name is used here for a muscle in *Varanus* that appears to be derived from a splitting of the genioglossus lateralis). Gnanamuthu failed to find a mandibulohyoideus III in the other lizards he examined (a gecko, a skink, a lacertid, a chameleon, and three agamids). In *Varanus* there is a somewhat similar muscle, but much more posteriorly placed (here called the prearticulohyoideus; see discussion of *varanus* below). The mandibulohyoideus III may be an iguanid specialization.

In *Ctenosaura* the *sternohyoideus* (as defined by Oelrich) arises from the interclavicle near the midline and extends forward to form two quite distinct insertions: (1) a more lateral insertion (the sternothyroideus of Camp, 1923 and other authors) along the posteromedial face of the first ceratobranchial; and (2) a more medial insertion (the sternohyoideus proper of most authors) on the second ceratobranchial. The *omohyoideus*, from the clavicle, adjacent lateral process of the interclavicle, and suprascapula, lies superficial to the sternohyoideus and inserts on the first ceratobranchial, immediately superficial to the "sternothyroideus" portion of the sternohyoideus. The medial edge of the omohyoideus is not sharply delimited from the lateral edge of the "sternohyoideus proper," and thus, although the omohyoideus and sternohyoideus are sharply distinct as, respectively, superficial and deep muscles at their insertion on the first ceratobranchial, they are continuous near the midline in the region of the second ceratobranchial (Camp, 1923 recognized the sternothyroideus as distinct, but considered the omohyoideus and sternohyoideus proper as a single, more superficial muscle under the name sternohyoideus). The sternohyoideus-omohyoideus complex retracts the tongue, including its posterior limbs, and is largely responsible for the tamping action of the tongue in swallowing.

THE CHEWING STAGE WITH RETRACTILE FORE-TONGUE

The Anguimorpha are set apart from the rest of living lizards by an absolutely diagnostic feature of the tongue; the foretongue is retractile within the hind-tongue at a *zone of invagination* just anterior to the attachment of the genioglossus medialis muscles to the hind-tongue (Fig. 3). This feature is found in all living members of the Anguimorpha and has been seen nowhere else among lizards. It is not to be confused with the ability to retract the base of the hindtongue into a pocket of the buccal floor beneath the larynx seen in chamaeleonids and in *Tupinambis* and related Tejidae, at least to a slight degree, and seen in some Anguimorpha in addition to the invaginability of the foretongue within the hind-tongue. The following families of living lizards belong to the Anguimorpha, as attested by their tongue structure: Anguidae, Xenosauridae (including *Shinisaurus*), Anniellidae, Helodermatidae, Varanidae, and Lanthanotidae. In addition to the living families, the Cretaceous families Aigialosauridae, Mosasauridae,.and Dolichosauridae are referred to the Anguimorpha on osteological evidence, although nothing can be observed of their tongue structure.

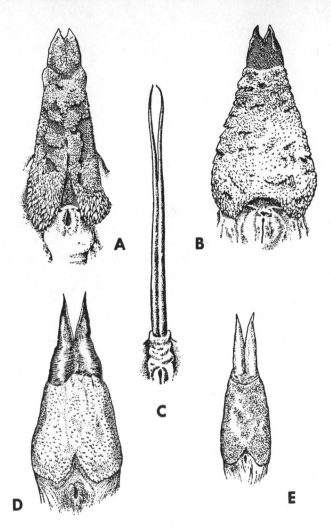

Fig. 3. Tongues, dorsal view, of some representative Anguimorphan lizards. A, Gerrhonotus multicarinatus *(Anguidae); B,* Shinisaurus crocodilurus *(Xenosauridae); C,* Varanus monitor *(=V.* bengalensis*), Varanidae; D,* Heloderma suspectum, *Helodermatidae; E,* Lanthanotus borneensis, Lanthanotidae *(From McDowell and Bogert, 1954)*

Among Anguimorpha, the anguoids (Anguidae, Xenosauridae, and Anniellidae) seem the most like nonanguimorphan lizards and, presumably, the most primitive. The tongue complex of the anguoids differs from that of nonanguimorphans primarily in: (1) the presence of a geniomyoideus muscle; and (2) the development of a zone of invagination between the fore- and hind-tongue. This latter feature is conventionally described as "foretongue retractile within the hind-tongue," but such description lays a false emphasis and might give the false impression that the anguoids are better equipped than nonanguimorphs for drawing the tongue backward into the oral cavity. In its resting, unextended state, the foretongue of an anguoid lies partially ensheathed in the hind-tongue, but its tip is no farther back in the mouth than is that of a non-anguimorphan lizard. A more accurate description of the anguoid tongue would be to say that a considerable amount of slack has been incorporated within it between fore- and hind-tongue, permitting increased extension.

The separation of foretongue from hind-tongue by a zone of invagination may have an additional functional value: allowing the frictional surface, borne mainly by the hind-tongue, to be drawn forward independently of the entire tongue when the tongue is depressed in the floor of the mouth by food and protraction of the entire tongue would be difficult or impossible. Frazzetta (1962) has recorded the movements of the jaws and tongue in the anguoid *Gerrhonotus coeruleus* feeding on mealworms and adult beetles. In the swallowing procedure, "the prey . . . is grasped in the mouth while the tongue . . . is slid forward beneath it." Then the lower jaw is depressed and the muzzle elevated while "the tongue pulls the prey upward and backward to disengage it from the mandibular teeth and to bring it further back into the mouth." The tongue then slides posteriorly past the prey, on which the mouth is closed. This is followed by a slow, hard bite, and then the jaws relax but do not gape. The jaws then open wider (to judge from the figure) and "the tongue is now slid forward beneath the prey, and the cycle is repeated." Frazzetta's figures, taken from tracings of cinema frames, show that forward motion of the bulge of the tongue is not accompanied by any projection of the tip.

The anguid *Gerrhonotus (Barisia) gadovi* (AMNH 98008) serves as an example of this stage in the evolution of the tongue complex.

The invaginable foretongue is narrower than in *Ctenosaura* and is quite distinctly forked, rather than merely nicked terminally, but it is similar to that of *Ctenosaura* in having smooth pallets confined to the ventral surface of the tips, with the papillose frictional surface covering the dorsal aspect. Other anguids, *Xenosaurus*, and *Shinisaurus* are similar, but in *Anniella* the dorsal surface of the foretongue is smooth or longitudinally wrinkled (Coe and Kunkel, 1907).

The hind-tongue is essentially as in *Ctenosaura*, and has large posterior limbs that flank the larynx and have broadly free lateral and posterior borders. The frictional surface is made up of soft and densely crowded papillae, much longer than those of the foretongue and particularly long on the posterior limbs. Other Anguidae, Xenosauridae, and *Anniella* are similar.

The ectochoanal fold (Fig. 4) is essentially as in *Ctenosaura*, but the fenestra vomeronasalis externa is a longitudinal, rather than transverse slit and the vomerine raphe is broader anteriorly and forms a triangular mound that fits the conspicuous triangular cleft in the tip of the tongue.

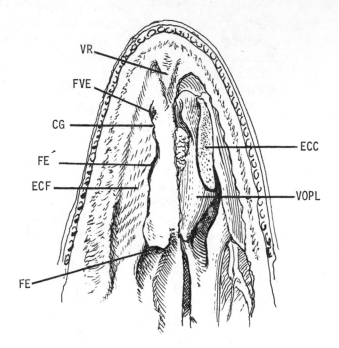

Fig. 4. Superficial palate of Gerrhonotus *(Barisia)* gadovi *AMNH 98008 with mucosa removed on reader's right. For abbreviations, see pp. 270-272.*

The hyobranchial skeleton is essentially as in *Ctenosaura*, but the second branchial arch is absent. In *Gerrhonotus* the anteriormost element of the hyoid arch is extended anterolateral to its articulation with the ceratohyal as a short process receiving some of the fibers of the genioglossus lateralis muscle, an unusual feature, and the long ceratohyal has a strong outwardly and dorsally directed flange at its middle; this flange lies opposite the hyoid attachment of the branchiohyoideus muscle but does not connect with any muscle from the lower jaw (unlike *Ctenosaura*, *Gerrhonotus* has no muscles running from the lower jaw to the ceratohyal). Besides loss of the second branchial arch, in a number of anguoids the hyoid arch is reduced, and as noted above (p. 197) this seems to be more associated with ear structure than with the structure of the tongue. Although the first branchial arch of *Gerrhonotus* is much like that of *Ctenosaura*, the dorsal process is absent in some Anguidae (*Anguis, Ophisaurus*) and in Xenosauridae; in *Anniella* the arch is represented only by a short ceratobranchial rod extending back from the lateral extremity of the body of the hyoid (Cope, 1900).

The anguoid throat musculature (Fig. 5) differs from that of nonanguimorphans in the presence of a *geniomyoideus* muscle (Camp, 1923). In *Gerrhonotus* this muscle originates at the symphysis region, anterior and *medial* to the origin

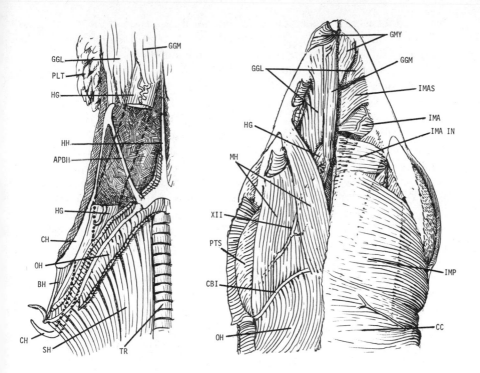

Fig. 5. Throat muscles of Gerrhonotus *(Barisia)* gadovi *AMNH 98008. The left-hand figure shows the deepest muscles and is enlarged in comparison to the right-hand figure; in the right-hand figure, the most superficial muscles have been removed on the reader's left side. For abbreviations see pp. 270-272.*

of the genioglossus medialis, and inserts on the skin of the anterior interramal region; the two genioglossus medialis muscles are thus separated from each other anteriorly by the geniomyoideus. In the vast majority of nonanguimorphan lizards, there is no suggestion of a muscle from the region of the mandibular symphysis to the skin of the throat; the only muscles in the symphysial region are the anterior ends of the paired genioglossi mediales, which are nearly or quite in contact. To judge from the figures and descriptions given by Camp (1923) and Gnanamuthu (1937), the exceptions to this are the following: (1) Gekkota, including Pygopodidae, and also some Agamidae and Chamaeleonidae have a broad intermandibularis anterior that extends forward to insert on the symphysial region, thus forming a group of diagonal fibers running forward and mediad from the lower jaw (lateral and posterior to the origin of the genioglossus medialis) to the symphysis; (2) *Amphisbaena* has a very powerful cervicomandibularis that runs forward, superficial to the throat muscles, to insert on the symphysis; and (3) in *Klauberina riversiana* (=*Xantusia riversiana* of Camp, 1923) and perhaps in other Xantusiidae, a few fibers from the body of the genioglossus run to the skin of the anterior throat. Even in these exceptions, no muscle fibers actually extend between the two genioglossi mediales and the anterior portions of the latter are in contact on the midline.

At its insertion, the geniomyoideus of *Gerrhonotus* is merged with the insertion of a cutaneous slip of the intermandibularis anterior, but this latter muscle slip originates from the lower jaw just posterior and lateral to the origin of the genioglossus medialis, and so is separated at its origin from the geniomyoideus by the origin of the genioglossus medialis. It is thus quite possible that the geniomyoideus is a specialized anteromedial extension of the intermandibularis (indeed, Langebartel, 1968 does not appear to differentiate between the geniomyoideus and intermandibularis anterior in *Anniella*); however, Camp (1923) may well be correct in regarding the geniomyoideus as a cutaneous slip of the genioglossus medialis. If Camp's interpretation is correct, then the geniomyoideus of anguoids would correspond to the most medial fibers of the genioglossus of nonanguimorphan lizards—that is, to the fibers inserting on the most anterior part of the tongue in nonanguimorphans. This would suggest that the geniomyoideus, which is characteristic of Anguimorpha, has been formed by further freeing of the foretongue to allow its greater retractility and permit its characteristic invagination within the hind-tongue. Haas (1960) has described a specimen of the anguoid *Xenosaurus grandis* (Family Xenosauridae) with the geniomyoideus arising from a tendinous inscription on the ventromedial surface of the genioglossus medialis, rather than from the mandible; this is reconcilable with derivation of the geniomyoideus from the intermandibularis, but fits better with a derivation from the genioglossus. All anguoids, including *Shinisaurus* (Haas, 1960), have a geniomyoideus.

The *intermandibularis* of *Gerrhonotus* is relatively simple and is divided into four portions: (1) the *intermandibularis anterior, superficial* portion, the most anterior portion, inserting with the geniomyoideus on the skin of the anterior interramal region; (2) the *intermandibularis anterior, principal portion*, entirely deep to the mandibulohyoideus and extending across the throat from jaw to jaw; (3) a narrow *intermandibularis anterior, interdigitating portion*, that passes between the two anterior heads of the mandibulohyoideus; and (4) a very broad but very thin *intermandibularis posterior*, entirely superficial to the mandibulohyoideus.

The thin *constrictor colli* of *Gerrhonotus* does not differ particularly from that of most nonanguimorphan lizards.

The *genioglossus medialis* of *Gerrhonotus* is narrower than that of *Ctenosaura* and is quite sharply set off from the genioglossus lateralis, but otherwise presents no notable difference. The *genioglossus lateralis* of *Gerrhonotus* gives off some delicate fibers to the lateral part of the hind-tongue, but most of the muscle inserts on the buccal floor beneath the root of the posterior limb of the tongue (probably the chief action of the muscle in protraction of the posterior limb of the tongue). At least in *G. gadovi*, a few fibers of the genioglossus lateralis attach to the hyoid arch (*sensu stricto*) at the angulation between the ceratohyal and the anterior process of the body of the hyoid.

The *hyoglossus* of *Gerrhonotus* presents no special peculiarities; it arises from the distal (lateralmost) end of the first ceratobranchial.

The *branchiohyoideus* of *Gerrhonotus* is similar to that of *Ctenosaura*, but in *Anniella* is absent, in accord with the absence of the hyoid arch (Langebartel, 1968).

The *mandibulohyoideus* of *Gerrhonotus* is relatively simple, with two mandibular insertions that interdigitate with the intermandibularis. To judge from Camp (1923), Haas (1960; *Xenosaurus* and *Shinisaurus*), and Langebartel (1968; *Anniella*), this simplicity of the mandibulohyoideus is a general feature of the Anguoidea.

The omohyoideus-sternohyoideus complex of *Gerrhonotus* is much as in *Ctenosaura*.

THE FRICTIONAL GULPING STAGE

This stage, represented by *Heloderma* and *Lanthanotus*, is advanced beyond the anguoids largely in the reduction of the usefulness of the tongue for swallowing small fragments and the increased ability to swallow rather large objects whole. The posterior limbs of the tongue are greatly reduced, without a free posterior edge to push food fragments down the gullet.

This reduction of the posterior limbs of the tongue characterizes all living Platynota (although it is not unique to them), and presumably obtained in the fossil platynotan families, as well. This reduction of the posterior limbs of the tongue is in accord with the other peculiarities of the group, such as an intramandibular hinge that permits distending the gape and the pointed and prehensile (rather than edged and cutting) teeth (secondarily crushing in one mosasaur and some species of *Varanus*), peculiarities that seem to increase the ability to swallow large prey whole, without chewing or breaking up the food.

Reduction of the posterior limbs of the tongue also permits the larynx to slide forward over the base of the tongue, useful in clearing the larynx away from the opening of the gullet.

The two genera showing this stage of modification of the tongue for feeding differ considerably, partly in the throat muscles, but most particularly in the modification of the foretongue for sensory purposes as a sample-collector for Jacobson's organ.

Heloderma

(The following account is based mainly on AMNH 74436, 74474, and 74475, all *H. suspectum* from Pima County, Arizona, and a specimen in the author's collection without locality.)

The foretongue of *Heloderma* (Fig. 6) is somewhat more deeply forked than in

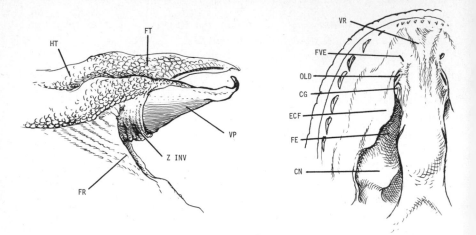

Fig. 6. Heloderma suspectum. *Left, tip of retracted tongue seen from right side; right, superficial palate. For abbreviations see pp. 270-272.*

Anguoidea, but otherwise very similar to that of *Gerrhonotus,* with a pair of ventral pallets that curve up onto the medial and lateral edges of the tines, but dorsally with a frictional surface of flattened papillae. When retracted and depressed the foretongue of *Heloderma* rests with these ventral pallets immediately dorsal to the sublingual plicae, presumably receiving from the plicae the secretion of the sublingual glands. The low degree of specialization of the tongue for serving Jacobson's organ does not indicate lack of importance for this function, since Bogert and Martín del Campo (1956) have presented observations indicating that the organ of Jacobson and tongue are important in food location in this genus. Both species of *Heloderma* (my own observation of captive specimens in the American Museum of Natural History) lap broken eggs with their tongues, and the presence of a frictional surface on the entire dorsal aspect of the foretongue is probably an important adaptation for lapping.

The posterior limbs of the tongue are greatly reduced, without free posterior edge, but the entire lateral edge of the hind-tongue is free. The rear of the hind-tongue is girdled by an unspecialized fold of the oral mucosa, with the larynx lying on the midline of this fold. The lateral portion of this mucosal fold overlies the angulation between the ceratohyal and the anterior process of the body of the hyoid. Since this angulation of the hyoid arch and the adjacent oral mucosa receive the insertion of the genioglossus lateralis, the pull of that muscle draws forward the larynx-bearing fold of mucosa, causing it to slide forward over the base of the tongue as a facultative sheath for the extreme rear of the tongue.

The frictional surface of the tongue of *Heloderma* is much like that of *Gerrhonotus* but is somewhat rougher, since the tips of the papillae are hard, presumably keratinized. Running a finger tip over the surface of the tongue readily demonstrates that the frictional resistance offered by the tongue papillae is considerably greater to an anteriorly directed stroke than to a stroke towards the gullet. Because of the thick frictional surface on the dorsal aspect of the tongue in *Heloderma*, the cross-folds marking the *zone of invagination* of the foretongue within the hind-tongue are largely confined to the ventral surface of the tongue, as in *Gerrhonotus*.

The *ectochoanal fold* of *Heloderma* (Fig. 6) is, by itself, essentially as in *Gerrhonotus*, but in *Heloderma* the fold touches the vomerine region only anteriorly, in the neighborhood of the anterior extremity of the vomer. This appears to be the result of an almost unique (but shared with *Varanus*) enlargement of the internal naris (fenestra exochoanalis), which is a broad oval opening that leaves the tip of the nasal concha fully exposed to palatal view. This choanal enlargement is at the expense of the vomer, which is narrow and does not underarch the choanal passage. The mucosa overlying the vomer is quite flat and the *fenestra vomeronasalis externa* opens onto a broad flat surface. The *opening* of the *lachrymal duct* is a long diagonal slit in normal position, just deep (dorsal) to the anterior end of the ectochoanal fold; the opening of the lachrymal duct is more broadly separated from the fenestra vomeronasalis externa than it is in *Gerrhonotus*.

The *body of the hyoid* is essentially as in *Gerrhonotus*, but the tip of the hypohyal process (which runs for the entire length of the hind-tongue) is only loosely bound to the muscles of the tongue. The hyoid arch is much as in *Gerrhonotus*, but with more gentle angulation between the ceratohyal and anterior process of the body of the hyoid, without a lateral flange on the ceratohyal, and with the dorsal process of the hyoid arch represented only by an outward curvature of the posterior end of the ceratohyal. The *first ceratobranchial* of *Heloderma* probably lacks a true dorsal process, for although the long ossified portion of the first ceratobranchial is continued distally by cartilage (as figured by Cope, 1900), this cartilaginous tip is not sharply angulated from the ossified portion. Although Camp (1923) lists *Heloderma* as having a free epibranchial II (=dorsal process of second ceratobranchial), neither Cope (1900) nor I have found any trace of a *second branchial arch* in *Heloderma suspectum*. I have never observed *Heloderma* to close the ear opening, and the heavy osteoderms in the skin behind the tympanic membrane are neither overlapped (so that they might slide over one another) nor separated by any considerable amount of soft tissue, so that it is unlikely that much deformation of the tissue around the ear opening is possible.

The *geniomyoideus* of *Heloderma* (Fig. 7) is even larger than in *Gerrhonotus*. The *intermandibularis* of *Heloderma* differs from that of anguoids in having three or four interdigitating portions of the intermandibularis anterior, passing between a corresponding number of slips of the mandibulohyoideus (by Camp's [1923] interpretation, *Heloderma* would be more primitive than any known

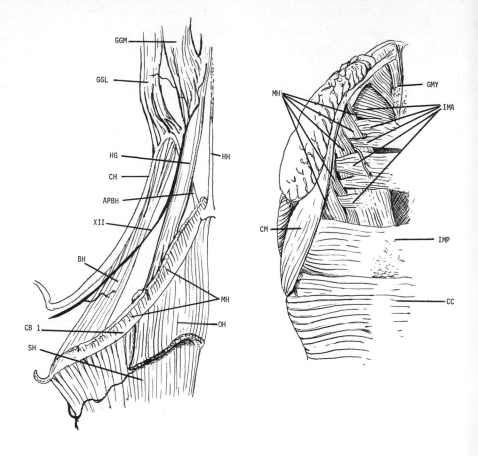

Fig. 7. Heloderma suspectum *AMNH 74475. Left hand, deep throat muscles; right hand, more superficial muscles (not to same scale). For abbreviations, see pp. 270-272.*

anguoid in this feature; indeed, more primitive than any other living Anguimorpha).

The *constrictor colli* of *Heloderma* is unusual in its thickness, forming a fleshy girdle around the neck with several layers of fibers, rather than the usual semitransparent muscle with a single layer of fibers. This probably reflects an increased importance as a swallowing muscle, serving to move a large food mass down the throat by a peristalsis-like action. The *cervicomandibularis* of *Heloderma* is better developed than in anguoids and, though slender, is fleshy for most of its length and is inserted on the ventral border of the lower jaw, probably assisting in broad gaping of the jaws.

The *genioglossus medialis* is as in *Gerrhonotus*, but the *genioglossus lateralis* of *Heloderma* differs from that of *Gerrhonotus* in that most of its fibers attach to the hyoid arch, at the flexure of the ceratohyal into the anterior process of the body of the hyoid, with only a minority of the fibers inserted onto the buccal floor. As noted above, the action of this muscle in *Heloderma* would seem to be drawing the fold of oral mucosa bearing the larynx forward over the base of the tongue. The *hyoglossus* is as in *Gerrhonotus*, and the *branchiohyoideus* is also similar to that of *Gerrhonotus*, but has a longer attachment along the hyoid arch. The *mandibulohyoideus* is as in *Gerrhonotus*, but with more interdigitations with the intermandibularis. The *omohyoideus-sternohyoideus* complex is as in *Gerrhonotus*.

Lanthanotus

The account of the tongue of *Lanthanotus* given by McDowell and Bogert (1954) is inaccurate in several details, most notably the failure to report the existence of well-developed, although cartilaginous, ceratohyals. The following account is based mainly on dissection of AMNH 87375, a female that died in the New York Zoological Park.

The foretongue (Fig. 8) is quite unlike that of the lizards described above in having a uniform, rather hard and smooth surface, both ventrally and dorsally, with a single row of papillae on each side from the level of the posterior end of the terminal cleft to the level of the zone of invagination. Just ventral to this row of papillae there is an obscure longitudinal groove. The foretongue is parallel-sided and rather narrow, with relatively slender terminal tines. In relaxed and retracted position, the foretongue lies in the floor of the mouth *between* the sublingual plicae, rather than on top of them, and probably the entire foretongue is bathed in the secretion of the sublingual glands.[1]

The hind-tongue shows even more reduction of the posterior limbs than does that of *Heloderma*, in that not only is there no free posterior edge, but the freedom of the lateral edge is considerably reduced. The hind-tongue appears to be but a raised and papillose pad on the floor of the mouth, with but little involution of the oral mucosa beneath its lateral edges except near its rear, where lateral lappets represent the posterior limbs of the tongue of most lizards. The *frictional surface* is confined to the hind-tongue and is more like that of anguids than that of *Heloderma* in being formed of soft and uncornified papillae. The softer texture of these papillae and the less freely movable tongue in *Lanthanotus* suggest that in this genus the tongue is less important than it is in *Heloderma* as an aid to swallowing, or else is used to swallow less bulky or less

[1] Since the above was written, the courtesy of Dr. W. King and Mr. P. Brazaitis has permitted me to observe a live *Lanthanotus* in the New York Zoological Society collection. The fore-tongue, which appeared white under a red light simulating darkness, was frequently extended and kept extruded for several seconds, as in snakes and *Varanus*, rather than flicked in and out as in amphisbaenids and *Tupinambis*, for example. Again as in snakes and *Varanus*, the tines were held in a divergent Y, rather than parallel as in amphisbaenids and *Tupinambis*. I did not observe any up-and-down waggling of the tongue such as seen in *Varanus* and most snakes.

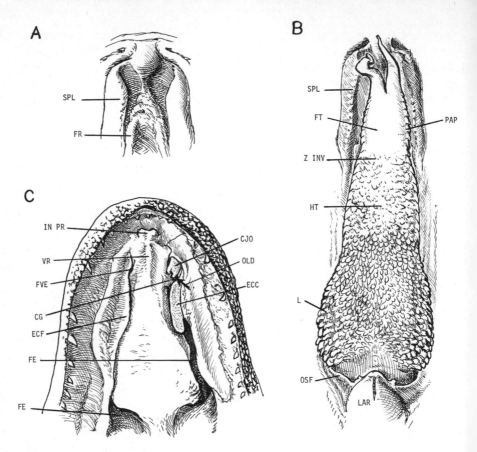

Fig. 8. Lanthanotus borneensis *(AMNH 87375), not to same scale. A, anterior part of floor of mouth; B, the tongue, dorsal aspect; C, superficial palate, with mucosa scraped away on reader's right. Abbreviations: OLD, arrow pointing to the nearly concealed opening of the (longer of two?) lachrymal duct(s); others on pp. 270-272.*

resistent food; unfortunately, nothing is known of the feeding habits in the wild of *Lanthanotus.*

The larynx-bearing fold of oral mucosa at the rear of the tongue is free to move forward over the base of the tongue as in *Heloderma*, forming a short facultative sheath for the base of the tongue. The mechanism for this facultative sheathing in *Lanthanotus* is as in *Heloderma*: the lateral ends of the larynx-bearing fold overlie the angulation between the anterior process of the body of the hyoid and the ceratohyal that is drawn forward by the genioglossus lateralis (Fig. 9).

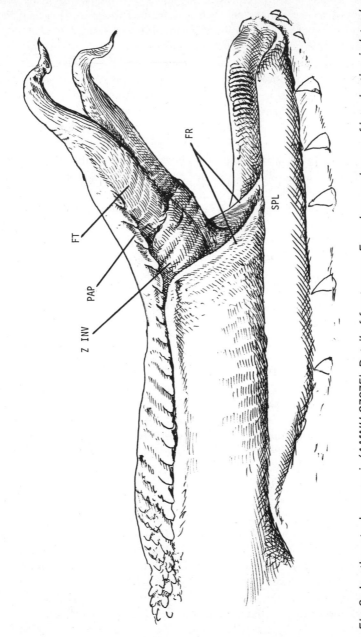

Fig. 9. Lanthanotus borneensis *(AMNH 87375), Detail of foretongue, Frenulum, and zone of invagination in lateral view. For abbreviations see pp. 270-272.*

The *ectochoanal fold* is essentially as in *Gerrhonotus,* and the vomer is not narrowed or the choana enlarged as it is in *Heloderma.* However, the anterior end of the ectochoanal fold of *Lanthanotus* is immediately adjacent to the *fenestra vomeronasalis externa*, a departure from all the lizards described above. *Lanthanotus* has two lachrymal foramina, as in *Varanus* but no other lizard (McDowell and Bogert, 1954), and presumably *Lanthanotus* possesses two *lachrymal ducts*, as in *Varanus.* Because dissection for a *shorter lachrymal duct* would involve extensive destruction of the snouth, such dissection was not attempted, and the only duct observed probably corresponds to the *longer lachrymal duct* of *Varanus.* The opening of this duct in *Lanthanotus* differs from that of the other lizards described above not only in its close approximation to the fenestra vomeronasalis externa but also in its form, as a tiny circular pore rather than a long slit.

The fenestra vomeronasalis externa opens into a narrow and groove-like depression, bounded laterally by the ectochoanal fold and lateral palatine stripe, and medially by the vomerine raphe. This groove-like depression is a nearly perfect mold of the dorsal aspect of the narrow tine of the foretongue; that the region of the fenestra vomeronasalis externa should fit the dorsal aspect of the tine of the tongue suggests that the tongue tip is not doubled over when it is wiped against the fenestra and that the dorsal surface of the tine of the tongue is useful as a sampler for Jacobson's organ.

The *body of the hyoid* of *Lanthanotus* is essentially as in *Heloderma* but has a shorter median hypohyal process that extends only through the posterior half of the hind-tongue, rather than through most of the length of the hind-tongue. The *hyoid arch* is much as in *Heloderma*, but the (cartilaginous) ceratohyal has an abtuse lateral process near its middle more as in *Gerrhonotus.* The tip of ceratohyal is quite free of the paroccipital process and there is no suggestion of a dorsal process (epihyal). The *first ceratobranchial* is bony for most of its length but ends in a cartilaginous portion that is in loose ligamentous connection with the paroccipital region of the skull. McDowell and Bogert (1954) interpreted the cartilaginous distal end as a first epibranchial (dorsal process of first branchial arch), but there is no angulation between the bony and cartilaginous parts *in situ*, and the distal cartilaginous end bears part of the origin of the mandibulohyoideus and most of the attachment of the branchiohyoideus, and much of the insertion of the sternohyoideus; these muscle attachments would indicate the cartilaginous portion is a continuation of the ceratobranchial rather than a dorsal process (epibranchial) element. There is no indication of a *second branchial arch.*

By the interpretation presented here, *Lanthanotus* totally lacks dorsal processes of the hyobranchial arches. This would be in keeping with the nature of the middle ear, in which the thick tympanic membrane is undifferentiated from the skin and not at all sunk inward, so that it is extremely unlikely that the ear is closed over (see McDowell, 1967 for an account of the middle ear).

The *geniomyoideus* (Fig. 10) is about as in *Heloderma*, but the diagonal fiber direction of the muscle in *Lanthanotus* is more suggestive of a specialized portion of the intermandibularis than suggestive of a part of the genioglossus. Indeed, the *superficial group of fibers of the intermandibularis anterior* is very closely associated at its insertion with the geniomyoideus, but has a more transverse direction of fibers. The superficial group is not clearly distinguishable from the principal (deep) portion of the intermandibularis anterior, and both arise from the lower jaw anterior to the intramandibular hinge, which in this genus is clearly defined as a vertical line of contact between the splenial and angular bones. There is a single interdigitating portion of the intermandibularis weakly divided into an anterior and a posterior slip. The intermandibularis posterior is broad but thin, arising from the entire ventral border of the lower jaw behind the intramandibular hinge, and inserting onto the median raphe of the throat; it nearly covers the interdigitating part of the intermandibularis anterior.

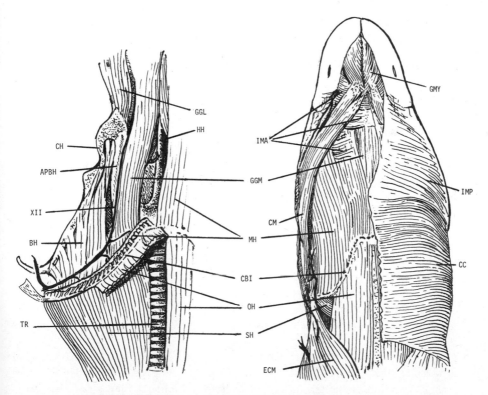

Fig. 10. Lanthanotus borneensis *(AMNH 87375). Left-hand sketch, the deep throat muscles; right-hand sketch, the more superficial muscles, with the most superficial muscles removed on reader's left. For abbreviations see pp. 270-272.*

It should be noted that in number of distinguishible portions separated by other muscles, the intermandibularis of *Lanthanotus* is more like that of *Gerrhonotus* than like that of *Heloderma*, and the *constrictor colli* of *Lanthanotus*, unlike the muscle of *Heloderma*, is very thin.

The *cervicomandibularis* of *Lanthanotus* is more complex than that of *Heloderma*. It arises high on the side of the neck, deep to the constrictor colli, and passes forward (deep to the intermandibularis posterior) to divide into three portions: (1) a lateral head inserted on the inner side of the rear of the dentary; (2) a middle head inserted on the surface of the rear of the geniomyoideus; (3) a medialmost head, inserted on the skin at the rear of the mental groove. Such a muscle could not only assist in wide gaping of the jaws, but could depress the anterior floor of the mouth, as well.

The *genioglossus medialis* of *Lanthanotus* is as in *Heloderma* and *Gerrhonotus*, but at its posterior attachment to the hyoglossus the two muscles blend much more smoothly than in the other lizards examined. The *genioglossus lateralis* of *Lanthanotus* is as in *Heloderma*, except that the attachment is entirely to the hyoid arch and there are no fibers to the buccal floor.

The *hyoglossus* of *Lanthanotus* is peculiar in the small degree of divergence of its posterior attachments, partly to the body of the hyoid and partly to the medial (anterior) end of the first ceratobranchial, medial and anterior to the attachment of the *branchiohyoideus*. The latter muscle in *Lanthanotus* does not differ appreciably from that of *Heloderma*, but because the ceratohyal is cartilaginous and pliable, the action of the branchiohyoideus is probably more to deform the hyoid arch than to approximate the hyoid and first branchial arches.

The *mandibulohyoideus* of *Lanthanotus* is like that of *Gerrhonotus* in that it is divided anteriorly into two slips, with an interdigitating portion of the intermandibularis anterior passing between them. In *Lanthanotus* the division of the mandibulohyoideus seems an adjustment to the intramandibular hinge (a hinge absent in *Gerrhonotus*), with the more anterior and medial slip of the mandibulohyoideus inserting on the jaw anterior to the hinge, the more posterior and lateral slip inserting on the jaw behind the hinge. Since the interdigitating portion of the intermandibularis anterior is divided into adjacent anterior and posterior slips, it is possible that the ancestor of *Lanthanotus* had a third, middle slip of the mandibulohyoideus passing between the two interdigitating intermandibularis slips, and that this (hypothetical) middle slip of the mandibulohyoideus has been lost fairly recently.

The *omohyoideus* and *sternohyoideus* of *Lanthanotus* are as in *Gerrhonotus* and *Heloderma*.

In the foretongue that is smooth except for a lateral fringe of papillae, and which sits between (rather than upon) the sublingual plicae, and also in the close approximation of the opening of the lachrymal duct to the fenestra vomeronasalis externa, *Lanthanotus* makes a closer approach to the condition seen in snakes than do the other lizards described above.

THE NONLINGUAL GULPING STAGE

Although in some particulars, mainly involving the throat muscles and hyobranchial skeleton, *Varanus* appears to represent a side-line rather than a stage in direct line of evolution of the tongue-complex of snakes, *Varanus* is snake-like in that the tongue has lost all swallowing function, as might be guessed from the absence of posterior limbs and of frictional surface, and as observed directly by Frazzetta (1962). The function of gathering particles for Jacobson's organ is retained, and the tongue has become considerably modified as a wholly sensory structure. Significantly, the tongue of *Varanus* is more snake-like than is that of any other lizard; so similar to that of snakes, in fact, that the excised tongue of *Varanus* is difficult to distinguish from that of a snake (in spite of some statements to the contrary, this cannot be said of any other known lizard).

The following account of *Varanus* is based on dissection of *V. bengalensis* (=*V. monitor*) AMNH 75321 and *V. varius* AMNH 27306, and examination without dissection of *V. dumerili* AMNH 61778, *V. tristis* AMNH 59956, *V. salvadori* AMNH 59932, and *V. prasinus* AMNH 59053. A very extensive description of the tongue, throat muscles, and hyobranchium of *V. monitor* has been given by Sondhi (1958).

Although it is much longer and more deeply cleft than that of *Lanthanotus*, the *foretongue* of *Varanus* (Fig. 11) is basically quite similar in having a uniformly hard and smooth surface and in resting between the sublingual plicae, so that probably its entire surface is bathed in the secretion of the sublingual glands. The foretongue of *Varanus* is even smoother than that of *Lanthanotus* and lacks even the reduced lateral fringe of papillae found in the latter genus.

Although it is well known that the tongue of *Varanus* is partially retractile into a sheath at its base, it does not seem to have been made clear in previous descriptions that the tongue of *Varanus* actually has two sheaths, an *inner sheathing fold* and an *outer sheathing fold*. The single sheath referred to in most general accounts of *Varanus* is the outer sheathing fold, but the sheath figured and described by Sondhi (1958) is the inner sheathing fold.

The *outer sheathing fold* is formed by the mucosa of the floor of the buccal cavity, and carries the larynx. The anterior and ventral ends of this mucosal fold are directly behind the sublingual plicae, and the relationships of the external sheath are essentially those of the larynx-bearing fold at the base of the tongue of *Heloderma* and *Lanthanotus*. However, in *Varanus* the ceratohyals are not intimately associated with this sheath, but folded over (sometimes crossing one another) on the ventral surface of the throat musculature when the throat is relaxed and unexpanded. Unlike the facultative sheath formed by the larynx-bearing fold in *Heloderma* and *Lanthanotus,* the outer sheathing fold of *Varanus* is readily perceived whatever the degree of extension of the tongue.

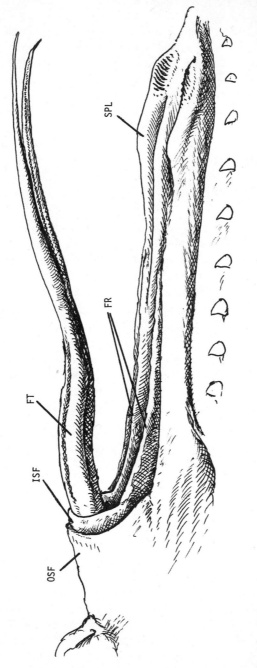

Fig. 11. Varanus bengalensis (AMNH 75321), tongue and floor of the mouth, lateral view. For abbreviations see pp. 270-272.

The *inner sheathing fold* is most clearly marked when the tongue is retracted; when the tongue is fully extended, this inner sheath is not at all distinguished from the surface of the tongue. This sheath is a thin and transparent membrane except for the genioglossus medialis muscles, which are constituents of the inner sheathing fold. Ventrally, the inner sheath is attached to the posterior termination of a median ridge on the floor of the mouth that runs between the sublingual plicae. The relations of the inner sheathing fold are, thus, those of the frenulum of *Heloderma* and *Lanthanotus*. However, the inner sheathing fold of *Varanus* forms a fold across the dorsal surface of the tongue, completely surrounding the posterior portions of the hyoglossus muscles, and is partly made up of the posterior ends of the genioglossus medialis muscles. This would indicate that the inner sheathing fold of the *Varanus* tongue is the homolog not only of the frenulum of *Heloderma* and *Lanthanotus*, but of the hind-tongue of these latter two genera, as well.

It appears, then, that in *Varanus* the *hind-tongue* has completely lost a frictional surface and is totally without posterior limbs, even as lateral lappets. That the inner sheathing fold is not visibly distinct on the fully protruded tongue of *Varanus* is in keeping with an homology of the inner sheathing fold with the hind-tongue. When the anguimorphan tongue is fully protruded, the foretongue and hind-tongue appear quite continuous, and it is only when the tongue is retracted that transverse folds set the two portions of the tongue apart, and show that the foretongue invaginates within the hind-tongue; in this facility, *Varanus* does not differ qualitatively from other Anguimorpha. The difference lies in the form of the hind-tongue, which is fleshy and with a frictional surface in most Anguimorpha, but is reduced to a mere membranous sheath for the foretongue in *Varanus*.

The circular furrow between the retracted foretongue and the surrounding inner sheathing fold of *Varanus* lies internal to the genioglossus medialis muscles and external to the hyoglossus muscles that form the core of the foretongue; thus, this circular furrow is morphologically anterior to the attachment of the genioglossus medialis to the hyoglossus and corresponds in its relations to the *zone of invagination* of the tongue of other Anguimorpha.

Sondhi (1958: p. 172) has noted that in *Varanus* the tip of the entoglossal (=hypohyal of Oelrich and present paper) does not lie between hyoglossus muscles in the flesh of the tongue, but instead enters the "tongue sheath" (=inner sheathing fold of present paper). This is the relationship to be expected if the inner sheathing fold represents the hind-tongue, and the entry of the tip of the hypohyal process into the inner sheathing fold of *Varanus* is strictly equivalent to the entry of the hypohyal process into the body of the hind-tongue in *Heloderma* and *Lanthanotus*, as well as other lizards.

Sondhi also found that only one distinct (paired) muscle exists in the tongue of *Varanus*, the hyoglossus; the various transverse and diagonal fibers, when traced backward and forward, can be seen to blend into the longitudinal hyoglossus. This description would probably fit the fore-tongue of *Heloderma* and *Lanthanotus*, and quite possibly the anterior tip of the tongue in quite a wide variety of lizards (compare, for example, Oelrich's [1956] account of the complex interweaving of hyoglossus fibers at the tip of the tongue of *Ctenosaura*). In both *Heloderma* and *Lanthanotus* the hind-tongue has a pulpy "cortex" of muscular tissue that seems to be continuous with the genioglossus. It is possible, therefore, that the simplicity of the musculature of the tongue in *Varanus* is the result of the great reduction of the hind-tongue.

The anterior portion of the superficial palate (i.e., the portion associated with Jacobson's organ) of *Varanus* (Fig. 12) is much as in *Lanthanotus*. The *fenestra vomeronasalis externa* lies at the anterior tip of the *ectochoanal fold*, and between the fenestra vomeronasalis externa and the vomerine raphe there is a long, narrow, and rather deep groove that extends well forward of the fenestra.

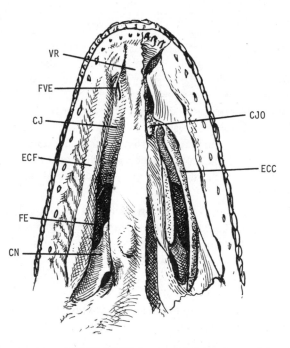

Fig. 12 Varanus varius *(AMNH 27306), superficial palate with mucosa scraped away on reader's right. For abbreviations see pp. 270-272.*

Bellairs (1949) does not describe the superficial palate of *Varanus* but his figure (4B) of a cross-section anterior to Jacobson's organ of a subadult *Varanus monitor* (=*V. bengalensis*) shows these grooves well, although they are unlabeled. From Bellairs's figure, it would appear that the epithelium in the groove is lower than elsewhere on the palatal surface.

Varanus has two lachrymal ducts (Bellairs, 1949), a feature probably true also of *Lanthanotus*, to judge from the dried skull, but otherwise known only in the fossil snake *Dinilysia*. The *shorter lachrymal duct* of *Varanus* opens into the choanal region in the neighborhood of the concha, but the *longer lachrymal duct* opens directly into the *fenestra vomeronasalis externa* (rather than immediately behind it as in *Lanthanotus*, or some distance behind it as in most lizards); this is as in most snakes (see discussion beyond), where the single lachrymal duct opens into the fenestra vomeronasalis externa. The shorter lachrymal duct retains the long and slit-like nature of its anterior orifice usual for the single anterior lachrymal orifice in most lizards. Very likely, the anteriormost (longer) lachrymal duct of *Varanus* and *Lanthanotus* has been developed as an accessory duct, required because the narrowness of the tongue-tips permits them to be placed in direct contact with the fenestra vomeronasalis externa without brushing against the choanal region; in the absence of a lachrymal duct opening in or immediately adjacent to the fenestra vomeronasalis externa the tongue-tip might be inserted in the organ of Jacobson with insufficient fluid to permit transfer of particles for sensation.

The choana of *Varanus* resembles that of *Heloderma* and differs from that of *Lanathanotus*, snakes, and most Squamata in general in being a large elliptical opening, directed downward between the maxilla and vomer for most of the posterior half of the snout-length, leaving much of the nasal concha exposed to palatal view.

Although the ectochoanal fold of *Varanus* is of about the same relative width as that of *Lanthanotus*, the narrow vomer of *Varanus* causes the ectochoanal fold to fail to reach the vomerine pad and, instead, to form merely a lateral pleat on the choanal margin. In *Varanus varius* AMNH 27306 the ectochoanal fold was supported by a tough tissue with essentially the form and position of the *ectochoanal cartilage* of *Lanthanotus*. Again as in *Lanthanotus*, the fenestra vomeronasalis externa was supported by a cartilage-like flap, here identified as the cartilage of Jacobson's organ. Bellairs (1949), working from serial sections, found similar cartilages in *V. monitor* (=*V. bengalensis*), but used a different terminology: what is here considered the cartilage of Jacobson's organ was termed the ectochoanal cartilage by Bellairs, while what is here considered the ectochoanal cartilage was termed by Bellairs, the "free posterior end of the lamina transversalis anterior." Pratt (1948), working with *V. bengalensis*, *V. niloticus*, and *V. salvator*, states that the ectochoanal cartilage is absent in *Varanus*.

The hyobranchial skeleton and its associated muscles have become quite complex in *Varanus*, principally as a result of modification of the ceratohyal to form a lever actively depressing the buccal floor and expanding the gullet (that is, expanding the gullet to receive large prey before the prey is introduced into the pharynx, rather than merely stretching in response to the pressure of prey in the pharynx). Live *Varanus* (my own observations are based mainly on *V. gouldi* captive in the American Museum of Natural History) can "puff out the throat" into a spacious receiving chamber for food (such as a whole white rat), and it is probably the peculiarly modified hyoid arch and its muscles which are responsible for this ability, although the precise functions of the individual skeletal and muscular elements is quite obscure.

Aside from the entry of the hypohyal process into the inner sheathing fold of the tongue, the *body of the hyoid* of *Varanus* is as in *Heloderma*, and even this difference really represents a modification of the hind-tongue to form the inner sheathing fold rather than a modification of the skeleton. The *hyoid arch*, however, is very peculiar and complex in *Varanus*, with an intrinsic musculature (running between the ceratohyal and the anterior process of the body of the hyoid) that is probably unique in lizards. The ceratohyal is ossified and is expanded anteriorly into a hook-like plate resembling an umbrella-handle. This ossified and expanded portion of the ceratohyal is joined to the anterior process of the body of the hyoid by a slender and folded cartilage, and when the throat is unexpanded the ossified portions of the ceratohyals lie across the throat (often across one another anteriorly), deep to the mandibulohyoideus musculature, in an inverted position (that is, with the surface homologous to the dorsal surface in other lizards facing ventrally). The ceratohyal has a lateral process as in *Gerrhonotus* and *Lanthanotus*, but the dorsal process of the hyoid arch (epihyal of most authors) is absent; there is no close association with the ear, and *Varanus* does not appear capable of closing over its ear opening.

The *first ceratobranchial* of *Varanus* is divided at its middle into a proximal and a distal portion, but the muscular attachments of the distal portion are those of a ceratobranchial and there is no (epibranchial) process (thus, the first branchial arch is as in *Lanthanotus*). There is no second branchial arch.

There is an extensive literature on the throat muscles of *Varanus* (Fig. 13); the most important references are: Camp (1923) on *V. nuchalis* (now regarded as a geographic race of *V. salvator*); Gnanamuthu (1937) on *V. bengalensis*; Langebartel (1968) on *V. monitor* (=*V. bengalensis*); and particularly Sondhi (1958) on *V. monitor* (=*V. bengalensis*).

Although Camp (1923) believed that *Varanus* lacks a *geniomyoideus*, the muscle discovered by Sondhi (1958) and termed by him "genioglossus portio minor" has all the positional relationships of a geniomyoideus except that it is concealed from ventral view unless the jaws are spread apart. This muscle is entirely medial to the genioglossus medialis and is attached to the buccal floor dorsal to the mental groove (rather than to the mental groove itself, as in other Anguimorpha). The fibers are diagonal, more longitudinal than those of the intermandibularis, but more transverse than those of the genioglossus; this ambiguity as to whether a specialized part of the genioglossus or a special slip of the intermandibularis, as well as its origin from the symphysis medial to the origin of the genioglossus medialis, is diagnostic of a geniomyoideus. It would seem that innervation could settle the question of its nature, since the

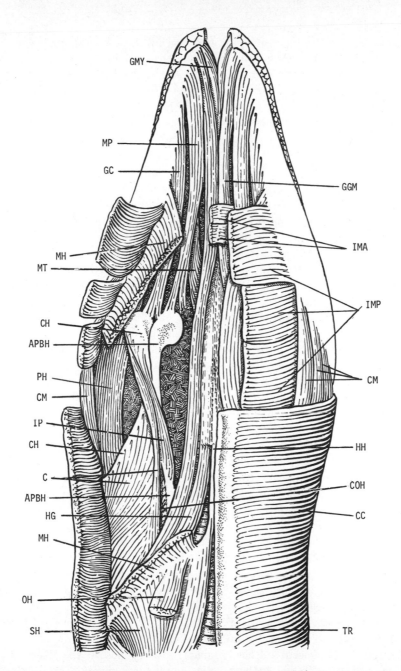

Fig. 13. Varanus bengalensis *(redrawn from Sondhi, 1958), throat muscles and hyo-branchium. The jaws have been artificially separated at the symphysis to expose the geniomyoideus (GMY), and the ceratohyal (CH) has been reflected at its anterior end. For abbreviations see pp. 270-272.*

intermandibularis is innervated by the trigeminal while the genioglossus is innervated by the hypoglossal; but the mylohyoid ramus of the trigeminal nerve and the hypoglossal nerve share a common sheath proximal to the supply of the geniomyoideus, and only a detailed tracing of the individual neurons, not yet attempted, will determine the innervation of this muscle. Thus, Sondhi finds the genioglossus, an undoubted hypoglossal muscle, to be innervated in *Varanus* by the anterior mylohyoid nerve (his ramus muscularis et glandularis).

The *intermandibularis* of *Varanus* is unusually simple for a lizard. The superficial group of the intermandibularis anterior is broad and rather posteriorly placed (almost or quite contiguous to the intermandibularis posterior) and is quite separate at its insertion from the geniomyoideus. The intermandibularis anterior principal portion has no interdigitation with the mandibulohyoideus (in spite of Gnanamuthu, 1937) but is divided into two contiguous narrow slips that are both deep to the mandibulohyoideus. (The intermandibularis anterior is termed the mentalis by Sondhi, 1958.) The intermandibularis posterior (mylohyoideus anterior of Sondhi, 1958 but not of other authors) is entirely superficial to the mandibulohyoideus, as usual, but is peculiar in being divided into two contiguous broad slips.

The *constrictor colli* of *Varanus* is unusually thick, even thicker than in *Heloderma* (the mylohyoideus posterior of Sondhi 1958 is the constrictor colli of other authors). Food taken into the mouth of *Varanus* forms a distinct bulge in the neck, a bulge which may be seen to pass backwards to the region of the shoulder girdle. Probably it is the constrictor colli which produces the peristalsis-like action moving food along the esophagus from the level of the ear opening to the level of the shoulder girdle.

The *cervicomandibularis* (geniolateralis of Sondhi, 1958) of *Varanus* is similar to that of *Heloderma* but is much stronger and divided anteriorly into three tendons that insert on connective tissue over the ventrolateral surface of the jaw and the skin of the lower lip; probably this muscle is an additional depressor of the jaw in broad gaping.

The *genioglossus medialis* of *Varanus* is essentially like that of *Heloderma, Lanthanotus*, and *Gerrhonotus*. As noted above, this muscle helps form the inner sheathing fold, which represents the hind-tongue, but does not give off any transverse fibers in the tongue. The *genioglossus lateralis* of other lizards appears to be represented in *Varanus* by three separate muscles, none of which inserts upon the tongue itself:

(1). The *mandibulotrachealis* (of Sondhi, 1958; = geniotrachealis of Langebartel, 1968), running back in the outer sheathing fold of the tongue to attach to the larynx and adjacent trachea, probably corresponds to the fibers of the genioglossus lateralis that insert on the buccal floor in *Heloderma*. As noted above, the genioglossus lateralis of *Lanthanotus* and *Heloderma* probably acts to pull the larynx forward indirectly, by pulling on the region of the hyoid arch underlying the larynx-bearing fold of the oral mucosa. The mandibulotrachealis of *Varanus* would seem to have a similar action, but has attained a direct attachment to the larynx, made necessary by the modification of the hyoid arch. This muscle is of considerable interest because a very similar and at least morphologically (if not phylogenetically) homologous muscle occurs in all snakes (see Langebartel, 1968) and no lizard other than *Varanus* is known to have a muscle extending from the symphysial region of the jaw directly to the larynx and trachea.

(2). The *mandibuloproximalis*, inserted on the anterior process of the body of the hyoid and adjacent buccal floor, probably corresponds to the more medial fibers of the genioglossus lateralis attached to the anterior angulation of the hyoid arch in *Heloderma* and *Lanthanotus*. The probable action of this muscle in *Varanus* is to aid in putting tension on the hyoid arch and help straighten it from its normal folded form, thus expanding the floor of the buccal cavity.

(3). The *genioceratoideus* (of Sondhi, 1958: = anterior slip of the genio-hyoideus of Langebartel, 1968; = anterior part of genioceratoideus of Gnan-amuthu, 1937), inserting partly on the anterior process of the body of the hyoid and mostly on the anterior end of the ceratohyal, probably corresponds to the more lateral of the genioglossus lateralis fibers that insert on the anterior angulation of the hyoid arch in *Heloderma* and *Lanthanotus*. In *Varanus* this muscle probably acts with the mandibuloproximalis to exert tension on the hyoid arch, straightening it, and thus expanding the floor of the buccal cavity.

The *hyoglossus* of *Varanus* is as in *Heloderma*, but longer, in accordance with the longer tongue. It arises from the extreme distal (lateralmost and posterior-most) tip of the first ceratobranchial, and thus the posterior ends of the two hypoglossi are broadly divergent from each other (in marked contrast to the nearly parallel posterior ends of the hyoglossi of *Lanthanotus*).

The *branchiohyoideus* of other lizards is represented in *Varanus* by three separate muscles: (1) the *ceratohyoideus*, extending from the first cerato-branchial to the ceratohyal; (2) the *cornuohyoideus*, extending from the first ceratobranchial to the anterior process of the body of the hyoid, deep to the ceratohyoideus; and (3) the *interportialis*, between the ceratohyal and the anterior process of the body of the hyoid. (Gnanamuthu, 1937 and Langebartel, 1968 regard all of these muscles as a single "ceratohyoideus".) The action of these muscles probably depends on the position of the first ceratobranchial when they contract, and the ceratohyoideus might function either to draw back the ceratohyal into the resting position, or—by making the hyoid arch parallel to a tensed and vertical first branchial arch—could aid in straightening the hyoid arch and expanding the buccal floor. Probably the interportialis functions to erect the ceratohyal from its inverted position in the relaxed and unexpanded throat, and thus could aid in initiating expansion of the buccal floor; but once the buccal floor is expanded, contraction of the interportialis would make the angle between the ceratohyal and the anterior process of the body of the hyoid more acute, thus constricting the throat and helping to squeeze food down the gullet.

The *mandibulohyoideus* (geniohyoideus of Sondhi, 1958, Gnanamuthu, 1937, and Camp, 1923; ceratomandibularis of Langebartel, 1968) is not perforated by interdigitating fibers of the intermandibularis in *Varanus*; in my material and Sondhi's (1958), the muscle is a broad sheet extending from the entire length of the first ceratobranchial and body of the hyoid to insert along almost the entire length of the lower jaw (but failing to reach the anterior and posterior extremities of the jaw). However, Langebartel (1968) found the muscle divided into a narrow medial portion, from the hypohyal process to the anterior part of the jaw, and a broad lateral portion, from the body of the hyoid and the first ceratobranchial to the middle third of the lower jaw. Except for the absence of the interdigitating intermandibularis, the mandibulohyoideus of Langebartel's specimen of *Varanus* would not differ greatly from that of *Lanthanotus*.

Varanus has a muscle from the rear of the lower jaw to the ceratohyal that has not been observed in any other anguimorphan lizard. Sondhi (1958) termed this muscle the mandibulohyoideus, but as that name is used here for the muscle called geniohyoideus by Sondhi, the name *prearticulohyoideus* is used here for the muscle that originates on the prearticular bone (behind the posterior mylohyoid foramen) and · inserts on the middle third of the ceratohyal. (Langebartel, 1968 considers this muscle a posterior slip of the geniohyoideus, the anterior slip of that muscle being the mandibuloproximalis of the present paper; the latter muscle is here considered a specialized slip derived from the genioglossus lateralis of other lizards.) Sondhi found the twig of the hypoglossal innervating the prearticulohyoideus and the twig innervating the mandibulo-hyoideus (my nomenclature) to arise from a common stem, and the prearticulo-hyoideus is entirely deep to the mandibulohyoideus. Probably the prearticulo-hyoideus has been formed from deeper fibers of the mandibulohyoideus that have gained attachment to the ceratohyal, rather than merely passing beneath the ceratohyal as in other Anguimorpha. The muscle called mandibulohyoideus III in *Ctenosaura* is roughly similar to the prearticulohyoideus of *Varanus* but is more anteriorly placed, arising from the lower jaw in front of the posterior mylohyoid foramen, and it seems more likely that the prearticulohyoideus of *Varanus* is an independent development associated with the complications of the hyoid arch. The action of the prearticulohyoideus would seem to be to draw forward the ceratohyal and orient it more vertically, helping to expand the buccal floor.

The *omohyoideus-sternohyoideus complex* of *Varanus* is essentially as in *Lanthanotus* and *Heloderma*.

In general, *Varanus* has much the most snake-like tongue known among lizards and also is the only lizard known to have a mandibulotrachealis muscle (a muscle found in all snakes); the presence of a lachrymal duct that opens directly into the organ of Jacobson is an additional snake-like feature. But in combination with these snake-like features, *Varanus* also has the most complex hyoid arch among lizards, with an elaborate hyoidean musculature, whereas in snakes the hyoid arch is probably quite absent (see below) and the hyoid arch muscles are absent.

The complexity of the hyoid arch and its muscles in *Varanus* appears to be a modification for active distension of the pharynx, quite usual for fish but unusual (at least to such degree) in a tetrapod. In fish, the hyoid arch is a major part of the mechanism for pharynx distension (see Tchernavin, 1953) and *Varanus* has become roughly convergent to actinopterygian fishes in making use of the hyoid arch as a lever to expand the gullet. However, *Varanus* has the hyoid arch inside out in the relaxed (undistended) state of the pharynx, and pharyngeal distension involves restoring the hyoid to normal morphological relations, whereas the bony fish *Chauliodus*, as described by Tchernavin (1953), turns the hyoid arch inside out in distending the pharynx and restores normal morphological relations in relaxing and contracting the gullet. The precise mechanism of pharyngeal distension in *Varanus* has yet to be described and it must be hoped that someone with access to live material will do so.

THE SNAKE STAGE

Snakes are like *Varanus* in that the tongue takes no part in swallowing, but is highly developed for collecting particles to be sensed by Jacobson's organ. Although snakes (apart from the Scolecophidia) agree with *Varanus* in being adapted to swallowing large prey whole, they do not actively expand the pharynx, but rather force food into the pharynx with movable tooth-bearing elements in the mouth and have a pharynx that is easily stretched to permit a passive accommodation to large prey. Scolecophidia (Anomalepididae, Typhlopidae, and Leptotyphlopidae) are small-mouthed forms feeding on small prey (usually termites), and with few toothed elements in the mouth, although the toothed elements present are highly motile (the toothed lower jaw of Leptotyphlopidae has the most motile intramandibular hinge known among Squamata, while the toothed maxilla of Anomalepididae and Typhlopidae is exceedingly free). The Alethinophidia (booid and colubroid snakes) normally feed on relatively very large prey and feed in a characteristic and unique way, advancing the tooth maxilary, palatine, pterygoid, and dentary bones of one side forward over the prey, while the toothed elements of the other side hold as an anchor; normally this is reciprocal, with the right and left sides alternating in advancing over the prey (see Gans, 1961).

As might be expected, considering the differences in feeding methods, Scolecophidia and Alethinophidia differ markedly in a number of features of the tongue complex; however, these differences are almost wholly confined to the hyobranchial skeleton and throat musculature, and there is a remarkable uniformity to the tongue in the strict sense among all snakes.

The following account is based mainly on:

Scolecophidia: Anomalepididae: *Anomalepis aspinosus* MCZ 14783; Typhlopidae: *Typhlops angolensis* AMNH 11627; Leptotyphlopidae: *Leptotyphlops
humilis* AMNH 68461.

Alethinophidia: Boidae: *Python molurus* AMNH unnumbered; *Loxocemus
bicolor* AMNH 68066; Colubridae: *Masticophis flagellum* AMNH unnumbered;
Coluber constrictor author's coll.; *Natrix rhombifera* author's coll. (Carolina
Biological Supply Co. prep.).

In addition to these direct observations, I have made use of a number of
well-illustrated published descriptions: Langebartel (1968)—wide variety of
snakes, with all families represented; Camp (1923)—*Typhlops congestus*;
Frazzetta (1966)—*Python sebae* and *P. molurus*; Gibson (1966)—*Boa constrictor*; Albright and Nelson (1959)—*Elaphe obsoleta*; Gans (1952)—*Dasypeltis*;
Sondhi (1958)—*Xenochrophis piscator*; and Gnanamuthu (1937)—*Atretium
schistosum*.

In spite of the near-uniformity in tongue structure, the differences in
hyobranchial skeleton and throat muscles make it most convenient to divide the
snakes considered here into three groups: (1) Anomalepididae, (2) Typhlopidae
and Leptotyphlopidae, and (3) Alethinophidia.

Anomalepis

The tongue of *Anomalepis* (Fig. 14) is not only shorter than that of any other
snake examined, but shorter than that of *Varanus* and is subequal to the skull in
length (about the relative length seen in *Gerrhonotus*, *Heloderma* and *Lanthanotus*).

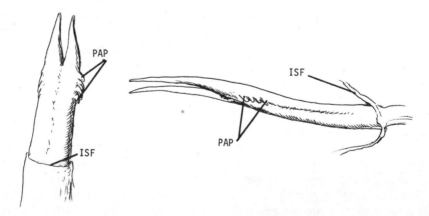

Fig. 14. Tongues of scolecophidians: left, dorsal view of the tongue of
Anomalepis aspinosus (MCZ 14783); right, lateral view of the tongue of
Leptotyphlops humilis (AMNH 68461). For abbreviations see pp. 270-272.

The foretongue is much as in *Varanus*, but is shorter and less deeply forked. There is an even closer resemblance to the foretongue of *Lanthanotus* in the presence of a row of about four papillae on each side, just behind the level of forking. As in both *Lanthanotus* and *Varanus*, the surface of the foretongue is otherwise smooth and rather hard, and the retracted tongue sits between the sublingual plicae, rather than on top of them, and so is probably bathed both dorsally and ventrally by the secretion of the sublingual glands.

The *hind-tongue* is reduced to an *inner sheathing fold*, precisely as in *Varanus*. The relations of the genioglossus medialis to this inner sheathing fold are as in *Varanus*, and the arguments for homology of the inner sheathing fold of *Anomalepis* with the hind-tongue of most lizards are as for *Varanus* (except that involving the hypohyal process, absent in *Anomalepis*). As in *Varanus*, the buccal mucosa bearing the larynx at the base of the tongue of *Anomalepis* has become permanently rolled forward over the rear of the tongue as an *outer sheathing fold*; however, in *Anomalepis* (as in snakes generally) the outer sheathing fold has been extended considerably farther anteriorly than in *Varanus*, bringing the larynx to the level of the choanal openings, into which the larynx is fitted (as clearly shown in figures 34 to 36 in Haas, 1968), facultatively separating the respiratory passage from the general buccal cavity, as in most snakes.

The *ectochoanal folds* (Fig. 15) are conspicuously pulpy and like those of *Lanthanotus* and *Gerrhonotus* in broadly underlapping the vomerine raphe (shown well in the figures of cross-sections of *Anomalepis aspinosus* presented by Haas, 1968 and of the closely related *Liotyphlops albirostris* presented by Haas, 1964). However, the *ectochoanal cartilage* is quite unconnected to the maxilla, an obvious adaptation to the motility of that bone. Further, the choanal opening dorsal to the ectochoanal fold is closed ventrally by a webbing of soft tissue that joins the vomerine pad to the dorsolateral base of the ectochoanal fold (that is, to the region of the *ectochoanal groove*); this webbing extends behind the level of the vomer and thus floors a short median *ductus nasopharyngeus* that is directly pressed against the larynx, as noted above. As shown by Haas's (1968) figures, the single *lachrymal duct* opens into the *fenestra vomeronasalis externa*, as does the longer of the two lachrymal ducts of *Varanus*.

The hyobranchium of *Anomalepis* (Fig. 16) and its close relatives *Liotyphlops*, *Helminthophis*, and *Typhlophis* differs from that of all other snakes in being shaped approximately like an *M*, with a forwardly concave middle section that continues into a pair of cornua that extend backward and outward and, at their distal ends, hook forward. The general form is that of the body of the hyoid (without median hypohyal process) and anterior processes of the body of the hyoid plus ceratohyals and dorsal processes of the ceratohyals of most lizards. Because of this shape, as considered *in isolation*, Smith and Warner (1948), McDowell and Bogert (1954), List (1966), and Langebartel (1968) interpret the

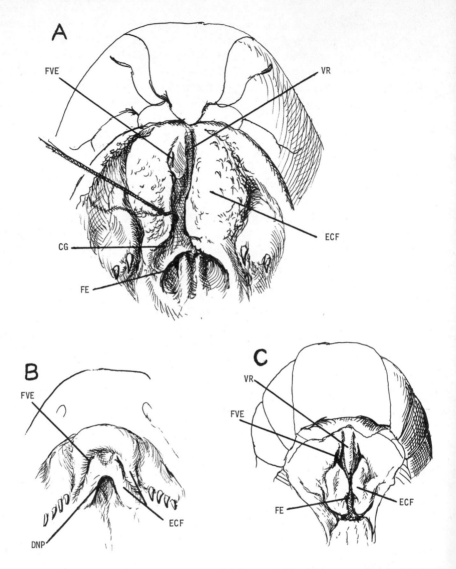

Fig. 15. Superficial palates of scolecophidians: A, Typhlops angolensis *(AMNH 11627); B,* Anomalepis aspinosus *(MCZ 14783); C,* Leptotyphlops humilis *(AMNH 68461). The right ectochoanal fold of* Typhlops *is shown as artificially reflected; in nature, it meets its fellow on the midline. A feature worth noting is that the tips of the maxillary teeth of* Typhlops *and* Anomalepis *are naturally exposed as in lizards, rather than covered by a loose fold of gum as in alethinophidians. For abbreviations see pp. 270-272.*

hyobranchium of Anomalepididae to be formed mainly or entirely from the hyoidean arch. This interpretation offers serious difficulties, however, because the muscle attachments (described by Warner, 1946 and Langebartel, 1968) are

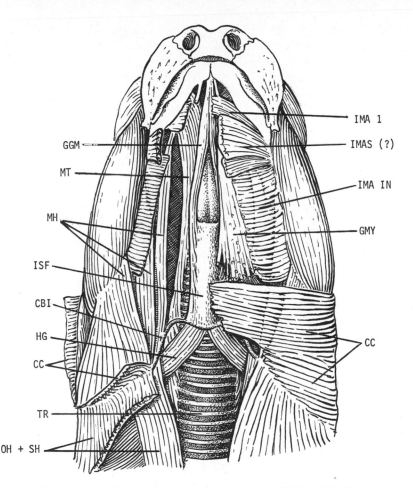

Fig. 16. Throat muscles of Anomalepis aspinosus *(MCZ 14783), with deeper muscles exposed on reader's left. For abbreviations see pp. 270-272.*

those of a first branchial arch. Thus, the hyoglossus arises from forwardly bent distal end of the hyobranchial cornu; in all other Squamata the hyoglossus arises from the first ceratobranchial and an origin of the hyoglossus from the hyoid arch is not reported elsewhere among tetrapods. I find three slips of muscle to extend from the hyobranchial cornu to the lower jaw, with part of the intermandibularis passing between the outer and middle of these slips; it is difficult to interpret this muscle as anything but the lizard mandibulohyoideus, a muscle arising from the first ceratobranchial and adjacent body of the hyoid. Furthermore, the hyobranchial cornua of *Anomalepis, Liotyphlops* (Lange-bartel, 1968), and *Typhlops* (Myers, 1967) receive a muscle arising from the skin, but otherwise similar to the lizard omohyoideus, a muscular attachment normal for a first ceratobranchial but quite unusual for a ceratohyal. Langebartel

(1968) noted these peculiarities of muscle attachment, but chose to identify the cornu as hyoidean on the basis of its shape and suggested the muscles of the first branchial arch became transferred to the hyoid arch; he explains the attachment of the hyoglossus muscles thus (p. 9): "The hyoglossal muscles attach only to the ceratohyals because these are the only parts of the hyoid available for attachment."

It seems implausable to me that a first ceratobranchial would be lost if it had an important muscle attachment, since the intermediate condition in the proposed transfer of the muscle would almost certainly be at a severe selective disadvantage. It must also be questioned that the *shape* of hyobranchium is even constant in an individual anomalepidid. This entirely cartilaginous structure is very thin and flexible and the middle hyobranchium is at the rear of the inner sheathing fold of the tongue, the precise point where the left and right hyoglossus muscles become free to diverge posteriorly; the posterior attachments of each hyoglossus muscle is to the cornu at the point where the latter bends forward. Possibly the Z-shaped bending of each cornu is the result of tension placed upon it by a contracted hyoglossus. Unfortunately, no anomalepidid with a fully extended tongue (and fully relaxed hyoglossus) is available.

Langebartel (1968: p. 9) cites as evidence for hyoid (*sensu stricto*) homology, "The fact that the recurrent cornua extend forward to the skull in at least some specimens, as reported by Smith and Warner, is surely more evidence for a 2nd arch derivation, since the 2nd arch hyoid derivatives in vertebrates commonly retain such a connection." However, in *Lanthanotus* it is the first cerato-branchial which is tied by a ligament to the paroccipital process, not the hyoid arch, and loose association with the skull is not diagnostic of any particular hyobranchial arch.

It seems unnecessary, therefore, to assume that muscle attachments have been shifted from one arch to another, and the hyobranchium of the anomalepidids seems most likely to consist of the body of the hyoid plus first ceratobranchials, with all other arches lost.

The *geniomyoideus* is probably represented by a muscle of *Anomalepis* (not described or figured for *Liotyphlops* by Langebartel 1968) that arises by a narrow tendon from the region of the mandibular symphysis just lateral to the tendon of genioglossus medialis and extending back, deep to the superficial portion of the intermandibularis anterior but superficial to the interdigitating portion, to fan out into a brush of fibers attached to the skin of the throat near the midline at the level of the jaw articulation. This muscle seems to be a cutaneous slip of the genioglossus medialis, thus fitting Camp's (1923) original definition of the geniomyoideus, but in its straight backward direction and in its origin just lateral (rather than just medial) to the origin of the genioglossus medialis, the muscle of *Anomalepis* differs from the geniomyoideus of the anguimorphan lizards.

The *intermandibularis* of *Anomalepis* has a broad interdigitating portion, passing deep to the outermost slip of the mandibulohyoideus and superficial to the rest of the mandibulohyoideus. I could find no part of the intermandibularis superficial to the entire mandibulohyoideus, and thus, by the definitions used here, the intermandibularis posterior would seem to be absent. The muscle of *Liotyphlops* so identified by Langebartel (1968) arises deep to the outer slip of mandibulohyoideus and would seem to be the superficial portion of the intermandibularis anterior. In *Anomalepis* the corresponding muscle arises anterior to the termination of the outer slip of the mandibulohyoideus and thus is not overlapped by that muscle. The anteriormost part of the intermandibularis of *Anomalepis* (here called intermandibularis anterior 1) is superficial to the innermost of the three mandibulohyoideus slips and is probably a specialized slip of the intermandibularis anterior superficial group, to which it is immediately adjacent. All the intermandibularis fibers are transverse in direction, and in having a single broad interdigitating portion, the intermandibularis of *Anomalepis* is most like that of *Gerrhonotus* and *Lanthanotus*.

The *constrictor colli* is thin; most fibers end on the superficial surface of the mandibulohyoideus, immediately overlying the course of the first ceratobranchial; the anteriormost fibers, however, continue across the throat. It is possible that only these anterior fibers forming a narrow collar represent the true constrictor colli and that the more numerous fibers ending directly over the first ceratobranchial represent the *cervicomandibularis*, which otherwise seems to be absent.

The *genioglossus medialis* is as in *Varanus*. The *genioglossus lateralis* is represented by the *mandibulotrachealis*, which is essentially as in *Varanus* but is unusually thick (much heavier and stronger than the genioglossus medialis). This great strength of the mandibulotrachealis was also observed in *Liotyphlops* by Langebartel (1968), who terms this muscle the geniotrachealis. The habits of the anomalepidids remain unknown, and it would be interesting to know why the muscle that pulls the larynx forward is so much stronger than the muscle that exserts the tongue. In the absence of the hyoid arch, the *mandibuloproximalis* and *genioceratoideus* of *Varanus* are absent, as is the *branchiohyoideus*.

Langebartel (1968) found a *hyotrachealis* in *Liotyphlops*, originating on the buccal floor and running forwardly and medially to insert on the trachea. This muscle is found only in snakes and according to Langebartel is innervated by the vagus, suggesting it is derived from the intrinsic laryngeal musculature.

The *hyoglossus* is as in *Varanus*, with strong posterior divergence of the left and right muscles, but differs in being entirely dorsal to the hyobranchium, a result of the absence of the hyoid arch (in lizards the hyoglossus passes ventral to the hyoid arch).

The *mandibulohyoideus* is divided into three slips in *Anomalepis*, all arising from the portion of the first ceratobranchial that runs backward and outward.

The most superficial and most lateral slip is also much the broadest, and inserts on the ventrolateral surface of the rear of the lower jaw; the middle slip is deep to the last and much narrower, and inserts on the ventromedial surface of the middle of the lower jaw; the third slip, deepest and most medial, is also the narrowest and inserts by a narrow tendon on the ventromedial surface of the anterior part of the lower jaw just behind the origin of the mandibulotrachealis. As noted above, the intermandibularis passes between the first and second of these slips. The figure of *Liotyphlops* given by Langebartel (1968) indicates that this genus has only two slips of the mandibulohyoideus, apparently corresponding to the first and second of the slips seen in *Anomalepis.*

Because the first ceratobranchial of *Anomalepis* extends diagonally for the full transverse width of the throat, the mandibulohyoideus is separated from the omohyoideus-sternohyoideus complex by the ceratobranchial, as in lizards. Langebartel (1968), does not interpret the muscle mass attached to the rear of the ceratobranchial as an omohyoideus-sternohyoideus complex, which should be innervated by the hypoglossal nerve, but as a forward extension of a spinally innervated cutaneous muscle, the costocutaneus superior. It is doubtful that a sharp distinction can be drawn between spinal innervation and hypoglossal innervation, and Langebartel himself (1968: p. 47) groups hypoglossal-innervated and spinal-innervated muscles of lizards together as an "hypobranchial-spinal group." In *Anomalepis* the muscles with the positional relationships of an omohyoideus-sternohyoideus complex form two distinct layers: (1) the more superficial layer, much the broader, inserted along most of the length of the first ceratobranchial, originating from the surface of the muscles of the vertebrae (the dorsal head) and from the external surface of the muscles of the ribs (the ventral head); (2) a deeper and much narrower layer, originating on the skin of the belly near the midline and inserted on the medial portion of the first ceratobranchial. Warner (1946) identified the dorsal head of the superficial muscle as an omohyoideus, the ventral head of the superficial muscle as a sternohyoideus, and figured the deeper muscle without label. The distinction of the dorsal head of the superficial muscle from the ventral head might, indeed, reflect former origin (before loss of the shoulder girdle) from the clavicular-scapular region and from the interclavicular-coracoid region, respectively, and thus correspond to the separation of omohyoideus from sternohyoideus; but more likely, this simply reflects that the ribs can move relative to the vertebrae, and thus a single broad origin from the surface of both the vertebral and costal regions would not be feasible. The relationships at the insertion onto the ceratobranchial suggest rather that the entire superficial muscle is an *omohyoideus* and the deeper muscle is a *sternohyoideus.*

Typhlops and *Leptotyphlops*

Although until recently the Anomalepididae were classified with the Typhlopidae, while the Leptotyphlopidae were kept apart, the genus *Typhlops* is much more like *Leptotyphlops* in the structure of its tongue complex than it is like anomalepidids.

So far as the tongue itself is concerned, *Typhlops* and *Leptotyphlops* (Fig. 14) are much as in *Anomalepis* and other snakes. The *hind-tongue* is reduced to an *inner sheathing fold*, with its relations to the genioglossus medialis as in *Anomalepis* and *Varanus*. The oral mucosa bearing the larynx is modified into a permanent *outer sheathing fold* that is extended far forward (as in *Anomalepis*) to bring the larynx into close contact with the internal narial opening. As in other snakes (as well as *Varanus* and *Lanthanotus*), the retracted *foretongue* lies on the floor of the mouth between the *sublingual plicae*. The foretongue of *Leptotyphlops* has a row of lateral papillae as in *Anomalepis* and *Lanthanotus*, but *Typhlops angolensis* has a completely smooth foretongue, as in *Varanus*; however, some other *Typhlops* (e.g., *T. braminus*) have long lateral papillae.

The *ectochoanal folds* (Fig. 15) are unusually pulpy in texture and nearly or quite meet each other on the midline beneath the vomer, concealing the interior of the nasal chamber from below. In *Typhlops*, the *fenestra vomeronasalis externa* is on the superficial surface of the palate, just lateral to the vomerine raphe, but the ectochoanal fold covers the fenestra from below. The vomerine raphe is exposed between the ectochoanal folds, but is extremely narrow and the grooves separating it from the fenestrae vomeronasales externae are closer together than are the tines of the forked tongue (this suggests that either the region of the fenestrae vomeronasales externae is stretched transversely when the tongue is introduced, perhaps through motion of the maxillae, or else only one tine of the tongue is brought against the palate at a time). As in *Anomalepis* (and most other snakes), the soft tissue dorsomedial to the ectochoanal fold extends to the vomer beneath the choana, closing the choanal passage to the level of the rear of the vomer, but unlike Anomalepididae (and most snakes), this flooring of soft tissue does not extend behind the level of the fenestrae exochoanales to define a ductus nasopharyngeus. Bellairs and Boyd (1950) have shown that the single *lachrymal duct* of *Typhlops* opens into the duct of Jacobson's organ (as does the longer of the two lachrymal ducts of *Varanus*).

Haas (1959) has described the very peculiar superficial palate of *Leptotyphlops*. In this genus the fenestra vomeronasalis externa does not open downward onto the palate, but (apparently) backward into the choana, in close proximity to the opening of the lachrymal duct. This is quite unlike the condition in other snakes, but it does not resemble any known lizard and it seems certain that this is a specialization of *Leptotyphlops*. Haas interprets this as a retention of an embryonic feature, but a different interpretation is possible. *Leptotyphlops* differs from other snakes and resembles most lizards in the absence of a webbing of soft tissue to close the slit-like anterior part of the choana between the ectochoanal fold and vomer. When the ectochoanal fold is reflected, the interior of the nasal chamber is exposed ventrally and, thus, there is no ductus nasopharyngeus. As noted by Haas (1964), the snout of

Leptotyphlops is "telescoped," with the front end strongly decurved. For this reason, the fenestra vomeronasalis externa faces backward, rather than downward. However, the prominent and bulbous ectochoanal folds do not take part in this flexure, but retain a straight and approximately horizontal course. The palatal orifice of *Leptotyphlops*, considered the choana by Haas (1959), does not really correspond to the fenestra exochoanalis of *Typhlops*, but to the more ventral chamber of *Typhlops* formed between the two ectochoanal folds and below the webbing that closes over the choana anteriorly. The absence of this webbing in *Leptotyphlops* leaves the true fenestra exochoanalis externa undefined from the more ventral chamber, which last represents the (essentially confluent) left and right *ectochoanal grooves*. What Haas calls the "choana" of *Leptotyphlops* is, instead, the confluent left and right ectochoanal grooves, and it is quite normal for the fenestra vomeronasalis externa of snakes (and some lizards) to open into the ectochoanal groove. If the webbing (i.e., roof of the ectochoanal groove) of *Typhlops* were cut away, the result of this dissection would be a palate much like that occurring in *Leptotyphlops*; however, in having the lachrymal duct open adjacent to the fenestra vomeronasalis externa, rather than directly into the fenestra, *Leptotyphlops* is more like *Lanthanotus* than like other snakes and *Varanus*.

In *Typhlops* and *Leptotyphlops* the *ectochoanal cartilage* is wholly free of the maxilla, as in Anomalepididae and other snakes. This freedom of the ectochoanal cartilage has an obvious functional explanation in *Typhlops*, where the maxilla is highly mobile and such mobility requires freeing the bone from the structures in the wall of the nasal chamber. But in *Leptotyphlops* the toothless maxilla is solidly connected to the other bones of the muzzle, as in a lizard; the explanation in best accord with the many special resemblances of *Leptotyphlops* to *Typhlops*, is that the lack of kinesis of the maxilla in *Leptotyphlops* is secondary and that the freedom of the maxilla from the ectochoanal cartilage is a vestige of former maxillary kinesis.

The *hyobranchium* of Typhlopidae and Leptotyphlopidae has been studied by List (1966). He finds three kinds: (1) A simple Y-shaped structure, with the apex of the Y directed forward (between the hyoglossus muscles) and with the posteriorly directed arms of the Y short but strongly divergent; (2) similar to above, but with a pair of separate and more or less parallel rods trailing behind the arms of the Y; (3) a pair of parallel rods, but without a Y-shaped element. All three of these types occur within the genus *Typhlops* as currently defined, but all *Leptotyphlops* examined by List were of type 1. List's interpretation is that type 2 is the most primitive and shows a *body of the hyoid* (the Y-shaped piece) and a pair of *first ceratobranchials*. Type 3 could be derived from type 2 by loss of the body of the hyoid, while type 1 could be derived from type 2 by either loss of the first ceratobranchials or their fusion with the body of the hyoid.

Whatever the type, the hyobranchium of *Typhlops* and *Leptotyphlops* is unusually far back, well behind the head (farther back than in alethinophidian snakes and much farther back than in Anomalepididae). The tongue, if measured from its tip to its hyobranchial attachment, is thus extremely long, in contrast to the relatively short tongue of *Anomalepis*. The median forward process of the hyobranchium is an obvious *hypohyal process* but because of the backward displacement of the hyobranchium, the tip of this hypohyal process is well posterior to the inner sheathing fold of the tongue (i.e., the homologue of the hind-tongue) and does not extend into the inner sheathing fold as it does in *Varanus*.

In contrast to the hyobranchium of Anomalepididae, that of Typhlopidae and Leptotyphlopidae is narrow and fails to extend for any considerable distance across the throat. It thus fails to separate the omohyoideus-sternohyoideus complex from the mandibulohyoideus, and these two muscle complexes are joined into a neurocostomandibularis, as in other snakes excepting Anomalepididae, and unlike lizards.

A possible *geniomyoideus* is represented in *Leptotyphlops* (Fig. 17) by a muscle arising from the anterior tip of the dentary, medial and ventral to the origin of the genioglossus medialis and concealing the latter from ventral view, and extending backwards and laterally to insert on the skin near the angle of the mouth. In *Typhlops angolensis* I found a similar muscle, but with its insertion more anterior, beneath the sublingual gland. Langebartel (1968) does not figure or note this muscle in *Leptotyphlops maximus* or *Typhlops bibroni* and *T. schlegeli*, but Camp (1923) figures it in *Typhlops congestus* as the "intermaxillaris" and notes its resemblance to the geniomyoideus of anguimorphan lizards. I identify this muscle as the geniomyoideus because of its origin medial to that of the genioglossus medialis on the tip of the mandible and because of the essentially lengthwise direction of its fibers. In extending backward and laterally, rather than backward and medially, it differs from the geniomyoideus of the lizards examined, but this is probably the result of loss of the mental groove in Typhlopidae and Leptotyphlopidae (the normal point of insertion of the geniomyoideus of anguimorphan lizards). In *Leptotyphlops* there is a very flexible intramandibular hinge, and this muscle probably serves to flex that hinge. In *Typhlops*, without hinge, the muscle probably acts to compress the sublingual gland.

The most superficial portion of the *intermandibularis* in both *Typhlops* and *Leptotyphlops* is a diagonal muscle that runs from the anterior interramal region to the skin and connective tissue at the angle of the mouth and rear of the lower jaw; posteriorly it is deep to the anterior end of the cervicomandibularis. Camp (1923) identifies this muscle in *Typhlops congestus* as a reflected or superficial portion of the mylohyoideus anterior (=intermandibularis anterior of the present paper), but in being attached to the lower jaw posteriorly, at the level of the angle of the mouth, and in being the most superficial of the intermandibularis muscles, it seems more likely to be an intermandibularis posterior with its medial

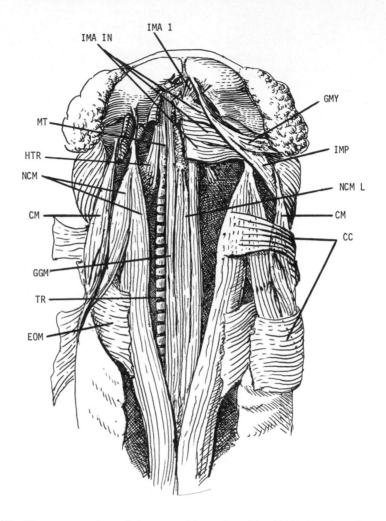

Fig. 17. Throat muscles of Leptotyphlops humilis *(AMNH 68461), deeper muscles shown on reader's left. For abbreviations see pp. 270-272.*

attachment unusually far forward as a result of the nearly transverse orientation of the mouth and consequently very short and broad interramal region. In *Leptotyphlops* the medial (anterior) end of this muscle is connected with the tendon of the geniomyoideus.

The remainder of the intermandibularis has transverse, rather than diagonal fibers and is divided into two portions, one deep to the narrow anterior tendon of the neurocostomandibularis, and the other superficial to that tendon. The anterior tendon of the neurocostomandibularis appears to be the homologue of the similar middle slip of the mandibulohyoideus of *Anomalepis*, and the transverse portion of the intermandibularis superficial to this tendon in *Typhlops* and *Leptotyphlops* seems to be the *interdigitating portion of the intermandibularis anterior*, differing from that of *Anomalepis* in not being overlain by another, more lateral, slip of the mandibulohyoideus. The transverse part of the intermandibularis deep to the tendon of the neurocostomandibularis appears to represent the *principal portion of the intermandibularis anterior.*

The *constrictor colli* of both *Typhlops* and *Leptotyphlops* appears to be in two parts, each thin but strong: an anterior portion, the narrower of the two, lies just posterior to the level of the quadrato-mandibular articulation, partially covering the cervicomandibularis; the posterior part overlies the anteriormost ribs, the origin of the cervicomandibularis, and the origin of the dorsal (omohyoideus-like) head of the neurocostomandibularis. I was unable to find the innervation of either muscle, and my identification is tentative; Langebartel (1968) regards the anterior portion as the constrictor colli and identifies the posterior as the obliquus abdominis internus; Camp (1923), on the other hand, identified the posterior muscle as the constrictor colli and identified the anterior muscle as the mylohyoideus (=intermandibularis) posterior.

The *cervicomandibularis* in both *Typhlops* and *Leptotyphlops* is a slender muscle attaching to the external surface of the rear portion of the lower jaw. (Langebartel, 1968 identifies this muscle as the neuromandibularis.) The muscle makes no approach towards the midline of the throat (as it does in *Lanthanotus*), nor is it split anteriorly (as in *Varanus*), and thus is perhaps most like that of *Heloderma* of the lizards studied.

The *genioglossus medialis* of *Typhlops* and *Leptotyphlops* is as in *Varanus* and *Anomalepis*. The *genioglossus lateralis* is represented in *Typhlops* and *Leptotyphlops* by the mandibulotrachealis (geniotrachealis of Langebartel, 1968), which is similar to that of *Anomalepis* but much more slender and is subequal in diameter to the genioglossus medialis.

The *hyoglossus* differs from that of *Anomalepis* in being much longer, a result of the backward displacement of the hyobranchium, and in having its left and right portions parallel and nearly in contact even at their posterior terminations on the hyobranchium, as in *Lanthanotus* and unlike the strong posterior divergence seen in *Anomalepis* and most lizards. The muscle is attached posteriorly to the arms of Y-shaped hyobranchium (the Typhlopidae and Leptotyphlopidae examined by both me and Langebartel, 1968 have all been forms with type 1 hyobranchium, and the precise attachments of the hyoglossi in *Typhlops* with type 2 or type 3 hyobranchium have not been described). In the forms I dissected (but not those examined by Langebartel, 1968), the backward displacement of the hyobranchium has brought the rear of the hyoglossus directly dorsal to part of the omohyoideus-sternohyoideus complex, as discussed below, and the hyoglossus receives a tendinous slip from the omohyoideus-sternohyoideus complex just before entering the inner sheathing fold.

The *hyotrachealis* muscle, known only in snakes, is reported by Langebartel (1968) to arise in *Typhlops* from the hypaxial muscles lying over the ends of the rib cage. In *Leptotyphlops* this muscle arises from the mucosa of the buccal floor.

As noted above, the *mandibulohyoideus* muscle and the *omohyoideus-sternohyoideus complex* blend together in *Typhlops* and *Leptotyphlops* to form a single muscle, the *neurocostomandibularis*, as a result of the failure of the hyobranchium to extend laterally and separate the two muscle groups. The anterior attachment in both *Typhlops* and *Leptotyphlops* is a narrow slip of muscle, between slips of the intermandibularis, inserting onto the anterior portion of the lower jaw; this attachment has the form and position of either the middle or medialmost slip of the mandibulohyoideus of *Anomalepis*. Traced backward, this muscle divides into a dorsolateral head, arising from the lateral surface of trunk muscles, and a ventromedial head, that extends back to the region of the hyobranchium; the dorsolateral head appears quite homologous with the dorsolateral head of the omohyoideus-sternohyoideus complex of *Anomalepis*, but differs in running directly into the muscle slip attaching to the jaw, rather than in attaching to the hyobranchial cornu; this difference is an obvious consequence of the reduced lateral extent of the hyobranchium and of the posterior displacement of the hyobranchium to a position posterior to the convergence of dorsolateral and ventromedial heads of the omohyoideus-sternohyoideus complex, so that the hyobranchium lies within the ventromedial head of the omohyoideus-sternohyoideus complex rather than between the mandibulohyoideus and the omohyoideus-sternohyoideus complex.

There does not appear to be any attachment to the lower jaw corresponding to the broadest and lateralmost slip of the mandibulohyoideus of *Anomalepis*; however, a broad cutaneous muscle of the interramal area in both *Typhlops* and *Leptotyphlops*, considered part of the costocutaneus superior by Langebartel (1968), may represent this portion of the mandibulohyoideus of *Anomalepis*, with its insertion transferred to the skin from the lower jaw.

In both *Typhlops* and *Leptotyphlops* there is a median pair of muscle slips, arising from the midline of the belly and running forward beneath the rear of the hyoglossus musculature and hyobranchium to insert (in my material) on the hyoglossus just behind the entry of the latter into the inner sheathing fold. Langebartel (1968) identifies this muscle as the sternohyoid and finds it to end on the hyobranchium in his material. In either case, this portion of neurocostomandibularis would seem to form a very powerful retractor for the tongue, running from the skin of much of the belly either to direct attachment on the hyoglossus or to attachment upon a hyobranchium that is little more than a calcified cartilaginous tip to the rear of the hyoglossus muscles.

Just why *Typhlops* and *Leptotyphlops* should be so much better provided than *Anomalepis* (or other snakes) in musculature for retraction of the tongue is unknown, but I offer the following conjecture. *Typhlops* and *Leptotyphlops* differ from other Serpentes in having only one pair of toothed bones in the mouth, without any opposing dentition to hold the prey while the maxilla (*Typhlops*) or dentary (*Leptotyphlops*) is advanced. Further, *Typhlops* and *Leptotyphlops* feed on very small arthropods of such small mass and inertia that the inertial method of feeding, as described for some lizards by Gans (1961), would be ineffective. The usual prey of *Typhlops* and *Leptotyphlops* is of a mass so small (relative to its surface) that it can be picked up by the surface tension of a drop of water on the end of a needle. If it be assumed that the salivary secretion of *Typhlops* and *Leptotyphlops* is at least equal to ordinary tap water in adhesiveness, than the saliva-covered tongue of these scolecophidians should be effective in capturing and ingesting the usual prey of these snakes. Indeed, the quite toothless Manidae, Myrecophagidae, and Tachyglossidae among mammals depend entirely on lingual adhesion in capturing prey similar to that of the Typhlopidae and Leptotyphlopidae. It should be emphasized, however, that this is quite conjectural, and no one has ever observed a typhlopid or leptotyphlopid to feed in anteater fashion with its tongue.

Alethinophidian (Booid and Colubroid) Snakes

The foretongue (Fig. 18) of all the alethinophidians examined is most like that of *Lanthanotus* in the presence of a row of papillae along each side behind the level of the terminal cleft, but is longer and more deeply cleft, and in these respects more like *Varanus*. As in the scolecophidians, *Lanthanotus* and *Varanus*, the retracted foretongue fits between (rather than upon) the *sublingual plicae*. In the alethinophidians examined, the median anterior end of the frenulum of the tongue is much higher and more conspicuous than the median ridge seen in *Varanus* and *Lanthanotus*, and forms a distinct tubercle. This median tubercle probably performs two functions: (1) it helps steer the tines of the tongue towards the sublingual plicae as the tongue is moved in and out; and (2) it helps bound a pair of grooves in which the secretion of the sublingual glands can collect, forming pools of secretion to bathe the tines of the tongue.

In the booids examined (*Loxocemus bicolor* and *Python molurus*), I could find no macroscopic trace of a gland within this median tubercle, and Baumeister (1908) could find no trace of a median sublingual salivary gland in serial sections of the uropeltine aniliid *Rhinophis planiceps*. However, in colubrids this median tubercle contains the orifice of a *median sublingual gland*, as described by Gnanamuthu (1937) for *Atretium schistosum*. According to Baumeister (1908), who terms this gland the glandula lingualis posterior, it originates from paired structures that fuse on the midline in "*Tropidonotus*" (=*Natrix*). Since the openings of this gland are within the outer sheath of the tongue, it seems likely that the median gland represents the rear portions of the paired sublingual glands of lizards, brought together within the outer tongue sheath as a result of the forward extension of the latter.

The *hind-tongue* of alethinophidians, as in scolecophidians is a facultative

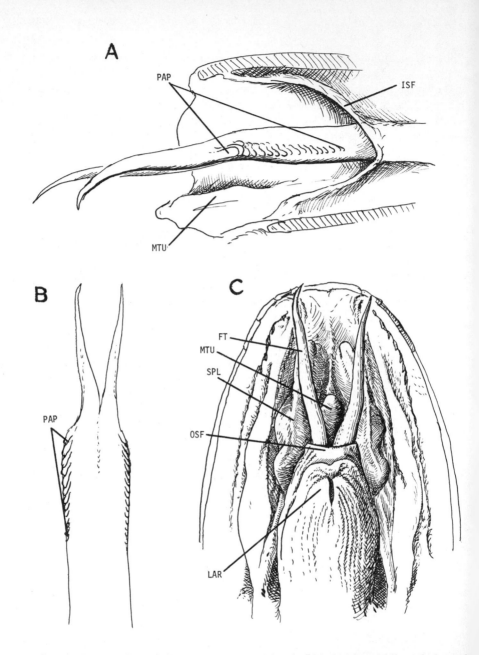

Fig. 18. Loxocemus bicolor *(AMNH 68069), a boöid alethinophidian: A, lateral view of tongue with sheathing folds slit open; B, dorsal view of foretongue; C, floor of mouth with the tips of the retracted tongue protruding from the sheath. For abbreviations see pp. 270-272.*

inner sheathing fold (Fig. 19). When the tongue is fully extended, the inner sheathing fold becomes the outer surface of the rear half (or more) of the tongue itself; when the tongue is fully retracted, the inner sheathing fold may be totally inverted and appear to be only an especially thin and smooth lining of the outer tongue sheath (as in Fig. 18A of the fully retracted tongue of *Loxocemus*); or a free edge of the doubled-over membrane may mark the inner sheathing fold as

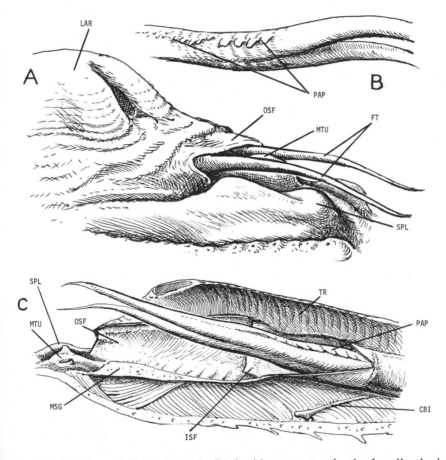

Fig. 19. Tongues of Colubridae. A, Diadophis punctatus *(author's collection), side view of the retracted tongue and adjacent floor of the mouth; B, detail of the tongue at the region of furcation, same specimen; C,* Masticophis flagellum *(AMNH unnumbered), retracted tongue with the sheathing folds slit open and the trachea and floor of the mouth hemisected slightly to the left of the midline. MSG, median sublingual gland; CB I, ceratobranchial I (or a replacement of that structure by the body of the hyoid?). For abbreviations see pp. 270-272.*

distinct from the outer sheath (as in Fig. 19C of *Masticophis*), but in such cases I am not sure the tongue is in maximum retraction. When the tongue is partially retracted, the inner sheathing fold is most conspicuous upon dissection, but seldom projects beyond the sheath formed by the outer sheathing fold. The relations of the inner sheathing fold of alethinophidians to the genioglossus medialis muscle is as in *Varanus* and scolecophidians. In those colubroids which have a forward median process of the hyobranchium (hypohyal process), this process lies in the floor of this tongue sheath (representing the hind-tongue) rather than the "body" of the tongue.

The *outer sheathing fold* of the tongue of alethinophidians bears the larynx and has longitudinal pleats continuous with those of the esophageal lining; it is quite obviously a forward extension of the buccal mucosa over the base of the tongue, as in *Varanus* and scolecophidians, and, as in those groups, it contains a mandibulotrachealis muscle that appears to be derived from the genioglossus lateralis of most lizards. As in scolecophidians, the outer sheathing fold of alethinophidians is extended far forward, to bring the larynx into direct contact with the opening of the ductus nasopharyngeus.

The superficial palate of alethinophidians (Fig. 20) is essentially as in scolecophidians, except that the *vomerine raphe* is broader, so that the narrow longitudinal grooves flanking the raphe form a natural mold of the tines of the tongue. The fenestra vomeronasalis externa opens into the longitudinal groove flanking the vomerine raphe. *Loxocemus* differs from the other alethinophidians examined in the presence of a curled flap of tissue (here called the *vomerine flap*) on the medial border of the posterior end of the groove. The vomerine flap is superficial to the rear of the vomer and bears considerable resemblance to the tough supporting tissue at the posterolateral angle of the vomer of *Lanthanotus*; but in *Loxocemus* the vomer extends lateral to the vomerine flap to meet the palatine, thus forming a complete bony false palate (quite unusual in snakes, but seen also in *Anilius, Cylindrophis*, and *Xenopeltis*).

Bellairs and Boyd (1950) have shown that the single[2] *lachrymal duct* of alethinophidian snakes opens directly into the fenestra vomeronasalis externa, and noted the similarity of the course of this duct to that of the longer of the two ducts in Varanus. Although Bellairs and Boyd (1950) state that the *choanal groove* is absent in snakes, the groove flanking the vomerine raphe noted above lies just dorsomedial to an ectochoanal fold and thus seems to be the homolog of the choanal groove of lizards, an homology in keeping with the entry of both the

---

[2] Although all living snakes have a single lachrymal duct, it would appear from the figures and description in Estes et al. (1970) that *Dinilysia* of the Upper Cretaceous had two lachrymal foramina, as in *Varanus* and *Lanthanotus*. Estes et al. identify the upper of the two as the "orbitonasal canal," a term usually reserved for a more medial passageway for the ethmoidal (V_1) nerve from the orbit to the posteromedial surface of the nasal capsule. Estes (letter) has informed me that their usage of the term "orbitonasal canal" was not in the usual sense, but that of Bahl (1937), who so identified the upper lachrymal foramen of *Varanus*.

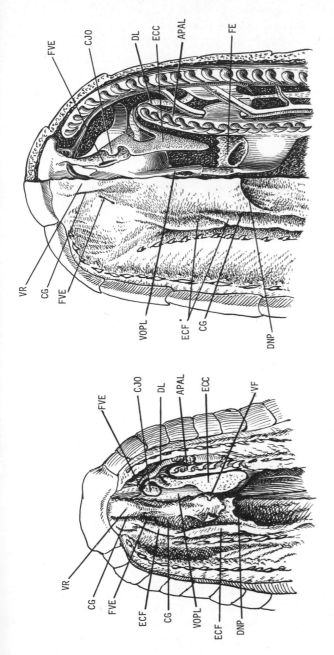

Fig. 20. Superficial palate of (left) the booid Loxocemus bicolor *(AMNH 68066) and (right) the colubrid* Thamnophis sauritus *(author's collection), both with the mucosa removed on reader's right side. APAL, anterior dentigerous process of palatine. For abbreviations see pp. 270-272.*

lachrymal duct and Jacobson's organ into this groove (by a single opening, the fenestra vomeronasalis externa). The ectochoanal fold is represented by a fleshy ridge lateral to this groove and is divided by a pleat into an anterior and a posterior portion, with the front of the posterior portion lying just medial to the rear of the anterior portion.

The differences between the ectochoanal fold of alethinophidians and that of lizards seems to be the result of differences in the form of the palatine bone. In alethinophidians, the palatine is extended forward lateral to the choana for a considerable distance (nearly or quite to the level of the fenestra vomeronasalis externa in the genera specially considered here). The palatine is not rigidly fixed to the adjacent bones, but capable of vertical and horizontal movement during capture and swallowing of prey. Because the lining of the mouth is only moderately extensible, the kineticism of the palatine in snakes is accompanied by pleating of the adjacent oral lining to allow for expansion. The division of the ectochoanal fold into anterior and posterior portions appears to be an example of such pleating.

The *ectochoanal fold* of snakes is supported proximally by an ectochoanal cartilage, so identified by Bellairs and Boyd (1957). However, in his earlier (1949) paper, Bellairs identified this cartilage as the "hypochoanal cartilage," and identified as the *ectochoanal cartilage* an extension of the cartilage of Jacobson's organ along the duct of that organ. The identification of the "hypochoanal cartilage" of snakes with the ectochoanal cartilage of lizards seems quite reasonable in terms of the position of the cartilage relative to the nasal capsule and the general form of the cartilage. Although the general form of the ectochoanal cartilage of *Loxocemus* is quite similar to that of *Lanthanotus*, the relations to the surrounding bones are rather different because of the modification of these bones in snakes for independent kinesis.

Even anterior to the palatine, the ectochoanal ("hypochoanal") cartilage of *Loxocemus* and other snakes does not attach to the maxilla, and this failure of attachment seems to be the result of greatly reduced medial extent of the maxilla associated with freeing of that bone from the rest of the skull to permit kinesis. In *Lanthanotus*, as in other lizards, the maxilla forms a broad shelf that supports the dental lamina, and the developing replacement teeth for the maxillary sockets sit upon this shelf in a vertical position. In *Loxocemus*, as in other snakes, the shelf of the maxilla for the dental lamina is absent and the dental lamina is tucked upward in a nearly vertical position without osseous support, so that the replacement teeth lie in soft tissue in a reclining position and swing up into a vertical position just before emplacement in the socket.

The development of the ectochoanal ("hypochoanal") cartilage of snakes has been described by Kamal and Hammouda (1965a), who give a full bibliography of earlier work. The cartilage arises as a quite separate element with the form of a diagonally placed rod. Subsequently, this cartilage fuses to the posterior end of a backward extension from the cartilage of Jacobson's organ. This backward extension of the cartilage of Jacobson's organ is the "ectochoanal cartilage" of Kamal and Hammouda, as well as most authors, and by such homology, the "hypochoanal cartilage" of snakes would have no counterpart in lizards. The suggestion of deBeer (1937) that the snake "hypochoanal cartilage" represented the posterior maxillary process of lizards (a posterolateral projection of the nasal capsule closely associated with the lachrymal duct) was put to rest by Kamal and Hammouda (1965b) when they found that in the boid *Eryx jaculus* there is both a posterior maxillary process of the capsule and a "hypochoanal cartilage."

An explanation of the "hypochoanal cartilage" and its initial independence in the embryo is suggested by a developmental abnormality described by Bellairs and Boyd (1957). They describe a *Eunectes* (Family Boidae) with a unilateral "hare-lip" and cleft palate, caused by failure of the frontonasal process (the lobe of the fetal face just anterior to the naris) to fuse with the maxillary process (the lobe of the fetal face just behind the naris). This failure left the "hypochoanal cartilage" isolated from the cartilage of Jacobson's organ, whereas on the opposite side, with normal fusion of the frontonasal and maxillary processes, there was normal fusion of the "hypochoanal cartilage" with the cartilage of Jacobson's organ. This strongly indicates that the "hypochoanal cartilage" merely represents the portion of the ectochoanal cartilage that develops within the maxillary process, and as such has a better claim to homology with the ectochoanal cartilage of most lizards than does the backward projection of the cartilage of Jacobson's organ.

The fleshy palate in alethinophidians continues backward for the entire length of the ectochoanal cartilage and even beyond, to fuse with its fellow on the midline behind the choanae and thus form a *palatal velum* defining the median *nasopharyngeal duct*, as in *Anomalepis*.

The hyobranchium of alethinophidians (Fig. 21) has only a single pair of cornua, but these cornua are of two types: (1) in most booid snakes, the cornua are divergent posteriorly and roughly parallel to the lower jaws; (2) in colubroids and a few booids, the cornua are slightly convergent posteriorly, but essentially parallel to the trachea. Langebartel (1968) interprets the cornua of most booids as first ceratobranchials, and the cornua of colubroids as second ceratobranchials; but it seems unlikely that two different arches are involved, since in both colubroids and booids the hyoglossus muscles arise from the single pair of cornua and the other muscular attachments are also closely similar. In colubroids (but usually not booids; see Langebartel, 1968) the cornua are joined anteriorly into a median piece, which usually has at least a short anteriorly directed median process; there is no disagreement that this much of the hyobranchium represents a body of the hyoid with a median hypohyal (entoglossal) process.

Kamal and Hammouda (1965b) have studied the development of the hyobranchial apparatus in the boid *Eryx jaculus* and find that at first (their stage I) there is a transverse median crescent of cartilage, with its tips directed backward and outward. In a later stage (their stage II, with complete

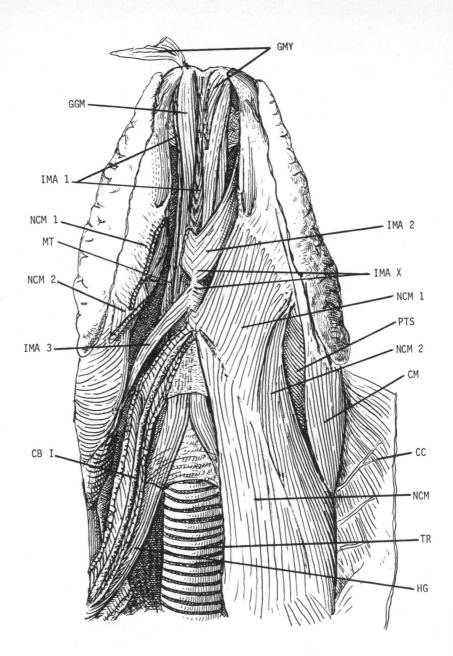

GMY

GGM

IMA 1

NCM 1

MT

NCM 2

IMA 3

CB I

IMA 2

IMA X

NCM 1

PTS

NCM 2

CM

CC

NCM

TR

HG

Fig. 21. Loxocemus bicolor *(AMNH 68066), throat muscles, with deeper muscles exposed on reader's left. For abbreviations see pp. 270-272.*

chondrocranium), the median part has been resorbed and the lateral ends have grown back as a pair of longitudinal and posteriorly divergent rods. Kamal and Hammouda (1965a) also studied the development of the hyobranchium in the colubrid *Psammophis sibilans* and find that here there is first an angulated median piece that is quite similar to the rudiment of the hyobranchium of stage I *Eryx*. However, in *Psammophis* this median piece persists and later develops a median forward projection that is fairly obviously the hypohyal process, even though it does not enter the tongue. Kamal and Hammouda identify the initial median rudiment of the hyobranchium in both *Eryx* and *Psammophis* as the "hyoid corpus" (body of the hyoid), an identification that seems correct beyond reasonable doubt. Most booids would seem to differ from colubrids in resorbing the body of the hyoid.

Kamal and Hammouda identify the cartilaginous rod growing back from the lateral corner of the body of the hyoid as a ceratohyal, without giving arguments for this identification. Such homology seems unlikely, both because it bears the posterior attachment of the hyoglossus (attached to the first ceratobranchial in other tetrapods), and because its shape is not like that of the hyoid arch of lizards (it lacks the forwardly bent "knee" between the anterior process of the body of the hyoid and the ceratohyal). No snake (aside from some *Typhlops*, noted above) shows a joint within the hyobranchium, and the development of the hyobranchium by backward extension from an initial median cartilage is in best accord with the interpretation given by List (1966), that the alethinophidian hyobranchium represents a body of the hyoid that has extended its posterolateral arms to replace a branchial arch; this interpretation also fits the fact that in all alethinophidian snakes, as in *Typhlops* and *Leptotyphlops*, the hyobranchium fails to isolate the mandibulohyoideus from the omohyoideus-sternohyoideus complex, and so these two muscle groups are joined together into a neurocostomandibularis. List's interpretation begs the question, however, of precisely which arch has been replaced by extension of the body of the hyoid. The muscle attachments, particularly of the hyoglossus, very strongly suggest that it is the first branchial arch that has been replaced by the extension of the body of the hyoid, with the other arches totally unrepresented. One of the lizards examined here (*Lanthanotus*) has a considerable portion of the hyoglossus arising from the body of the hyoid, and extension of the body of the hyoid to usurp the entire origin of the hyoglossus would not involve any major dislocations in such a lizard as *Lanthanotus*.

Gnanamuthu (1937), working with *Atretium* (Colubridae), and Sondhi (1958), working with *Xenochrophis* (Colubridae), recognized the "intermaxillaris" as a distinct muscle in alethinophidians, characterized by its origin from the extreme anterior end of the dentary and its insertion on the "intermaxillary ligament" (the elastic sheet of connective tissue forming the anteriormost part of the buccal floor and connecting the tips of the lower jaws); this insertion on the "intermaxillary ligament" might also be described as an insertion on the anterior end of the mental groove. Frazzetta (1966), Gibson (1966), and Albright and Nelson (1959) do not recognize the "intermaxillaris" as a distinct muscle in *Python, Boa,* and *Elaphe,* respectively, but describe a bundle of nearly longitudinal fibers (almost parallel to the genioglossus medialis and just superficial to that muscle) that run from the tip of the mandible to the mental groove; they term this bundle of fibers either the intermandibularis anterior (Frazzetta), or the medial head of the intermandibularis anterior (Gibson), or the pars cutaneomandibularis of the intermandibularis anterior (Albright and Nelson). Langebartel (1968) makes no distinction between an "intermaxillaris" and the intermandibularis anterior.

In the colubrids (*Thamnophis, Natrix, Masticophis,* and *Diadophis* [Fig. 22]) I examined, the details are as figured by Albright and Nelson (1959) for *Elaphe,* with the "intermaxillaris" merging with the intermandibularis anterior, but in *Loxocemus* (Fig. 21) the "intermaxillaris" is quite separate, as a very thin muscle originating at the extreme tip of the jaw (anteromedial to the origin of the genioglossus medialis) and running longitudinally to an insertion on the skin in the vicinity of the mental groove. The fibers of this muscle cover the ventromedial surface of the genioglossus medialis and at first glance appear to be a part of that muscle. This muscle appears to correspond to the "pair of muscles [which] runs from the lower surface of the dentaries' tips and attaches to the skin folds between the first pair of chin shields at their [the shields'] posteriormost point of junction" described by Gans (1952) in *Dasypeltis.* This muscle has the same position and fiber direction as the geniomyoideus of *Lanthanotus* and *Heloderma,* and is, further, like the geniomyoideus of anguimorphan lizards in the ambiguity as to whether it is a cutaneous slip of the genioglossus medialis or an unusually anterior part of the intermandibularis. When the tips of the jaws of a snake lie in contact (the obligatory position in lizards) this muscle appears to be longitudinal, and it is only when the jaw tips are spread broadly apart (the possibility of this, without dissection, is characteristic of Alethinophidia) that the muscle becomes transverse. It should be emphasized that the arguments for the presence of a geniomyoideus in snakes are the same as those for the presence of a geniomyoideus in *Lanthanotus,* and whatever the precise homologies may be, the pattern of muscle fibers in the region of the mandibular symphysis (*Lanthanotus*) or "intermaxillary ligament" (alethinophidians) is very similar in the two groups.

Although variations in proportions have led to a confusing synonymy in the literature, the *intermandibularis* of the alethinophidians I have examined consists of three or four parts that form a diagnostic X-like pattern:

(1) *Intermandublaris anterior pars anterior,* often joining with the genio-myoideus as noted above, but a thicker and deeper muscle that is closely associated with the paired sublingual gland and arises from the dentary *posterior*

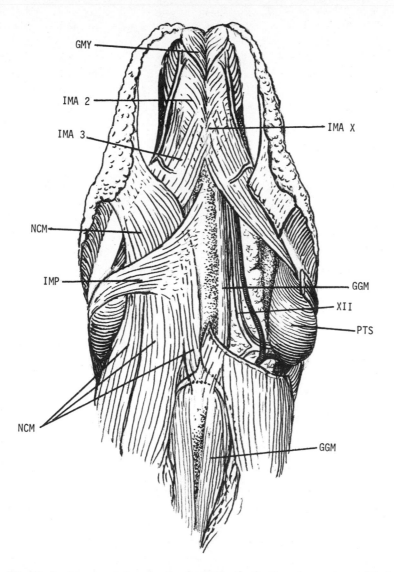

Fig. 22. Diadophis punctatus *(author's collection), throat muscles, with inter-mandibularis posterior (IMP) and anterior part of neurocostomandibularis (NCM) partially removed to expose deeper structures on reader's right. For abbreviations see pp. 270-272.*

to the origin of the genioglossus medialis; it inserts on the connective tissue underlying the median frenulum of the tongue. This muscle seems to be the homolog of the anteriormost slip of the intermandibularis of most lizards and resembles the anteriormost intermandibularis fibers of *Lanthanotus* in being closely associated with the geniomyoideus.

(2) The *intermandibularis anterior pars medialis*, not always well distinguished from the pars anterior just described, and like the pars anterior in being closely associated with the paired sublingual gland. In *Loxocemus*, it arises from the region of the splenial and dentary just anterior to the intramandibular hinge and runs backwardly and medially to insert on a pad of connective tissue just beneath the orifice of the outer sheathing fold of the tongue. This muscle is deep to the anterior portion of the neurocostomandibularis (i.e., deep to the equivalent of the lacertilian mandibulohyoideus).

(3) The *intermandibularis anterior pars posterior* is like the preceding two parts in being deep to the neurocostomandibularis, and shares its medial insertion, on the connective tissue just beneath the orifice of the outer sheathing fold of the tongue, with the pars medialis. However, the lateral origin of the pars posterior is far back on the compound bone of the mandible, immediately adjacent to the belly of the pterygoideus superficialis. The direction of the fibers of the pars posterior is thus forward and medially, approximately perpendicular to the direction of the pars medialis fibers. Because of this perpendicularity, and because of the common point of insertion of the pars medialis and pars posterior, the left pars medialis and right pars posterior lie nearly in a straight diagonal line crossing a corresponding diagonal formed by the right pars medialis and left pars posterior. The X-shaped figure thus formed by the partes mediales and partes posteriores of the intermandibularis anterior is a diagnostic feature of the Alethinophidia and is here called the *intermandibular chiasma*; its functional significance is discussed below. The pars posterior is here considered a part of the intermandibularis anterior because it is deep to the neurocostomandibularis, but because of the extreme posterior position of its lateral origin, this muscle is called the intermandibularis posterior by many authors, such as Langebartel (1968) and Frazzetta (1966).

(4) The *intermandibularis posterior* is here restricted to the single transverse trigeminal-innervated muscle that is superficial to the neurocostomandibularis. It is often absent and is very thin when present. I did not find it in *Loxocemus* or in *Python molurus*, nor does Frazzetta (1966) note any part of the intermandibularis superficial to the neurocostomandibularis in *P. sebae*.

It will be noted that in Alethinophidia the intermandibularis muscle does not interdigitate with the mandibulohyoideus (represented by the anterior portion of the neurocostomandibularis); instead, it is either mainly deep to the mandibulohyoideus with one superficial slip (the intermandibularis posterior) or, when the intermandibularis posterior is absent, is entirely deep to the mandibulohyoideus. The one reported exception is a specimen of the hydrophiine elapid *Aipysurus eydouxii* (CNHM 11572) reported by Langebartel (1968: p. 78, and Fig. 17, pp. 140-141). The relatively advanced phylogenetic position of *Aipysurus* make it seem likely that this interdigitation is secondary, particularly since it is accompanied in this specimen by a unique feature: attachment of the intermandibularis to the hypohyal process of the hyobranchium. The lack of interdigitation between intermandibularis and mandibulo-hyoideus is not a true resemblance to nonsquamate gnathostomes, where the intermandibularis is entirely superficial to the hypoglossal-innervated muscula-ture, but rather is an extreme of the trend begun in lizards for the intermandibularis to form deep attachment to the lower jaw, *internal* to the attachments of some of the fascicles of the mandibulohyoideus. Nor does it seem likely that loss of interdigitations between the mandibulohyoideus and the intermandibularis has taken place in quite the same way in alethinophidians as in *Typhlops* and *Leptotyphlops*. In the latter two genera the overlapping slip of the mandibulohyoideus (present in *Anomalepis*) has either been lost or else transformed into a cutaneous muscle, so that the interdigitating portion of the intermandibularis is left fully superficial to the recognizable mandibulohyoideus. But in alethinophidians it seems to be the deeper slip of the mandibulohyoideus that has been lost, so that (*Aipysurus eydouxii* excepted) all of the interman-dibularis anterior is deep to (or else anterior to the level of) the mandibulo-hyoideus.

The intermandibular chiasma is not suggested in lizards and scolecophidians, where the left and right jaws are joined at the symphysis and the interman-dibularis fibers run transversely. The chiasma appears to be an adaptation to the peculiar feeding mechanism of alethinophidians (see Gans, 1961 for analysis) in which the left and right lower jaws alternately move forward over the prey and, during such advancement, one jaw may be displaced far anterior to its fellow on the opposite side. When the jaws are in such a position, a transverse intermandibularis (such as found in lizards and scolecophidians) would be pulled into a diagonal position, lessening its efficiency as a transverse constrictor of the throat; but the two diagonals of the alethinophidian intermandibular chiasma would alternately each be transverse during the alternate advancement of the left and right jaws.

The *constrictor colli* of *Loxocemus* was thicker than in the other alethin-ophidians examined, but even in *Loxocemus* the muscle is thin and so thoroughly fixed to the skin that it has virtually become a dermal muscle (in contrast to the unusually thick muscle of *Varanus* and *Heloderma*). The *cervicomandibularis* of *Loxocemus* has been well figured by Haas (1955) as the "musculus cutaneus." The muscle is relatively thick and strong and extends to the quadratomaxillary ligament, to the fascia over the temporal region, and to the region of the quadratomandibular joint; I could not find any definite fleshy extension onto the throat. I was unable to find the muscle at all in *Diadophis*. Gans (1952) shows a fleshy continuation of the depressor mandibulae in *Dasypeltis* extending down onto the throat; such a continatuation of the depressor mandibulae probably represents a cervicomandibularis.

The *genioglossus medialis* of Alethinophidia is as in *Varanus, Anomalepis, Typhlops,* and *Leptotyphlops* and is attached extensively to the inner sheathing fold of the tongue, as in those genera. The *genioglossus lateralis* is represented in

Alethinophidia by the mandibulotrachealis, which is as in *Varanus, Typhlops,* and *Leptotyphlops* and much more slender than in *Anomalepis.*

In the absence of the hyoid arch, the *genioceratoidesu* and *mandibuloproximalis,* as well as the *branchiohyoideus,* are absent, as in Scolecophidia.

As in *Typhlops* and *Leptotyphlops,* there is a *hyotrachealis* muscle in Alethinophidia that does not appear to have a counterpart in lizards.

The *hyoglossus* muscles of Alethinophidia are much as in *Varanus,* but diverge more posteriorly (most booids) or do not diverge at all (Colubroidea and such booids as *Tropidophis*), a resemblance to *Lanthanotus*; the left and right hyoglossi run side-by-side on the midline between the first ceratobranchials (or the extensions of the body of the hyoid replacing the first ceratobranchials; see discussion of hyobranchium above) rather than running lateral to the first ceratobranchials as in *Varanus*; the hyoglossus of alethinophidians is quite definitely dorsal (deep to) the hyobranchium, probably because there is no hyoid arch (*sensu stricto*) that the muscle must pass beneath. In the colubroid snakes with an hypohyal process, this process is entirely ventral to and free of the hyoglossus muscles (in contrast to *Typhlops* and *Leptotyphlops*), and so the hypohyal process appears to be free of the tongue; however, the hypohyal process lies in the floor of the inner sheathing fold of the tongue (representing the hind-tongue of lizards) and this apparent freedom of the hypohyal process is an illusion resulting from the extreme reduction of the hind-tongue.

As noted above, the mandibulohyoideus and the omohyoideus-sternohyoideus complex are joined together into a neurocostomandibularis in Alethinophidia. In *Boa* (Gibson, 1966) and *Python* (Frazzetta, 1966) the anterior attachment, obviously representing the lizard mandibulohyoideus, is a broad and simple one to the outer side of the lower jaw, but in *Loxocemus* this attachment is clearly divided into a superficial insertion on the outer side of the dentary and a deep insertion on the compound bone of the lower jaw, behind the intramandibular hinge; this suggests division of a broad muscular sheet to adapt to the hinge within the mandibular ramus rather than the splitting of the lizard mandibulohyoideus by an interdigitating portion of the intermandibularis, for in the lizard condition (retained in *Anomalepis*) the anterior portion has a deeper insertion than the posterior. The entire anterior attachment of the alethinophidian neurocostomandibularis appears to represent only the lateral most (broadest) head of the mandibulohyoideus of *Anomalepis.* All the colubroids examined at least approached *Loxocemus* in the differentiation of the mandibular attachment of the muscle into prehinge and posthinge heads, and Sondhi (1958) gave the name "geniohyoideus" to the prehinge portion in *Xenochrophis* and termed the posthinge head the "genio-lateralis."

The posterior attachment of the neurocostomandibularis of Alethinophidia is divided into a dorsal head, from the surface of the musculature over the vertebrae, and a ventral head from the surface of the muscles of the ribs, as in *Anomalepis.* Just as in *Anomalepis,* it is tempting to identify the dorsal head with the lizard omohyoideus and the ventral head with the lizard sterno-hyoideus; but just as in the case of *Anomalepis*, it is more realistic to consider the two heads as a separation necessitated by the fact that the ribs can move relative to the vertebrae.

TONGUE STRUCTURE AND THE ORIGIN OF SNAKES

The preceding section outlines the morphological stages in converting a normal lizard tongue to the characteristic tongue of snakes (Fig. 23 summarizes most of this material). In general summary, this conversion has involved the progressive reduction of the part of the tongue involved in swallowing as the relative size of the object to be swallowed increases beyond the capacity of that part to be useful. At the same time, the sensory function of the tongue, as a collector for Jacobons's organ, seems to be increased, perhaps because limitations on tongue structure imposed by the requirements of its swallowing functions have been removed. The tongue of snakes (and of *Varanus*) is like the auditory ossicles of mammals in being a purely sensory structure that has been allowed to perfect itself for this function by becoming freed from the feeding apparatus.

When the homology of the inner sheathing fold of the snake tongue with the hind-tongue of lizards is appreciated, snakes are seen to share with the anguimorphan lizards the diagnostic feature of that group: ability to retract the foretongue within the hind-tongue. One living genus of Anguimorpha, *Varanus*, has developed a tongue that is nearly identical with that of snakes in both form (the excised tongue of *Varanus* is difficult to distinguish from that of a snake) and in function (the tongue of *Varanus* is not used in swallowing but is of great sensory importance as a collector for Jacobson's organ).

In this resemblance to snakes, *Varanus* is unique in degree among Squamata, but some other lizards make an approach to snakes. *Tupinambis* of the leptoglossan family Tejidae continuously flicks its tongue in and out in very snake-like fashion and approaches snakes and *Varanus* functionally. Underwood (1957) even says, "*Varanus* has a long protractile snake-like tongue which can however be matched in *Tupinambis*." Bellairs and Underwood (1951) also note similarity between snakes, *Varanus*, and *Tupinambis*: "The circulatory mechanism of Jacobson's organ has been investigated by Pratt (1948), and may be similar in snakes and in lizards such as *Tupinambis* and *Varanus* where the structure of the tongue (Gnanamuthu, 1937) resembles the ophidian condition."

In spite of the functional similarities, I believe resemblance between snakes and *Tupinambis* (Fig. 24) has been exaggerated, and considerable insight into the morphology of the tongue of snakes can be gained by noting the features in which the tongue of *Tupinambis* is not snake-like. In *Tupinambis* and its close relatives the posterior limbs of the tongue are considerably reduced and tapered posteriorly, but not quite so reduced as in *Heloderma* and *Lanthanotus*, and of course not so reduced as in snakes and *Varanus*, where the posterior limbs are

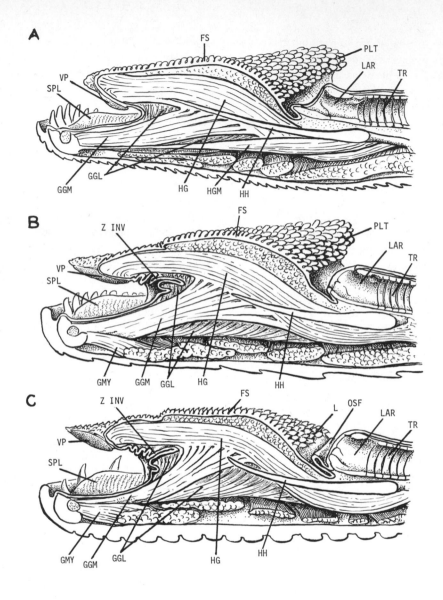

Fig. 23. Diagrammatic longitudinal hemisections of the tongue and floor of the mouth of: A, Ctenosaura, a generalized lizard, with well-developed posterior limbs of the tongue (PLT) and ventral pallets (VP) on the foretongue that lie upon the sublingual plicae (SPL), the entire dorsal aspect of the tongue being covered by the frictional surface (FS); the medial hyoglossus (HGM) extending to the chin is an inguanid specialization. B, Gerrhonotus, a primitive anguoid (diploglossan), with the differentation of a geniomyoideus muscle (GMY) and with the foretongue retractile within the hind-tongue at a zone of invagination (Z INV). C, Heloderma, a primitive platynotan, with the posterior limbs of the

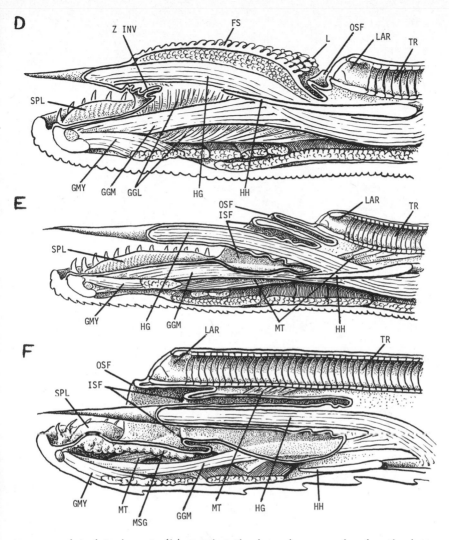

tongue reduced to lappets (L), so that the buccal mucosa bearing the larynx (LAR) can slide forward over the base of the tongue as a facultative outer sheathing fold (OSF). D, Lanthanotus, with the frictional surface (FS) lost from the foretongue, which rests betwen the sublingual plicae. E, Varanus, with the outer sheathing fold (OSF) a permanent structure and the genioglossus lateralis (GGL) of more generalized forms A-D represented by a mandibulotrachealis (MT) inserted directly on the trachea (TR); the hind-tongue is reduced to an inner sheathing fold (ISF) that lies anterior to the juncture of the genioglossus medialis (GGM) with the hyoglossus (HG); the inner sheathing fold thus lies in the position of the zone of invagination (Z INV) of forms B-D and receives the tip of the median hypohyal process (HH). F, a colubrid snake, essentially like Varanus, but with more anteriorly extended outer sheathing fold (OSF) and with a median sublingual gland (MSG).

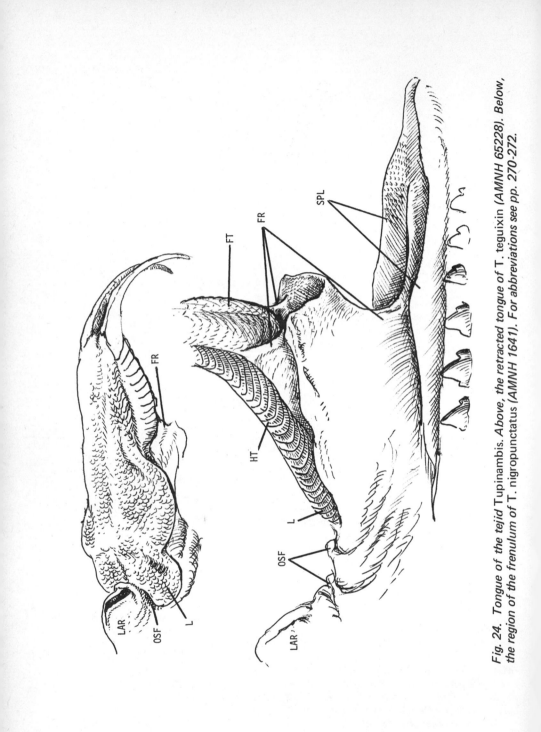

Fig. 24. Tongue of the tejid Tupinambis. Above, the retracted tongue of T. teguixin (AMNH 65228). Below, the region of the frenulum of T. nigropunctatus (AMNH 1641). For abbreviations see pp. 270-272.

quite absent. This tapering of the posterior limbs allows the fold of buccal floor mucosa bearing the larynx to slide forward over the base of the tongue and form a temporary (facultative) "outer sheathing fold" for the rear of the tongue. This is an approach to *Lanthanotus* and *Heloderma*, but falls considerably short of the degree of perfection of the outer sheathing fold seen in snakes and *Varanus*. In snakes and *Varanus* the outer sheathing fold is a permanent, rather than temporary, structure and contains a muscle, the mandibulotrachealis, which runs from the tip of the jaw to a direct attachment on the trachea. As argued in the previous pages, the mandibulotrachealis seems to be a modified slip of the genioglossus lateralis, originally a tongue-protracting muscle lying ventral to the tongue proper; in snakes and *Varanus*, apparently uniquely, the posterior end of this muscle has moved dorsal to the tongue to attach to the trachea.

In *Tupinambis* there is nothing to suggest the inner sheathing fold of snakes and *Varanus*. As argued above, this fold appears to represent the hind-tongue of diploglossans (anguoids), *Heloderma,* and *Lanthanotus*, and receives the genioglossus medialis muscle and the tip or even the entirety of the hypohyal (entoglossal) process, as might be expected of a hind-tongue but not to be expected of a fold formed of buccal mucosa. The development of a telescoping transverse fold within the tongue is diagnostic of the Anguimorpha among lizards, a group to which *Varanus* certainly belongs, not only as evidenced by some of its own structural features (e.g. method of tooth-replacement), but as shown by the morphologically intermediate genus *Heloderma*. In all Anguimorpha the hind-tongue is a sheath for the retracted foretongue, and *Varanus* differs in this respect from other Anguimorpha only in that the hind-tongue has lost all its other functions. *Tupinambis* is a scincomorphan lizard and there is no reason to believe its ancestors ever had a transverse fold within the tongue to permit telescoping of the anterior end within the base. It would be more surprising for such a fold to arise *de novo* in *Tupinambis* than for the usual saurian method of tongue retraction to be accentuated and exaggerated; and it is the latter which seems to have occurred.

If the remarkably close agreement between snakes and *Varanus* in sheathing of the tongue is totally convergent, then it is a truly astounding example of convergence, but it is not necessary to assume that the tongue of snakes is evolved directly from one like that of *Varanus*. The inner sheathing fold, as just noted, is present in all Anguimorpha, and the outer sheathing fold is at least facultative in all living Platynota (and, therefore, may reasonably be assumed to have been present in the fossil families). The particularly close resemblance between *Varanus* and snakes can mostly be attributed to the total loss in both groups of the posterior limbs of the tongue and of the frictional surface, losses that can be explained as the result of adaptation to feeding on prey too large to be moved by the tongue.

However, loss of the (quite highly developed) frictional surface of the tongue of *Tupinambis* would not result in a snake-like tongue-sheath, for the only sheathing suggested in *Tupinambis* is the *outer* sheathing fold, posterior and external to the attachment of the genioglossus medialis to the tongue. The inner sheathing fold, anterior and internal to the attachment of the genioglossus medialis to the tongue, would be absent and the tongue would be attached to the floor of the mouth by the frenulum (in snakes and *Varanus* the tongue appears at first glance to lack a frenulum, because the part of the tongue to which the frenulum attaches has become the inner sheathing fold).

The tongue of *Tupinambis* contains the hypohyal, which is not in any way associated with the sheathing fold, but is dissociated from the rest of the hyobranchial skeleton (Jollie, 1960), an adaptation to tongue retractility unique to *Tupinambis* and its immediate relatives.

Thus, while I think it unnecessary to derive snakes from Varanidae in order to account for the resemblance in tongue structure, I think it is demanding too much of evolutionary convergence to derive snakes from lizards without the diploglossan tongue characteristic of Anguimorpha.

PLATYNOTAN FEATURES OF SNAKES

That all snakes should have a feature diagnostic of the Anguimorpha among lizards is powerful evidence that the snakes are derived from an anguimorphan ancestor, and it is not the only bit of evidence for such an ancestry of the Serpentes. Most snakes have a hinge within the lower jaw (Gans, 1952; McDowell and Bogert, 1954; Albright and Nelson, 1959; Frazzetta, 1966) and a backward extension of the narial opening to separate the nasal and prefrontal bones. These are diagnostic marks of a group within the Anguimorpha, the Superfamily Varanoidea or Platynota, containing the Helodermatidae, Varanidae, Lanthanotidae, Dolichosauridae, Aigialosauridae, and Mosasauridae. All three living genera of Platynota (personal observation) further agree with Serpentes in having the heart far back from the head, so that the carotids are very long, and in lacking a ductus caroticus connecting the dorsal ends of the carotid and systemic aortic arches. However, the Amphisbaenia also show this circulatory pattern, and Chamaeleonidae lack the ductus caroticus, although they do not show carotid elongation or backward displacement of the heart.

The snakes also agree with the platynotans in their method of tooth replacement; the old tooth is shed by breakdown of its bony ankylosis to the jaw-bone and the new tooth moves into the socket without ever lying in a fossa excavated by resorption of the base of the old tooth. McDowell and Bogert (1954) followed Camp (1923) and termed this type of tooth replacement "interdental." They cited it as a diagnostic characteristic of the Anguimorpha, terming the type of replacement found in nonanguimorph lizards (where the new tooth lies for some time in a fossa resorbed in the base of the old and directly proximal to the old crown) "successive" replacement. Edmund (1960) has given new terms for these two methods of replacement, calling the first the "varanid type" and the second the "iguanid type." Edmund's terms are preferable, because the terminology of Camp and of McDowell and Bogert, intended to describe the replacement at a single socket, might be misunderstood to refer to the rhythm of replacement throughout the dental series. Edmund also finds traces of the "iguanid type" of replacement on jaws of some Anguidae and Xenosauridae, indicating that the diagnostic value of this feature is not so great as implied by McDowell and Bogert. It must be noted that although not all Anguimorpha show the snake-like method of tooth replacement throughout the dentition, it is *only among the Platynota* that Edmund found loss of the old tooth to involve, as in snakes, the resorption of only the bone (cement) attaching the tooth to the socket, and the entry of the new tooth into the socket only subsequent to loss of the old tooth.

The derivation of snakes from anguimorphan lizards—more precisely, from the Platynota—was the generally accepted belief of most herpetologists and anatomists, and also of many paleontologists, particularly Nopcsa, who was familiar with the early Cretaceous Dolichosauridae from deposits near Trieste. Nopcsa (1908) derived the snakes from the Dolichosauridae.

However, Bellairs and Underwood (1951) questioned the generally accepted affinity between the Platynota and the Serpentes and concluded (p. 232) that the evidence was inadequate to establish close relationship between the snakes and any known platynotan types. They conceded that the origin of snakes from unknown platynotans during the early Mesozoic remains a possibility. They also held it most probable that the ophidian ancestors were "fossorial rather than above-ground or aquatic in habits."

Although it was not apparent in 1951, platynotan origin of snakes is not exclusive of burrowing origin. Nor is burrowing origin exclusive of aquatic origin, in spite of the contrast in the English language between the words "fossorial" and "aquatic." Thus, the primitive snakes *Anilius* (=*Ilysia*) and *Cylindrophis* are cited as burrowing snakes, and their family, the Aniliidae, is considered, by Bellairs and Underwood "especially on grounds of cranial anatomy, to be the most primitive ophidian family now existing." But *Cylindrophis* can as easily be considered an aquatic snake as a burrower. M. A. Smith (1943: 97) says: that *Cylindrophis rufus* takes readily to water and its food consists of other snakes and eels. Schmidt (1928) records a specimen taken in a salt water lagoon near Hué, Vietnam. As to *Anilius,* Prado (1945: 67) says that in Brazil it is called *Coral dágua* because of its fondness for wet places.

Lanthonotus in captivity (Mertens, 1964) is both a highly aquatic (freshwater) lizard, which swims by serpentine locomotion but also may walk on the bottom with the aid of its much reduced limbs, and also an efficient burrower that has been collected in holes in the ground (Harrison and Haile, 1961). So far as general body form and proportions are concerned, the Lower Cretaceous

Dolichosauridae from marine deposits near Trieste are much like *Lanthanotus* and may well have had similar habits. (Compare the plate of *Adriosaurus suessi* given by Nopcsa, 1908, and the plate of *"Hydrosaurus"* [=*Pontosaurus*] *lesinensis* given by Kornhuber, 1873, with the X-ray of *Lanthanotus* given by McDowell and Bogert, 1943.) Indeed, comparison of *Lanthanotus* with *Adriosaurus* suggests the "Lanthanotidae" should be merged with the Dolichosauridae.

It is thus unlikely that "burrowing" and "aquatic" are genuinely alternative, and the borrowing origin of snakes favored by Bellairs and Underwood need not be in direct conflict with the marine origin favored by Nopesa and other paleontologists. Just as eels are often considered snake-like fishes, snakes can as well be regarded as eel-like reptiles; most eels are crevice-inhabiting or fossorial, although marine. On the other hand, the chief reason for postulating such a burrowing origin of snakes was to account for degeneration of the eye, with subsequent rebuilding of the eye in a radically different pattern from that of the lizard. I see no necessity for postulating a burrowing origin for this, since adaptation to nocturnalism, to muddy water, or to deep water would seem just as effective as adaptation to burrowing. Some fishes, such as the Mormyridae, have quite small and degenerate eyes, and eels could be considered snake-like in having lost scleral ossicles and cartilage.

Although Bellairs and Underwood criticise the view of a special relationship between snakes and platynotans, they do not suggest any other phyletic group of lizards with a greater probability of ancestry to snakes. Underwood (1957) undertook to show that the Gekkota at least equalled the Platynota in resemblance to the snakes. As Underwood concedes, the tongue of Gekkota differs greatly from that of snakes, but I believe he seriously understates the resemblance between snakes and Platynota.

It is impossible to arrange the living anguimorphans in a single series that demonstrates progressive acquisition of the snake-like condition for every one of the structures considered. Obviously, some "parallelism" has taken place, and any attempt to estimate the phylogeny without making allowance for parallelism is doomed. However, it seems a necessary rule of procedure to make our estimate of phylogeny rely on "parallelism" to a minimum. It also seems reasonable to believe that parallel and convergent evolution are most frequent in the loss of some structure and least frequent in reproducing some complex and intricate structural pattern.

A further complication is presented by the fact that only the living forms allow study of the soft structures under discussion, but it is only the fossil families, particularly the Dolichosauridae, which have any realistic claims to consideration as snake ancestors. Of the living lizards, *Lanthanotus* comes closest in osteological features to the Cretaceous Dolichosauridae (in which it might well be included), Aigialosauridae, and Mosasauridae, and it is probably a reasonable approximation to assume that the tongue of the Cretaceous families was similar to that of *Lanthanotus*.

REASONS FOR NOT REGARDING THE VARANIDAE AS TRUE ANCESTORS OF SNAKES

Although the living *Varanus* is the most snake-like of lizards in the general form of its tongue, some details in the morphology of *Varanus* and its fossil relatives suggest that *Varanus* is not so close to the true ancestry of snakes as is *Lanthanotus*.

The Palate and Frictional Surface of the Tongue

Living *Varanus* has a toothless palate, but the fossil varanids of the subfamily Saniwinae had small pterygoid teeth. It is hard to imagine what could have pressed food against such teeth, or freed food from these teeth, unless it was a frictional surface of the tongue. It should be noted that palatal teeth in lizards (including Saniwinae) are unlike the palatal dentition of alethinophidians in being much smaller than the teeth on the margins of the jaws and presumably replaced much less frequently, since replacement teeth are rarely encountered in the palatal dentition of lizards. The palatine and pterygoid teeth of alethinophidians (absent in some) are essentially similar to the mandibular and maxillary teeth in form and size, with similarly well-developed batteries of replacement teeth (but these lie lateral, rather than medial, to the functional row). The ophidian palatal dentition is similar to the marginal dentition in function, as well (see Albright and Nelson, 1959; Gans, 1961; and Frazzetta, 1966), acting to pull prey back into the gullet by alternate left and right engagement, retraction, and disengagement of the palatal arcades. No such function is possible for the palatal dentition of lizards, and here the palatal dentition is merely a rough shagreening that acts as a frictional surface of the palate. It seems unlikely that *Saniwa* and its relatives would retain a palatal frictional surface and at the same time lose the opposing frictional surface of the tongue.

All living snakes have a tongue without frictional surface, and it would seem reasonable that the frictional surface was lost in the common ancestor of the scolecophidians and the typical snakes. However, there is one small bit of evidence that hints the earliest Serpentes may have retained a frictional surface. The Upper Cretaceous Patagonian snake *Dinilysia* (see Estes et al., 1970) lacks any dentigerous forward extension of the palatine, and has, in general, a lizard-like palate without apparent modification for alternate backward movement of the left and sides (there is an unusually firm attachment of the palatine to the vomer, even in comparison to lizards). Yet there are small pterygoid and palatine teeth of the type found in many lizards, forming a frictional surface for the palate. As argued above in the case of the fossil Varanidae, the presence of a frictional surface on the palate of *Dinilysia* suggests the possibility that an opposing frictional surface was present on the tongue of this early snake.

The Lateral Lingual Papillae

Although the presence of a frictional surface of papillae and the fleshy nature of the hind-tongue make the tongue of *Lanthanotus* less snake-like in appearance than is the tongue of *Varanus*, the row of papillae along the lateral margin of the otherwise smooth foretongue seems to be a feature unique to *Lanthanotus* and the great majority of snakes.

The Relation of the Lachrymal Duct to the Maxilla

Although there is a remarkable similarity between the ventral duct of *Varanus* and the single duct of living snakes, particularly in the direct entry into the duct of Jacobson's organ, the extension of the maxilla along this duct to lie in the wall of the capsule of Jacobson's organ is a feature in which this genus is less snake-like than *Lanthanotus*, where the maxilla is not bound to Jacobson's organ. The motility of the maxillary bone in snakes demands that it be free of the Jacobson's organ, and it would be easier for such motility to arise in a form without such connection than in a form such as *Varanus*.

The Hyoid Arch

The extraordinary complication of the hyoid (*sensu stricto*) arch and its musculature in *Varanus* seems to be a modification for active expansion of the throat to receive food, or perhaps for respiration. None of the other lizards discussed here, or snakes, show any indication of exceptional ability to distend the throat actively (as opposed to a passive yielding to the stretching force of food entering the gullet).

The Constrictor Colli

Varanus seems to be much like *Heloderma* in heavy development of the constrictor colli. In the thin, almost membranous, nature of the constrictor colli, *Lanthanotus* is more snake-like than are *Varanus* and *Heloderma*, but no particular weight can be given to this because *Lanthanotus* is like the majority of lizards in this respect.

The Choanal Opening

The unusually large choanal opening of *Varanus* suggests a special affinity with *Heloderma* apart from the more general platynotan affinity. *Lanthanotus* has no suggestion of an enlarged choanal opening and, instead, resembles most lizards and snakes in this region.

The Interdigitations of the Mandibulohyoideus and Intermandibularis

The throat muscles of the scolecophidians would seem to indicate that the immediate ancestor of snakes has at least one interdigitating portion of the intermandibularis anterior. Very likely there were at least two mandibular slips of the mandibulohyoideus, one deep and anterior to the interdigitating slip of the intermandibularis, the other superficial and posterior to the interdigitating slip. The scolecophidian *Anomalepis* shows the most lizard-like arrangement, with a broad interdigitating slip of the intermandibularis passing between the outer two of the three slips of the mandibulohyoideus.

The great simplification of interdigitations between the mandibulohyoideus and intermandibularis seen in *Varanus* is a resemblance to higher snakes, but seems to be the result of parallelism, because the scolecophidians would seem to be derived from an ancestor with more complex interdigitations than are seen in *Varanus*.

In throat musculature, *Lanthanotus* retains interdigitating slips of the intermandibularis, lost in *Varanus* and higher snakes, but retained in the Scolecophidia. As in the case of the papillae on the foretongue, the throat muscles of *Lanthanotus* thus seem more like those to be expected in an ancestor of snakes. *Varanus* seems to have overshot the condition of primitive snakes and paralleled the higher snakes.

CONCLUSIONS: THE TONGUE AS A "CONSERVATIVE TAXONOMIC CHARACTER"

Although the preceding account has emphasized changes in tongue structure, we should remember the point made at the very beginning: that the tongue is essentially constant throughout snakes and is nearly or quite constant in structure in large groups of lizards (such as the Scincidae, Iguanidae, and Gekkonidae). Even in the transitional stages discussed here, the tongue is constant for each family involved, but the families are moderately small (Anguidae, Varanidae) to very small (Helodermatidae with two living species, Lanthanotidae with one species). This constancy does not extend to the throat muscles and hyobranchial skeleton, which show at least a moderate degree of variation within families with any considerable number of species.

Such constant structures as the tongue of snakes and of the various lizard groups are of enormous practical value to taxonomy for quick diagnosis of relationships. Although it is a truism that evolutionary relationships should be determined from many characters rather than from a single character, all experienced taxonomists are aware that in most groups of animals there are certain "single characters" that are more reliable indicators of relationships than are large assemblages of other characters. (Some examples: the Weberian ossicles of ostariophysan fishes; the amniotic and chorionic membranes of reptiles, birds, and mammals; the notochord of chordates). Because of their diagnostic value, these characters have been termed "conservative taxonomic characters." The tongue of snakes, and the diploglossan tongue of anguimorph lizards are "conservative taxonomic characters."

At one time, the constancy of "conservative taxonomic characters" was explained as a result of their lack of selective advantage or disadvantage. Aside from the point that many "conservative taxonomic characters" (including the examples cited above) can be demonstrated to be of major importance in the biological functions of the organisms possessing them, the implied assumptions about the genetics of these characters no longer seem reasonable. If a morphological character is the same in a large number of related species and is under the control of the same genes in all these species, these genes must be of a very wonderful sort. Such genes must be capable of achieving the same results in regulating a process as complex as metazoan development against almost any genetic background! Genetics is full of surprising discoveries, but I am skeptical of the discovery of any such amazing genes as these. That "conservative taxonomic characters" are the result of genes that have been "ignored" by natural selection and left undistrubed since the origin of the character is one of the least probable of all possible explanations. Much more likely, the "conservative taxonomic characters" are the result of homeostatic selection (as discussed by Mayr, 1963), and the phenotypes have been far more stable (and hence, more "basic") than the genes and developmental mechanisms at present responsible for them.

An examination of the "conservative taxonomic characters" discussed in this paper, the tongue structures characteristic of certain lizard families and of snakes, does not suggest that the structural features of the tongue of a given group are functionally unimportant; instead, quite the reverse is true, and for each group a balance has been struck between the demands of the organ of Jacobson and the demands of the feeding mechanism in determining the form of the tongue: both the organ of Jacobson, a food-locating and possibly also a mate-locating organ, and the feeding mechanism are most unlikely to be selectively neutral. However, although these structural features of the tongue are of great importance in detecting and (in most lizards) in engulfing food, they are of a general value and not closely related to any specific item of diet; a tongue structure advantageous for feeding on beetles would seem equally good for feeding on crickets. Hence, a large number of related species, each with its own unique niche and each with a unique set of resource species on which it is dependent, can all operate efficiently with the same tongue apparatus.

An examination of the transitional forms (most particularly *Heloderma* and *Lanthanotus*, but the anguoids might also be considered as transtiional between the majority of lizards and the platynotans) reveals that when a change in feeding habits changes the functional demands upon the tongue, the "conservative taxonomic characters" change in the same manner that other characters do under the influence of natural selection; there is no indication that the characters of the tongue that are so stable in large groups of lizards are inherently unable to change. The stability of the product (the tongue) has been a response to the demands of the market (as represented by natural selection) rather than the limitations of production (as represented by developmental mechanisms and their molecular control).

The transitional forms make a surprisingly good series, considering that only living forms are available for consideration, in which facultative structures of one stage become permanent structures in later stages, and in which morphological relationships (e.g., medial to, external to, etc.) of the structural elements to one another remain the same, but proportions change (including reduction to total absence) to such a degree as to produce qualitative differences.

At no point in this transition is there a stage that might be considered "inadaptive." Not only can each structural innovation be explained as an adaptation to a change in functional demands, but each of the transitional stages demonstrates by its survival that it is not only better adapted for its niche than more primitive forms, but is also better adapted (and better "morphologically integrated") for this niche than more specialized forms. *Heloderma* coexists with the less specialized anguids and with the more specialized snakes, and has successfully defended its niche from both quarters. *Lanthanotus* of Borneo is sympatric with *Varanus* and numerous snakes, both of which groups are more specialized in tongue structure than is *Lanthanotus* but are on the same line of "evolutionary trend," but neither *Varanus* nor any snake has dislodged *Lanthanotus* from its niche.

At the same time, the diploglossan tongue, although a specilization beyond most lizards, does not appear to have conferred on its possessors any remarkable power to usurp the niches of lizards without the ability of invaginating the foretongue within the hind-tongue. In terms of number of species, the Anguimorpha are only modestly successful (less successful than iguanids, tejids, scincids, or geckos). However, the specializations of the anguimorphans, when exaggerated and augmented with additional innovations, led to the Serpentes, a group so successful that the number of species of snakes is probably about equal to the number of species of all groups of lizards put together.

There is no evidence, from the present study, of the evolution of an adaptive complex of characters that any stage passed through an "adaptive valley." But there seems to have been a transition through isolated "adaptive peaks" and "small ranges" until an "adaptive cordillera" was reached. In the long run, "limited success" is perhaps equivalent to failure, for while the intermediate forms are able to defend their own niches from more progressive stages, they do not demonstrate any marked ability to take over *new* niches, and it is probable (although not certain) that all anguimorphan lizards will become extinct before all snakes have done so, and thus will appear[3] in hindsight as a relatively unsuccessful "transition" stage.

It is unlikely that the great success of snakes can be attributed to their tongue structure. More likely, the tongue structure is a concomitent of the general advantage enjoyed by the alethinophidian snakes: they are able to be unusually small relative to the size of their prey, and thus each species can split up its biomass into an unusually large number of individuals. The biomass available to predator species is limited by the biomass of the resource species upon which it feeds, and normally there is an enormous step-by-step decrease in number of individuals as one proceeds from initial resource species to primary predator to secondary predator and so on. Because of their ability to be not much larger than their prey, as well as their economical metabolism which does not dissipate food resources as heat in maintaining a body temperature, snakes are probably better able than most predatory animals to obtain the security of large population sizes.

Acknowledgments

I am most grateful to Dr. C. M. Bogert and Dr. R. G. Zweifel of the American Museum of Natural History (AMNH), and to Dr. E. E. Williams of the Museum of Comparative Zoology, Harvard University (MCZ) for the use of specimens in their collections. I am additionally indebted to Dr. Willaims for opportunity to see the manuscript and figures of Estes, Frazzetta, and Williams (1970) before publication and to see first hand the skull of *Dinilysia.* I am also most appreciative of the advice of a number of people, including Professor A. d'A. Bellairs, Dr. G. Underwood, Dr. K. C. Sondhi, and Professor C. Gans who read this manuscript in various stages.

Abbreviations Used on Figures

APAL	anterior process of palatine
APBH	anterior process of body of hyoid
BH	branchiohyoideus
CB I	ceratobranchial I
C	ceratohyoideus
CC	constrictor colli
CG	choanal groove
CH	ceratohyal
CJO	cartilage of Jacobson's organ
CM	cervicomandibularis
CN	concha nasalis
COH	cornuohyoideus
DL	lachrymal duct
DNP	ductus nasopharyngeus

[3]To whom it will "appear" I leave open, for by the argument here presented, it is unlikely that man will outlast either all species of snakes or all species of Anguimorpha.

ECC	ectochoanal cartilage
ECF	ectochoanal fold
ECM	episternocleidomastoideus
EOM	external oblique muscle (of trunk)
FE	fenestra exochoanalis, main portion
FE'	fenestra exochoanalis, slit-like forward continuation
FR	frenulum
FS	frictional surface of tongue
FT	foretongue
FVE	fenestra vomeronasalis externa
GC	genioceratoideus
GGL	genioglossus lateralis
GGM	genioglossus medialis
GMY	geniomyoideus
HG	hyoglossus
HGM	medial hyoglossus
HH	hypohyal
HT	hind-tongue
HTR	hyotrachealis
IMA	intermandibularis anterior
IMA 1	intermandibularis anterior, pars anterior
IMA 2	intermandibularis anterior, pars medialis
IMA 3	intermandibularis anterior, pars posterior
IMA IN	intermandibularis anterior, interdigitating portion
IMAS	intermandibularis anterior superficialis
IMA X	intermandibular chiasma
IMP	intermandidularis posterior
INPR	incisive process
IP	interportialis
ISF	inner sheathing fold
L	lappet representing posterior limb of tongue
LAR	larynx
MH	mandibulohyoideus
MP	mandibuloproximalis
MSG	median sublingual gland
MT	mandibulotrachealis
MTU	median tubercle
NCM	neurocostomandibularis
NCM L	neurocostomandibularis, lingual slip
NCM 1	neurocostomandibularis, superficial anterior slip
NCM 2	neurocostomandibularis, deep anterior slip
OH	omohyoideus
OLD	opening of lachrymal duct
OSF	outer sheathing fold
PAP	row of papillae on foretongue
PH	prearticulohyoideus
PLT	posterior limb of tongue
PTS	pterygoideus superficialis
SH	sternohyoideus
SPL	sublingual plica
TR	trachea
VF	vomerine flap

VOPL	plate of vomer
VP	ventral pallet of tongue
VR	vomerine raphe
XII	hypoglossal nerve
Z INV	zone of invagination

REFERENCES

Albright, R. G., and E. M. Nelson. 1959. Cranial kinetics of the generalized colubrid snake *Elaphe obsoleta quadrivittata*. J. Morph., 105:193-291.

Bahl, K. N. 1937. Skull of *Varanus monitor* (Linn.). Rec. Indian Mus., 39:133-174.

Barrows, S., and H. M. Smith. 1947. The skeleton of the lizard *Xenosaurus grandis* (Grey). Univ. Kansas Sci. Bull., 31:227-281.

Baumeister, L. 1908. Beiträge zur Anatomie und Physiologie der Rhinophiden. Integument, Drüson der Mundhohle, Augen und Skeletsystem. Zool. Jahrb; 26(Morph.): 423-526.

Bellairs, A. d'A. 1949. Observations on the snout of *Varanus*, and a comparison with that of other lizards and snakes. J. Anat., 83:116-146.

    and J. D. Boyd. 1950. The lachrymal apparatus in lizards and snakes.—II The anterior part of the lachrymal duct and its relationship with the palate and with the nasal and vomeronasal organs. Proc. Zool. Soc. London, 120:269-310.

    and J. D. Boyd. 1957. Anomalous cleft palate in snake embryos. Proc. Zool. Soc. London, 129:525-539.

    and G. Underwood. 1951. The origin of snakes. Biol. Rev. Cambridge Philos. Soc., 26:193-237.

Bogert, C. M., and R. Martín del Campo. 1956. The Gila Monster and its allies. Bull. Amer. Mus. Nat. Hist., 109:1-238.

Camp, C. L. 1923. Classification of the lizards. Bull. Amer. Mus. Nat. Hist., 48:289-481.

Coe, C. W., and B. W. Kunkel. 1907. Studies on the California limbless lizard, *Anniella*. Trans. Connecticut Acad., 12:349-396.

Cope, E. D. 1900. The crocodilians, lizards, and snakes of North America. Rept. U. S. Nat. Mus., 1898:153-1294.

deBeer, G. 1937. The Development of the Vertebrate Skull. Oxford, Oxford University Press.

Edmund, A. G. 1960. Tooth Replacement Phenomena in the Lower Vertebrates. Toronto, Royal Ontario Museum.

Estes, R. 1962. A fossil gerrhosaur from the Miocene of Kenya (Reptilia: Cordylidae). Breviora, 158:1-10.

    T. H. Frazzetta, and E. E. Williams. 1970. Studies of the fossil snake *Dinilysia patagonica* Woodward: Part I. Cranial morphology. Bull. Mus. Comp. Zool. (Harvard) 140(2):25-74.

Frazzetta, T. H. 1962. A functional consideration of cranial kinesis in lizards. J. Morph., 111:287-320.

    1966. Studies on the morphology and function of the skull in the Boidae (Serpentes). Part II. Morphology and function of the jaw apparatus in *Python sebae* and *Python molurus*. J. Morphol., 118:217-296.

Gans, C. 1952. The functional morphology of the egg-eating adaptations of the snake genus *Dasypeltis*. Zoologica (New York), 37:209-244.

    1961. The feeding mechanism of snakes and its possible evolution. Amer. Zool., 1:217-227.

Gibson, F. W. 1966. Head muscles of *Boa constrictor*. Zoologica (New York), 51:29-48.

Gnanamuthu, C. P. 1937. Comparative study of the hyoid and tongue of some typical genera of reptiles. Proc. Zool. Soc. London, 107(B):1-63.

Haas, G. 1955. The systematic position of *Loxocemus bicolor* Cope (Ophidia). Amer. Mus. Novitates, 1748:1-8.

1959. Bemerkungen über die Anatomie des Kopfes und des Schädels der Leptotyphlopidae (Ophidia), speziell von *L. macrorhynchus* Jan. Vierteljahrschrift Naturforsch. Ges. Zurich, 104:104.

1960. On the trigeminus muscles of the lizards *Xenosaurus grandis* and *Shinisaurus crocodilurus*. Amer. Mus. Novitates, 2017:1-54.

1964. Anatomical observations on the head of *Liotyphlops albirostris* (Typhlopidae, Ophidia). Acta Zool., 45:1-62.

1968. Anatomical observations on the head of *Anomalepis aspinosus* (Typhlopidae, Ophidia). Acta Zool., 49:63-139.

Harrison, T., And N. S. Haile. 1961. A rare earless monitor lizard from Borneo. Nature (London), 218(4782):1213.

Jollie, M. T. 1960. The head skeleton of the lizard. Acta Zool. 41:1-64.

Kamal, A. M. and H. G. Hammouda. 1965a. The development of the skull of *Psammophis sibilans*. J. Morphol., 116:197-310.

1965b. The chondrocranium of the snake *Eryx jaculus*. Acta Zool., 46:167-208.

Kornhuber, A. 1873. Ein neuen fossilen Saurier aus Lesina. Abh. K. K. Geol. Reichsinst. Wien, 5:75-90.

Langebartel, D. A. 1968. The Hyoid and its Associated Muscles in Snakes. Illinois Biol. Monogr. No. 38. Urbana, University of Illinois Press.

List, J. C. 1966. Comparative Osteology of the Snake Families Typhlopidae and Leptotyphlopidae. Illinois Biol. Monogr., No. 36. Urbana, University of Illinois Press.

Mayr, E. 1963. Animal Species and Evolution. Cambridge, Mass., Belknap Press of Harvard University Press.

McDowell, S. B. 1967. The extracolumella and tympanic cavity of the "earless" monitor lizard, *Lanthanotus borneensis*. Copeia, 1967: 154-159.

And C. M. Bogert. 1954. The systematic position of *Lanthanotus* and the affinities of the anguimorphan lizards. Bull. Amer. Mus. Nat. Hist., 105:1-142.

Mertens, R. 1964. Beobachtungen an Taubwaranen (*Lanthanotus borneensis*) in Terrarium. Datz, 6:179-183.

Myers, C. W. 1967. The familial position of *Typhlophis* Fitzinger (Serpentes). Herpetologica, 23:75-77.

Nopcsa, F. 1908. Zur Kenntnis der fossilen Ediechsen. Beitr. Paläont. Öster.-Ungarns, 21:5-62.

Oelrich, T. M. 1956. The anatomy of the head of *Ctenosaura pectinata* (Iguanidae). Misc. Publ. Mus. Zool., No. 94. Ann Arbor, University of Michigan.

Prado, A. 1945. Serpentes do Brazil. São Paulo, Sitios e Fazendas.

Pratt, C. W. McE. 1948. The morphology of the ethmoidal region of *Sphenodon* and lizards. Proc. Zool. Soc. London, 118:171-201.

Rooij, N. de. 1915. The Reptiles of the Indo-Australian Archipelago. I. Lacertilia, Chelonia, Emydosauria. Leiden, E. J. Brill.

Schmidt, K. P. 1928. Notes on the herpetology of Indo-China. Copeia, 1928:77-80.

Smith, H. M., and R. Warner. 1948. Evolution of the ophidian hyobranchium. Herpetologica, 4:189-193.

Smith, M. A. 1943. The Fauna of British India Ceylon and Burma, Including the Whole of the Indo-Chinese Sub-Region. Reptilia and Amphibia. Vol. III. Serpentes. London, Taylor and Francis.

Sondhi, K. C. 1958. The hyoid and associated structures in some Indian reptiles. Ann. Zool., 2:155-239.

Tchernavin, V. V. 1953. The feeding mechanisms of a deep sea fish *Chauliodus sloani* Schneider. London, British Museum [Natural History].

Underwood, G. 1957. On lizards of the family Pygopodidae. J. Morph., 100:207-268.

Warner, R. 1946. Pectoral girdles vs. hyobranchia in the snake genera *Liotyphlops* and *Anomalepis*. Science, 103:720-723.

9

The Trisulcate Petrosal Pattern of Mammals

GILES TERNAN MACINTYRE

Department of Biology
Queens College of the City University of New York
Flushing, N. Y. 11367

INTRODUCTION

New facts about the roots of major adaptive radiations have an obvious interest for students of evolution, but the beginnings of the great radiation of the Class Mammalia have a special significance in this dedicatory volume.

The great diversification of the placental and marsupial mammals, which traditionally characterized the Age of Mammals (geologically the Cenozoic era), is well known to have begun during the Age of Reptiles (the Mesozoic era). The common ancestral group from which both marsupials and placentals arose during the Cretaceous period generally resembled the smaller living opossums and tree shrews. Their known remains are mostly teeth, which are usually isolated and often broken. These teeth were nevertheless recognizable when first discovered as those of ancestral mammals, because they showed a characteristic primitive pattern postulated years before.

This chapter presents the view that there is also a primitive pattern of the petrosal bone just as characteristic of placental and marsupial mammals as is the primitive pattern of their teeth.

The petrosals are the paired bones of the mammalian skull that contain the hearing organs and the organs of balance and orientation in space. These ear bones are inconspicuous parts of the base of the cranium, just behind the jaw joint. They are usually covered, in most modern mammals, by a bony shell, the tympanic bulla, formed in various ways from parts of the tympanic bone and others in the region. Nearby, the internal carotid artery to the brain enters the skull, and the internal jugular vein drains out. Several important cranial nerves

275

pass through various openings in and around the petrosal, and one of them is solely concerned with carrying impulses to the brain from the complex organs inside the petrosal itself. This region is obviously anatomically important; its importance in terms of the broader questions of organic evolution perhaps can best be assessed after some recapitulation of familiar terms and concepts in what Simpson (1953) calls "Four-Dimensional Biology."

Recognition of a primitive pattern means, first of all, seeing familiar structures in a new way. The act of recognition implies full awareness of what is being recognized and why recognition is not trivial. Even now, many evolutionary hypotheses are concerned with primitive characters, because understanding evolution involves understanding genetic relationships (usually observed via phenotypic manifestations). Thus, contemporary taxa are normally taken to be genetically related if they share various primitive phenotypic characters. They are *not* normally taken to be *closely* related if *all* the shared characters are primitive.

Modern biologists understand that the primitive characters of a given group are those conditions presumably present in the ancestry. Such characters are commonly recognized as those found widespread among otherwise diverse organisms. When early members of diverse groups share characters that converge backward in time toward some common form, we can reasonably believe that to be the primitive form for all these groups.

However, because the term "primitive" is always relative to some other condition (expressed or implied), characters that are primitive at one level of organization are also specialized at the same time relative to a lower level of organization. That is to say, the primitive state of a character must also have been a viable, specialized adaptation, shaped by the usual processes of mutation and selection, at some time in the ancestral line. For example, the dentary-squamosal jaw articulation, a character primitive for mammals, was a specialized character among therapsid reptiles.

Clearly, if we are not to avoid the error of using the term "primitive" as an absolute, we need to judge it by its place in time. Circumstantial evidence such as geographical distribution for evolutionary sequences may be valid, but material evidence for occurrence in time comes from the fossil record. It should be obvious that evolutionary studies (even of Recent organisms) involve the time dimension to the extent that they involve the premise that the course of evolutionary events, as deduced from conditions observed in the present, actually did occur in the more or less remote past. Hence, unless the investigator has a complete series of breeding members of each generation preserved entire, statements of evolutionary relationships are by necessity speculative and arbitrary to some extent. This is not to say that such statements are invalid, but merely that, strictly speaking, they refer to probabilities.

Because of the necessary involvement of the time dimension, the discovery of an adequate fossil record constitutes a kind of experimental test of phylogenetic hypotheses and is hence much to be desired. Further, evolutionary or taxonomic hypotheses that conflict with a known fossil record should prompt a searching review of the evidence. To be sure, the fossil record is imperfect, but then so are other kinds of records, and paleontologists are usually well aware of the limitations of their material.

It is a truism that some characters are not observable in fossils. The term "character" in practice includes any observable fact about a given taxon, so that such things as prehistoric scents, sounds, and body temperatures are gone forever. Study of fossils is therefore anatomical study, usually of the parts left after the soft tissues have vanished (sometimes leaving marks on the hard parts), but having room for as much cautious speculation about behavioral or physiological characters as one may reasonably build upon the structures preserved.

Caution is sometimes made necessary by the nature of the character itself, which may be clear cut, like number of ribs, or continuously variable, like body size. Such characters are easy to measure or count, but others may be more subtle (e.g., shade of fur color), and there is no necessary correlation between the significance and the convenience for study of different characters. Bone structures are often subtle and variable in this way.

Complex characters, with several interrelated parts, may themselves be integrated with other character complexes, so that a change in one part may have far-reaching consequences. For example, reduction of the dentition in the termite-eating hyena (*Proteles*, the aard-wolf of Africa) is correlated with reduction of the jaw muscles and consequently of the muscle attachments on jaws and skull, resulting in a very different appearance from those parts in other hyenas. In contrast, the skull and teeth of *Acinonyx* (cheetahs) are unmistakably cat-like, but the feet and legs lack the sharp, retractable claws which other cats use for gripping; the cheetah foot and leg pattern is rather dog-like (for that matter, so is that of hyenas, including *Proteles*). Neither cheetahs nor hyenas are derived from dogs, of course, and there is no real difficulty in sorting out the groups in question, because associations are made on the basis of the totality of characters of the teeth, feet, arrangement of certain skull foramina, and many other factors, including the way in which the tympanic bulla forms around the petrosal.

From this example, it may be seen why, in order to detect underlying relationships and thus work out true evolutionary sequences, it is wise to examine carefully chosen sets of characters. Character complexes that are *not* functionally integrated with other such character complexes are particularly useful in this regard, because, although convergence in function for one such complex (e.g., feet) may result in close resemblance of individual parts, convergence in two such complexes (e.g., feet and teeth) is less likely, and for three (e.g., feet, teeth, and bullae) still less so. The probability of several unrelated systems converging is very small, but then, there is a limit to the systems that *can* be independent in a living organism. In any case, knowledge of the primitive state of each complex is a prerequisite to proper interpretation, and, against this background, the discovery of the primitive state of such a character complex for all mammals becomes a matter of interest from several points of view.

In order to sustain a claim that one has discovered a character complex primitive for all mammals, it seems necessary at this point to make clear what one includes in all mammals. To start with, I do not agree that Mammalia should be included under Reptilia (Von Huene, 1948), or submerged into Sarcopterygii, together with all tetrapods (Nelson, 1969), either. It may be logical to equate taxonomic units arising at the same time or from the same dichotomy (Hennig, 1965) but it is neither reasonable nor practical to do so in all cases; as Simpson pointed out (1945, p. 218): "There are other essential logical considerations, for instance, the desirability of approximate balance as to evolutionary status and distinctness."

Without going into details best elaborated elsewhere and omitting the well-known characters of living mammals that cannot be applied to fossils, the term "mammal" is here restricted to placentals, marsupials, and their immediate common ancestry. These true mammals are distinguishable from their Mesozoic near-mammalian relatives by a combination of four characteristics:

(1). A dentary bone free of all three middle ear bones in adults, and
(2). A cochlea of the inner ear with at least one full coil, and
(3). Mesozoic fossils with tribosphenic or pretribosphenic cheek teeth, and
(4). Living forms with a surpraspinous fossa on the scapula bone.

This diagnosis (no more arbitrary than the dentary-squamosal articulation formerly accepted, and believed to be unambiguous and less inconvenient than other proposed diagnoses) includes the vast majority of fossils now regarded as mammalian as well as all living mammals, excepting the peculiar, egglaying, platypus and echidnas of Australia, Tasmania, and New Guinea. As mammals, the monotremes are distinctly anomalous (being practically toothless, their relationships to Mesozoic groups are obscure; the ear region, as Simpson (1938) described it, is not of the therian type and I think not derivable from the primitive mammalian pattern), but as surviving therapsid reptiles they are perfectly comprehensible, although of course more like living mammals than like living lizards or turtles.

The fossil groups excluded by this diagnosis comprise a variety of totally extinct lines, of quasi-mammalian, borderline status, not directly ancestral to living placental or marsupial mammals, plus a more or less complete series of known or suspected members of that ancestral line back to the level of primitive fish.

The division of a continuous evolutionary spectrum is not likely to provoke instant agreement on all sides, but is to be hoped that my proposal will be considered from the standpoint of its expression of biological reality and practical applicability (keeping in mind the slow but seemingly inevitable improvement of the fossil record).

As a very general conclusion of this very general introduction, if we accept the very broad definition of systematics offered by Simpson (1961), the guiding principles remain biological and evolutionary. That more restricted facet of systematics, the art of classification, retains its relevance to the real world of life by following the same principles. Even though the investigator is dealing with the preserved remains of dead organisms from one time plane, he now thinks in terms of living populations, dynamically interconnected and changing constantly through time. This habit of mind leads one to examine those characteristics commonly used for sorting from the standpoint of biological significance in four dimensions; the groups arrived at by this means are most likely to be useful to other biologists.

HISTORICAL REVIEW

The ear region of the mammalian skull is a complicated anatomical domain which has been recognized by a growing number of students of mammalian evolution as the kind of independently evolving complex particularly useful for study. At least a score of active vertebrate paleontologists and surely many times that number of students of ear anatomy in Recent mammals have published contributions in the past 10 or 15 years, but at this writing, I am constrained to mention only the largest and most general works. Most of the past literature has not been on the petrosal proper, and fortunately most of it has been summarized in the detailed, structure-by-structure survey of the tympanic bulla by Van der Klaauw (1931), who often quotes the classic work by Van Kampen (1905). The embryology of the ear region has been discussed as part of the general development of the vertebrate skull by de Beer (1937), and various aspects of ear region anatomy are covered in general works such as Starck (1967). The morphology of the acoustic organs has recently been reviewed by Neubert and Wüstenfeld (1962), and Thenius (1969) has included practically all the shorter papers of interest here in his extensive review of mammalian paleontology. Because they apply to the ear regions of relatively primitive mammals or near-mammals, and also summarize a significant amount of previous work, certain short papers are particularly helpful starting points for study of fossil mammalian ear regions: Butler (1948, 1956, 1969), Crompton (1964), Hopson (1964), McDowell (1958), Olson (1944), and Simpson (1937, 1938) lead a long list of such works. There are dozens of other papers by these and other authors, but this brief review of the literature is not claimed to be exhaustive, nor does it cover the numerous studies of ear anatomy in Recent mammals. However, it should be clear that there has been a reversal of bygone conditions once observed by Matthew (1909, p. 334): "It is an unfortunate fact that the attention of paleontologists has been so exclusively centred upon the teeth of fossil mammals, that they have often failed to realize that these alone are an unsafe guide, especially in ordinal relationships."

Matthew (1909, 1937) and Gregory (1910) customarily used the ear region of the skull in arriving at their taxonomic conclusions, incidentally providing much information on the petrosals of primitive forms in which the bulla is reduced and easily detached. Although a primitive pattern for the petrosal bone was implicit in much of their studies, they never made it explicit. Again, in his classic book on the structure and development of vertebrates, Goodrich (1930, Fig. 490) illustrates the ear region of "a mammal" which (following van Kampen) contains most of the structures that one can actually observe or infer on the real fossil petrosal bones from Bug Greek Anthills Quarry (Late Cretaceous of Montana).[1] These fossils are much more abundant, cleaner, and much older than any placental mammal petrosals available before 1963, and they have made it possible for me not only to reconstruct the internal anatomy of the ear region in these Late Cretaceous mammals, but also to recognize in them the trisulcate pattern, which is here claimed to be primitive for all mammals (as defined above), in the same way that the very different character complex of the molar teeth of mammals permits recognition of a primitive pattern.

In the late 1930's G. G. Simpson reduced the cumbersome designation "tritubercular-tuberculosectorial" for the primitive molar tooth pattern to the short, euphonic, but descriptive term, *tribosphenic*. It was with the deliberate intention of recalling that felicitous and mnemonic name that I have chosen the term *trisulcate* to refer to the newly recognized primitive petrosal bone pattern. The three sulci, or grooves, to which my term refers are present on all the petrosal bones of primitive mammals of the Cretaceous, Paleocene, and Eocene known to me. Admittedly, these grooves (for the facial nerve, for the stapedial artery, and for the inferior petrosal vein) may be marked to varying degrees, but they are a convenient peg to hang a short, easily remembered name upon, not a truly vital component of the pattern. The details of that pattern concern us next.

DESCRIPTION

If one thinks of a relatively primitive mammal (e.g., dog) skull as being roughly the shape of a half-cone with the nose at the apex and the neck attached to the semicircular base, the petrosal bones would be exposed at the corners of that base. They are medial and ventral to the squamosals, ventrolateral to the

---

[1] Details of this quarry and represented fauna were published by Sloan (1964, 1969) and Sloan and Van Valen (1965).

supraoccipital, lateral and anterior to the exocipitals, dorsolateral to the basioccipital, and posterolateral to the exoccphenoid bones.

The overall shape of a trisulcate petrosal is neither simple nor any more regular than that of the skull itself, but may be geometrically visualized as irregularly tetrahedral, with four apices and four sides (Fig. 1). The side usually exposed on the posterolateral corner of the skull may be called the *lambdoid* side; the side

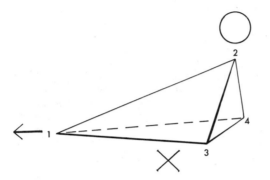

Fig. 1. Tetrahedron, to illustrate the general shape of a trisulcate petrosal. 1, rostral apex; 2, dorsal apex; 3, paroccipital apex; 4, mastoid apex. The arrow points in the anterior direction, the cross marks the medial side, the circle marks the dorsal side.

usually visible on the inside of the skull is here called the *cerebellar side*; the *squamosal side* and the *tympanic side* face the squamosal and tympanic bones, respectively. The *rostral apex* is at the pointed end of the *petrous portion* and points toward the optic chiasma. The *dorsal apex* ("apex" of authors) is the highest point of the *mastoid portion* and points upward along the nuchal crest of the skull. The *paroccipital apex* is posteromedial, close to the suture with the exoccipital bone, and posterolateral to the *sulcus jugularis*. The *mastoid apex* is more lateral and corresponds to the most ventral extension of the *mastoid process*. The two portions of the petrosal bone may be conveniently recognized in these primitive forms as a flattened ovoid (*petrous*) portion, fused at the larger end to one corner of a roughly pyramidal (*mastoid*) portion (Fig. 2). Fossils collected by washing and screening may lose the more fragile mastoid portion; the remaining petrous portion then resembles an apple or orange seed, perforated on both sides and at the blunt end.

Certain striking features make identification of the sides reasonably simple, even in isolated specimens, and the orientations suggested are based on study of the osseous labyrinth.

The cerebellar side faces dorsomedially toward the brainstem, tends to be more or less concave, and is marked by two conspicuous openings: the *internal auditory meatus* in the petrous portion—primitively shallow and subdivided into

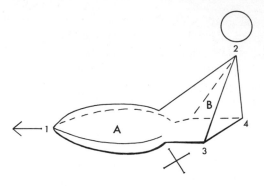

Fig. 2. Relationship of petrous portion (A) to mastoid portion (B) of the petrosal bone as seen from cerebellar side; other parts coded as in Fig. 1. Side 1, 2, 3 is the cerebellar side; 2, 3, 4 is the lambdoid side; 1, 3, 4 is the tympanic side; 1, 2, 4 is the squamosal side. The crista petrosa runs from (2) toward (1); the cross on the medial side indicates the jugular notch, and the lower edge of (A) from this notch to (1) is the crista promontorii medioventralis. Diagram, not to scale.

several smaller pits; and the *subarcuate (parafloccular) fossa* in the mastoid portion—primitively deep and simple.

The squamosal side faces anterolaterally, tends to be more or less vertical and comparatively flattened. It is bounded dorsally by a crest (*crista petrosa*) which extends from the rostral apex toward the dorsal apex along the lateral boundaries of the internal auditory meatus and the subarcuate fossa. The ventral edge of the squamosal side is turned ventrally and thins out into a relatively sharp crest (usually broken) which passes from the rostral apex toward the mastoid apex. The alisphenoid and squamosal bones may have been in contact with some parts of this edge. There is no indication of a pyriform fenestra as described for soricoid insectivores by McDowell (1958). Strictly speaking, the thin, laterally directed shelf of the *tegmen tympani* is not developed primitively (see McDowell, 1958, for a convenient list of definitions and sources), but this ventrally directed crest could be a precursor, in part.

The tympanic side faces ventrolaterally, forming the roof and part of the wall of the tympanic cavity. It tends to be more or less convex and is marked by the semi-ovoid bulge of the *promontorium cochleae*, being the ventral side of the petrous portion. The prominent crest of the *crista facialis petrosi* (bearing the tympanohyal at its most posteromedial extremity and the *processus mastoidei* laterally) defines a somewhat excavated area, the *fossa mesotympanicae* which includes a lateral area of excavation (shared with the squamosal), the *recessus epi-tympanicas*. Opening into this area are the facial canal, the oval opening for the foot plate of the stapes (*fenestra ovalis vestibuli*), and the *fenestra cochleae* ("*rotunda*" of man but not primitively rounded) at the posterior end of the promontorium. Posterior to the fenestra ovalis and immediately posterolateral to the fenestra cochleae is a rounded pit for the stapedius muscle, the *fossa muscularis minor*, and skirting the lateral rim of that pit is a groove (*sulcus facialis*) leading from the facial canal toward the posterior end of the mastoid portion. At the posterior end of this groove, a hook-like projection (*tympanohyal*) may be seen in well-preserved specimens; growing ventrally and medially, it defines a semicircular passage known as the *foramen stylo-mastoideum primitivum* (even though it is not primitively a foramen in the strict sense, but a sulcus). Van der Klaauw (1931) has provided an exhaustive discussion of this and similar details, without indicating the primitive conditions. In summary, the tympanic side is the most complex.

The *lambdoid side* faces posteriorly and laterally, tends to be flattened, and is marked by the relatively more rugose surfaces, with various pits and ridges, associated with muscular attachments. Because of the effect which muscles have upon bone, molding and modeling it with glacial slowness but just as much implacability, the lambdoid side tends to be the most variable, both ontogenetically and phylogenetically. In consequence, the mastoid portion of the petrosal is likely to be more useful in separating related genera than in recognizing primitive patterns.

The general features can be summarized as those of a vaguely tetrahedral bone, roughened somewhat for muscle attachment on the outer side, rather complex on the base, marked by two big holes on the inner side, and practically featureless on the fourth side. The dense, smooth, seed-shaped petrous portion is distinguishable from the more porous, gnarled, pyramidal, mastoid portion, but more because of their contents than any sharp morphological boundary, surely *not* because there is any trace of a pro-otic versus opisthotic homology. The two ancestral halves of the late therapsid periotic were anterior and posterior, indistinguishably fused long before the essentially dorsal and ventral moieties of mastoid and petrous portions could be distinguished.

The fundamental character of the petrosal is largely dictated by the important sensory apparatus which it contains (Fig. 3). When the bone is reduced, as in some living bats and shrews, this effect is striking. The *membranous labyrinth* is a set of tubes within tubes, the inner set comprising the *endolymphatic system*, derived from the original ectodermal invagination of the otic vescicle and containing the modified thigmoreceptors of the sensory nerves, which detect and differentiate gravity, head motions, and sound vibrations in association with the sacculus, utriculus, semicircular canals, and cochlea. This set of tubes and chambers is almost completely enveloped in a mesodermal casing, the *perilymphatic* system, which fits tightly around the cochlear duct, more loosely around the semicircular canals, and so spaciously around the sacculus, utriculus, and connecting ducts that only a vague *vestibular cavity (cavum vestibuli)* can be inferred in the *osseous labyrinth*. In contrast, the osseous labyrinth rather faithfully mirrors the perilymphatic system in bone.

As revealed by randomly fractured fossils of Late Cretaceous placental

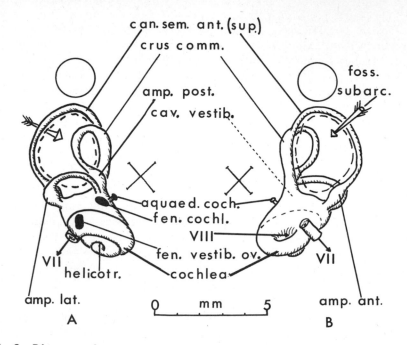

can. sem. ant.(sup.)

crus comm.

foss.
subarc.

amp. post.
cav. vestib.

aquaed. coch.
fen. cochl.
VIII
fen. vestib. ov.

VII

VII
helicotr.   cochlea

amp. lat.   0   mm   5   amp. ant.

A   B

Fig. 3. Diagram of reconstructed left osseous labyrinth in Late Cretaceous mammal, (A) seen from the posterolateral and somewhat ventral aspect; (B) from the anteromedial and somewhat dorsal aspect. The arrow passes posteriorly into the outline of the fossa subarcuata. The pointer for the cavum vestibuli also indicates the approximate location of the base of the aquaeductus vestibuli (for endolymphatic duct), but not actually observed by me. VIII and VII indicate the main passages for the acoustic and facial nerves, respectively. The labeled ampullae also indicate the corresponding anterior (superior), posterior (inferior), and horizontal (lateral) semicircular canals. The circle indicates the dorsal, the cross the medial side. Abbreviations: amp. ant., ampulla of anterior semicircular canal: amp. lat., ampulla of lateral (horizontal) semicircular canal; amp. post., ampulla of posterior (inferior) vertical semicircular canal; aquaed. coch., cochlear aqueduct for perilymph; can. sem. ant. (sup.), anterior (superior) vertical semicircular canal; cav. vestib., position of cavum vestibuli; crus comm., crus commune; fen. cochl., fenestra cochleae; fen. vestib. ov., fenestra vestibuli ovalis; foss. subarc., fossa subarcuata; helicotr., helicotrema of cochlea.

mammals (from Bug Creek, Montana) the structure of the inner ear is hence shown in detail proportionate to the tightness of fit of the osseous labyrinth around the endolymphatic system. This permits a reasonable reconstruction of the labyrinth from fossils, with some limits.

The sound detectors of the cochlea are contained within the petrous portion, the detectors of motion in the semicircular canals are inside the mastoid portion, and the gravity detectors are generally near the junction between the two regions.

Due to the loose fit of the cavum vestibuli, the gravity detectors (utriculus and sacculus) together with the fine ducts connecting them with the other parts of the endolymphatic labyrinth cannot be traced in fossils. The *crus commune*, which is usually attached directly to the utriculus, is seen to be much as usual in Recent mammals—an essentially vertical tube uniting the *superior* and *inferior semicircular* canals. These two semicircular canals primitively were at right angles to each other and to the lateral semicircular canal; the latter is horizontal when the head is in a neutral attitude, while the other two are normally at a 45° angle to the sagittal plane of the head, and to a vertical transverse plane bisecting the crus commune of the right as well as that of the left ear. Once the position of the canals is determined, therefore, it is convenient to use them in reconstructing the original orientation of isolated petrosal bones.

Turning to the cerebellar side of the bone (Fig. 4), the fossa subarcuata is bounded in large part by the semicircular canals. The slight swelling (gyrus) of the bone covering the anterior (superior) canal forms the dorsal lip of the opening to the subarcuate fossa. Within the medial lip of the broadly open fossa, this anterior canal joins the crus commune. The posterior (inferior) canal curves backward from the upper end of the crus commune. Carefully focused, narrow-beam illumination into the fossa will show its gyrus within the posteromedial wall, and the gyrus of the horizontal (lateral) canal in the floor, of the subarcuate fossa. Because these canals thus define this large cavity primitively, and because the paraflocculus of the brain is a rather variable structure without any experimentally verified function (and absent in humans and other species, hence functionless in those species at least) the terms "parafloccular," or "floccular fossa" of authors seem inappropriate to me.

Orientation of petrosals may also be aided by the observation that the ventral *gyrus* of the horizontal canal is primitively visible as the rounded rim of the cavity (*fossa muscularis minor*) (Fig. 5) giving origin to the stapedius muscle. This shallow fossa lies opposite the bar of bone separating the fenestra ovalis vestibuli from the fenestra cochleae. It is usually skirted laterally by the sulcus facialis. In small petrosal bones the roof of the fossa muscularis minor and the floor of the fossa subarcuata are separated by a layer of bone thin enough to be transluscent. This area of near-contact of the two cavities in such specimens provides another feature useful in orientation, because if the thin spot is down, the canal around it must be more or less horizontal.

Comparison of the relationships of the three semicircular canals described here for Cretaceous mammals with those of any Recent mammal will show a clear consistency of pattern. Anything else would be surprising, since the same structures in practically any gnathostone vertebrate reveal the remarkably conservative nature of this part of the system. No significant differences appear in the cavum vestibuli between Cretaceous and Recent, but inferences here are limited, as previously noted.

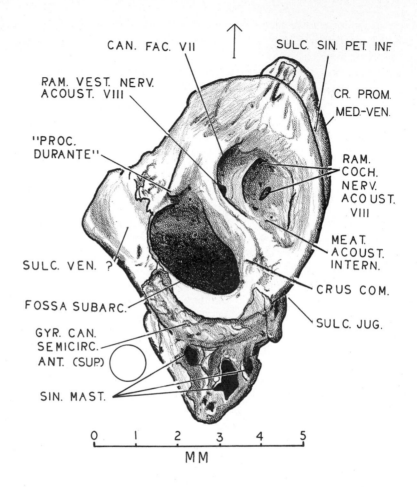

CAN. FAC. VII

SULC. SIN. PET. INF

RAM. VEST. NERV.
ACOUST. VIII

CR. PROM.
MED.-VEN.

"PROC.
DURANTE"

RAM.
COCH.
NERV.
ACOUST.
VIII

MEAT.
ACOUST.
INTERN.

SULC. VEN. ?

CRUS COM.

FOSSA SUBARC.

SULC. JUG.

GYR. CAN.
SEMICIRC.
ANT. (SUP)

SIN. MAST.

0   1   2   3   4   5

MM

Fig. 4. Cerebellar side of trisulcate petrosal. ("Ferungulate" variety from Late Cretaceous of Montana.) Arrow at anterior end; circle on dorsal side. Abbreviations: CAN. FAC. VII, facial canal or area facialis. CR. PROM. MED.-VENT., crista promontorii medioventralis. CRUS COM., crus commune. FOSSA SUBARC., fossa subarcuata. GYR. CAN. SEMICIRC. ANT. (SUP.), gyrus of anterior vertical (superior) semicircular canal. MEAT. ACOUST. INTERN., internal acoustic meatus. "PROC. DURANTE," proboscis-shaped process. RAM. COCH. NERV. ACOUST. VIII, foramina for cochlear ramus of acoustic (auditory) nerve or area cochleae. RAM. VEST. NERV. ACOUST. VIII, foramen for vestibular ramus of acoustic nerve. SIN. MAST., mastoid sinuses. SULC. JUG., jugular notch. SULC. SIN. PET. INF., groove for inferior petrosal sinus vein. SULC. VEN.?, probable course of postglenoid branch of internal jugular vein.

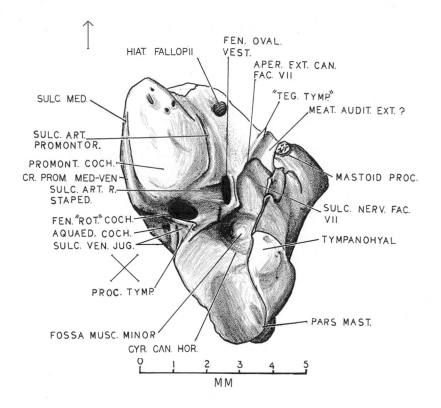

Fig. 5. Tympanic side of trisulcate petrosal. ("Ferungulate" variety from Late Cretaceous of Montana.) Arrow at anterior end; cross on medial side. Abbreviations: *APER. EXT. CAN. FAC. VII*, external opening of facial nerve canal. *AQUAED. COCH.*, opening for perilymphatic duct. *CR. PROM. MED.-VEN.*, medioventral crest of promontorium. *FEN. OVAL. VEST.*, fenestra ovalis vestibuli. *FEN. "ROT." COCH.*, fenestra "rotundum" cochleae. *FOSSA MUSC. MINOR*, fossa for stapedius muscle. *GYR. CAN. HOR.*, gyrus of horizontal semicircular canal. *HIATUS FALLOPII*, exit for great superficial ramus of facial nerve. *MASTOID PROC.*, processus mastoideus. *MEAT. AUDIT. EXT.?*, possible location of external auditory meatus. *PARS MAST.*, mastoid portion of petrosal bone. *PROC. TYMP.*, tympanic process. *PROMONT. COCH.*, promontorium of cochlea. *SULC. ART. R. STAPED.*, sulcus for the stapedial branch of the internal carotid artery. *SULC. MED.*, sulcus medialis, probably for medial ramus of internal carotid artery. *SULC. NERV. FAC. VII*, sulcus for the facial nerve. *SULC. VEN. JUG.*, jugular notch. "*TEG. TYMP.*," possible incipient tegmen tympani. *TYMPANOHYAL*, area of attachment for hyoid arch.

The *cochlea* contains the specialized organ of hearing (*organ of Corti*) enclosed within an ectodermal duct (*scala media*) of wedge-shaped cross section, but these leave no traces on the bone.

The scala media is enfolded partly within two mesodermal ducts, one below (*scala tympani*) and the other partly above (*scala vestibuli*). These mesodermal ducts join at the small end (*helicotrema*) of the cochlea, but for most of their length they are separated by a sharp shelf of bone (*lamina spiralis osseae*) attached to the hollow core (*modiolus*) of the cochlear helix (the result is not unlike the thread of a short, fat, wood screw). In living mammals, the *basilar membrane* joins the outer wall of the cochlea with the spiral lamina, completing the roof of the scala tympani and forming the floor of the scala media under the organ of Corti.

The base of the spiral lamina contains a helical canal (*canalis spiralis modioli*), which houses the spiral ganglion of the acoustic nerve (VIII) and this communicates with the many branches of the cochlear ramus of that nerve via the sieve-like *tractus spiralis foraminosus*. This spiral tract of foramina forms part of the wall of the *area cochleae*, one of the conspicuous pits within the internal auditory meatus.

In all Late Cretaceous mammal petrosals having breaks in the promontorium, the cochlea is visibly coiled. Specimens broken across show that there were at least two coils, and one specimen (Fig. 6) fractured across the facial canal (which passes close to the vestibular cavity near the beginning of the cochlea) and almost exactly through the helicotrema (the end of the cochlea), makes a reconstruction of the true shape of the cochlea possible, as well as revealing the finer details just described. This reconstruction shows that the left cochlea had two turns, counterclockwise downward, decreasing in diameter as usual toward the helicotrema. No living mammals have fewer than one turn to the cochlea and most mammals have only one or two additional turns. Platzer and Firbas (1966) have shown that some living shrews have just two turns, and more general data may be found in Neubert and Wüstenfeld (1962).

In summary, there has been relatively little change (except for lengthening in most but not all mammals) in the cochlea during the last 65 million years, perhaps longer. Fernandez and Schmidt (1963) found striking similarities of cell structure and cochlear function among living placental and marsupial mammals, an indication that structures that the fossil record cannot show were probably little changed well back into the Cretaceous. I have no facts that contradict their view that the basic cochlear structure was probably evolved before the placental-marsupial differentiation occurred. They also point out that the presence of a macula lagenae at the end of the monotreme cochlea is more primitive than its absence in the cochlea of placentals and marsupials, another of the many facts emphasizing the isolated, anomalous position of the monotremes.

Having discussed the labyrinth, we turn to a number of surface features of the primitive trisulcate petrosal which are significant (Fig. 7).

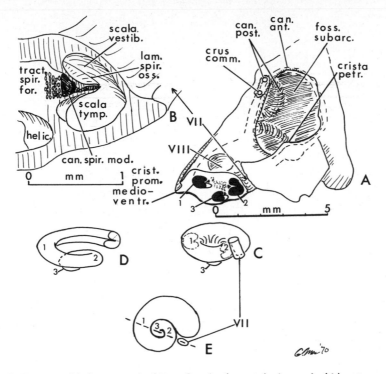

Fig. 6. Fractured left petrosal of Bug Creek placental, shown in (A) anteromedial and somewhat dorsal view (compare Fig. 3,B), with (B) enlarged detail of cochlear cross-section. (C) Reconstruction of cochlear relation to facial canal VII. (D) Reconstruction of cochlear coil, indicating direction of coil from (1) to (3), counterclockwise downward in left ear. (E) Reconstructed plan of cochlea, showing line of break (dashes) across helicotrema in coil (3) and facial canal (VII) just beyond beginning of cochlea. Abbreviations: can. ant., can. post., anterior and posterior vertical semicircular canals. can. spir. mod., canalis spiralis modioli. crista petr., crista petrosa. crist. prom. medio-ventr., crista promontorii medioventralis. crus comm., crus commune. fossa subarc., fossa subarcuata; helic., helicotrema. lam. spir. oss., lamina spiralis osseae. scala tymp., scala tympani. scala vestib., scala vestibuli. tract. spir. for., tractus spiralis foraminosus. VII, canalis facialis. VIII, area cochleae meatus auditorius internus.

There are four openings which appear to be primitive for mammals from the vestibular cavity to the outside of the petrosal: *fenestra ovalis vestibuli, fenestra cochleae, aquaeductus cochleae* and *aquaeductus vestibuli*. The *fenestra ovalis vestibuli* is a conspicuous oval opening on the lateral face of the promontorium, and opens out from the proximal end of the scala vestibuli. In life, the footplate of the stapes (*basic stapedis*) fills the fenestra, thus connecting it to the incus, the malleus, and the tympanic membrane ultimately. None of the isolate ossicles of any Cretaceous mammal have been discovered yet. If a stapes should be found, it will probably be unsurprising in form, to judge from the clues available.

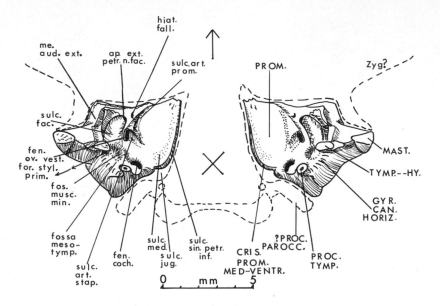

Fig. 7. Diagram of restored Late Cretaceous mammalian basicranium of type referred provisionally to unguiculate affinities. Dashed outlines are hypothetical. Compare Figs. 5 and 8.

There is a marked socket around the external rim of the fenestra ovalis vestibuli indicating that it fitted closely around a footplate with semicircular ends and straight sides. The presence of a definite groove (*sulcus arteriae stapediae*) leading directly across the fenestra ovalis vestibuli indicates that there was a well-developed stapedial branch of the internal carotid artery passing through the stapes. The presence of a *fossa muscularis minor* posterior to the fenestra ovalis indicates that the *musculus stapedius* originated there, and we may reasonably imagine that it inserted on the nearest leg (*posterior crus*) of the stapes, as usual.

Just at the posterior end of the promontorium, medial to the fossa muscularis minor, is the second largest opening to the vestibule, actually opening at the distal end of the scala tympani. This opening is the *fenestra cochleae*, which in life is closed by the *membrana tympanica secunda*, a compensating membrane to relieve the rapid changes in hydraulic pressure caused by the vibrating stapes. Long-term pressure changes in the *perilymph* (fluid filling the spaces between the mesodermal and ectodermal labyrinth) are evidently adjusted via the *aquaeductus cochleae*, a short passage primitively opening into the jugular notch just dorsal and medial to the fenestra cochleae. The small *vena cochleae* (cochlear vein) travels with this aqueduct.

The *aquaeductus vestibuli*, a longer and narrower passage opening more dorsally in Recent mammals, has not yet been surely identified in my specimen of primitive trisulcate petrosals, but Clemens (1966) has identified it in *Didelphodon*, a marsupial discussed below. In living mammals it carries the slender *ductus endolymphaticus*, from the vestibular cavity near the base of the crus commune, providing a compensating mechanism for the *endolymph* (a sea-water-like fluid, similar to perilymph, filling the ectodermal labyrinth).

The *sulcus jugularis* is a broad, rather smooth and shallow, nearly vertical notch in the medial edge of the petrosal, at the rear end of the promontorium. Together with a corresponding slight indentation in the exoccipital bone, it forms half of the *foramen jugulare* (usually called *foramen lacerum posterius*) for the internal jugular vein and cranial nerves IX, X, and XI. No separate imprints of these structures are visible on the bone, but the invariable association in living mammals of these structures leaves little doubt that such was true of Cretaceous mammals.

Passing forward from the sulcus jugularis along the smooth, nearly straight medial edge of the promontorium is a distinct groove for the inferior petrosal sinus vein (*suleus sini petrosi inferior*). In living mammals that vein connects the venous sinus (*sinus cavernosus*) encasing the arterial circle of Willis (around the pituitary gland and optic chiasma) with the internal jugular vein just before it emerges from the jugular foramen. In primitive trisulcate petrosals there is a crest just dorsal to this sulcus and a more prominent crest immediately ventral to it. Between this prominent crest (which I will call the *crista promontorii medioventralis*) and the bulge of the promontorium proper, another, fainter sulcus is visible on the ventral surface, possibly for the medial branch of the primitive entocarotid artery. This medial ramus may have run concurrently or even coaxially with the inferior petrosal sinus vein (as does the human carotid), but because it could well have followed a separate and more ventral path, that groove may be called the *sulcus medialis* without prejudice.

The presence of the stapedial artery has already been inferred; diverging from the most ventral part of the sulcus arteria stapedia on trisulcate petrosals, a similar, but longer and somewhat less distinct groove can be seen, curving around toward the rostral end of the promontorium. This groove (*sulcus arteriae promontorii*) probably marks the passage of the promontory ramus of the entocarotid artery, which is "the carotid" of primates. The promontory ramus is therfore technically the mainstream of the carotid artery. The groove for the arteria promotorii is usually small and may be absent in early placentals as it is in all marsupials, indicating that it was not primitively the mainstream artery, but rather a small branch of the stapedial, which itself if a branch of the medial entocarotid discussed above.

It is therefore necessary to remember that the three sulci of the primitive trisulcate petrosal were for the facial nerve, the stapedial artery, and the inferior petrosal sinus vein; there may have been three branches of the carotid artery in primitive placentals, which could have left additional grooves.

On the cerebellar side, dorsal to the opening of the subarcuate fossa, there was probably a sinus jugularis lateralis, which arched over the opening and connected posteromedially with the inferior cerebral vein near the jugular foramen, while connecting anterolaterally with the transverse sinus, draining ventrally through the postglenoid foramen. However, there is not sufficient clarity or uniformity in the possible pathways of these veins to warrant including their vague and variable sulci as part of the primitive pattern.

Projecting ventrally from the lip of the jugular sulcus, a transversely oriented bony strut (*processus tympanicus*) partly conceals but does not occlude the fenestra cochleae. When well developed it may have supported the posterior part of the ectotympanic ring. There is no evidence suggesting fusion of this processus tympanicus with the tympanohyal in primitive trisulcate petrosals, but the two processes may have nearly completed the ring around the foramen stylomastoideum primitivum; all available specimens in which this might have occurred have one or the other of these relatively delicate processes somewhat damaged. Specimens in which the processus tympanicus is reduced appear to have it in vestigial form rather than incipient form, but although its *presence* is probably a primitive character, great development of this process represents a specialization.

Following the sulcus facialis *inward* from the foramen stylomastoideum primitivum, it appears as a well defined, curving groove which skirts the rim of the fossa muscularis minor (for the stapedius muscle), bends medially and passes, dorsal to the fenestra ovalis vestibuli, through the *apertura externa canalis facilis petrosi*. This opening is a little dorsal and anterior to the fenestra ovalis; it leads to a straight passage which ends anteriorly in another foramen (*hiatus fallopii*). Primitively opening on the ventral side of the petrosal, near the point where the bulge of the promontorium meets the edge connecting the rostral apex with the mastoid apex, the hiatus fallopii (in living mammals) is the exit for a nerve (*ramus petrosus superficialis major* VII) which branches off from the facial nerve. After joining with the *nervus petrosus profundus major* (a nerve of the sympathetic system branching from the *nervus carotidis interni*) the great superficial petrosal nerve is known as the vidian nerve and ultimately joins the sphenopalatine ganglion. The facial nerve proper (homologous with the ancestral fish *ramus hyomandibularis* VII) and its anterior branch are thus connected within a short, straight tunnel, thinly covered with bone. If this bone is broken (as usual in fossils), a large canal at right angles to the surface tunnel can be seen, and careful study indicates a slight enlargement of the canal at this point, undoubtedly a fossa for the geniculate ganglion. In living mammals the great superficial petrosal nerve leaves the ganglion on the anterior side, while the facial nerve proper turns sharply in the posterior direction toward the sulcus facialis. The facial nerve root canal may be traced inward from the ganglion straight into the internal auditory meatus on the cerebellar side of the petrosal.

The *meatus auditis internus* is a shallow opening in the cerebellar face of the petrous portion of the trisulcate petrosal. It is subdivided into two deeper pits by a strong crest (*crista transversa*) oriented toward the rostral apex of the petrosal, more or less parallel to the crista petrosa. The larger of the pits (*area cochleae*) is more ventromedial, showing a helical band of small foramina for the clochlear ramus of the auditory nerve (cranial nerve VIII, also called *acusticus*)—previously described in connection with the cochlea. The posterior part of the area cochleae also contains small foramina for parts of the *ramus vestibuli* of the auditory nerve going to the sacculus, utriculus, and the posterior ampulla. Dorsal to the crista transversa are two more foramina in the *area facialis*. The larger and more anterior foramen is the beginning of the facial canal, already described. The smaller, more dorsal of the two openings carries branches of the vestibular ramus of the acoustic nerve to the anterior and lateral ampullae of the corresponding semicircular canals.

It is usual, in living mammals, for practically all foramina to carry a vein and an artery as well as a nerve; presumably the major nerve foramina have accompanying small blood vessels, just as the larger arteries are accompanied by small nerves, and the larger veins often have a concurrent arterial supply.

The *fossa subarcuata* is primitively large and spheroidally rounded; the few significant details of its structure have already been discussed in connection with the semicircular canals.

The lambdoid side of petrosals is the side least likely to be well preserved and the most likely to be variable. As a fossil skull disintegrates, the more exposed and delicate mastoid portion is more likely to break up before the denser, more protected petrous part. In life, the details of muscular attachments arc probably more subject to comparatively rapid ontogenetic and phylogenetic changes than structures associated with the nervous and sensory systems. Interpretation of such muscle attachments is not conveniently done on isolated petrosals, moreover, and in order to avoid speculation, this paper will include only rather general remarks on possible muscular attachments in this region of the skull.

There are two major muscular processes associated with this region of the skull: paroccipital and mastoid. The paroccipital process may involve the adjacent part of the mastoid region with this basically exoccipital outgrowth. The digastric muscle and related depressors of the mandible originate from the extreme tip of the paroccipital process in such a wide variety of mammals (Turnbull, 1970, shows this for *Didelphis, Echinosorex, Felis, Equus, Odocoileus, Ovis, Sciurus, Rattus,* and *Hystrix*) that it is hard to believe that this muscle could have primitively been attached to the mastoid. Muscles that turn the head and neck, or elevate or depress the head on the neck, on the other hand, are attached either to the paroccipital process (*rectus capitis lateralis*—nods head downward) or to both paroccipital and mastoid processes (*obliquus capitis anterior*—both working together toss head up; singly flex to side) or are attached to the mastoid and the nuchal crest (*splenius*—together raise head and neck; singly flex to side) as well as to the wing of the atlas and the transverse processes of some other cervical vertebrae, or possibly to the mastoid process alone (*longissimus capitis et atlantis*—extend head and neck; singly flex head and neck laterally, or rotate atlas). The mastoid process thus is a point of origin or insertion for muscles that move the head and neck but not the jaws, while the paroccipital process (which may be partly formed in the basal region by the mastoid portion of the petrosal) is mainly an attachment point for muscles of the head and neck, and gives origin to mandibular depressor muscles only at or near the extreme tip.

From the foregoing, it may reasonably be deduced that ventral enlargement of the mastoid region posterior to the sulcus jugularis would be the result of enlargement of the paroccipital process or of its forward movement relative to the petrosal; this in turn would be due to a change in the jaw-opening muscles or the head and neck movement muscles, or both. Enlargement of the mastoid process, located close to the lateral side of the skull, just behind the external ear opening (*meatus auditis externus*) is associated with the enlargement of neck muscles. The *processus mastoideus* (properly so-called) is a ventral projection, but in primitive mammals, with relatively large jaw muscles and small braincases, there is a lateral component, attached to a corresponding lateral expansion of the post-tympanic process of the squamosal bone (which forms the dorsal rim of the external ear opening and which I will call the *lateral mastoid flange, apophysis lateralis mastoideus*). The lateral mastoid flange is a laterally directed, vertically oriented extension of the nuchal or occipital crest. It is characteristically roughened for muscle attachment and commonly shows the suture between the squamosal and mastoid portions along its edge.

The mastoid process of the primitive trisulcate petrosal is distinct and has some lateral expansion, but the exact size and shape of the process is variable. Primitively, trisulcate petrosals probably had no special involvement in the paroccipital process of the exoccipital bone, and this process was primitively distinct from the mastoid process.

Because the primitive trisulcate petrosal was probably not covered by a bony bulla of any great extent (except for the partial protection of membranes and a presumably rather simple ectotympanic ring) no special bullar attachments of the mastoid or paroccipital processes were present.

The *processus tympanicus*, which supports the ectotympanic bone, is a structure found only in mammals because the mammalian ectotympanic is not the homologue of a reptilian cranial bone but a jaw bone, the angular. This process may not have evolved in mammals until after the petrosal had assumed its characteristic trisulcate form, but when it did appear it was in the form of a ventrally directed outgrowth of the petrosal in the region just posterior to the fenestra cochleae ("rotundum"), lateral to the sulcus jugularis and medial to the fossa muscularis stapedius (fossa muscularis minor).

DISCUSSION

When a complex morphological pattern is discovered repeatedly in a variety of mammals from the Eocene and Paleocene, converging toward a common form as we trace them back into the late Cretaceous, that morphological pattern may reasonably be regarded as primitive for mammals in general. Once a morphological complex can be thus recognized as primitive, all derivative types can be compared with it, with increasing economy and clarity of description.

The primitive trisulcate pattern described here may be compared with numerous examples illustrated by Matthew (1909, 1937) of Eocene and Paleocene mammals, which will be found to preserve much the same arrangement. Of special interest here is the ear region of *Didelphodon* (senior synonym of "*Didelphops*," "*Stagodon*," "*Ectoconodon*," "*Thlaeodon*," and "*Diaphorodon*"), a large and peculiarly specialized marsupial of the late Cretaceous of Lance Creek, Wyoming, described by Clemens (1966). *Didelphodon* is not really a primitive marsupial, being the largest mammal of the late Cretaceous (about badger-size) and having oddly bulbous premolar teeth. Its ear region conforms to the trisulcate pattern generally but differs strongly from the primitive living dasyuroid and didelphoid ear regions in some details. It is nevertheless the only complete Cretaceous marsupial ear region known and is therefore very important. Fortunately, Clemens' description is very full and well illustrated, requiring only a few comments on the characters of the petrosal of *Didelphodon*, which are here regarded as specializations and not part of the primitive pattern. Assessment of the significance of the epitympanic sinus in the squamosal is not within the scope of this paper, but I accept Clemens' judgement that this structure in *Didelphodon* and *Eodelphis* (the petrosal of the latter is represented by a few useless scraps of bone attached to a fragment of the squamosal) is similar to structures found in later marsupials. I would add only that such cavities are not uncommon (but usually smaller) among placental mammals, and that large epitympanic sinuses are not necessarily primitive and certainly are not so if developed in the petrosal.

The great development of the lateral mastoid flange in *Didelphodon* is as usual in very large, primitive mammals and converges remarkably with the similar development in the large placental *Mesonyx* of the Middle Eocene, for example (compare Fig. 56b of Clemens,1966 with Fig. 93 of Matthew, 1909).

The unusually pronounced development of the *sulcus medialis*, which in *Didelphodon* is actually a tunnel along the ventromedial rim of the promontorium, is a peculiar specialization. Clemens believes it carried a branch (which I think was the medial entocarotid) of the internal carotid artery. The inferior petrosal sinus vein undoubtedly ran in the sulcus (visible but not labeled in Clemens' Figure 56 b) medial to the carotid tunnel.

The *crista promontorii medioventralis* is therefore the blunt crest medial to the arterial tunnel and lateral to the venous groove on the *Didelphodon* petrosal, and the prominent crest lateral to the arterial tunnel represents, as Clemens says, part of an ossified bulla, attached to " . . . a plate of bone covering part of a trench beginning lateral to the fenestra vestibuli and extending posteriorly past the fenestra cochleae, which opens into this cul-de-sac." I believe that the "trench" (in part, at least) includes the fossa muscularis minor (visible but not labeled in Clemens' figure 56 c), and the "plate of bone" behind the fenestra cochleae would then correspond to the processus tympanicus visible in the Cretaceous placental petrosals described above. In living marsupials, the alisphenoid forms a major part of the bulla, but nothing is known of this part of Cretaceous marsupial anatomy. The only Cretaceous alisphenoid fragment so far described (MacIntyre, 1967) does not show any bullar wing.

Clemens reports " . . . a groove in the petrosal starts at a point near the fenestra vestibuli, parallels the course of the canalis facialis, and probably pierced the bulla. Otherwise the surface of the petrosal is gently undulating and has no ridges or grooves indicating courses of vessels or nerves." The use of the word "petrosal" is clearly meant to mean "promontorium," because the petrosal is elsewhere replete with carefully drawn and labelled grooves, which Clemens obviously identified correctly. It seems clear that "parallels the course of the canalis facialis" means that it passes rostrally and hence "probably pierced the bulla" anteriorly. The promontory artery is unknown in marsupials, and this groove is too far lateral on the promontorium for that, anyway. Just anterior to the medial chamber of the epitympanic sinus, a break is indicated in Clemens' Figure 56c, with a curved groove apparently ending abruptly at that break. If there was a foramen there, it would be near the usual position for the foramen admitting the superior ramus of the stapedial artery to the braincase; the groove, which parallels the facial canal, could possibly have been for the inferior ramus of the stapedial artery. Although my examination of the *Didelphodon* petrosal at the kind invitation of Dr. Clemens was too brief to permit recall of every detail seen several years ago, my recollection of a *sulcus arteria stapedia* crossing the fenestra vestibuli seems to be partly confirmed by a groove visible in Clemens' Figure 56c. Under the circumstances, I hesitate to disagree with Dr. Clemens, so I will just say that if *Didelphodon* did not have a stapedial artery, this was another of its unusual specializations.

Because of its specialized nature, the petrosal of *Didelphodon* is not necessarily a certain guide to the primitive position of the minute passage for the endolymphatic duct (the *aquaeductus vestibuli*), which Clemens indicates as emerging from a point near where the base of the crus commune should have joined the cavum vestibuli, but in the absence of other evidence this position for the aquaeductus vestibuli is acceptable.

The aquaeductus cochleae in *Didelphodon* emerges in the sulcus jugularis (a term I prefer over its synonym "foramen lacerum posterium," when discussing isolated petrosals) and this position can be demonstrated by insertion of a bristle in several Bug Creek Cretaceous petrosals, so that point is fully confirmed as the primitive positon.

Lest this detailed list of minor disagreements seems to redound to the discredit of Dr. Clemens, let me say that I consider his description admirable on the whole. I only mention the few places where we might differ, in preference to repeating the much longer list of structures that I think he has described correctly. Despite the peculiarly specialized nature of the *Didelphodon* petrosal, I am inclined to agree with Clemens on practically every point.

The most remarkable thing about this *Didelphodon* petrosal is that there is such a broad area of agreement in structure and general appearance with the much smaller placental mammal petrosals from Montana, although *Didelphodon* is a much larger and more specialized animal than any of the therians from Bug Creek.

In discussing the Bug Creek fossils it is unfortunately impossible to make a confident association of particular petrosals with particular genera, because there appears to be a strong bias in preservation or collection, which has distorted the original ratio of teeth to ear bones. According to the analysis of some 6,000 teeth and jaws recovered from Bug Creek Anthills Quarry (Sloan and Van Valen, 1965), almost 75% of those specimens represented multituberculates (nearly 43% *Mesodma* and nearly 36% *Stigemys*, with six other genera among the remainder), but only a minority of the ear regions recovered were those of multituberculates. The fact that there were some was clearly indicated by their definite resemblance to the ear region of *Ptilodus* described by Simpson (1937), and to those of Mongolian Cretaceous multituberculates (Kielan-Jaworowska, 1970), but the general similarity of the majority of the petrosals from Bug Creek Anthills to those of Paleocene and Eocene mammals familiar from the works of Matthew (1909, 1937) and even to some Recent mammals such as *Solenodon* (Gregory 1910, Fig. 18) leaves no doubt that they were therian. Moreover, the presence of a sulcus for the promontory artery indicates that they were eutherian (i.e., placental) in nature. Among these placental mammal petrosals, two forms are clearly represented, as Table 1 makes clear.

There are 5 specimens in the group here referred to the ferungulates (substantially equal to the ancestral Ferungulata of Simpson, 1945) (Figs. 4 and 5) and 14 among the unguiculate group (Figs. 6 and 7), but this is a tentative assignment and the proportions of teeth and jaws in the collection do not agree with it. The most obvious ferungulate found at Bug Creek is the arctocyonid *Protungulatum* and this genus is the most heavily represented by dentitions (16.70% of the total) among the true mammals, so it should be represented by the most petrosals, yet only 5 out of 19 seem to fit this concept. The available arctocyonid and condylarth petrosals of the Paleocene are not so perfectly preserved nor were they so delicately prepared that certainty about their morphology is assured, but I am reasonably confident of the assignment made here. The condition of the specimens in skulls seldom permits description of the

Table 1. Comparison of Two Bug Creek placental petrosal
varieties and Lance Creek marsupial *Didelphodon*

Feature	"Unguiculate"	"Ferungulate"	*Didelphodon*
facial canal bridge	narrow	broad	very broad
hiatus fallopii	ventral	ventral	ventral? (broken)
tympanohyal—size	moderate	small? (broken)	large? (broken)
tympanohyal—relation to mastoid	closely attached	separate, on ridge	separate at base?
fossa muscularis minor	small, rounded	small, rounded	large, bean-shaped
promontorium—profile	rounded—high	rounded—low	flattened—low
promontorium—surface	smooth	slightly uneven	irregular
fossa subarcuata	large, rounded	large, rounded	large, rounded
tympanic process—size	large (broken)	vestigial	large? (broken)
mastoid process	relatively small	relatively large	relatively small
lateral mastoid flange	moderate	relatively large	very large
rostral apex	pointed	bluntly pointed	bluntly pointed
ventromedial promontory crest	sharp	dull	dull
sulcus sini petrosi inferior	moderately deep	shallow, but clear	very deep
sulcus arteriae stapediae	moderately deep	moderately deep	doubtful (present
sulcus arteriae promontorii	shallow	shallow	absent
sulcus medialis	broad	narrow	very deep and bridged over

details of the two exits for the facial nerve branches, but the promontorium of arctocyonids and primitive ungulates is characteristically bluntly pointed, rounded rather than sharp medially and lacking a conspicuous tympanic process behind the fenestra cochleae. The tympanic process, on the other hand, is found among a variety of living lipotyphlous insectivores (Insectivora in the strict sense) as a prominent crest of the mastoid region covering the fenestra cochleae, a condition which McDowell (1958, p. 205) regarded as a specialization of the Lipotyphla. While it is undoubtedly true that development of this process to any great degree is a specialization away from the primitive condition, the mere presence of such a processus tympanicus may be primitive for placentals.

It seems obvious that the unguiculate group is distinct from the ferungulate group, but equally clear that the differences were not very extensive at that time (Fig. 8).

As Lillegraven (1969) has pointed out, late Cretaceous mammals show a paleoryctid grouping which probably includes the ancestors of carnivores, creodonts, and arctocyonids (the last named being ancestral in turn to the ungulates) and a second group of leptictid affinities, which probably gave rise to the primates, rodents, and true (lipotyphlous) insectivores. He also cites similar conclusions based on the characters of the fetal membranes. Lillegraven's own study is based largely on dentitions, and without associated ear regions, positive statements at this stage would be premature, but it may well turn out that the ferungulate petrosal type corresponds to the paleoryctid side and the unguicu-

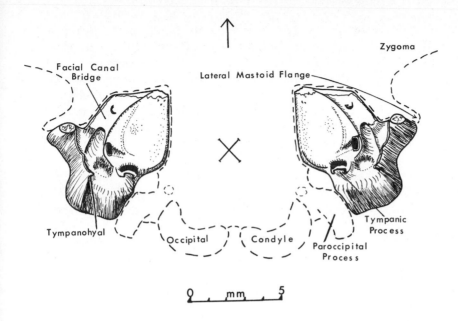

Fig. 8. Diagram of restored Late Cretaceous mammalian basicranium of group referred provisionally to ferungulate affinities. Dashed outlines are hypothetical. Compare Figs. 5 and 7.

late petrosals belong to the leptictid side of this division. McKenna (1969) gives a brief but comprehensive summary of possible relationships among ancestral mammals, also indicating a paleoryctid-leptictid split, with a possible third division represented by the Mongolian Cretaceous genus *Zalambdalestes* Gregory and Simpson (1926). McKenna's (1969, Fig. 4) association of *Hyotheridium* Gregory and Simpson with *Kennalestes* Kielan-Jaworowska (1969) is not supported by specific evidence, but he promises (McKenna 1969, p. 229) to discuss the dentition and relationships in a later paper, now that removal of the jaws from the skull have made this possible. The forthcoming description of the ear regions of both *Kennalestes* and *Zalambdalestes* likewise promised by Kielan-Jaworowska (1969) should be of great interest. The affinities of late Cretaceous mammals to their descendants cannot of course be deduced solely on the basis of ear region anatomy, but certainly provide supporting evidence in conjunction with teeth and other features. The affinities of creodonts and condylarths have been clear for many years; as Matthew stated (1909, p. 333) " . . . the approximation between the less specialized Creodonts and Condylarths is equally marked in the characters of the teeth, of the skull, of the feet, and other parts of the skeleton. These resemblances, extending to all parts of the skeleton, will bear the most careful scrutiny and comparison, and indicate a common origin of Creodonta and Condylarthra at no remote period."

Even if we restrict the term Creodonta to the families of hyaenodontids, oxyaenids, and their near relatives as some recent authors have done (MacIntyre, 1966; McKenna, 1969), the differences between the ear regions found in the late Cretaceous are perceptable, like the differences in the dentitions from the same age, but they likewise point to a common origin of all placental mammals "at no remote period." Those characters of the ear regions here grouped as ferungulate were so designated because they appear to be much the same in the Paleocene arctocyonid condylarths of North America (Matthew, 1937), and of Europe (Russell, 1960; Weigelt, 1960) as well as in the hyaenodontids, oxyaenids, mesonychids, and miacids, of the Eocene (Matthew, 1909). Among many more specialized offshoots of this basal stock, some such as *Meniscotherium* (Gazin, 1965) had distinctively modified the basic pattern by Early Eocene time; others such as *Hyracotherium* were relatively conservative in petrosal anatomy. Despite the large numbers of specimens collected over a period of more than a century, *Hyracotherium* is still represented by only one well preserved ear region, part of a skull in the American Museum of Natural History (AMNII 4831) described by Kitts (1956). The specimen is not completely cleaned out, so that the exact position of the facial nerve foramina is unclear, but the exposed parts generally conform to the ferungulate style of trisulcate pattern, differing in a more rounded, somewhat irregular, bluntly pointed promontorium (misidentified by Kitts as the tympanic bulla, which was as usual lost postmortem), a low, rounded tympanic process just posterior to the fenestra cochleae, and no feature that could not have been derived from the presumably arctocyonid ancestors represented at Bug Creek by *Protungulatum.*

Because the emphasis here is on the persistance of the primitive pattern of the petrosal into the Eocene, it must be pointed out that there are naturally some differences in detail between the petrosals of different taxa. The purpose of this paper is to point out the primitive pattern that makes for a certain similarity between all early mammal petrosals; the elucidation of differences has already been done in part by others, and more work along these lines is needed in the future.

The foregoing account of the primitive petrosal pattern as currently understood is of course not as complete as could be wished. It provides sufficient information for the pattern to be recognizable to students of fossil mammals, however, and it will be followed by other papers describing representatives of the post-Cretaceous mammalian radiation that show the trisulcate pattern of the petrosal.

SUMMARY

Studies of the ear region of the skull, including the petrosal, have systematic and evolutionary significance because, as a complex and highly characteristic anatomical domain, ear structure often provides clues to relationships not available from the study of teeth alone. For several reasons known to most students of phylogeny, knowledge of the primitive states of such independently evolving character complexes is a vital component in their proper interpretation, but up to now, no underlying primitive pattern for the petrosal bone has been identified.

The mammals (defined here as restricted to the placental and marsupial mammals and their immediate common ancestry) of the early Cenozoic and late Cretaceous show a number of features of the petrosal bone in common, so that it is now possible to postulate a primitive petrosal pattern. Here called the *trisulcate* petrosal pattern (analogous to, but quite independent of, the tribosphenic pattern of mammalian molar teeth), this character complex undoubtedly owes its underlying uniformity to the relatively conservative anatomy of the membranous labyrinth contained within it. The details of external anatomy of the known specimens of trisulcate petrosals from the late Cretaceous of North America are discussed in full, and the features common to all are stressed. Because the single specimen of a Cretaceous marsupial belonged to a large and relatively specialized genus, discussion of the differences between groups has been confined to those observed in the isolated trisulcate petrosals from the latest Cretaceous of Montana. There appear to be two major kinds of placental mammals represented there by petrosal bones. One group fits in with known ear regions of arctocyonids, creodonts, and carnivores, the other group seems closer to primates, rodents, and lipotyphlous insectivores. Such differences in detail, however, do not obscure the striking similarity of overall pattern, which indicates that there was a close common ancestry for all placentals and a clear community of origin for all true mammals as well.

Acknowledgments

It is a pleasure to acknowledge the specimens I have received from K. Kowalski, M. C. McKenna, and R. E. Sloan, for facilities and equipment provided by the American Museum of Natural History, Queens College of the City University of New York, and Royal Holloway College of the University of London (where this paper was written), and for the many profitable discussions I have had over the years with D. Baird, S. B. McDowell, M. C. McKenna, J. Mellett, B. Patterson, and more recently with P. M. Butler and S. B. Cox, about various aspects of ear region evolution. My debt to George Gaylord Simpson is a special one, for, by helping me through a crucial time of my graduate studies and providing me with so much tolerant guidance during the years that followed, he has built the foundation for the best part of my work. This paper gives me a welcome opportunity to express my deep feelings of affectionate respect for him.

REFERENCES

Butler, P. M. 1948. On the evolution of the skull and teeth in the Erinaceidae, with special reference to fossil material in the British Museum. Proc. Zool. Soc. (London), 118(2):446-500.

——1956. The skull of *Ictops* and the classification of the Insectivora. Proc. Zool. Soc. (London), 126(3):453-481.

——1969. Insectivores and bats from the Miocene of East Africa: new material. *In* Leakey, L.S.B., ed., Fossil Vertebrates of East Africa, Vol. 1:1-37. London and New York, Academic Press.

Clemens, W. 1966. Fossil mammals of the type Lance Formation, Wyoming. Part 2. Marsupialia. Univ. California Pub. Geol. Sci., 62:1-122.

Crompton, A. W. 1964. On the skull of *Oligokyphus*. Bull. Brit. Mus. (Nat. Hist.) Geol., 9:70-82.

De Beer, G. 1937. The Development of the Vertebrate Skull. Oxford, Clarendon Press.

Fernandez, C. and R. S. Schmidt. 1963. The opossum ear and the evolution of the coiled cochlea. J. Comp. Neurol., 121:151-160.

Gazin, C. L. 1936. A taeniodont skull from the Lower Eocene of Wyoming. Proc. Amer. Philos. Soc., 76:597-612.

——1953. The Tillodontia: an early Tertiary order of mammals. Smithsonian Misc. Coll., 121:1-110.

——1965. A study of the early Tertiary condylarthran mammal *Meniscotherium*. Smithsonian Misc. Coll., 149:1-98.

Goodrich, E. 1930. Structure and Development of the Vertebrates. London, MacMillan, Ltd.

Gregory, W. K. 1910. The orders of mammals. Bull. Amer. Mus. Nat. Hist., 27:1-524.

——and G. G. Simpson. 1926. Cretaceous mammal skulls from Mongolia. Amer. Mus. Novit., 225:1-20.

Hennig, W. 1965. Phylogenetic systematics. Ann. Rev. Entom., 10:97-116.

Hopson, J. 1964. The braincase of the advanced mammal-like reptile *Bienotherium*. Postilla, 87:1-30.

Kielan-Jaworowska, Z. 1969. Results of the Polish-Mongolian paleontological expeditions. Part 1. Preliminary data on the upper Cretaceous eutherian mammals from Bayn Dzak, Gobi Desert. Paleontologia Polonica, 1968(19):171-191.

——1970. Unknown structures in multituberculate skull. Nature (London), 226:974-976.

Kitts, D. B. 1956. American *Hyracotherium* (Perissodactyla, Equidae). Bull. Amer. Mus. Nat. Hist., 110:1-60.

Lillegraven, J. A. 1969. Latest Cretaceous mammals of upper part of Edmonton Formation of Alberta, Canada, and review of marsupial-placental dichotomy in mammalian evolution. Univ. Kansas Paleont. Contrib., Art. 50 (Vert. 12): 1-122.

MacIntyre, G. 1966. The Miacidae (Mammalia, Carnivora). Pt. 1. The systematics of *Ictidopappus* and *Protictis*. Bull. Amer. Mus. Nat. Hist., 131:115-210.

——1967. Foramen pseudovale and quasi-mammals. Evolution, 21:834-841.

Matthew, W. D. 1909. The Carnivora and Insectivora of the Bridger Basin. Mem. Amer. Mus. Nat. Hist. 9(6),289-567.

——1937. Paleocene faunas of the San Juan Basin, New Mexico. Trans. Philos. Soc. Philadelphia (n.s.), 30:1-510.

McDowell, S. 1958. The Greater Antillean insectivores. Bull. Amer. Mus. Nat. Hist., 115(3):117-214.

McKenna, M. C. 1969. The origin and early differentiation of mammals. Ann. N. Y. Acad. Sci., 167:217-240.

Nelson, Gareth J. 1969. Gill arches and the phylogeny of fishes, with notes on the classification of vertebrates. Bull. Amer. Mus. Nat. Hist., 141:475-552.

Neubert, K. and E. Wüstenfeld. 1962. Morphologie des akustischen Organs, Hdb. der Zool. (Kükenthal–Krumbach), Bd. 8, Teil 8, lief. 29: Beitrag (3):1-44. Berlin, De Gruyter.

Olson, E. C. 1944. Origin of mammals based on the cranial morphology of therapsid suborders. Spec. Papers Geol. Soc. Amer., 55:1-136.

Platzer, W. and W. Firbas. 1966. Die Cochlea der Soricidae. Anat. Anz., 118(2):1-113.

Russell, Donald E. 1960. L'anatomie cranienne de deux Créodontes du Paléocene de France. Bull. Soc. Géol. France (7ᵉ serie), 2:195-199.

Simpson, G. G. 1937. Skull structure of the Multituberculata. Bull. Amer. Mus. Nat. Hist., 73:727-763.

_____ 1938. Osteography of the ear region in monotremes. Amer. Mus. Novit., 978:1-15.

_____1945. Principles of classification and a classification of the mammals. Bull. Amer. Mus. Nat. Hist., 85:1-350.

_____1953. The Major Features of Evolution. New York, Columbia University Press.

_____1961. Principles of Animal Taxonomy. New York, Columbia University Press.

Sloan, R. 1964. Paleoecology of the Cretaceous-Tertiary transition in Montana. Science, 146:430.

_____1969. Cretaceous and Paleocene terrestrial communities of western North America. Proc. N. Amer. Pal. Conv. Part E., Chicago.

_____and L. Van Valen. 1965. Cretaceous mammals from Montana. Science, 148:220-227.

Starck, D. 1967. Le crane des mammifères. In Grassé, P. ed., Traité de Zoologie, T. 16, Fasc. 1: Mammifères. Téguments, Squelette: 405-549. Paris, Masson et Cie.

Thenius, E. 1969. Stammesgeschichte der Säugetiere. Hdb. der Zool. (Kükenthal–Krumbach) Bd. 8, Teil 2, Lief. 47 & 48: Beitrag (1):1-722. Berlin, De Gruyter.

Turnbull, W. 1970. Mammalian masticatory apparatus. Fieldiana: Geology, 118(2):149-356.

Van der Klaauw, C. J. 1931. The auditory bulla in some fossil mammals, with a general introduction to this region of the skull. Bull. Amer. Mus. Nat. Hist., 62:1-352.

Van Kampen, P. N. 1905. Die Tympanalgegend des Säugetierschädels. Morphol. Jahrb., 34:321-722.

Von Huene, F. R. 1948. Short review of the lower tetrapods. Robert Broom Commem. Vol. Cape Town, Roy Soc. S. Apro, pp. 65-106.

Weigelt, I. 1960. Die Arctocyoniden von Walbeck. Freiberger Forsch. H. & Rte. (Berlin) 77:1-214.

10

Holarctic Evolution and Dispersal of Squirrels (Rodentia: Sciuridae)

CRAIG C. BLACK

Department of Systematics and Ecology
University of Kansas, Lawrence, Kansas

Both the geographical distribution and the ecological relationships of animals are outcomes of evolution . . . Where animals are and what they do there are results of historical processes and events. G. G. Simpson—Condon Lectures, 1953.

INTRODUCTION

Members of the rodent family Sciuridae occur on all continents except Australia. Squirrels are one of the few families of mammals to have such a nearly cosmopolitan distribution. However, patterns of dispersal and evolution within the family have only recently come under study (Moore, 1959, 1961; Black, 1963; Gromov eta l., 1965). Recent paleontolegical data (Black, 1963, 1965b, 1966; Bruijn and Mein, 1968; Mein, 1970; Sulimski, 1964) and chromosome studies of living squirrels (see Nadler, 1969; Voronstov and Lyapunova, 1970), taken together with Moore's (1959) morphological studies and his classification of living squirrels exclusive of flying squirrels, now provide a basis for a reconstruction of "historical processes and events" within the family. Such is the intent of the present paper. Evolution within the Sciuridae and exchange between the Nearctic and Palearctic will be considered for the most part at the generic level. This is done for two reasons: fossil and living genera are more nearly equivalent taxonomic categories; and, too little is known about mid- and late-Pleistocene species of squirrels in Eurasia to allow for discussion of species dispersal in most groups.

Darlington (1957) was unable to determine the zoogeographic history of the Sciuridae because of inadequate data on the living members of family. Moore (1961), after a detailed morphological study of the living forms, proposed a history of dispersal for the Holarctic sciurids. He was well aware of the then

305

inadequate state of knowledge of the geological history of the Sciuridae when he wrote (Moore, 1961, pp. 2-3) "the present paper seeks to give such an explanation [of the existing geography of sciurids] for the Holarctic and Neotropical members now living, without attempting to assess how the poorly understood fossil record bears on the various problems." Unfortunately, explanations of zoogeographic patterns that can not, or do not, consider the evolutionary history of the group being studied quite often bring about improbable or incorrect dispersal patterns. Moreover, Moore based his scheme on what has proved to be a misunderstanding of the relationships among Old and New World *Marmota* and *Spermophilus*.

BASIC ADAPTIVE TYPES

Throughout the history of the Sciuridae, two basic adaptive types can be distinguished primarily on characters of the cheek teeth, jaw morphology, and certain cranial characters (Fig. 1). Both types are correlated with distinct food and habitat preferences. In general the skulls of tree squirrels, flying squirrels, and chipmunks are more convex than those of ground squirrels, marmots, and prairie dogs, with a greater flexion of the basicranial axis in the former group than in the latter. The diastema is longer and shallower in the ground squirrel group than it is in tree squirrels. Chipmunks are closer to ground squirrels in this character than they are to tree squirrels. Occlusal patterns of the cheek teeth again separate tree squirrels, flying squirrels, and chipmunks from terrestrial squirrels. M^1-M^2 are subquadrate with expanded protocones, indistinct meta-conules, and low complete lophs in the tree squirrels, while in ground squirrels M^1-M^2 are usually triangular with large metaconules, high lophs, and incomplete metalophs. M_1-M_2 are rectangular to square in occlusal outline in tree squirrels, whereas they are rhomboidal with narrower lingual than buccal margins in ground squirrels. In tree squirrels the posterior lophs of the cheek teeth are low and there is generally a quite distinct cusp at the postero-internal corner of each tooth but this cusp is absent or indistinct in the various ground squirrel types, in which the posterior lophs are elevated and rounded posterointernally.

These morphological characters readily separate almost all modern Holarctic species of sciurids and are also quite useful in determining relationships among fossil forms. The low crowned, heavier dentition of tree squirrels and their allies reflects the primary crushing function of the dentition, while the higher crowned, sharper-lophed dentition of the ground squirrels is adapted to a greater cutting action necessitated by their herbaceous diet. Tree squirrels, flying squirrels, and chipmunks are primarily seed, nut, and berry feeders, while ground squirrels, marmots, and prairie dogs are primarily grazers and browsers.

Various other trends are of course recognizable within these two main types. Flying squirrels developed loose folds of skin between their wrists and ankles and became gliders. The dentition of some of the Chinese and Malaysian flying

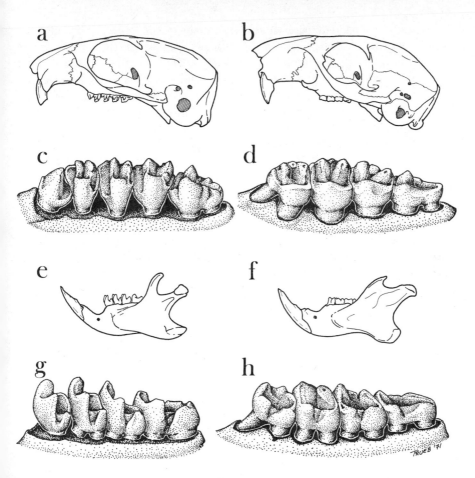

Fig. 1. The two main Holarctic sciurid adaptive types are shown. The figures on the right are of Sciurus niger while those on the left are of Spermophilus (Spermophilus) richardsoni. From top to bottom: a and b are lateral views of the skulls; c and d are oblique views of P^4-M^3 crown pattern (anterior end to left and buccal side to the top); e and f are lateral views of the left mandibles; and, g and h are oblique views of P_4-M_3 crown pattern (anterior end to the left and buccal side to the bottom). The figures are not to scale.

squirrels is highly modified, becoming high crowned and developing exceedingly complex occlusal patterns. While the diet of flying squirrels normally consists of fruits, nuts, seeds, and buds, they also occasionally take insects and meat. Certain ground squirrels develop an essentially shearing or chopping type of dentition. Some ground squirrels and tree squirrels have become quite insectivorous in their diet. Another group of ground squirrels has become highly fossorial with consequent skeletal and cranial modifications.

Since postcranial material of squirrels is extremely rare in the fossil record and since complete skulls are also only infrequently encountered, most of the inferences regarding relationship and habit of sciurids throughout the Tertiary must be made on characters of the mandible and the cheek teeth. Fortunately, such inferences appear to be based upon reasonably firm ground, as analysis of modern character complexes shows good correlation with observed habitat and dietary preferences.

Cytotaxonomic evidence (Hoffmann and Nadler, 1968; Nadler. 1969; Nadler and Hoffmann, 1970) establishes the basic chromosome number within the subfamily Sciurinae as evidently $2n = 38$ to 40. This $2n$ predominates in members of the tribes Xerini and Sciurini, among chipmunks and marmots, and among the more generalized species of the ground squirrel subgenus *Spermophilus (Otospermophilus)*.

Earlier (Black, 1963) I stressed the intermediate position of chipmunks both in habit and structure within the family Sciuridae. Although such a position is supported by chromosome studies (Nadler et al., 1969) which reveal a diploid number of $2n = 38$ for *Tamias* and *Eutamias*, several species of *Sciurus* also have $2n = 40$ (Nadler, 1969, Fig. 13), and the possibility that the earliest squirrels were arboreal and more tree-squirrel- than chipmunk-like can not be ruled out. Whatever the earliest sciurid morphotype may have been, it is certain that the earliest late Eocene or early Oligocene members of the family evolved in what was probably a broadleafed evergreen to mixed deciduous hardwood forest (Axelrod, 1966) environment and that they were arboreal to semiarboreal nut, seed, and berry feeders. It is within this framework then that we may proceed to any analysis of the fossil record of Holarctic members of the family Sciuridae.

THE FOSSIL RECORD

The fossil record of the Sciuridae is woefully inadequate when one attempts to trace the evolution and dispersal of the varied types of arboreal squirrels, both tree squirrels and flying squirrels, through the Tertiary. The record is also inadequate for specialized fossorial forms. There are occurrences in Europe of fossil tree squirrels and flying squirrels, often associated with fissure deposits, which were probably open and acting as traps in deciduous forest situations. In North America there are one or two occurrences of flying squirrels and a few more of tree squirrels but these are the chance, fragmentary occurrences in stream or flood plain deposits, and the specimens were probably transported some distance from any large area of suitable habitat. For the various types of ground squirrels, the record is much better, and certain phyletic sequences and patterns of dispersal can be traced with some assurrance.

The earliest rodents of Europe and North America, members of the family Ischyromyidae, were probably quite similar to one another in structure and habits on both continents. Several of the same genera occurred in the early

Eocene of Europe (Michaux, 1968) and of North America (Wood, 1962). These were very generalized types of rodents with unspecialized dentitions and masseter muscle complexes. As far as we can tell, they were scansorial to perhaps semiarboreal with few of the special modifications which have made the order so highly successful today. Unfortunately, we know nothing of the early history of rodents in Asia.

After this initial rather considerable similarity between rodents of the early Eocene in Europe and North America there was a rapid divergence of rodent types in the two areas. By the late Eocene, approximately 40 million years ago, there was essentially no generic similarity between the rodents of known European and North American faunas. Eight genera of rodents belonging to four families are known for the European late Eocene; six genera of three families for Asia; and eighteen genera of five families for North America (Table 1). There are no genera in common between any of the three areas. Of the nine families of rodents presently recognized from the Holarctic late Eocene, only two have species living today, the Ctenodactylidae of North Africa (four genera) and the Gliridae of Eurasia and North Africa (seven genera).

Table 1. Numbers of Genera of Late Eocene Holarctic Rodents

	North America	Asia	Europe
Ischyromyidae	10	3[a]	2
Gliridae	0	0	1
Eomyidae	3	0	0
Pseudosciuridae	0	0	3
Sciuravidae	2	2	0
Cylindrodontidae	2	0	0
Ctenodactylidae	0	1	0
Protoptychidae	1	0	0
Theridomyidae	0	0	2
Total genera	18	6	8

[a]Dawson (1964) described two different ischyromyids but without generic assignment, and Li (1963) described one.

[b]*Advenimus* Dawson (1964) is here considered to be a primitive ctenodactylid rather than a sciuravid.

The late Eocene endemism of rodent assemblages in the various Holarctic regions continues into the Oligocene with theridomyids, cricetids, glirids, and eomyids dominating the European faunas, cylindrodontids and cricetids in Asia, and in North America advanced ischyromyids, heteromyids, eomyids, and cricetids as the major rodent elements. It is during the Oligocene that the first members of the squirrel family, Sciuridae, appear. They are few in number and poorly known during the Oligocene but at least two and possibly three types are represented in the late Oligocene of both North America and Europe.

The exact age of the earliest European sciurid is unknown. Two specimens of "*Sciurus*" *dubius* from the Phosphorites du Quercy in France provide the earliest record of the family in Europe but the age of these specimens can be narrowed only to the early to mid-Oligocene. "*Sciurus*" *dubius* resembles members of the genus *Protosciurus*, which is known in North America from the early Oligocene to early Miocene. This type of sciurid is more typically tree-squirrel-like in its dental morphology than are the other Oligocene sciurids. In addition, Vianey-Liaud (1969, p. 229) reports five sciurid teeth from deposits in the Phosphorites, which he says correspond in age to the zone of La Sauvetat, which is middle Oligocene in age. The occlusal pattern of these teeth compares well with that of the cheek teeth of *Palaeosciurus feignouxi* of the European Miocene; the Oligocene specimens are smaller, however.

In the late Oligocene of Europe at localities in West Germany and France are found the first members of the present-day African ground squirrels of the tribe Xerini. These earliest xerines are all placed in the genus *Heteroxerus* (Black, 1965b; Bruijn and Mein, 1968; Hugueney, 1969). Evolution of several xerine lineages can be traced through the Miocene and early Pliocene of Spain and France. Species of *Heteroxerus* are quite common in many European faunas, and members of the extinct African genus *Getuloxerus*, first described from the "Upper Miocene" of Morocco, are also found in Spain during the Miocene (Bruijn and Mein, 1968, p. 84). *Getuloxerus* is quite close and possibly ancestral to the living *Atlantoxerus*. No fossil xerine sciurids are known outside Western Europe and Africa and it appears almost certain that this group of squirrels originated in, and was possibly confined to, this region throughout their history, although the· Recent *Spermophilopsus* of Afghanistan, Turkestan, and Iran is considered to be a xerine ground squirrel by Moore (1959, p. 184).

No sciurids other than *Heteroxerus*, the few teeth assigned to ?*Paleosciurus*, and the problematic "*Sciurus*" *dubius* are known from the Palearctic before the beginning of Aquitanian or Miocene time. There is no Oliogocene record for the family in Asia. In North America the first sciurid is found in the early Oligocene; species of *Protosciurus* of this age are known from Montana and Nebraska (Black, 1963; 1965a). *Protosciurus* shows very little advance over the Eocene ischyromyids but some changes in the zygomasseteric structure and in the masticatory muscles allow its placement among the sciurids rather than in the ancestral Ischyromyidae. Like "*Sciurus*" *dubius*, species of *Protosciurus* all display the more generalized tree squirrel dental characters.

At least one and possibly two other sciurid lineages had developed in North America by the late Oligocene. An undescribed specimen collected in 1969 from the top of the Brule formation at the Three Tubs in Goshen Hole, Wyoming, and now in the Carnegie Museum collections represents the earliest known occurrence of *Miospermophilus*, the first of the true ground squirrels, which was ancestral to the modern *Spermophilus*. A second specimen from the late Oligocene of California (Black, 1963, p. 227) is referable to the family Sciuridae but little more can be said about this record.

By the end of the Oligocene, therefore, several distinct types of sciurids can be recognized in Europe and in North America. The earliest known member of the family Sciuridae appears in the North American early Oligocene and by the end of the epoch two distinct and different ground squirrel lineages had evolved, xerines in the Palearctic and spermophilines in the Nearctic. In addition primitive spermophilines may also have been present in western Europe during the latter part of the Oligocene.

MIOCENE

The Miocene record of sciurids is by far the most complete both in the Old and the New Worlds. Table 2 lists the genera of sciurids found in the fossil record of Europe, Asia, and North America. More genera of sciurids are recognized during the Miocene in Europe and in North America than during any other period in the fossil record of the family. The European Miocene record is heavily weighted with genera of flying squirrels (Mein, 1970) while the North American record has more ground squirrel types (Black, 1963). Grasslands and open savannah parklands were evidently much more commonly represented in the North American Miocene record than during the same epoch in Western Europe. Unfortunately, the large areas of Eurasia which might be expected to have habitats more similar to those in North America during the Miocene are not represented in the fossil record to any appreciable extent.

Mein (1970) has reviewed the European flying squirrels. A fossil record for this group of sciurids in North America is nearly absent until the Pleistocene; two species referred to *Sciuropterus* (=*Cryptopterus* of Mein) are known from the late Miocene to early Pliocene of southern California (James, 1963) but there is no other Tertiary record of flying squirrels in North America. Mein recognizes three groups of flying squirrels in western Europe, each with an independent history back into the Miocene. He also suggests (1970, p. 53) independent origin for flying squirrels and all other sciurids, the two sciurid groups evolving from two different subfamilies of ischyromyids. I have elsewhere (1963, p. 126) suggested independent origin for different flying squirrels from different tree squirrels in various geographic areas. The fossil record, however, is totally inadequate for choosing between these alternatives, although recent chromosome studies (Nadler, 1969, p. 301) tend to confirm the close relationship between North American *Sciurus* and *Glaucomys*. Because of these uncertainties, most discussion of distribution and migration patterns will be limited to members of the subfamily Sciurinae. However, genera of flying squirrels are listed in Table 2 as they occur in the Tertiary record.

Table 2. Occurrence of Sciurid Genera in the Tertiary and
Pleistocene of the Holarctic

	North America	Asia	Europe
Pleistocene	*Sciurus* *Tamiasciurus* *Tamias* *Glaucomys* *Spermophilus* *Ammospermophilus* *Cynomys* *Marmota* †ᵃ*Paenemarmota*	*Sciurus* *Sciurotamias* *Tamias* *Spermophilus* *Marmota*	*Sciurus* *Tamias* †*Petauria* *Petaurista* *Petinomys* *Spermophilus* *Marmota*
Pliocene	*Sciurus* *Tamias* †*"Sciuropterus"* *Spermophilus* †*Protospermophilus* ?*Ammospermophilus* *Marmota*	*Sciurus* *Tamias*	*Sciurus* *Tamias* †*Cryptopterus* †*Pliopetaurista* †*Blackia* †*Pliopetes* †*Petinomys* †*Spermophilinus* †*Heteroxerus* †*Getuloxerus*
Miocene	*Sciurus* †*Miosciurus* †*Protosciurus* †*"Sciuropterus"* (=?*Cryptopterus*) *Tamias* †*Miospermophilus* †*Protospermophilus* *Spermophilus* †*Palaearctomys* †*Arctomyoides*	Sciurid indet.	*Sciurus* *"Ratufa"* †*Cryptopterus* †*Pliopetaurista* †*Miopetaurista* †*Blackia* †*Forsythia* †*Petinomys* †*Getuloxerus* †*Heteroxerus* †*Spermophilinus* †*Palaeosciurus*
Oligocene	†*Protosciurus* †*Miospermophilus* sciurid indet.		*"Sciurus"* †*Heteroxerus* †?*Palaeosciurus*

ᵃ† = extinct.

Although the radiation of ground squirrels in western Europe was nowhere near as extensive or complex as the radiation of that group in North America, two groups of ground-squirrel-like sciurids, each represented by two genera, are found in the European Miocene sequence. The two xerine genera, *Getuloxerus* and *Heteroxerus*, evolved from the late Oligocene *Heteroxerus* stock (see above). By Vindobonian time, there was considerable diversity of species of *Heteroxerus* (Bruijn and Mein, 1968). The second group is first represented by *Palaeosciurus feignouxi* from the early Miocene of Saint-Gérand-le-Puy. Characters of the skull, mandible, and dentition ally this species with the ground squirrels rather than with the tree squirrels. The dorsal profile of the skull is not convex, the diastemal region of the mandible is quite long and does not drop abruptly anterior to P_4, the mandible is rather light and shallow, and the pattern of the upper and lower molars is much closer to that of ground squirrels than tree squirrels. Although this lineage may have been present in Europe by the mid-Oligocene (Vianey-Liaud, 1969), *Palaeosciurus* is not well known until Miocene time. *Palaeosciurus feignouxi* was probably ancestral to *Palaeosciurus fissurae*, known from deposits of Burdigalian age in Germany, and representatives of this lineage are now known after Burdigalian or middle Miocene time in western Europe.

Palaeosciurus is distinguished from a second genus, *Spermophilinus*, by its larger size, and by differences in the zygomasseteric structure and the infraorbital foramen (Bruijn and Mein, 1968). However, characters of the dentition and mandible again clearly demonstrate that *Spermophilinus* is much more a ground squirrel than a tree squirrel; it first appears in the early Vindobonian of France and persists into the Pliocene of Spain.

There are a few scattered records of tree squirrels from various localities through the Miocene of Europe. In all cases, however, the material is too fragmentary to provide any insight into the evolution of tree squirrels during this time. This situation is quite comparable to that found in North America for *Sciurus*. Dehm (1950, p. 347) has reported the occurrence of the genus *Ratufa* in the middle Miocene of Germany. Reference of a partial lower jaw and several isolated teeth to this modern Malaysian genus is, in my opinion, somewhat dubious. That these specimens represent a rather large generalized tree squirrel is all that can be clearly substantiated at the present time.

Gromov et al. (1965, p. 54) report the occurrence of a Miocene species of *Tamias* (?) from Priirtish'e, Siberia. No description or illustration of this specimen is presented. It is therefore impossible to evaluate this report but it would not be surprising to find chipmunks as well as other sciurid types in northern Asia during the Miocene. On the basis of the known distribution of terrestrial squirrels of the genera *Miospermophilus, Palaeosciurus,* and *Spermophilinus* in Europe and North America during the Miocene, it is a certainty that ground squirrels were present and probably diverse in Asia during this period.

The fossil record of sciurids during the Miocene in North America is much more extensive and complex than that found in Europe. Exclusive of flying squirrels, nine genera are recognized in North America; five of these are ground squirrels, one is a chipmunk, and three are tree squirrels. Species of *Protosciurus, Miosciurus,* and *Sciurus* are relatively common in the early Miocene but the history of tree squirrels after this time is essentially a blank until the Pleistocene.

There is a considerable diversity of ground squirrels throughout the Miocene in North America. Two separate lineages arising from within *Miospermophilus* can be distinguished. One of these gave rise to several species of the genus *Protospermophilus*, which first appears in the early Miocene. The skull structure of *Protospermophilus* suggests that these animals were terrestrial as does their abundance in stream channel and flood plain deposits where arboreal forms are completely absent. However, species of *Protospermophilus* evidently paralled tree squirrels in their food preferences. The dentition in this lineage remains low crowned and quite heavy, suggesting that these animals fed primarily on seeds and nuts much as do the modern tree squirrels. As grasslands became more and more extensive during the Miocene, particularly in the Great Plains, the genus *Protospermophilus* was evidently replaced by members of the modern genus *Spermophilus*. *Spermophilus* arose independently from *Miospermophilus* sometime during the early mid-Miocene (Black, 1963, p. 236). These modern ground squirrels probably evolved in response to increasing aridity through the Miocene in North America and the development of extensive grassland areas during the latter part of the Miocene. They had undergone a considerable radiation by the early Pliocene.

Two additional sciurid genera, *Palaearctomys* and *Arctomyoides*, are known from the late Miocene of Montana. Both show cranial and dental specializations which foreshadow characters seen in marmots. *Arctomyoides* is somewhat more specialized than *Palaearctomys* and probably diverged from *Protospermophilus* somewhat earlier in time than did *Palaearctomys*. It is not known whether *Arctomyoides* was fossorial or not. The skull of *Palaearctomys*, however, does suggest fossorial adaptation. Each of these genera is represented by only a single species and is not known to persist beyond the Miocene.

The last group of squirrels found in the Miocene of North America is known by only the sparsest of records. Chipmunks, assigned to the genus *Tamias*, are recorded from localities of early, middle, and late Miocene age. However, in every instance, the material is so fragmentary that nothing more can be said other than that chipmunks do occur during this time interval.

PLIOCENE

The Pliocene record in both Europe and North America is much less complete for the family Sciuridae than it is in the preceding epoch. This record is also difficult to evaluate because of problems in correlation of the European and North American Pliocene sequences. For this discussion, the Vallesian faunas of Spain (Bruijn and Mein, 1968) and the Marktl fauna of Bavaria (Black, 1966) are considered to be early Pliocene in age. The relative ages of the Polish Pliocene faunas follows Kowalski (1963), with Podlesice being of late middle Pliocene and Weze of late Pliocene age.

The European sequence is again dominated by a number of forest-dwelling forms with *Sciurus* plus five genera of flying squirrels (Mein, 1970) recognized in the Pliocene. Species of *Sciurus* are found in the early Pliocene in Spain and in Germany. Undescribed species are also present in collections of middle Pliocene (Podlesice) and of late Pliocene (Weże) age in Poland. Ground squirrels of the genera *Spermophilinus* and *Heteroxerus* are known from several early Pliocene localities in Spain. Both genera are not known after the early Pliocene. A third ground squirrel genus, *Getuloxerus*, has been described from the Spanish early Pliocene (Bruijn and Mein, 1968) and is also known to have occurred in somewhat earlier Spanish faunas (Bruijn, in press). Whether *Getuloxerus*, originally described by Lavocat (1961) from Morocco, is an African emigrant into Europe or whether this lineage originated in Europe and migrated into North Africa is a question that can not be answered on present evidence. No terrestrial squirrels are known in the Palearctic between the early Pliocene and the Pleistocene.

Chipmunks have been reported from the late Pliocene of Poland (Sulimski, 1964) and from the late Pliocene of China (Chardin and Young, 1931, p. 4). The material from Weże was described as *Eutamias orlovi* by Sulimski (1964, p. 165). Teeth of *Eutamias orlovi* are also present in the Podlesice fauna of middle Pliocene age, which is under study at the present time. Although it is difficult to be certain of a chipmunk identification on the basis of isolated teeth and a partial lower jaw, it does seem quite probable that Sulimski was correct in his assignment of Polish material to the genus *Eutamias* or perhaps more properly the genus *Tamias* (Nadler et al., 1969, p. 869). *Tamias* sp., described by Teilhard de Chardin and Young (1934) from the Reddish Clay of locality 5 in North China, was based on identification of a partial lower jaw with well-worn cheek teeth. These authors suggested reference to *Tamias wimani* described from the early Pleistocene, Choukoutien fauna. On the basis of the Polish and Chinese material it is entirely probable that chipmunks were present in Eurasia during most of the Pliocene.

The North American Pliocene record is somewhat better documented than that in Europe, particularly for ground squirrels. This is due, in large measure, to a greater number of Pliocene localities in North America and to a better understanding of the age relationships of these faunas. The influence of the extensive, open grassland, savannah type of environment also introduces an obvious bias in the North American record. This influence is even stronger than that observed during the Miocene. Remains of the tree squirrel, *Sciurus*, are extremely rare during Pliocene time, while chipmunks are known from the early Pliocene faunas but are absent from the record during the middle and latter part of the Pliocene. Flying squirrels referred to *"Sciuropterus"* (=?*Cryptopterus* of Mein, 1970) are also known from the Claredonian of California but otherwise flying squirrels do not appear in the North American Pliocene record.

The Pliocene record is primarily one of ground squirrel and marmot diversification and evolution. During Claredonian time, several species of *Spermophilus (Otospermophilus)* are known from the Great Plains (Black, 1963) and from the Great Basin (Shotwell, 1970). Members of the subgenus *Otospermophilus* are considered to be the most primitive of spermophiles (Bryant, 1945; Black, 1963) and other subgenera of *Spermophilus* probably evolved from this group. One specimen from the early Pliocene of Nebraska may represent the earliest record of the more advanced *Spermophilus (Spermophilus)* group of ground squirrels (Black, 1963, p. 221), and by Hemphillian time, this subgenus is definitely present, represented by a species in Oregon, *Spermophilus (Spermophilus) mckayensis.* There are, in addition, a variety of species of *Spermophilus (Otospermophilus)* known from the Great Plains and from the Great Basin. Antelope ground squirrel of the genus *Ammosphermophilus* may have differentiated by early Pliocene time, although Shotwell (1970) questions this. No species of the other subgenera of *Spermophilus* are known to occur in the Pliocene.

A second Pliocene radiation of terrestrial squirrels occurred in North America, this in the genus *Marmota.* The first marmots appear in the early Pliocene, probably having evolved from the protospermophiline ground squirrels. Two species are known from the middle Pliocene, and it is probable that a third lineage, which was ancestral to the Pleistocene genus *Paenemarmota*, was present during the late Pliocene.

TERTIARY DISPERSAL PATTERNS

The first representatives of the Sciuridae are found in the early Oligocene of North America. These first sciurids evolved from some late Eocene ischyromyid, again probably in North America. The great diversity of ischyromyids in North America, as contrasted with their rather restricted occurrence in Europe and Asia, lends some support to the hypothesis of North American origin for the family Sciuridae. Sometime shortly after the Sciuridae first appeared in North America, a species that was most probably tree-squirrel- or chipmunk-like in appearance and habit migrated into Eurasia and spread rather rapidly into Western Europe. The next exchange between the Nearctic and the Palearctic occurred during the late Oligocene and involved the first terrestrial squirrels. Whether the migration occurred from east to west or west to east is difficult to determine on present evidence. Species of *Miospermophilus* in North America and *Paleosciurus* in Europe are ground squirrels in general morphological appearance. It is possible that members of this group first appeared in northern Asia where there were probably large areas of unforested, open habitat. It is unlikely that the first ground squirrels appeared in Europe, since no large areas of suitable habitat are known there during the mid-Tertiary. A North American origin for the earliest ground squirrels can not be ruled out, however; and open plains areas were certainly present by late Oligocene time in North America as well as in Asia. That such open habitats were much more prevalent in North America than in Europe during the Tertiary is amply attested to by the much greater diversity of Miocene and Pliocene ground squirrels in North America than in Europe.

Interchange between the North American and European faunas during the late Arikareean is rather well established (Wilson, 1960). During this exchange a species of *Miospermophilus* evidently moved into the Palearctic. This population underwent further differentiation in Asia and then spread into Western Europe, where it was ancestral to *Spermophilinus* known from the late Miocene and Pliocene of western Europe.

While both *Tamias* and *Sciurus* had evolved by early Miocene times, their place of origin remains unknown. On present evidence it would appear most probable that *Tamias* migrated from North America into Eurasia sometime during the middle Pliocene. Marmots and ground squirrels are unknown in Eurasia before the Pleistocene or possibly latest Pliocene (Gromov et al., 1965). In North America these genera have a rather long and complex Miocene and Pliocene history. Discussion of dispersal patterns in these groups will be considered with treatment of the Pleistocene forms. (See Figs. 2, 3.)

PLEISTOCENE

No attempt will be made here to consider the Pleistocene record of the Sciuridae in any detail. This record is much too extensive and in need of critical revision, particularly at the species level, to make any such evaluation possible. Certain general trends and patterns are discernable at the generic level, however, and these do provide insight into Holarctic dispersal patterns. One other factor which complicates an understanding of the Pleistocene picture of migration of various sciurid lineages is the lack of agreement between authors on correlation of North American and European faunas (Repenning, 1967; Kurtén, 1963).

Modern ground squirrels of the genus *Spermophilus* are first known in the Palearctic at the beginning of the Pleistocene (Gromov et al., 1965). *Spermophilus primigenius* and *S. nogaici*, both known from the early Pleistocene of eastern Europe, are species of the subgenus *Urocitellus* (Gromov et al., p. 172 and 178), one of the more advanced subgenera of the genus. No species of the more primitive terrestrial squirrels of the subgenus *Otospermophilus*, so common in the Nearctic Pliocene, are known from the Palearctic. The same pattern is also seen among marmots, with no specimens of *Marmota* known in the Palearctic before the early Pleistocene or possibly latest Pliocene. This earliest occurrence is based upon a record (cited by Repenning, 1967, p. 299) of the presence of a species of *Marmota* in the Tologoi fauna of Siberia. Repenning gives the age of this specimen as late Pliocene but Yerbayeva (1966 not seen in the original; cited from Zimina and Gerasimov, ms.) considers it to be early Pleistocene. Marmots

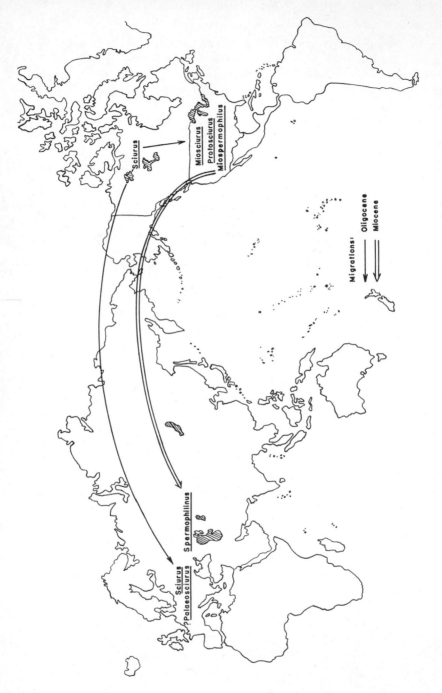

Fig. 2. Some of the probable Holarctic sciurid dispersal patterns during the Oligocene and early Miocene.

318

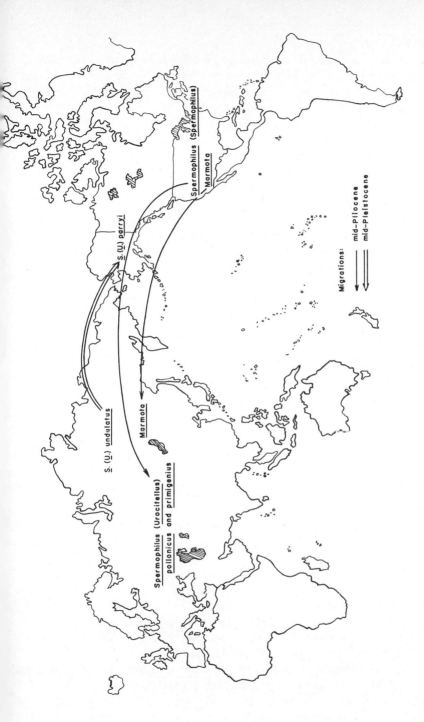

Fig. 3. Some of the probable Holarctic sciurid dispersal patterns during the Pliocene and Pleistocene.

319

are otherwise known only from middle and late Pleistocene faunas in Asia, with only one extinct species, *Marmota primigenius*, having been described from the Palearctic. It is quite possible that *Spermophilus* and *Marmota* crossed the Bering land bridge into Asia together, sometime during the latest Pliocene. As Moore (1961, p. 20) has shown, the present Palearctic distribution of *Spermophilus* and *Marmota* is closely sympatric and there is no reason to suspect it has not been so since these two phyla entered the Old World. Hoffmann and Nadler (1968) have considered *Marmota monax* of North America to be the least specialized ecologically of all marmot species and has suggested that this species is probably closest to the ancestral condition for the group.

The Pleistocene history of *Tamias* and *Sciurus* is extremely unclear. *Tamias* and *Sciurus* are both present in the Villafranchian faunas of Poland and China as well as in a number of North American Pleistocene faunas. Whether these early Pleistocene species evolved in place independently in the Palearctic and Nearctic, or migrated from one region to another, is not known. On karyotypic evidence, Nadler et al. (1969) have suggested that Nearctic species of *Tamias* have evolved from Palearctic immigrants of *Tamias sibericus*, a species they characterize as more ecologically and morphologically varaiable than other species of the genus. Both Asian and North American *Tamias* have $2n = 38$ but the North American species have a much smaller Y chromosome, which is thought to have been reduced from the larger Y of the Eurasian *Tamias sibericus*. Karyotype studies are not as conclusive for dispersal patterns among species of *Sciurus*; the two Eurasian species and those studied in North America have $2n = 40$ (Nadler and Hoffmann, 1970). Moore (1961, pp. 8-9) has suggested two and possibly more invasions of Palearctic *Sciurus vulgaris* into North America and subsequent divergence there to produce at least some of the species endemic to the New World. Present evidence is insufficient, however, to be certain of the place of origin of *Sciurus* itself as well as of the Recent species.

CONCLUSIONS

(1). Members of the Sciuridae first appear in North America during the early Oligocene.

(2). By the mid-Oligocene, sciurids are found in Europe and North America and both ground squirrels and tree squirrels had evolved by the late Oligocene.

(3). Probably as a result of differing depositional environments, the European squirrel record is dominated by flying squirrel remains, while that in North America shows a predominance of terrestrial squirrel types.

(4). One, and possibly two, lineages of terrestrial squirrels entered Europe from North America in the Tertiary but each became extinct.

(5). Modern ground squirrels, genus *Spermophilus*, and marmots, genus *Marmota*, entered Eurasia in the latest Pliocene or early Pleistocene from North America.

(6). Chipmunks, genus *Tamias*, entered Asia from North America in the middle Pliocene. One or two lines may have reinvaded North America in the early Pleistocene or chipmunks may have evolved independently in the Nearctic and Palearctic since mid-Pliocene time.

(7). Tree squirrels, genus *Sciurus, sensu latissimo*, are known in both North America and Eurasia since the Miocene. The center of origin for modern *Sciurus* is unknown.

(8). North America has been the center of terrestrial squirrel radiation since the origin of the family.

Acknowledgments

I wish to thank Dr. Robert Hoffmann for his critical review of the manuscript and Dr. Kazimierz Kowalski for allowing me to study the undescribed sciurid material from the Pliocene and Pleistocene of Poland.

The opportunity to examine the European material was provided by support from National Science Foundation grants GB-1266 and GB-4089.

REFERENCES

Axelrod, D. I. 1966. A method for determining the altitudes of Tertiary floras. Palaeobotanist, 14:144-171.
Black, C. C. 1963. A review of the North American Tertiary Sciuridae. Bull. Mus. Comp. Zool., 130(3):109-248.
———1965a. Fossil mammals from Montana. Pt. 2. Rodents from the early Oligocene Pipestone Springs local fauna. Ann. Carnegie Mus., 38(1):1-48.
———1965b. New species of *Heteroxerus* (Rodentia, Sciuridae) in the French Tertiary. Verh. Naturf. Ges. Basel, 76(1):185-196.
———1966. Tertiary Sciuridae (Mammalia: Rodentia) from Bavaria. Mitt. Bayer. Staats-samml. Paläont. Hist. Geol., 6:51-63.
Bruijn, H. 1971. Gliridae, Scuiridae and Eomyidae (Rodentia, Mammalia) from Calatayud (prov. Zaragossa, Spain) and their bearing on the biostratigraphy of the area. Bol. Inst. Geol. Min. España. (in press)
——— and P. Mein. 1968. On the mammalian fauna of the *Hipparion*-Beds in the Calatayud-Teruel Basin (prov. Zaragoza, Spain). Proc. Kon. Neder. Akad. Wet. [B], 71(1):73-90.
Bryant, M. D. 1945. Phylogeny of Nearctic Sciuridae. Amer. Midl. Natural., 33(2):257-390.
Chardin, Pierre Teilhard de, and C. C. Young. 1931. Fossil mammals from the late Cenozoic of northern China. Palaeont. Sinica, [C], 9(1):1-89.
Darlington, P. J., Jr. 1957. Zoogeography: the Geographical Distribution of Animals. New York, John Wiley and Sons.
Dawson, M. R. 1964. Late Eocene rodents (Mammalia) from Inner Mongolia. Amer. Mus. Novit., 2191:1-15.
Dehm, R. 1950. Die Nagetiere aus dem Mittel-Miocän (Burdigalium) von Wintershof-West bei Eichstätt in Bayern. Neues Jahr. Min. Paläont., Abh., 91(B):321-428.
Gromov, I. M., D. I. Bibikov, N. I. Kalabukhov, and M. N. Meier. 1965. Fauna SSSR, 3(2):1-467 (in Russian).

Hoffmann, R. S., and C. F. Nadler. 1968. Chromosomes and systematics of some North American species of the Genus *Marmota* (Rodentia:Sciuridae). Experientia, 24:740-742.

Hugueney, M. 1969. Les rongeurs (Mammalia) de l'Oligocène superiur de Coderet-Bransat (Allier). Doctoral thesis, University of Lyons.

James, G. T. 1963. Paleontology and nonmarine stratigraphy of the Cuyama Valley badlands. California. Part 1. Geology, faunal interpretations, and systematic descriptions of Chiroptera, Insectivora, and Rodentia. Univ. Calif. Publ. Geol. Sci., 45:1-171.

Kowalski, K. 1963. The Pliocene and Pleistocene Gliridae (Mammalia, Rodentia) from Poland. Acta Zool. Craco., 8(14):533-567.

Kurtén, B. 1963. Notes on some Pleistocene mammal migrations from the Palaearctic to the Nearctic. Eiszeitalter Gegenwart, 14:96-103.

Lavocat, R. 1961. Le gisement de vertébrés miocènes de Beni Mellal (Maroc). Étude systématique de la Raune de mammiféres et conclusions générales. Notes Mém. Serv. Geol. Maroc, 155:29-120.

Li, Chuan-kuei. 1963. Paramyid and sciuravids from North China. Vert. Palasiatica, 7:151-160.

Mein, P. 1970. Les sciuroptères (Mammalia, Rodentia) Neogènes d'Europe Occidentale. Geobios (Lyon), 3(3):7-77.

Michaux, J. 1968. Les Paramyidae (Rodentia) de l'Eocène inférieur du bassin de Paris. Palaeovertebrata, 1(4):135-193.

Moore, J. C. 1959. Relationships among living squirrels of the Sciurinae. Bull. Amer. Mus. Nat. Hist., 118(4):153-206.

—— 1961. The spread of existing diurnal squirrels across the Bering and Panamanian land bridges. Amer. Mus. Novit., 2044:1-26.

Nadler, C. F. 1969. Chromosomal evolution in rodents. *In* Benirschke, K., ed., Comparative Mammalian Cytogenetics, pp. 277-309. Heidelberg, Springer-Verlag.

—— and R. S. Hoffmann. 1970. Chromosomes of some Asian and South American squirrels (Rodentia:Sciuridae). Experientia, 26:1383-1386.

—— R. S. Hoffmann, and D. M. Lay. 1969. Chromosomes of the Asian chipmunk *Eutamias sibiricus* Laxmann (Rodentia: Sciuridae). Experientia, 25:868-869.

Repenning, C. A. 1967. Palearctic-Nearctic Mammalian dispersal in the late Cenozoic. *In* Hopkins, D. M., ed., The Bering Land Bridge, pp. 289-311. Palo Alto, Stamford University Press.

Shotwell, J. A. 1970. Pliocene mammals of southeast Oregon and adjacent Idaho. Bull. Mus. Nat. Hist. Univ. Oregon, 17:1-103.

Simpson, G. G. 1953. Evolution and geography. An essay on historical biogeography with special reference to mammals. Condon Lectures, 1953:1-64.

Sulimski, A. 1964. Pliocene Lagomorpha and Rodentia from Weże 1 (Poland). Acta Palaeont. Polonica, 9(2):149-240.

Vianey-Liaud, M. 1969. Rongeurs de l'Oligocène moyen provenant de nouvelles fouilles dan les Phosphorites du Quercy. Palaeovertebrata (Montpellier), 2(5):209-239.

Vorontsov, N. N., and E. A. Lyapunova. 1970. Chromosome numbers and speciation in the Sciuridae: Xerinae and Marmotinae of Holarctica. Bull. Mus. Soc. Natural., Ser. Biol., 5(3):122-136.

Wilson, R. W. 1960. Early Miocene rodents and insectivores from northeastern Colorado. Univ. Kansas Paleont. Contrib. Vertebrata, 7:1-92.

Wood, A. E. 1962. The early Tertiary rodents of the Family Paramyidae. Trans. Amer. Philos. Soc., 52(1):1-261.

Young, C. C. 1927. Fossile Nagetiere aus Nord-China. Palaeont. Sinica, [C], 5(3):1-92.

Zimina, R. P., and I. P. Gerasimov (ms.) The periglacial expansion of marmots (*Marmota*) in Middle Europe during the Upper Pleistocene.

11

Relationships, Origins, and History of the Ceboid Monkeys and Caviomorph Rodents: A Modern Reinterpretation

ROBERT HOFFSTETTER

*Institut de Paléontologie, Muséum National
d 'Histoire Naturelle, Paris*

This modest essay is dedicated to Dr. George Gaylord Simpson, to acknowledge my admiration for the man and his work. The reading of his publications has been for me very enriching. But, more than his discoveries and the results of his studies, both considerable, I appreciate his rigorous and penetrating mentality, his courageous attitude with respect to ideas received, his scientific honesty which obliges him to reconsider syntheses in the light of new facts. This is why I have chosen a theme where, following the line of conduct of which he is an example, I have voiced some opinions which diverge from those he has defended and which I myself have long adopted.

INTRODUCTION

For a long time, biogeographical studies have drawn attention to groups that are essentially austral in distribution. Among tetrapod vertebrates, Leptodactylidae, Pipidae, Chelidae, Ratites, and Marsupialia can be mentioned. Other examples not less significant could be chosen among fishes, invertebrates, and plants.

To account for these distributions, former authors have been led to imagine an ancient austral continent, fragmented now by large subsidences. Such subsidences seeming unaccountable, in consideration of their width, some people have advocated the temporary emerging of transoceanic "bridges", whose number has increased to absurdity, in order to account for the geographical distribution of each animal or vegetable group. It is to the credit of W. D. Matthew and G. G. Simpson to have pointed out the improbability of those hypothetical constructions.

For a while Wegener's theory of continental drift raised the hope of explaining faunal exchanges between the large austral lands without appealing to such "land bridges." But the fragmentation of the Gondwana continent and the subsequent drift of its parts, while being denied by some authors, have been considered by others as too ancient a phenomenon to take a part in the biogeographical history of modern groups such as angiosperms, frogs, lizards, birds, or mammals.

As a natural reaction, and considering the ideas that prevailed then in geological circles, Matthew and Simpson and most authors after them did agree that oceans and continental masses practically have not changed since the middle Cretaceous, and especially in the austral hemisphere. Owing to the fact, direct faunal exchanges between austral continents were considered as highly improbable, not to say impossible, even by rafting, in view of the hugeness of interposed marine barriers. Invertebrate zoologists and botanists showed some reluctance in admitting such ideas. But as regards mammals, it was generally agreed that the center of origin and dispersion of most groups could only be the Holarctic region (North America and Eurasia). The different austral continents would have been populated by migrants of northern origin. Local differentiations subsequently gave to each of these austral faunas its peculiar characters. Resemblance between some African, South-American, and Australian faunal elements could be explained by phenomena of parallelism or convergence. The same opinion still appears in the conclusion to the Symposium on The Evolution of Mammals on Southern Continents, which took place in Washington (1963) during the XVIth International Congress of Zoology. According to Simpson (1966): "the southern continents Africa, Australia and South America have in common that they are dead ends as far as expansion of land mammals is concerned. . ." This clearly implies that mammals would never have reached Antarctica.

This statement was the logical outcome of the paleogeographical premises that discarded in fact any other hypothesis. Moreover, it had the agreement of nearly all the paleomammalogists. It was, in any case, a fruitful working hypothesis, as it instigated research in various branches in view of corroborating or invalidating it.

As a consequence of these researches in chorology, paleontology, comparative anatomy, parasitology, etc., a certain number of divegent opinions have been expressed during the last few years. But it was modern geophysical studies, above all, which brought new support to the theory of continental drift, with the intervention of sea-floor spreading. At present it has been practically demonstrated that the width of the oceans and, in consequence, relative positions of continental masses, have undergone considerable variations during geologic time. Some land areas may have changed in latitude and, consequently, passed from one climatic zone to another (this is particularly important for Antarctica). Such a phenomenon does not concern only old geological periods but also Cretaceous, Cenozoic and Recent times; thus, it must be taken into account in the history of modern animal and plant groups.

In fact, the whole history of the mammals, their migrations and consequent geographical segregations, must be reconsidered (see Hoffstetter 1970a, b, and in press.)

In the present essay, we consider only the mammalian exchanges that may have occurred between the austral continents whose paleontological documentation is richest, that is to say, South America and Africa. The problem as posed here concerns essentially the platyrrhine monkeys and caviomorph rodents, which suddenly appear in South America in the early Oligocene. First of all I shall briefly present the faunistic successions observed in South America, the arrival of groups here considered representing only an episode of this history. I shall sum up then the various pieces of information that shed some light on the question of phyletic and geographical origin of the Caviomorpha and the Platyrrhina.

As we shall see further on, this is the most striking example of the conflicts that arose between zoological classification (as given by the study of living and fossil forms) and restraints introduced by paleogeography (or at least the accepted ideas at a given time on this subject).

MAJOR FEATURES OF SOUTH AMERICAN MAMMALIAN HISTORY

The Paleogeographic history of South America is not yet perfectly known. During a large part of the Tertiary, at least from the middle Paleocene to the middle Pliocene, it was isolated from the rest of the world by oceanic barriers. Patterson and Pascual (1968) think that this isolation goes back much further, but this is not confirmed by stratigraphical observations on isthmian Central America (Costa Rica and Panama), where the late Eocene rests nearly everywhere in discordance upon the late Cretaceous volcanic and marine sediments. But it is true that a branch of the sea may have existed at this time in northwestern Colombia, where stratigraphical data are still rather obscure.

As far as South American mammals are concerned, Simpson distinguishes three major episodes corresponding to three faunal strata[1], which he considers as resulting from immigrations of northern origin, some by terrestrial ways, others by "sweepstake routes." The first immigration, which he believes to have occurred at the beginning of the Tertiary or at the extreme end of the Cretaceous, could have brought marsupials, edentates, and ungulates: this is the ancient stock. The second one, which took place roughly at the Eocene-Oligocene boundary, corresponds to the arrival of "island hoppers"—caviomorph

---

[1] Reig (1962) proposes to use rather the term *cenochron*, to underline that the immigrant groups became integrated, at a given time in a given area, into preexisting communities.

rodents and platyrrhine monkeys. In Neogene layers, formerly thought to be late Miocene but recently recognized as Pliocene in age, procyonid Carnivora appeared, also coming by rafting; they are sometimes connected with the second stratum, but it is more satisfactory to consider them as forerunners of the third one. Finally, the third stratum starts at the end of the Pliocene and increases through the Quaternary; it corresponds to faunal exchanges, massive and bilateral, that occurred between North and South America, thanks to the emersion of the Panamanian isthmus.

ANCIENT MAMMALIAN STOCK AND ARRIVAL OF THE EARLIEST NEOTHERIDA IN SOUTH AMERICA

The ancient mammalian stock of South America is known from fossiliferous localities of different geological ages: Laguna Umayo (Peru) for the latest Cretaceous; Rio Chico (Patagonia) and Itaborai (Brazil) for the late Paleocene; Casamayor and Musters (Patagonia) and maybe Ciococa (Peru), Tama and Gualanday (Colombia) for Eocene. Contrary to what is currently admitted, I think that these faunas are the results of long local histories. As far as mammals are concerned, there is little probability that South America was an empty continent until the latest Cretaceous. Indeed, some presently unknown (or unpublished) Theria, and non-Theria as well, may have inhabited it before this time. Strictly indigenous faunas may have existed originally. Moreover, one or several migrations have probably brought allochthonous elements which have undergone local differentiation and may have eliminated some indigenous forms. Therefore it seems better, when mentioning the known portion of this ancient stock, to avoid such usual terms as "initial stock," "first faunal stratum," "ancient immigrants," and "cenochron," some of these terms denying the possible existence of previous faunas, others postulating a single biogeographical history for all the constituant elements.

Be that as it may, during the time from which mammal-bearing deposits are known, this ancient stock consists only of marsupials and "paleotherid"—or better, "henotherid" (nomen novum)[2] —placentals, the latter including xenarth-

---

[2] The term "Palaeotherida" as created by Broom in 1927 in opposition to "Neotherida" applies to mammals that have but three bony elements in their basicranial axis. This term seems unsuitable for two reasons. Firstly, it may be mistaken, especially when in adjectival form, for its near homonym "Palaeotheriidae" (a family based on the genus *Palaeotherium*). Secondly, in its original meaning, this taxon includes monotremes, marsupials, several placental orders (Xenarthra, Artiodactyla, Perissodactyla, Proboscidea, Sirenia), and probably some extinct mammalian groups. This is certainly not a natural grouping.

Actually the neotherid disposition (acquisition of a fourth basicranial axial element) seems to result from an early dichotomy of placentals (see Hoffstetter, 1970a); if this hypothesis proves to be right, the two resulting stems (superorders) may be designated Neotherida Broom (1927) and Henotherida nom. nov. (from Greek 'Ένος 'old,' One 'beast'), the latter for placentals that have not yet acquired the neotherid structure (excluding therefore nonplacental mammals). Furthermore, the affinities and taxonomic position of some aberrant groups (Chrysochloridae, Hyracoidea, Cetacea) still have to be debated.

ran edentates, and a complex of ungulates and and paenungulates. All of them belong to groups where the basicranial axis includes only three bony elements.

With the Deseadan (Early Oligocene), two placental orders, previously unknown for that continent, suddenly appear in South America: Rodentia and Primates, respectively represented by the Caviomorpha and the Platyrrhina (= Ceboidea). These are Neotherida whose basicranial axis includes four bony elements. It should be pointed out that the Neotherida seem to represent a monophyletic assemblage apparently originating in Laurasia from ancestral placentals ("insectivores" with three bony elements in the basicranial axis). But they undergo rapid diversification in the holarctic region. Successively there appear true Insectivora, Carnivora s.l. = Ferae (first represented by the Deltatheridia), and Primates in the late Cretaceous; Palaeanodonta (ascribed to Pholidota by Emry, 1970), Rodentia, and Lagomorpha in the Paleocene; Chiroptera and Tubulidentata in the Eocene.

The Neotherida are completely absent in the old South American stock. On this continent, their first representatives are, indeed, caviomorph rodents and ceboid primates, known from the Deseadan but whose arrival may have been a little earlier (see below). Anyway, at that time South America was geographically isolated by oceanic barriers. Therefore it was by passive transportation, probably thanks to natural rafts and maybe by means of island relays, that these immigrants ("island-hoppers" of Simpson) found it possible to reach South America. Their place of origin has been and is still controversial. In any case, it cannot be elsewhere than North America or Africa (the latter more or less connected with Eurasia).

The problems raised by the affinities and origin of both groups are astonishingly similar and have probably the same explanation. Similar, too, are the successive approaches that have been made to these questions, so that it is possible to consider them together.

FORMER CLASSIFICATIONS

Caviomorpha all possess the so-called hystricomorph structure (a very enlarged infraorbital canal giving passage to the deep layer of the masseter; Figure 1, *Myocastor*). Thus it has been natural to include them in the suborder Hystricomorpha Brandt 1855, together with similar Old World forms. This is still the position of Simpson (1945), who keeps the classical threefold division of rodents, and divides Hystricomorpha into one or two strictly African superfamilies (Hystricoidea and perhaps Bathyergoidea); three South American (Erethizontoidea, Cavioidea, and Chinchilloidea); and one composite (Octodontoidea, in which families from both continents are assembled).

In the same way, since the earliest zoological studies, South American primates were considered as monkeys but authors have distinguished them under the names of Platyrrhina Hemprich 1820 or Ceboidea Simpson 1931. Simpson's classification still remains conservative since his suborder Anthropoidea (in

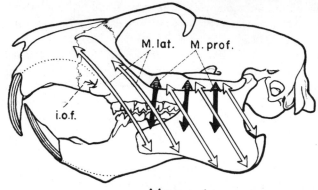

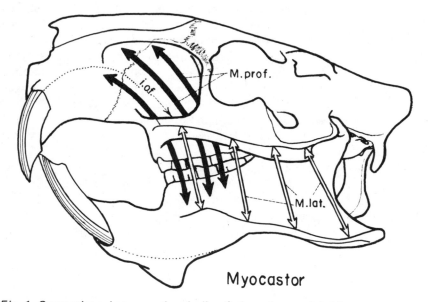

Fig. 1. Comparison between the skulls of the sciuromorph Marmota marmota *and the caviomorph* Myocastor coypus, *x 4/5. The latter displays the "hystrico-morph" disposition; the* Masseter profundus *(M. prof., black arrows) has spread forward through an enlarged infraorbital foramen (i.o.f.) onto the snout.*

opposition to Prosimii) groups together Ceboidea, Cercopithecoidea, and Hominoidea.

However, it seems convenient to emphasize that in his explicative notes (Review of Mammalian Classification), Simpson (1945) states that he was obliged to adopt for these groups a morphological classification which does not necessarily reflect phylogenetic relations. Nevertheless, the same author (Simpson, 1961, Fig. 28E, p. 213) proposes a phylogenetic scheme for Primates, in which the Anthropoidea (including Ceboidea) clearly appear as a monophyletic group.

TRANSOCEANIC MIGRATIONS OR PARALLELISM?

The classical systematic arrangements led very naturally to a search for an African origin for the Caviomorpha and the Platyrrhina, since Africa was the place where the nearest forms, at least morphologically, were found.[3] It implies transoceanic migrations from Africa to South America, raising serious problems. The first hypotheses (the emerging of continents or of transoceanic "bridges" followed by subsidences) has been at last abandoned: not only were they lacking in geological support, but they did not take into account the characteristics of the migrations considered, which appear to be unilateral and limited to two mammalian groups. On the other hand, we have said already that geophysicists and geologists did not favorably receive Wegener's theory. Thus, Matthew being lead to formulate his own fixist conception of paleogeography, there remained no more than two hypotheses to try to explain the resemblances between the primates and the rodents on both sides of the Atlantic. Either both groups crossed the Atlantic by means of natural rafts (this possibility was still considered in the case of Hystricomorpha by Matthew himself in 1915, and by Romer in 1945), or monkeys and Hystricomorpha arose respectively from Holarctic stocks and the likeness between New and Old World forms is attributable to parallelism and not to direct phylogenetic relations.

The immensity of the Atlantic barrier, in its present dimensions, makes very improbable a successful transportation by rafts; thus most authors have rallied to the second hypothesis (which, let us repeat, also postulates the rafting of immigrants from North America, or at least from nuclear Central America, to South America).

In order to support this hypothesis, workers have approached this problem in two ways: (1) by searching in North America for possible ancestors of the Caviomorpha and the Platyrrhina; (2) by trying to discover some anatomical criteria allowing a demonstration of the phylogenetic independence of both neotropical groups with respect to the Old World ones.

THE SEARCH FOR NORTH AMERICAN ANCESTORS

If the Caviomorpha did not arise in Africa, we are obliged to seek their ancestry in North America. But the only recent North American Hystricomorpha are a few late immigrants originating from South America, and the rich Tertiary faunas of North America have never yielded hystricomorph rodents. It

---

[3]Some authors, in particular Ameghino, have considered an opposite filiation, from South American to African forms, but such an hypothesis encounters so many difficulties that we won't discuss it here.

was consequently among nonhystricomorph forms that workers have been led to search for ancestors of the Caviomorpha. The results have been disappointing. Of course there is no objection to deriving the Caviomorpha from the Paramyidae, a Holarctic family generally considered as the ancestral group of all the rodents. Wood (1949, 1950, 1962) has even pointed out in this family several genera (*Reithroparamys*, *Rapamys*) exhibiting some "hystricomorph tendencies," but taking into account their geological age, these genera are not enough advanced in the hystricomorph way to take place in the direct line leading to Caviomorpha.

The problem raised by ceboid monkeys is astonishingly similar. There are no monkeys, alive or extinct, in North America. The only extinct primates discovered there are Prosimii. Consequently, it is among these latter that workers were led to look for direct ancestors for the Ceboidea. It has been suggested that the stem stock could correspond to the Omomyoidea, the Holarctic group from which Old World monkeys are equally supposed to have arisen.

In both cases, no intermediate has ever been found between the supposed North American ancestral stocks and the first known representatives of the Caviomorpha and the Ceboidea. It was then assumed that these unknown intermediates lived in Central America during the Eocene epoch. Yet this is but a weak hypothesis. One cannot understand why these hypothetical Central American groups, which are supposed to have crossed southwards a large marine barrier in order to colonize all of South America, would not have spread northwards. And this is particularly unlikely for the rodents, which are well known for their aptitudes in adapting to different environments.

In fact, there is no ground for asserting a direct filiation, for either the Ceboidea or for the Caviomorpha, from North American stocks. Yet we need conclusive arguments to support an hypothesis which, once adopted, would lead to profound changes in classification. The concept of monkeys (and even of Simiae = Anthropoidea) should be abandoned in zoology if it were proved that it includes two stems independently originated from Prosimii. In the case of rodents, the situation is still worse since it results in putting at the end of the list a series of superfamilies and families incertae sedis! (See Wood's classification as adopted by Romer, 1966). That state of things seems to betray the inadequacy either of the criteria or of the phylogenetic conceptions used.

ANATOMICAL ARGUMENTS FOR AND AGAINST AN AFRICAN ORIGIN OF THE CAVIOMORPHA AND THE PLATYRRHINA

Comparative anatomical studies dealing with Caviomorpha and Old World Hystricomorpha were undertaken by various researchers in order to choose between affinity and parallelism as an explanation of the observed similarities.

As the result of his studies on the Deseadan genus *Platypittamys*, Wood (1949,

1950) thought he had discovered a relevant odontological criterion. According to him, the caviomorph cheek teeth would arise from a tetralophodont pattern, where as the Old World Hystriocomorpha are fundamentally pentalophodont. On the other hand, Stehlin and Schaub (1951) and later Schaub (1953, 1958) still classified the Caviomorpha (= Nototrogomorpha) among the Pentalophodonta, while Wood (1955, 1959, 1965) and Wood and Patterson (1959) keep their own position. New material from the Deseadan of Bolivia (Hoffstetter, 1968) gives strong evidence in support of a fundamental pentalophodonty in the Caviomorpha (Hoffstetter and Lavocat, 1970). Besides, it shows that *Platypittamys* does not deserve the meaning ascribed to it by Wood: several features considered as primitive by him do in fact result from secondary simplifications, and are found in other South American and African forms as well. Of course these grounds are not sufficient to infer a relationship between the Caviomorpha and the African Hystricomorpha (since pentalophodonty is found also among some nonhytricomorph rodents). Yet, the feature put forward by Wood is not relevant for excluding the possibility of such a relationship.

Landry (1957) noticed an impressive number of features common to the Caviomorpha and the Old World Hystricomorpha, but his conclusions are not always convincingly supported. Nevertheless, his contribution was real and deserved a reception quite different from the one that was given to it.

Brundin (1966), when adopting Hennig's ideas on phylogenetic systematics, has violently attacked the classical conceptions mainly from a methodological point of view. All of his assertions are not acceptable; but Hennig's ideas contribute a certain number of positive elements that Patterson and Pascual (1968) should not have discarded without discussion.

In fact our knowledge has considerably increased during the last years. African fossils have been studied by Wood (1968) for the Oligocene, and by Lavocat (in press) for the Miocene. We are now well acquainted with the Deseadan rodents in Patagonia (Wood and Patterson, 1959) as well as in Bolivia (Hoffstetter and Lavocat, 1970, and works in progress).

Presently there is no doubt that the hystricomorph structure of the orbitotemporal region arose among various independent branches and that the former suborder Hystricomorpha must be dismembered. In 1899, Tullberg already suggested that, from a phylogenetical point of view, the mandibular structure is far more relevant. Lavocat took up and strengthened this idea by supporting it with solid arguments. The Caviomorpha are both hystricomorph (by their infraorbital foramen; Figure 1, *myocaster*) and hystricognath (a mandibular specialization [see Figures 2, 3] well studied by Waterhouse, (1839, 1848), Tullberg (1899), Landry (1957), and Lavocat (in press), to which can be added more or less correlative features such as the perforation of the pterygoid fossae). To the Old World forms showing both features, i.e., the Phiomyidae and other related extinct families, the Thryonomyidae (including Petromurinae), the

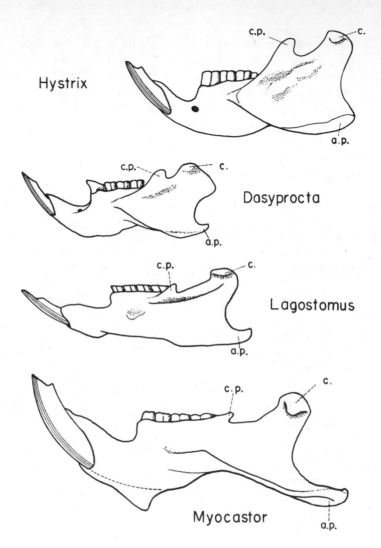

Fig. 2. Lateral view of hystricognath lower jaws of Old World Phiomorpha (Hystrix longicauda) and New World Caviomorpha (Dasyprocta aguti, Lagostomus viscaccia, Myocastor coypus), x 4/5. These few examples show various degrees of lowering of the condyle (co), reduction of the coronoid process (c.p.), as well as backward and lateral expansion of the angular process (a.p.) See also Fig. 3.

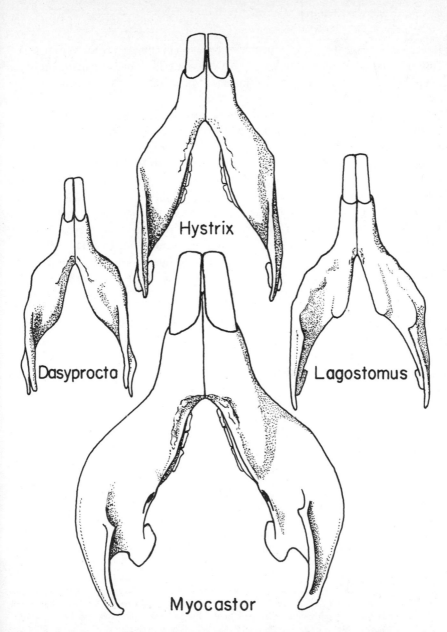

Fig. 3. Ventral view of hystricognath lower jaws, x 4/5: same specimens as in Fig. 2. The hystricognathy is characterized by the lateral position of the angular process in relation to the plane defined by the outer side of the incisor.

Hystricidae, and the Bathyergidae[4], Lavocat (in press) gives the name of Phiomorpha. The other Old World "hystricomorph" forms (Theridomorpha, Ctenodactylidae, Pedetidae, Anomaluridae), all of them sciurognath, obviously belong to distinct lineages.

So it is between Caviomorpha and Phiomorpha, and more especially between Caviomorpha and Thryonomyoidea (Hystricidae and Bathyergidae being branches too specialized), that a comparative study ought to be done. Lavocat undertook it with, at first, the hope of supporting Wood's thesis (which he shared at the time) of a parallel evolution of two independent groups. His results, therefore, are all the more significant. In spite of a thorough study, he was not able to disclose any character, osteological or dental, that allowed a clear distinction between the two groups. Still better, he observed among South American and African forms such anatomical similarities (including the otic region) as can hardly be explained without appealing to a true relationship. He concludes, therefore, that the Caviomorpha and the Phiomorpha do constitute a natural group (suborder), for which he utilizes the term Hystricognatha as created by Tullberg in 1899.

The study of the present problem might take into account researches concerning the soft anatomy (myology, circulatory apparatus, endocrine glands, fetal membranes, and so forth), the histology, cytogenetics, serology[5], and physiology. Unfortunately the works till now published, on the whole, do not concern a sufficient variety of taxa in order to lead to clear conclusions. It must be noticed, however, that Guthrie's studies (1963, 1969) on the arterial system disclose relevant similarities between the Caviomorpha and the Phiomorpha. On the other hand, Mossman and Luckett (1968) state: "Nidation and fetal membrane morphogenesis in *Bathyergus* (a fossorial African phiomorph) are, except in minor details, like those of the New World hystricomorphs *Erethizon*, *Cavia*, *Dasyprocta*, *Chincilla*, and *Myocastor*, and not like those of any known sciuromorph or myomorph." They conclude: "The Bathyergidae are closely related to New World hystricomorphs. Is there a geologic explanation?"

In summary, it seems that no anatomical argument opposes a possible relationship between primitive Phiomorpha and the Caviomorpha.

---

[4] In fact, the Bathyergidae present a secondarily reduced infraorbital canal but, as was showed by Tullberg (1899), Landry (1957), and Lavocat (in press), on the whole their characters are clearly consistent with their belonging to Hystricognatha.

[5] As far as serology is concerned, the limited researches made by Moody and Doniger (1955) are not conclusive. According to them the North American and African porcupines [*Erethizon* and *Hystrix*] "have but slight serological similarity," and "that similarity is of about the same order of magnitude as that shown by either porcupine to the guinea pig [*Cavia*] and the agouti [*Dasprocta*]". These first results emphasize the ancientness of these various phyletic lines, which are zoologically separated at least since early Oligocene. They do not exclude a common ancestry for the whole. More definite conclusions would need a deeper research, with crossed tests, using antisera prepared from a great variety of rodents (Caviomorpha, Phiomorpha, and non-hystricognath groups).

The problem raised by the Platyrrhina is similar but more simple. A comparative study shows some anatomical differences between the living Platyrrhina and the Recent Catarrhina, differences which are also found in the Neogene representatives of both groups. The former are distinguished principally by the presence of three premolars, by their simple ectotympanic not prolonged in the form of an ossified external auditory meatus, and by the retention of an auditory bulla (Figure 4). All of these features give to the Platyrrhina a relatively primitive character, which for a long time has prevented them from being considered as descended from the Catarrhina.

Nevertheless, Simons' work (1967a, b) has disclosed the existence of extinct African monkeys provided with three premolars (*Apidium, Parapithecus*) and shown that the earliest Catarrhina lacked a completely ossified auditory meatus. He has also noted among the primates from the Fayum (Egypt) other ceboid features concerning the humerus, the tail, etc. Simons (1967) concludes that although these African primates are already true monkeys in their general features, they nevertheless correspond to a rather primitive stage more or less comparable to that of the living South American monkeys. He did not hesitate to qualify the Parapithecidae as a "primitive New-World monkey-like" family. It would certainly be rash to infer a direct filiation from Parapithecidae to Ceboidea. But these observations give some likelihood to an African origin of Ceboidea. It is not impossible that the African stem-stock correponds to a prosimian grade. But the observations of Simons already quoted lead rather to suppose the existence of Eocene African monkeys, which gave rise to the Neotropical Platyrrhina and the African Catarrhina.

PARASITOLOGICAL EVIDENCE

Cameron (1960, p. 83) gives the following conclusion, based on a study of the parasites of the Platyrrhina and the Catarrhina: "The evidence suggests that both groups of monkeys evolved in common in Africa until a comparatively advanced stage—possibly until the second half of the Tertiary [sic] ". Such an affirmation cannot be defended, but its basic promises have found some echo (Reig, 1968, p. 225). However, according to A. G. Chabaud and J. C. Quentin (pers. comm.), these bases themselves are very debatable and correspond perhaps to accidental infestations in captive animals. In fact, it is not possible to conclude anything from the distribution of the filarid *"Acanthocheilonema"* (= *Dipetalonema*) and of the cestode *Bertiella*; both of them attack many mammalian groups in the Old and New Worlds. The oxyures that infest the Platyrrhina do not belong to the genus *Enterobius* (which is localized in the Old World), but to a very different genus *Trypanoxyuris*. Cameron reports the same species of the nematode *Subulura* in both groups of monkeys; this indication is erroneous or else it rests upon a case of accidental infestation. In fact, the Subuluridae parasitizing monkeys belong to the genus *Primasubulura* (distinct from *Subulura*), subdivided into two subgenera, the more primitive of which (*Platysubulura*) attacks

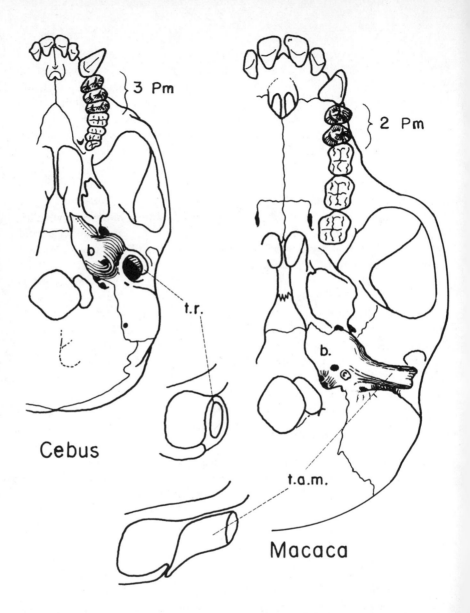

Fig. 4. Basal aspect of the skull in Platyrrhina (Cebus) and Catarrhina (Macaca), x1. In the modern Catarrhina, the following features are characteristic: only two premolars (Pm) instead of three; auditory bulla (b) not inflated; ectotympanic bone (or tympanic ring: t.r.) developed in the form of a tubular auditory meatus (t.a.m.). The latter differentiation is illustrated too in the diagrammatic section (below), modified after Le Gros Clark.

only the Platyrrhina, but the other (*Primasubulura* s.s.) is present only in the Catarrhina. Such a distribution does not allow one to go so far as Cameron does, but it speaks in favor of a common origin for the Platyrrhina and Catarrhina, because the genera that infest the Prosimii are different: *Subulura*, in Lemuroidea, and *Tarsubulura*, in Tarsioidea.

In the parasitological research concerning the Caviomorpha, an outstanding work, still in progress, on heligmosomid nematodes is being done by Durette-Desset (1971). A phylogenetic interpretation leads her to distinguish in this family several natural groups ("lineages"), of which two infest the Caviomorpha. One of these groups (Heligmonellinae—Pudicinae of Durette-Desset), issued from African forms like *Heligmonella* (parasitizing the phiomorph genera *Thryonomys* and *Atherurus*), is found in five families of Caviomorpha (Erethizontidae, Echimyidae, Myocastoridae, Capromyidae, and Dasyproctidae) and also in Neotropical Sciuridae. The other group (Viannaiinae of Durette-Desset), strictly South American, infests Neotropical marsupials and (secondarily) four families of Caviomorpha, distinct from the first ones (Caviidae, Hydrochoeridae, Cuniculidae, and Chincillidae), as well as some cebid monkeys. Such a distribution is interesting. The presence, in five families of Caviomorpha, of Heligmosomidae closely related to African parasites of Phiomorpha, suggests an African origin for these Caviomorpha. In this hypothesis, the latter would have arrived in South America bringing their own parasites. The second group of the Caviomorpha, on the contrary, would have been contaminated, after its arrival, by parasites already present, at that time, in South American marsupials. If we consider that these two groups of rodents are completely distinct from one another, and if we note that the second group corresponds to the forms that are the most hypsodont[6], we may suppose that they would derive from two distinct colonizations, independent but not necessarily different in age. This is an important point asking for confirmation (see later).

DATES AND NUMBER OF
PALEOGENE COLONIZATIONS IN SOUTH AMERICA

The arrival of the rodents and the primates in South America goes back at least to the early Oligocene (Deseadan), since they are found beginning at this date in Patagonia (rodents), in Bolivia (rodents and primates), and possibly in Colombia (Peneyita rodent). Nevertheless, the initial diversity of the Caviomor-

---

[6] Unhappily, we lack information about some families of the Caviomorpha, notably the Octodontidae, Abrocomidae, and Ctenomyidae. Moreover, referral of the Dasyproctidae to the first group and the Cuniculidae (pacas) to the second one needs a confirmation or a particular explanation if these two families are closely related, as is generally accepted. It is true that some authors, especially Ellerman (1940) and Schaub (1958), do not share this opinion. According to them, the Dasyproctidae are not closely related to the Cuniculidae; they may have some support from parasitology.

pha, in Boliva as well as in Patagonia, suggests an earlier colonization, perhaps in the late or even middle Eocene. Wood and Patterson (1959) and also Patterson and Pascual (1968) are of the opinion that this arrival occurred during the interval between the Mustersan and the Deseadan. But oddly enough, rodents fail to appear in the Divisadero Largo fauna, which is situated precisely in this interval. Were the Caviomorpha confined for a time to the intertropical zone owing to their climatic requirements? Were the first immigrants cut off by a geographical barrier? Maps proposed by Schaffer (1924, Fig. 544, p. 443; reproduced in Kurtén, 1966) and by Cameron (1960, Fig. 2) suppose the existence of arms of the sea that in the Paleogene would have fragmented the South American continent. But there is no evidence of continuous marine sediments that would justify such an hypothesis. Landry (1957) suggests the existence of Antillean relays that could have served as centers of diversification prior to the Oligocene. Only the discovery of Eocene intertropical fossil localities will allow an elucidation of this problem.

It is possible that the Platyrrhina arose from a single stock, since the teeth of the Hapalidae as well as of the Cebidae may be derived from those of *Branisella* (Hoffstetter, 1969).

In the same way, Wood and Patterson (1959, p. 396) suppose that the Caviomorpha, as a whole, have diversified from a single invasion. But we have seen that parasitological evidence conveys more the impression of two different colonizations in South America. If this is proved to be the case, the Caviomorpha could no longer be regarded as a monophyletic group. But we must not make hasty conclusions. Maybe both the groups of Caviomorpha distinguished by Durette-Desset by their parasites, are in fact the result of an *ecological* segregation from a single South American stem-stock. Certain paleontological observations seem to support this last hypothesis. In Bolivia I know two Deseadan fossiliferous localities. All the rodents from one of these—Salla-Luribay—possess brachyodont or feebly hypsodont teeth (see Hoffstetter and Lavocat, 1970) and belong to the first of Durette-Desset's groups. The other locality—Lacayani (still unpublished)—is of the same age (presence of *Trachytherus, Glyptatelus*, etc.) but with a different facies (absence of *Pyrotherium, Rhynchippus*, etc.). The rodents from the latter locality are very hypsodont and all belong to one or another of the families Chinchillidae and Eocardiidae (unknown from Salla); that is to say, to the second group distinguished by Durette-Desset. These two associations or rodents suggest distinct ecological control: it seems that the food sources supplied by the vegetation of Lacayani were more abrasive than that of Salla.

POSSIBILITY OF TRANSATLANTIC MIGRATIONS DURING THE PALEOGENE

It is therefore in Africa where we are obliged to seek the direct ancestors of the Caviomorpha and the Platyrrhina. We come back then to the former conceptions which have been dismissed for a long time because of paleogeographical reasons. Modern geophysical studies have restored with solid evidence the theory of continental drift, which is now admitted as a fact. During the Paleogene the Atlantic was far from having reached its present width, yet it already constituted a considerable barrier (see Le Pichon. 1968; Funnell and Smith, 1968; Dietz and Holden, 1970). It must be stressed, however, that the probability of a successful rafting depends perhaps more on marine currents than on the distance to cover. During the Paleogene, the Atlantic and Pacific oceans communicated by a large branch of the sea, which was probably swept from east to west by the equatorial current. The latter rendered very improbable the transportation by rafting between the two Americas. On the contrary, the same equatorial current could carry African rafts westward only, toward the coasts of Brazil (thus accounting for the one-way direction of observed migrations).

Romer (1945, p. 504) at first admitted that "it is hard to escape the conclusion that the hystricoids, by some means or other, made a successful western crossing of the South Atlantic." Later on, he came to consider such a migration as impossible because, according to him (1968, p. 225), "the South Atlantic is a long swim for a necessarily pregnant female." Presented in this form, the argument is peremptory. Indeed, nobody will ever admit that it should be possible for a gravid female to cross the Atlantic (even if it were of a reduced width) by swimming. It is clear that, in order to give an ironical touch to an objection he wanted impressive, Romer deliberately limited himself to the most improbable hypothesis. In fact we can conceive other modes of transportation and colonization. Tropical rivers sometimes do carry veritable floating islands made up of entangled trees. Such rafts can harbor small populations of rodents and/or primates and, under propitious circumstances, may successfully transport them fron one continent to another. Moreover, some island relays, made up by volcanoes such as are known since the Cretaceous in the South Atlantic ocean (see Deitz and Holden, 1970; maps, pp. 37-38), may have facilitated this crossing.

Nevertheless, even in this form, the success of such rafting remains very problematical. In most cases, the raft will disintegrate and the harboured animals die of thirst, starvation, or by drowning. However in the case considered, a feeble probability would be sufficient to account for one single successful crossing (by means of a raft bearing together rodents and monkeys) or even two or three successes (as distinct implantations of founding colonies, one of primates, one or two of rodents). The chances of success, still appreciable at the beginning of the Tertiary, diminished as the Atlantic Ocean grew wider. This is in accordance with the failure of any African faunal element to settle in South America since the beginning of the Oligocene, that is to say, during the last 40 millions of years.

CONCLUSIONS

In brief, the African origin of the Caviomorpha and the Platyrrhina is by far the most probable hypothesis. It is the only one to account satisfactorily for the totality of the evidence presented by paleontology, comparative anatomy, parisitology, and chorology. Immigrants probably arrived by rafting towards the end of the Eocene. Such an origin, if we accept it, requires a reconsideration of the phylogenetic and biogeographic history of the rodents and the primates.

The rodents are known since the late Paleocene in North America (Paramyidae). We know neither their ancestors—probably neotherid Insectivora—nor their place of origin.

I would incline to the belief that the Sciurognatha and the Hystricognatha are the result of an early dichtomy caused by geographical segregation. As a matter of fact, the former are essentially Laurasian, the latter, essentially African. The two groups are clearly distinguished one from another by their mandibular structure. Hystricognathy represents an excellent apomorph character (according to Hennig's terminology), and makes it possible to contrast the group defined by Tullberg (1899) and Lavocat (in press) with the other rodents as a whole, which are all sciurognath and include the oldest representatives of the order.

In fact, the Hystricognatha are known only since the Oligocene, but, on the one hand, they are the only rodents described from Africa of that epoch, and, on the other hand, no other representative of them is known at that time in the rest of the Old World. Their ancientness is not known exactly, but they could have differentiated in Africa at the beginning of the Tertiary, our ignorance of their first representatives being due to the lack of African fossil-bearing deposits of adequate age. Towards the end of the Eocene, primitive Phiomorpha (Phiomyidae ?) succeeded in crossing the Atlantic ocean and settling in South America to give rise to the Caviomorpha[7]. These, first confined to the South American continent, reached the West Indies probably in the Neogene, and some of them passed to Central America, then to North America, after the emersion of the Isthmus of Panama.

In a parallel fashion, the Phiomorpha that remained in Africa gave rise to the central group Thryonomyoidea and also to the specialized families Hystricidae and Bathyergidae, the history of which is poorly known. Two famlies, (Thryonomyidae and Hystricidae) passed to Eurasia near the Miocene, but did not reach Australia or even Madagascar. (See Figures 5, 6.)

---

[7] If I interpret Lavocat's observations correctly, the terms Phiomorpha and Caviomorpha enable a distinction to be made between two biogeographical assemblages, but these cannot be separated by anatomical diagnoses. So, the distinction would not be valid from a taxonomic point of view.

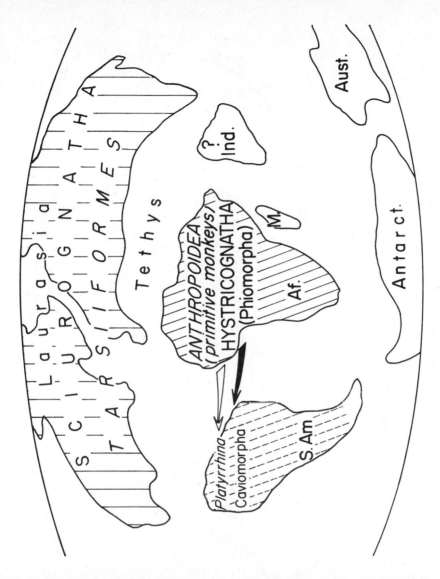

Fig. 5. Place of origin and early expansion of the hystricognath rodents and the anthropoid primates, following the present interpretation. In the early Tertiary both groups differentiated in Africa (Af.: oblique lines), whereas their respective sister-groups—Sciurognatha and Tarsiformes—differentiated in Laurasia (vertical lines). Towards the late Eocene, both African groups crossed the South Atlantic (arrows) giving rise to Caviomorpha and Platyrrhina in South America (S.Am.: dashed oblique lines). The sketch indicates approximately the position of the land masses in the Eocene.

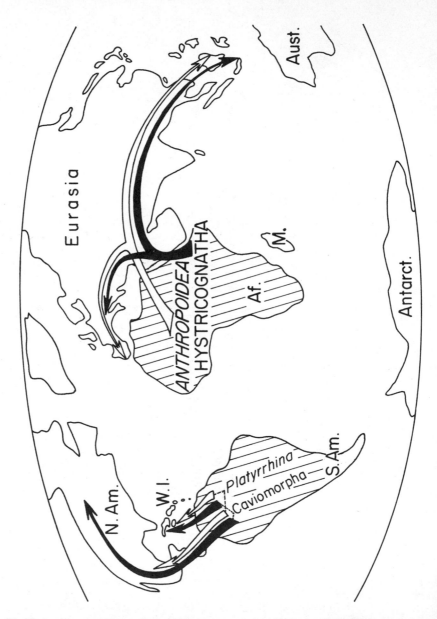

Fig. 6. Later migrations of the Hystricognatha and the Anthropoidea (excluding man): starting from Africa, penetration into Eurasia during and after the Miocene (after the Alpine orogenic phase of the late Oligocene); from South America, (a) rafting to the West Indies during the Neogene, (b) invading of Central America (and North America as regards the Caviomorph) during the Pleistocene, after emergence of the Panamanian isthmus. Geographic disposition of the land masses as at present.

It is more difficult to draw a picture of the history of the Sciurognatha, the initial radiation of which was extraordinarily rapid and led to precociously individualized branches, whose interrelationships are obscure. Convergences and parallelisms appear (groups with a "hystricomorph" orbitotemporal region, with pentalophodont molars, etc.), which explains the mistakes committed by certain authors. It is worth observing that the Sciurognatha, first confined to Laurasia, penetrated several times into Africa, at least since the Miocene, and the earliest colonizations gave rise to strongly endemic groups such as the Anomaluridae and the Pedetidae. Only later, some modern groups reached Madagascar (Cricetidae), Australia (Muridae), and South America (numerous Cricetidae since the Pliocene; a few Sciuridae since the latest Pleistocene; and one recently arrived heteromyid).

Thanks to the numerous works which have been devoted to the primates (see Valois, 1955; Piveteau, 1957; Le Gros Clark, 1959; Genet-Varcin, 1963, 1969; Wilson, 1966; McKenna, 1967, Simons, 1967a, b, and references cited by these authors), and taking in account the monophyletism of monkeys here advocated, the history of this order becomes rather clear, at least in its general features.

The primates are known since the latest Cretaceous of North America (*Purgatorius*). They arose from Insectivora probably soon after the acquisition of the neotherid disposition by the latter. They gave rise precociously to an offshoot, the Plesiadapoidea, an aberrant group with chisel-like incisors, known only in the Paleocene and the early Eocene of North America and Western Europe.

The main stock of the primates seems to have undergone an early dichotomy, giving rise to the two groups for which Hill (1953) reinstates the old names of Strepsirhini and Haplorhini.

The Strepsirhini, better known as Lemuriformes or Lemuroidea, represent the plesiomorph group of this dichotomy (Hennig's terminology). They spread over all the continents, except Australia and South America. But their history is only fragmentarily known. In fact, they have been found: (1) in the Eocene of Europe, North America, and Eastern Asia (Adapidae, incl. Nothartidae),; (2) in the Pleistocene and Recent of Madagascar and neighboring islands (Lemuridae, incl. Indriidae; and Daubentoniidae, related to the former, but showing a very specialized dentition recalling that of the Plesiadapoidea); (3) in the Miocene of Africa and in the Recent of Africa and Southern Asia (Lorisidae, the very peculiar otic structure of which indicates a very early separation from the common trunk). All this suggests a long history, insufficiently illustrated, in which there acted climatic requirements (abandonment of the Holarctic zone after the Eocene), geographic segregations (origin of the Lorisidae), substitutions, and also refuges of which Madagascar is a typical example. But, in that last case, we do not even know whether the Lemuridae reached Madagascar from Africa or from India.

The Haplorhini, apomorph sister group of the former (Hennig's terminology) underwent in their turn an early dichotomy which seems to correspond to a geographic segregation. The Tarsiiformes (plesiomorph branch), which include the Omomyoidea and the Tarsioidea, differentiated in Laurasia; they lasted up to the lower Miocene in North America, up to the Eocene in Europe, and they survive nowadays with the genus *Tarsius*, which took refuge in islands of Indonesia and Philippines. The Anthropoidea = Pithecoidea = Simiae = Simii (apomorph branch) were certainly born in Africa but one unfortunately does not know their first representatives. Again, they subdivided by geographic segregation. Primitive monkeys, having crossed (I suggest) the Atlantic ocean by rafting towards the end of the Eocene, gave rise to the Platyrrhina = Ceboidea = New World monkeys (plesiomorph subdivision), which tardily reached Central America and also Jamaica (*Xenothrix*). The Catarrhina (apomorph subdivision) that remained in Africa include a primitive group (the Parapithecidae, which Genet-Varcin, 1969, refers to as "Protocatarhiniens"), still nearly related to the Platyrrhina; and two progressive groups, the Cercopithecoidea (Old World monkeys) and the Hominoidea (apes, *Oreopithecus*, and hominids). These two last groups reached Eurasia: the apes in the Miocene, probably at the same time as the mastodonts did, the monkeys in the Pliocene (or before) and the Hominidae in the Quaternary. Finally, man conquered the entire world.

As we can see, the genealogic tree of the Primates is rather clearly drawn, but there is no general agreement about taxonomy. One will notice, in particular, that the phylogenetic relationships brought out above lead to the suppression of the concept Prosimii, a composite (or better, "paraphyletic" in Hennig's terminology) assemblage, which are not correct in contrasting with that of the Anthropoidea, if we want the classification to express the phylogeny.

The present interpretation, which seems coherent, brings out an astonishing analogy between the history of the Hystricognatha and that of the Anthropoidea. These two groups are of African origin. Both arise from a dichotomy resulting from a geographic segregation, their respective sister-groups being at the beginning localized in Laurasia. Both succeeded in crossing the Atlantic, maybe simultaneously, and in settling in South America. They penetrated only later on into northern continents: about the Miocene coming from Africa, the Pleistocene coming from South America. They did not reach Madagascar any more than Australia (we except the special case of man). So numerous coincidences concerning two groups, independent phylogenetically, could not be fortuitous. It is clear that both groups, all along their history, have been stopped by the same biogeographic obstacles and have availed themselves of the same opportunities of expansion.

ADDENDUM

After the writing of the present essay, Wood and Patterson published a paper (dated 1970, but published in 1971) answering Lavocat's note (1969). This paper would deserve a detailed analysis. I only shall express my agreement with the following conclusion of the authors: ". . . we must continue to stress the importance, in dealing with fossil rodents, of making no assumptions of the relationships of fossil forms (especially from areas widely separated, geographically) without a transitional series of fossils." However, this statement is valuable too for the other zoological groups, and must apply to the various possible hypotheses. Now, let us repeat that the respective ancestors of the Caviomorpha and the Platyrrhina had to cross a wide barrier, wherever they came from: Africa or North America. On the other hand, the lack of "transitional series of fossils" is particularly flagrant in the hypothesis of a filiation from the North American Paramyidae and Omomyidae, respectively, to the South American Caviomorpha and Platyrrhina. The anatomical gap is slight in the assumption of an African origin for the two latter groups.

REFERENCES

Broom, R. 1926. On the mammalian presphenoid and mesethmoid bones. Proc. Zool. Soc. 1926: 257-264.

———— 1927. Some further points on the structure of the mammalian basicranail axis. Proc. Zool. Soc. London, 1927: 233-244.

Brundin, L. 1966. Transantarctic relationships and their significance, as evidenced by Chironomid midges. K. Svenska Vetensk. Akad. Handl., (4. ser.) 11(1):472 pp.

Cameron, T. W. M. 1960. Southern intercontinental connections and the origin of the southern mammals. In Evolution: its science and doctrine (Symposium Roy. Soc. Canada, 1959). 79-89. Toronto, University of Toronto Press.

Clark, W. E. LeGros. 1959. The Antecedents of Man. Edinburgh, University of Edinburgh Press.

Darlington, P. J. 1965. Biogeography of the Southern End of the World. Cambridge, Mass., Harvard University Press.

Dietz, R. S., and J. C. Holden. 1970. The breakup of Pangaea. Sci. Amer., 223(4):30-41.

Durette-Desset, M. C. 1971 (unpublished). Essai de classification des Nématodes Heligmosomes. Corrélations avec la paléobiogéographie des hôtes. Thése Doctorat Sc. Nat., Univ. Paris (Orsay) Sud.

Ellerman, J. R. 1940. The Families and Genera of Living Rodents. Vol. 1, Rodents other than Muridae. London, British Museum (Nat. Hist.).

Emry, R. J. 1970. A North American Oligocene pangolin and other additions to the Pholidota. Bull. Amer. Mus. Nat. Hist., 142(6):455-510.

Funnell, B. M., and A. G. Smith, 1968. Opening of the Atlantic Ocean. Nature (London), 219:1328-1333.

Genet-Varcin, E. 1963. Les Singes Actuels et Fossiles. Paris, Boubée & Cie.

———— 1969. A la Recherche du Primate Ancêtre de l'Homme. Paris, Boubée & Cie.

Guthrie, D. A. 1963. The carotid circulation in the Rodentia. Bull. Mus. Comp. Zool., 128(10):457-481.

———— 1969. The carotid circulation in the Aplodontia. J. Mammal., 50:1-7.

Hennig, W. 1966. Phylogenetic Systematics. Urbana, Chicago, and London, University of Illinois Press.

Hill, W. C. O. 1953-1966. Primates, Comparative Anatomy and Taxonomy. 6 vols. Edinburgh University Press.

Hoffstetter, R. 1954. Les Mammiféres fossiles de l'Amérique du Sud et la biogéographie. Rev. Gén. Sci., 51(11-12):348-378.

—— 1968. Un gisement de Mammiféres déséadiens (Oligocéne inférieur) en Bolivie. C. R. Acad. Sci. (Paris) [D], 267:1095-1097.

—— 1969. Un Primate de l'Oligocéne inférieur sud-américain: *Branisella boliviana* gen. et sp. nov. C. R. Acad. Sci. (Paris) [D], 269:434-437.

—— 1970. Radiation initiale des Mammiféres Placentaires et biogéographie. C. R. Acad. Sci. Paris [D], 270:3027-3030.

—— 1970b. L'historire biogéographique des Marsupiaux et la dichotomie Marsupiaux-Placentaires. C. R. Acad. Sci. (Paris) [D], 271-388-391.

—— (in press). Le peuplement mammalien de l'Amérique du Sud. Rôle des continents austraux comme centres d'origine, de diversification et de dispersion pour certains groupes mammaliens. An. I Simposio Brasil. Paleont. (Rio de Janeiro, Sept. 1970) = suppl. An. Acad. Brasil. Ciencias.

—— and R. Lavocat, 1970. Découverte dans le Déséadien de Bolivie de genres pentalophodontes appuyant les affinités africaines des Rongeurs Caviomorphes. C. R. Acad. Sci. (Paris) [D], 271:172-175.

Kurtén, B. 1966. Holarctic land connexions in the early Tertiary. Comment. Biol. Soc. Sci. Fenn., 29(5):1-5.

Landry, S. O. 1957. The interrelationships of the New and Old World hystricomorph Rodents. Univ. Calif. Publ. Zool., 56:1-118.

Lavocat, R. 1969. La systématique des Rongeurs hystricomorphes et la dérive des continents. C. R. Acad. Sci. (Paris) [D], 269:1496-1497.

—— (in press). Affinités systématiques des Caviomorphes et des Phiomorphes et origine africaine des Caviomorphes. An. I Simposio Brasil. Paleont. (Rio de Janeiro, Sept. 1970) = suppl. An. Acad. Brasil. Ciencias.

—— (in press). Les Rongeurs du Miocéne d'Afrique orientale. *In* Leaky, L. S. B., ed. Fossil Vertebrates of Africa. London and New York, Academic Press.

Le Pichon, X. 1968. Sea-floor spreading and continental drift. J. Geophys. Res., 73(12):3661-3697.

McKenna, M. C. 1967. Classification, range and deployment of the prosimian primates. Colloq. Intern. C.N.R.S., n 1963, Problémes actuels de Paléontologie, Evolution des Vertébrés (Paris, Juin 1966):603-610.

Matthew, W. D. 1915. Climate and evolution. Ann. New York Acad. Sci., 24:171-318.

Moody, P. A. and E. D. Doniger. 1955. Serological light on porcupine relationships. Evolution, 10(1):47-55.

Mossmann, H. W. and W. P. Luckett. 1968. Phylogenetic relationship of the African mole rat, *Bathyergus janetta*, as indicated by the fetal membranes. Amer. Zool., 8:806.

Patterson, B., and R. Pascual, 1968. The fossil mammal fauna of South América. Quart. Rev. Biol., 43(4):409-451.

Piveteau, J. 1957. Primates. *In* Piveteau, J., ed., Traté de Paléontologie, Vol. 7. Paris, Masson et Cie.

Reig, O. A. 1962. Las Integraciones cenogenéticas en el desarrollo de la fauna de Vertebrados tetrápodos de América del Sur. Ameghiniana, 2(8):131-140.

—— 1968. Peuplement en Vertébrés tétrapodes de l'Amérique de Sud. *In* Delamare-Deboutteville, C., and E. Rapoport, eds., Biologie de l'Amérique Australe, IV:215-260, Paris (C.N.R.S.).

Romer, A. S. 1945. Vertebrate Paleontology, 2d ed., Chicago and London, University of Chicago Press.

—— 1966. Vertebrate Paleontology, 3d ed., Chicago and London, University of Chicago Press.

—— 1968. Notes and Comments on Vertebrate Paleontology. Chicago and London, University of Chicago Press.

Schaffer, F. X. 1924. Lehrbuch der Geologie, II. Teil, Grundzüge der historischen Geologie. Leipzig and Vienna, Franz Deuticke.

Schaub, S. 1953. Remarks on the distribution and classification of the "Hystricomorpha". Verh. Naturf. Ges. Basel, 64:389-400.

_____ 1958. Simplicidentata (= Rodentia). *In* Traité de Paléontologie, VI-2:659-818. Paris, Masson et cie.

Simons, E. L. 1967a. New evidence on the anatomy of the earliest catarrhme Primates. *In* Starck, D., R. Schneider, and H. -J. Kuhn, eds. Neue Ergebnisser der Primatologie. First Congr. Intern. Primat. Soc., Frankfurt a. M., 26-30, July, 1966, pp. 15-18. Stuttgart, G. Fischer.

_____ 1967b. The earliest apes. Sci. Amer., 217(6):28-35.

Simpson, G. G. 1945. The principles of classification and a classification of mammals. Bull. Amer. Mus. Nat. Hist., 85(1):xvi + 350 pp.

_____ 1950. History of the fauna of Latin America. Amer. Sci., 38:361-389.

_____ 1961. Principles of Animal Taxonomy. New York, Columbia University Press. 247 pp.

_____ 1965. The Geography of Evolution. Philadelphia and New York, Chilton books.

_____ 1966. Mammalian evolution on the Southern continents. N. Jahrb. Geol. Paläont. Abh., 125 (Festband Schindewolf):1-18.

_____ 1967. The Tertiary lorisiform primates of Africa. Bull. Mus. Comp. Zool. 136(3):39-61.

_____ 1969. South American mammals. *In* Fitkau, E. J., J. Illies, H. Klinge, G. H. Schwabe, and H. Sioli, eds., Biogeography and Ecology in South America, 2:879-909. The Hague, W. Junk.

Stehlin, H. G., and S. Schaub. 1951. Die Trigonodontie der simplicidentaten Nager. Schweiz. Paläont. Abh., 67:1-385.

Tullberg, T. 1899. Ueber das System der Nagethiere, eine phylogenetische Studie. Nov. Acta Reg. Soc. Sci. Upsal., (3)18:1-514, A1-A18.

Valois, H. 1955. Ordre des Primates. *In* Grassé, P. -P., ed., Traité de Zoologie. 17-2:1854-2206.

Waterhouse, G. R. 1839. Observations on the Rodentia. Mag. Nat. Hist., (n.s.) 3:90-96, 184-188, 274-279, 598-600.

_____ 1848. A Natural History of the Mammalia. Vol. 2, Rodentia. London, H. Bailliére.

Wilson, J. A. 1966. A new primate from the earliest Oligocene, West Texas, preliminary report. Folia Primat. (Basel), 4:227-248.

Wood, A. E. 1949. A new Oligocene rodent genus from Patagonia. Amer. Mus. Novit., 1435:54 pp.

_____ 1950. Porcupines, paleogeography and parallelism. Evolution, 4:87-98.

_____ 1955. A revised classification of the rodents. J. Mammal., 36:165-187.

_____ 1959. Eocene radiation and phylogeny of the rodents. Evolution, 13(3):354-361.

_____ 1962. The early Tertiary rodents of the family Paramyidae. Trans. Amer. Philos. Soc., (n.s.) 52(1):1-261.

_____ 1965. Grades and clades among rodents. Evolution, 19(1):115-130.

_____ 1968. Early Cenozoic mammalian faunas, Fayum province, Egypt. The African Oligocene Rodentia. Bull. Peabody Mus. Nat. Hist., 28:23-105.

_____ and B. Patterson, 1959. The rodents of the deseadan Oligocene of Patagonia and the beginnings of South American rodent evolution. Bull. Mus. Comp. Zool., 120(3):279-428.

_____ and B. Patterson. 1971. Relationships among hystricognathous and hystricomorphous rodents. Mammalia, 34(4):628-639.

12

Human Evolution

S. L. WASHBURN

Department of Anthropology
University of California
Berkeley, California 94720

INTRODUCTION

Recently Simpson (1966, p. 10) has stated, "We are no longer concerned with *whether* man evolved, because we know he did. We are still very much concerned with *how* he evolved, with what is most characteristically human about him and how those characteristics arose." Clearly, man is separated from the contemporary nonhuman primates primarily by the functions of the brain (intelligence, language, degree of memory, planning, and social behaviors), and the fossil record shows that these followed long after the evolution of bipedalism, the use of stone tools, and the evolution of human dental characteristics (Simpson, 1966). Recent discoveries in southern Ethiopia (Howell, in press) and northern Kenya (R. E. Leakey, in press) show that the antiquity of stone tools is far greater than previously thought—probably at least twice as old as the assemblage from Olduvai Gorge for which these tools are named. These earliest tools are diversified in form (M. D. Leakey, 1967) and continued without improvement for at least 2 million years, and probably much longer.

The question of *how* man evolved is divided into two parts, two major adaptations. The first involved tool-using, bipedalism, and a change in dental morphology. The second adaptation occurred millions of years later, wherein one species of the early hominids evolved complex tools, a larger brain, and ultimately, language and all the behaviors which now separate man and ape. It must be stressed that what evolved was a whole new successful way of life. Bipedal locomotion, early tools, and modified teeth evolved in a complex feedback relation. Later, an expanding brain, complex tools, social life, and language evolved as a successful pattern of adaptation. The patterns of life are only very sparingly reflected in the fossil record, and there is no way to escape

349

the problems arising from the difficulties of reconstruction. For example, chimpanzees make use of tones, branches, twigs, leaves, etc. (van Lawick-Goodall, 1968). In the fossil record such unworked stones could not be identified as tools, nor would any of the other utilized objects such as wood be preserved at all. It is my bias that if members of the genus *Australopithecus* were making stone tools for some millions of years, we should think of their use of objects as including a wide range of things which are not preserved. It is likely that their principal tools were of wood, and the main importance of stone tools may have been for woodworking.

The "how" of evolution does not come directly from the record, and this is one of the reasons that controversies have been, and will continue to be, intense. In the study of human evolution progress comes from limiting the alternatives, making the choices narrower. As an instance, for a long time many denied that a creature with as small a brain as *Australopithecus* (used here in the widest sense, including large and small forms and specimens extending over some 2 or more million years) could have made stone tools, but no other hominid is associated with the early stone tools. However, there is still no agreement on questions dealing with diet, hunting, bone tools, and a wide range of other problems whose solution is essential in the reconstruction of the adaptive behaviors of our ancestors and their closest relatives.

With this major qualification in mind, this paper will consider recent developments and how they affect our notions of the "how" of human evolution.

THEORY

Until the 1940's the study of human evolution was dominated by typological thinking, orthogenesis, belief in the importance of nonadaptive characters, and with minimum dependence on reliably dated fossils. Whole schools of thought depended on reconstructing evolutionary history from types abstracted from contemporary populations. The rise of population genetics and the synthetic theory of evolution removed much of the theoretical and methodological base from traditional physical anthropology. The synthetic theory substituted population for type, adaptation over time for orthogenesis, and real history for reconstruction. Huxley's *Evolution: The Modern Synthesis* (1942) marks the advent of the new era in evolutionary thinking, and, in this country the influence of Simpson, Dobzhansky, and Mayr has revolutionized the ways of thinking about human evolution. Simpson's *The Meaning of Evolution* (1949) made the new synthesis available to all in readable form and this book has been widely used in courses on human evolution. *Behavior and Evolution*, edited by Roe and Simpson (1958) developed the notion of the importance of behavior in adaptation and evolution, and this is summarized by Simpson, *ibid.*, pages 507-535.

In light of the synthetic theory, it is clear that understanding the "how" of human evolution involves gaining insights into the behavioral stages which have led to man and which account for his evolutionary survival. It is for this reason that the understanding of human evolution necessarily contains a large element of reconstruction. The behavior of our ancestors as such is not available for study, but must be inferred from the fossils, from associated fauna and objects, and from our knowledge of the contemporary primates.

TIME

During the last two years stone tools associated with bones of *Australopithecus* have been found east of Lake Rudolf (northern Kenya) by Richard Leakey (in press) and in southern Ethiopia by F. Clark Howell (in press). The earliest stone tools are more than 3 million years old and teeth are even older. These finds add at least a million years to the earliest evidence of man in Olduvai Gorge (1.8 million years). The teeth belong to the genus *Australopithecus* (using the term in the broadest sense), and the tools are of the Oldowan type. The ones from East Rudolf are remarkable for their variety and skill of manufacture. It seems probable that by 3 million years ago there were at least two species of the genus *Australopithecus* making stone tools and that the separation of the lineages leading to man and to the African apes must have occurred a considerable time before that. Radiometric dating indicates that the origin of the small-brained *Australopithecus* and stone tool-making occurred millions of years earlier than complex stone tools (full Acheulian) and *Homo erectus* (Clark, 1970).

The chronometric dating methods discussed by Clark (1970) have provided evidence for much longer spans of time than the previous informed guesses on the length of the Pleistocene in general and on the East African deposits in particular (Hay, 1967). Prior to the potassium-argon dating method the early part of the Pleistocene was considered to be short, which made it appear that once stone tools appeared they evolved quite rapidly. Now it is apparent that there was a very long time in which small-brained men made stone tools with little evolution either in brain or in tools. Chronometric dating methods have allowed the separation of this long australopithecine phase of human evolution from the later phase associated with *Homo erectus*. As long as the evidence came primarily from South Africa, where rocks suitable for chronometric dating are not associated with the fossils and where the fossils are from cave deposits which are extremely difficult to date by other methods, a long stage of australopithecine evolution could not be proved. It is the East African K-A dates (supported by fission track, reversal of the magnetic field, stratigraphy, and associated fauna) which prove that the genus *Australopithecus* lasted for a long period of time and was in existence millions of years before *Homo erectus*.

MOLECULAR BIOLOGY AND IMMUNOLOGY

Simpson (1966) has stated that "Man evolved from apes also ancestral to chimpanzees and gorillas, but less specialized than the latter." This is a conclusion with which I thoroughly agree, and which was clearly stated by Huxley in 1863. However, many other points of view are held by competent authorities, and almost every conceivable theory of human origin has been suggested from a separation of the lineage leading to man of 50 million years (Hürzeler, 1968), to less than 5 million years ago (Wilson and Sarich, 1969). Perhaps the most widely held point of view has been an early Miocene separation, something on the order of 20 million years. According to Pilbeam (1970) the lines leading to man and the great apes separated in the late Oligocene, some 25 to 30 million years ago, with chimpanzee and gorilla separating only a little later. Whatever the ultimate solution may be, it is apparent that the fossils are sufficiently fragmentary and the traditional methods of comparative anatomy sufficiently unconvincing so that no agreement is likely to emerge.

Fortunately, in the last few years the methods of immunology have been refined and the data of molecular biology have been added to the traditional methods of comparison.

Table 1 presents some of the information comparing the differences between man and chimpanzee and man and Old World monkey (macaque). The comparison of DNA, sequence of amino acids in hemoglobin or fibrinopeptides, or immunological distance in albumin, transferrin, carbonic anhydrase, or gamma globulin—*all* show that man and chimpanzee are far more similar than man and monkey. As Goodman (especially, 1963 and 1968) has pointed out for years in numerous publications, the order of relationship among the existing primates is: man, chimpanzee and gorilla, orangutan, gibbon, Old World monkeys, New World monkeys. This is the traditional view based on comparative anatomy and agrees precisely with the phylogenetic tree based on DNA (Kohne, 1970). The same arrangement is supported by extensive analysis of the primate albumins (Wilson and Sarich, 1969; Sarich, 1970). The main issues of primate relationship are settled, and there can be no further reasonable doubt that man and the African apes are closely related, sharing a common ancestor long after the separation of apes (Pongidae) and monkeys (Cercopithecidae).

It should be stressed that accepting the conclusions of molecular biology and immunology as settling many long-term controversies does not mean that the fossil record is unimportant. For example, the fact of the close relationship between man and the African apes tells us nothing of the reasons for the separation of man and ape. It might have been found that the large brain evolved first, changing the entire interpretation of the course of human evolution. Also there were many fossil forms which have no surviving relatives. The whole

Table 1. Some Biochemical Comparisons Between Man
and Chimpanzee, and Man and Macaque

	Man-Chimp	Man-Macaque	
DNA	2.5%	10.1%	(Kohne, 1970)
Hemoglobin	0.	15. Mut. dist.	(Reviewed by Wilson and Sarich, 1969)
Fibrinopeptides	0.	7. Mut. dist.	(Doolittle and Mross, 1970)
Albumin	7.	35. ID units	(Wilson and Sarich, 1969)
Transferrin	3.	30. ID units	(Wilson and Sarich, 1969)
Carbonic anhydrase	4.	50. ID units	(Nonno et al., 1969)
Albumin	0.	3.7	(Goodman, 1963)
Transferrin	0.	3.7	(Goodman, 1963)
Gamma globulin	.19	3.4	(Goodman, 1963)

ecological setting of primate evolution requires study of the past, and the study of immunology would give no understanding of the evolution of primate behavior. What the new data do, is to permit a quantifiable assessment of primate relationships which makes some taxonomic relationships vastly more probable than others.

Returning to the subject of time, biochemical evolution seems to be more regular than would have been anticipated on the basis of traditional morphological studies or Darwinian evolution. How the regularities should be interpreted is now under debate (King and Jukes, 1969). The question of biological clocks has been discussed by Wilson and Sarich (1969), and it will be possible to determine the probable dates of the separations of the groups of primates from the proteins alone. To what extent this is possible at the present time is a matter of controversy. The least that can be said at present is that the order of difference seen between man and chimpanzee cannot represent a long period of time as compared to the differences between man and monkey. The fossil record makes a separation of man and ape of less than 5 million years improbable, and the immunological and molecular information make a separation of more than 10 million years highly improbable. With the biochemical information accumulating so rapidly, this issue should be largely settled in the next two or three years.

BEHAVIOR

Although some aspects of molecular evolution may proceed in a nonadaptive manner, the evolution of behavioral complexes is controlled by natural selection. The fossil record gives clues to the kinds of behaviors which led to success, or extinction, in times past. Study of the structure and behaviors of the contemporary primates gives many insights which could not be gained from the fossils alone, and it is essential to remember that the bones were parts of living creatures when they were important. If the phylogeny suggested by the molecular and immunological data is combined with information from the fossils and the contemporary primates, it is possible to understand the major events of the behavioral stages leading to man. This order will be briefly discussed, but it must be remembered that except for jaws and teeth, there are few primate fossils, and neither the details of phylogeny nor behavior can be fully reconstructed. Here we are concerned only with attempting to understand the major events.

Australopithecus was a biped, as shown by the foot (Napier, 1967) and the pelvis, and it has long been recognized that in the origin of bipedalism lay one of the main keys to the origin of man. Continuing Simpson's (1966) emphasis on the "how" of human evolution, the question to be considered is how did bipedalism evolve? Man's closest living relatives (chimpanzee and gorilla) are knuckle-walkers. Traditionally, human precursors have been regarded as arboreal apes or even quadrupedal monkeys (Straus, 1968), but the close relationships of man and the living apes suggests that the ancestors of *Australopithecus* may have been more similar to the African apes than to quadrupedal monkeys in their locomotor patterns. There is some direct fossil evidence. The hominid hand, found in Olduvai bed I by L. S. B. Leakey, is intermediate between that of contemporary man and the gorilla (Napier, 1962). Tuttle (1967) has noted that the phalanges show similarities to those of the African terrestrial apes. Less than two million years ago the hands of our ancestors had small thumbs, massive fingers, and it now seems that the form of the human hand is a product of the later phases in human evolution, and is the result of new selection pressures which came with tool-using. A long and massive humerus attributed to the large species of *Australopithecus* found near Lake Rudolf (R. E. Leakey, 1971) also suggests that the arms of *Australopithecus* may have been much longer relative to the legs than have heretofore been shown in reconstructions. This evidence supports that of the hand, essentially that the arm may have retained many ape-like features after the legs had become adapted to bipedalism. The adaptations to bipedalism were not complete, especially in the pelvis (Zihlman and Hunter, in press).

Knuckle-walking is a unique method of locomotion and it used to be regarded as merely a makeshift way of getting around. But Tuttle (1967, 1969) has shown that many of the features of the hand of the African apes correlate with this way of locomoation, which sharply differentiates the African apes from the orang and gibbons. Most primates cannot adopt a knuckle-walking position, and it is an interesting fact that man occasionally adopts the knuckle-walking position under special circumstances—professional football linemen, for example. Human legs are too long for this posture to be used normally, but some lecturers adopt the position, leaning forward on a table. In rising from a sitting position one friend of ours uses his fingers so much that he has callouses on his knuckles. In short, the close relationship of man to the African apes, the features of some fossils, and the behavior of man, all suggest that the ancestors of *Australopithecus* may have had a locomotor pattern not very different from that of the contemporary chimpanzee.

If our Pliocene ancestors were knuckle-walkers, then coming to the ground does not account for the origin of man, any more than it does for the origion of chimpanzee or gorilla. They are largely terrestrial, using a highly specialized method of locomotion. The problem of human origin becomes how a knuckle-walker became a biped, rather than how an arboreal ape became terrestrial. The whole history of the study of the origin of man has centered on the discussion of coming to the ground, and usually the explanation has been in terms of desiccation and the reduction of the forests—but knuckle-walkers on the forest floor would have had their habitat reduced by desiccation.

The behavior of the chimpanzee gives many clues to the possible behaviors of knuckle-walking ancestors (van Lawick-Goodall, 1968; Dolhinow, pers. comm.). Chimpanzee rather than gorilla behavior is stressed because there is so much more information—the differences between the two species are not great. In contrast to monkeys, chimpanzees mature slowly (Schultz, 1969), and there is as great a difference between monkeys and chimpanzees as between chimpanzees and man. The importance of this protracted period for protected learning for manual and social skills has been stressed by Dolhinow and Bishop (1970). In marked contrast to monkeys, chimpanzees play with objects, use objects in displays, throw stones, and use sticks as tools. Objects are carried in the hand, while the animal walks on its knuckles. (The whole literature on carrying and its importance in human evolution assumes that the ancestral form placed the palm down in locomotion. Knuckle-walkers can carry objects with minimum locomotor interference.) "Fishing" for termites involves selection of the time and place of the activity, selection and some preparation of the fishing implement (stick or grass), and substantial learning by the young chimpanzees. Leaves are used for cleaning and getting water. Chimpanzees hunt monkeys and some other small animals with as many as four males cooperating in the hunting, and the activity may cover a long distance. The contrast between monkey and chimpanzee is particularly clear in the Gombe Stream Reserve where the monkeys, especially baboons, have precisely the same opportunities, and so the contrast is clear.

Obviously, the contemporary chimpanzee is not a human ancestor, but equally clearly the study of chimpanzee behavior provides many clues as to the behavior of our ancestors. Behaviorally, they are more similar to man than to monkeys, suggesting the same phylogeny as the immunological data. Traditionally, man was supposed to be distinguished from the apes by such factors as ground-living, object using, hunting, and meat-eating. But these are all behaviors of the chimpanzee. The key to the origin of man is in the evolution of bipedalism from knuckle-walking and a possible explanation of this concerns conditions which favored more bipedalism, more use of objects, more hunting, and more. cooperation.

Selection for more of the whole pattern may have occurred at the edge of the forests. Chimpanzees must still flee into the trees when danger threatens, and they do not range far from trees. Moving onto the savanna may have freed ancestral species from competition with the other knuckle-walkers and provided a new habitat in which there would be increased selection for hominization. During the early Pliocene there were apes in India and presumably in the whole vast area of the Middle East between India and Africa, and it may well have been in this area that, over millions of years, a tool-using biped evolved from ancestral knuckle-walking apes. It would not be surprising to find creatures that would be classified as apes on the basis of teeth and pelvis and limb proportions which were making stone tools. If a minimum use of objects can be as adaptive as it is in the chimpanzee way of life, relatively little more in a savannah setting might have initiated the evolution of man as a distinct adaptive radiation.

ANATOMY

Comparative anatomy is compatible with the derivation of man from ape (Hominidae from Pongidae). This was not only the traditional point of view supported by a wide range of evidence, but the recent study of the wrist by Lewis (1969) shows the close similarity to the African apes. Lewis demonstrates that the similarities are far too close to be due to parallel evolution. The general similarities of man and ape have been reviewed recently (Washburn, 1968), but the traditional anatomical approach has been unable to force agreement among scientists. The anatomical differences can neither be counted nor quantified, as is the case with the molecular and immunological data. There are no rules which govern the way anatomical comparisons are made, and this allows the widest divergences in the interpretation of the data. This is why we say that the anatomical data is compatible with the phylogeny derived from the other kinds of data, but anatomy alone has been subject to a wide variety of interpretations.

PALEONTOLOGY

As mentioned earlier, the course of evolution can be determined only from the fossil record. Even if the time of separation of man and ape can be approximately determined by the study of the proteins, and the relationship between man and ape demonstrated, the reasons for the separation cannot be understood without recourse to the fossil data. Unfortunately, although hundreds of fossils of monkeys and apes are known, they are mostly limited to teeth and fragments of jaws. For example, the structure of the proximal end of the humerus is particularly important in determining the differences in locomotion between quadrupedal monkeys and apes. The climbing-feeding adaptation of the apes evolved during the Miocene, long after the dental evidence shows that monkeys and apes were evolving separately. In *Pliopithecus* the proximal end of the humerus is like that of a quadrupedal monkey. In the published descriptions of *Proconsul* this part is reconstructed. As the record stands, the similarities in the trunk and arms that man shares with the apes did not evolve before the later part of the Miocene (Washburn, 1968). Granting the nature of the record, the fossil evidence is compatible with the phylogeny suggested by Huxley (1863) and Goodman (1963), or the DNA studies of Kohne (1970)—although this is not the opinion of those who know the fossils best.

For example, Pilbeam (1970) suggests that the common ancestors of apes and man were late Oligocene, and that the lineages ultimately leading to orang, African apes, and man separated at that time. The chimpanzee and gorilla are viewed as separating in the early Miocene some 25 million years ago. Such an early separation of the chimpanzee and gorilla is unusual, but an Oligocene separation of man and ape is not unusual. The ancestral monkeys and apes of the late Oligocene were quadrupedal forms, and even an ape living millions of years later (*Pliopithecus*) had a long tail, long lumbar region, and was essentially still a monkey-like creature, with gibbon-like characters primarily limited to the teeth and skull (Zapfe, 1958). Separations would demand an extraordinary parallel evolution in the viscera, trunks, teeth, skulls, and limbs. It may be fairly stated that these very early separations simply do not fit the evidence of comparative anatomy, behavior, or immunology. At the present time it is not clear how these major differences of interpretation can be resolved.

THE LAST MILLION YEARS

Homo erectus is thought to have evolved from one of the species of *Australopithecus*, and the origin of much of what we think of as human appears to have taken place since that dichotomy, long after the appearance of stone tools and the separation of man and ape. It is for this reason that we have divided the "how" of human origins into two parts, an early adaptive radiation of at least two (and probably several) species of *Australopithecus* and a later stage, *Homo erectus*, which probably never divided into separate species. With the transition to *Homo erectus* the brain doubled in size, the bipedal adaptation was completed, and human skills showed themselves in complex tools (Acheulian), killing many large animals, fire, and the occupation of the whole temperate and tropical Old World by a single species. It was with *Homo erectus* that man became so adaptable and effective that there is no further evidence of speciation, and this was probably the result of greatly improved intelligence and technology. Obviously, the transition did not occur at one time or place and may have taken half a million years, but in this second phase of man's evolution lies the origin of the large-brained, adaptable hunter and gatherer. His tools are found in vast quantities over a huge area, which attests to both his skills and to the effectiveness of his social and technical adaptation.

These tools and their makers evolved very slowly until some 50 to 35 thousand years ago. Then there is a great acceleration in the rate of technical evolution, and local cultures replace the formerly very widespread ones. There are evidences of shelters, burials, and art. Bows and arrows, boats, fishing, use of shellfish all appear. By 10,000 B. C. the first evidences of agriculture appear, marking the beginning of the modern era.

The archeological information suggests that there are three major phases in the evolution of man: (1) a primary phase when there were several species of stone tool-making bipeds with many ape like features in brain, hands, and probably in other less well known parts of the anatomy. This lasted for some millions of years and from it evolved (2) a large brained, much more effective *Homo erectus*, who replaced the other forms and was a successful form of life for some hundreds of thousands of years. (3) Then circa 50 to 35 thousand years ago *Homo sapiens sapiens* appears, conquers the arctic, enters Australia, comes to the New World, and cultural evolution proceeds at a vastly accelerated rate.

As Simpson (1966) has pointed out, perhaps the most important distinguishing character of modern man is language. The sounds of the nonhuman primates are controlled by the primitive brain (limbic system). Human language is a new system based on the cortex (Robinson, 1967). Language is so important, that it is hard to think of a species of men who could not talk, yet this probably was the case. Human language takes a great deal of cortex and there is no suggestion that such a system could be housed in the skull of *Australopithecus*. Several linguists (the late Morris Swadesh; Lenneberg, 1967) have suggested that human language as we know it today has an antiquity of something on the order of 50 to 30 thousand years. Foster (1969) has suggested that all contemporary languages may have derived from a single language much more recently than has been thought. The same notion is clearly implied in Chomsky's theories of universal grammar (1968). This does not mean that there might not have been simpler linguistic systems prior to 30 to 50 thousand years ago, but that the evolution of languages of the extraordinary adaptability of those we know, was late. This would suggest that brains that can learn languages with such ease are late in human evolution. Obviously, the time of origin of languages is difficult to prove because they leave no direct traces in the fossil record, but the great acceleration of change which comes in the last 50,000 years suggests that some new behavioral dimension had been added. However the origins of language may be timed, language represents a remarkable, new human ability which makes possible modern civilization.

From the fossil record, it appears that the human brain is a product of the human way of life—or to put the matter differently, the brain and the human way of life, evolved in a complex feedback relation with each other. The primitive emotional brain is still there, but it is under control of the new cortex, and it is the newer parts of the brain which make possible technical skills, planning, control of emotions, and language. Art, religion, and social complexity are all a part of human social-biology made possible by the biological evolution of man. As Simpson (1966) has put it,

> Like other animals, man develops, is born, grows, reproduces and dies. Like other animals, he eats, digests, eliminates, respires, locomotes. He bends the qualities of nature to his own ends, but he is fully subject to nature's laws as is any other animal and is no more capable of changing them. He lives in biological communities and has a niche and an ecology, just as do robins and earthworms. Let us not forget those aspects of man's nature. But let us also remember that man stands upright, builds and makes as never was built or wrought before, speaks and may speak truth or lie, worships and may worship honestly or falsely, looks to the stars and into the mud, remembers his past and predicts his future, and writes (perhaps at too great length) about his own nature.

SUMMARY

The understanding of how man evolved depends on the reconstruction of the behavioral stages, of the way of life of our ancestors. Recently chronometric dating methods have shown that stone tools and genus *Australopithecus* are much older than previously thought, and that the Pliocene is much shorter. Molecular and immunological data prove man to be remarkably close to the African apes. It is probable that man's ancestors were knuckle-walkers, and the origin of man was the evolution of a ground-living ape into a bipedal form (*Australopithecus*). This view is in accord with what is known of the behavior of the contemporary primates and primate anatomy. It is not in agreement with theories demanding an early separation of the evolutionary line leading to man.

Tool-using, savanna living, bipedalism, and changes in the dentition very likely evolved as an interrelated complex—separating man more and more from the forest-living apes. Much later *Homo erectus* evolved, and this adaptive complex included complex tools, much larger brains, fully human teeth and locomotor patterns, more hunting, fire, and a very much wider distribution. The final phases of human evolution involved language, complex social life, art, religion, and accelerating technical progress. Most of man's unique characteristics evolved in response to human conditions, millions of years after the separation of man from ape.

Acknowledgments

This paper is part of a program on primate behavior supported by the United States Public Health Service (Grant No. MH 08623). I particularly want to thank Dr. Phyllis Dolhinow and Mr. Henry Wesselman for advice and help in the preparation of this paper and Mrs. Alice Davis for editorial assistance.

REFERENCES

Chomsky, N. 1968. Language and Mind. New York, Harcourt, Brace, and World.

Clark, J. D. 1970. Prehistory of Africa. London, Thames and Hudson.

Dolhinow, P. J., and N. Bishop. 1970. The development of motor skills and the social relationships among primates through play. Minnesota Symposia on Child Psychology, 4:141-198. University of Minnesota Press.

Doolittle, R. F., and G. A. Mross. 1970. Identity of chimpanzee with human fibrinopeptides. Nature (London), 225:643-644.

Foster, M. L. 1969. Ten postulates for primordial language reconstruction. Paper presented at American Anthropological Association meeting, 1969 (unpublished).

Goodman, M. 1963. Man's place in the phylogeny of the primates as reflected in serum proteins. In Washburn, S. L., ed., Classification and Human Evolution, pp. 204-234. Chicago, Aldine Publishing Co.

_____ 1968. Phylogeny and taxonomy of the catarrhine primates from immunodiffusion data. I. A review of the major findings. In Chiarelli, B., organizer, Taxonomy and Phylogeny of Old World Primates with References to the Origin of Man, pp. 95-107. Turin, Rosenberg and Sellier.

Hay, R. L. 1967. Hominid-bearing deposits of Olduvai Gorge. In National Academy of Sciences Publication 1469, Time and Stratigraphy in the Evolution of Man, pp. 30-42. Washington, D. C.

Howell, F. C. Recent advances in human evolutionary studies. In Washburn, S. L., and P. Dolhinow, eds., Perspectives on Human Evolution II. New York, Holt, Rinehart and Winston. (In press)

Hürzeler, J. 1968. Questions et reflexions sur l'histoire des anthropomorphes. Ann. Paléont. 59:195-233.

Huxley, J. S. 1942. Evolution: The Modern Synthesis. New York, Harper.

Huxley, T. H. 1863. Evidence as to Man's Place in Nature. London, William and Norgate.

King, J. L. and T. H. Jukes. 1969. Non-Darwinian evolution. Science, 164:788-798.

Kohne, D. E. 1970. Evolution of higher-organism DNA. Quart. Rev. Biophy., 3:327-375.

Leakey, M. D. 1967. Preliminary survey of the cultural material from Beds I and II, Olduvai Gorge, Tanzania. In Bishop, W. W., and J. D. Clark, eds., Background to Evolution in Africa, pp. 417-446. Chicago, University of Chicago Press.

Leakey, R. E. 1971. Further evidence of Lower Pleistocene hominids from East Rudolf, North Kenya. Nature (London), 231:241-245.

_____ In press. In Washburn, S. L., and P. Dolhinow, eds., Perspectives on Human Evolution II. New York, Holt, Rinehart and Winston. (in press)

Lenneberg, E. H. 1967. Biological Foundations of Language. New York, John Wiley and Sons.

Lewis, O. J. 1969. The hominid wrist joint. Amer. J. Phys. Anthrop., 30:251-268.

Napier, J. R. 1962. Fossil hand bones from Olduvai Gorge. Nature (London), 196:409-411.

_____ 1967. The antiquity of human walking. Sci. Amer., 216:56-66.

Nonno, L., H. Herschman, and L. Levine. 1969. Serologic comparisons of the carbonic anhydrases of primate erythrocytes. Arch. Bioch. Biophys., 136:361-367.

Pilbeam, D. R. 1970. The Evolution of Man. New York, Funk and Wagnalls.

Robinson, B. W. 1967. Vocalization evoked from forebrain in Macaca mulatta. Physiol. Behav., 2:345-354.

Roe, A., and G. G. Simpson (eds.) 1958. Behavior and Evolution. New Haven, Yale University Press.

Sarich, V. W. 1970. A protein perspective. In Napier, J. R., and P. N. Napier, eds., Old World Monkeys, pp. 175-226. New York, Academic Press.

Schultz, A. H. 1969. The Life of Primates. London, Weidenfeld and Nicolson.

Simpson, G. G. 1949. The Meaning of Evolution. New Haven, Yale University Press.

_____ 1966. The biological nature of man. Science, 152:472-478.

Straus, W. L. 1968. Huxley's *Evidence as to Man's Place in Nature*—a century later. *In* Stevenson, S. G., and R. P. Multhauf, eds., Medicine, Science and Culture, pp. 161-167. Baltimore, The Johns Hopkins Press.

Tuttle, R. H. 1967. Knuckle-walking and the evolution of hominoid hands. Amer. J. Phys. Anthrop., 26:171-206.

_____ 1969. Knuckle-walking and the problem of human origins. Science, 166:953-961.

van Lawick-Goodall, J. 1968. The behavior of free-living chimpanzees in the Gombe Stream Reserve. Anim. Behav. Monogr., 1:161-311.

Washburn, S. L. 1968. The Study of Human Evolution. Condon Lectures. Eugene, University of Oregon Press.

Wilson, A. C., and V. M. Sarich. 1969. A molecular time scale for human evolution. Proc. Nat. Acad. Sci. U.S.A., 63:1088-1093.

Zapfe, H. 1958. The skeleton of *Pliopithecus (Epipliopithecus) vindobonenis* Zapfe and Hürzeler. Amer. J. Phys. Anthrop., 16:441-455.

Zihlman, A. L. and W. Hunter. Internal rotation in the interpretation of the pelvis of *Australopithecus*. (in press)

13

Differential Fertility and Human Evolution

JAMES V. NEEL AND WILLIAM J. SCHULL

Department of Human Genetics
University of Michigan Medical School
Ann Arbor, Michigan 48104

INTRODUCTION

Human biological evolution, like evolution in any other species, is ultimately dependent on two phenomena, namely, changes in the gene pool of the species due to genetically based differences in the survival of individuals, and changes due to genetically based differences in reproductive performance. The higher the early mortality rates in a population, and the greater the spread in number of children reared to maturity by those reaching maturity, then the greater the rate at which genetic change can occur, given that there is some genetic basis for either of these phenomena. The truism was more elegantly and more mathematically stated by Fisher (1930) as follows: "The rate of increase in fitness of any organism at any time is equal to its genetic variance in fitness at that time." This Fundamental Theorem of Natural Selection, as he termed it, measures fitness in terms of reproductive value, that is, as the intrinsic rate of increase associated with a given genotype. This intrinsic rate of increase he has called the Malthusian parameter.

It is amazing how little we know about the genetic component in the probability of survival of the average child or the reproductive performance of the average adult. In this article we propose to discuss just one of these two phenomena, namely, the genetic aspects of differential fertility, and the implications of these data for human evolution. Obviously, it will not be possible

Presented at the Symposium on Human Evolution of the First National Biological Congress, November 10, 1970, in Detroit, Mich. The investigations of the authors have been greatly facilitated by the financial support of the U. S. Atomic Energy Commission.

363

to cover all aspects of the matter. Accordingly, we will concentrate on four interrelated topics, namely, (1) an effort to establish a diachronic perspective on differential fertility, (2) a discussion of the opportunity for genetic change in present-day fertility differentials, (3) a description of an example of the complexity of the genetic factor in reproductive differentials, and (4) a discussion of some of the possible consequences for human evolution of stabilizing human numbers.

AN HISTORICAL PERSPECTIVE ON DIFFERENTIAL FERTILITY

Differential fertility is an old phenomenon in the history of our species. In connection with this statement, it seems important to recognize a commonly held misconception, namely, that primitive man was so beset by disease and so preyed upon by beasts that the female of the species had to reproduce at near capacity in order to maintain population numbers. We cite as evidence to the contrary our own data on two relatively unacculturated Indian tribes of South America, presented in Table 1. Small and imperfect though the samples are (cf. Neel and Chagnon, 1968), it is clear that the average woman is reproducing well below her innate capacity, with abundant opportunity for "reproductive compensation" (see below). We recognize that these tribes are not to be equated with the hunters and gatherers of a million years ago, but suggest these statistics are more representative of prehistoric man than are the statistics of the fixed, agricultural populations of recent Africa and India.

In order to provide a standard for comparison, we present in Table 2 a summary of the Xavante-Yanomama data together with comparable figures on several other types of populations. It is surprising how sparse are the data on what we might term "agricultural man." The three sets of data presented all suffer from the imperfection that they are based on women living to complete the age of reproduction. By contrast, our data on the two Indian tribes represent an effort to reconstruct the more significant data, on a cohort of women entering the reproductive period. For examples of the populations of more industrialized nations, we present the data on numbers of children born to United States white and nonwhite women aged 45 to 49 at the time of the 1960 census (U. S. Department of Health, Education, and Welfare, 1966) and previously unpublished data on an agricultural-fishing community of rural Japan for marriages contracted during 1890-1919. The figures for the United States suffer from the same defect as do those for agricultural man, whereas the Japanese data, although married women are represented whether or not they lived to complete the reproductive period, fail to include the small proportion of women who remain unmarried. The eight series have been selected because estimates of mortality between birth and the age of reproduction are also available; the reasons for this will be apparent shortly.

Table 1. Number of Liveborn Offspring to Xavante and Yanomama Females Whose Reproduction Had Been Completed Either Because of Age (> 40 years) or Death After Reaching Adulthood but Prior to Age 40.

Tribe	Number of Women	Number of Children												Mean Number of Children	Variance (σ^2)
		0	1	2	3	4	5	6	7	8	9	10	11		
Xavante															
Alive (> 40 years)	35	—	1	—	6	3	9	7	1	4	1	1	2	5.7	5.5
Dead (est. <40 years)	25	—	6	4	3	5	2	2	3	—	—	—	—	3.4	4.3
Total	60	—	7	4	9	8	11	9	4	4	1	1	2	4.7	6.1
Yanomama															
Alive (> 40 years)	33	1	1	5	7	10	4	3	1	1	—	—	—	3.8	2.9
Dead (est. <40 years)	31	8	12	5	3	2	1	—	—	—	—	—	—	1.4	1.8
Total	64	9	13	10	10	12	5	3	1	1	—	—	—	2.6	3.7

Table 2. A Comparison of the Reproductive Performance and Frequency of Death Prior to About age 15, for a Variety of Populations, Together with a Computation of Crow's Index of Potential Selection for these Same Populations

	Early Man		Agricultural Man			Man of Industrialized Countries			
	Xavante	Yanomama	Uganda, Basoga Bantu (Roscoe, 1950)	Nygasaland, Yao (Mitchell, 1949)	Gold Coast, Ashanti (Meyers, 1954)	Contemporary U.S. Dept. (U.S. Dept. HEW, 1966) White	Nonwhite	Rural Japan (Schull, et al., 1968)	"Replacement man"
Mean live births per female reproduction complete ($M \pm \sigma^2$)	4.7±6.1[a]	2.63±3.7[a]	7.0±7.2[b]	5.4±9.7[b]	6.5±10.0[b]	2.2±4.3[c]	2.7±9.8[c]	5.1±9.5[d]	2.1±1.7
Estimated percentage dying prior to age 15	ca. 0.33	ca. 0.18	ca. 0.64	ca. 0.24	ca. 0.44	ca. 0.03	ca. 0.05	0.22[d]	ca. 0.05
Index of Potential Selection									
I_m	0.49	0.22	1.78	0.32	0.79	0.03	0.05	0.28	0.05
I_f	0.41	0.66	0.42	0.43	0.43	0.92	1.41	0.76	0.41
I_t	0.90	0.88	2.20	0.75	1.22	0.95	1.46	1.04	0.46

[a]Based on an effort to reconstruct a cohort of women reaching the age of reproduction.
[b]Based on women living through the reproductive period, i.e., to age 40 or 45.
[c]Based on women completing their 44th year, who, because of low mortality ages 20-44, approximate a cohort.
[d]Based on all marriages contracted in 1920-1939 represented by a living spouse residing on Hirado in 1964.

What, now, are the implications of these data for natural selection? A comparison of the eight sets of figures is greatly facilitated by the Index of Potential Selection Intensity developed by Crow (1958). This Index is

$$I_t = \frac{V}{\overline{w}^2}$$

where V is the variance in the number of born children per female, and w is the mean number. This index has two components, I_m, due to mortality prior to the age of reproduction, and I_f due to fertility differences among women reaching the age of reproduction. $I_m = P_d/P_s$, where P_d is the proportion of all births dying before the reproductive period, and P_s is the proportion surviving. Ideally, P_d should include all zygote loss between conception and reproduction, but measurements of the early loss, between fertilization and seven month's gestation, remain so inadequate that no investigator has yet attempted to introduce early loss into his calculations. $I_f = (V_f/x^2)/P_s$, where x_s is the mean number, and V_f is the variance in the number of births per women reaching the age of reproduction. (I_f has, with Crow's concurrence, been slightly modified from the original definition.)

Table 2 also presents the results of computing Crow's Index for the data presented therein. The data are so unsatisfactory in so many respects that these Indices must be considered only as first approximations. It must at this point be emphasized strongly that Crow's Index is for *potential* rather than *realized* selection. Only if in all cultures all prereproductive mortality and differential fertility were firmly rooted in the genetic constitution of the individual would the Index provide a reliable means of comparison. Let us then proceed with due caution. When adequate data are available, I_t will probably be found to be higher for "agricultural" than "primitive" man, due to increases in I_m. Incidentally, there are reasons to suspect that relatively isolated though these Indian tribes have been, the prereproductive mortality rates may have increased recently, in consequence of the introduction of new causes of mortality by direct and indirect contact with representatives of Western culture. I_f appears about the same for the two groups, but since the data for "agricultural" man are not based on the cohort approach, these must be underestimates of I_f—how great is impossible to say. We note also that I_t is today about the same for U. S. Caucasins as it was for the Japanese population studied and the two Indian tribes, but that these four values are exceeded by that for the U. S. nonwhite population. However, differential fertility in both U. S. groups now contributes relatively much more to the Index than was true for the Indian populations. For a concise discussion of how rapidly in the past several centuries the components of I_t have altered in tne United States (and presumably other western countries), the reader is referred to Kirk (1968). Our first point, then, is that although there have probably been marked fertility differences between individuals throughout all human history and prehistory, in recent years (i.e., the past several thousand) both the *relative* and *absolute* significance of these differentials as agents of potential genetic change, as judged by female reproductive performance, has probably increased.

As we have strongly emphasized, this Index has significance to our thinking only in proportion to the genetic contribution to its components. If, for instance, fertility is in no way related to genotype, then although by force of chance and socioeconomic circumstances one genotype could make a greater contribution to the next generation than another, differential fertility would have no real impact on the gene frequencies of the next generation. If, furthermore, the basis for reproductive success, although invariant for any one generation, changed rapidly from one generation to the next, so that selective differentials were not maintained, differential fertility might also result in relatively little genetic change. In other words, if there is no apparent consistent genetic contribution to fertility differences from generation to generation, then differential fertility will have relatively little genetic impact.

It is surprising how little we know of the heritability of fertility, that is, of the proportion of variability in fertility ascribable to genetic variation. Pearson and Lee's much quoted study (1899) utilized data "from Foster's *Peerage and Baronetage*, Burke's *Landed Gentry*, some family histories and a collection of family data." In this heterogeneous assemblage, the correlation between size of mother's sibship and number of her offspring was 0.04, while for fathers the corresponding correlation was 0.05. For the Peerage data alone, which is probably the most complete, the correlation for mothers was 0.21 but for fathers, 0.07. Fisher in 1930 could apparently find no better data than those of Pearson and Lee, but in developing his argument utilized only the Peerage mother-daughter correlation.

With respect to subsequent studies of mother-daughter correlations in number of offspring, Huestis and Maxwell (1932) reported a correlation between size of mother's sibship and number of her children of 0.12 in a sample of 638 families ascertained through a child attending the University of Oregon. Bresard's (1950) data on French families clearly indicated a similar correlation, but they are not presented so that a precise calculation can be made. Berent (1953) found a correlation of 0.19 in a sample of British women. Duncan et al. (1965) reported a regression coefficient of 0.11 for United States wives 47 to 61 years old, for size of their completed families on size of their "sociological" sibship. The correlation is presumably somewhat larger since the variance in "sociological" sibship size is undoubtedly greater than the square root of the product of the variance in size of completed families and variance in "sociological" sibships. When duration of marriage and wife's education were controlled, however, the regression (and hence correlation) was substantially less. Finally, Imaizumi et al. (1970) found a correlation of 0.01 in a rural Japanese population. As the various authors recognize, each of these series departs from the ideal in one way or another.

Aside from the early data of Pearson and Lee (1899) only the series of Duncan et al. (1965) and Imaizumi et al. (1970) present comparable relationships for fathers. In the data of Duncan et al. (1965) the corresponding regression is 0.10, with a comparable reduction to that observed for mothers after control for duration of marriage and wife's education. In the data of Imaizumi et al. (1970) the corresponding correlation is -0.03. Moberg (1950) found no significant or consistent correlation between number of children born to Swedes who had completed the "matriculation examination" (predominantly males) and size of student's sibship, and although Berent (1953) does not present a correlation, the data suggest a greater correlation of number of children with wife's sibship size than with husband's. Finally, although the specialized nature of the data and the compartmentalized nature of the presentation of the Indianapolis Study of Fertility render generalizations impossible, there is a small positive relationship of husband and wife's sibship size with number of children and "the data in some respects are consistent with the hypothesis that the wife's family of origin exerts a stronger influence on a couple's fertility than the husband's family or origin, but the influence in both cases is so minor as to make the comparison fairly meaningless" (Kantner and Potter, 1954). More data on the correlation between fathers's sibship size and number of his offspring are urgently needed, since husband-wife differences in the magnitude of this correlation point strongly to nongenetic maternal influences in fertility.

In none of these studies have the women been reproducing at near capacity, so that the existing data deal with "social fertility" rather than "natural fertility." A group which provides an especially good test of the latter is the Amish religious sect. From published geneaologies of Amish families residing, for the most part, in Ohio and Indiana (Hostetler, 1912), we have calculated another set of correlations for marriages contracted between approximately 1820 and 1879. Here the correlation between mother's sibship size and her completed reproduction is 0.09; the comparable figure for fathers is 0.07. It is worth noting that the mean size of mother's sibship was 9.74 and of father's sibship was 9.57. Little birth control would seem to be involved, but the correlations remain small.

We can now add to the literature two new sets of data regarding the heritability of fertility. With respect to the Indian populations mentioned earlier, Dr. Jean MacCluer has developed a complex, Monte Carlo simulation of the breeding structure of the Yanomama, which permits modeling the fate of the population over periods up to 400 years. In the course of developing that model, difficulties were encountered with respect to the frequency of marriages between first cousins. After several hundred years of simulation, these frequencies fell below those observed in the actual population, in those instances where we had the necessary genealogical depth to permit accurate determination of this type of consanguineous marriage. The reasons for the discrepancy finally became clear when Dr. MacCluer contrasted the observed number of *grand-children* per Indian male surviving to age of reproduction, with the number predicted by the computer program after several hundred years of simulation. In the real population, some males had more grandchildren than the largest number appearing in the simulation program. Since first-cousin marriages are between the grandchildren of a given individual, it was clear that here was the reason for the discrepancy. The simulation had been based on the assumption of no correlation in fertility between generations. Reexamination of the data revealed an actual correlation of 0.26. When the program was altered to give males from large sibships a proper advantage in obtaining wives, the distribution of grandchildren (and first-cousin marriages) now agreed satisfactorily with observation.

As an aside, we feel a strong case can be developed for regarding a large portion of this correlation as cultural rather than biological in origin. These are polygynous societies, with the village headmen usually enjoying the higher degrees of polygyny. Competition for the position of headman is vigorous, with the headman appearing to achieve his position through a combination of aggressiveness, skills in hunting and war, knowledge of tribal lore, and leadership abilities. It is also important that through marriage he has created certain alliances that support his position. It is the impression of Dr. Napoleon Chagnon, the anthropologist member of the team working on the Yanomama, that an able, alert, aggressive son of a headman, who because of his father's exceptional polygyny has more half sisters than the average Indian, can—especially if his father dies relatively young—manipulate the marriages of his sisters so as to form alliances and improve his own chances of obtaining multiple wives. Obviously not all the sons of a headman can take similar advantage of this situation—there would appear to be an interaction between biological and cultural factors, with an able son of a headman in a position to manipulate the system so as to enjoy a fertility greater than an equally able individual born to a nonpolygynous father.

The other set of new data regarding the heritability of fertility came from Hirado, the aforementioned Japanese island, and is an outgrowth of a study of the effects of inbreeding and consanguinity on mortality, morbidity, and fertility (Schull, Komatsu, et al., 1968). More specifically, these data stem from an island-wide census in 1964, which sought to enumerate the reproductive performances of all marriages then represented by at least one spouse alive and residing on Hirado. The Japanese National Census of 1960 revealed Hirado to have a population of slightly more than 40,000 individuals; the *ad hoc* census disclosed a somewhat smaller number. In all, the reproductive performances of some 10,530 marriages were obtained; about 15% of these marriages involve spouses who are biologically related. Available on most of these marriages is a variety of observations of a socioeconomic and attitudinal nature; these include such items as education, occupation, religion, size of household and number of persons within the home, income, land holdings, expenditures on food, desirable size of family, and attitude toward the artificial interruption of pregnancies. Finally, as intimated in the enumeration of the socioeconomic variables, these marriages are subdivisble on religious grounds into Buddhist, Catholic, and *kakure*, the latter a syncretic religion incorporating elements of Buddhism, Catholicism, and Shintoism. These three religious communities differ markedly in respect of a number of variables of interest in the study of fertility differentials. Among these are frequency of consanguineous marriages, socio-economic level, and attitude toward birth control.

Two observations warrant especial mention. First, prereproductive mortality among liveborn children in Hirado increases significantly with parental consanguinity, presumably as a consequence of homozygosity for sublethal and subvital genes. However, the increased reproductivity of the consanguineous marriage largely offsets the increased mortality among the issue from such unions, and thereby dampens the rate of elimination of deleterious genes and the loss of genetic variability (Schull et al., 1970). The commonness of such reproductive compensation is not known, but it could be an important factor in the maintenance of genetic variability, particularly in those populations where mean family size is small and most prereproductive mortality occurs in the first year of life. Second, the heritability of fertility appears small. Table 3 sets out the means of father's and mother's sibship sizes and the correlations between these sibship sizes and their reproductive performances for Hirado for three decades. The decades indicated are those in which the marriages of father and mother were contracted, and were selected to ensure that families would have been minimally

Table 3. Means of Sibship Sizes and Correlations in Sibship Sizes for Hirado for the Stated Decades of Marriage. The Number of Observations are Indicated Within the Parentheses.

	1890-1899	1900-1909	1910-1919	Pooled
MEAN TOTAL BIRTH NUMBER				
Father's sibship	5.84 (32)	6.41 (140)	6.81 (237)	6.59 (409)
Mother's sibship	6.41 (27)	6.67 (130)	6.80 (246)	6.73 (403)
Children	4.92 (59)	3.73 (270)	3.95 (483)	3.95 (812)
CORRELATION IN SIBSHIP SIZES				
Father-offspring	0.089 (32)	−0.129 (140)	0.001 (237)	−0.043 (409)
Mother-offspring	0.122 (27)	0.001 (130)	0.019 (246)	0.019 (403)

disrupted by the events of World War II, which, because of the degree of Japanese mobilization, led to long separations of spouses. The pooled correlation estimates are −0.043 (father-offspring) and 0.019 (mother-offspring); these correspond to regression coefficients of −0.049 and 0.022, respectively. It will be noted that these values are very similar to those obtained by Imaizumi et al. (1970) in Kumamoto Prefecture, and when mothers are used as the reference parent, result in an estimate of heritability of 4 to 5%. The authors just cited report a somewhat higher heritability, 12%, if the correlation in sibship sizes is based upon numbers of survivors rather than total births; presumably the same would obtain for Hirado in view of the comparability of the other findings in the two studies.

Our second major point, then, is that although as noted earlier, recently the potential role of differential fertility as an agent of genetic change is relatively greater than previously; in general the evidence suggests that under the present conditions of human reproduction the genetic contribution to fertility differentials is relatively small.

THE POSSIBLE RATES OF GENETIC CHANGE INHERENT IN FERTILITY DIFFERENTIALS

Having presented something of a perspective on differential fertility, and some evidence concerning its heritability, we propose next to present some simple calculations concerning its possible genetic consequences. We will in these calculations eschew the extremes of eugenic fancy, such as complete selection against a dominant or a recessive trait, and consider, rather, some of the potentialities inherent in the present patterns when multifactorial traits are the objects of selection. As the first approximation we shall presume that the heritability of fertility is about 10%. This value seems reasonable on prior considerations as well as on the basis of the data previously cited. Certainly, granted the limitations on fertility imposed by the physiology of human reproduction, it seems unlikely, that heritability, after centuries of selection, would be large, for presumably with selection would come a measure of genetic uniformity, and hence the observed differences in fertility would be more likely to reflect differences in environments rather than genes. This statement would not necessarily hold if the genetic basis for fertility differences was changing rapidly. Be this as it may, we ask how much would selection, natural or otherwise, alter population composition with time?

In order to provide a simple, uncomplicated answer to this query, we argue as follows: Assume that the genetic contribution to fertility is mediated through a large number of loci, the average effects of which are small and approximately additive. Let $\bar{x}$ be the mean of the particular character of interest (fertility) in the generation before selection, and x_i be the fertility of some subset of individuals, say the ith, in the same generation. We wish to know what effect on fertility there would be if all of the breeding individuals in a particular generation were drawn from the subset with fertility x_i. Simple linear regression theory states that the fertility expected for this subset in the next generation, $\hat{y}_i$, is merely the mean of the fertility of a generation to which all subsets contribute, $\bar{y}(=\bar{x})$. plus the product of the regression of y on x (offspring on parent) and the deviation of the ith subset from the mean of the parental generation before selection, that is,

$$\hat{y}_i = \bar{y} + b(x_i - \bar{x}).$$

The latter may be rewritten

$$(\hat{y}_i - \bar{y}) = b(x_i - \bar{x}).$$

The left side of this equality has been termed the selection response, R_e, for it is the amount by which a generation derived entirely from parents with fertilities x_i would deviate from a generation to which all subsets of parents contributed, presumably in proportion to their representation in the parental generation. The right side, it will be noted, is the product of the regression coefficient and the difference, say S, between the mean of those individuals selected for parenthood and the mean of the population from which they are to be selected. Finally, since the regression coefficient is a measure of the extent to which y is "caused" by x, and the latter depends upon the degree to which fertility is inherited,

$$R_e = bS = h^2 S,$$

a well-known result in quantitative genetics, for heritability, h^2, in the narrow sense, is by definition the ratio of the additive genetic variance to the total phenotypic variance. This latter ratio can be shown, in the case of the regression of offspring on parent, to be twice the regression coefficient associated with the observed values. In essence, this result implies that the only portion of the genetic variability that is readily transferable from one generation to the next is the one attributable to additive inheritance.

Before we turn to a numerical illustration, one further observation needs to be made, and this concerns correlated selection responses. Suppose, for example, that intelligence is either positively or negatively correlated with fertility, and that selection for fertility occurs. Intuitively, one would expect some selection for intelligence also. It can be shown that the effect on intelligence is simply the selection response with respect to fertility multiplied by the regression of the genetically controlled deviations in intelligence on the genetically controlled deviations in fertility, i.e., the ratio of the genetic covariance for the two characters and the genetic variance in fertility. If the genetic variances in fertility and intelligence are the same, then this ratio is the correlation in the genetic determination of the two characters, intelligence and fertility in this example. While this correlation is not precisely known, it would appear to be small and possibly negative. There is certainly no reason to believe that it would exceed -0.10, on the one hand, or $+0.10$, on the other.

But to return to fertility, imagine a population with a mean number of livebirths per female of 2.7, somewhat more than that in the United States. Assume that within this population there is a large subset with mean fertility of 3.6, that is, a third larger than the population mean. If the heritability of fertility is only 10%, then with complete selection for this more fertile subset (i.e., reproduction only from this subset), mean fertility would change from 2.7 in one generation to about 2.8 in the next. To the extent that selection is less than complete the shift in the mean from one generation to another will be even smaller. Insofar as man is concerned, and with only natural selection involved, it is unlikely that selection for a quantitative character would be more than 10% effective. If this conjecture is reasonable, then the change in mean fertility would be more nearly 2.7 to 2.71, that is, less than 0.05% of the mean of the parental generation. Admittedly a change of this magnitude might contribute substantially to the population problem, but it would do little to alter the genetic composition of the population insofar as fertility is involved.

Clearly if one's concern were not with fertility but rather with some characteristic associated with fertility, such as intelligence, the effect on the latter characteristic would be vanishingly small. Some numeric substance can be given this remark if we assume that (1) selection is only 10% effective, (2) the correlation between fertility and intelligence lies between −0.10 and +0.10, and (3) the mean I.Q. of the population before selection is 100. We hastily add that this is no brief for intelligence tests but merely an attempt to provide a value against which the effect of selection can be evaluated. Under these circumstances, the correlated effect on intelligence of selection for fertility would be 0.001 in absolute measure, or at most 0.1 I.Q. points per generation relative to a mean I.Q. of 100. It would seem clear, then, that some of the recent arguments which, assuming a genetic basis for ethnic differences in intelligence, predict imminent significant declines in human intelligence because of individual and ethnic differences in fertility are specious. Otherwise stated, in view of the foregoing demonstration, it is difficult to see how the present (temporary) socioeconomic and ethnic differences in fertility, which will presumably largely disappear as we achieve a truer democracy, can have a truly significant impact on human intelligence.

Lest these calculations seem to denigrate the role in evolution of differential fertility, it is important to reiterate that these are effects on quantitative characteristics, presumably due to many genes, and measured over successive generations. In the time scale of human evolution, even small differentials can produce significant results. Thus, for example, given three genotypes *AA, Aa,* and *aa*, with fitnesses 1, 1, and 0.99, and an initial gene frequency of *a* of 0.5, at the end of 10 generations the frequency of *a* will be 0.488; at 50, 0.44; and at 100, 0.39. Even 100 generations is short in the scale of human evolution, of course.

AN EXAMPLE OF THE COMPLEXITY OF GENE-BASED
FERTILITY DIFFERENTIALS

Just how genotype influences fertility is, except in the extreme case of severe mental defect or extreme physical disability, essentially unknown, and needs to be a subject of intensive investigation. As we have just seen, over long periods of time fertility differentials of 1 or 2% between two phenotypes based on genetic differences can be highly effective in evolution. Unfortunately, the sample sizes necessary to demonstrate fertility differences of that magnitude are almost prohibitively large, unless the human biologist is ready to think on an order of magnitude greater than has been his custom—and can command support for his new thinking. It is thus unlikely that the immediate future will yield insights into fertility differences related to common genes, where one would expect selection differentials of the above-mentioned magnitude.

However, studies of phenotypes associated with rare genes may be instructive. Some years ago we undertook a rather extensive study of multiple neurofibromatosis (von Recklinghausen's disease) in the State of Michigan, with the objective of understanding the balance between mutation and selection in this disease (Crowe, et al., 1956). This condition is characterized by abnormal patches of brownish pigmentation, termed café-au-lait spots, and multiple tumors in association with the peripheral nervous system. These tumors are usually benign, but occasionally undergo malignant degeneration. They may also be life threatening if, though benign, they occur as space-occupying lesions in certain critical areas. There is a special type of diffuse, plexiform neurofibroma, which may be quite disfiguring or crippling. Finally, a higher-than-usual number of persons with the disease are mentally defective.

Our studies revealed that the reproductive expectancy of affected individuals at birth was approximately half normal. This was based on a comparison with their normal siblings. In another later study, on Huntington's chorea, we have found that unaffected siblings may not be satisfactory controls (Reed and Neel, 1959), but the nature of our findings suggests that the points to be made would not be invalidated even if siblings were not an entirely satisfactory control group. A determined effort was made to analyze how this gene resulted in a reduced fertility. The results are presented in Table 4.

We can discern the operation and interplay of three kinds of selection in this table plus the associated data at our disposal. First, note that whereas the fertility of all affected individuals is 53% of normal, the fertility of married affected individuals is 80% of normal. Since this is by comparison with their siblings, it is clear that the expectancy of marriage is decreased in this disease. This is in part directly due to defect which would be incompatible with marriage in any community: life-threatening tumors, plexiform neurofibromas, severe mental defect. We may call this "selection due to gross defect."

Table 4. The Relative Fertility of Various Subgroups
of Individuals With Multiple Neurofibromatosis,
Expressed as a Proportion of the Fertility of
Unaffected Siblings.

Fertility of all affected individuals	0.527
Fertility of all affected males	0.413
Fertility of all affected females	0.748
Fertility of all married affected individuals	0.795
Fertility of all married affected males	0.620
Fertility of all married affected females	0.887

Secondly, the reduction in marriage rates appears to be greater than can be accounted for by gross defect. This is perhaps because of the cosmetic effects of the disease, perhaps because of the effects of the gene on I.Q. (even when not resulting in institutionalization). We can term this "selection for social reasons." Presumably this would not be so strongly operative in many primitive or agricultural economies, where the pressure for marriage is greater than in the contemporary United States.

Thirdly, however, even after marriage, fertility is reduced, more so in males than in females. The reason for this is not clear, but this cause of fertility reduction seems different from the other two; we shall simply label it as "selection due to reduced intrinsic fertility," a selection much more effective in males than females. Finally, now, the data show that the reduction in marriage rate is proportionately greater in males than females, perhaps pointing to sexual selection.

It should be emphasized that many of the differences we are discussing are not statistically significant. Extensive though the study was, the smallness of the sample on which we base these impressions would appall a demographer. We present these interpretations as material for consideration rather than established fact. On the other hand, there is little doubt that the reduction in fertility associated with possession of this gene is complex, and that other genetically based fertility differences may be equally complex.

THE CONSEQUENCES OF STABILIZING POPULATION NUMBERS

The most important single issue facing our species today is reconciling population numbers with the world's resources. This can be accomplished by limiting population size and/or increasing food production. Let us assume that the solution remains in our hands, that tragic events such as war and famine do not impose their own solution. Let us then not gamble on the "green revolution," but take the most drastic steps our society will accept to limit population growth. If population numbers are too great, how should they be limited?

There are two obvious alternatives. In either event the gross birth rate is fixed, but in one case it is done with an attempt at "quality control," in the other case not. There is at present neither the knowledge nor wisdom to formulate an equitable system of quality control. The only realistic and acceptable approach is the enunciation of some type of quota system, such that each adult woman is encouraged to bear a certain fixed number of children. We would visualize the system as voluntary, but with certain built-in incentives to abide by it.

It seems virtually certain that something of this nature is developing. In view of our earlier considerations, let us consider the implications of this for human evolution. We will agree for the moment that we wish a replacement type of population, wherein each female at birth has an average reproductive expectation of two children. If in fact each and every female born had exactly two pregnancies both of which survived, then although there might be small random changes in the frequencies of specific genes from one generation to the next because of the nature of the genetic sampling process between generations, in the large populations of today these changes would be small, and not systematic. In other words, human evolution would virtually come to a standstill, save for the input of mutation, and this at a time when, because of the rapidly changing environment, the need of the human species to accelerate the rate of genetic adaptation was probably never greater. Faced with the need to meet the population crisis, as balanced against the desirability of ongoing human evolution, we as geneticists would unhesitatingly vote for a simple quota system for all human reproduction for the present.

In fact, however, the choices are perhaps not so polarized as they may appear to be. Each woman may not want exactly two children, or if she does, she may for social or biological reasons be unable to fulfill her wishes. It was in recognition of that fact, and on the assumption that the world was not yet ready to consider actually reducing the number in the next generation through stringent birth control, that earlier we suggested that even if the average couple thinks in terms of an "ideal" family of three (with provision for voluntary sterilization immediately after the birth of that third child), population stabilization could be accomplished. It was felt that failure to reproduce or voluntary limitation below three would reduce the realized average to about two (Neel, 1970).

Let us now extend that earlier thought, to the implications for natural selection. We will assume that in a cohort of newborn, liveborn females, mortality prior to the age of reproduction is 5%. This is slightly higher than the present figure for United States whites, and reflects a certain pessimism concerning the standard of living and the quality of life in the years ahead. We will assume that approximately 10% of women in the cohort remain unmarried, and for practical if not moral reasons, fail to reproduce. We will also assume that some 10% of married women in the cohort are unable to conceive. These figures are slightly higher than the actual values today, and significantly higher than in primitive cultures. If inability to conceive is a poorly understood biological response to our changing environment, the frequency may well go higher in the near future. We will further assume that among the remainder, 10% of the original cohort for various reasons have one child, 10% two, 50% three, and 5% somehow manage to have four. This latter feat is probably best accomplished by placing for adoption a child born out of wedlock, followed by marriage and three children. On these assumptions, even if half of the women reaching adult life have three liveborn children, we still have a "replacement" population. What now are the opportunities for selection? Expressed again as Crow's Index, I_f is 0.05, I_m is 0.41, and I_t is 0.46. The Index has, to be sure, fallen, but I believe most of us would agree, not as much as the concept of a uniform quota system would at first thought suggest.[1]

It must again be emphasized that this is an index of *potential* selection. It is impossible to predict whether the genetic contribution to this Index under the above-described circumstances will be relatively greater or less than at present or in the time of primitive man. It is tempting to argue that it will probably be greater, because individuals in whose family there occurs known genetic disease will be more prone to limit family size than others. On the other hand, the low heritability of human fertility suggests the need for extreme caution in the use of this Index.

CONCLUSIONS

It seems clear that with present trends in infant and childhood mortality, differential fertility is the principal phenomenon through which natural selection can operate. On the basis of sparse data, the extent of differential fertility among women appears to be somewhat greater today than in the time of primitive man. However, the genetic contribution to differences in reproductive performance seems small. Only in the extreme case of certain rare, inherited diseases such as multiple neurofibromatosis do we have data on exactly how genotype influences reproduction. It is estimated that when a country achieves a replacement-type reproductive pattern (average family size of two surviving children), the index of potential genetic selection will be approximately half the present value for United States whites.

REFERENCES

Berent, J. 1953. Relationship between family sizes of two successive generations. Milbank Mem. Fund Quart., 31:39-50.

[1] For those who feel that with the above "policy" the population will still continue to expand, and that the emphasis should be on a family size of two, we suggest a possible compromise slogan: "Three is all right, but two is better."

Bresard, M. 1950. Mobilité sociale et dimension de la famille. Population, July-September (3):533-566.

Crow, J. F. 1958. Some possibilities for measuring selection intensities in man. Hum. Biol., 30:1-13.

Crowe, F. W., W. J. Schull, and J. V. Neel. 1956. A Clinical, Pathological and Genetic Study of Multiple Neurofibromatosis. Springfield, Illinois, Charles C Thomas.

Duncan, O. D., R. Freedman, J. M. Coble, and D. P. Slesinger. 1965. Marital fertility and size of family of orientation. Demography, 2:508-515.

Fischer, R. A. The Genetical Theory of Natural Selection. Oxford, Clarendon Press.

Fortes, M. 1954. A demographic field study in Ashanti. *In* Lorimer, F. ed., Culture and Human Fertility, pp. 253-324. Paris, UNESCO.

Hostetler, H. 1912. Descendants of Jacob Hochstetler. The Immigrant of 1736. Elgin, Illinois, Brethren Publishing House.

Huestis, R. R., and A. Maxwell. 1932. Does family size run in families? J. Hered., 23:77-79.

Imaizumi, Y., M. Nei, and T. Furusho. 1970. Variability and heritability of human fertility. Ann. Hum. Gent., 33:251-259.

Kantner, J. F., and R. G. Potter. 1954. Social and psychological factors affecting fertility. XXIV. The relationship of family size in two successive generations. Milbank Mem. Fund Quart., 32:294-311.

Kirk, D. 1968. Patterns of survival and reproduction in the United States: Implications for selection. Proc. Nat. Acad. Sci. U.S.A., 59:13-21.

Mitchell, J. C. 1949. An estimate of fertility in some Yao hamlets in Luwanda District of Southern Nyasaland. Africa, 19:293-308.

Moberg, S. 1950. Marital status and family size among matriculated persons in Sweden. Population Studies, 4:115-127.

Neel, J. V. 1970. Lessons from a "primitive" people. Science, 170:815-822.

—— and N. A. Chagnon. 1968. The demography of two tribes of primitive relatively unacculturated American Indians. Proc. Nat. Acad. Sci. U.S.A., 59:680-689.

Pearson, K., and A. Lee. 1899. On the inheritance of fertility in mankind. Philos. Trans. Roy. Soc. London, [A], 192:279-290.

Reed, T. E., and J. V. Neel. 1959. Huntington's chorea in Michigan. 2. Selection and mutation. Amer. J. Hum. Genet., 11:107-136.

Roscoe, J. 1915. The Northern Bantu. Cambridge, Cambridge University Press.

Schull, W. J., T. Furusho, M. Yamamoto, H. Nagano, and I. Komatsu. 1970. The effect of parental consanguinity and inbreeding in Hirado, Japan. IV. Fertility and reproductive compensation. Humangenetik, 9:294-315.

—— I. Komatsu, H. Nagano, and M. Yamamoto. 1968. Hirado: Temperal trends in inbreeding and fertility. Proc. Nat. Acad. Sci. U.S.A., 59:671-679.

United States Department of Health, Education and Welfare, Public Health Service. 1966. Vital Statistics of the United States, 1964, Volume II, Part A. Washington, D. C., Government Printing Office.

14

The Apportionment of Human Diversity

R. C. LEWONTIN

Committee on Evolutionary Biology,
University of Chicago,
Chicago, Illinois

INTRODUCTION

It has always been obvious that organisms vary, even to those pre-Darwinian idealists who saw most individual variation as distorted shadows of an ideal. It has been equally apparent, even to those post-Darwinians for whom variation between individuals is the central fact of evolutionary dynamics, that variation is nodal, that individuals fall in clusters in the space of phenotypic description, and that those clusters, which we call demes, or races, or species, are the outcome of an evolutionary process acting on the individual variation. What has changed during the evolution of scientific thought, and is still changing, is our perception of the relative importance and extent of intragroup as opposed to intergroup variation. These changes have been in part a reflection of the uncovering of new biological facts, but only in part. They have also reflected general sociopolitical biases derived from human social experience and carried over into "scientific" realms. I have discussed elsewhere (Lewontin, 1968) long-term trends in evolutionary doctrine as a reflection of long-term changes in socioeconomic relations, but even in the present era of Darwinism there is considerable diversity of opinion about the amount or importance of intragroup variation as opposed to the variation between races and species. Muller, for example (1950), maintained that for sexually reproducing species, man in particular, there was very little genetic variation within populations and that most men were homozygous for wild-type genes at virtually all their loci. On such a view, the obvious genetical differences in morphological and physiological characters between races are a major component of the total variation within the species.

Dobzhansky, on the other hand (1954) has held the opposite view, that heterozygosity is the rule in sexually reproducing species, and this view carries with it the concomitant that population and racial variations are likely to be less significant in the total species variation.

As long as no objective quantification of genetic variation could be given, the problem of the relative degree of variation within and between groups remained subjective and necessarily was biased in the direction of attaching a great significance to variations between groups. This bias necessarily flows from the process of classification itself, since it is an expression of the perception of group differences. The erection of racial classification in man based upon certain manifest morphological traits gives tremendous emphasis to those characters to which human perceptions are most finely tuned (nose, lip and eye shapes, skin color, hair form and quantity), precisely because they are the characters that men ordinarily use to distinguish individuals. Men will then be keenly aware of group differences in such characters and will place strong emphasis on their importance in classification. The problem is even more pronounced in the classification of other organisms. All wild mice look alike because we are deprived of our usual visual cues, so small intergroup differences in pelage color are seized upon for subspecific identification. Again this tends to emphasize between-group variation in contrast to individual variation.

In the last five years there has been a revolution in our assessment of inherited variation, as a result of the application of· molecular biological techniques to population problems. Chiefly by use of protein electrophoresis, but also by immunological techniques, it has become possible to assess directly and objectively the genetic variation among individuals on a locus by locus basis. The techniques do not depend upon any *a priori* judgments about the significance of the variation, nor upon whether the variation is between individuals or between groups, nor do they depend upon how much or how little variation is actually present (Hubby and Lewontin, 1965). As a result, the original question of how much variation there is within populations has now been resolved. In a variety of species including Drosophila, mice, birds, plants, and man, it is the rule, rather than the exception, that there is genetic variation between individuals within populations. For example, Prakash et al. (1969) found 42% of a random sample of loci to be segregating in populations of *D. pseudoobscura*, producing an average heterozygosity per locus per individual of 12%. A study of a number of populations of *Mus musculus* by Selander and Yang (1969) gave almost identical results. Two analyses for man, one on enzymes by Harris (1970) and one on blood groups by Lewontin (1967), give respective estimates of 30% and 36% for polymorphic loci within populations, and 6% and 16% for heterozygosity per gene per individual.

The existence of these objective techniques for the assessment of genetic variation, and their widespread application in recent years to large numbers of populations, in conjunction with older information on the distribution of human blood group genes, makes it possible to estimate, from a random sample of genetic loci, the degree of variation within and between human populations and races, and so to put the comparative differentiation within and between groups on a firm quantitative basis.

THE GENES

Of the 35 or so blood group systems in man, 15 are known to be segregating with an alternative form in frequency greater than 1% in some human populations. (For a summary, see Lewontin, 1967.) Of these, 9 systems have been characterized in enough populations to make them useful for our purposes. They are listed in Table 1 together with the extremes of gene frequency known over the whole range of human populations. I use the concept of "system" rather than "gene" here since it is uncertain whether the MNS system is a single locus with four alleles (as I treat it here) or two closely linked loci with two alleles each. The same ambiguity exists for the Rhesus group, which, again, I treat as a single locus with multiple alleles. For the Rh system, there are many more alleles known than the six listed, but most studies have not had available the full range of antisera, especially anti-D^u, anti-e and anti-d, so that the six classes used here include some confounding of subclasses. All the blood group data upon which the present calculations have been made are taken from Mourant (1954), Mourant et al. (1958), and Boyd (1950).

A second group of loci that have more recently been surveyed are serum proteins and red blood cell enzymes (Table 1). In contrast to the blood groups, which are detected by immune differences, the serum proteins and RBC enzymes are studied by electrophoretic techniques, different alleles producing proteins with altered electrophoretic mobility. A full discussion of these methods is given by Harris (1970), who was the first to use it for population genetic purposes in man; and by Giblett (1969), who also gives extensive information on the distribution of alleles in different human populations. It is from this latter source that the data for this paper are taken.

THE SAMPLES

The amount of world survey work carried out for the different genes obviously varies considerably. For Xm only four populations are reported: a Norwegian, a U.S. white, a U.S. black, and an Easter Island sample; while for the ABO system literally hundreds of populations in all regions of the world had been sampled by the time Mourant's 1954 compilation was made. In the case of the better known blood groups such as ABO, Rh, and MNS, there is an *embarras de richesse*, and some small sample of population is included in the present calculation. Since our object is to look at the distribution of genic diversity

Table 1. Human Genes or "Systems" Included in this Study
and Extremes of Allele Frequency in Known Populations

Locus		Allele	Frequency Range	Extreme Populations
Haptoglobin	(Hp)	Hp^1	.09 - .92	Tamils-Lacondon
Lipoprotein	(Ag)	Ag^X	.23 - .74	Italy-India
Lipoprotein	(Lp)	Lp^a	.009- .267	Labrador-Germany
	(Xm)	Xm^a	.260- .335	Easter Is.-U.S. Blacks
Red Cell Acid Phosphatase	(APh)	p^a	.09 - .67	Tristan da Cunha-Athabascan
		p^b	.33 - .91	Athabascan-Tristan da Cunha
		p^c	0- .08	Many
6-phosphogluconate dehydrogenase	(6PGD)	PGD^A	.753-1.000	Bhutan-Yucatan
Phosphoglucomutase	(PGM$_1$)	PGM_1	.430- .938	Habbana Jews-Yanomama
Adenylate kinase	(AK)	AK^2	0- .130	Africans, Amerinds-Pakistanis
Kidd	(Jk)	JK^a	.310-1.000	Chinese-Dyaks, Eskimo
Duffy	(Fy)	Fy^a	.061-1.000	Bantu-Chenchu, Eskimo
Lewis	(Le)	Le^b	.298- .667	Lapps-Kapinga
Kell	(K)	K	0- .063	Many-Chenchu
Lutheran	(Lu)	Lu^a	0- .086	Many-Brazilian Amerinds
P		P	.179- .838	Chinese-West Africans
MNS		MS	0- .317	Oceanians-Bloods
		Ms	.192- .747	Papuans-Malays
		NS	0- .213	Borneo, Eskimo-Chenchu
		Ns	.051- .645	Navaho-Palauans
Rh		CDe	0- .960	Luo-Papuans
		Cde	0- .166	Many-Chenchu
		cDE	0- .308	Luo, Dyak-Japanese
		cdE	0- .174	Many-Ainu
		cDe	0- .865	Many-Luo
		cde	0- .456	Many-Basques
ABO		I^A	.007- .583	Toba-Bloods
		I^B	0- .297	Amerinds, Austr. Abo.-Toda
		i	.509- .993	Oraon-Toba

throughout the species, I have tried to include what would appear to be *a priori* representatives of the range of human diversity. But how does one do that? Do the French, the Danes, and the Spaniards, say, cover the same range of density as the Ewe, Batutsi, and Luo? How many different European nationalities should be included as compared with how many African peoples or Indian tribes? There is, morever, the problem of weighting. The population of Japan is vastly larger than the Yanomama tribes of the Orinoco. Should each population be given equal weight, or should some attempt be made to weight each by the proportion of the total species population that it represents? Such weighting would clearly decrease any total measure of human diversity since it would reduce effectively to zero the contribution of all of the small, isolated and usually genetically divergent groups. It would also decrease the proportion of all human diversity calculated to be between populations, for the same reason. In this paper I have chosen to count each population included as being of equal value and to include, as much as possible, equal numbers of African peoples, European nationalities, Oceanian populations, Asian peoples, and American Indian tribes. Both of these choices will maximize both the total human diversity and the proportion of it that is calculated betweeen populations as opposed to within populations. This bias should be born in mind when interpreting the results.

A second methodological problem arises over the question of racial classification. In addition to estimating the within-and between-population diversity components, I attempt to break down the between-population components into a fraction within and between "races." Despite the objective problems of classification of human population into races, anthropological, genetical, and social practice continues to do so. Racial classification is an attempt to codify what appear to be obvious nodalities in the distribution of human morphological and cultural traits. The difficulty, however, is that despite the undoubted existence of such nodes in the taxonomic space, populations are sprinkled between the nodes so that boundary lines must be arbitrary. No one would confuse a Papuan aboriginal with any South American Indian, yet no one can give an objective criterion for where a dividing line should be drawn in the continuum from South American Indians through Polynesians, Micronesians, Melanesians, to Papuans. The attempts of Boyd (1950) and Mourant (1954) to use blood group data and other genetic information for racial classification illustrate that, no matter what the form of the data, the method of classification remains the same. Obvious and well differentiated stereotypes are set up representing well-differentiated population groups. Thus, the inhabitants of Europe speaking Indo-European languages, the indigenes of sub-Saharan Africa, the aborigines of North and South America, and the peoples of mainland East and Southeast Asia, become the modal groups for Caucasian, Negroid, Amerind, and Mongoloid races. Then by the use of linguistic, morphological, historical, and cultural information, all those not yet included are assorted by affinity into these original classes or, in the case of particularly divergent groups like the Australian aborigines, set up as separate races or subraces. In such a scheme, some populations always create difficulties. Are the Lapps Caucasians or do they belong with the Turkic peoples of Central Asia to the Mongoloid race? Linguistically they are Asians; morphologically they are ambiguous; they have the ABO and Lutheran blood group frequencies typical of Europeans but their Duffy, Lewis, Haptoglobin, and Adenylate-kinase gene frequencies are Asian. Their MNS blood group is clearly non-Asian but also is a very poor fit to European frequencies. Similar great difficulties exist for Hindi-speaking Indians and Urdu-speaking Pakistanis. They are, genetically, the mixture of Aryans, Persians, Arabs, and Dravidians that history tells us they should be.

For the purpose of this paper there are two alternatives. Racial classification could be done entirely from evidence external to the data used here (i.e., linguistic, historical, cultural, and morphological). This convention would then decrease the calculated diversity between races and increase the within-race, between-population component, since it would lump together, in one race, groups that are genetically divergent. The alternative would be to use internal evidence only and establish the racial lines that maximize the similarity of the populations with races. The difficulty of such a procedure is that it has no end. The between-race component would be maximized if every population were made a separate race! Even a reasonable application of this method would require that Indians and Arabs each be made separate races and that Oceania be divided into a number of such groups. I have chosen a conservative path and have used mostly the classical racial groupings with a few switches based on obvious total genetic divergence. Thus, the question I am asking is, "How much of human diversity between populations is accounted for by more or less conventional racial classification?" Table 2 shows the racial classification used in this paper. I have made seven such "races" adding South Asian aborigines and Oceanians to the usual four races, also segregating off the Australian aborigines with the Papuan aborigines. Not all the populations listed under each race are sampled for every gene, but the racial classification was, of course, consistent over all genes.

THE MEASURE OF DIVERSITY

The basic data are the frequencies of alternative alleles at various loci (or supergenes) in different populations. The problem is to use these data to characterize diversity. One ordinarily thinks of some sort of analysis of variance for this purpose, an analysis that would break down genetic variance into a component within population, between populations, and between races. A moment's reflection, however, will reveal that this is an inappropriate technique for dealing with allelic frequencies since, when there are more than two alleles at one locus, there is no single well-ordered variable whose variance can be calculated. If there are two alleles at a locus, say A_1 and A_2, they can be assigned random variable values, say 0 and 1, respectively, and the variance of the numerical random variable could be analyzed within and between populations. If there are three alleles, however, this trick will not work, for if we assigned random variable values, say 0, 1, and 2 to three alleles A_1, A_2, and A_3, we would get the absurd result that a population with equal proportions of A_1 and A_3 would have a greater variance than are those with equal proportions of A_1 and A_2, and A_2 or A_3.

Table 2

Inclusive List of All Populations Used For Any Gene
in this Study by the Racial Classification Used in this Study

Caucasians

Arabs, Armenians, Austrians, Basques, Belgians, Bulgarians, Czechs, Danes, Dutch, Egyptians, English, Estonians, Finns, French, Georgians, Germans, Greeks, Gypsies, Hungarians, Icelanders, Indians (Hindi speaking), Italians, Irani, Norwegians, Oriental Jews, Pakistani (Urdu-speakers), Poles, Portuguese, Russians, Spaniards, Swedes, Swiss, Syrians, Tristan da Cunhans, Welsh

Black Africans

Abyssinians (Amharas), Bantu, Barundi, Batutsi, Bushmen, Congolese, Ewe, Fulani, Gambians, Ghanaians, Hobe, Hottentot, Hututu, Ibo, Iraqi, Kenyans, Kikuyu, Liberians, Luo, Madagascans, Mozambiquans, Msutu, Nigerians, Pygmies, Sengalese, Shona, Somalis, Sudanese, Tanganyikans, Tutsi, Ugandans, U.S. Blacks, "West Africans," Xosa, Zulu

Mongoloids

Ainu, Bhutanese, Bogobos, Bruneians, Buriats, Chinese, Dyaks, Filipinos, Ghashgai, Indonesians, Japanese, Javanese, Kirghiz, Koreans, Lapps, Malayans, Senoy, Siamese, Taiwanese, Tatars, Thais, Turks

South Asian Aborigines

Andamanese, Badagas, Chenchu, Irula, Marathas, Naiars, Oraons, Onge, Tamils, Todas

Amerinds

Alacaluf, Aleuts, Apache, Atacameños, "Athabascans", Ayamara, Bororo, Blackfeet, Bloods, "Brazilian Indians," Chippewa, Caingang, Choco, Coushatta, Cuna, Diegueños, Eskimo, Flathead, Huasteco, Huichol, Ica, Kwakiutl, Labradors, Lacandon, Mapuche, Maya, "Mexican Indians," Navaho, Nez Percé, Paez, Pehuenches, Pueblo, Quechua, Seminole, Shoshone, Toba, Utes, "Venezuelan Indians," Xavante, Yanomama

Oceanians

Admiralty Islanders, Caroline Islanders, Easter Islanders, Ellice Islanders, Fijians, Gilbertese, Guamians, Hawaiians, Kapingas, Maori, Marshallese, Melanauans, "Melanesians," "Micronesians," New Britons, New Caledonians, New Hebrideans, Palauans, Papuans, "Polynesians," Saipanese, Samoans, Solomon Islanders, Tongans, Trukese, Yapese

Australian Aborigines

Any measure of diversity ought to have the following characteristics: (1) It should be a minimum (conveniently, 0) when there is only a single allele present so that the locus in question shows no variation. (2) For a fixed number of alleles, it should be maximum when all are equal in frequency—this corresponds to our intuitive notion that the diversity is much less, for a given number of alternative kinds, when one of the kinds is very rare. (3) The diversity ought to increase somehow as the number of different alleles in the population increases. Specifically, if all alleles are equally frequent, then a population with ten alleles is obviously more diverse in any ordinary sense than a population with two alleles. (4) The diversity measure ought to be a *convex function* of frequencies of alleles; that is, a collection of individuals made by pooling two populations ought always to be more diverse than the average of their separate diversities, unless the two populations are identical in *composition*. It is the identity of *composition*, not of diversity which matters here. Hence, a population with alleles A_1 and A_2 in a 0.70:0.30 ratio, and a population with A_1 and A_2 in a 0.30:0.70 ratio ought to have identical diversity values, but a collection of individuals from both populations ought to have a higher diversity.

There are two measures that immediately suggest themselves as qualifying under the four requirements. One is simply the proportion of heterozygotes that would be produced in a random mating population or assemblage. If the frequency at the ith allele at a locus is p_i, then

$$(1) \qquad h = \sum_{i,\, j=1}^{n} p_i\, p_j \qquad\qquad i \neq j$$

is the herterozygosity, and it can be verified that h, so defined, satisfies requirements (1) to (4) above.

A second measure, which bears a strong resemblance numerically to h, is the Shannon information measure

$$(2) \qquad H = -\sum_{i=1}^{n} p_i\, \ln_2 p_i.$$

This latter measure is widely used to characterize species diversity in community ecology, and since I am performing a kind of taxonomic analysis here, I will use H. The calculation of H is somewhat eased by published tables of $p\ln_2 p$ (Dolanský and Dolanský, 1952). In line with our requirements for a diversity measure,

$$H = 0 \quad \text{if} \quad \begin{aligned} p_k &= 1 \\ p_i &= 0 \quad i = 1,2,...,k\text{-}1,k\text{+}1,...,n \end{aligned}$$

$$H_{max} = \ln_2 n \quad \text{if} \quad p_i = \frac{1}{n} \quad \text{for all } i.$$

H has been calculated at three levels for gene frequencies. For each gene, H has been calculated for each population. This within-population value is designated H_O and its average over populations within a race is designated H_{pop}. Second, for each gene, H has been calculated on the *average gene frequency* over all populations within a race. This value, designated as H_{race}, is greater than the average H_O for the race, H_{pop}, by virtue of the convexity of the measure H. The difference between H_{race} and H_{pop} is the added diversity that arises from considering the collection of all populations within a race. It is the between-population, within-race component of diversity.

Third, H is calculated on the average gene frequencies at a locus over all the populations in the species. This value, $H_{species}$, is the total species diversity at that locus and will be greater than the average H_{race} over all races. The difference between $H_{species}$ and $\bar{H}_{race}$ is a measure of the added diversity from the factor of race. It is the between-race component of diversity.

The calculation of H_{pop}, $\bar{H}_{pop}$, H_{race}, $\bar{H}_{race}$, and $H_{species}$ involves some convention on how each population shall be weighted. I have already indicated that each population in the sample is given equal weight, so that H_{pop} is the unweighted average of all H_O within a race, and H_{race} is calculated on the unweighted average gene frequency within each race. $\bar{H}_{pop}$ and $\bar{H}_{race}$ are averaged over all races weighted by the number of populations studied in each race, and $H_{species}$ is likewise calculated on the average gene frequency of the whole species counting each population once. These latter conventions are necessary to be constant with H_O and H_{pop}, and to make the total diversity add up. The effect of these conventions is to overestimate the total human diversity, $H_{species}$, since small populations are given equal weight with large ones in the calculation of the average gene frequency, $\bar{p}_{species}$, of each allele. These conventions also overestimate the proportion of the total diversity that is between populations and races as opposed to within populations since it gives too much weight to small isolated populations and to less numerous races like the Amerinds and Australian aborigines, both of which have gene frequencies that differ markedly from the rest of the species.

THE RESULTS

Table 3 shows the results in detail for the 17 genes included in the study. For each gene the number of populations in each race, N, the gene frequency p for each race, the value of H_{race} based on each gene frequency $\bar{p}$, the average within-population H_{pop} for each race separately, and the ratio H_{pop}/H_{race} for each race separately, are given. Where there are only two alleles at a locus known, one of them is arbitrarily chosen for $\bar{p}$, which contains all the information. Where more than two alleles are known, separate $\bar{p}_i$ are given for each allele. Separate race components have not been calculated for lipoprotein Ag, lipoprotein Lp, and protein Xm, because too few populations were available.

Table 3. Gene Frequencies and Diversity Components for 17 Genes in 7 Races.
See Text for Detailed Explanation

	Caucasians	African	Mongoloid	S. Asian Aborigines	Amerinds	Oceanians	Australian Aborigines	Total	$\bar{H}_{species}$	$\bar{H}_{race}$	$\bar{H}_{pop}$
Haptoglobin											
N	25	21	12	6	21	15	1	101			
$\bar{p}$	.354	.563	.303	.157	.581	.565	.200		.456		
H_{race}	.938	.989	.885	.627	.981	.988	.722		.994		
H_{pop}	.912	.934	.873	.586	.900	.913	.722			.938	
H_{pop}/H_{race}	.972	.944	.986	.935	.917	.924	–				.888
Lipoprotein Ag											
N	4	0	3	0	0	0	0	7			
$\bar{p}$	–	–	–	–	–	–	–		.453		
H_{race}	–	–	–	–	–	–	–		.994		
H_{pop}	–	–	–	–	–	–	–			.829	
Lipoprotein Lp											
N	5	2	0	0	2	1	0	10			
$\bar{p}$	–	–	–	–	–	–	–		.162		
H_{race}	–	–	–	–	–	–	–		.639		
H_{pop}	–	–	–	–	–	–	–			–	.600
Xm											
N	2	1	0	0	0	1	0	4			
$\bar{p}$	–	–	–	–	–	–	–		.290		
H_{race}	–	–	–	–	–	–	–		.869		
H_{pop}	–	–	–	–	–	–	–			–	.866

Red Cell Ap H

N	7	3	4	0	7	3	0	24
$\bar{p}_1$	.276	.203	.310	—	.376	.280	—	.302
$\bar{p}_2$	.693	.767	.685	—	.621	.713	—	.683
$\bar{p}_3$	.051	.015	.005	—	.003	.007	—	.014
$\bar{p}_4$	.000	.015	.000	—	.000	.000	—	.001
H_{race}	1.035	.942	.936	—	.983	.912	—	.989
H_{pop}	.973	.919	.912	—	.878	.886	—	.977
H_{pop}/H_{race}	.940	.975	.974	—	.893	.971	—	.917

6 PGD

N	5	4	5	0	3	0	0	17
$\bar{p}$	.961	.914	.905	—	.999	—	—	.940
H_{race}	.238	.423	.453	—	.011	—	—	.327
H_{pop}	.231	.410	.411	—	.007	—	—	.305
H_{pop}/H_{race}	.971	.969	.907	—	.636	—	—	.286

PGM

N	6	4	4	0	7	0	0	21
$\bar{p}$	.690	.785	.769	—	.863	—	—	.781
H_{race}	.893	.751	.780	—	.576	—	—	.758
H_{pop}	.842	.750	.751	—	.564	—	—	.739
H_{pop}/H_{race}	.942	.999	.963	—	.979	—	—	.714

Adenylate kinase

N	9	6	4	0	2	0	0	21
$\bar{p}$	.055	.003	.016	—	0	—	—	.028
H_{race}	.311	.029	.095	—	0	—	—	.184
H_{pop}	.297	.028	.004	—	0	—	—	.160
H_{pop}/H_{race}	.955	.966	.042	—	—	—	—	.156

Table 3. Gene Frequencies and Diversity Components for 17 Genes in 7 Races. (continued)

	Caucasians	African	Mongoloid	S. Asian Aborigines	Amerinds	Oceanians	Australian Aborigines	Total	$\bar{H}_{species}$	$\bar{H}_{race}$	$\bar{H}_{pop}$
Kidd											
N	2	2	2	0	4	0	0	10			
$\bar{p}$	.520	.757	.655	—	.615	—	—				
H_{race}	.999	.800	.930	—	.961	—	—		.411	.930	
H_{pop}	.999	.798	.446	—	.688	—	—		.977		.724
H_{pop}/H_{race}	1.000	.998	.480	—	.716	—	—				
Duffy											
N	7	2	4	4	5	3	0	25			
$\bar{p}$	.410	.072	.784	.715	.826	1.000	—				
H_{race}	.977	.373	.753	.862	.667	0	—		.645	.695	
H_{pop}	.835	.370	.680	.671	.586	0	—		.938		.597
H_{pop}/H_{race}	.854	.992	.903	.778	.879	—	—				
Lewis											
N	5	0	6	0	0	5	0	16			
$\bar{p}$	.459	—	.432	—	—	.483	—				
H_{race}	.995	—	.987	—	—	.999	—		.456	.993	
H_{pop}	.994	—	.935	—	—	.956	—		.994		.960
H_{pop}/H_{race}	.999	—	.947	—	—	.957	—				
Kell											
N	9	4	5	0	0	1	0	19			
$\bar{p}$	.040	.016	.025	—	—	0	—		.029		
H_{race}	.242	.118	.169	—	—	0	—		.189	.184	

								Total
Kell (continued)								
H_{pop}	.240	.101	.135	—	—	0	—	.170
H_{pop}/H_{race}	.992	.856	.799	—	—	—	—	
Lutheran								
N	5	4	3	4	4	0	2	22
$\bar{p}$	.028	.027	.011	0	.051	—	0	.022
H_{race}	.184	.179	.087	0	.291	—	0	.153
H_{pop}	.177	.166	.081	0	.137	—	0	.139
H_{pop}/H_{race}	.962	.927	.931	—	.471	—	—	.106
P								
N	18	4	5	6	4	4	0	41
$\bar{p}$	.533	.693	.433	.388	.431	.572	—	.509
H_{race}	.997	.890	.987	.963	.986	.985	—	1.000
H_{pop}	.980	.812	.934	.931	.971	.969	—	.978
H_{pop}/H_{race}	.983	.912	.946	.967	.985	.984	—	.949
MNS								
N	13	12	6	6	5	4	2	48
$\bar{p}_1$	.246	.140	.072	.188	.227	.002	.009	.158
$\bar{p}_2$	.320	.434	.554	.456	.585	.356	.224	.420
$\bar{p}_3$	.084	.060	.090	.080	.041	.057	.052	.070
$\bar{p}_4$	.350	.366	.284	.306	.147	.585	.715	.353
H_{race}	1.854	1.695	1.574	1.785	1.609	1.236	1.112	1.746
H_{pop}	1.819	1.648	1.443	1.611	1.465	1.181	1.045	1.663
H_{pop}/H_{race}	.981	.972	.917	.903	.911	.956	.940	1.591
Rh								
N	16	13	9	3	9	10	1	61
$\bar{p}_1$	.469	.096	.766	.813	.506	.831	.585	.518

Table 3. Gene Frequencies and Diversity Components for 17 Genes in 7 Races. (continued)

	Caucasians	African	Mongoloid	S. Asian Aborigines	Amerinds	Oceanians	Australian Aborigines	Total	$\bar{H}_{species}$	$\bar{H}_{race}$	$\bar{H}_{pop}$
Rh (continued)											
$\bar{p}_2$	.019	.024	.001	.055	.029	.001	.129		.020		
$\bar{p}_3$	.097	.075	.137	.088	.392	.123	.201		.148		
$\bar{p}_4$	.006	.004	.035	0	.009	0	0		.009		
$\bar{p}_5$	.060	.608	.049	.020	.018	.045	.085		.166		
$\bar{p}_6$	.342	.192	.016	.023	.035	0	0		.139		
H_{race}	1.763	1.659	1.175	1.020	1.509	.805	1.600		1.900	1.420	
H_{pop}	1.679	1.537	.994	.855	1.307	.716	1.600				1.281
H_{pop}/H_{race}	.952	.926	.846	.838	.866	.899	—				
ABO											
N	22	11	10	6	10	10	1	70			
$\bar{p}_1$	.258	.154	.216	.174	.226	.247	.306		.223		
$\bar{p}_2$	.117	.134	.200	.187	.009	.092	0		.117		
$\bar{p}_3$	.625	.712	.583	.639	.765	.661	.694		.660		
H_{race}	1.290	1.154	1.396	1.304	.842	1.210	.889		1.241		
H_{pop}	1.276	1.132	1.334	1.219	.667	1.141	.889			1.204	
H_{pop}/H_{race}	.989	.981	.956	.935	.792	.943	—				1.126

The last three columns show the value of $H_{species}$ calculated on grand average gene frequency of the species, $\bar{H}_{race}$ and $\bar{H}_{pop}$ average over all races and populations.

There are several interesting details. Where aboriginals, Amerinds, and Oceanians have been studied, they are usually the groups with the lowest H_{race}. Particularly striking examples are the very low diversities for Amerinds in 6PGD, Ak, and ABO; for aborigines in Lutheran, MNS, and ABO; and for Oceanians in Duffy, Kell, and Rh. The only cases where one of the three large races is low in diversity are the Africans for Duffy and the Mongoloids for Lutheran. Since H_{race} measures also the heterozygosity within the race, the low diversities in Aborigines, Amerinds, and Oceanians suggest an effect of genetic isolation and small breeding size for these races. Such effects must apply to the race as a whole, however, and not simply to the breeding structure of each population within it. If a race consists of many small isolated populations, the homozygosity within each population should be high, so that H_{pop} should be low for the race; but different alleles would be randomly fixed in different populations, so that H_{race} would not be especially low. The effect of subdivision of a race into many small populations would be a small ratio, H_{pop}/H_{race}. The only striking example of such a small ratio is for Lutheran in the Amerinds. There is a general tendency for Oceanian and Amerind ratios to be smaller than for the three main races, and Caucasians tend to have the highest ratios, but much of this difference arises from arbitrarily classifying certain populations together in one race. Allowing for this uncertainty, we must conlude that there is no internal evidence that sparse aboriginal populations are more genetically isolated from their neighbors than are more continuously distributed large races.

The lower H_{race} values for the aboriginal populations must reflect something about their early history rather than their general breeding structure. It is generally assumed that both the Amerinds and Australian aborigines became isolated, as groups, rather early and stemmed from a small number of respective ancestors. The genetic evidence of low H_{race} strongly supports this view. The Oceanians are more of a surprise since there appears to be more genetic homogeneity within the group than might have been expected from the variety of physical types.

Table 4 summarizes the results of Table 3 in a form relevant to the main problem I have posed. The first column gives the value of $H_{species}$ for each gene. The next three columns show how this total diversity is apportioned to within-population, between-population, and between-race components, calculated as follows from Table 3:

$$\text{Within populations} = \frac{H_{pop}}{H_{species}}$$

$$\text{Between populations in races} \quad = \quad \frac{H_{race} - H_{pop}}{H_{species}}$$

$$\text{Between races} \quad = \quad \frac{H_{species} - H_{race}}{H_{species}}$$

Table 4. Proportion of Genetic Diversity Accounted for Within and Between Populations and Races

Gene	Total $H_{species}$	Within Populations	Within Races Between Populations	Between Races
Hp	.994	.893	.051	.056
Ag	.994	.834	–	–
Lp	.639	.939	–	–
Xm	.869	.997	–	–
Ap	.989	.927	.062	.011
6PGD	.327	.875	.058	.067
PGM	.758	.942	.033	.025
Ak	.184	.848	.021	.131
Kidd	.977	.741	.211	.048
Duffy	.938	.636	.105	.259
Lewis	.994	.966	.032	.002
Kell	.189	.901	.073	.026
Lutheran	.153	.694	.214	.092
P	1.000	.949	.029	.022
MNS	1.746	.911	.041	.048
Rh	1.900	.674	.073	.253
ABO	1.241	.907	.063	.030
Mean		.854	.083	.063

The results are quite remarkable. The mean proportion of the total species diversity that is contained within populations is 85.4%, with a maximum of 99.7% for the Xm gene, and a minimum of 63.6% for Duffy. Less than 15% of all human genetic diversity is accounted for by differences between human groups! Moreover, the difference between populations within a race accounts for an additional 8.3%, so that only 6.3% is accounted for by racial classification.

This allocation of 85% of human genetic diversity to individual variation within populations is sensitive to the sample of populations considered. As we have several times pointed out, our sample is heavily weighted with "primitive" peoples with small populations, so that their H_O values count much too heavily compared with their proportion in the total human population. Scanning

Table 3 we see that, more often than not, the H_{pop} values are lower for South Asian aborigines, Australian aborigines, Oceanians, and Amerinds than for the three large racial groups. Moreover, the total human diversity, $H_{species}$, is inflated because of the overweighting of these small groups, which tend to have gene frequencies that deviate from the large races. Thus the fraction of diversity within populations is doubly underestimated since the numerator of that fraction is underestimated and the denominator overestimated.

When we consider the remaining diversity, not explained by within-population effects, the allocation to within-race and between-race effects is sensitive to our racial representations. On the one hand the over-representation of aborigines and Oceanians tends to give too much weight to diversity between races. On the other hand, the racial component is underestimated by certain arbitrary lumpings of divergent populations in one race. For example, if the Hindi and Urdu speaking peoples were separated out as a race, and if the Melanesian peoples of the South Asian seas were not lumped with the Oceanians, then the racial component of diversity would be increased. Of course, by assigning each population to separate races we would carry this procedure to the *reductio ad absurdum*. A *post facto* assignment, based on gene frequencies, would also increase the racial component, but if this were carried out objectively it would lump certain Africans with Lapps! Clearly, if we are to assess the meaning of racial classifications in genetic terms, we must concern ourselves with the usual racial divisions. All things considered, then, the 6.3% of human diversity assignable to race is about right, or a slight overestimate considering that H_{pop} is overestimated.

It is clear that our perception of relatively large differences between human races and subgroups, as compared to the variation within these groups, is indeed a biased perception and that, based on randonly chosen genetic differences, human races and populations are remarkably similar to each other, with the largest part by far of human variation being accounted for by the differences between individuals.

Human racial classifcation is of no social value and is positively destructive of social and human relations. Since such racial classification is now seen to be of virtually no genetic or taxonomic significance either, no justification can be offered for its continuance.

REFERENCES

Boyd, W. C. 1950. Genetics and the Races of Man. Boston, D. C. Heath and Co.

Dolanský, L., and M. P. Dolanský. 1952. Table of $\log_2$ $1/P$, $p \cdot \log_2$ $1/p$, and $p \cdot \log_2$ $1/p + (1-p) \cdot \log_2$ $1/(1-p)$. Technical Report 227, Research Laboratory of Electronics. Cambridge, Massachusetts Institute of Technology

Dobzhansky, Th. 1954. A review of some fundamental concepts and problems of population genetics. Sympos. Quant. Biol., 20:1-15.

Giblett, E. R. 1969. Genetic Markers in Human Blood. Oxford and Edinburgh, Blackwell.

Harris, H. 1970. The Principles of Human Biochemical Genetics. Amsterdam, North Holland Publishing Co.

Hubby, J. L., and R. C. Lewontin. 1965. A molecular approach to the study of genetic heterozygosity in natural population. Genetics, 54:577-609.

Lewontin, R. C. 1967. An estimate of the average heterozygosity in man. Amer. J. Hum. Genet. 19:681-685.

———— 1968. The concept of evolution. The International Encyclopedia of the Social Sciences, 5:202-209.

Mourant, A. E. 1954. The Distribution of the Human Blood Groups. Oxford, Blackwell.

———— A. C. Kopeć, and K. Domaniewska-Sobczak. 1958. The ABO Blood Groups. Oxford, Blackwell.

Muller, H. J. 1950. Our load of mutations, Amer. J. Human. Gent., 2:111-176.

Prakash, S., R. C. Lewontin, and J. L. Hubby. 1969. A molecular approach to the study of genic heterozygosity in natural populations. IV. Patterns of genic variation in central, marginal and isolated populations of *Drosophila pseudoobscura*. Genetics, 61:841-858.

Selander, R. K., and S. Y. Yang. 1969. Protein polymorphism and genic heterozygosity in a wild population of the house mouse (*Mus musculus*). Genetics, 63:563-667.

15

Polygenic Inheritance and Human Intelligence

I. MICHAEL LERNER

*Department of Genetics and Institute of Personality
Assessment and Research
University of California,
Berkeley, California 94720*

INTRODUCTION

Inheritance of human intelligence is a subject which has received an increasing amount of attention from human geneticists, psychologists, educators, sociologists, and others. Not only has the development of a methodology to study this trait been vigorously pursued, but in some instances consequences for the future of mankind and conclusions regarding changes needed in our educational system have been drawn. The relevant literature is vast. It is not the purpose of this paper to review it, nor is there any intention to discuss the controversies which are currently rife on many aspects of the subject (see, e.g., Hirsch, 1970).

This contribution rather attempts to consider the broad problem viewed to some extent from the outside, partly as an audodidactic exercise, and partly as an expression of the outlook of an animal breeder who is trying to become a behavioral geneticist. Though I have done some work on the behavior of flour beetles and am currently involved in designing studies of genetics of personality in man, most of my career has been spent in the company of the domestic fowl, *Gallus gallus*. Hence, just as some animal behavior students adopt an anthropomorphic approach, so in talking of human intelligence, I plan to use what may be called a *gallomorphic* one.

Modified from a talk given at a symposium on Human Evolution at the First National Biology Congress of the American Institute of Biological Sciences in Detroit, November, 1970.

In the general evolutionary context, the principal dimension that might seem relevant to the problem is, of course, time. Evolutionary processes have a past, a present, and a future (even if it means extinction for some species). But with respect to the intelligence of *Homo sapiens*, if one is restricted to microevolution, factual information on the past is virtually unobtainable, despite the unfortunate and unprovable assertions by some, e.g., Li (1970), that "It is an irrefutable evolutionary fact that man's intelligence has been increasing over the entire history of man, from the primitive to the modern"; that about the future is conjectural; that about the present is beclouded by mists of prejudice, emotion, and characterized by vast areas of ignorance not only of facts but of the methodology of dealing with observations.

The very first points that one presumably must take up in any discussion of the subject of polygenic inheritance and human intelligence are the meaning of the terms (to reverse the order) (a) human intelligence, and (b) polygenic inheritance.

DEFINITION OF HUMAN INTELLIGENCE

One may possibly escape a rigorous definition of the first by substituting the term I.Q. for it, and then specifying that we shall discuss whatever it is that the I.Q. measures. We might even say that, because phenotypic correlations of relatively high magnitude between certain I.Q. tests and some measure of scholastic achievement exist, it is the latter which we are talking about. But when dealing with a broad evolutionary perspective this switch of terms (which, in some guise I shall most certainly pull) produces difficulties. Certainly, data on such tests as the Stanford-Binet, the Otis, or the Wechsler scale, are not available for our Stone Age ancestors, nor (to play it safe, one may say, with a few exceptions) very meaningful when applied to whatever survivors there are in comparable primitive cultures today. This is probably also true of nonverbal approaches such as the Raven test and others, despite the assertions of some psychometricians that they are culture-fair. Here, I am inclined to agree with Eckland (1967), who in his monumental review of the role of genetics in sociology expressed his disbelief in the existence of such tests. However, his reductionism in looking forward to a somewhat distant day when direct biochemical measurements or even close correlates of genetic determinants of intelligence become available, is perhaps overoptimistic (of course, cases of mental retardation such as in PKU are in a different category). At least, this is probably true for anything of use to those alive today. Nor is it certain that, even reduced to the level of codons specifying sequences of amino acids that are eventually reflected in something loosely described as intelligence, all properties high on a value scale today will also be high twenty generations hence. I feel that this is an important point especially in discussing any programs of genetic action with respect to human intelligence, though as noted in the next section there are opposing views.

The discussion to follow hence is based on a somewhat amorphous concept of intelligence. For the present purposes it could mean a number of things: scholastic aptitude should one wish to say so, some measure of success in life, degree of motivation either in actual pursuit of happiness or in taking some psychometric test, the limits of achievement dictated either by genotype or by phenotype, or any number of other possibilities which it would take a competent psychologist to list in full. That is, for the present purposes, intelligence could be factor-analytic, hierarchical, facet-oriented, fluid, crystallized, something couched in terms of central neural processes mediating between input of information and output of reaction, Piaget's hierarchical developmentally sequential outlook, or any number of other approaches (Bouchard, 1968). And it may also involve processes of thinking, reasoning, and abstracting, or the overall criterion of "adequacy of behavior," the ability to maintain operations under conditions of disturbance and privation, performance in verbal reasoning, numerical fluency, and general knowledge (H. Gough, personal communication).

This looseness in viewing intelligence is made possible simply because in a gallomorphic way one can hide behind generalities about some sort of a number on a scale, which can be manipulated analytically for determination of heritability or for selection, just as the number of eggs laid by a chicken is treated. This number may, in practically oriented situations, be used as a statistic without reference as to how it was arrived at physiologically. That is not to say that the physiological components of egg production, i.e., hormone levels or sensitivities, degree of broodiness, clutch size, rate of sexual maturity, and others contributing to the number of eggs cannot themselves be similarly handled. And, no doubt, further subdivision of each of these traits is either actually or potentially possible. In brief, intelligence for our purposes may be defined as a number in order to examine it in an evolutionary or, perhaps, genetic perspective.

The reason that intelligence is to be considered in such a nonspecific fashion is first of all to make it possible to point out why it is that such a trait is actually different from characters used in animal breeding to which various kinds of inteligence have been compared. Also, contrary to some opinions expressed, it needs to be shown that in dealing with intelligence we are dealing with polygenic inheritance (this term shall be considered in a less cavalier, and, at least in a little more precise, fashion than intelligence), and that our estimates of the heritable fraction of the variation observed when these numbers standing for intelligence are plugged into various formulas are accurate only in terms of general magnitude. Finally, the loose use of the term "human intelligence" will permit speculation, in a few sentences, about the future.

In plant and animal breeding the main purpose of analysis of traits of economic significance lies in the possibility of *predictions* of future behavior of a population subjected to one or another selection technique. *Understanding* of the processes underlying some trait selected for is only peripheral to the main goal of the investigator and if attained (usually partially) is a bonus of the goal of *predictability*. In essence, the purposes of study of these traits in animal breeding are part of operational research leading to what has been called *engineering optimization*, which in animal improvement refers to the process of increases in amount or efficiency of food and fiber production. This goal reflects one important difference in the application of the methodology of polygenic inheritance in plants and animals on the one hand, and human behavioral traits, on the other.

It is true that the proponents of eutelegenesis, that is, improvement of the human gene pool by selective breeding, have often drawn on the success of animal breeders as an example of what could be done with mankind, but the analogy is, perhaps, somewhat far-fetched. Animal breeders had to meet certain conditions before they were truly successful with respect to characters that were (a) nontrivial, (b) polygenically determined, and (c) of relatively low heritability. We may examine some of the conditions for success in the improvement of economic traits in animals by selection with annotation as to why they are not necessarily met in human populations.

SELECTION IN ANIMAL IMPROVEMENT

The first one of these is a clear definition of the goals desired. Thus, dairy cattle breeders had first to agree on the desirability of the direction of selection, and secondly, to devise, for example, measurements of the butterfat content of milk, before a sensible program of selection could be made efficient. And even then, there are instances of decisions on what is desired which had to be reversed for economic reasons.

One example is in the selection for back fat in Danish pigs (Figure 1). Before World War I, the British export market for Danish breeders called for lard. After the war, lean bacon pigs were desired. The graph is reasonably self-explanatory. In this instance, reversal of direction was possible because an adequate reserve of genetic variability was still available, and the success of later endeavors than those portrayed also became dependent on the invention of new tools for accurate measurement of the character on live animals. It is difficult to believe that very many specific aspects of human behavior are predictable with respect to their desirability 1000 years, or let us say 30 to 35 generations ahead, when we do not even know what we want in a pig.

It should, however, be noted that some psychologists hold the view that intelligence, contrary to the uncertainty about the permanence of the scale of values that may be applied to it expressed in the foregoing, may be conceptualized as a sort of transcendental quality impervious to fashions or historical changes. Furthermore, I have also been enjoined (H. Gough, personal communication) not to push the difference between humans and animals, on the

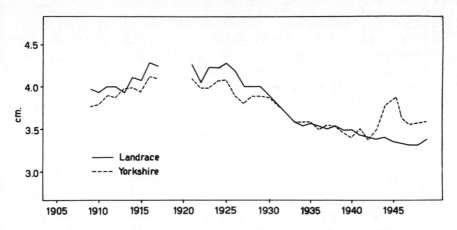

Fig. 1. Progress of selection for thickness of back fat in two Danish breeds of swine (Lush, 1936, and 1951). Reproduced from "Genetic Homeostatis" by I. Michael Lerner (1970) by permission of Dover Publications, Inc., New York, through permission of the publisher.

grounds that while breeding cannot be controlled in man, intelligence can be measured in animals!

In the second place, the objective of animal breeders has been uniformity of the population, a fact which led, in some instances, to fixation of type by levels of inbreeding not tolerated in human society (such as in dog breed formation), and to development of inbred lines for production of uniform crosses displaying hybrid vigor. If there is any desideratum in human populations which may be considered reasonable beyond serious dispute, it is that of human diversity and not complete uniformity (Dobzhansky, 1962).

Thirdly, much of the success of breeding plants and animals depends on progeny or sib testing. This is a technique which permits more accurate evaluation of genotypic properties from phenotypic measurements than is available from the direct phenotypic measurement on the animal itself. In practice, let us say in dairy cattle breeding, this method involves production of thousands of individuals for purposes of evaluating their sires. But the price paid is the coincident condemnation of tester individuals or their relatives, which failed on the basis of the test to prove their genotypic merit, to celibacy and childlessness.

Fourthly, control of the mating system, that is, a programmed decision as to which successful male is bred to which females (the fact that patterns of mating in animals are polygamous is not an important point at issue), is also involved in efficient animal breeding improvement, a measure which human society may not as yet be prepared to adopt, except in the trivial instance of artificial insemination in highly advanced societies.

Fifthly, animal breeding with a relatively short intergeneration interval permits constant revision of parameters entering what is called the *selection index* (a measurement of genotypic worth when selection is directed towards several objectives), necessary because of changes in the degree of heritability generated by selection itself, changes in environment, changes in the relative weights to be assigned to different traits, changes induced by so-called responses (side effects on traits themselves not necessarily under selection, because of the break-up of previously established genetic correlations) and other factors.

Even if not all of these conditions are always met in animal breeding practice, it requires faith in the constancy of the parameters listed, of environment and of value judgments, and in the possibility that all desirable traits are positively correlated, to support the notion that lessons from knowledge of the consequences of polygenic inheritance in plants and animals are *directly* applicable to programs of eugenic control of complex multigenically determined behavioral traits in man, traits which include whatever it is that various psychometric tests purports to measure.

POLYGENIC INHERITANCE

It is, perhaps, appropriate at this time to come to grips as to what I want to call polygenic inheritance. The first thing that may be said about polygenic inheritance is that, technically speaking, there are no such entitites as polygenes, though unfortunately this shorthand term has often been used in talking of genes that exercise effects on polygenically determined phenotypes. *Polygenicity*, to coin a term, is primarily the property of phenotypes. In no sense does it imply that gene action at the primary level of producing given substances is not specific. In other words, polygenic inheritance simply refers to the control of phenotype variation of some trait by an unspecified number of loci, acting like any other Mendelian unit, but having interchangeable effects on the *phenotypic* level. Thus, for instance, for human melanic pigmentation, four or five loci may be postulated to account for the variation in skin reflectance between the extreme expressions of the phenotypes of White and Black Americans. Each gene at these loci may do its own thing at the biochemical level (though some may be truly redundant), but the phenotypic effects on this metrically measurable trait may be interchangeable, so that it is possible to have identical phenotypes produced by completely different genotypes. Reciprocally, environmental differences can of course cause identical genotypes to express themsleves as different phenotypes.

There are several other properties of polygenic systems which have been postulated, practically entirely on empirical grounds. They may have no bearing on ontogenetically trivial traits, such as bristle number in fruit flies, though this character has only too often been used as a model in pilot studies of polygenic inheritance. They include: the possibility that substitution of alleles at any given locus has small phenotypic effects relative to the variation in a population; the fact (already implied) that phenotypic expressions of polygenic traits are often (but not always, as, for instance, in the cited case of melanism in man) subject to permanent modification by varying environmental stimuli in the course of development of the phenotype; and possession by most populations of a considerable store of genetic reserves. Finally, another important property may be found in the frequently observed mandatory reduction in reproductive fitness of stocks in which selection has been directed to some specific metric trait. More generally, it has been observed in many instances that the genes involved are organized into cohesive, so-called *coadapted*, systems which may break up under the pressure of artificial selection for some single or compound trait, but which also have a tendency to regain such structure when natural selection is permitted to operate so as to return the various components involved to a coadapted state.

HERITABILITY

We may next ask as to what property or parameter of the polygenic system is of particular interest to the breeder. There are really several, but if we were to single out one for particular attention it would be that of *heritability*. We shall provisionally, and not entirely accurately, define this term as the proportion of the phenotypic variance observed in the population that is traceable to the variance between genotypes (heritability in the broad sense), with the balance being attributable broadly to differences between the environments in which each genotype develops.

In actual fact, heritability thus defined is of less interest to the breeder than a related measure, heritability in the narrow sense, to be designated here as h^2, which is the property of the population that permits at least prediction of the results of selection on the performance of successive generations.

The difference between the two kinds of heritability lies in the fact that interactions between genes in any given generation of genotypes are broken up because of Mendelian segregation. Hence, the enduring genetic effect between generations is based on what is called the additively genetic effects, which, in a crude way, can be thought of as the average differences between alternative alleles irrespective of the genotypic combinations in which they are found. Thus, effects attributable to dominance interactions (though only in some circumstances), that is interaction between the alleles at a given locus, and epistatic interactions (those between alleles at different loci), which enter broad heritability, are not present in narrow heritability (h^2) and do not contribute to changes in the average genotype produced by selection. In ordinary schemes of determination of narrow heritability, the nonadditive effects are precipitated into the environmental fraction of the phenotypic variance.

Figure 2 shows schematically the predicted changes from selection on the basis of different narrow heritability values. Should the variance of a phenotypic trait be entirely determined by additively genetic variability, the mean of the offspring of a group of selected parents would be expected to equal that of the selected group. Conversely, if no additively genetic variance is involved, no matter from what part of the distribution curve the parents were selected for reproduction, the mean of the offspring, all other conditions being equal, would not differ from that of the unselected parental generation. Most traits, of course, show an intermediate heritability.

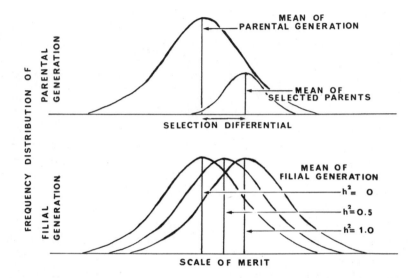

Fig. 2. A schematic illustration of the effect of variation in heritability (h². The upper part of the diagram represents the distribution of the whole parental generation with respect to some metric trait and the more restricted distribution of individuals that are actually selected to be parents of the next generation. When h² = 0, the filial generation will retain the same distribution as the parental generation. When h² = 1.0, the mean of the offspring will be the same as that of the actual parents, should these show no variation in fitness. An intermediate h² will show a mean intermediate in value between the total and the selected parental generation. Reproduced from "Population Genetics and Animal Improvement" by I. Michael Lerner (1950) by permission of Cambridge University Press.

Figure 3 shows an experimental situation, which gives a concrete example of the effects of differences in this parameter. For our purposes, we do not need to enter the operational consequences of the difference shown, except to note that they refer to the methods of evaluating superior genotypes. In the case of the high h^2, the phenotype of the individual itself is an adequate and efficient measure of its additive genotype; when h^2 is low, phenotypic performance of the individual is a poor predictor of genetic performance, and reliance on family

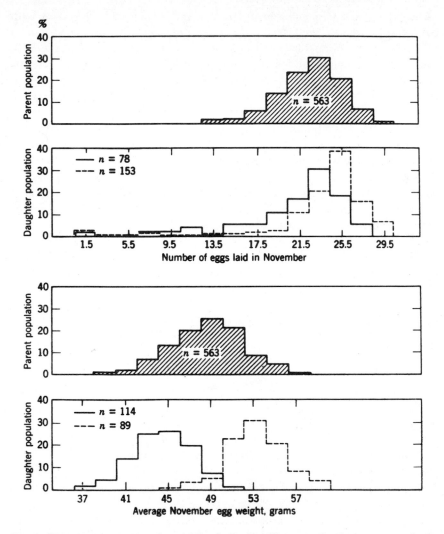

Fig. 3. The consequences of variation in heritability on selection progress. In the upper part of the graph, the character under selection, egg number in November, has a relatively low heritability: the offspring from parents selected for low egg number (solid line) and those selected for higher number (dashed line) show a considerable degree of overlap. The lower part of the graph refers to a trait of high heritability, average egg weight: the offspring of parents selected in opposite directions show very little overlap in their distributions. Reproduced from "The Genetic Basis of Selection" by I. Michael Lerner (1958) copyright © 1958, by permission of John Wiley and Sons, Inc.

testing (for instance, average performance of sibs or half-sibs) has to enter the selective process in order to ensure efficient gains.

There is no need to enter here into the precise details of the heritability concept as applied to intelligence. A recent comprehensive analysis of a number of human behavior traits is to be found in the study of Jinks and Fulker (1970), which may be consulted for this purpose. This work is admirable in most respects but one, and that is the virtual disregard of the fundamental work of Sewall Wright (1921), which underlies much of the thinking on the subject, and the complete neglect of the contributions to it by Jay Lush (1945), in whose laboratory the very term heritability orignated (it has proved to be impossible to pinpoint the precise time the word was coined).

In any case, the paper of Jinks and Fulker is a must for any serious student of the subject. For one thing, it lays to rest on statistical grounds (rather than on *a priori* ones regarding the nature of intelligence) suggestions which have been made that the range of variation of normal human intelligence (that is, excluding specific metabolic blocks that produce mental retardation) can be explained by differences at few loci. In fact, their analysis of the various types of intelligence tests (e.g., Stanford-Binet, Otis, the Wechsler scale, and others) seem to indicate that at least 20-odd, and, much more likely, 100 or so genes are involved. If this be the case, the alleged localization of polygenically acting genes on Drosophila bristle number appears to be irrelevant to the details of the mechanism of inheritance of intelligence by any reasonable definition.

DETERMINATION OF h^2

The actual techniques of estimating h^2 in animals may be found in many papers and books (e.g., Falconer, 1960; Lerner, 1950, 1958). Generally speaking, they are based on (a) empirically observed correlations between phenotypes of relatives; (b) the magnitude of correlations between genetic values of relatives, postulated on basis of Mendelian correlations; and (c) theoretical or observed correlations between mates.

The important point is that the phenotypic correlations in turn depend on the degree of correlation between the genotypes of mates as well as between the environments. In animal experimentation it is possible to minimize the latter. Thus in chickens, sibs may be hatched in incubators and raised in randomized environments, independent of the environment of each and of the parents. The only source of environmentally induced resemblance between such sibs would lie in the community of the source of embryonic nutrition supplied by the eggs in which they develop. For many traits, this makes the environmental correlation zero.

Similarly, the possibility that different genotypes will respond in a differential fashion to different environments (i.e., existence of a genotype-environment interaction) may be minimized experimentally, or at least, detected. In human populations, especially in behavioral traits, neither this interaction nor the environmental correlation is subject to measurement. One notable example is found in a set of behavioral traits for which, because of interpersonal interaction, monozygotic twins reared apart may resemble each other more than those reared together (Shields, 1962; see also Wilde, 1970).

These technical difficulties are compounded in the human population by still another term, that is, the possibility of covariation between genotype and environment. Thus, parents with a "superior" genotype may be expected to produce genetically "superior" offspring, but at the same time they may be able to provide their children with a more favorable environment (for example, maternal nutrition, cultural enrichment, education, etc.). All these factors make estimates of heritability in the narrow sense of intellectual capacities from empricially observed phenotypic correlations a precarious, to say the least, procedure even within groups alleged to be homogeneous for factors assumed to be statistically controllable (ethnic origin, socioeconomic status, race). And comparisons based on field data between mean genetic values of groups differing in these and many other aspects which enter the complex patterns determining variation are not only precarious, but plainly foolhardy.

HERITABILITY AND INTELLIGENCE

What then can we say about evolutionary aspects of the purported topic of this paper? There are four points beyond those already mentioned that may be made. They refer to: (a) the use of other measures than h^2 for estimating degree of additively genetic determination of human capabilities; (b) the essentially qualitative nature of estimations based on degrees of resemblance between relatives and nonrelatives which have been tabulated by so many observers; (c) an example from investigations on cattle of the uncertainty of quantitative estimation of heritability in such comparisons, and finally, (d) a brief comment on the future course of human intelligence.

The first of these points relates to various statistics that, though meaning different things, none of which is precisely h^2, have been masquerading under the letter H. I do not want to, nor am I, indeed, capable of evaluating all these, but the fact is that in a variety of studies on human behavior traits, the symbol H, often described as heritability (thus confusing it with h^2), has been employed by different investigators. Thus, in studies contrasting monozygotic and dyzygotic twins, this symbol has been used for a variety of different indexes of genetic determination. However, in the paper by Jinks and Fulker (1970) translations into terms of h^2 for a number of these symbols can be found.

In general, the fact that these measures differ from h^2 does not deny their validity. Indeed, the area of communality between the H's and h^2 may be greater than the area of their divergence. But it is important to realize that it is not entirely valid to directly apply to man conclusions claimed on the basis of the assumption that the various H's are, indeed, exactly equivalent to h^2 in experimentally controlled populations.

The next point to be noted is simply an affirmation that while exact quantitative conclusions regarding h^2 of human intelligence within groups are not possible, a qualitative statement that the genotypic component of phenotypic variance *within groups* is high, is inescapable, as shown by a summary of the variety of studies on relatives and nonrelatives with respect to the degree of their resemblance in I.Q. (Figure 4). More recent studies, including that of Jinks and Fulker, are in general agreement with the trend of these figures.

But it is fundamentally important to remember that heritability is a fraction, and changes in components of either the denominator or the numerator will change its value. Heritability, then, is neither a property of an individual, nor is it expected to be a constant over generations even in a homogeneous population. Changes in mating system or selection may reduce or increase genetic variation, just as changes in environment may reduce or increase environmental variation, not to mention the covariance and interaction terms. Heritability at any given time depends on both components of these fractions. They vary between populations at a given time, and vary within populations from generation to generation. Furthermore, the fact that some selection for intelligence components has gone on at least between our primate ancestors and ourselves (forgetting Li's [1970] incautious statement for the moment), while h^2 is still high, would argue for changes in fitness values of various components of intelligence as a whole.

Finally, Figure 5 shows that while ranking of heritability estimates remains the same in four different methods of estimation, their values change in a highly significant and systematic fashion depending on the method used. Especially important is the spread in the midrange show, the range within which it may be expected that the properties of man that concern us fall. The differences between the estimates shown for controlled environments and field studies are precisely due to (as noted in the previous section) the unavoidability of removing the covariance, interaction, and nonadditive terms in the latter. And, of course, it is the field data which provide the bulk of information on man. Studies on identical twins must then be interpreted in the light of the differences portrayed in the figure.

IN CONCLUSION

The final issue to be considered very briefly is the future with reference to the possible erosion of human intellectual faculties because of differential reproductive rates of individuals differing in intelligence. There are many prophets of doom who take the view that any advance in technology, in treatment of disease, in improvement of environment, place mankind in jeopardy of losing the race against deterioration and erosion of intelligence, health, and other human properties, generally deemed to be of value. There are others who see no cause for immediate worry, who find no discernible trend in this direction, or in fact find evidence to the contrary.

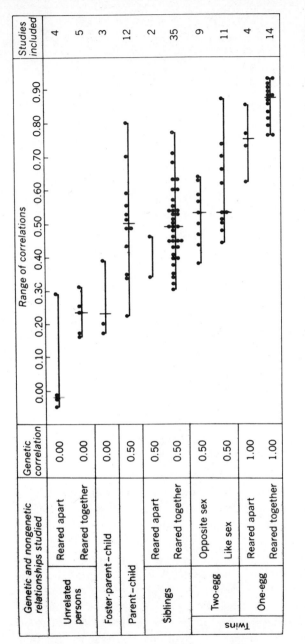

Fig. 4. A summary of phenotypic correlation coefficients between measures of intelligence of unrelated and related persons. Ranges of individual studies are indicated. Compilation by Erlenmyer-Kimling and Jarvik (1963). Reproduced from "Heredity, Evolution and Society" by I. Michael Lerner (1968); copyright© 1968 by W. H. Freeman and Company.

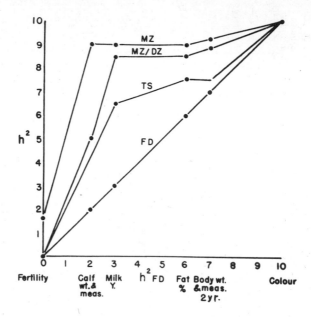

Fig. 5. A classical demonstration of the variation in h^2 *values depending on the methods of estimation used. Heritability values of six traits of dairy cattle estimated from monozygotic twin data (MZ), the difference between mono- and dizygotic (MZ/DZ) twins, half-sisters at testing stations (TS) in which environment is randomized, and field data (FD) comparable to that found in human populations under uncontrolled environment are plotted against* h^2 *estimates obtained by the last of the methods. It may be seen that at extreme values of* h^2 *the various estimates show reasonable agreement. In the middle of the range, however, MZ estimates may be double those of FD estimates. Reproduced from Donald (1959) by permission of author and publisher (see list of references).*

Choosing sides in this issue is mostly a matter of taste or of faith, but in part a matter of evaluation of the operational consequences of what is known. Although there is a substantial amount of literature on the subject, I shall forbear discussing it here. The several longitudinal studies on the changes in I.Q. in human populations (e.g., for that of Scottish children see Population Investigation Committee, 1949 and *seq.*) and the recent reconciliation of data on reproductive patterns of families of different sizes (see Reed, 1965) suggest a guarded optimism. At the worst, it seems that the urgency in preserving or improving the quality of the human gene pool with respect to polygenic traits affecting intelligence seems less than that in establishing ethical and moral guidelines for genetic manipulation. But this is a problem of much wider significance than the ambit of this article includes.

Here, we may only mention some of the pitfalls in attempting a prognosis for the global future of man with respect to his intelligence. In brief, they include:

(a) as already noted, lack of any technique to estimate genetic differences in intelligence between groups, be they ethnic, socioeconomic, or geographic, a deficiency which at the moment seems impossible to overcome, although one may hope that fresh approaches by statisticians and others may remedy it in the future: (b) a change in values of Darwinian fitness of different genotypes, which is one of the ongoing processes of evolution; (c) the uncertainty of the very future of *H. sapiens*, less because it may be replaced by a superior species (a contingency unlikely in the face of conformity pressures) and more because of environmental factors unleashed by the galloping and as yet uncontrolled advances in technology; (d) the general acceleration in the rate of cultural evolution and its feedback to organic evolution, which greatly increases the relative effects of nonbiological factors on the expression of behavioral phenotypes, and many others.

In conclusion then, it merely needs to be pointed out (a) that extrapolation to man of the techniques developed for specific purposes and based on experimental domestic animal material is not directly possible for purposes of predictive uses in human behavior and human intelligence, (b) that the subject of inheritance of human intellectual faculties is still in the exploratory stages, (c) that in spite of the spate of literature on the subject, there is only a little that can be said with confidence about it, and (d) that hopefully the minds of physical scientists, mathematicians, and statisticians brought to bear on problems of human behavior, even if the data deal with soft rather than hard facts which these superior beings are used to dealing with, must be drawn upon if breakthroughs in both understanding and prediction in this area are to be expected.

REFERENCES

Bouchard, J. 1968. Current conceptions of intelligence and their implications for assessment. Advances Psychol. Assessment, 1:14-33.

Dobzhansky, Th. 1962. Mankind Evolving. New Haven, Yale Univ. Press.

Donald, H. P. 1959. Evidence from twins on variation in growth and production of cattle. Proc. X Intern. Cong. Genet., 1:225-235. Toronto, University of Toronto Press.

Eckland, B. K. 1967. Genetics and sociology: a reconsideration. Amer. Sociol. Rev., 32:173-194.

Erlenmeyer-Kimling, L., and L. F. Jarvik. 1963. Genetics and intelligence: a review. Science, 142:1477-1479.

Falconer, D. W. 1960. Introduction to Quantitative Genetics. Edinburgh, Oliver and Boyd.

Hirsch, J. 1970. Behavior-genetic analysis and its biosocial consequences. Seminars in Psychiatry, 2:89-105.

Jinks, J. L., and D. W. Fulker. 1970. Comparison of the biometrical, genetical, Mava, and classical approaches to the analysis of human behavior. Psychol. Bull., 73:311-349.

Lerner, I. M. 1950. Population Genetics and Animal Improvement. Cambridge, Cambridge Univerity Press.

_____ 1958. The Genetic Basis of Selection. New York, John Wiley & Sons.

_____ 1968. Heredity, Evolution and Society. San Francisco, W. H. Freeman and Company.

_____ 1970. Genetic Homeostatis. New York, Dover.

LI, C. C. 1970. Human genetic adaptation. *In* Hecht, M. K. and W. C. Steere, eds., Essays in Evolution and Genetics in Honor of Theodosius Dobzhansky pp. 545-577. New York, Appleton-Century-Crofts.

Lush, J. L. 1936. Genetic aspects of the Danish system of progeny-testing swine. Iowa Agric. Exp. Sta. Res. Bull., 204:108-196.

_____ 1945. Animal Breeding Plans. 3rd ed. Ames, Iowa, Collegiate Press.

_____ 1951. Genetics and animal breeding. *In* Dunn, L. C., ed., Genetics in the 20th Century, pp. 493-525. New York, Macmillan.

Population Investigation Committee of the Scottish Council for Research on Education. 1949. The Trend of Scottish Intelligence. London, University of London Press.

Reed, S. C. 1965. The evolution of human intelligence. Amer. Sci., 53:317-326.

Shields, J. 1962. Monozygotic Twins Brought up Apart and Brought up Together. London, Oxford University Press.

Wilde, G. J. S. 1970. An experimental study of mutual behavior initiation and person perception in MZ and DZ twins. Acta Genet. Med. Gemellol., 19:273-279.

Wright, S. 1921. Systems of mating. Genetics, 6:111-178.

16

On the Evolutionary Uniqueness of Man

THEODOSIUS DOBZHANSKY

Department of Genetics,
University of California,
Davis, California 95616

INTRODUCTION

The purpose of this article is to review the unique features of the evolutionary process which gave rise to the human species. These unique features are examined in the light of our modern understanding of the methods which bring evolution about. No originality is claimed for any of the ideas presented in the article. The general conception of the nature of human evolution may nevertheless be controversial. If so, the author hopes to have a powerful ally in George G. Simpson, many of whose writings seem to indicate that we are in a general agreement on most, though not on all subjects, and to whom this article is dedicated with admiration and affection on his 70th birthday.

Charles Darwin published "The Descent of Man" a century ago, in 1871. In this book Darwin spelled out clearly that man had evolved from ancestors who were not men. As usual with Darwin, the conclusion was buttressed by an impressive array of supporting evidence. The idea of man's origin from animal ancestors was, however, accepted by pioneer evolutionists earlier. It was expounded by Herbert Spencer in his "Principles of Biology" (1863), and by T. H. Huxley in "Evidence as to Man's Place in Nature" (1863). It was, in fact, adopted by Darwin himself more than a decade before "The Descent of Man." The penultimate page of Darwin's "On the Origin of Species" (1859) contains

Variants of this article were included in the Herbert Spencer Lecture, given in Oxford on November 27th, 1970; in a lecture to the Teilhard de Chardin Association of Great Britain and Ireland, given in London on November 30th, 1970; and also in lectures at Sarah Lawrence College, The University of Texas at Austin, and Stanford University.

this not very cryptic sentence: "Light will be thrown on the origin of man and his history." The light of evolution elicited, however, hostility from many of Darwin's contemporaries. Evolutionists were obliged to assemble nothing less than overwhelming evidence that man is a part of nature and kin to all life.

They succeeded thoroughly. The opinion that man appeared at once in his present state, rather than evolved from animal ancestors, now has few adherents. To be sure, this opinion is still the vogue in some places. In a dwindling minority of schools in provincial U.S.A., biology textbooks are preferred that do not mention these two dangerous topics: evolution and sex.

In September of 1969 I was party to a kind of Wilberforce-Huxley debate in miniature, in Delphi, Greece. Most surprisingly, the part of Wilberforce was played not by an ignorant fanatic but by a professor at the University of Athens, Marcos Siotis. Rather less surprising is the success of a reactionary politician, Max Rafferty, who headed for a time the Department of Education of the state of California. He promulgated a ruling obliging the schools to give equal attention to the supposedly still questionable theory of evolution and to the alternative of divine creation. How often the teachers obey this rule is not known.

It would be waste of effort to gather, in order to convince the doubters, still more evidence that man has evolved. Their doubts come not so much from lack of knowledge as from resistance to knowledge. That man, like other biological species, is a product of evolution, is now platitudinous. It is more interesting that human evolution is in some respects basically different from others. As George C. Simpson (1964) put it, man "is another species of animal, but not just another animal. He is unique in peculiar and extraordinarily significant ways." J. S. Huxley has rightly noted (1939) that "Man's opinion of his own position in relation to the rest of the animals has swung pendulum-wise between too great and too little a conceit of himself, fixing now too large a gap between himself and the animsls, now too small . . . The gap between man and animals was here reduced not by exaggerating the human qualities of animals, but by minimizing the human qualities of men. Of late years, however, a new tendency has become apparent."

Classical evolutionists strove to prove that mankind was like other biological species; the outstanding problem now is to find out in what ways it is unlike other species. A century ago, the demonstration that man shares common ancestry with apes, monkeys, and even with fishes and amoebae, altered man's view of himself and of his place in the universe. Understanding of his evolutionary uniqueness may also usher in a change of some importance in man's image.

INDIVIDUAL UNIQUENESS

In the living world, there are uniquenesses of different orders. Monozygotic multiple births excepted, every individual human has a unique genetic endowment, his genotype. The same is true of individuals of other sexually reproducing and outbreeding species. The basis of this uniqueness is that an individual heterozygous for n genes has the potentiality of forming 2^n kinds of sex cells with different constellations of his genes. It has become increasingly evident in recent years that in man and other higher organisms, n is of the order of at least thousands. The number of potentially possible genotypes is, therefore, vastly greater than can ever be realized. No genotype is likely to arise in more than a single zygote. Whoever does not have a monozygotic twin brother or sister is a carrier of a unique genotype, a singular biological "nature." Mankind is an array of unique, unprecedented, and nonrecurrent human "natures."

There is no generalized ideal man, so dear to many philosophers from Plato onward; there are only individual men, who resemble each other in some respects, and differ in other respects. This raises some difficulties which should be mentioned, even though they are only indirectly related to the topic of this article. If the archetypal man does not exist, what becomes of the inalienable human rights, human dignity, and sacredness of human life? Can one always decide who is or is not human?

The boundaries of mankind as a biological species are not in doubt. A sexual species has a corporate genetic endowment, a gene pool. Any individual whose genes are derived from mankind's gene pool belongs to the human species. Some genetic diseases and malformations make the afflicted individuals seemingly lose all semblance of humanness. Others behave in ways which we would have liked to believe men cannot behave. But there is no escape from considering them our conspecifics. They have all human rights, including the right to be judged according to their contributions to society.

FAMILIES, POPULATIONS, AND RACES

Any aggregate of human beings consists of genetically unique individuals, and is consequently also unique. Children do not inherit the genotypes of their parents. They inherit only one half of their genes. In the process of development the contributions of each gene do not stand alone; they interact. The morphological, physiological, and psychological individualities are emergent products of the gene constellation in the genotype. This limits the predictability of an individual's characteristics. If both parents carry a recessive gene for phenylketonuria in heterozygous condition, each of their children has a 25% chance of being a homozygous phenylketonuric. Man's personality, is, however, a composite trait of utmost complexity; many genes and environmental influences contribute to its formation; he will be a foolhardy geneticist who ventures to predict the personalities of even his own children.

Mankind is, considered genetically, a single inclusive Mendelian population. Yet within it, there is a most intricate array of subordinate Mendelian populations—clans, tribes, social, economic, occupational, religious, linguistic, national, and racial subdivisions. Mankind is a genetically closed system; it receives no genes from, and contributes none, to the gene pool of any other species. The subordinate populations are open systems. A marriage of a Bushman to an Eskimo has not, as far as I know, been recorded. It is nevertheless certain that gene exchange does take place between populations of geographically remote countries, through a chain of geographically intermediate populations.

No species matches mankind in the complexity of its geographically and socially maintained subdivisions. It must, however, be stressed that the genetic differences between them are entirely, or at least predominantly, quantitative rather than qualitative. No gene is known that would be present in every individual of one race and absent in every individual of another. Races differ in gene frequencies, not in presences and absences. Of course, no native of the Congo has a light skin like natives of Sweden, and no Swede a dark skin like a Congolese. The skin color is, however, a product of several, at least four but possibly more than twice that many, genes with additive effects. It is not at all unlikely that European populations have scattered genes for dark, and African populations for light skin colors. A breeder probably could obtain a dark-skinned clan of Swedes, and a light-skinned clan of Congolese. Be that as it may, the main point is that race differences are compounded of genetic constituents in which individuals within a race, and siblings within a family, may also differ. Interpopulational and intrapopulational variations are basically consubstantial.

MANKIND AS A SPECIES

The central issue in this essay is not the uniqueness of individuals, but that of mankind as a species. An explanation is needed at this point. Evolutionary uniqueness is the property of most biological species, in the sense that a species arises only once. Only so-called allopolyploid species, which originate by doubling of the chromosome set in hybrids between preexisting species, may be produced repeatedly. The concern felt by nature lovers for rare and endangered species is warranted because the extinction of a species is irreversible. If mankind were to commit suicide, as it is technologically capable of doing, it would not be reestablished by evolution from apes, or monkeys, or anything else. Existence of extraterrestrial humans is sheer fantasy. However, it is not the quasi-universal uniqueness of most biological species which interests us here. To parody a well-known witticism, that though all men are equal some are more equal than others, I say that although most species are unique, the human species is the most unique of all. Furthermore, its most outstanding unique properties are predominantly not in the morphological or physiological, but in the psychological realm.

Linnaeus classified living beings according to their externally visible characteristics; biological classification is still based preponderantly on external morphology and anatomy. The bones of the skeleton furnish an abundance of usable traits. Classification of fossils rests perforce on such traits, since soft parts of the body are rarely preserved. Though he was a believer in special creation, Linnaeus recognized that man is a member of the order of primates and of the class of mammals. Modern taxonomy uses more categories than Linnaeus did, such as suborder, superfamily, family, subfamily, etc. It recognizes (among the rest) two coordinate families, Hominidae with a single living representative, *Homo sapiens*, and Pongidae, the great apes. The point which I wish to make is that if the classification were based on psychology rather than on morphology, man would have to be considered an organism sharply differentiated from all others. Though sharing common descent with representatives of the family Pongidae, man has diverged very greatly from them.

Simpson (1964) lists 22 characteristics of the human species, 12 of them structural or morphological, and the remainder psychological. I shall not copy his list here; it is more interesting to consider these traits not separately but in their interrelations. In Simpson's words, "The most crucial single anatomical point is acquisition of upright posture and strictly bipedal locomotion. Most of the other main peculiarities of human anatomy either follow from that or are coadapted with it. . . As posture is focal for consideration of man's anatomical nature and tools are for consideration of his material culture, so is language focal for his mental nature and his non-material culture. Language is also the most diagnostic single trait of man: all normal men have language; no other now living organisms do."

There were many debates as to which of the distinctive human traits appeared first in the evolutionary history, and which were secondary. Did our ancestors first acquire the erect posture, and then start to employ their hands for using and making tools? Or did the tool use put a selective premium on freeing the hands from locomotor duties, and hence on erect posture? Neither possibility can be ruled out, since there are largely bipedal animals not using tools, and tool-using but not bipedal ones. Did communication by symbolic language make possible the transmission of culture, or did the increase of cultural tradition stimulate the evolution of the genetic basis that made language feasible? It is now fairly generally realized that such alternatives are illusory. The evolutionary repatterning that transformed an animal into man involved feedback processes within and between the morphological and the physchological spheres. Inception of tool use favored the emancipation of the anterior extremities from walking, and increasing manual dexterity made possible greater and greater dependence on tools. Making tools according to a traditionally set pattern requires an organization of psychological faculties, which makes also possible the development of symbolic language. It is nevertheless not an idle question to ask in what characteristics and abilities has the human species departed farthest from its animal ancestors and cousins. I agree with Simpson (1969) that "language is the most entirely unique, the most completely diagnostic characteristics of *Homo sapiens*. From an evolutionary point of view, language is a biological adaptation essential in the way of life specific for that species."

LANGUAGE

Many, indeed most, animals communicate with conspecific individuals at least occasionally (e.g., at mating time) by signals of various kinds—auditory, visual, chemical, etc. Particularly in mammals and birds, these signals reach a degree of elaborateness which makes tempting comparisons with human languages. It is therefore necessary to distinguish clearly between so-called animal "languages" and human languages. Hockett (1959) considers the combination of the following six characteristics essential in language:

1. Duality of patterning. Words and sentences are patterns of sounds or phonemes, which by themselves have no meaning but are components of meaningful utterances.

2. Productivity. In our speech we frequently utter phrases which neither the speaker nor the hearer ever made or heard before, and yet the meaning of these utterances is understood usually without difficulty.

3. Arbitrariness. Words are socially agreed-upon symbols, most of them having no "iconicity", i.e., no similarity to the shapes, colors, sounds, or smells of the objects or qualities for which they stand. From their sounds, one would not know to which animals the words "dog" and "cat" refer; one must learn this from speakers of a given language.

4. Interchangeability. Any speaker of a language is theoretically capable of saying anything that he can understand when someone else says it.

5. Displacement. We often speak of things and events out of sight, of past and future, and even of imaginary and nonexistant situations.

6. Cultural transmission. Language is learned from, and taught by, other speakers of the same language.

Some of the above characteristics, at least in rudimentary forms, are not exclusively human; they are found scattered here and there in the animal kingdom. Their presence in nonhuman animals is, to an evolutionist, eloquent testimony that the building blocks from which the "humanum" was compounded exist outside the human species. Their combination in fully developed form is, however, uniquely human.

Hockett and Ascher (1964) say that "The proto-hominids did not have the power of speech. The most that we can validly ascribe to them in this respect is a call system similar to that of modern gibbons. These apes have approximately six vocal signals, indicating discovery of food, danger, the whereabouts of the signaling individual, etc. In a given situation, an animal can only emit the appropriate call, or remain silent. Gibbon calls thus lack the quality of productivity." Hockett and Ascher speculate that this quality may have evolved by "opening of the call system," i.e., by combining the whole or parts of the original fixed calls, thus giving rise to numerous "blends." The blends then acquired socially agreed-upon meanings, and became a "pre-language." A further surmise is that prelanguages and languages appeared in our ancestors at least one million years ago, and played a role in the establishment of the morphological changes which gave rise to the organs of speech now found in *Homo sapiens*.

Several experimenters have attempted to teach apes in captivity to speak. Most successful among such experiments were those of Hayes (1951) and Hayes and Hayes (1954). An infant chimpanzee was being brought up as though she were a human child. The animal learned more or less easily many human behavior patterns that quite assuredly no chimpanzee in its natural habitats ever did. Learning to speak was, however, a conspicuous exception. After much effort, the ape acquired a "vocabulary" of only three short words. What is the reason for this failure? It is not only that uttering the sounds of which human language is composed is difficult for a chimpanzee. The situation is more comparable to the condition in man known as aphasia, the inability to speak caused by injury to the speech centers in the brain of a person, otherwise physically and mentally healthy.

Human language consists of acoustic signals. Gardner and Gardner (1969) reasoned that the failure of an ape to master even the rudiments of acoustic language is no evidence of its inability to learn some other forms of symoblic communication. They adopted the American Sign Language, invented for and used by the deaf. Instead of sounds, it consists of manual configurations and gestures, which stand for different objects and concepts. The success was remarkable. After 22 months of training, a female chimpanzee learned to use, appropriately and often spontaneously, at least 30 signs. Some of these stood for demands and others for objects. The ape learned to use signs as symbols or names for objects, an ability hitherto considered uniquely human. She also used combinations of two or more signs.

The great interest of these experiments is indisputable. Yet they do not mean that the particular chimpanzee with which the Gardners worked became a user of human language, still less that chimpanzees in their natural habitats utilize symbolic language. Bronowski and Bellugi (1970) point out that the acquisition of language by a human child involves "not just the capacity to learn names as they are specifically taught by the humans around the child in the early stages. Far more basic and important is the child's ability to analyze out regularities in the language, to segment novel utterances into component parts as they relate to the world, and to understand these parts again in new combinations." The chimpanzee has not mastered this art of analysis and synthesis.

LANGUAGE AND CULTURE

In a very perceptive article Lenneberg (1964) points out that "man may be equipped with highly specialized, biological propensities that favor and, indeed, shape the development of speech in the child, and that roots of language may be as deeply grounded in our natural constitution as, for instance, our predisposition to use our hands." Language is not a special gift of any particular race or population. It is a universal faculty of the human species. It is the universal foundation of culture, which is likewise species-wide.

Biological species other than mankind evolve adaptations to their environments through changes in their genes. Genetic changes occur also in human evolution, but they are subsidiary to cultural innovations and modifications. Birds, bats, and certain other animals became fliers when they developed wings; man became the most powerful flier of all when he developed aircraft. Animals resist cold by evolving warm fur, by hibernation in an inactive state, or by migration to warmer lands. Man dominates cold by heating his dwellings and dressing in warm garments. Indisputably, culture is the most potent method of adaptation that has emerged in the evolutionary history of the living world. It is perhaps astonishing that only a single species, mankind, has become the user of this device for adaptedness. It is further noteworthy that every nonpathological representative of the human species partakes of this method of adaptedness. It is indispensable for survival, of mankind as a species as well as of humans as individuals.

Although symbolic language is its salient trait, culture includes much more. It has technological, sociological, and ideological components. Taylor defined culture a century ago as "That complex whole which includes knowledge, belief, art, morals, law, custom, and any other capabilities and habits acquired by man as a member of society." Kluckhohn's more recent definition (1965a) is "The total life-way of a people, the social legacy the individual acquires from his group." Man is a tool-user and tool-maker. Tool-using is found sporadically in several groups of animals; tool-making has long been regarded man's unique achievement. Making tools presupposes a higher order of brain development than using them. In Oakley's (1961) words, "Man can see a tool in a formless lump of stone." He can also see a canoe in a treetrunk, a painting on an empty canvas, and himself under circumstances which will arise in the future or in completely imaginary circumstances. Even rudiments of tool-making are exceedingly rare among animals. Kohler observed long ago that chimpanzees in captivity could fit together sticks to obtain food that was otherwise out of reach. Lawick-Goodall (1965) discovered that chimpanzees in nature prepared sticks by stripping them of leaves, and used them to extract termites from the nests of the latter. Man not only uses and makes tools, but also prepares tools to make other tools.

An interesting and provocative attempt has been made by Holloway (1969) to find a common psychological denominator in symbolic language and tool-making activities. Already Geertz (1964) before him had characterized culture as "imposition of an arbitrary framework of symbolic meaning upon reality." Holloway phrases this almost identically: "imposition of arbitrary form upon the environment." He argues that man differs from other animals in possession of higher intelligence, motor skills, and an ability to delay the reactions to stimuli received from the environment. These are, however, differences in degrees only. Natural selection favored the development of these abilities because of their immediate survival values but, as it turned out, it has thus prepared the ground for the "human revolution," i.e., for the origin of truly unique human ability. The consummation of the "revolution" became possible with the appearance of a new faculty, namely the ability to structure the environment arbitrarily. The cognitive processes involved in language as well as in tool-making presuppose this ability.

According to Holloway, natural selection "favored the cognitive structures dependent on brain organization and social structure which resulted in both language and tool-making." And further: "Through social rules, shared frames of reference, socially transmitted strategies for producing structure, arbitrary form was imposed on the environment, and rules imposed upon the society's members." He also contends, I believe needlessly, that we learn nothing about the origin of human culture from studies on the behavior of nonhuman primates and other animals. His emphatic reassertion that culture is "a human domain" and "something unique to man" is nevertheless useful.

SELECTION BY AND FOR CULTURE

In having given rise to man, biological evolution has transcended itself. Mankind is the only species which is engaged in two evolutions at the same time—the biological and the cultural. The two evolutions are distinct in principle. Biological inheritance is transmitted by genes in the sex cells, cultural inheritance by instruction and learning. Bodily modifications acquired by an individual during his lifetime are not transmitted to his progeny. The genetic transmission is exclusively from parents to their offspring. No such constraint exists upon cultural transmission. Culture is wholly acquired in each generation, and cultural acquisitions can be passed to other persons, irrespective of the genetic relationships. Cultural "heredity" is really a metaphor that can be misleading if taken literally.

The contrasting properties of the cultural and biological domains are evident. Apparently a large majority of social scientists believe these domains to be wholly disconnected, and this view is adopted by many intellectuals and the educated public. It has even been asserted that in having acquired culture, mankind has escaped biology. This is certainly an illusion. Culture and biology are connected by feedback relationships. Cultural changes have genetic consequences. To give a single example: control of malarial fevers has decreased, and may have reversed, the adaptive values of several genes which caused resistance to these diseases. It is probable that man is in the process of transforming his biology by his culture, and it is possible that he may learn to do so deliberately and in the direction of his choosing.

Cultural evolution is a prolongation and a sequel of the biological, and human genetic endowment is the precondition of culture. A human child takes easily to the process of enculturation or socialization, which confers upon him the competence to function as a member of a human society. A chimpanzee child can be trained to do many things, but it is refractory to enculturation. Barring gross pathology, the receptivity to socialization is species-wide in mankind. It was made species-wide at the dawn of human cultural evolution by the unrelenting pressure of natural selection. The genetic variants that were deficient in receptivity must have been eliminated, because their Darwinian fitness did not suffice for survival and perpetuation of their kinds in nascent human societies. We also find that culture is species-wide. Peoples in different parts of the world have evolved a variety of cultures, as they evolved a variety of languages. A cultureless human population would be unlikely to survive for long, even if it were sheltered from competition with better endowed neighbors. This is because mankind as a species is adaptively specialized for a way of life unlike that of any other animal species. Man is committed by his genetic endowment to live in societies with other men, to communicate with them by means of symbolic language, and to secure his livelihood by using, and at least from time to time by making, tools.

The genetic basis of man's psyche, no less than that of his physique, has been shaped in the evolutionary history of our species. It has often been claimed that mankind is genetically adapted to live in the environments in which our ancestors lived, rather than in the environments created by the civilization in which we live. Up to a point, this claim is plausible. A population of any species is, in any given generation, most likely to be adapted best to the environment of the generation that preceded it. While natural selection has done what it could in the ancestral generation, it is only in the process of working on the generation now living. In man's case, the retardation of the evolutionary adaptive process may be of greater consequence than elsewhere, because of the rapid and accelerating transformations of the environments by culture.

Are we, then, adapted by our genetic constitution to the way of life of our cave-dwelling ancestors? Are the environments "natural" for us those of the tribes of hunter-gatherers, or of Ice Age men, or maybe those of the australopithecines? A bewildering variety of opinions have been, and are being put forward again and again, concerning the ways of life and the modes of behavior towards which men are supposedly driven by the imaginary force called "human nature." The dour Calvinistic assumption of an innate depravity of man emanating from the Original Sin does not lack its supporters. Man, we are told, is saddled with something called "the territorial imperative," which is "genetic and ineradicable"; and so, "we are predators, of course, and from time to time we shall go out looting and raping and raising general havoc in the surrounding countryside" (Ardrey, 1966). Authorities from Nietzsche to Hitler, Mussolini, and Keith found war desirable and glorious because man is innately a warrior, and "we are in fact the spawn of the winners of millions of years of war" (Bigelow, 1969). Even the gentler Lorenz (1966) ascribes to man innate aggressiveness, "that is to say the fighting instinct in beast and man which is directed against members of the same species."

The *tabula rasa* theory appeals most to social scientists and to not a few psychologists, although probably only a minority would now readily subscribe to the famous statement of Watson (1924): "Give me a dozen healthy infants, well formed, and my own special world to bring them up in, and I'll guarantee to take any one at random and train him to become any type of specialist I might select—doctor, lawyer, artist, merchant-chief, and yes, even beggar and thief, regardless of his talents, penchants, tendencies, abilities, vocations, or race of his ancestors." And finally, Montagu (1955) is the ablest modern exponent of the assumption of an innate goodness of man: "It is not evil babies who grow up into evil human beings, but an evil society which turns good babies into disordered adults, and it does so on a regimen of frustration. Babies are born good, and desirous of continuing to be good."

All these views are vitiated by the same oversight. They fail to take into consideration the pivotal adaptive strategy characteristic of human evolution, and of human evolution alone. Without question this is culture. Culture is acquired, it is not innate or inborn. What is vouchsafed by the genes is not a culture but the ability to acquire one. Man's genes make him a ready receptor of enculturation and training. They enable man to profit from experience, to visualize alternative courses of action with their consequences, to choose those he finds most advantageous, and to leave the others in abeyance. Natural selection has favored cultural receptivity not in some populations and at some times only, but in the whole species and ever since the formative stages of humanity. If Holloway (see above) is right that the same cognitive structures underlie communication by symbolic language as well as tool-making, this selection may have been at work for at least two million years. As theoretical possibilities, one can envisage that man might be genetically determined as aggressive or submissive, warlike or peaceful, territorial or wanderer, selfish or generous, mean or good. Are any of these possibilities likely to be realized? Would the fixation of any of these dispositions, so that they become uncontrollable urges or drives, increase the adaptedness of a species which relies on culture for its survival? I believe that the answers to these questions are in the negative.

Man is the creator and the creature of his culture. The point I wish to stress is simple but, I believe, fundamental. It has to do with time. Let us take the estimate of 2,000,000 years as the time during which the selection for cultural receptivity has operated, and 20 to 25 years as the average length of human generation over this time span. Some 80,000 to 100,000 generations were, then, subject to the selection for receptivity to enculturation. The Neolithic Revolution, which inaugurated crop raising and village settlements, occurred less than 10,000 years, or 400 to 500 generations ago. The civilization in Mesopotamia and Egypt began some 5,000 to 6,000 years ago. The Industrial Revolution, counting from the invention of the steam engine by Watt, is a mere two centuries old in England and some western European countries. It is still under way, or only commencing in the developing countries.

Were men selected genetically for these cultural developments? Or were they adapting themselves to new modes of securing their livelihood by being brought up in different ways? The ways of life of hunters and gatherers, of peasants cultivating the soil, of herdsmen tending their herds, and of industrial workers operating machines, are evidently distinct. In all probability, both genetic selection and appropriate teaching have operated, but the latter was vastly more efficacious than the former. Genetic selection is a slow process; while in contrast, teaching and learning are relatively very rapid. Improved genes can be passed only to the progenies of the individuals selected; improved techniques and new ideas can be taught to anybody, regardless of genetic relationship. The length of a human generation makes the establishment of superior genetic qualities too dilatory in human populations to be an effective agency in cultural change. Furthermore, the heritability of human behavioral characters and of special abilities is generally low; indeed it is so low that providing conclusive evidence that they are heritable at all is notoriously difficult.

Western civilization has shown itself capable of evolving particularly rapidly. Millions upon millions of industrial workers the world over are sons, grandsons, and great-grandsons of peasants who tilled the soil, or of craftsmen skilled in some trades. Many of them changed their occupation within a single generation, without waiting for many generations of genetic selection to qualify them, or their progenies, for the new employments. Those among us who have reached middle or old age have experienced, or at least seen, our living environments change more or less radically, sometimes almost beyond recognition. Whether these changes were good or bad is immaterial for our argument here—all kinds can be exemplified. What we do know for certain is that we have become adjusted to these changes by mastering new skills and becoming habituated to them, not by undergoing genetic mutations.

INDIVIDUALS AND SOCIETIES

Peoples in different parts of the world have evolved a variety of cultures and languages. Despite this diversity, the capacity for enculturation is a universal trait of mankind. At least as a child, any individual free of gross pathology can learn to speak any language and become a competent member of any culture. At the same time, every individual has a unique and nonrecurrent genetic endowment. He is not a reflection or a copy of some universal human nature, but a bearer of his own singular nature. Although the receptivity to enculturation is species-wide, it need not be an all-or-none trait. How wide and how consequential are the variations in this receptivity is a topic of many investigations and many more, often acrimonious, polemics. The heritability of the IQ, the intelligence quotient, has a most voluminous literature devoted to it. Data that are suggestive, though mostly inconclusive, have also been obtained on the genetic components of the variance of temperaments, special abilities, and some forms of deviant behavior.

The work of Jensen (1969) has become the center of some lively polemics. Having reviewed and competently analyzed a mass of relevant data, Jensen concluded that individual differences in IQ test scores have a strong genetic component. Something close to 80 percent of the variance is found to be genetic. This analysis tells us little or nothing about the heritability of the differences between the IQ *averages* for socioeconomic classes, castes, and racial groups. In human societies, relatives tend to "inherit" not only similar genes but also similar environments. Environmental differences between socioeconomic classes may be far greater than between siblings in the same family, or between families of the same socioeconomic level. The great bulk of the data analyzed by Jensen comes from middle class white families; how relevant are these data for estimation of the genetic components of the differences between class and race means? Jensen attempts to overcome the difficulty in comparing the IQ scores of black and white children of supposedly the same socioeconomic levels. It is however questionable whether the criteria of socioeconomic status adequately measure the quality of the environments, particularly of the white and black people in the United States. Their families may have the same incomes, similar housing, and even attend the same schools. Yet the simple fact of being visibly, identifiably, black exposes black people to discrimination. A lower heritability of the IQ scores among the blacks has been demonstrated particularly clearly in the recently published work of Scarr-Salapatek (1971).

These problems assuredly deserve all the attention that they have had, as well as further careful and extensive studies. Yet such studies do not tell the whole story of the relationships between biological and cultural evolutions. Moreover, what they miss is at least as crucial as what they reveal. An individual man meets in his lifetime multifarious environments. Different men meet and have to contend with at least in part different repertories of environments. From the inception of the human forms of social organization, and increasingly with their historical developments, the aspects of the environments that mattered most were not the physical but the cultural. We must cope with vicissitudes of climate, weather, and infections. What our survival and success, biological or social, depend mainly on are, however, our relations with other people individually, and collectively as represented by the social order in which we live. Any human society, and a civilized society much more than a primitive one, can function only because most human genetic endowments assure a flexibility in acquisition of different patterns of behavior, different skills, and competence for different employments, occupations, and roles which the society is in need of.

Traditionally, political conservatives have stressed genetic differences among people, which liberals have deemphasized or overlooked. One could plausibly argue that it should be the other way round. Man is born certainly not a *tabula rasa*. He is born with a genetically secured capacity to become a member of any human society, and to be trained for many, though not necessarily for all, roles in that society. Individuals may be genetically best endowed to achieve proficiency or excellence in some particular sphere. Some have absolute pitch, and others are tone deaf; some have a good singing voice, which others lack. I probably could have been trained to play some music, but no training would have made me a musical virtuoso. Mozart probably could have learned biology or engineering or soldiering, but most likely he would have played music whenever he had the slightest opportunity. I see nothing repugnant in supposing that some populations may be better endowed on the average in some respects, and other populations in other respects. What is significant is, however, that in most or in all respects the best endowed individual of any population is always superior to the mean of all other populations, and the least well endowed members of any population are inferior to all other population means.

Human equality is an ethic, a moral, or religious precept, not a biological goal, still less a biological fact. Human equality does not aim to make everybody alike. Quite the contrary, it endeavors to provide an equality of opportunity that would enable people to realize their different potentialities and to follow their different tastes and preferences. If all men were born *tabulae rasae*, or if all were genetically as nearly alike as monozygotic twins, equality would be meaningless and superfluous. It is justified and necessary because every person has an ineluctable individuality. Denial of equality will make him suffer or revolt.

It often happens in evolution that a species responds to the same challenge of its environment by evolving not one but two or several adaptive mechanisms which reinforce each other. The human species can exist in a variety of sociocultural environments, and can have individuals specializing for different positions, occupations, and employments, because of (a) its genetically secured educability, and (b) genetic variety. Which of these two adaptive strategies is the more efficacious and therefore more important? One should not belittle either, but there can be, in my view, not the slightest doubt that the cultural evolution of mankind has been, and probably will continue to depend mainly on the unique organization of man's psyche, which enables him to acquire, store, and transmit information about the world in which he lives. Man uses his knowledge, understanding, and technology to modify or create new environments to fit his genes. A reverse process may also become feasible: man may learn to modify his genes to fit the environments which he wittingly or unwittingly creates. Man's science and, hopefully, his wisdom should be better guides towards deliberate and planned genetic change than the blind force of natural selection was in the past.

CONCLUDING REMARKS

It was Herbert Spencer, not Darwin, who introduced the term "evolution" in its present sense. Before Spencer, "evolution" meant the unfolding of preexisting rudiments, as in a bud or in an embryo. It applied mainly to ontogeny, not to phylogeny. Seen from the vantage point of present knowledge, Herbert Spencer's greatest distinction was the recognition of the universality of evolution. To Spencer, evolution was inherent in the very nature of the universe. The evolution of man and his cultures was a prolongation of the biological evolution, and biological evolution an extension of the inorganic or cosmic evolution. Among modern authors the universality of evolution is stressed, starting from philosophic postulates very different from those of Spencer, by Teilhard de Chardin (1959).

The stream of evolution does not, however, flow uniformly at the same rate. From time to time the continuity is broken by radical transmutations, when there emerge some novel configurations of phenomena, and new fields of hitherto nonexistent processes and regularities are opened up. In retrospect, we can discern two salient turning points in the evolution of the universe. The first was the origin of life from lifeless matter. The second was the origin of man from his prehuman and nonhuman ancestors.

The first came to pass some three billion years ago, and as far as known for certain only on a single planet in an otherwise unremarkable solar system. This evolutionary transcendence was the starting point of organic evolution, which became superimposed on the evolution of inert matter. Life is a particular pattern of physicochemical phenomena; living organisms are machines, but machines of a very special sort. Biological laws are not imcompatible with physics or chemistry, they are merely irrelevant in the nonliving world. The second transcendence was the origin of man, tentatively reckoned as about two million years ago. The cultural evolution, the human evolution proper, became superimposed on the biological and the cosmic evolutions. Man is subject to biological laws, like any other biological species. He does, however, possess unique mental abilities; humans communicate by means of symbolic languages, and the societies in which they live are predicated upon their members having self-awareness, and being responsible for their actions because they can foresee the consequences of these actions.

The cosmic, biological, and cultural evolutions are now under way. Whither are they going? Is another transcendence in prospect? Teilhard de Chardin (1959) has confidently predicted one. These questions are, however, outside the limits of competence of scientists; at any rate, they are outside my competence.

REFERENCES

Ardrey, R. 1966. The Territorial Imperative. New York, Atheneum.
Bigelow, R. 1969. The Dawn Warriors. Boston, Little, Brown, and Company.
Bronowski, J., and U. Bellugi, 1970. Language, name and concept. Science, 168:669-673.
Darwin, C. 1859. On the Origin of Species. London, Murray. (Facsimile edition, Cambridge, Harvard University Press, 1964.)
——— 1871. The Descent of Man. 2 vols. London, Murray.

Gardner, R. A., and B. T. Gardner. 1969. Teaching sign language to a chimpanzee. Science, 165:664-672.

Geertz, C. 1964. The transition to humanity. *In* Tax, S., ed., Horizons of Anthropology. Chicago, Aldine.

Hayes, C. 1951. The Ape in Our House. New York, Harper.

Hayes, K. J., and C. Hayes. 1954. The cultural capacity of chimpanzee. Hum. Biol., 26:288-303.

Hockett, Ch. F. 1959. Animal "languages" and human language. In Spuhler, J. N., ed., The Evolution of Man's Capacity for Culture, pp. 32-39. Detroit, Wayne University Press.

——— and R. Ascher. 1964. The human revolution. Current Anthropol., 5:135-168.

Holloway, R. L. 1969. Culture, a human domain. Current Anthropol., 10:395-412.

Huxley, J. S. 1939. Man in the Modern World. New York, Harper.

Huxley, T. H. 1863. Evidence as to Man's Place in Nature. New York, D. Appleton and Co.

Jensen, A. R. 1969. How much can we boost IQ and scholastic achievement? Harvard Educational Rev., 39:1-123.

Kluckhohn, C. 1945. The concept of culture. *In* Linton, R., ed., The Science of Man in the World Crisis. New York, Columbia University Press.

Lawick-Goodall, J. van. 1965. New discoveries among Africa's chimpanzees. Nat. Geogr., 128:802-821.

Lennenberg, E. H. 1964. The capacity for language acquisition. *In* Cohen, Y. A., ed., Man in Adaptation to Biosocial Background. Chicago, Aldine.

Lorenz, K. 1966. On Aggression. New York, Harcourt, Brace.

Montagu, M. F. A. 1955. The Direction of Human Development. New York, Harper.

Oakley, K. P. 1961. On man's use of fire, with comments on tool-making and hunting. *In* Washburn, S. L., ed., Social Life of Early Man. Chicago, Aldine.

Scarr-Salapatek, S. 1971. Race, social class, and IQ. Science 174:1285-1295.

Simpson, G. G. 1964. This View of Life. New York, Harcourt, Brace.

——— 1969. Biology and Man. New York, Harcourt, Brace.

Spencer, Herbert. 1863. Principles of Biology. London, Williams.

Teilhard de Chardin, P. 1959. The Phenomenon of man. New York, Harper.

Thorpe, W. H. 1965. Science, Man and Morals. London, Methuen.

Washburn, S. L., and C. S. Lancaster. 1968. The evolution of hunting. *In* Washburn, S. L., and Ph. C. Jay, eds., Perspectives on Human Evolution. New York, Holt, Rinehart and Winston.

Watson, J. B. 1924. Behaviorism. New York, W. W. Norten & Company, Inc.

Author Index

Subject Index

437

438 Subject Index

Contents of Previous Volumes

Volume 4 (1970)

Supplementary Volume (1970)[1]

[1] Essays in Evolution and Genetics in Honor of Theodosius Dobzhansky: A Supplement to Evolutionary Biology, edited by M. K. Hecht and W. C. Steere.

Volume 5 (1972)